Queer Economics

Queer Economics is the examination of and response to the effects of heteronormativity both on economic outcomes and on economics as a discipline. The editors of this reader fill an empty niche both by defining the field of queer economics and by bringing together into one volume many of the salient early articles in the field as well as important recent contributions.

A brief introductory essay sets out the reasons for and aims of the project. No book currently exists that consolidates what has been published up to this point in the field; nor does any other book try to define the field of queer economics. The reader consists of nine sections: why queer economics?, barriers to the study of queer economics, queer demography, queer political economy, queer economic history, queer labor economics, queer consumer economics, queer urban economics, and queer political finance. Each section contains a short introduction that defines the topic at hand and provides an introduction to each of the key readings.

The field is related both to a broader literature in economics that considers the economic outcomes of various minority and oppressed groups, as well as to the growing literature in queer studies, most of which does not address economics at all, or only tangentially. This book is necessary reading for students in research areas including political economy, urban studies, economics, economic history and demographic economics.

Joyce P. Jacobsen is Andrews Professor of Economics at Wesleyan University, Connecticut, USA.

Adam Zeller is Manager of Digital Merchandizing and Marketing, Starz Media, New York, USA.

Queer Economics

A Reader

Edited by

Joyce Jacobsen and Adam Zeller

Routledge
Taylor & Francis Group

LONDON AND NEW YORK

First published 2008
by Routledge
2 Park Square, Milton Park, Abingdon, Oxon OX14 4RN

Simultaneously published in the USA and Canada
by Routledge
270 Madison Ave, New York, NY 10016

Routledge is an imprint of the Taylor & Francis Group, an Informa business

Typeset in Perpetua and Bell Gothic by
RefineCatch Limited, Bungay, Suffolk
Printed and bound in Great Britain by
Antony Rowe Ltd, Chippenham, Wiltshire

British Library Cataloguing in Publication Data
A catalogue record for this book is available from the British Library

Library of Congress Cataloging in Publication Data
Queer economics : a reader / edited by Joyce Jacobsen and Adam Zeller.
    p. cm.
    Includes bibliographical references and index.
1. Gays—United States—Economic conditions.   2. Gay consumers—United States.
3. Lesbian consumers—United States.   4. Homosexuality—Economic aspects.
I. Jacobsen, Joyce P.   II. Zeller, Adam.
    HQ76.3.U5Q43 2007
    330.086'64—dc22

                                                                2007011487

ISBN 10: 0–415–77170–6 (hbk)
ISBN 10: 0–415–77169–2 (pbk)
ISBN 10: 0–203–93945–X (ebk)

ISBN 978–0–415–77170–2 (hbk)
ISBN 978–0–415–77169–6 (pbk)
ISBN 978–0–203–93945–1 (ebk)

Adam: *To Ryan*
Joyce: *To Bill, Catherine, and Kenneth*

Contents

Acknowledgements

The publishers would like to thank the following for permission to reprint material:

M. V. Lee Badgett and Rhonda M. Williams, "The Economics of Sexual Orientation: Establishing a Research Agenda," originally published in *Feminist Studies*, vol. 18, no. 3 (Fall 1992): 649–57, by permission of the publisher, *Feminist Studies*, Inc.

M. V. Lee Badgett, "Gender, Sexuality, and Sexual Orientation: All in the Feminist Family?" originally published in *Feminist Economics*, vol. 1, no. 1 (Spring 1995): 121–39, by permission of the publisher, *Feminist Studies*, Inc. <http://www.tandf.co.uk/journals>.

Colleen Lamos, "Opening Questions," *Feminist Economics*, vol. 1, no. 2 (Summer 1995): 59–62, by permission of the publisher, *Feminist Studies*, Inc. <http://www.tandf.co.uk/journals>.

Marieka M. Klawitter, "Why Aren't More Economists Doing Research on Sexual Orientation?" *Feminist Economics*, vol. 4, no. 2 (Summer 1998): 55–9, by permission of the publisher, *Feminist Studies*, Inc. <http://www.tandf.co.uk/journals>.

Kyle D. Kauffman, "Uncovering a Quantitative History of Gays and Lesbians in the United States," *Feminist Economics*, vol. 4, no. 2 (Summer 1998) : 61–4, by permission of the publisher, *Feminist Studies*, Inc. <http://www.tandf.co.uk/journals>.

Dan Black, Gary Gates, Seth Sanders, and Lowell Taylor, "Demographics of the Gay and Lesbian Population in the United States: Evidence from Available Systematic Data Sources," *Demography*, vol. 37, no. 2 (May 2000):

139–54, by permission of the authors and the Population Association of America.

Voon Chin Phua and Gayle Kaufman, "Using the Census to Profile Same-Sex Cohabitation: A Research Note," *Population Research and Policy Review*, vol. 18, no. 4 (1999): 373–86. © Kluwer Academic Publishers. Reprinted by permission of Kluwer Academic Publishers.

Prue Hyman, "Lesbians and Gay Men Flirting with/Disengaging from Vital Statistics: Same Sex Relationships and the NZ Census 1971/2001," *Hecate*, vol. 29, no. 2 (2003): 248–60. Reprinted by permission of publisher and author.

Richard R. Cornwall, "Queer Political Economy: The Social Articulation of Desire," in *Homo Economics: capitalism, community, and lesbian and gay life*, eds Amy Gluckman and Betsy Reed. © Routledge 1997. Reprinted by permission of the publisher.

Jeffner Allan, "Lesbian Economics," in *Sinuosities, Lesbian Poetic Politics*. © Indiana University Press, 1996. Reprinted by permission of Indiana University Press.

John D'Emilio, "Capitalism and Gay Identity," in *Powers of Desire: the politics of sexuality*, eds Ann Snitow, Christine Stansell, and Sharon Thompson. © Monthly Review Press, 1983. Reprinted by permission of Monthly Review Press.

Julie Matthaei, "The Sexual Division of Labor, Sexuality, and Lesbian/Gay Liberation: Towards a Marxist-Feminist Analysis of Sexuality in U.S. Capitalism," in *Homo Economics: capitalism, community, and lesbian and gay life*, eds Amy Gluckman and Betsy Reed, Routledge, 1997. Original version in *Review of Radical Political Economics*, vol. 27, no. 2 (1995): 1–37. © *Review of Radical Political Economics*, 1995. Reprinted by permission of Sage Publications, Inc.

M. V. Lee Badgett, "The Wage Effects of Sexual Orientation Discrimination," *Industrial and Labor Relations Review*, vol. 48, no. 4 (1995): 726–39. © Cornell University. Reprinted by permission of Cornell University.

Erik Plug and Peter Berkhout, "Effects of Sexual Preferences on Earnings in the Netherlands," *Journal of Population Economics*, vol. 17, no. 1 (2004): 117–31. © Springer-Verlag. Reprinted by permission of Springer-Verlag.

Doris Weichselbaumer, "Sexual Orientation Discrimination in Hiring," Reprinted from *Labour Economics*, 10: 629–42. © 2003, with permission from Elsevier.

Amy Gluckman and Betsy Reed, "The Gay Marketing Moment," in *Homo Economics: capitalism, community, and lesbian and gay life*, eds Amy Gluckman and Betsy Reed, Routledge, 1997. Original version in *Dollars & Sense*, November/December (1993). Reprinted by permission of *Dollars & Sense*, a progressive economics magazine <www.dollarsandsense.org>.

Lisa Peñaloza, "We're Here, We're Queer, and We're Going Shopping! A Critical Perspective on the Accommodation of Gays and Lesbians in the U.S. Marketplace," in *Gays, Lesbians, and Consumer Behavior: theory, practice, and research issues in marketing*, ed. Daniel L. Wardlow, *Journal of Homosexuality*, vol. 31, no.1/2 (1996): 9–41. © The Haworth Press. Reprinted by permission of The Haworth Press, Binghamton, New York.

Andrew S. Walters and Maria-Cristina Curran, "Excuse Me, Sir? May I Help You and Your Boyfriend?": Salespersons' Differential Treatment of Homosexual and Straight Customers," in *Gays, Lesbians, and Consumer Behavior: theory, practice, and research issues in marketing*, ed. Daniel L. Wardlow *Journal of Homosexuality* vol. 31, no. 1/2 (1996): 135–52. © The Haworth Press. Reprinted by permission of The Haworth Press, Binghamton, New York.

Lawrence Knopp, "Gentrification and Gay Neighborhood Formation in New Orleans: A Case Study," in *Homo Economics: capitalism, community, and lesbian and gayl life*, eds Amy Gluckman and Betsy Reed, Routledge, 1997. Reprinted from *Political Geography*, 9, Lawrence Knopp, "Theoretical Implications of Gay Involvement in an Urban Land Market," 337–52. © 1990, with permission from Elsevier.

Gill Valentine and Tracey Skelton, "Finding Oneself, Losing Oneself: The Lesbian and Gay 'Scene' as a Paradoxical Space," *International Journal of Urban and Regional Research*, vol. 27, no. 4 (2003): 849–66. © Blackwell Publishing. Reprinted by permission of Blackwell Publishing.

James Alm, M. V. Lee Badgett, and Leslie Whittington, "Wedding Bell Blues: The Income Tax Consequences of Legalizing Same-Sex Marriage," *National Tax Journal*, vol. 53, no. 2 (June 2000): 201–14. Reprinted by permission of *The National Tax Journal*.

David L. Chambers, "What If? The Legal Consequences of Marriage and the Legal Needs of Lesbian and Gay Male Couples," *Michigan Law Review*, vol. 95, no. 2 (1996): 447–91. Reprinted by permission of author and *Michigan Law Review*, Ann Arbor.

INTRODUCTION

■ Joyce Jacobsen and Adam Zeller

THIS READER ORIGINATED AS THE OUTPUT from a tutorial in queer economics proposed by Adam and supervised by Joyce at Wesleyan University during Spring 2000. Adam wrote the initial commentary and selected the original articles. We have subsequently reworked and expanded the project to incorporate additional readings, discussion, and web links. We originally planned the project as a freestanding website aid for students who wanted to take a tutorial in queer economics. Subsequent to a conversation with Rob Langham, Routledge's Senior Editor for Economics, we realized that the project might serve in this pedagogical role better as a published reader that would include the full text of original articles on the various topics.

This brief introduction sets out the reasons for and aims of the project. No other book currently exists that consolidates what has been published up to this point in the field; nor does any book try to define fully what comprises the field of queer economics. However, this is a field poised to take off, and there has been an increased number (though still small) of research contributions in this area, indicating a substantial uptick of interest in the topics contained herein. We consider this field as related both to a broader literature in economics that considers the causes and consequences of differential economic outcomes for various minority and otherwise disadvantaged groups, as well as related to the growing literature in queer studies, most of which addresses economics not at all or only tangentially. Thus the reader fills an empty niche in publishing both by aiding in defining the field of queer economics and by bringing together into one volume many of the salient early articles in the field as well as some of the important recent contributions and some lesser-known contributions.

We (hesitantly) define queer economics as the examination of and response to the effects of heteronormativity both on economic outcomes and on economics as a discipline. Queer economics can be thought of as having the same relationship to the economics of sexual orientation as, say, the related area of feminist economics has to the economics of gender. It implies a more active critique of the field of economics rather than a simple description of a subdivision of interest within economics. Nonetheless, one cannot exist without the other. Without first knowing something of the patterns and policies that exist in the world, one cannot begin to question why these patterns and policies have occurred and why they may be so resistant to change. Hence the two types of economics are intertwined and treated at some times by some writers as synonymous when the distinction is less important to draw. At other times the distinction is key, particularly when the topic turns to power; that is, to the realm of political economy.

The reader consists of nine sections, as sketched below, each of which contains a short introduction that defines the topic at hand and introduces the two or three readings in the section. A few broad discussion questions are included in each section's introduction that can serve to motivate discussion in class settings, as well as indicate the themes we find to be of interest for each section. Each section's introduction also references related readings and web sources.

Section One, "Why Queer Economics?," considers why there is a need for examining markets and government policies for evidence of heteronormative biases and outlines how leading scholars in the area have attempted to begin their studies.

Section Two, "Barriers to the Study of Queer Economics," outlines the types of problems scholars have faced in studying the questions of interest to queer economics, and the types of solutions some have devised, as well as the increasing availability of data for answering these questions.

Section Three, "Queer Demography," provides some background both of the types of patterns we are beginning to understand regarding the demography of sexual orientation and of the approaches scholars have taken to developing our understanding of these demographics.

Section Four, "Queer Political Economy," addresses directly the effects both on the economics discipline and on society in general of heteronormative thinking, and considers how an alternative to heteronormativity could be structured and what effects such an alternative might have on research and on outcomes.

Section Five, "Queer Economic History," considers how one might understand past economic history through the queer economics lens and also how the past affects the present and how past analytical techniques affect present analytical techniques.

Section Six, "Queer Labor Economics," outlines results in this very active area of current research regarding differential labor market outcomes (including employment, earnings, and occupational representation) by sexual orientation and issues regarding the effects of being "out" in the workplace.

Section Seven, "Queer Consumer Economics," describes and discusses differential consumption patterns and differential marketing by sexual orientation, as well as considering the issues surrounding the desirability of such differences.

Section Eight, "Queer Urban Economics," discusses location and home ownership patterns by sexual orientation, and documents the existence and nature of enclaves, or groupings, related to sexual orientation, as well as their causes and consequences.

Section Nine, "Queer Public Finance," considers the interaction of the legal system with the market and touches upon numerous public policy issues with economic consequences, such as the expansion of laws regarding marriage and partnership rights to same-sex couples, including inheritance, pensions, child raising, and family benefit coverage.

We titled these sections so as to correspond to some of the traditional areas of interest within economics so as to show how in each of these areas queer issues and topics may be incorporated. We do not consider these nine subdivisions as the limits of the scope of queer economic analysis, though they give some indication of where many researchers' interests have been to date.

We see this reader as having a place not only as a reference source for those researchers interested in seeing the early articles in this area but also as a supplementary text for economics courses covering discrimination and gender-related topics when instructors might want to broaden their coverage into this area. The reader can also be used in various interdisciplinary studies courses (e.g., American studies, queer studies, gender studies) that want to cover social science work in the area of queer studies. While all of the articles were written in English and many discuss US patterns, several of the articles explicitly consider patterns in other countries and this is a likely area of further research in the years to come; thus the book has potential international appeal as well.

We thank all the authors of the included pieces for having the vision that led them to write these works and for carrying through on that vision. We also thank Wesleyan University for long-standing intellectual support; Rob Langham for his encouragement and support of this project; Henry Abelove, Claire Potter, and Diana Strassman for their bibliographic suggestions; Dustin Schur for his research assistance; Margaret Milnes for her contractual consultation; and our families and friends for their influences on what we have accomplished in our lives, of which bringing forth this reader is a salient part.

Why queer economics?

M ANY USEFUL STUDIES IN ECONOMICS that utilize gender, race, ethnicity, socio-economic status, age, disability status, and countless other categorizations of the human race have been conducted, resulting in remarkable insight being gained on these subjects. But sexuality and sexual orientation, if considered at all, have often been considered as sidebars to gender studies and, until recently, this state of discourse has been generally accepted.

Sexuality has long been a misrepresented field in economics. Simply addressing this topic as a gender-related issue creates a viewpoint that does not allow for the complete consideration of the aspects unique to this field. The typical dual-type male–female or man–woman model used in most economic applications (when sex or gender is even considered at all) does not apply perfectly to situations involving lesbians, gays, transgenders, transsexuals, bisexuals, and other categorizations that do not fit neatly into a dual-type framework. For one thing, we cannot assume that the choices and opportunities for these various types of individuals are identical sets. In addition, where the "family unit" is concerned, even larger discrepancies can be found between types of family units as governments, conventional social structures, and the community as a whole place various limitations on the ability of various units to form and prosper.

The readings in this section explicate the need for more work on the economics of sexuality and sexual orientation. They argue that a dissection of existing heterosexist models reveals that rather than attempting to fit homosexuality in an existing train of thought, a new mold must be created. However, while gender, sexuality, and sexual orientation are separate categories of inquiry, there is no denial of the connection between the categories. Only through the study of the fields individually can the borderline be drawn clearly, and this is exactly why the lens of Queer Economics is essential.

In the first chapter in this section, "The economics of sexual orientation: establishing a research agenda" (1992), M. V. Lee Badgett and Rhonda Williams illustrate some of the issues within the economics profession regarding the study of gender, sexuality, and sexual orientation by describing the first economics conference session on the economics of sexual orientation, held at the American Economic Association meetings in January 1992. From their descriptions of the four papers at that session (none of which, to our knowledge, has been published subsequently), one can see the initial points of disagreement with conventional economics as applied to issues of sexual orientation

The other two chapters in this section create dialogue around the question of the relationship between research focused on gender and research focused on sexuality and sexual orientation. "Gender, sexuality, and sexual orientation: all in the feminist family?" (1995) was published in the inaugural issue of the pathbreaking journal *Feminist Economics*. In this chapter (which refers to the 1992 conference session), M. V. Lee Badgett argues that gender is not a sufficient focus for developing an economics of sexuality and sexual orientation. In particular, families that develop on the basis of same-sex couples need to be conceptualized as having a different nature than male–female couples, including potentially different patterns of task specialization within the household. "Opening questions" (1995), by Colleen Lamos, was published in the following issue of *Feminist Economics*. While Lamos echoes a number of Badgett's points regarding the importance of investigating diverse family structures, she also argues that Badgett does not acknowledge the gendered nature of division of labor that occurs within same-sex couples and other family units. Lamos brings up an interesting point: if domestic partners benefits are made widely available for same-sex couples, does this tend to encourage development of ossification into assigned roles within these families, much as it may have within heterosexual couples?

Readers who want to examine further the issues surrounding introduction and definition of this new field of endeavor can consult a number of other pieces. Badgett, one of the leading researchers in the area of queer economics, has contributed a number of other pieces (some with co-authors) that help to define the field and summarize relevant literatures, including works from related disciplines (Badgett 1995, 1998, 2001; Badgett and Hyman 1998; Cornwall and Badgett 1999). *Feminist Economics* has published a number of pieces in the area of queer economics, including a section which serves as an introduction to the area and the work to date in one of its early (1998) issues; several of the pieces appear later in this reader and others can also serve as background (Badgett 1998; Badgett and Hyman 1998; Cornwall 1998; Patterson 1998). An early anthology focusing on queer political economy and economic organization issues is Gluckman and Reed (1997), which contributes three pieces to the current collection. For professional economists, a leading event in making them aware of gender and sexual orientation issues was the public discussion by leading economist Donald (now Deirdre) McCloskey of coming to terms with his/her crossgender orientation (McCloskey 1995).

Readers desiring additional background in the general area of queer studies may want to consult one of a number of recent compendia/handbooks/readers in this area (Dynes 1990; Abelove 1993; Duberman 1997; Richardson and Seidman 2002; Stein 2003; Valocchi and Corber 2003). Key single-author books include Butler (1999), Escoffier (1998), and Abelove (2005). Two key journals in the area are *GLQ* and *Journal of Homosexuality*. Cornwall and Badgett (1999) give a quick, economist-oriented introduction to sexual orientation; Stein (1999) provides a thorough discussion. Those desiring more reading specifically in the area of queer theory also have several recent comprehensive books available (Warner 1993; Turner 2000; Sullivan 2003; Wilchins 2004).

DISCUSSION QUESTIONS

1   How do you define the three terms of gender, sexuality, and sexual orientation?
2   How do the dynamics of gender, sexuality, and sexual orientation differ and, as a result, do they require separate analyses? If so, how might the analyses differ?
3   How might standard economic models of human behavior, including models predicting division of labor within households, be challenged by newer models that take sexuality and/or sexual orientation into consideration?
4   In what areas of economics do you expect that a differentiation between gender, sexuality, and/or sexual orientation will prove important to make?
5   Can existing studies that take gender into account assist in designing studies of sexual orientation? If so, in what ways?

REFERENCES

Abelove, H. (ed.) (1993) *The Lesbian and Gay Studies Reader*, London and New York: Routledge.

—— (2005) *Deep Gossip*, Minneapolis: University of Minnesota Press.

Badgett, M. V. L. (1995) "The last of the modernists?," *Feminist Economics*, 1: 63–5.

—— (1998) "Some readings related to lesbian and gay economics: an annotated bibliography," *Feminist Economics*, 4: 111–16.

——(2001) *Money, Myths, and Change: the economic lives of lesbians and gay men*, Chicago and London: University of Chicago Press.

Badgett, M. V. L. and Hyman, P. (1998) "Introduction: towards lesbian, gay and bisexual perspectives in economics: why and how they may make a difference," *Feminist Economics*, 4: 49–54.

Butler, J. (1999) *Gender Trouble, tenth anniversary edition*, New York and London: Routledge.

Cornwall, R. R. (1998) "A primer on queer theory for economists interested in social identities," *Feminist Economics*, 4: 73–82.

Cornwall, R. and Badgett, M. V. L. (1999) "Sexual orientation," in M. Lewis and J. Peterson (eds) *Encyclopedia of Feminist Economics*, Cheltenham, UK, and Northampton, Mass.: Edward Elgar.

Duberman, M. (ed.) (1997) *A Queer World: the Center for Lesbian and Gay Studies reader*, New York: New York University Press.

Dynes, W. R. (ed.) (1990) *Encyclopedia of Homosexuality*, New York: Garland Press.

Escoffier, J. (1998) *American Homo: community and perversity*, Berkeley, Calif.: University of California Press.

GLQ: A Journal of Lesbian and Gay Studies, Durham, N.C.: Duke University Press (<http://glq.dukejournals.org/>).

Gluckman, A. and Reed, B. (eds) (1997) *Homo Economics: capitalism, community, and lesbian and gay life*, New York: Routledge.

Journal of Homosexuality, Haworth Press, (<http://www.haworthpress.com/>).

McCloskey, D. N. (1995) "Some news that at least will not bore you," *Eastern Economic Journal*, 21: 551–3.

Patterson, P. L. (1998) "Including gays and lesbians in the economics curriculum," *Feminist Economics*, 4: 65–72.

Richardson, D. and Seidman, S. (eds) (2002) *Handbook of Lesbian and Gay Studies*, London and Thousand Oaks, Calif.: Sage Publications.

Stein, E. (1999) *The Mismeasure of Desire: the science, theory, and ethics of sexual orientation*, Oxford: Oxford University Press.

Stein, M. (ed.) (2003) *Encyclopedia of Lesbian, Gay, Bisexual, and Transgender History in America*, New York: Scribners.

Sullivan, N. (2003) *A Critical Introduction to Queer Theory*, New York: New York University.

Turner, W. B. (2000) *A Genealogy of Queer Theory*, Philadelphia, Pa.: Temple University Press.

Valocchi, S. and Corber, R. J. (2003) *Queer Studies: an interdisciplinary reader*, Oxford and Malden, Mass.: Blackwell.

Warner, M. (ed.) and Social Text Collective (1993) *Fear of a Queer Planet: queer politics and social theory*, Minneapolis: University of Minnesota Press.

Wilchins, R. (2004) *Queer Theory, Gender Theory: an instant primer*, Los Angeles: Alyson Books.

Chapter 1

M. V. Lee Badgett and Rhonda M. Williams

THE ECONOMICS OF SEXUAL ORIENTATION: ESTABLISHING A RESEARCH AGENDA

From *Feminist Studies* 1992, 18 (3): 649–57

> *"Economics has gained the title of queen of the social sciences by choosing solved political problems as its domain."*
>
> — Abba Lerner, 1972

MORE SO THAN MOST SOCIAL THEORISTS, neoclassical economists have managed to pursue their research and policy agendas untouched by a generation of feminist scholarship. And Abba Lerner, in the above quotation, succinctly articulates the self-understanding with which mainstream economists shield themselves from conceptual scrutiny. It is also a standpoint which renders orthodox economics profoundly hostile to feminist arguments that socially constructed forms of gendered and racialized power affect the workings of existing capitalist economies.

Within the economics profession, those critical of the neoclassical commitment to methodological individualism[1] – institutionalists, post-Keynesians, neo-Ricardians, neo-Marxists, and Marxists – labor under the incomplete hegemony of the orthodoxy. Yet the political economists, including some feminists, persist, building their own professional organizations and research institutions, organizing and writing in their own journals. Feminist economists know too well the political and policy influence wielded by our profession. We know that leaving the formation of public policy and the construction of political discourse to the queens of social science is a dangerous strategy.

January 1992 witnessed the coming out of an emergent community of scholars who join feminists in challenging the overtly androcentric and heterosexist content of neoclassical theorizing and research. Some of these challengers organized the first session on "The Economics of Sexual Orientation: Establishing a Research Agenda" for the meetings of the American Economic Association held in New Orleans.[2] Robert Anderson began the session with a discussion of "Economic Issues Related to Sexual Orientation" and was followed by Richard Cornwall's presentation of "Notes on a Research Agenda for Economists Inspired by the Coming Out of Lesbian, Gay, and Bisexual Communities: The Role of Markets in the Social Construction of Identities." Kathryn Larson addressed "The Economic Status of Lesbians: The State of the Art," and M.V. Lee Badgett discussed "Labor Market Discrimination: Economic Issues for Gay Men and Lesbians." Heidi Hartmann and Rhonda M. Williams were discussants.

Cornwall's theoretical analysis challenged two long-standing neoclassical tenets: that competitive markets decrease social inequality and that individual preferences, or "tastes," are both exogenous to their models and are unchanged by market, community, political, or familial life. Specifically, he explores the economic implications of community, here defined as a group of people that share "a significant amount of connectedness in their social relations," embrace a common set of social norms, and are more likely to interact with one another than with persons outside the community. Communities are economically significant because they form and maintain "social capital," a structure of social relations which enhances productivity. Communities sustain their social connectedness via the articulation of distinct voices, the "attitudes and perspectives based on a distinctive experience which has been shared, not in totality, but in large part, by members of the community."

Social capital includes the relations which enhance information exchanges, self-esteem levels, credibility, and/or levels of trust. Cornwall argues that social capital is economically significant for two reasons. First, it determines the costs of organizing and maintaining economic transactions; second, it creates incentives to distinguish insiders from outsiders.

Consider a lesbian in search of employment as a legal assistant. She can reduce her search costs by beginning with the paralegals and lawyers in her lesbian support group or biking club. Conversely, in a broader heterosexist community, the price for access to the nonlesbian career networks could be the denial of the same woman's voice as a lesbian. Moreover, virulent heterosexism hinders the formation of lesbian and gay communities, thus constraining the formation of queer-specific social capital. Cornwall concludes that "the formation of community and the articulation of voice appear to be interdependent and simultaneously determined."

The creation and deployment of social capital creates community members and nonmembers. Insofar as nonmembers are sociopolitical subordinates to members, the existence of social capital mediates community members' decisions whether to cooperate or take advantage of outsiders. Cornwall employs game theory to demonstrate an intuitively compelling proposition: the superordinate insiders (straights) have material incentive – the ability to restrict access to social capital – to collaborate with the reproduction of social hierarchies and social identities that define outsiders. Those outside the community are fair game for exploitation. Community members can take advantage of them with impunity at least, and under certain circumstances (e.g., the existence of a limited supply of high-wage jobs) actually benefit. Hence, economic interactions construct social identities and communities, and individuals have incentives to cooperate with members, exploit outsiders, and enforce the definition of community via the sanctioning of defectors.

Cornwall's work is significant in its incorporation of the social nature of economic life. Economists working within the traditions of political economy have long embraced the notion that the social nature of production significantly affects exchange relations Cornwall's analysis is an invitation to mainstream theorists to address systematically political economy's insights.

Kathryn Larson finds that conventional neoclassical economists have naught to say about the economic status of lesbians. The "state of the art" is currently in "no state": there is no body of economic literature on lesbian households. It is this very absence that Larson addresses via a systematic consideration of lesbian invisibility and a discussion of the implications of visibility for theorizing gender inequality. Institutionalized heterosexuality has, of course, restricted women's economic activities, although the precise form of these constraints reflects the historical complexities of women's kinship relations across classes and racial ethnic communities.

Larson's work presupposes basic familiarity with the mainstream theory of household economics and its assumed heterosexuality, which can be summarized as follows. Neoclassical theorists explain women's subordinate labor market status as a consequence of either women's assumed preferences for the unpaid work of species reproduction or the heterosexual couple's rational response to the gender wage gap. Because economists emphasize the relationship between specialization and efficiency – the former promotes the latter gender-based differences in tastes explain men's "specialization" in market activities and women's confinement to the domestic sphere. Orthodox theorists employ this model to explain a variety of phenomena. Women pursue education not to increase earning power but in order to marry high-earning men; because women know that they will have sporadic labor force participation due to child and elder care responsibilities, we choose occupations that do not penalize such absences.

These occupations also tend to have low wage-growth rates, thus explaining the gender earnings gap.

Liberal and feminist economists have waged theoretical and empirical battles against the explanatory power of this paradigm for more than a decade.[3] However, as Larson observes, they have not addressed the growing numbers of women who live/choose a lesbian life or women who never choose the wife/mother route. Like their orthodox colleagues, the liberals and feminists to date have not theorized women's economic behavior in households without men. The "new" home economics and critiques thereof clearly bear the marks of heterosexual hegemony.

Lesbian sociocultural invisibility carries over into social science data. As Larson observes, the absence of large panel data sets which include information on lesbians clearly inhibits the development of an applied research agenda for those who might wish to study lesbian lives statistically. Census data obstruct researchers interested in sorting lesbians from nonlesbian households and individuals. The 1990 census will enable researchers to identify lesbian and gay households who chose to report their status. For those who did not report, the census will again count single lesbians as single women/one-person households and lesbian households as female-headed families or nonfamilies (depending on the presence of children or persons related to the first person listed).

Data gathered by noneconomists suggest the importance of making the above distinctions. Larson's survey of existing studies reveals prima facie evidence that lesbians and nonlesbians may differ significantly in rates of labor force participation, levels of education, household income, and demand for children, just to name a few characteristics. For example, surveys from the early 1980s report that more lesbians than wives and cohabiting women worked full time; a 1991 survey reported that the lesbian household's average income is higher than the U.S. average. All studies to date indicate a more equitable sharing of household work by lesbians than heterosexuals. However, many of the existing surveys must be approached with caution, given small sample sizes and oversampling of whites.

The existing studies clearly suggest that lesbians are not just like single straight women and men or heterosexual parents in regard to economic behavior. At the very least, that hypothesis warrants testing. Larson offers several questions conducive to such tests. For example, what factors affect the stability of lesbian household formation? Do lesbians systematically differ from nonlesbians in their household division of labor and demand for children? How have urbanization and increased economic opportunities for women changed the relative economic costs of living a nonheterosexual life? How do lesbians differ from one another and from nonlesbians along lines of race, class, ethnicity, religion, and nationality?

Larson's solution to the data problem is to develop a questionnaire of her own which she is circulating through an extended network of personal and professional contacts. The nonrandom nature of such a sampling technique will prohibit generalizations, but her data will provide the foundations for more hypothesis generation and a basis for future comparisons.

M.V. Lee Badgett's paper explores the role of sexual orientation in determining an individual's employment status and income. Although she approaches the topic from an academic perspective, Badgett's ultimate concern is public policy, because the possibility of discrimination puts lesbian, gay, and bisexual workers at a disadvantage in the labor market. Antidiscrimination policies cover sexual orientation in six states,[4] some local jurisdictions, and many private companies. Such policies protect some employees, as does the judicial chipping away of the employment-at-will doctrine that has traditionally allowed private employers to hire and fire as they please. This protection is meager, however, and is neither widely applicable nor reliable.

When surveyed, many lesbians and gay men have said that they have been fired, harrassed, not hired, or not promoted because of their sexual orientation. A measure often used to demonstrate sex or race discrimination – individual or household income – reveals an unexpected pattern. Surveys that collect such data usually find incomes for the lesbian and/or gay respondents that are *higher* than national averages. Assessing both kinds of evidence is difficult given problems with sampling methods. Other characteristics of those surveyed show that mainly highly educated, urban, white lesbians and gay men return surveys or identify themselves as lesbian or gay when asked by pollsters. Badgett and Larson reach the same conclusion: none of these surveys is representative of the population of people identifying as lesbian or gay (or bisexual in some surveys) or of people with same-sex sexual partners.

Interpreting and extending these survey results requires a more thorough understanding of how sexual orientation affects one's labor market position, and this understanding must be developed in the context of other structural factors determining individuals' labor market choices and positions, that is, race, class, and gender. Badgett follows Jeffrey Escoffier and Beth Schneider in developing a theoretical framework centered on workplace disclosure of sexual identity. Because the social dimensions of work environments vary, someone may choose an occupation or job that allows her/him a desired degree of passing or of disclosure. Once in a work situation, the worker's disclosure decisions are likely to be influenced by the social environment and by a decision-making process that could be characterized as a cost-benefit or investment process. Costs include the potential loss of job and/or income and would be weighted by the likelihood that coworkers or bosses would react adversely to disclosure and by the lesbian or gay worker's ability to manage adverse reactions. Potential benefits from disclosure include psychological benefits (e.g., enhanced self-esteem) and political or economic benefits (e.g., removing heterosexist biases in compensation).

This already complex hypothesized process is further complicated when placing it in the context of persistent discrimination by race and sex. Gay white men may have developed particular strategies of disclosure well-suited to their economic position as white men. Dealing with sexism and/or racism places women and men of color and white women in different situations regarding costs and benefits, and the effects of economic inequality are likely to be evident both in workplace strategies and in the willingness to give reliable answers to survey questions on sexual orientation Differences in adaptations and economic position should also inform policy debates, particularly the consideration of affirmative action for lesbians and gay men.

Given these complex relationships, the usual econometric method for detecting discrimination – adding a dummy variable for sexual orientation to a multiple regression explaining income or employment – will not properly capture the effect of being lesbian, gay, or bisexual. Badgett suggests more appropriate research strategies that range from more sophisticated econometric modeling to case studies of workplaces to matched pair testing, all of which are designed to detect some form of employment discrimination. Data collection must be designed with attention to the distinction between behavior and identity and with some way of estimating sample selection and response biases.

Anderson's paper broadens the focus on public policy to economists' potential contributions to a number of issues related to lesbians and gay men. He first asks how much lesbians and gay men, who pay taxes, actually benefit from the existing distribution of public resources to areas including the arts, health services, and substance abuse treatment, among others. A second area involves further economic analysis of the HIV/AIDS epidemic. Work by economists in this area has largely focused on the costs of treatment and aggregated estimates of the economic cost of the epidemic. Notable exceptions also provide examples of other useful kinds of economic research. Robert M. Anderson and John M. Quigley[5] have done economic analyses of California referenda on AIDS policy (Propositions 64 and 102), showing that these proposed policies, for example, reporting, contact tracing, and quarantines, would result in large costs to taxpayers without significant public health benefits.

A third area addressed by Anderson is the extension of employee benefits to domestic partners of lesbians and gay men. Anderson's cost-benefit study of domestic partner benefits in San Francisco[6] is an example of the value of economic analysis. An important part of this analysis was a survey mailed to a random sample of city employees asking about partnership status and the demand for various benefits. Responses were anonymous and the return rate was high (35 percent). With these data, Anderson was able to estimate that allowing partners to purchase health insurance (the city only covers employees) would cost San Francisco $1.1 million.

At the most general level, all the papers presented at the January 1992 panel took some standard economic techniques or approaches into an area almost completely untouched by economists.[7] All showed that economists' tools and perspectives are potentially useful in understanding the economic dimensions and decisions in the lives of lesbian, gay, and bisexual people.

But expanding the agenda of economics to include these questions also challenges the underpinnings of the discipline itself. Larson's analysis of lesbian invisibility challenges economic theory to pick apart its assumptions about the nature and behavior of families and households and to rebuild on a more inclusive and nonsexist, nonheterosexist foundation. Using conventional economic assumptions and methodologies, Cornwall shows that market behavior both affects and is affected by social identities. Badgett shows how nonmainstream theories and empirical methods are necessary to situate sexual orientation in its fuller social context, going beyond the individualistic, narrowly constructed approach of mainstream discrimination models.

As the panel participants noted, a common issue in future work concerns data availability and reliability. Anderson has shown that useful data can be collected, although his experience was at a very local level with a limited population. Larson is currently conducting her own survey of lesbian households using traditional snowball-sampling techniques. Construction of a larger, more representative survey remains a distant goal, but Badgett suggests that anticipation and accommodation of potential problems can allow analysts to adjust for sample selection problems.

One of the goals of this panel was to inspire other economists to add issues related to sexual orientation to their own research agendas. The discussions during and after the presentations in New Orleans generated new ideas and energy for many involved, but getting others with already established agendas to move in new directions will be difficult. This difficulty is compounded, of course, by the existence of homophobia and heterosexism within the economics profession.

Two of the panelists plan to present future work at next year's Allied Social Science Associations' meetings. Larson will be analyzing her survey data, and Badgett has collected some existing data sets that provide information on sexual orientation and labor market outcomes. A panel discussing this research and related work by Julie Matthaei (comparing neoclassical and Marxist feminist theories of the family) was proposed to the American Economic Association (AEA) and rejected. The fact that two panels proposed by the recently formed International Association for Feminist Economics were also rejected by the AEA suggests that the AEA program committee may be more interested in the political content than the quality of the panels.

Notes

1   Methodological individualism is the notion that economic outcomes are the result of impersonal market mechanisms balancing the behaviors of freely choosing, autonomous, and self-interested individuals.

2   Readers interested in the original papers can contact the authors at their respective institutions. Cornwall is at Middlebury College, Middlebury, Vermont; Larson teaches at Elon College, Elon, North Carolina; Anderson at the University of California at Berkeley; and Badgett at the University of Maryland. Other signs of movement against the mainstream include the forthcoming 1993 publication of Marianne Ferber and Julie Nelson's "Beyond Economic Man: Feminist Theory and Economics" (University of Chicago) and the July 1992 convening of the First Annual Conference on Feminist Economics by the International Association for Feminist Economics.

3   Empiricists have noted, for example, that there are no differences between the occupational distribution of women with more continuous labor market experience and women with less. Theorists have noted how the aforementioned model presupposes an absence of sex discrimination, which could account for women's labor market outcomes. Moreover, they have noted the circularity in arguments which assert that, on the one hand, women earn less because of their "preferences," and, on the other hand, women specialize in home work because of the gender wage gap.

4   The states are Connecticut, Hawaii, Massachusetts, New Jersey, Vermont, and Wisconsin.

5   Robert M. Anderson and John M. Quigley, "The Economic Impact of the Adoption of Proposition 64, the Larouche Initiative," *Working Paper*, No. 119 (Graduate School of Public Policy, University of California, Berkeley, August 1986). See also Anderson and Quigley's "The Economic Impact of the Adoption of Proposition 102, the Dannemeyer Initiative," *Working Paper* No. 153 (Graduate School of Public Policy, University of California, Berkeley, September 1988).

6   This survey and analysis are contained in "Approaching 2000: Meeting the Challenges to San Francisco's Families: *The Final Report of the Mayor's Task Force on Family Policy, June 13, 1990*" (San Francisco: Mayor's Office, 1990).

7   In addition to work by economists already cited, Richard Posner considers "homosexuality" from an explicitly neoclassical perspective in his recently published *Sex and Reason* (Cambridge: Harvard University Press, 1992).

Chapter 2

M. V. Lee Badgett

GENDER, SEXUALITY, AND SEXUAL ORIENTATION: ALL IN THE FEMINIST FAMILY?

From *Feminist Economics* 1995, 1 (1): 121–39

Introduction

DURING A LIVELY DISCUSSION of the economic relationships between women and men within families at the first IAFFE conference in 1992, I reminded my fellow participants that not all families are based on a heterosexual married couple. In addition to single-parent families, lesbians and gay men also form families that do not conform to the traditional male–female marital model. Kathryn Larson expanded on this point later in the conference in discussing the near complete invisibility of lesbian couples and households within economic theory and in empirical research on women and families.

Although neither of our comments generated much of a discussion at the time, their modest impact became apparent in other ways. In particular, in more than one subsequent presentation of a model of family economic behavior that weekend, the presenters specifically noted that their models could be applied to any kind of family, whether heterosexual or homosexual. While I welcomed the greater acknowledgment of lesbian and gay families, I have remained skeptical of the idea that economic models developed to explain the behavior of heterosexual families can be simply transferred to explain lesbian and gay families.

At the time of the conference, I had hoped that this initial acknowledgment was a harbinger of more inclusive feminist economic models to come. My intense interest in these questions is undoubtedly related to the fact that, as a lesbian, I must deal with these issues in a personal way every day. And as a feminist, I see the questions raised by considering sexual orientation as pointing to a need to rethink much economic and feminist thought on many topics. But in the two years since that conference, only a few economists – most of us self-identified feminists – appear to have made efforts to consider seriously whether existing theories are good explanations of the economic lives of lesbian, gay, and bisexual people, or to contemplate the broader implications of sexuality for economic theorizing.[1]

In the meantime, many economists who are feminists have continued to collectively and self-consciously identify our work as having some common feminist thread, even though we may come from different economic methodological perspectives. For example, Marianne Ferber and Julie Nelson (1993:9) support the practice of many feminist economists and social scientists of using gender rather than biological sex as the primary analytical category to understand women's experiences, where "gender is the *social meaning* given to biological differences between the sexes." Simply adding gender as an additional analytical category, however, risks universalizing "women," forgetting the very different experiences of women of different racial, ethnic, and class backgrounds and of different sexual orientations. Rhonda Williams (1993) warns of this universalizing tendency in some recent definitions of feminist economics which ignore important racial differences among women. Nancy Folbre suggests that "the real contribution of feminist theory lies in its efforts to reconceptualize the relationship between different forms of social inequality, rather than simply to empower women" (Folbre 1994: 268). Folbre analyzes social reproduction in the context of many different dimensions of collective action where groups (defined by gender, age, sexual orientation, race, class, and/or nation) act within "structures of constraint," or "sets of asset distributions, rules, norms, and preferences that empower given social groups" (p. 51). All of this is not to say that gender as an analytical category and feminism as a way of using that category to understand and break down the suppression of women have no uses. But to understand and facilitate change in the material circumstances of women requires a nuanced analysis incorporating the "divided loyalties and competing interests" (cf. Folbre 1994) of different groups of women and men.

In the next section of this essay, I argue that a focus on gender (and the use of gender-based family models) is, first of all, inadequate for the development of the economics of sexuality (broadly defined) because of important differences between "gender" and "sexuality" as analytical categories. Also, without separate attention to sexual orientation, which I use to refer to the aspect of sexuality based on the gender of one's sex partners, the experiences of lesbians as women and gay men as men may remain invisible even within a feminist economic model.[2] Later in the paper, I will demonstrate the extent of this invisibility by analyzing examples from prominent economists who study gender and families, with a particular emphasis on the work of Gary Becker. Becker has explicitly used his family model to "explain" some aspects of gay people's family lives, making him one of the few economists to acknowledge the existence of such families (Larson 1992). Barbara Bergmann's work while feminist, reflects economists' general inattention to possible differences in the concerns, interests, and behaviors of lesbian, gay, and bisexual people. As I will show, the gender-centered models of Becker and most other economists are seriously inadequate once the existence of sexual orientation as an issue is acknowledged.

Making lesbian, gay, and bisexual people visible within economic theory requires more than forcing them into standard economic conceptions of family based on gender differences alone. I will argue that lesbian, gay, and bisexual people do not emulate the heterosexual marriage model when creating interpersonal relationships characterized by love, commitment, sacrifice, and interdependence, in other words, in creating what we might commonly think of as a "family." One consequence of the academic homogenization of families is that economists tend to overlook the important legal, political, and cultural differences that shape the economic position and behavior of families formed by lesbian, gay, and bisexual people. Acknowledging this common limitation of economic modeling should encourage us to open up our research on families to consider how variations in sexual orientation might direct us to rethink the influence of gender norms and family legal institutions on economic behavior.

Recently I have seen first-hand another consequence of homogenizing lesbian and gay families. While feminists – both heterosexual and homosexual – have been busy theorizing about the family, lesbian, gay, and bisexual activists have been successfully organizing and lobbying for new legally and socially recognized forms of family relationships, often right under our academic noses in colleges and universities across the United States. These newly recognized family relationships, commonly called "domestic partnerships," represent an important step forward for gay people, both socially and materially. However, the structure and implementation of these new relationships are generally quite conservative, being modeled on a property-based heterosexual marriage ignoring potentially powerful feminist principles and underpinnings. Using the domestic partner movement in colleges and universities as a case study, I argue that the relatively conservative outcomes are at least partly the result of a failure of collective action in the form of heterosexual free-riding on the efforts of the lesbian, gay, and bisexual activists. This active rewriting of family definition and policy presents an important opportunity for feminists of all sexual orientations to affect what a "family" means and does.

Gender, sexuality, and sexual orientation

Why should feminist economists think about sexual orientation? How should feminist economists think about sexual orientation? One possible answer is that issues of gender and of sexuality are not just intertwined but are inseparable. In that case, a focus on gender-based economic theories will provide the essential tools for understanding sexuality, making issues related to sexual orientation a subfield of feminist economics. This would be a useful integration if sexuality explains a large part of gender oppression, and if gender oppression is at the root of oppression against lesbian, gay, and bisexual people. I will argue, however, that gender and sexuality constitute two separate analytical axes, and that simple gender-based economic models seriously misinterpret or implicitly omit the lives of lesbian, gay, and bisexual people.

To the extent that women's economic choices and well-being are limited by or structured around reproduction, the economic effects of gender and sexuality are closely connected. Even economists with empirically flawed and incomplete theories recognize some relationship between sexuality and gender. Posner's rational choice model of sexuality, for example, traces family organizational forms back to biologically determined differences between the sexes, mainly in terms of sex drive and reproductive roles.[3] (See Robert Anderson 1993 for a critique of Richard Posner's analysis and his use of questionable empirical information.) Outside of a family and reproductive context, sexuality has an important influence on women's labor market opportunities and experiences: both sexual harassment and employers' assumptions about women's likely fertility decisions have limited women's job opportunities.

Further, sexuality has an important influence on the social and legal treatment of individuals of differing sexual orientations. In one important article, for instance, Adrienne Rich (1983: 191) addresses the interactions between sexuality and gender in explaining the status of lesbians and heterosexual women:

> But whatever its origins, when we look hard and clearly at the extent and elaboration of measures designed to keep women within a male sexual purlieu, it becomes an inescapable question whether the issue we have to address as feminists is not simple "gender inequality," nor the domination of culture by males, nor mere "taboos against homosexuality," but the enforcement of heterosexuality for women as a means of assuring male right of physical, economical, and emotional access.

Similarly, a gender-based analysis which considers sexual orientation would be essential to understand the often troubled political and social relationships between lesbians and gay men.

One very concrete example of the connection between sexuality and gender is the argument that discrimination against lesbians and gay men is simply a form of gender discrimination: lesbians face discrimination because they love women instead of men, and gay men face discrimination because they love men instead of women. Using this interpretation to frame employment discrimination against gay men and lesbians as an illegal practice under Title VII has been unsuccessful, however (*Harvard Law Review* Editors 1991: 68–70). Judges have generally turned the sex discrimination argument around, pointing out that lesbians and gay men are treated in the same way, so no gender discrimination exists.[4] A plausible but as yet untried variant of this gender-based legal strategy argues that employment discrimination against lesbians and gay men is rooted in their violation of traditional gender roles, particularly those related to reproduction (*Harvard Law Review* Editors 1991: 17–18 and 70–1). A gender-based analysis was successful in one recent and potentially significant marriage case, however. The Hawaii Supreme Court ruled that marriage laws forbidding same-sex marriages violate the state's constitutional prohibition of sex discrimination. A lower court must now decide whether a compelling state interest exists for such a violation (Steven Homer 1994). Even with the possibility of one significant victory, the overall lack of success of this legal strategy has helped to make acquiring explicit protections against sexual orientation discrimination a priority of the lesbian and gay civil rights movement.

Although the failure of a particular legal strategy does not negate the possibility of a gender-based analysis of sexual orientation, the crucial question remains: can the study of sexuality be made equivalent to or be subsumed by the study of gender? Noted literary critic Eve Kosofsky Sedgwick argues persuasively that sexuality should constitute a separate analytical axis because many aspects of sexuality do not overlap with gender:

> An objection to this analogy [of sexuality with race or class as an analytic axis] might be that gender is *definitionally* built into determinations of sexuality, in a way that neither of them is definitionally intertwined with, for instance, determinations of class or race. It is certainly true that without a concept of gender there could be, quite simply, no concept of homo- or heterosexuality. But many other dimensions of sexual choice (auto- or alloerotic, within or between generations, species, etc.) have no such distinctive, explicit definitional connection with gender; indeed, some dimensions of sexuality might be tied, not to gender, but *instead* to differences or similarities of race or class.
>
> (Sedgwick 1990: 31; emphasis in the original)

According to this view, sexuality is too complex to be explained adequately with a simple gendered analysis. Bisexuals' sexuality cannot be defined simply by the gender of their sex partners, for instance (see Steven Seidman 1993 on challenges to gender-based sexual identities). And as Sedgwick notes, the race or class of a sex partner might be more important than gender for some people, suggesting that an analysis of sexuality must include interactions with many potentially eroticized characteristics.

Considering sexual orientation, in particular, Sedgwick then argues that even when gender is a *necessary* component of the analysis (as in Rich's argument, for example), gender analysis is not *sufficient*. Sedgwick suggests that gender analysis is inherently incapable of revealing the subtle underpinnings of the differential status and treatment of gay people:

> . . . [T]he ultimate definitional appeal in any gender-based analysis must necessarily be to the diacritical frontier between different genders. This gives heterosocial and heterosexual relations a conceptual privilege of incalculable consequence. . . . It is unrealistic to expect a close, textured analysis of same-sex relations through an optic calibrated in the first place to the coarser stigmata of gender difference [pp. 31–2].

For economists, this point implies that attempts to graft models of heterosexual families onto families formed by lesbian, gay, and bisexual people will perpetuate heterosexist assumptions about the appropriate form of families and will neither explain nor transform the lives of lesbian, gay, and bisexual people's families. (While some might argue that no existing economic theory provides a "close, textured analysis" of opposite-sex relations, many economists have sought and continue to seek a better model.)

Examples of the failure of a gendered economic analysis to explain the behavior and economic situations of lesbians and gay men are easy to find in the work of both feminist and nonfeminist economists. Sometimes the failures are particularly egregious. Economic models of fertility, for example, generally ignore how sperm and egg actually connect. Economists clearly consider the mode of conception to be obvious, given the implicit assumption that all families contain a man and a woman. Even when economists are more specific, heterosexual blinders often lead to incorrect conclusions:

> Indeed, their [men's and women's] times are *complements in sexual enjoyment*, the production of children, and possibly other commodities produced by the household. Complementarity implies that households with men and women are more efficient than households with only one sex, but because *both sexes are required to produce certain commodities* complementarity reduces

the sexual division of labor in the allocation of time and investments.

(Becker 1991: 39; emphasis added)

Even assuming that Becker means making babies rather than making love when he refers to the production of "certain commodities," his reasoning curiously ignores the fact that sperm – not the physical presence of a man in a household – is the necessary complementary good for lesbians seeking to conceive, and sperm is available in various forms and from many different sources, e.g. friends or sperm banks. As anthropologist Kath Weston points out in her study of lesbian and gay families, "New reproductive technologies have collided with ideologies that picture a child as the 'natural' product of the union of a woman and a man in an act of sexual intercourse that gives expression to contrasting gender identities" (Weston 1991: 169–70).

But neoclassical economists are not the only ones to universalize and privilege the male–female-based family. Some feminist economists, in their attacks on neoclassical models' assumptions and policy implications, have criticized those models while continuing to locate the roots of women's unequal economic position within the gender dynamics of a heterosexual family structure:

One way to achieve equity between the sexes – very possibly the only way – would be for women and men to take similar economic roles. By social custom husbands and wives would do the same amount of family-care work and devote the same time and energy to paid employment.

(Bergmann 1986: 266)

Indeed, the very concept of "the sexual division of labor" – the focus of many feminist economists – is rooted in a division *between* the sexes, i.e. it assumes a male–female distinction within the family. Although Bergmann's perspective might advance heterosexual women's status, the invisibility of same-sex couples (and of individuals not in a couple) within feminist economists' ideas of "a family" leads to an incomplete political agenda. Even though an improvement in heterosexual women's economic position is likely to improve lesbians' economic position relative to both heterosexual and gay men, lesbians and bisexual women (and gay and bisexual men) might still face a labor market disadvantage because of their sexual orientation, just as women of color will still face race and ethnicity discrimination (see Badgett 1995). A "feminist" policy agenda based on the male–female couple will not address the legal, social, and economic disadvantages of gay families' households, and such an agenda risks perpetuating important inequities.

Learning about *all* families from lesbian, gay, and bisexual people's families

Some might argue that since lesbian couples and gay male couples often appear similar to heterosexual couples – each being a relationship between two people characterized by long-term commitment, emotional and physical intimacy, and economic interdependence – existing economic models of families (whether based on maximizing a single family utility function or on bargaining within the family) can still be used to explain some aspects of lesbian and gay household members' behavior. Those models of household production and distribution, it might be argued, do not necessarily require a male–female couple, even though they have been historically developed out of concern for heterosexual families.

Certainly many lesbian, gay, and bisexual people form a relationship with one person of the same sex in a way that seems comfortingly similar to heterosexual married couples.[5] But too little representative or detailed analysis of lesbian and gay families exists to make me comfortable with any sweeping generalizations. For instance, in her study of lesbian and gay male kinship (structures that she calls "families we choose"), Weston (1991: 109) finds that

> In the Bay Area, families we choose resembled networks in the sense that they could cross household lines, and both were based on ties that radiated outward from individuals like spokes on a wheel. However, gay families differed from networks to the extent that they quite consciously incorporated symbolic demonstrations of love, shared history, material or emotional assistance, and other signs of enduring solidarity. Although many gay families included friends, not just any friend would do.

Economists' forcing such complex family structures into a narrow heterosexual tradition simply reproduces the problems associated with equating gender and sexual orientation as categories of analysis, and in particular makes invisible the distinct experiences of lesbian, gay, and bisexual people and their families.

On a more theoretical level, a lively political debate continues among lesbian, gay, and bisexual people about the nature and form of relationships. Some writers advocate the right of same-sex couples to marry (e.g. Thomas Stoddard 1989) and see such marriages as desirable (e.g. Richard Mohr 1994). Others warn that marriage would undermine "the affirmation of gay identity and culture; and the validation of many forms of relationships" (Paula Ettelbrick 1989). Ruthann Robson (1994) argues for resisting even the idea of "family," warning that lesbians should not enter into the "redefining the family" debate. Robson worries that even liberal redefinitions

of "family" will inevitably result in the application of traditional heterosexual forms, assumptions, and legal regulations to lesbian relationships,
destroying the diversity and complexity of lesbian relationships. She
argues for resistance to the category of "family" and for a thorough
reconceptualization of categories of relationships between individuals:

> Thus, rather than lesbians requesting inclusion into the privil-
> eged legal category of "family," what if lesbians advocated the
> abolition of benefits based on family status, the reconsidera-
> tion of what constitute "benefits," or even the abolition of the
> category "family" itself?
>
> (Robson 1994: 992)

Of course, one might argue that lesbians (and gay men and bisexuals) are
not the only people whose complex relationships are delegitimized and
disadvantaged by existing legal definitions of family relationships. In the
same way, the standard economic model of "a family" privileges one
increasingly uncommon form and ignores many other forms of family
organization. Feminist anthropologists and sociologists have studied the
diversity of family forms in the United States that result from "women's
resistance to and negotiation of the structure that subordinate them" (Barrie
Thorne 1992: 7). While not rejecting the entire category of "family," Jane
Collier et al. (1992) view "The Family, not as a concrete institution
designed to fulfill universal human needs, but as an ideological construct
associated with the modern state." They provide some useful guidance for
theorizing about families:

> What we can begin to ask is what we *want* our families to do.
> Then, distinguishing our hopes from what we have, we can
> begin to analyze the social forces that enhance or undermine the
> realization of the kinds of human bonds we need.
>
> (Collier et al. 1992: 34)

While the task of reconceptualizing "family" from a broad feminist perspective is certainly a large and daunting one, feminist economists moving
beyond a narrow critique of existing family models to new conceptualizations have several possible starting points. Expanding the economic theory
of the family should involve *analyzing* that which is normally *taken as given*
in economic models, i.e. the range of functions performed by families, the
legally and culturally sanctioned idea of what constitutes a family, and the
roles of individuals within the family. In this project, variation in the
sexual orientations of individuals collected into something called "a family"
or household provides a way to study the impact of legal and social institutions and norms on the formation and economics of all families, not just
heterosexual ones. Thus rather than dealing with sexual orientation by

either squeezing one form of gay family (the same-sex couple) into the heterosexual model or by developing an entirely separate model of gay families, feminist economists could contribute to the development of a theory explaining the existence and dynamics of *many* kinds of family structures.

Sketching out a few examples illustrates the usefulness of this approach. Take, for instance, a question of central concern to feminist economists: is the sexual division of labor a product of rational choice or a product of gender norms about appropriate work for men and women? The neoclassical model of the family's allocation of time starts with the household maximizing one aggregate utility function by combining time and market goods in the production of commodities for consumption. An efficient household (of any size and regardless of gender composition) allocates its members' time between market and nonmarket production based on their comparative advantage in one or the other, leading to specialization by most or all household members (Becker 1991: 33–6). For heterosexual couples, biological differences and wage discrimination give a comparative advantage to women in nonmarket work and to men in market work, leading to the observed sexual division of labor. Specialization leads to dependence on other household members, giving rise to the institution of marriage for male–female couples, defined by Becker as "a written, oral, or customary long-term contract between a man and a woman to produce children, food, and other commodities in a common household" (Becker 1991: 43), and reinforcing the existing division of labor.

Would we expect rational lesbian, gay, and bisexual people and their families to specialize in the same way? Becker argues that same-sex households cannot take advantage of what he (inaccurately) cites as complementarities exclusive to opposite-sex couples (producing children and sexual enjoyment). In Becker's model, the absence both of those complementarities and of within-couple gender wage differentials should reduce specialization within same-sex couples. Given differences in education, upbringing, and tastes, however, it seems likely that gay individuals' marginal products in home and market production vary, making comparative advantage of potential equal relevance for same-sex households. (Also, some gay people's families and households might include men *and* women and possibly people of differing sexual orientations.) Becker's model therefore implies that specialization would also be efficient in lesbian, gay, and bisexual people's families when the individuals share the same physical households.

Other factors normally taken as given in economic models suggest that gendered patterns of specialization would be much rarer among lesbian or gay households. The first factor is the impact of gender norms on the division of labor. Sociologists Philip Blumstein and Pepper Schwartz (1983: 14) argue that comparisons of heterosexual couples (both married and unmarried) and gay couples constitute a natural experiment for studying gender roles:

> By contrasting homosexual couples with both types of hetero-sexual couples, we can see how relationships function when there are no male/female differences to contend with. By com-paring gay men to lesbians, we explore differences in male and female contributions to relationships.

Within same-sex couples or households, a strictly gendered division of labor is simply not possible. Further, as Letitia Anne Peplau (1991) points out, research in other social sciences reveals that same-sex couples typically reject gendered roles. In their study of a nonrandom sample of couples, Blumstein and Schwartz discovered relatively little market–nonmarket specialization within lesbians and gay male couples, and they found that respondents' personal values were a major influence on the market labor supply of both individuals in same-sex couples, most of whom believed that both partners should engage in market work (pp. 127–31). And while such comparisons have focused on couples, similar questions could be asked of larger households.

The second reason which might be expected to decrease the extent of specialization in gay couples is that the legal and social institutions support-ing heterosexual couples and families are not accessible to gay people's families. For example, legal marriage is limited to heterosexual couples, making people in homosexual couples legal strangers to each other (Robson 1992), a distinction absent from Becker's analysis. The absence of legal marriage increases uncertainty about pooling assets and income, since the division of assets would not be governed by the rules applicable in the case of marital divorce. Gay couples and their lawyers have created some imperfect substitutes for marriage, including contracts regarding mutual support and division of property, wills, and the assignation of powers of attorney (*Harvard Law Review* Editors 1991). However, the transaction costs of such substitute arrangements are higher than those of marriage, so all couples may not have such agreements. Further, such contracts are some-times ruled unenforceable (William R. Rubenstein 1993: 439). Families of adults extending beyond a couple have no options for establishing a legally recognized set of family relationships.[6]

Tax policies and the widespread practice of tying employment benefits to marriage (supported by tax policy) also have differential consequences for specialization in gay families. The federal income tax system still includes a marriage penalty for couples whose incomes are similar and therefore reinforces traditional divisions of labor, with men doing market work and women doing (untaxed) nonmarket work. With the option of marriage closed off, same-sex couples (and larger lesbian, gay, and/or bisexual households) will not have this tax incentive for such specialization.

Employment-based health care (and other) benefits for employees, their legal spouses and their children also encourage market work by all lesbian, gay, and bisexual people. Because employers rarely extend family benefits to the partners (and in some cases the children) of lesbian and gay employees, specialization in nonmarket work would likely carry the additional consequence of no benefits for gay partners.[7]

Thus analyzing the impact of differences in legal and social norms and institutions for gay families provides new research strategies for understanding the division of labor within households generally, and the sexual division of labor in heterosexual households in particular. And Kathryn Larson suggests that heterosexual couples will also have an alternative model for the division of household work from studies of gay families (Larson 1992: 252).

In addition to the household division of labor, economic models of the family also attempt to explain fertility and the demand for children. Becker (1991: 330) and many others assume that lesbians and gay men are not likely to have children. Two surveys, one a random sample of the U.S. (Rex Briggs 1994) and the other a random sample of voters (M. V. Lee Badgett 1994a), both showed that lesbians are just as likely as heterosexual women to have children in their homes, although gay men are much less likely than heterosexual men to have children.[8] But even if lesbians and gay men have fewer children, this difference is unlikely to be simply the result of a lower demand for children. Lesbian, gay, and bisexual people who want to raise children face institutional and legal constraints that few heterosexuals need to consider (see *Harvard Law Review* Editors 1991: 119–50). Some states prohibit adoption or foster care by gay people. A biological parent (such as a former spouse) or other relative may successfully challenge a lesbian or gay parent's right to child custody. The relationship between biological parents and nonbiological co-parents is ill-defined and subject to legal challenge. Some state laws restrict lesbians' access to reproductive technologies. Given these conditions, gay families could have the same "demand curve" for children as heterosexual couples but have fewer children (either biological or adoptive) because they face a far higher price of conceiving or adopting and raising children.

Children are also important in the context of another subject of family models, the stability of marriage and relationships. Becker argues that "investment in children" is the main form of "marital-specific" capital for heterosexual couples, an investment that partially determines the likelihood of divorce. Becker cites one study of a nonrandom sample that showed homosexual couples were less stable than married couples (Becker 1991: 330), and he attributes this lesser stability to the gay couples' lower number of children, less stark division of labor, and fewer investments in relationship-specific capital, circumstances which would, in his opinion, also reduce the stability of marriages and tend to become self-fulfilling prophecies.[9] However, he again fails to recognize the role of underlying legal and social institutions that treat heterosexual and homosexual couples differently and may account for all of any difference in stability.[10] Regarding larger household configurations, Becker argues that the possibility of shirking and the loss of individual privacy reduce the stability of those arrangements, again without reference to the lack of legal ties that might encourage more permanent bonds (1991: 48–53).

Because it ignores the impact of strong social norms related to the division of labor as well as exclusionary institutions (and their historical development), the neoclassical model of family decision-making is left open to justifiable criticism from feminists. Furthermore, feminists could develop a more damaging empirical challenge to Becker's model (and similar models) by using comparisons among families differentiated by the sexual orientations of their adult members. Such a feminist research agenda would serve dual purposes: learning more about an under-studied group of people as well as furthering our understanding of how *all* families work. Both goals will be increasingly important as policy-makers are compelled to respond to changing family structures and to the rapidly developing political efforts of lesbian, gay, and bisexual people.

Political lessons from lesbian and gay families are opportunities for feminists

Just as consideration of sexual orientation could lead to an expansion of feminist economic theory, the experiences and successes of lesbian, gay, and bisexual activists demonstrate that changes in public policy and employment practices related to the family are possible. The movement to recognize "domestic partners" (or "spousal equivalents") shows that new legal family structures *can* be created to respond to changing family concepts and needs. At the same time, though, the domestic partner issue reveals the power of tradition to mold and limit debate. The resulting domestic partner policies are often relatively conservative reforms that do not include all of the diverse family structures of either gay *or* heterosexual people. As I will argue, without more active involvement of heterosexual feminists, the material gains will mainly go to some gay people – still a positive outcome, of course – but we feminists will have missed an opportunity for more direct shaping of family policy.

This historic movement to create new legally and socially recognized relationships is found in many places. Denmark and Sweden have created an alternative form of marriage for same-sex couples. Some municipalities and employers in the United States also recognize committed same-sex relationships for purposes ranging from hospital visitation rights to employment benefits (Charles Gossett 1994).

Institutions of higher education are a rapidly growing source of domestic partner benefits for employees. Since 1992, over twenty-five colleges and universities have agreed to cover domestic partners of employees and their children in employer-provided health care plans, for instance (Badgett 1994b). Other campuses extend more limited benefits to partners of employees. As my own university took up the domestic partner issue in spring 1994, I conducted a study of colleges and universities with domestic partner policies and of other campuses engaged in active discussion of those policies. The study revealed some important patterns in the development of domestic partner policies that should concern feminists, whether heterosexual, bisexual, or homosexual.[11]

As on my own campus, the collective action of lesbian, gay, and bisexual employees has been the motivating force behind the consideration and adoption of domestic partner policies at most universities. Whether working through layers of campus bureaucracy, lobbying high-level officials, or taking their employers to court, lesbian and gay employees have diligently progressed through the basics of collective action: collecting information, strategizing paths, calling in favors, marshalling allies, and educating co-workers. According to all of the interviews conducted during the study, heterosexual allies played important roles although those vocal allies were rarely heterosexuals with domestic partners, as will be discussed below.

What was the underlying motive of the activists? As with other gay political struggles, some gay civil rights activists see the domestic partnership effort as a step toward the equal treatment of lesbians and gay men with heterosexuals. In this view, basing benefits on legal marriage blatantly discriminates against gay people, who cannot marry. Domestic partnerships, then, are an interim step on the way to larger goals, such as legalization of same-sex marriage. As noted earlier, however, other activists (call this the "liberation" perspective) seek not the right to participate in the institution of marriage, but an expansion of the options for validating relationships (Ettelbrick 1989). In the view of this camp, tying employment benefits to marriage discriminates against all unmarried couples, and domestic partnerships constitute an alternative to marriage that should be open to *all* couples, straight or gay. In practice, many groups started off advocating the extension of domestic partner recognition to both same-sex and opposite-sex couples. But out of the twenty-five schools studied, only five offered benefits to opposite-sex partners (Badgett 1994b).

Limiting eligibility to same-sex partners resulted in part from administrators' resistance to the higher costs of including heterosexual domestic partners. The leadership of lesbian and gay employees and the "free riding" of heterosexual employees with domestic partners may have also influenced the limitation of eligibility to same-sex partners. Unmarried heterosexual couples do not appear to have developed a self-conscious identity or sense of community on the campuses studied – perhaps the cause of their low participation in most organizing efforts. In contrast, lesbian, gay, and bisexual faculty and staff often organize to deal with diverse issues, including campus safety, curricular changes, social events, research seminars, and campus political issues. Partnered heterosexuals may also fear homophobic reactions to their advocacy of an issue so closely associated with gay people. Gay activists often reveal their (stigmatized) sexual orientation in the course of lobbying, either directly or through the assumptions of co-workers, often risking their careers in the effort, but a sense of solidarity and community may reduce gay employees' apprehension or reluctance. At the campuses in the study, the greatest collective involvement from heterosexuals with unmarried partners came at the end of the process, in the form of complaints about an announced domestic partner policy for same-sex couples only.

Other elements of the domestic partner policies studied reveal a fundamentally traditional modeling on heterosexual marriage. For instance, the formal definition and eligibility standards are usually based on an idealized vision of marriage, with time requirements (to establish commitment), shared assets and debts, and a joint residence. Although none of those elements are required for legal marriage, they are nevertheless identified as characterizing a "real" marriage. In two cases (Dartmouth and Smith Colleges), partners must even attest that they would marry if legally allowed to do so.

During this rare time of active rewriting of the most basic element of family – defining relationships between adults – the underlying traditionalism and the limits of current collective action should serve as a warning to feminists interested in family matters. In the lesbian and gay staff and faculty group at my own campus, for example, theory has influenced practice: heterosexual domestic partners would most likely have been dropped from our political goal (and probably from the official proposal under consideration by our university), without the persuasive efforts of myself and other self-identified feminists, who were committed to the general principle of equitable treatment for employees regardless of marital status.

Many universities, however, are likely to remain resistant to counting opposite-sex partners as domestic partners, even with active efforts from heterosexual feminists, since such inclusion could increase the cost of the policy. But feminists of all sexual orientations can learn from and contribute to these efforts in important ways, starting with posing some important questions for active consideration: What functions does marriage serve that should be preserved and extended to other family formations? Why should two adults in a couple receive privileges that two single individuals would not receive? What impact should children have on the legal status of their parents? This moment in the development of domestic partner policies and debate seems particularly ripe for opening up these broader issues in a way that could lead to meaningful advances in the status and economic position of all women and their families.

Towards an economics incorporating sexual orientation

Some scholars have already begun to consider sexuality and sexual orientation in the context of economic theory and policy. Folbre's (1994) framework for understanding how individual and collective interests shape economic behavior provides the most comprehensive vision of how gender and sexuality fit together along with race, class, age, nationality, and other identities. Because economics has lagged significantly behind other social sciences attending to both sexuality and sexual orientation, even less ambitious undertakings addressing sexual orientation may make important contributions, both to academia and to lesbian, gay, and bisexual people more generally. Although gender and sexuality might constitute separate analytical axes, they are complementary and interdependent rather than mutually exclusive. My hope is that feminist economics will be inspired by the opportunities for fruitful inquiry that an economic analysis of sexual orientation will provide, influencing the economics profession, economic theory, and public policy.

Acknowledgments

I thank Rhonda Williams, Richard Cornwall, June Lapidus, Diana Strassmann, and participants at the 1994 IAFFE summer conference for making helpful suggestions and asking provocative questions. Two anonymous referees also offered valuable comments and suggestions.

Notes

1   For a review of the early offerings, see M. V. Lee Badgett and Rhonda M. Williams (1992).
2   Terminology is contested terrain in discussions of sexuality. In general, I use "sexual orientation" to distinguish between heterosexual, homosexual and bisexual people. Because a long history of using "gay" to refer to both lesbians and gay men perpetuated the invisibility of lesbians, and because bisexual people often share a common cause, history, and culture with lesbians and gay men, I collect nonheterosexual people under the "lesbian, gay, and bisexual" umbrella whenever practical. No blanket term has achieved widespread acceptance ("queer" currently tends to provoke readers of all sexual orientations), so I will occasionally lump all three groups into the term "gay," with the understanding that this refers to all three groups unless I specifically refer to "gay men."
3   Posner's ambitious project is weakened by his taking as exogenous important

gender-related factors, a reminder of the important interactions between gender and sexuality:

> . . . Much of the variance among different eras, cultures, social classes, races, and the sexes themselves in behavior, attitudes, customs, and laws concerning such aspects of sexuality . . . can be explained, and changes in them predicted, by references to the handful of variables that the theory identifies as likely to be significant. The principal variables are the occupational profile of women and . . . women's economic independence, plus urbanization, income, the sex ratio, and scientific and technological advances relating to the control of fertility and to the care of mothers and infants.
>
> (Posner 1992: 5)

4   *DeSantis v. Pacific Telephone & Telegraph Co.*, 608 F. 2d 327 (9th Cir. 1979).

5   The scope of this paper prevents going into detail about the similarities and differences of same-sex and opposite-sex *couples*. For first-person accounts of ceremonies and commitments of lesbians and gay men, see Sherman (1992). For more comparisons of the division of labor, etc., between gay couples and heterosexual married and unmarried couples, see Blumstein and Schwartz (1983); Larson (1992); and Lawrence A. Kurdek (1993).

6   In California, larger nontraditional families are allowed to register as private associations, but those registrations have no practical value as yet (Rubenstein 1993: 442–3).

7   Also, these social and economic institutions will influence any specialization that occurs, resulting in perhaps unexpected patterns. For instance, Phyllis Burke describes her family's decision that she would stay home to care for her young son while her partner, who was the biological and, therefore, legal mother of their child, returned to her job to provide health insurance for herself and the child. Because Burke was not a legal parent at the time, her employer's health insurance would not have covered their son (Burke 1993: 31).

8   The surveys do not ask what the legal relationship is to the child. Also, at least some of lesbians' children may have been conceived while one of the mothers was in a heterosexual relationship.

9   Becker and Posner offer two other reasons more intrinsically related to homosexuality that would reduce the stability of gay relationships. Without documenting his claims, Becker suggests that high search costs result in poorer matches (Becker 1991: 330). But from another perspective, high search costs would also reduce the gains from "divorce" to search for another mate, increasing the stability of couples (Larson 1992: 254). Posner argues that "the male taste for variety in sexual partners makes the prospects for sexual fidelity worse in a homosexual than in a heterosexual marriage" (Posner 1992: 306), an effect that would destabilize gay male couples but not lesbian couples, of course. Anderson counters this conclusion with an alternative prediction that such tastes "could lead to an understanding about allowable infidelity that would make the relationship *more* stable than that of a couple whose members disagree on the desirability of variety" (Anderson 1993: 197).

10   Becker also likens gay couples to heterosexual trial marriages when he points out that the lower legal costs of ending relationships might reduce stability, but he fails to mention the difference in the ability to marry in the first place.

11   Of the twenty-five colleges or universities that offered (or planned to offer) health care benefits to domestic partners as of April 1994, I was able through personal and professional networks to contact and interview activists closely involved in the approval process at twelve of those campuses. I also interviewed activists at three

campuses that do not yet have such policies. In addition to the interviews, I collected documents (official forms, press releases, news articles, etc.) from most of the twenty-five campuses. More details of the study are available in Badgett (1994b or 1994c).

References

Anderson, Robert M. 1993. "EP Seeks EP: A Review of *Sex and Reason* by Richard A. Posner." *Journal of Economic Literature* 31 (March): 191–8.

Badgett, M. V. Lee. 1994a. "Civil Rights and Civilized Research." Presented at the 1994 Association for Public Policy Analysis and Management Research Conference.

——, 1994b. "Equal Pay for Equal Families." *Academe*, May/June 80(3): 26–30.

——, 1994c. "Lesbian and Gay Campus Organizing for Domestic Partner Benefits," *Proceedings 22nd Annual Conference*. The National Center for the Study of Collective Bargaining in Higher Education and the Professions, Baruch College, CUNY.

——. 1995 (forthcoming). "The Wage Effects of Sexual Orientation Discrimination." *Industrial and Labor Relations Review*.

—— and Rhonda M. Williams. 1992. "The Economics of Sexual Orientation: Establishing a Research Agenda." *Feminist Studies* 18(3) (Fall): 649–57.

Becker, Gary. 1991. *Treatise on the Family*, enlarged edn. Cambridge: Harvard University Press.

Bergmann, Barbara. 1986. *The Economic Emergence of Women*. New York: Basic Books.

Blumstein, Philip and Pepper Schwartz. 1983. *American Couples: Money, Work, Sex*. New York: William Morrow.

Briggs, Rex. 1994. Data from *Yankelovich Monitor*, telephone interview.

Burke, Phyllis. 1993. *Family Values: Two Moms and Their Son*. New York: Random House.

Collier, Jane, Michelle Z. Rosaldo and Sylvia Yanagisako. 1992. "Is There a Family? New Anthropological Views," in Barrie Thorne with Marilyn Yalom (eds) *Rethinking the Family: Some Feminist Questions*, revised edn. Boston: Northeastern University Press.

Ettelbrick, Paula. 1989. "Since When is Marriage a Path to Liberation?" *OUT/LOOK National Gay and Lesbian Quarterly* 6(9) (Fall): 14–17. (Reprinted in Rubenstein 1993 and Sherman 1992.)

Ferber, Marianne A. and Julie A. Nelson (eds). 1993. "Introduction: The Social Construction of Economics and the Social Construction of Gender," in Marianne A. Ferber and Julie A. Nelson (eds) *Beyond Economic Man: Feminist Theory and Economics*, pp. 1–22. Chicago: University of Chicago Press.

Folbre, Nancy. 1994. *Who Pays for the Kids? Gender and the Structures of Constraint*. London: Routledge.

Gossett, Charles. 1994. "Domestic Partnership Benefits: Public Sector Patterns." *Review of Public Personnel Administration* 14(1): 64–84.

Harvard Law Review Editors. 1991. *Sexual Orientation and the Law*. Cambridge: Harvard University Press.

Homer, Steven. 1994. "Against Marriage." *Harvard Civil Rights–Civil Liberties Law Review* 29(2): 505–30.

Kurdek, Lawrence A. 1993. "The Allocation of Household Labor in Gay, Lesbian, and Heterosexual Married Couples." *Journal of Social Issues* 49(3): 127–39.

Larson, Kathryn. 1992. "The Economics of Lesbian Households," in Third Women's Policy Research Conference Proceedings, Institute for Women's Policy Research, Washington, D.C.

Mohr, Richard. 1994. *A More Perfect Union: Why Straight Americans Must Stand Up for Gay Rights*. Boston: Beacon Press.

Peplau, Letitia Anne. 1991. "Lesbian and Gay Relationships," in *Homosexuality: Research Implications for Public Policy*, pp. 177–96. Newbury Park, CA: Sage.

Posner, Richard. 1992. *Sex and Reason*. Cambridge: Harvard University Press.

Rich, Adrienne. 1983. "Compulsory Heterosexuality and Lesbian Existence," in Ann Snitow, Christine Stansell and Sharon Thompson (eds) *Powers of Desire: The Politics of Sexuality*, pp. 177–205. New York: Monthly Review Press.

Robson, Ruthann. 1992. *Lesbian (Out) Law: Survival Under the Rule of Law*. Ithaca: Firebrand Books.

——. 1994. "Resisting the Family: Repositioning Lesbians in Legal Theory." *Signs: Journal of Women in Culture and Society* 19(4): 975–95.

Rubenstein, William R. (ed). 1993. *Lesbians, Gay Men, and the Law*. New York: New Press.

Sedgwick, Eve Kosofsky. 1990. *Epistemology of the Closet*. Berkeley: University of California Press.

Seidman, Steven. 1993. "Identity and Politics in a 'Postmodern' Gay Culture: Some Historical and Conceptual Notes," in Michael Warner (ed) *Fear of a Queer Planet: Queer Politics and Social Theory*, pp. 105–42. Minneapolis: University of Minnesota Press.

Sherman, Suzanne (ed). 1992. *Lesbian and Gay Marriage: Private Commitments, Public Ceremonies*. Philadelphia: Temple University Press.

Stoddard, Thomas. 1989. "Why Gay People Should Seek the Right to Marry." *Out/Look* 6 (Fall): 9–13. (Reprinted in Rubenstein 1993 and Sherman 1992.)

Thorne, Barrie. 1992. "Feminism and the Family: Two Decades of Thought," in Barrie Thorne with Marilyn Yalom (eds) *Rethinking the Family: Some Feminist Questions*, revised edn. Boston: Northeastern University Press.

Weston, Kath. 1991. *Families We Choose: Lesbians, Gays, Kinship*. New York: Columbia University Press.

Williams, Rhonda M. 1993. "Race, Deconstruction, and the Emergent Agenda of Feminist Economic Theory," in Marianne A. Ferber and Julie A. Nelson (eds) *Beyond Economic Man: Feminist Theory and Economics*, pp. 144–53. Chicago: University of Chicago Press.

Chapter 3

Colleen Lamos

OPENING QUESTIONS

This essay is a comment on M. V. Lee Badgett's article, "Gender, Sexuality and Sexual Orientation: All in the Feminist Family?" [Chapter 2 in this volume]

From *Feminist Economics* 1995, 1 (2): 59–62

BADGETT'S GROUND-BREAKING ESSAY is an excellent introduction to the issues that lesbian and gay family structures raise for feminist economists. Lucidly written, her article explains the ways in which feminist theory, insofar as it relies upon a gender-based analysis, excludes specific consideration of sexual orientation. Badgett's impressive discussion of the advantages and disadvantages of the familial or marital model of lesbian and gay relationships concludes in a call for further thought regarding the economic functions of the institution of marriage and for its extension to other, namely homosexual, family formations.

Badgett does an excellent job of urging feminists to go beyond the analysis of gender difference. She argues that gender difference, heretofore the conceptual axis of feminism, has had little purchase on an understanding of homosexuality; in fact, a gender-based analysis implicitly accords privilege to heterosexuality. The aim of Badgett's essay is thus to render same-sex relationships visible for economists, to examine the limitations of existing economic theories for an analysis of those relationships, and, in turn, to consider the challenges that same-sex relationships pose for traditional economic models of the family.

This is a tall order, and thus it is not surprising that Badgett falters on some of the specific points of her argument. One of her major claims is that the concept of the sexual division of labor within the family assumes a male-female complementarity that does not obtain within same-sex couples. Rather idealistically, she argues that "same-sex couples typically reject gendered roles."

Badgett's assertion ignores the widespread practice among same-sex couples of adopting conventionally masculine or feminine tasks within relationships, ranging from butch/femme sexual styles and division of household chores to deciding who pursues a career and who sacrifices one for the sake of the relationship, although these roles may alternate or be flexibly adopted. In short, however actively same-sex couples may resist the customary sexual division of labor, economic exigencies more often than not enforce gendered patterns of specialization, regardless of the biological sex of those involved. The ways in which socio-economic determinates of gender override biological sex might prove to be an important area of investigation for feminist economists.

Badgett's confidence that same-sex family formations escape gender specialization apparently stems from her faith in an essential distinction between homosexuality and heterosexuality – that is, upon the popular belief that certain people "really" are gay while others "really" are straight. Thus, her assertion that, "within same-sex couples or households, a strictly gendered division of labor is simply not possible" collapses biological sex and socio-economic gender, for a gendered division of labor would be impossible in gay households only if sex necessarily entails gender.

Badgett's forgetting of the most crucial lesson of feminism follows from her belief that lesbians and gay men really are different, and from an idealization of lesbian relationships common in the 1970s and early 1980s. Much of the burden of recent lesbian and gay theory has been to show the ways in which homosexuality and heterosexuality are inter-implicated, and thus to call into question the assumption of a clearcut differentiation of people on the basis of sexual orientation. Indeed, one could argue that the categories of homosexual and heterosexual are themselves based upon a fear of same-sex desire. From this perspective, feminist economists might pose a different set of questions, including asking how putatively hetero- sexual or nonsexual relations are involved in a range of economically decisive homosocial affiliations.

Nevertheless, Badgett cogently argues against forcing lesbian and gay family relationships into what she calls "a narrow heterosexual tradition," claiming that the "diversity and complexity" of those relationships may cast into a different light our understanding of family structures in general. As the film *Go Fish* and other contemporary social documents attest, lesbian and gay relationships are based not upon the enclosed and rigidly struc- tured nuclear family but upon a more fluid web of relations that defy contemporary economic models. An examination of lesbian and gay familial structures has the potential to offer a critical perspective upon economic models that are based upon the closed household, especially if same-sex relations are considered not as a marginal aberration but as directly implicated with other-sex relations.

Perhaps the most compelling aspect of Badgett's essay is her demonstration of how institutional structures, such as the federal tax code, entrench traditional divisions of labor between men and women. Her attentiveness to the economic factors that reinforce heterosexual relations thus renders her criticism of Gary Becker's analysis of homosexual family structures somewhat off the mark. As Badgett notes, Becker attributes the instability of homosexual couples to the absence of an "investment in children" as well as to the lack of a specialization of the sexual division of labor and to fewer investments in relationship-specific capital. Badgett criticizes him for ignoring the legal and social homophobia that disrupts gay relationships. She argues quite rightly that feminists should investigate lesbian and gay families in order to develop comparative models; indeed, the absence of empirical research on lesbian and gay relationships is deplorable and renders any firm conclusions regarding them at this stage highly speculative. Yet Becker's arguments concerning the instability of lesbian and gay relationships focus upon the lack of economic constraints within such couples, which, in turn, results in the sort of fluidity and diversity of family configurations that Badgett praises.

There is a Catch-22 here: the more social acceptance that lesbians and gay men gain, including the extension of benefits to domestic partners, the more their relationships will likely come to resemble heterosexual marriages; while the social, legal, and economic barriers to lesbians and gays have produced what Badgett applauds as unsettled yet heterogeneous family formations that offer alternatives to traditional marriage.

As a consequence, Badgett's conclusion regarding the advisability of advocating domestic partners benefits for gay employees is ambivalent. Her call for the extension of such benefits to unmarried heterosexual couples as well as to gay couples is qualified by her criticism of the former as getting a free ride from the efforts of gay activists. Although she claims to favor "the general principle of equitable treatment for employees regardless of marital status," this principle would entail the abolition of all partner benefits, not the extension of them to quasi-married gay couples.

The current debate concerning gay domestic partners benefits is nonetheless a useful site for the examination of familial norms. If this controversy results only in a broadening of the concept of the family to include a wider range of structures, it will at least have opened up a host of significant questions for economic theorists regarding this supposedly natural yet most ideologically saturated of all social arrangements.

Barriers to the study of queer economics

OVER THE PAST FIFTY YEARS the study of marginalized groups has come to the forefront of academic study. The civil rights movement that African Americans and their allies fought, as well as the emergence of feminism as a mainstream ideology, has brought the history and sociology of these groups to the colleges and universities of the world. Similarly, New York City's 1969 Stonewall Riots created the same atmosphere for queer theory. Yet the field of economics has virtually ignored the study of this population, apart from the efforts of a handful of economists. Hence, a fair amount of the queer economics literature focuses on why more economists are not studying gay and lesbian aspects of their field.

This section contains two chapters that explore these questions. In Marieka Klawitter's article, "Why aren't more economists doing research on sexual orientation?" (1998), the academic institution itself is questioned. Klawitter asserts that if there were more accepting atmospheres in those institutions, with negligible discrimination, there would be a greater interest in the topic. The interest would, in turn, create more data sets, and the field would grow. Kyle Kauffman voices a different perspective on the issue in his article, "Uncovering a quantitative economic history of gays and lesbians in the United States" (1998). He cites the major problem in the field of queer economics as being a lack of reputable data to begin with, and assumes that the field will grow as more reliable data become readily available, particularly from the government.

It is the case, as we will see in the following sections of this book, that more economists are doing research on sexual orientation, and that additional data have become available. A few economists have even recently written their dissertations on topics in the economics of sexual orientation (Jepsen 1998; Blandford 1999; Comolli 2005). However, the problems of economic historians interested in sexual orientation topics will likely persist, considering the difficulty of retroactive data collection.

DISCUSSION QUESTIONS

1   Is discrimination or a lack of data the driving force behind the lack of academic economic literature in this area?

2   What types of issues do you see regarding collection of useful survey data to study the economics of sexual orientation? What types of questions would you want to ask in such surveys?

3   Why might people be likely to hide their sexual orientation, and how might you get people to answer interviewers and/or surveys truthfully regarding their sexual orientation?

4   In what ways can economists who want to study queer issues legitimize their projects?
5   Can the problem of getting more economists to study queer economics be compared to the formation of other subfields in economics or other fields (for example, in economics, the study of economics of gender, the economics of racial and ethnic minorities, or the economics of disability)? Why or why not?

REFERENCES

Blandford, J. M. (1999) "Sexual Orientation's Role in the Determination of Earnings and Occupational Outcomes: theory and econometric evidence," Dissertation, South Bend, Ind.: University of Notre Dame.

Comolli, R. (2005) "The Economics of Sexual Orientation and Racial Perception," Dissertation, New Haven, Conn.: Yale University.

Jepsen, L. K. (1998) "Essays on the Economics of Marriage: an empirical study of same-sex and opposite-sex couples," Dissertation, Nashville, Tenn.: Vanderbilt University.

Chapter 4

Marieka M. Klawitter

WHY AREN'T MORE ECONOMISTS DOING RESEARCH ON SEXUAL ORIENTATION?

From *Feminist Economics* 1998, 4 (2): 55–9

[. . .]

What's so interesting about sexual orientation?

THE CULTURAL AND POLITICAL context of sexual orientation has changed dramatically in the last thirty years, offering up many quasi-experimental opportunities for researchers. Culturally, mainstream public opinion about homosexuality has become more benign, if not accepting (David Moore 1993). Also, sexual minorities have expanded or created supportive subcultures and communities (John D'Emilio 1993). In the U.S., public policies regarding employment discrimination, sodomy, benefits for domestic partners, adoption, and child custody all provide ample variation over time and geography to serve empirical researchers. In addition to the effects of changing culture and public policies, research opportunities abound in the mechanisms of discrimination, the economics of HIV/AIDS, the effects of sexual orientation on household decision-making, and the influence of culture on economic decisions.

With all this material, why aren't more economists working on issues of sexual orientation? In my view, the barriers to research on sexual orientation include: discrimination against sexual minorities, lack of interest or knowledge, the absence of support for the work, and scarcity of appropriate models and data. While each of these barriers is partly explained by lingering discrimination, each can exist without overt hostility toward sexual minorities.

First, a word about the kinds of research and researchers I am referring to. I use "sexual minorities" to include people who identify as homosexual, gay, lesbian, bisexual, queer, transgender, or transsexual, or who participate in same-sex sexual or affectional behaviors.[1] That's certainly a large and diverse category, but I group these people as sexual minorities because I believe that they face many of the same kinds of discrimination and barriers based on their sexual or gender identities.[2] Also, these groups have formed similar and often overlapping cultural and political communities. Perhaps predictably, we don't all get along, and there are many fractures between groups and heated arguments about which sexualities are legitimate and deserving of respect by mainstream culture and institutions. I won't address these debates here, except to say that I feel that we all gain by advocating for more acceptance of research on issues of sexual orientation.

Discrimination against sexual minorities

Discrimination or intolerance can stifle work on sexual orientation in many ways. First, sexual minorities probably do most of the research on sexual orientation. If economics or public policy departments discriminate in admissions or hiring there will be fewer sexual minorities to do research on these issues.[3] Second, if departments create unsupportive environments for sexual minorities, then fewer economists of any kind will study sexual orientation. Even if trained and hired, closeted sexual minorities are unlikely to work on issues of sexual orientation because of the fear of being exposed in an unsupportive environment. In addition, heterosexuals are unlikely to work on sexual orientation if sexual minorities are stigmatized. While some white economists study race, and male economists have long worked on gender-related projects (or have at least used data on women), few of these economists have worried about being misidentified as a person of color or as a woman. How many straight economists would not flinch at being mistaken for being gay or lesbian? To underline the obvious – mistaken identity wouldn't matter if homosexuality were not stigmatized.

Recent surveys of sociologists and political scientists have documented the perceptions of discrimination by gay and lesbian faculty (Verta Taylor and Nicole C. Raeburn 1995; Committee on the Status of Lesbians and Gays in the Profession of the American Political Science Association 1995). Among gay and lesbian faculty, 43 percent of sociologists and 32 percent of political scientists felt that they had been discriminated against because of their sexual orientation. Discrimination might be limited (and further evidenced) by the fact that only about 45 percent of the sociologists and 40 percent of the political scientists are "out" to all their colleagues.

The levels of discrimination in economics departments have probably decreased over time, mirroring the trends in general public opinion.[4] Though I know of no studies of the level of discrimination in economics, I would guess it to be similar to sociology and political science. Research on sexual orientation is likely to increase if economics departments, and the colleges and universities around them, become more tolerant or supportive.

Interest and knowledge

Many economists know little or care little about sexual minorities or sexual orientation. The salience of sexual orientation is likely to be low for people without personal or professional experience with sexual minorities. In addition, the relatively small population of sexual minorities and the popular notions of gays as wealthy might lead some researchers to attach low importance to the issues.[5] A more supportive environment in the field and a critical mass of research on sexual orientation would foster further research by increasing salience and knowledge.

Support

Support for research comes in many forms: job offers or promotions, internal or external research funds, and cross-fertilizing teaching opportunities. Most of us consider how our work will affect our ability to get, keep, or be promoted in jobs. Departments and funders may view research on sexual orientation as too interdisciplinary, overly political, or nonobjective, especially when done by sexual minorities (like feminist theory developed by women). In addition, departments may not want to be associated with this kind of work, and by extension, with sexual minorities. If departments and institutions don't "count" this work, then few economists will risk it.[6] In addition to "credit," funding for projects in this area is especially important for collection of original data because secondary data are hard to come by.[7] Finally, opportunities to teach on issues of sexual orientation are scarce, especially for people in traditional economics departments. Teaching creates opportunities for "joint production" and allows time for the interdisciplinary reading necessary for working in a field like this. The support of departmental and granting decision-makers is key to facilitating research.

As an adviser once told me, "We're in the business of getting publications." It takes a brave researcher (and a thrill-seeking untenured researcher) to risk an investment in a project which may not be publishable, even with departmental support. Published articles on the economics of sexual orientation (of which there are few) would evidence journals' willingness to seriously consider this type of research and thereby leverage new work in the area.

In addition to perusing publications, I think that most of us find inspiration from the work of colleagues through hallway talk, informal networks, and conference presentations. An active network and visible presence at conferences would feed additional work. The problem, then, is how to establish that critical mass of research and researchers. Some of the seeds have already emerged, but additional support may come from feminist economists and the new work on sexual orientation in the humanities and other social sciences.

Raw material

Theories and data are the raw materials of economics. Theories might be adaptable or expandable to issues of sexual orientation, but access to data is still severely limited. Most national surveys don't collect information on sexual orientation or behavior. Even if they did, many would need to over-sample sexual minorities to obtain a workable sample size. There are, however, several sources of U.S. data including the U.S. Census (for same-sex couples), the General Social Survey (includes measures of sexual behavior), voter survey data (Voter Research and Surveys Exit Polls include questions on sexual identity), and some convenience samples collected for special projects.[8] New data sets that combine information on sexual identity and behavior with economic variables would draw researchers.

Against the odds

So what has attracted people to research on sexual orientation in spite of the barriers? Probably the same things that ultimately drive other research projects – intellectual curiosity, personal salience, and opportunity. Like early feminist scholars, many of us have found the work irresistible because of the connections to personal and political events. However, the support of colleagues, departments, universities, grantors, and data collectors could greatly leverage our efforts to advance the scholarship on sexual orientation.

Notes

1   The personal identities chosen by people are not always consistent with the labels used by researchers or the public. Edward O. Laumann, John H. Gagnon, Robert T.

Michael, and Stuart Michaels (1994), in the National Study of Health and Sexual Behavior Survey, found imperfect overlap in homosexual desire, behavior and identity of their respondents.

2   I am very willing to draw a line between these categories and others; I would not include in my list of "protected" sexual minorities pedophiles or others whose sexual behavior involves beings who lack the willingness or ability to consent.

3   Although there are places and institutions with anti-discrimination policies, coverage is far from universal or perfectly enforced.

4   Interestingly, Taylor and Raeburn reported increases in perceptions of discrimination between 1981 and 1992 (from 27 percent to 43 percent). However, at the same time, they found large increases in the number of gays and lesbians who were out at work (30 percent in 1981 and 45 percent in 1992 were out to most colleagues).

5   Rand National Defense Research Institute (1993) found estimates of the size of the homosexual population from 2 to 10 percent of the U.S. population. M. V. Lee Badgett (1995) and Marieka Klawitter and Victor Flatt (1997) estimate that, on average, gay men earn less than straight men, and that lesbians earn about the same as straight women (among full-time workers).

6   Most political science department chairs surveyed expressed acceptance of faculty presenting papers on lesbian/gay topics (86 percent), but were less likely to view the department or institution as accepting (81 percent and 73 percent, respectively). However, 22 percent of gay and lesbian faculty reported being discouraged (not necessarily by the chair) from researching gay or lesbian topics, and 38.9 percent reported avoiding research in this area because of concern that it would not be taken seriously as political science (Committee on the Status 1995).

7   One source of funding available to economists (as well as other behavioral and social scientists) is the American Psychological Foundation's Wayne F. Placek Award. Information is available from APF, 750 First Street NE, Washington DC 2002–4242.

8   The 1990 U.S. Census includes information for same-sex couples. The General Social Survey includes measures of sexual behavior (for past year and five years) for the years 1988–91, 1993. The Voter Research and Surveys Exit Polls include questions on sexual identity beginning in 1992.

References

Badgett, M. V. Lee. 1995. "The Wage Effects of Sexual Orientation Discrimination." *Industrial and Labor Relations Review* 48(4): 726–39.

Committee on the Status of Lesbians and Gays in the Profession of the American Political Science Association. 1995. "Report on the Status of Lesbians and Gays in the Political Science Profession." *PS* (September): 561–74.

D'Emilio, John. 1993. "Capitalism and Gay Identity," in William B. Rubenstein (ed.) *Lesbians, Gay Men, and the Law*, pp. 26–31. New York: The New Press (reprint).

Klawitter, Marieka M. and Victor Flatt. 1997. "The Effects of State and Local Anti-discrimination Policies for Sexual Orientation." *Journal of Policy Analysis and Management* (forthcoming).

Laumann, Edward O., John H. Gagnon, Robert T. Michael, and Stuart Michaels.

1994. *The Social Organization of Sexuality: Sexual Practices in the United States.* Chicago: University of Chicago Press.

Moore, David W. 1993. "Public Polarized on Gay Issue." *Gallup Poll Monthly* (April): 31–4.

Rand National Defense Research Institute. 1993. *Sexual Orientation and U.S. Military Personnel Policy: Options and Assessment.*

Taylor, Verta and Nicole C. Raeburn. 1995. "Identity Politics as High-Risk Activism: Career Consequences for Lesbian, Gay, and Bisexual Sociologists." *Social Problems* 42(2): 252–73.

Chapter 5

Kyle D. Kauffman

UNCOVERING A QUANTITATIVE ECONOMIC HISTORY OF GAYS AND LESBIANS IN THE UNITED STATES

From *Feminist Economics* 1998, 4 (2): 61–4

GAY AND LESBIAN HISTORY has become a "hot" topic in history departments of late. A number of books, both scholarly and popular, have been published on many different topics related to gay history.[1] Most, however, have been social histories focusing primarily on documenting the existence of gay men and lesbians in the past and the social institutions that arose to meet their needs. Of course any discussion of gays in history brings up the issue surrounding the various forms that same-sex sexuality took over time. While definitions of what constitutes sexuality are at the heart of the controversy, I agree with John Boswell (1990) in being interested in documenting and studying same-sex sexuality (broadly defined) in different periods. Thus, I would define the term "gay" as anyone whose sexual interest is predominantly directed toward his or her own gender. For a good introduction to this essentialist/constructionist debate see Edward Stein (1990).

With all of the apparent interest in history departments, why, then, have economic historians completely avoided researching *economic* issues involving gays and lesbians?[2] It would appear to be an obvious topic of interest to economic historians. For instance, there has been much work done on the economic history of labor market discrimination against other minorities, such as African-Americans and Asian-Americans.[3] Has there been no mainstream economic history of gay and lesbian workers in the United States because economic historians believe the topic to be uninteresting or unimportant, or rather is it a simple case of homophobia? The answer, I believe, has more to do with standards of appropriate research methodology and use of evidence than with an inherent bias against doing research on these groups.

Discrimination against gays and lesbians in the labor market should be intrinsically interesting to many economic historians. The plot and cast of characters is essentially the same as in much of the good and valuable research done by economic historians on wage and occupational discrimination. There is a sizable, and thus economically important, group of people to research. The exact size of this group is certainly a matter of debate, but if we assume a relatively conservative number of 3 to 5 percent of the population, this number is similar to that of other minority groups in United States history who have received much more attention. For example, in 1900 African-Americans were 11.6 percent of the population and "all other races" were only 0.5 percent.[4] Lesbians and gay men have been socially and politically stigmatized to varying degrees, like blacks and many minority immigrant populations. They are also a group who, according to many social histories, accumulated above-average levels of human capital, similar to certain Asian communities (whom studies have found earned less than their white counterparts after controlling for other factors). For reasons such as these, the basic topic of gay and lesbian history *should* be of interest to economic historians.

The new economic history that developed in the late 1950s and early 1960s, which became known as "Cliometrics," is based firmly on the notion of using reliable and accurately collected data to answer an interesting economic question from the past. Much of the data used by economic historians come from federal and state government documents such as the Census, Bureau of Labor Statistics Reports, and so on.[5] The basic problem is that in the past, and for the most part still today, the government did not collect economic data on gays and lesbians.

The problem of a lack of obvious data sources has, however, been circumvented in many other instances in economic history research. For instance, much of what we know about the workings of the slavery system is derived from plantation records, ship manifests, and contemporary newspaper reports. These and many other creative methods of data collection have increased our knowledge in several areas of economic history. In order to break the logjam in the development of an economic history of gays and lesbians, we need to be equally creative in the use of historical data sources. These could include such things as matching the names of men and women from member lists of gay social clubs or the names of men arrested in bar and bath raids from police and court records to census data; studying historically "gay ghettos" in large cities in which large proportions of gay men and lesbians lived; and matching same-sex cohabiters in the census. All such methods invariably will be imperfect, but could serve as a first step in developing a foundation of credible data on which a legitimate economic history of both gay men and lesbians can be built. These sorts of methods could potentially provide a quantitative economic history going back to the first census of 1790.

Without the development of credible data sets, research on the economic history of gays and lesbians simply will not be accepted for publication in journals such as the *Journal of Economic History* and *Explorations in Economic History*, the discipline standard bearers. The challenge to develop a Cliometric-style economic history of gays and lesbians is significant. Just as it took much time, cleverness, and ingenuity to uncover appropriate data to understand other seemingly elusive topics, so too will it take patience and effort to uncover data appropriate to the task of writing an economic history of gay men and lesbians.

Acknowledgments

For helpful comments and discussions I thank Lee Badgett, Richard Cornwall, Prue Hyman, Sumner LaCroix, Julie Matthaei, Deirdre McCloskey, Martha Olney, Ann Velenchik and an anonymous referee. Any remaining inelegancies or errors in judgment are due to me.

Notes

1   Particularly noteworthy books include Martin Duberman, Martha Vicinus, and George Chauncey (1989), Elizabeth Lapovsky Kennedy and Madeline D. Davis (1993), George Chauncey (1994), and John Boswell (1994). In addition, a number of prestigious university presses, such as the University of Chicago and University of Illinois Presses, have established entire series devoted to the topic of homosexuality.

2   Interestingly, many social histories of gays and lesbians spend a great deal of time discussing economic issues. While some of these researchers have an impressive grasp of the issues they discuss, others unfortunately obviously lack competency and sophistication in economics.

3   This is one of many economic topics that one could explore within the gay and lesbian community. Others include capital accumulation, savings rates, and labor supply issues among others.

4   U.S. Bureau of the Census (1975), Series A91–A104. "All Other Races" in the 1900 Census included Indians, Japanese, and Chinese.

5   While most of the evidence used by "cliometric" economic historians is quantitative, qualitative evidence can be both informative and revealing. The use of oral histories, such as by Kennedy and Davis (1993), often provide an important starting point for future research. The ultimate goal, it would seem, is to move beyond an anecdotal history of gays and lesbians to a body of research that is more generalizable and universal.

References

Boswell, John. 1990. "Categories, Experience and Sexuality," in Edward Stein (ed.) *Forms of Desire: Sexual Orientation and the Social Constructionist Controversy*, pp. 133–73. New York: Garland.

—— . 1994. *Same-Sex Unions in Pre-Modern Europe*. New York: Villard.

Chauncey, George. 1994. *Gay New York: Gender, Urban Culture, and the Making of the Gay Male World*. New York: Basic Books.

D'Emilio, John. 1983. "Capitalism and Gay Identity," in Ann Sintow, Christine Stansell, and Sharon Thompson (eds.) *Powers of Desire: The Politics of Sexuality*, pp. 100–13. New York: Monthly Review Press.

Duberman, Martin, Martha Vicinus, and George Chauncey (eds.). 1989. *Hidden from History: Reclaiming the Gay and Lesbian Past*. New York: Meridian.

Kennedy, Elizabeth Lapovsky and Madeline D. Davis. 1993. *Boots of Leather, Slippers of Gold: The History of a Lesbian Community*. New York: Routledge.

Stein, Edward (ed.). 1990. *Forms of Desire: Sexual Orientation and the Social Constructionist Controversy*. New York: Garland.

United States Bureau of the Census. 1975. *Historical Statistics of the United States*. Washington, DC: Government Printing Office.

Queer demography

THE DATA COLLECTION and resulting calculation of statistics concerning sexual orientation and the characteristics of households and individuals by sexual orientation have not been a major concern of the US Bureau of the Census or most other data collection agencies and projects. Much of the historic information that is available contains sampling, question construction, or interviewing biases and must be evaluated meticulously in order to obtain any relevant and dependable findings. Researchers have developed a new interest in the field, and attempts at careful observation are now being made that we can increasingly trust for statistical inference purposes. This work is important because it opens society's eyes to the fact that homosexuality is more than anomaly and that there is a considerable percentage of the population that falls into this category.

Annual incomes, socio-economic positions, and job market concentration are all areas of interest in the study of queer demographics. Many myths concerning these figures for gay and lesbian households have their origin in erroneous data and require scrutiny for flawed assumptions and inferences (Hewitt 1995; Badgett 1997, 2000, 2001; Carpenter 2004). One such falsehood was that incomes for gays were substantially higher than those of their heterosexual counterparts.

Dan Black and his co-authors for "Demographics of the gay and lesbian population in the United States: evidence from available systematic data sources" (2000) present statistical characteristics of the gay and lesbian population. This chapter shows the types of characteristics that may be of interest, including the cities with the highest concentration of gays, death rates, military service, marriage rates and presence of children in the home, to name just a few. It also discusses the US surveys that provide various comparisons between homosexual and heterosexual groups, the General Social Survey, the National Health and Social Life Survey, and the Census. This chapter is important both for its definitions of the characteristics of interest and in its discussion of how one might explore the demographics of sexuality using nationally representative survey data in the absence of a direct survey question regarding sexual orientation.

Voon Phua and Gayle Kaufman, in "Using the census to profile same-sex cohabitation: a research note" (1999), directly tackle a difficult issue – namely, how to identify same-sex cohabiters. They consider one way to proxy for same-sex cohabiters, namely using 1990 US Census data on people who report living with a nonrelated person of the same sex, and discuss the pros and cons of using this methodology. This methodology will likely continue to be important for other surveys, particularly for many European countries, where cohabitation and formal non-marriage partnerships are increasingly considered to be normal household structures and questions asked to distinguish married from cohabiting heterosexual couples.

In a less-well-known piece about a less-well-known country – New Zealand, "Lesbians and gay men flirting with/disengaging from vital statistics: same sex relationships and the NZ Census 1971/2001" (2003), Prue Hyman creatively discusses the question of how to manage visibility and whether it is desirable in all circumstances. This piece contrasts to the previous two both in its non-US focus and its less sober tone.

Looking forward, the ability to observe the demographics of same-sex couples has improved greatly. While other researchers have used the 1990 US Census data as well (e.g., Jepsen and Jepsen 2002, 2006; Jepsen 2007), other sources of information about same-sex households have also been used, in part to compare the Census estimates of same-sex household prevalence (Carpenter 2004) and also to study epidemiological topics such as HIV infection prevalence and its relation to risky sexual behavior (Auld 2006).

The 2000 US Census is also now available for comparison with the 1990 results (Gates and Ost 2004), and allows for additional attempts to distinguish cohabiters from roommates (Jepsen 2007). Recent US reports (e.g. Black *et al.* 2007) using these newer Census data have focused on more specific topics and on population subsamples, including the number and location of same-sex couples raising children (Bennett and Gates 2004a; Sears *et al.* 2005), the number of gay, lesbian, and bisexual seniors (Bennett and Gates 2004b), the interaction of minority racial or ethnic status with same-sex orientation (Gates and Sears 2005), and homeownership rates (Leppel 2007). More reports are starting to come out for other countries as well – for instance, countries that have regis-tered partnership data (e.g. Norway and Sweden – see Andersson *et al.* 2006).

However, it is important to realize the ongoing challenges of getting accur-ate demographics with regards to household composition by sexual orientation for all countries. In particular, without a direct question as to sexual orienta-tion it is not possible to determine the composition of non-couple households with regards to this factor. Other surveys that have asked more detailed questions regarding sexual orientation, or that have focused specifically on same-sex couples, have been suspect regarding their representativeness (for instance, if a magazine survey is used, responses are limited to those who choose to send in answers). While internet sampling shows promise, particularly in reduced sam-pling costs and maintained anonymity and privacy while responding, results from such surveys must be carefully examined for selection bias (Koch and Emrey 2001). And a number of questions remain understudied, including the nature and extent of extended family and community networks by sexual orien-tation (Rose and Bravewomon 1998). Thus it continues to be a challenge to collect, analyze, and disseminate accurate data regarding the relative numbers of people by sexual orientation and to analyze different groups' characteristics.

And as well, the question of whether visibility is indeed desired and, if so, on what terms, continues to exist, even as recent public policy matters such as the question of legalizing same-sex marriage have tended to push this issue to the back of current debates.

DISCUSSION QUESTIONS

1   What are some problems concerning data collection regarding sexual orientation and how can they be minimized?
2   Are there significant demographic differences between same-sex and heterosexual couples?
3   On what dimensions have the relative economic positioning of queer and heterosexual individuals been compared? Can you think of other dimensions that would be of interest?
4   What kind of statistics would be pertinent to current political debates, and why?
5   Why might invisibility be desirable? If desirable, how can that be reconciled with the desire for accurate statistics to inform public policy?

REFERENCES

Andersson, G., Noack, T., Seierstad, A., and Weedon-Fekjaer, H. (2006) "The demographics of same-sex marriages in Norway and Sweden," *Demography*, 43: 79–98.

Auld, M. C. (2006) "Estimating behavioral response to the AIDS epidemic," *Contributions to Economic Analysis & Policy*, 5: 1–27.

Badgett, M. V. L. (1997) "Beyond biased samples: challenging the myths on the economic status of lesbians and gay men," in A. Gluckman and B. Reed (eds) *Homo Economics: capitalism, community, and lesbian and gay life*, New York: Routledge.

—— (2000) "Income inflation: the myth of affluence among gay, lesbian, and bisexual Americans," Joint publication of the Policy Institute of The National Gay and Lesbian Task Force and The Institute for Gay and Lesbian Strategic Studies.

—— (2001) *Money, Myths, and Change: the economic lives of lesbians and gay men*, Chicago and London: University of Chicago Press.

Bennett, L. and Gates, G. J. (2004a) "The cost of marriage inequality to children and their same-sex parents," Human Rights Campaign Foundation Report, Washington, DC: Human Rights Campaign.

—— (2004b) "The cost of marriage inequality to gay, lesbian and bisexual seniors,"

Human Rights Campaign Foundation Report, Washington, DC: Human Rights Campaign.

Black, D. A., Sanders, S. G., and Taylor, L. J. (2007) "The economics of lesbian and gay families," *Journal of Economic Perspectives*, 21: 53–70.

Carpenter, C. (2004) "New evidence on gay and lesbian household incomes," *Contemporary Economic Policy*, 22: 78–94.

Gates, G. and Sears, R. B. (2005) "Asians and Pacific Islanders in same-sex couples in California," California Center for Population Research On-Line Working Paper Series, no. CCPR–021–05, Los Angeles: UCLA.

Gates, G. J. and Ost, J. (2004) *The Gay and Lesbian Atlas*, Washington, DC: Urban Institute Press.

Hewitt, C. (1995) "The socioeconomic position of gay men: a review of the evidence," *American Journal of Economics and Sociology*, 54: 461–79.

Jepsen, C. A. and Jepsen, L. K. (2006) "The sexual division of labor within households: comparisons of couples to roommates," *Eastern Economic Journal*, 32: 299–312.

Jepsen, L. K. (2007) "Comparing the earnings of cohabiting lesbians, cohabiting heterosexual women, and married women: evidence from the 2000 Census," *Industrial Relations*, forthcoming.

Jepsen, L. K. and Jepsen, C. A. (2002) "An empirical analysis of the matching patterns of same-sex and opposite-sex couples," *Demography*, 39: 435–53.

Koch, N. S. and Emrey, J. A. (2001) "The internet and opinion measurement: surveying marginalized populations," *Social Science Quarterly*, 82: 131–8.

Leppel, K. (2007) "Homeownership among married and unmarried, opposite- and same-sex couples," *Feminist Economics*, forthcoming.

Rose, N. and Bravewomon, L. (1998) "Family webs: a study of extended families in the lesbian/gay/bisexual community," *Feminist Economics*, 4: 107–9.

Sears, R. B., Gates, G., and Rubenstein, W. B. (2005) "Same-sex couples and same-sex couples raising children in the United States: data from Census 2000," report, the Williams Project on Sexual Orientation Law and Public Policy, Los Angeles: UCLA School of Law.

Chapter 6

Dan Black, Gary Gates, Seth Sanders, and Lowell Taylor

DEMOGRAPHICS OF THE GAY AND LESBIAN POPULATION IN THE UNITED STATES: EVIDENCE FROM AVAILABLE SYSTEMATIC DATA SOURCES[1]

From *Demography*, May 2000, 37 (2): 139–54

[. . .]

THE EMERGENCE OF SOLID demographic studies describing the gay and lesbian population marks an important change for social science research. Historically, few sizable surveys of this population were available, and many previous surveys that provided large samples of gays and lesbians utilized "convenience sampling," as in samples drawn from readers of particular magazines or newspapers, or responses solicited from Internet sites or in gay bars. Researchers have been properly reluctant to draw general inferences about the gay and lesbian population from these samples. Recently, however, a number of scholars have begun to study economic and social issues in the gay and lesbian population using sizable samples with known properties – samples drawn from the General Social Survey, the National Health and Social Life Survey, and the 1990 U.S. census.

We view this recent emergence of careful, systematic empirical work on the gay and lesbian population as valuable on two fronts. First, this work can usefully inform public policy. The past decade has been marked by a significant amount of public debate and legislation regarding gay and lesbian Americans. Issues include initiatives designed to prohibit discrimination or, conversely, to prohibit civil rights protection based on sexual orientation; public policy concerning provision of domestic partnership benefits (including health insurance) to gay and lesbian couples; the U.S. military policy prohibiting openly gay and lesbian individuals from serving in the armed forces; the legalization of same-sex marriage; and gay and lesbian parental rights and suitability for adoption. Informed policy analysis about these issues requires accurate demographic information about the gay and lesbian population. For example, the city of San Francisco was unable to estimate the number of partnered households or the rate at which one domestic partner was not covered by benefits. This situation led Carol Piasente, a spokeswoman for the San Francisco Chamber of Commerce, to comment, "We don't have a clue about costs. That's the problem. Nobody knows" ("S.F. Seeks Equal Treatment" 1996:3b).

Second, careful empirical analysis of the gay and lesbian population holds promise for helping social scientists understand a wide array of important questions – questions about the general nature of labor market choices, accumulation of human capital, specialization within households, discrimination, and decisions about geographic location.

Our work provides an overview of available data currently used by social scientists to study the gay and lesbian population in the United States; in doing so, it provides interesting and policy-relevant statistics about this population. We focus on what can be learned about the gay and lesbian population from three large data sets: the General Social Survey (GSS), the National Health and Social Life Survey (NHSLS) and the U.S. census. In particular, we examine four characteristics of the gay and lesbian population: their geographical distribution, their veteran status, the family structure of their households, and their education, earnings, and wealth.

We begin by reviewing the limited economic and demographic literature that investigates gays and lesbians using the NHSLS, the GSS, or 1990 census data. We then discuss the three data sources, emphasizing how gays and lesbians can be identified in each survey. We pay special attention to confirming that the sample of gays and lesbians identified is not simply the result of recording error. In the next section, we provide a comparison of findings from the data sets (and in some instances, comparisons with other available information). In doing so, we develop a statistical portrait of the gay and lesbian population that is broadly consistent across data sources. We close with concluding remarks.

Literature review

The National Health and Social Life Survey (NHSLS) served as the basis for two well-known books, *Sex in America: A Definitive Study* (Michael et al. 1994) and *The Social Organization of Sex: Sexual Practices in the United States*

(Laumann et al. 1994). The latter book features a chapter (Chapter 8) on gays and lesbians that focuses on the definition of homosexuality and the prevalence of gay, lesbian, and bisexual behavior in the United States. One of the main issues addressed by Laumann et al. is how varying definitions of homosexuality affect the measured incidence rates. The authors show that whereas the incidence rate of homosexual desire is 7.7% for men and 7.5% for women, the rate at which men identify themselves as gay is 2.8%, and the rate at which women identify themselves as lesbians is 1.4%. These figures are similar to the rates at which men and women have exclusively same-sex sex (3.0% and 1.6%).

The authors' findings are important for two reasons. First, they demonstrate the importance of sampling from a known population. There exists a widespread belief, based largely on Kinsey's pioneering research (e.g., Kinsey et al. 1948), that "10 percent of males are more or less exclusively homosexual." This statement is not supported in the careful work of Laumann et al. (1994).[2] Second, they highlight the ambiguity of the very definition of homosexuality. Those who acknowledge homosexual desires may be far more numerous than those who actually act on those desires. Nonetheless, gays and lesbians show substantially different behavior than other individuals on some important dimensions: For example, they are less likely to enter into traditional marriages.

In addition to standard economic and demographic data, the NHSLS collects by far the most extensive information on sexual practices and sexual partners. Among the data sets we examine, the NHSLS is the only data set that gathers information on sexual practices over the life course – an important advantage because sexual behavior regarding the sex of one's partner is not immutable. Any inferences about gays and lesbians drawn from this sample, however, are based on very small samples. For example, in a sample of 3,432 American men and women, only 12 women identified themselves as lesbians and only 27 men identified themselves as gay. As we discuss below, far more men and women than indicated by these figures have had same-sex experiences.

A second data source is the General Social Survey. To our knowledge, Badgett's (1995) study of earnings and sexual orientation, based on pooled 1989–1991 GSS data was the first work exploiting the GSS to systematically compare gays and lesbians with heterosexual counterparts. For most of her analysis, Badgett (1995) defines lesbians, gays, and bisexuals as individuals having more same-sex sexual partners than opposite-sex sexual partners since age 18. Using this definition and conditioning on a variety of characteristics, she finds that gay men earn 28% less than heterosexual men, but that sexual orientation has no statistically significant effect on women's earnings.

Black et al. (1998) provide a similar analysis using GSS, data from 1988–1991, 1993, 1994, and 1996. They find that the effect of sexual orientation on earnings depends to some degree on the definition of sexual orientation that is used. One general finding in their work confirms Badgett's earlier finding for men: Gay men appear to earn substantially less than other men with equal skills. Lesbian women, however, earn 20% to 35% more than other equally skilled women; this difference is statistically significant.

Pooling the GSS samples over eight years produces a reasonable sample of gays and lesbians, between about 150 and 450 individuals (depending on the definition used), along with several thousand other men and women. Though obviously more satisfactory than the sample taken from the NHSLS, this is still quite small.

A third data source, the 1990 U.S. census, allows a sample of more than 13,700 gays and lesbians to be identified. In taking the decennial census, the Census Bureau designates as the head of household (the householder) "the member (or one of the members) in whose name the home is owned, being bought, or rented." The Census Bureau then collects information on all the members of the household and identifies each member by his or her relationship to the householder. Before 1990, couples living outside marriage in marriage-like relationships were not identified separately from individuals living together as roommates. Demographers, however, had noticed an increasing prevalence of the former type of household. Bumpass and Sweet (1989), for example, report that only 3% of women born between 1940 and 1944 had ever cohabited by age 25; among women born 20 years later, 37% reported cohabiting by age 25. Because of this trend, the Census Bureau changed the survey instrument for the 1990 census to allow unmarried partners to be identified separately from roommates.

Fortunately the census instrument allows household heads to report an unmarried partnership regardless of the partner's sex. In contrast, many previous surveys (e.g., the National Longitudinal Study of the Class of 1972) explicitly restricted cohabitation questions to heterosexual partnerships. In the public use samples of the 1990 census, we can identify a sample of more than 6,800 gay and lesbian households. Clearly, this is not a random sample of people who would identify themselves as gay or lesbian, nor is it a sample of those who have engaged in same-sex sex, because the sample contains only individuals who are involved in a cohabiting relationship. Exploring the nature of this sample is a major contribution of this paper.

To our knowledge, the 1990 census data were first used to study a group of gays and lesbians by Lisa Krieger (1993), a reporter for the *San Francisco Examiner*. Since then, these data have proved useful for several academic studies. Black et al. (1997) examined the effects of sexual orientation on men's wages. They found that men in gay couples earn substantially less than other men, with controls for earnings-related characteristics such as potential experience, education, and demographic traits (e.g., race). Much of this wage differential, however, may be explained by the occupational choices of the coupled gay men.

Klawitter (1997) studied the effects of sexual orientation on earnings among women. She found that women in lesbian couples earn substantially more than other women, but that much of this difference is attributable to differences in earnings-related characteristics. Klawitter and Flatt (1998), investigating the effects of state and local antidiscrimination policies for sexual orientation, found little evidence that these policies are correlated with higher earnings for gay men.

Black et al. (1999), who studied the geographic distribution of gay men, argued that gay men are more willing to pay for amenities not related to children, and provided evidence that this trait influences gay men to locate in unusually attractive locations. Jepsen (1998) and Jepsen and Jepsen (1999) studied assortative mating and labor market specialization of gay and lesbian couples.

Although these papers constitute a useful advance in understanding gays and lesbians in the United States, the reliability of their principal data source has not been investigated systematically.

Identifying gays and lesbians in social science data sets

The General Social Survey (GSS) and the National Health and Social Life Survey (NHSLS)

The GSS is designed to measure social indicators of opinions and attitudes over time in the United States. It uses a multistage area probability sampling design, in which a randomly selected adult from each household in selected geographic areas is asked to participate. Approximately 1,500 adults were sampled annually from 1972 through 1994 (except in 1981 and 1992). Since 1996, the sample size has been doubled but the survey has been conducted only every two years.

In 1992, when the GSS was not fielded, the resources were dedicated to fielding the NHSLS. The NHSLS was drawn using the same sampling frame as the GSS, and many of the same questions are asked, so that the two surveys can be combined for analysis. The NHSLS is restricted to individuals ages 18–59; the GSS samples adults at any age over 18.

In comparing gays and lesbians with other men and women, one cannot avoid the complicated question of what it means to be gay or lesbian. The GSS and the NHSLS contain a common set of questions on sexuality that allows several ways of defining sexual orientation. Beginning in 1988 the GSS has asked several questions about the sex of individuals with whom the respondent has had sex: Respondents were asked, "Have your sex partners in the last 12 months been exclusively male, both male and female, exclusively female?" Beginning in 1991, a parallel question has been asked about a respondent's sex partners in the five years prior to the survey. In each year since 1989 the GSS has asked both male and female respondents, "Now thinking about the time since your 18th birthday (including the past 12 months), how many male partners have you had sex with?" A parallel question is asked about the number of female partners.

In combination with the respondent's sex, these questions can be used to classify a respondent's sexual orientation by four different definitions. The first and second definitions, "having ever had a same-sex sex partner" and "having had at least as many same-sex as opposite-sex sex partners since age 18," rely on information about the sex of sex partners since age 18. The third and fourth definitions, "having had exclusively same-sex sex over the last year" and "having had exclusively same-sex sex over the last five years," rely on the sex of sex partners over the last year or last five years. The first definition is employed in Laumann et al. (1994), Badgett (1995), and Black et al. (1998). The second definition is used in Badgett (1995) and Black et al. (1998). The third and fourth definitions are used in Laumann et al. (1994) and Black et al. (1998).

In Table 1 we report the incidence rates and sample counts of gay and lesbian status based on these four different definitions, using a sample that pools data from the 1989–1991, 1993, 1994, and 1996 GSS and NSHLS. Like Laumann et al., we find that the incidence rate of homosexuality varies greatly depending on how homosexuality is defined. For example, 4.7% of men in the combined samples have had at least one same-sex experience since age 18, but only 2.5% of men have engaged in exclusively same-sex sex over the year preceding the survey. Similarly, 3.5% of women have had at least one same-sex sexual experience, but only 1.4% have had exclusively same-sex sex over the year preceding the survey. Table 1 also shows that

Table 1 Sample sizes (and incidence) of gays and lesbians for various definitions in the combined 1988–1991, 1993, 1994, and 1996, GSS and NHSLS[a]

	Women		Men	
Definition of homosexuality	Lesbian	Bisexual	Gay	Bisexual
1 At least one same-sex partner since age 18[b]	260 (3.6%)		260 (4.7%)	
Total observations	7,125		5,536	
2 More same-sex than opposite-sex partners since age 18	123 (1.8%)		164 (3.1%)	
Total observations	6,826		5,239	

3 Same-sex and opposite-sex sex partners over the last year	–		29 (0.5%)	–		33 (0.6%)
Exclusively same-sex sex partners over the last year[c]	88 (1.4%)		–	139 2.5%		–
Total observations		6,414			5,519	
4 Same-sex and opposite-sex sex partners over the last 5 years	–		66 (1.2%)	–		72 (1.6%)
Exclusively same-sex sex partners over the last 5 years[c,d]	78 (1.5%)		–	115 (2.6%)		–
Total observations		5,361			4,430	
5 Self-identified gay, lesbian, or bisexual[e]	12 (0.6%)		10 (0.5%)	27 (1.8%)		11 (0.7%)
Total observations		1,921			1,511	

[a]   Excluded from the analysis are all individuals who showed an inconsistency suggesting that their recorded sex or sexual history might be in error. The GSS asked the respondent's sex and then the sex of each member of the household. If the GSS recorded different sexes for the respondent in these two parts of the survey, the observation was not used. In addition, if an individual indicated having had sex with a person of a particular sex over the last year (or last five years), but also reported never having had sex with a person of that sex since age 18, the observation was excluded from analysis. Similarly, if a respondent reported having had a child born to him or her, but reported never having had opposite-sex sex, the observation was dropped from analysis.

[b]   Questions on the number of male and female partners of the respondent since age 18 were asked beginning with the 1989 survey.

[c]   Categories include exclusively same-sex sex, exclusively opposite-sex sex, sex with both men and women, and no sex during the relevant period. More individuals may have had exclusively same-sex sex over the last five years than over the last year, as more individuals have had sex at all over the last five years than over the last year.

[d]   Asked in the GSS since 1991.

[e]   Asked only in the NHSLS.

regardless of definition, the samples of gays and lesbians are small in the GSS and NHSLS, even when we combine seven years of data.

Table 2 shows that the definitions of homosexuality are not correlated as highly as one might think, particularly for women. For example, we find that among women who had at least one female sex partner since age 18,

Table 2 Fraction of men and of women with same-sex sexual experience who are gay or lesbian by various definitions, combined 1988–1991, 1993, 1994, and 1996, GSS and NHSLS

	2 More same-sex than opposite-sex sex partners since age 18	*3 Exclusively same-sex sex partners over the last year*	*4 Exclusively same-sex sex partners over the last 5 years*
Men			
1 At least one same-sex sex partner since age 18	0.61 ($n=249$)	0.42 ($n=209$)	0.43 ($n=173$)
2 More same-sex than opposite-sex sex partners since age 18		0.68 ($n=111$)	0.69 ($n=98$)
3 Exclusively same-sex sex partners over the last year			0.83 ($n=80$)
Women			
1 At least one same-sex sex partner since age 18	0.42 ($n=233$)	0.28 ($n=196$)	0.21 ($n=170$)
2 More same-sex than opposite-sex sex partners since age 18		0.51 ($n=78$)	0.49 ($n=53$)
3 Exclusively same-sex sex partners over the last year			0.66 ($n=44$)

Source: Authors' compilations from the GSS-NHSLS data.

Notes: The denominator for each fraction is the number of individuals ever with a same-sex sexual experience since age 18 who could be classified as gay or lesbian by the relevant definition. For definitions based on sex of sex partners over the last year and over the last five years, the risk set consists of all individuals who had exclusively same-sex sex, who had exclusively opposite-sex sex, or who had sex with both men and women over the relevant period. Excluded are individuals who did not have sex over the relevant period, as well as individuals who did not answer the question. For the definition based on having had at least as many same-sex as opposite-sex sex partners, the risk set includes only individuals who reported an exact number of men and of women with whom they had had sex since age 18. People who refused to answer either question or who answered in a range (e.g., "more than one") are excluded.

only 28% have been involved, over the past year, in exclusively same-sex sexual relationships. Similarly, only 42% of men who have had a male sexual partner since age 18 have had exclusively same-sex sex over the year before the survey.

The NHSLS has two unique features that make it far more valuable than simply an additional year of GSS data. First, it is the only large probability survey that asks respondents directly about their sexual orientation. The questionnaire asks, "Do you think of yourself as heterosexual, homosexual, bisexual, or something else?" Table 1 shows that the incidence rate of homosexuality is slightly lower by this definition than by the definition of having had exclusively same-sex sex over the past year. Because of the low incidence rate (and the modest sample size of the NHSLS), only 12 women and 27 men report thinking of themselves as homosexual.

A second unique feature of the NHSLS is that the survey records detailed data on sexual partners and on living arrangements between the respondent and all sexual partners over his or her lifetime. As we make clear below, understanding partnership is crucial to understanding the sample of gays and lesbians identified in the 1990 census data. In the NHSLS data we can define gay and lesbian respondents as "partnered" if, at the time of the NHSLS survey, they were cohabiting with a partner with whom there was a sexual relationship.

Unfortunately the GSS includes only limited information on sex partners and on cohabitation. In the GSS we know only the respondent's current household structure; identifying a household member as an "unmarried partner" is not an option. Since 1988, however, the GSS has asked respondents, "Was one of your partners (in the last 12 months) your husband, wife or regular sex partner?" In the GSS we can define a respondent as "partnered" if he or she either has a spouse in the household (for gays and lesbians, a spouse of the same sex), or lived with an unrelated adult in the household and also reported having had sex with a "husband, wife or regular sex partner."[3]

Table 3 presents the partnership rates among men and women who had exclusively same-sex sex over the year preceding the survey. From the combined GSS and NHSLS data, we estimate that 28.4% of gay men and 44.1% of lesbians are partnered at the time of the survey. Then, using the NHSLS, with its rich cohabitation history, we find that 67.9% of gay men and 93.8% of lesbians lived with a same-sex sex partner at some time. Finally, we present the same statistics for the set of men and women in the NHSLS who self-identify as gays and lesbians. Although the samples are small, we find that the partnership rates among gays and lesbians who self-identify are quite similar to the rates for gays and lesbians defined by their sexual experience over the year before the survey.

Our first four definitions of sexual orientation in the GSS rely on accurate recording of the respondent's sex, as well as accurate recording of the sex of the respondent's partners. In general, accurate recording of sex is not an issue in social science data. Because only a small fraction of the U.S. population is gay or lesbian, however, inaccurate reporting of sex becomes a salient issue. To understand the issue at hand, consider an individual with one partner. Let the recorded sex of a respondent, S, and

Table 3 Partnership rates among gays and lesbians in the NHSLS and GSS

	Sample size	Percentage currently partnered	Percentage ever partnered
Same-sex sex last year			
(GSS and NHSLS)	161	34.2	NA
Gay	102	28.4	NA
Lesbian	59	44.1	NA
Same-sex sex last year			
(NHSLS Only)	44	34.1	77.3
Gay	28	28.6	67.9
Lesbian	16	43.8	93.8
Self-identified gay			
(NHSLS only)	39	25.6	66.6
Gay	27	18.5	59.3
Lesbian	12	41.6	83.3

Source: Authors' compilations from the GSS-NHSLS data.

the recorded sex of a respondent's partner, P, take on one of two values, M or F (male or female). Let S^* and P^* be respectively the respondent's true sex and the true sex of a respondent's partner (that is, sex in the absence of recording error). We focus on the following question: Given that there is inevitably some recording error in S and P, among men who were recorded "gay" (have same-sex partners), how many in fact are gay? A simple Bayes's rule calculation is helpful here:

$$\Pr(S^* = M, P^* = M \mid S = M, P = M)$$
$$= \frac{\Pr(S^* = M, P^* = M) \times \Pr(S = M, P = M \mid S^* = M, P^* = M)}{\sum_{s\varepsilon\{M,F\}} \sum_{p\varepsilon\{M,F\}} \Pr(S^* = s, P^* = p) \times \Pr(S = M, P = M \mid S^* = s, P = p)}. \quad (1)$$

Suppose, for example, that a respondent's sex is recorded incorrectly with the same frequency as is the sex of a respondent's partner. If, in addition, incorrect recording of sex is independent of a respondent's sexual orientation, Eq. (1) reduces to

$$\Pr(S^* = M, P^* = M \mid S = M, P = M)$$
$$= \frac{\Pr(S^* = M, P^* = M) \times \Pr(S = M \mid S^* = M) \times \Pr(P = M \mid P^* = M)}{\sum_{s\varepsilon\{M,F\}} \sum_{p\varepsilon\{M,F\}} \Pr(S^* = s, P^* = p) \times \Pr(S = M \mid S^* = s) \times \Pr(P = M \mid P^* = p)}.$$
$$(2)$$

Evidence suggests that the fraction of gays in the population, $\Pr(S^* = M, P^* = M)$, is approximately 2.5%; the fraction of lesbians in the population, $\Pr(S^* = F, P^* = F)$, is approximately 1.5%; and the remaining 96% of the population is divided approximately evenly between heterosexual men, $\Pr(S^* = M, P^* = F)$, and heterosexual women, $\Pr(S^* = F, P^* = M)$. To complete our example, suppose that 0.5% of own and partner's sex is in error. Then Eq. (2) indicates that 16% of the sample classified as gay is not gay and that 24% of the sample classified as lesbian in fact is not lesbian.

No study has been conducted to validate the accuracy of the demographic variables in the GSS or NHSLS.[4] The internal consistency of the GSS data can be checked in several ways, however. For example, the survey asks each respondent his or her sex twice, once to collect the respondent's background characteristics and again to collect the relationship between persons living in the same household. For the 1988–1996 surveys, these two reports of sex agree in 96.13% of all cases in which the respondent was the head of household or a spouse; this percentage suggests an error rate of about 1.97%.[5]

Similarly, there are multiple reports of the sex of the respondent's sex partners. During the 1989–1996 surveys, for example, 4,105 respondents reported having sex with a man over the last year, and also reported the number of men with whom they had sex since age 18. Clearly, if the respondent reported having sex with a man in the last year, but then reported never having had sex with a man since age 18, one of the reports is in error. This occurred in only 0.8% (33) of the cases, yielding an error rate of 0.4%. If the rate at which sex is recorded incorrectly is 1.97% and the rate at which partner's sex is recorded incorrectly is 0.4%, Eq. (2) suggests that 32% of respondents classified as "gay" in fact are not gay and that 44% of respondents classified as "lesbian" are not lesbian. Because of the nature of the recording error, most respondents coded mistakenly as gay are heterosexual women with their sex miscoded, and most respondents recorded mistakenly as lesbians are heterosexual men with their sex miscoded.

It is important to understand the implication of this misclassification. For example, women generally earn less than men in the labor market. Given this, it would be easy to infer that men recorded as gay in our sample earn less than other men, even if gay men's average earnings are the same as other men's. In drawing conclusions about differences between gay men and other men, or lesbian women and other women, it is paramount that this measurement issue be addressed.

There is no infallible method for addressing this problem with the GSS. One reasonable approach is to use only observations in which the two reports of the respondent's sex agree. A second approach is to attempt to combine the various measures of sexual orientation into one reliable measure. For example, Black et al. (1998) examine the robustness of their analysis of gays and lesbians as follows: They start with the observation that only a small fraction of heterosexual men and women ever have sex with a member of the same sex (as indicated in Table 1). Gay men, however, typically have had sex with a woman, and lesbian women typically have had sex with a man, at some time since age 18. Black et al. (1998) thus suggest that one way of limiting the intrusion of sex misclassification is to exclude all men recorded as currently "gay" who have not had sex with a woman at some time since age 18. (Similarly, they exclude all women recorded as lesbians who have not had sex with a man at some time since age 18.) The cost of such a procedure is that a gay man who has never experimented with opposite-sex sex will be excluded from the gay sample. The benefit is that virtually all women who have been coded mistakenly as men will be eliminated from the sample of gay men. (The only women in the gay sample would be women whose sex is miscoded and who have had same-sex sex. In the sample sizes used here, this would be a very small number of individuals, probably zero.)

The 1990 census public use microdata samples

Next we explore how the combination of the 5% and 1% Public Use Microdata Samples (PUMS) of the 1990 census can be used to construct a sample of gays and lesbians. In the 1990 census, as we have discussed, gay and lesbian respondents can identify themselves as unmarried partners (but not as married). These are the households we wish to study.

We begin with a sample of 6,632,090 households. Of these, we excluded 293,471 group quarters and 807,558 vacant housing units, as well as 205,494 households in which some household member's relationship to the householder was imputed.[6] Figure 1 displays our scheme for classifying the remaining 5,325,565 households in the 1990 census.

The double-outlined boxes represent our three relationship categories: households in which the head has no apparent marriage-like relationship (A), households in which the head has a marriage-like relationship (B), and households in which the head appears to have multiple marriage-like relationships (C). A "marriage-like relationship" refers to a married couple or a partnered couple (either opposite- or same-sex). Each marriage-like relationship is divided into subgroups. Subgroups in boxes with solid outlines are, in principle, observable from the data, whereas subgroups in boxes with broken outlines are unobservable.

We find just over 2 million households with no marriage-like relationship. (We immediately exclude 57,321 of these households either because the householder was under 18 or because the householder's age was allocated.) The majority of these households with no marriage-like relationship are single adults (1.5 million). Obviously some of these individuals are gay or lesbian, but the census does not ask questions about respondents' sexual orientation, so they cannot be identified.

Of the remaining households, 131,598 are composed of three or more adults (A.3). Another 260,929 households consist of two related adults, which we also do not characterize further (A.2.1). Of the 124,519 households with two unrelated adults (A.2.2), 48,380 are of mixed sex (A.2.2.2), divided between opposite-sex roommates and cohabiting couples who chose not to identify themselves as unmarried partners, while 39,407 are two-male (A.2.2.1) and 36,732 are two-female (A.2.2.3) households. These households include heterosexual and homosexual individuals, but there is no means of identifying the respondents' sexual orientation.

About 3.2 million households contain one marriage-like relationship. (We immediately exclude 64,591 households with allocated age or sex and households in which either the partner or the householder was under 18.) Over 3 million are heterosexual married couples (B.1), 151,358 are opposite-sex couples who are unmarried partners (B.2), and, finally, 6,863 are same-sex unmarried partners: 3,800 male couples (B.3.1) and 3,063 female couples (B.3.2) (in boxes with bold outlines). These are same-sex couples with each partner over age 18. By excluding all households with any age allocation, any sex allocation, and any relationship-to-householder allocation, we can be assured that respondents indeed indicated that they were in a same-sex unmarried partnership.

Two important questions about our sample arise immediately. First, are same-sex partners identified in the sample indeed gay or lesbian, or instead are they nonpartnered individuals who were measured in error? Although the samples of gay and lesbian households are quite large, they account for only about 0.1% of all households in the census. Thus even small levels of misclassification of unmarried partnership status might lead to erroneous classification of a large fraction of same-sex couples in B.3.

Second, even if these 6,863 households are gay and lesbian, how do they relate to the population of gays and lesbians more generally? Obviously this sample necessarily excludes gays and lesbians not living in partnered relationships; furthermore, it is likely that the census greatly undercounts partnered gays and lesbians.

Our first concern is establishing an a priori case that the same-sex partners we observe are not predominantly the product of measurement error. Below we discuss how partnered gays and lesbians differ from non-partnered gays and lesbians, and how the census sample of partnered gays and lesbians differs from a random sample of partnered gays and lesbians drawn from the GSS.

One case that clearly shows some sort of measurement error is among households classified as containing multiple marriage-like relationships (C).[7] The extent and type of error recorded in such cases provides an

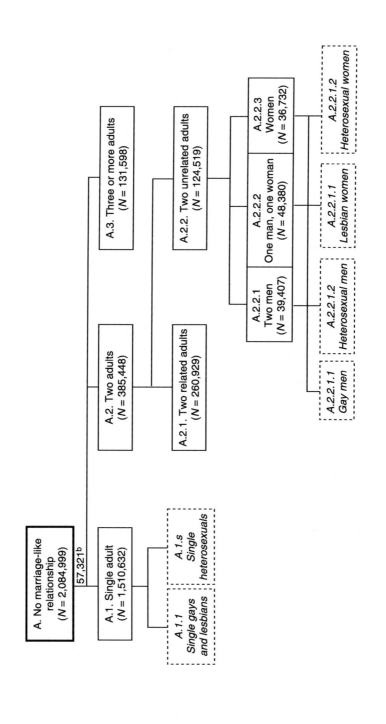

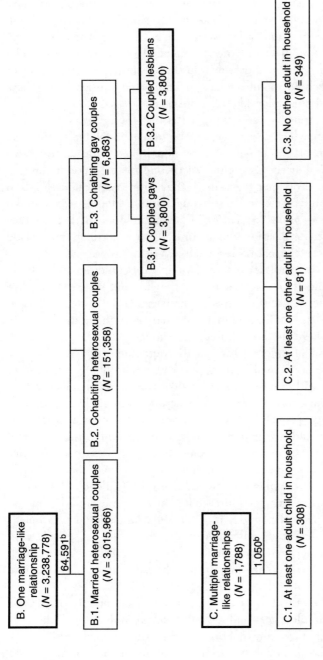

Figure 1 Classification of households into marriage-like relationships for a sample with nonimputed relationship to householder for all household members: public use microdata samples, 1990 census[a]

[a] The total number of households in the PUMS is 6,632,090. In 205,494 households, at least one household member had his or her relationship to the householder imputed by the Census Bureau. The sample contains 293,471 group quarters and 807,558 vacant households. Two households contain coding errors.

[b] Households with age allocated, sex allocated, or householder or partner under age 18.

important clue about the extent and type of measurement error we might expect to face elsewhere in the data (particularly in B.3). The most prevalent reason for apparent multiple partnerships is that a child is classified as a partner or that a household member's age or sex was allocated. Of the 1,788 apparent multiple marriage-like relationships, 1,050 households show one of the partners under age 18 or with an allocated age or sex. This type of error will not affect our measurement of gay and lesbian couples because in all of our same-sex partnerships in B.3, both partners are 18 or older and all household members have nonallocated age and sex. There remain 738 multiple marriage-like relationships.

The first hypothesis we can investigate is that these errors are simply mistakes – cases in which a very small number of individuals randomly "checked the wrong box." If we examine households with exactly three adults, we find 86 households composed of one married couple and an additional partner. Altogether there are 450,717 three-adult households in which two of the adults are married. If we accept that spouses are identified correctly, then, since only 86 of 450,717 householders marked another adult as an unmarried partner, the error rate in recording "unmarried partner" among these households is trivial: less than 0.02%.

If we perform a similar exercise among households containing no married couples, the error rate is somewhat higher, but still very low. We find that among the 109,690 three-adult households without a marriage, 229 identify two of the adults as unmarried partners of the householder. In these cases, we believe the householder occasionally "checked the wrong box." This suggests a 0.2% error rate for this outcome.

These calculations provide strong evidence that the error present among households with multiple marriage-like relationships does not take the form of random error ("checking the wrong box"), which affects all individuals with equal probability. Instead, a small but nontrivial number of individuals in households with no married couple apparently "misinterpret" the meaning of *unmarried partner*. For example, a respondent may consider his two roommates "partners" if household resources are shared. If this is the form of the error, it is easy to calculate its incidence. Altogether 153,048 households in our sample contain three or more adults but no married couples (this is the sum of the 131,598 households with no partnerships, 20,858 households with one partnership, 540 households with two unmarried partners recorded, and 52 with more than two unmarried partners). There are 592 errors among these households, for an error rate of 0.39%.

We consider even this low rate an upper bound on the rate of misclassification for our sample of gay and lesbian couples. Among the 592 errors by households with three or more adults but no married couple, 540 indicate that the householder has exactly two unmarried partners. We suspect that most of these cases are not the consequence of misinterpreting the meaning of *unmarried partner* per se; rather, we believe they entail the mistaken recording of relationships by a householder who lives with other adults, two of whom in fact are unmarried partners. The mistake made here by the householder is failure to recognize that he must mark his own relationship to each household member.

Further evidence of this type of error comes from the 308 households in which an adult child lives at home (C.1 in Figure 1). Inspection suggests that in many of these cases the heterosexual unmarried partner of an adult child is recorded mistakenly as the householder's unmarried partner. (In the most common pattern, a husband and wife live with a child and an adult partner close in age to the child.) These sorts of error, however, are not likely to occur in our sample of same-sex couples, because only 15% of gay and lesbian couples live with any other adult in the household, and only 4% live with an adult child.

In sum, we read the evidence as suggesting that virtually none of the misclassification of "unmarried partner" status is due to random error or to confusion about the term; instead it is the result of mistakes concerning an individual's relationship to the householder. If in fact "unmarried partner-ship" was generally interpreted correctly, then misclassification is neg-ligible when (as in the great majority of gay and lesbian couples) there are only two adults in the household. Even the worst possible case, however, in which about 0.4% of nonmarried householders mistake the meaning of *unmarried partner*, is not particularly serious for our analysis. Our sample contains just over 76,000 two-adult households in which both adults are of the same sex. If 0.4% of these householders mistakenly marked "unmarried partner," only about 305 couples would be identified mistakenly as gay or lesbian couples. In contrast, we actually identify nearly 7,000 cohabiting same-sex couples in our sample (B.3 in Figure 1).

As for sex miscoding, we can look to the 1970 census for validation. The Census Bureau studied the accuracy of the 1970 census data by match-ing the 1970 short- and long-form data to the 1970 Current Population Survey. Because many questions are the same in the CPS as on the census form, this matched file constituted a sample of over 20,000 cases. The Bureau reports that the error rate for sex among adults is less than 0.2% (U.S. Census Bureau 1975).[8]

Of course, a problem remains: The gays and lesbians in B.3 are only a fraction of all gays and lesbians in the population. One can calculate roughly how accurately the sample of same-sex partners identified in the census represents the gay and lesbian population in general. Suppose we adopt the reasonably narrow definition of *gay* and *lesbian* to be individuals who have engaged exclusively in same-sex sex over the last year. Then, according to Table 1, 2.5% of men are gay and 1.4% of women are lesbian. Given the estimated partnership rates for gays and lesbians of 28.4% and 44.1% respectively, we would estimate that in the United States, 0.71% of adult males are in gay-partnered households and 0.62% of women are in lesbian-partnered households. Our census sample contains 2,921,421 men age 18 to 60, of whom 7,287 are partnered gays, and 3,207,702 women age 18 to 60, of whom 5,762 are partnered lesbians. These latter statistics suggest that the number of households that self-report as same-sex couples in the 1990 U.S. census is considerably lower than the number counted in the GSS and NHSLS samples. It would appear that roughly 35% of men living as partnered same-sex couples are recorded in the census; for women the corresponding fraction is 29%.

Given that only about one-third of cohabiting same-sex couples identify themselves as such in the census, extreme care is needed in drawing general inferences about the population of gay and lesbian couples. We certainly cannot rule out a priori the possibility that a householder's propensity to indicate that a same-sex partner is indeed an "unmarried partner" is correlated with individual characteristics such as age and education. We pursue one avenue for addressing this problem in the next section, comparing demographic characteristics of gay and lesbian couples in the census sample with corresponding information in the GSS and NHSLS (which are much closer to true random samples). Other researchers may find it useful to employ the data to form bounds on parameters of interest.

Beyond this, researchers must use informed judgment as to the suitability of the census data for addressing particular questions. In estimating wage regressions, for example, Klawitter (1997) implicitly assumes that, after conditioning on a variety of characteristics (such as education and potential experience), self-identification by cohabiting lesbian women is not correlated with their wages in the labor market. We find this to be a reasonable working assumption, especially because the alternative is simply to abandon the important goal of studying the role of sexual orientation in labor market outcomes.

Characteristics of gays and lesbians in the United States: results from two data sources

In examining the characteristics of the gay and lesbian population, we focus on four issues that are relevant for current discussions in public policy: the geographic distribution of gays and lesbians, military service, family structure, and earnings and earnings-related characteristics. As discussed above, great care is needed in interpreting results because gays and lesbians are defined differently in each data source. In addition, one must be sensitive to the likelihood that at least some persons in the sample of "gays" and "lesbians" are heterosexuals who have been miscoded (especially in the GSS). In this section we look for differences between gay men and other men, and between lesbian women and other women, that are qualitatively consistent across data sources. The presence of consistent differences between gays and lesbians and other individuals also helps establish the validity of the data sources.

Geographic concentration

Our first use of the census sample is to provide some information about the geographic distribution of gay and lesbian couples in the United States. This information is interesting in its own right, and it is helpful also for providing further evidence that our sample of same-sex couples does not consist predominantly of misrecorded opposite-sex couples. If opposite-sex couples constituted the bulk of the sample, one would expect the geographic distribution of same-sex couples to be similar to the distribution of the population in the United States as a whole. This is very clearly not the case, however. In Table 4 we list the 20 cities in the United States with the largest populations of gay couples, and present a similar list for lesbian couples, along with the percentage of the total census sample contained in each city. The 20 cities with large numbers of gay couples, which are home to less than 26% of the U.S. population, contain nearly 60% of our sample of gay men. Clearly gay men are concentrated in a selected number of urban areas. Lesbian women are somewhat less geographically concentrated.

Comparison of columns (2) and (3) for men and of columns (5) and (6) for women shows that some cities have atypically high concentrations of gays and lesbians. For example, a randomly selected gay man in our sample is about 12 times more likely to live in San Francisco than are other individuals in the U.S. population. Other cities with especially high concentrations of gays include Los Angeles, Washington, DC, and Atlanta. High concentrations of lesbian women are found in San Francisco, Seattle, and Minneapolis. When we look at concentrations of gay and lesbian couples in smaller cities (e.g., 200,000 to 700,000), we find a disproportionate number of "college towns" such as Ann Arbor and Madison. (For both gays and lesbians, seven of the 10 smaller cities with high concentrations contain a major university.) Inference about the gay and lesbian population in smaller cities, however, is severely limited by small sample sizes.

Unfortunately there exist no reliable data, other than the census, suitable for calculating even the most rudimentary statistics on the location of the gay and lesbian population. (We cannot report the geographic distribution of gays and lesbians from the GSS because this information is confidential.) Thus we cannot compare our results with findings from other samples.

We can gain some confirmatory evidence, however, by investigating the spatial distribution of AIDS deaths in 1990. In that year, an overwhelmingly

Table 4 Twenty cities (PMSAs) with the largest gay/lesbian-couple populations, 1990 census

Cities ordered by number of gay couples (1)	Percentage of gay sample in the city (2)	Percentage of U.S. population in the city (3)	Cities' orders by number of lesbian couples (4)	Percentage of lesbian sample in the city (5)	Percentage of U.S. population in the city (6)
1 Los Angeles, CA	9.77	3.57	New York, NY	6.03	3.39
2 New York, NY	8.37	3.39	Los Angeles, CA	5.35	3.57
3 San Francisco, CA	7.90	0.65	San Francisco, CA	3.27	0.65
4 Washington, DC	4.42	1.54	Minneapolis, MN	2.90	0.92
5 Chicago, IL	3.65	2.44	Washington, DC	2.84	1.54
6 Atlanta, GA	2.60	0.98	Seattle, WA	2.51	0.79
7 San Diego, CA	2.56	1.01	Boston, MA	2.48	1.08
8 Oakland, CA	2.54	0.84	Chicago, IL	2.47	2.44
9 Boston, MA	2.30	1.08	Oakland, CA	2.46	0.84
10 Seattle, WA	1.85	0.79	Philadelphia, PA	2.14	1.95
11 Dallas, TX	1.76	1.03	Sacramento, CA	1.69	0.59
12 Houston, TX	1.66	1.30	Atlanta, GA	1.55	0.98
13 Philadelphia, PA	1.61	1.95	San Diego, CA	1.53	1.01
14 Anaheim, CA	1.46	0.97	Baltimore, MD	1.39	0.95
15 Minneapolis, MN	1.31	0.92	Tampa, FL	1.33	0.83
16 Fort Lauderdale, FL	1.20	0.51	Portland, OR	1.31	0.47
17 Tampa, FL	1.17	0.83	Houston, TX	1.16	1.30
18 Phoenix, AZ	1.09	0.85	Phoenix, AZ	1.08	0.85
19 Denver, CO	1.07	0.63	Denver, CO	1.06	0.63
20 Sacramento, CA	1.04	0.59	San Jose, CA	0.93	0.60
Total	59.33	25.86	Total	45.48	25.38

Source: Authors' compilations from the 1990 U.S. census, 5% PUMS.

Note: Results in this table are drawn only from the 5% PUMS because the MSA definitions are not completely consistent across the 5% and 1% samples.

large fraction of men who died of AIDS were gay.[9] Using the 1990-detail mortality file (a complete enumeration of deaths in the United States), we calculated the total number of deaths and the number of deaths by AIDS for white men ages 25–44 in 300 SMSAs. Of 2,151,890 deaths in 1990, 74,600 occurred to white men ages 25–44; of these deaths, 12,844 were diagnosed as due to AIDS. For each of the identified SMSAs in the first panel of Table 4, we construct an AIDS death concentration ratio: the fraction of AIDS deaths in a city divided by the corresponding fraction of all deaths in the city. We find that this index is highly correlated with a "gay concentration index," formed by dividing the figures in column (2) by the corresponding figures in column (3). In particular, among the 20 cities containing the largest numbers of gay men, the correlation between the gay concentration index and the AIDS death index is 0.89 (significantly different from zero at the 0.01 level). Fifty-nine percent of same-sex male partners live in the 20 cities listed; 54% of all deaths from AIDS to white men ages 25–44 occurred in these 20 cities.

Veteran status

In regard to the interesting issue of military service among gays and lesbians, Table 5 provides for a comparison of military service for same-sex partners and other men and women. Although it appears that partnered gay men are much less likely than other men to be veterans, a substantial proportion (17.3%) of the sample are veterans, in the reserves, or on active duty in the military (compared with 36.8% for other men). For comparison, we conducted the same analysis with the GSS-NHSLS data and obtained similar results: 16.9% of gay men and 32.3% of heterosexual men are veterans. Among women, statistics based on census data show that 6.6% of the lesbian sample have served in the military, compared with 1.4% of other women. Again, estimates from the GSS–NHSLS data yield similar results: Military service rates are 8.1% for lesbian women and 1.4% for other women.[10]

The lower panel of Table 6 shows an interesting pattern. Gay men who reached draft age (age 18) during the World War II and Korean War eras served in the military at nearly the same rate as other men. In addition, during this period, gay men who were in the military served on average only slightly fewer years than other men. The rate of military service has been declining for men in general over the past several decades, and has decreased more rapidly for gay men than for other men. During the current era it appears that the fraction of gay men in the military is substantially lower than the fraction of other men, and that gay men are serving fewer years than other men.

Among women in same-sex partnerships who reached enlistment age (18) during the World War II and Korean War eras, over 10% served at

Table 5 Percentage veterans for partnered gays/lesbians and other men/women, U.S. Gensus

	Partnered gay men		Other men		Partnered lesbian women		Other women	
Military service for individuals Ages 18–67								
Any military service	17.3		36.8		6.6		1.4	
Veteran	15.5		31.1		5.1		1.0	
Reserves	1.6		4.2		1.2		0.2	
Military service and years served for cohorts reaching age 18 during specific eras	Percentage with any military service	Average number of years served	Percentage with any military service	Average number of years served	Percentage with any military service	Average number of years served	Percentage with any military service	Average number of years served
World War II era (1941–1947)	72.7	3.0	75.0	3.5	10.2	1.6	1.6	0.8
Korean War era (1950–1954)	60.6	3.6	64.3	3.9	11.9	1.0	1.0	0.6
Between Korean and Vietnam War eras (1955–1964)	38.6	3.0	49.9	3.6	6.1	0.9	0.9	0.6
Vietnam War era (1965–1974)	17.3	3.1	30.6	3.5	6.7	1.4	1.4	1.2
Post-Vietnam War era (1975–1980)	6.9	2.6	14.6	3.7	7.2	1.9	1.9	1.4
Current era (1981–1990)	7.0	1.7	14.0	2.6	5.1	1.7	1.7	1.0

Source: Authors' compilations from the 1990 U.S. census, 5% and 1% PUMS.

some time in the military. Among other women in this cohort, 1.0% to 1.6% served at some time. Women in same-sex partnerships who served in the military accumulated far more years of duty than other women. In fact, until the post-Vietnam cohort, the number of years of service for lesbians who served in the military was similar to the number of years served by men. More recently, there has been a narrowing in the large differences between lesbian women and other women in military service rates, perhaps as a result of changes in military policy that previously barred married women and pregnant women from service.

Family structure

Although adoption and parental rights policy for gay and lesbian couples is an intensely debated topic, we have virtually no empirical evidence regarding the current presence of children among gay and lesbian couples. The census sample provides the first reliable statistics on this matter. As shown in Table 6, these data indicate that a substantial number of same-sex couples, especially lesbian couples, currently have children present in the home: about 21.7% of partnered lesbians and 5.2% of partnered gays. Most of these children are relatively young: 71% of the children in lesbian households and 76% of those in gay households are under age 18. The combined GSS–NHSLS data tell a more dramatic story. These data, which of course include single gays and lesbians, and gays and lesbians who are married (and may still live with their spouses), indicate that over 14% of gays and over 28% of lesbians have children in the household.

Table 6   Presence of children in households, U.S. census: children at home by relationship status (percentages)

	Partnered gay/ lesbian	Partnered heterosexual	Married	Not partnered
Men				
No children	94.8	63.8	40.8	95.2
1 child	3.0	18.1	22.4	2.9
2 children	1.2	11.0	23.0	1.4
≥ 3 children	1.1	7.1	13.8	0.5
Women				
No children	78.3	63.8	40.8	77.9
1 child	12.6	18.1	22.4	10.1
2 children	5.0	11.0	23.0	7.6
≥ 3 children	4.1	7.1	13.8	4.5

Source: Authors' compilations from the 1990 U.S. census, 5% and 1% PUMS.

Table 7 Current and past marital status for gays and lesbians, GSS (1988–1996) and NHSLS (1992) data and census data (percentages)

Marital status	GSS/NHSLS			(Census)
	Gay/lesbian	Gay/lesbian with household screening	Gay/lesbian with opposite-sex experience	Partnered gay/lesbian
Men				
Currently married	20.1	18.3	14.6	1.3
Widowed, separated, or divorced, and not currently married	11.6	11.5	11.1	17.2
Never married	68.4	70.2	74.6	81.4
(Sample size)	(139)	(131)	(63)	(7,567)
Women				
Currently married	23.9	13.9	6.5	1.2
Widowed, separated, or divorced, and not currently married	21.6	22.2	32.6	28.7
Never married	54.6	63.9	60.9	70.1
(Sample size)	(88)	(72)	(46)	(6,081)

Source: Authors' compilations from the GSS–NHSLS data and the 1990 U.S. census, 5% and 1% PUMS.

Many of the children in gay and lesbian households recorded in the census were probably born in previous marriages. In the census sample, nearly 20% of men in gay partnerships and 30% of women in lesbian partnerships were married previously or (in a small number of cases) are currently married. (See the far right-hand column of Table 7). Among gays and lesbians more generally, as measured in the GSS–NHSLS, an even higher proportion are previously or currently married: possibly as many as 30% of the gay men and 46% of the lesbians (see Table 7).

Yet these measured rates decline somewhat when we make sample adjustments designed to reduce classification error. In particular, it seems very likely that a married gay or lesbian individual will have had opposite-sex experience. Thus readers may wish to focus on the third column in Table 7, which shows that about 25% of gay men and 40% of lesbian women are married or previously were married.

Education, earnings, and wealth

Education. The gays and lesbians in the census sample appear to be highly educated, span the distribution of ages, and are similar in racial makeup to the population as a whole. Table 8 indicates that same-sex partners generally have achieved higher levels of education than other individuals. (This is true of all the cohorts we examine, although in Table 8 we provide data only for ages 25–44.) The GSS–NHSLS data reveal a very similar pattern: For example, 13.0% of gay men have postcollege education and a further 23.7% have earned college degrees. The corresponding rates for married men are 10.3% and 17.0%. Among lesbian women, 13.9% have postcollege education and 25.0% have college education; comparable rates for married women are 6.1% and 16.0%.

The high educational levels of gays and lesbians in the census data may reflect poorly educated gays' and lesbians' relative unwillingness to indicate an unmarried partnership status on the census form; a similar selection bias may occur in the GSS–NHSLS data. Addressing this issue properly is a not a trivial matter. Here we pursue only one of the potential avenues for examining this type of selection in the GSS.

It is well known that an individual's education is correlated with his parents' education. Suppose we take as a working assumption that the relationship between an individual's education and his father's education is the same for gay men as for other men. Now consider the null hypothesis that educational attainment is the same for gay men as for other men. (Under this null hypothesis, gay individuals' educational levels are relatively high in the GSS because highly educated gay men are more willing than poorly educated gay men to report same-sex sexual relationships.) Given our working assumption, we would expect that the gay individuals in the

Table 8 Educational attainment by age and relationship status, U.S. Census (percentages)

Level of education	Men				Women			
	Not partnered	Heterosexual partnered	Gay partnered	Married	Not partnered	Heterosexual partnered	Lesbian partnered	Married
Age 25–34								
Some high school	8.72	21.56	5.57	13.59	14.87	17.95	7.03	11.83
High school diploma	24.80	34.36	14.99	31.57	25.74	31.46	12.58	32.10
Some college	30.84	27.69	36.84	30.39	33.31	32.46	33.62	33.36
College degree	25.39	12.64	29.47	17.66	19.25	14.26	31.17	17.86
Postcollege	10.25	3.75	13.13	6.79	6.83	3.87	15.60	4.85
(Sample size)	(119,820)	(60,048)	(2,963)	(608,533)	(167,914)	(59,112)	(2,302)	(711,537)
Age 35–44								
Some high school	10.10	19.44	4.44	11.76	11.21	18.69	5.02	11.65
High school diploma	22.64	30.14	9.26	24.88	24.44	32.45	10.31	31.70
Some college	32.08	31.12	30.22	30.72	34.27	32.02	26.86	31.00
College degree	21.53	12.50	31.82	19.28	17.61	10.97	28.50	16.62
Postcollege	13.65	6.80	24.26	13.36	12.47	5.87	29.31	9.03
(Sample size)	(108,534)	(35,364)	(2,358)	(731,765)	(143,346)	(31,554)	(1,909)	(737,449)

Source: Authors' compilations from the 1990 U.S. census, 5% and 1% PUMS.

GSS sample would have disproportionately well-educated fathers. Under the null hypothesis, the true distribution of father's education is the same for the gay population as for other men, but the observed distribution of father's education will be skewed toward higher levels of education because of selection bias (because fathers of poorly educated gay men are less likely to appear in the sample).

Empirically, however, we find no evidence of such a pattern. Instead we find that the distribution of education among gays' fathers is almost identical to that among other men's fathers in the GSS–NHSLS data. In turn, this finding provides tentative evidence that the gay men in fact accumulate more education than other men. (Similar analysis for women is hampered by small sample sizes.)

Earnings. Given the high levels of education among the gays and lesbians in both the census and the GSS–NHSLS data, it would not be surprising to find that gays and lesbians do relatively well in earnings. More important, there is evidence that sexual orientation affects earnings, even with conditioning on age and education. In Table 9 we present the mean annual earnings by age category, educational level, and relationship status for the census data.

Two obvious empirical regularities are present. First, partnered gays earn substantially less than married men. Second, lesbian women earn substantially more than married women. Furthermore, lesbians in the census data generally earn more than single women and heterosexually partnered women. Patterns in the GSS–NHSLS data are remarkably similar. A parametric approach employed by Black et al (1998) provides strong evidence that this pattern is statistically significant and robust to various definitions of sexual orientation. Black et al. suggest two possible interpretations for the observed effects of sexual orientation on earnings: One interpretation is based on Becker's (1981) model of specialization in the family, and the other is consistent with a subtle model of sex/sexual orientation discrimination.

Wealth: Homeownership. The census contains only limited information about household wealth. One important exception is homeownership. Two obvious patterns emerge in an analysis of homeownership and value by age category and relationship status. First, regardless of age category, the rate of homeownership is lower for partnered gays' and lesbians' households than for married-couple households. Second, conditional on owning a house, lesbian couples appear to have somewhat more expensive homes than their heterosexual counterparts, and gay couples appear to have much more expensive homes than their heterosexual counterparts. Consider, for example, individuals age 35–44: Sixty percent of partnered gay men own homes, and over 67% of those who do so have homes valued at $100,000 or more. Similarly, about 65% of partnered lesbian women own homes, and 55% of these women have homes worth $100,000 or

Table 9 Mean earnings by age, education, and relationship status, U.S. census

Level of education	Men				Women			
	Not partnered	Heterosexual partnered	Gay partnered	Married	Not partnered	Heterosexual partnered	Lesbian partnered	Married
Age 25–34								
Some high school	16,784	14,660	12,579	18,450	9,178	9,029	12,243	9,018
High school diploma	21,313	19,178	18,777	24,010	13,987	13,512	17,473	11,988
Some college	23,886	22,254	21,039	27,298	18,085	16,977	18,932	15,101
College degree	30,729	29,162	28,618	35,851	26,012	23,409	24,265	21,348
Postcollege	36,090	36,072	32,465	42,292	29,955	28,011	26,028	26,580
(Sample size)	(100,234)	(48,693)	(2,563)	(520,392)	(122,971)	(44,829)	(2,001)	(475,580)
Age 35–44								
Some high school	18,449	17,051	19,646	21,883	11,207	10,994	13,901	10,877
High school diploma	24,344	23,389	20,253	28,884	17,179	16,236	18,961	13,567
Some college	28,588	27,533	26,636	34,094	21,727	20,734	25,023	17,071
College degree	37,468	38,629	36,054	46,424	29,174	28,734	28,387	21,448
Postcollege	47,261	49,251	42,339	59,031	35,115	34,395	34,427	29,633
(Sample size)	(84,815)	(26,709)	(1,915)	(600,135)	(110,335)	(23,591)	(1,580)	(488,047)
Age 45–54								
Some high school	20,171	19,198	18,717	24,705	12,915	12,181	19,106	11,545
High school diploma	27,129	27,219	26,047	32,060	18,119	17,001	21,698	14,351
Some college	33,057	33,650	33,750	39,218	22,872	21,962	24,999	17,920
College degree	43,748	46,448	47,541	55,623	29,298	27,910	30,653	21,927
Postcollege	52,339	59,440	48,467	59,440	35,410	35,211	43,106	31,090
(Sample size)	(45,234)	(11,415)	(776)	(412,883)	(60,693)	(9,006)	(487)	(307,676)

Source: Authors' compilations from the 1990 U.S. census, 5% and 1% PUMS.

more. By way of comparison, homeownership rates are about 80% for both married men and women, but only about 45% of these homeowners have homes valued at $100,000 or more. In view of the differences in education levels are documented above, this finding simply may reflect the fact that gay and lesbian couples are more highly educated on average than heterosexuals (and thus have relatively high earnings). When we repeat the analysis for a set of individuals who have obtained a college degree, the magnitude of the differences between gay and lesbian couples and their heterosexual counterparts is reduced, but the basic pattern remains.

Conclusion

The three data sets that we examined here can be used by scholars to produce demographic research on the gay and lesbian population. The GSS and NHSLS provide a fairly small random sample of gay and lesbian individuals in the United States. We document a number of measurement-error problems that can produce misclassification of sexual orientation by researchers using the GSS–NHSLS, and we suggest some solutions. The 1990 U.S. census provides a much larger sample of gays and lesbians, but only partnered gays and lesbians can be studied. Our analysis of these data suggests that nearly all of the same-sex couples identified in the census data are in fact same-sex partners (not misclassified heterosexual couples). We estimate, however, that only about one-third of gay and lesbian couples report themselves as such in the census; thus selection bias is a potential concern.

Together these data allow us to offer a more complete statistical portrait of the gay and lesbian population than was previously available. Empirical observations along dimensions such as veteran status, education, and earnings are remarkably similar in the GSS–NHSLS and the census. This fact increases confidence in the quality of the data sources and in the reported results in general. The findings of this paper include the following:

Sixty percent of partnered gay men in the United States are concentrated in only 20 cities, especially in cities such as San Francisco, Washington, DC, Los Angeles, Atlanta, and New York. A very high correlation exists between the cross-city distribution of gay couples, as measured in the 1990 U.S. census, and 1990 death rates of AIDS among young men; this correlation increases the face validity of the findings. Partnered lesbian women are somewhat less concentrated in large cities than are gay couples.

Gay men historically have served in the military in relatively large numbers. Gays who were young during the World War II and Korean War eras were about as likely as other men to serve in the military. More recently, gay men have been less likely than other men to serve. In contrast, lesbian women are much more likely than other women to have served in the military, though this difference apparently has declined over the past five decades.

Many gay men and lesbian women have children. Non-negligible fractions of gay and lesbian people are currently married.

Gay and lesbian individuals have higher educational levels than other men and women. Suggestive evidence from the GSS–NHSLS indicates that this finding is not the result of selection bias.

Gay men generally earn less than other men, whereas lesbian women generally earn more than other women. Future research on this topic may provide important clues about the nature of specialization in households, discrimination, and labor market outcomes.

Perhaps the most useful contribution of this paper is that it demonstrates the viability of doing credible empirical work on the gay and lesbian population with existing data sources. As the GSS provides additional waves and as the Census Bureau collects the 2000 census, considerably more data will become available for this purpose. (In addition, researchers have not yet exploited the confidential one-in-six files of the 1990 census for the study of the gay and lesbian population.)

The increasing body of research on gays and lesbians holds promise for improving the understanding of a population that previously has undergone little systematic research based on large samples. In addition, we believe, careful theoretical and empirical work that pays close attention to sexual orientation can help us to understand questions about the general nature of labor market choices, accumulation of human capital, specialization within households, and many other issues of interest to social scientists.

Notes

1   Dan Black, Center for Policy Research, Syracuse University, Syracuse, NY 13244, dablac01@maxwell.syr.edu. Gary Gates, Heinz School of Public Policy and Management, Carnegie Mellon University; Seth Sanders, Department of Economics, University of Maryland; Lowell Taylor, Heinz School of Public Policy and Management, Carnegie Mellon University. The authors gratefully acknowledge financial support from NICHD Grant HD3703–01 430. We are also grateful to Hoda Makar for research and editorial assistance, and to Jason Fields, Gregory Lewis, Robert Little, Jane Mauldon, Susan Newcomer, and participants in demography workshops at the University of California, Berkeley and the University of Maryland for useful comments.

2   Kinsey's subjects were all recruited purposefully, not drawn from a known sampling frame. As is still common in research on gays, Kinsey selected his subjects from many venues, including institutions such as prisons and reform schools.

3   This definition of partnership may be inaccurate if, for example, a gay respondent is living with a male roommate who is not his sexual partner. Unfortunately the GSS consistently reports only that there is an unrelated adult in the household; it does not consistently report whether this unrelated adult is a partner or a roommate.

When a gay or lesbian person lives with an unrelated adult of the same sex, however, we find that the probability of that individual's having a regular sexual partner is close to 1. For example, of the 29 lesbians who were partnered by this definition, 27 had a regular sexual partner. (By comparison, fewer than half of the lesbians who were not partnered by this definition had a regular sexual partner.) Because of this ambiguity, we consider a gay or lesbian as partnered only if he or she lives with a person of the same sex identified as a spouse or an unrelated adult, and reports having a regular sexual partner.

4   Tom Smith, director of the GSS, gave us this information. It seems almost impossible that own or partner's sex is recorded incorrectly in the NHSLS. Many questions in the NHSLS are sex-specific. Therefore, if sex was recorded incorrectly, many of the responses to questions would be nonsensical, an error unlikely to go unnoticed.

5   We limit our analysis to respondents who were recorded as the head of household or the spouse of the household head. If we assume that the two sex reports are independent and that error rates are symmetric, then the two reports disagree whenever one records the respondent's sex correctly and the other does not. That is, the error rate = $0.0387 = (1 - 0.96130) = 2 \times Pr(P = M \mid P^* = F) \times (1 - Pr(P = M \mid P^* = F))$, so $Pr(P = M \mid P^* = F) = 0.0197$.

6   We exclude households in which any member's relationship to the householder is allocated because this individual's exact relationship to the householder is unclear; as a result, the exact nature of the household structure is also unclear. In doing this, we recognize that we also exclude some households with gay and lesbian partnerships in which an individual was identified as the "spouse" of a same-sex householder. Through a rather complex census recoding procedure, either the "spouse" in these same-sex couples was allocated into a different relationship status (such as roommate, unrelated adult, or possibly unmarried partner) or his/her sex was changed. In either case, the data in the PUMS do not allow the researcher to identify the specific reasons why an allocation of either relationship status or sex occurred. We are most grateful to Jason Fields, research analyst at the U.S. Census Bureau, for his assistance in researching the allocation process of same-sex spouses in the 1990 census.

7   We assume that polygamy or polyandry is negligible in our sample.

8   No similar matched file exists for the 1990 census. In a second census study, the "Content Reinterview Survey," several thousand households from the 1990 long form roster were interviewed again six months after the original census survey to validate the 1990 census data. Although data on sex and partnership status were collected, the accuracy of these two data items is not reported in the Bureau's report (see U.S. Census Bureau 1993).

9   The following statistics are taken from the web site for the U.S. Centers for Disease Control and Prevention (http://wonder.cdc.gov/aids00.shtml), for white men aged 25–44: 86.7% who were diagnosed with AIDS in 1990 were infected as a result of same-sex male sexual contact alone or a combination of same-sex male sexual contact and injection drug use; 87.1% of those who subsequently died belonged to the same two risk categories; and 90% diagnosed with AIDS in the 1980s came from these two risk categories.

10   For the GSS–NHSLS calculations we conducted a "household roster check" to eliminate households for which sex identification is uncertain. We were left with quite small samples for gays ($n = 77$) and especially for lesbians ($n = 37$).

References

Badgett, M.V.L. 1995. "The Wage Effects of Sexual Orientation Discrimination." *Industrial and Labor Relations Review* 48: 726–39.

Becker, G.S. 1981. *A Treatise on the Family*. Cambridge: Harvard University Press.

Black, D.A., G. Gates, S. Sanders, and L. Taylor. 1997. "The Effects of Sexual Orientation on the Wages of Men." Working paper, Heinz School of Public Policy and Management, Carnegie Mellon University.

———. 1999. "Why Do Gay Men Live in San Francisco?" Working paper, Heinz School of Public Policy and Management, Carnegie Mellon University.

Black, D.A., H. Makar, S. Sanders, and L. Taylor. 1998. "The Effects of Sexual Orientation on Earnings." Working paper, Heinz School, Carnegie Mellon University.

Bumpass, L.L. and J. Sweet. 1989. "National Estimates of Cohabitation." *Demography* 26:615–25.

Jepsen, L. 1998. *Essays on the Economics of Marriage: An Empirical Study of Same-Sex and Opposite-Sex Couples*. PhD dissertation, Department of Economics, Vanderbilt University.

Jepsen, L. and C. Jepsen. 1999. "An Empirical Analysis of Same-Sex and Opposite-Sex Couples: Do 'Likes' Still Like 'Likes' in the '90s?' Working paper, Northwestern University.

Kinsey, A.C., W.B. Pomeroy, C.E. Martin, and P.H. Gebhard. 1948. *Sexual Behavior in the Human Male*. Philadelphia: Saunders.

Klawitter, M.M. 1997. "The Effects of Sexual Orientation on the Determinants of Earnings for Women." Working paper, Graduate School of Public Affairs, University of Washington.

Klawitter, M.M. and V. Flatt. 1998. "The Effects of State and Local Antidiscrimination Policies on Earnings for Gays and Lesbians." *Journal of Policy Analysis and Management* 17: 658–86.

Krieger, L.M. 1993. "S.F. Remains a Mecca for Gay Couples: Census Data Reveal Same-Sex Households Abound in the City." *San Francisco Examiner*, September 12, pp. A1, A10.

Laumann, E.O., J.H. Gagnon, R.T. Michael, and S. Michaels. 1994. *The Social Organization of Sexuality: Sexual Practices in the United States*. Chicago: University of Chicago Press.

Michael, R.T., J.H. Gagnon, E.O. Laumann, and G. Kolata. 1994. *Sex in America: A Definitive Study*. Boston: Little, Brown.

"S.F. Seeks Equal Treatment." 1996. *San Jose Mercury News*, December 29, p. 3b.

U.S. Census Bureau. 1975. "Accuracy of Data for Selected Population Characteristics as Measured by the 1970 CPS-Census Match." *1970 Census of Population and Housing, Evaluation and Research Program Report*. Washington, DC: U.S. Government Printing Office.

———. 1993. "Content Reinterview Survey: Accuracy of Data for Selected Population and Housing Characteristics as Measured by Reinterview." *1990 Census of Population and Housing, Research and Evaluation Report, CPH-E-1*. Washington, DC: U.S. Government Printing Office.

Chapter 7

Voon Chin Phua and Gayle Kaufman

USING THE CENSUS TO PROFILE SAME-SEX COHABITATION: A RESEARCH NOTE

From *Population Research and Policy Review* 1999, 18: 373–86

Introduction

MOST STUDIES ON COHABITATION that address issues such as the couples' transition to marriage, dissolution of marriage and their attitudes towards marriage have focused on opposite-sex partners (e.g., Bumpass & Sweet 1989a; Mare 1991; Schoen & Weinick 1993). Opposite-sex cohabitation is often seen either as a prelude or alternative to marriage. The legal problems and controversies of same-sex marriage as well as the stigma associated with gay and lesbian relationships have resulted in the exclusion of same-sex partners in the research of cohabitation. Given the contextual differences, the motivations and factors surrounding same-sex cohabitation are likely to be different from those of opposite-sex cohabitation.

In this paper, we have two goals: (1) to explore the use of census data in examining same-sex cohabitation, and (2) to examine same-sex cohabitation in comparative terms. In the first case, we address the technical and conceptual usefulness of the 'unmarried partners' variable in the census. As an exploratory study, we use the 1990 US census 5% sample to provide a socio-economic profile of householders. We use the New York metropolitan area as a case study in order to avoid the nationwide diversity in housing options and costs. Householders are selected as the focus for comparisons and are divided into five mutually exclusive groups: (1)

householders with a same-sex unmarried partner, (2) householders with an opposite-sex unmarried partner, (3) householders who are married, (4) unmarried householders living with others, and (5) persons living alone.

The meanings of cohabitation

Three reasons are often used to explain why people cohabit: a precursor to marriage (e.g., Gwartney-Gibbs 1986; Oppenheimer 1988; Willis & Michael 1994; Nock 1995); an alternative to marriage (e.g., Bachrach 1987; Landale & Fennelly 1992); and an alternative to being single (e.g., Thornton 1988; Jacobsen & Pampel 1989; Rindfuss & VandenHeuvel 1990). Researchers who posit cohabitation as a precursor to marriage view cohabitation as part of the courtship process (e.g., Tanfer 1987) or as a trial marriage, a time to 'test' a potential marriage partner to make sure that the couple is compatible (e.g., Bumpass et al. 1991; Willis & Michael 1994). Bumpass et al. (1991) note that three-quarters of cohabitors plan or expect to marry their partner.

Other researchers argue that cohabitation is an alternative to being married (Landale & Fennelly 1992). The fact that cohabitors are more likely to expect a birth within five years than non-cohabitors or currently married women may indicate some kind of union stability for cohabitors. Women who are cohabiting are also more likely to plan pregnancy than single women who are not cohabiting (Manning 1992). Many children born into so-called single-parent families are really born with two cohabiting parents (Bumpass & Sweet 1989b; Landale & Hauan 1992; Bumpass & Raley 1995).

A third view posits cohabitation as an alternative to singlehood. Jacobsen & Pampel (1989), for example, suggest that cohabitation is another non-family living arrangement, which is related to a lack of economic resources among unmarried adults – those who live alone rather than with a partner are comparatively disadvantaged economically. According to a study by Rindfuss & VandenHeuvel (1990), characteristics such as school enrollment, home ownership, and dependency on parental financial support are usually more similar for cohabitors and those who are never married than for cohabitors and those who are married. Similarly, Thornton (1988), looking at entrance into marriage or cohabitation, finds that by age 23, 60% of women and 45% of men had entered a union, with between one-third and one-half via cohabitation. He concludes that cohabitation is not always a step to marriage nor a substitute for marriage.

Macklin (1986) expands the range of cohabitation definitions by including time as a factor: (1) temporary casual convenience, (2) affectionate dating–going together, (3) trial marriage, (4) temporary alternative to marriage, and (5) permanent alternative to marriage. What cohabitation means to a person is not necessarily constant through the life course but varies depending on his or her situation (e.g., economic status, race, and age). White cohabiting women are more likely to marry their partners than black cohabiting women (Schoen & Owens 1992). In her study, Manning (1993) concludes that for whites, cohabitation is a precursor to marriage for those in their twenties, whereas for blacks and teenage whites, cohabitation is an alternative to being single. Landale & Forste (1991) posit that cohabitation is a more viable option than marriage for men with poor economic situations. Sweet & Bumpass (1990) find weak evidence that cohabitation may be an alternative to marriage when the latter is not seen as feasible.

While researchers acknowledge the various meanings of cohabitation among persons of different economic and racial backgrounds as well as examining the different characteristics of married and cohabiting couples (e.g., Glick & Spanier 1980), few researchers have considered same-sex cohabitation. Studies of cohabitation as a life transition often are directly or indirectly linked to marriage. The legal problems and controversies of same-sex marriage as well as the stigma of homosexuality have resulted in the exclusion of same-sex partners in the research of cohabitation. However, researchers who do not explicitly view cohabitation as a life transition have studied issues surrounding same-sex couples. These studies include legal issues (e.g., Anderson 1987–88 on property rights), relational dynamics (e.g., Jones & Bates 1978 on satisfaction; Kurdek 1992 on stability and satisfaction; Deenen et al. 1994 on intimacy), as well as an expansion of the meaning of family (Poverny & Finch 1988; Scanzoni & Marsiglio 1991).

Few studies, however, have provided comparisons across groups (e.g., Cardell et al. 1981; Kurdek & Schmitt 1987). The lack of comparative studies partly reflects the politics of sexuality, such as some gay and lesbian scholars' resistance against using heterosexual as a reference in comparative studies as well as their assertion of the legitimacy and independence of same-sex relationships. A discussion of the politics of sexuality is beyond the scope of this paper. In this paper, we assume that different living arrangements (same-sex and opposite-sex couples) reflect nominal variations.

Using census data

The U.S. census provides extensive information on housing conditions and costs, their geographical locations, and intra-household relationships. Within each household, the census also provides information on individual economic resources and other individual characteristics such as immigration status and racial and ethnic identification. In the 1990 census, more extensive questions were asked to distinguish the specific relationship of non-relatives to the householder. Unlike earlier censuses, the 1990 census differentiates between a room-mate and a partner in order 'to specify who is living together as opposed to simply rooming together' (Barrett 1994: 17). With this distinct category of unmarried partners, researchers presumably will be able to measure the level of cohabitation. Unintentionally, the 1990 census also allows researchers to examine same-sex cohabitation. In this light, however, three issues are raised. First, using census data, we can only identify cohabitors in reference to the householder. One of the partners must be the householder, or they cannot be identified as a cohabiting couple. Nonetheless, the census provides a good source of data to examine cohabitors who are householders and more importantly, the data allow for comparative studies of persons in different living arrangements.

Second, a more general question surrounds the interpretation of the phrase 'unmarried partner'. The census defines an unmarried partner as 'a person who is not related to the householder and who shares living quarters, and who has a close personal relationship with the householder' as opposed to a housemate or room-mate who 'is not related to the householder and who shares living quarters primarily in order to share expenses' as well as to a roomer, a boarder, or a lodger of the householder (U.S. Bureau of the Census 1992: B15). However, we are unsure whether persons view a close personal relationship necessarily to be one of a sexual nature. Would two good friends who co-own a home report one as the householder and the other as the unmarried partner? In our New York data, we have found at least three outcomes reflecting unconventional interpretations of what unmarried partners meant. Some householders reported (1) having unmarried partners who are younger than 18 years old, (2) having more than one unmarried partner, and (3) being currently married (with and without spouse presence) and having unmarried partners. To simply dismiss these variations as misreporting would be superimposing our interpretation of what 'unmarried partners' meant to these individuals.

The third issue is more critical, as well as politically charged. Are same-sex unmarried partners synonymous with gay and lesbian couples? To address this question, we have to first understand who gay men and lesbians are. Studies have pointed to at least two ways of categorizing gays and lesbians: by behavior or identity. Questions have been raised on the implications of such modes of categorization: behavior assumes the process of labeling others, whereas identity involves the process of self labeling. The latter is more empowering than the former in light of identity politics. While it is not the intention of this paper to debate identity politics or define who gay men and lesbians are, it is important to understand that in using the census data, we cannot assert that same-sex cohabitors are either gay men or lesbians. This is particularly true when there might be more than one interpretation of what unmarried partners mean, as we have shown earlier. Even without labels, same-sex cohabitors present us with a variation of living arrangement that is worthy of examination.

A socio-economic profile of householders

Using the 1990 U.S. Census 5% public use micro-sample, we explore the socio-economic characteristics of same-sex unmarried partners in the New York metropolitan area (see Table 1 for selection criteria). Using house-holders as comparison units, we describe the socio-economic profile of same-sex cohabitors relative to those in other living arrangements, focusing especially on the comparison with the contrast between same-sex cohabi-tors and opposite-sex cohabitors and married householders.

While same-sex cohabiting householders comprise only a small frac-tion of our sample, we are still left with large numbers in this group (N = 10,438). A greater proportion of these cohabiting householders is male (65%) than female (35%). The average age of same-sex cohabiting householders is 38 for males and 41 for females, below the averages for other householders, with the exception of opposite-sex cohabiting house-holders. Blacks make up a disproportionately large part of opposite-sex cohabitors and those with other living arrangements (e.g., single parents), while they are under-represented among the group of same-sex cohabiting householders.

Table 2 contains information on income and home ownership. Same-sex cohabiting male householders have higher personal and household incomes than other male householders. Their personal income is somewhat higher than that of married male householders, yet closer to married than opposite-sex cohabiting male householders' income. When we examine household income, the differences become much wider. Same-sex cohabit-ing householders have the highest mean household income at over $70,000, compared to $55,600 for married householders and $45,600 for opposite-sex cohabiting householders. Finally, same-sex cohabiting male house-holders contribute more equally to their households than other male

---

Table 1 Definition of living arrangements (householders[a] as the anchor)

Same-sex cohabitors: Persons who are not currently married and have only one
    unmarried partner of the same sex who is older than 18 years old.
Opposite-sex cohabitors: Persons who are not currently married and have only one
    unmarried partner of the opposite sex who is older than 18 years old.
Married couples: Persons who are currently married (including both with spouse
    present and absent) and have no unmarried partners.
Persons living alone: Persons who are not currently married and are living alone.
Persons living with others: Persons who are not currently married, do not have any
    unmarried partners, and are not living alone.

---

[a]   We have excluded householders who (1) have more than one unmarried part-
    ner, (2) are currently married and have unmarried partners, or (3) have an
    unmarried partner who is under the age of 18 years old.

Table 2   Economic characteristics of householders by living arrangement

Living arrangement	Mean personal income	Mean household income	Personal income as proportion of household income	% own home
Male householders				
Same-sex cohabitors	40,810	70,860	0.57	31.13
Opposite-sex cohabitors	28,587	45,583	0.62	20.22
Married	37,790	55,576	0.69	50.95
Alone	29,528	29,528	1.00	22.02
Other	25,498	43,405	0.61	27.37
Female householders				
Same-sex cohabitors	28,629	53,784	0.52	25.19
Opposite-sex cohabitors	18,866	41,590	0.48	17.16
Married	19,043	51,390	0.55	37.61
Alone	20,038	20,038	1.00	25.10
Other	16,294	28,618	0.68	21.57

householders. Same-sex cohabiting male householders' personal income makes up the smallest mean proportion of their household income compared to that of other male householders. While the personal income of same-sex cohabiting male householders comprises 57% of their household income, opposite-sex cohabiting male householders contribute 62% and married male householders 69% to their household incomes. This suggests a more equal balance of resources in same-sex cohabiting households. Of course, by definition these households consist of two men and given men make more money than women, the result is not surprising. In addition, some of the differences in household income and proportion of household income may be due to the relative absence of children in same-sex cohabiting male households. In these households, neither partner is likely to stop working or work less in order to care for children. We later address this issue more fully.

Therefore, it may be more informative to look at women, and in fact, the same patterns emerge for women as for men. Same-sex cohabiting female householders have higher personal and household incomes than other female householders. Unlike men, opposite-sex cohabiting and married female householders have similar personal incomes ($19,000) while same-sex cohabiting female householders earn two-thirds more ($28,600). On the other hand, while same-sex cohabiting female householders have higher household incomes, married female householders are not far behind. Again, if we consider the fact that men earn more than women, it is likely that husbands and male partners will contribute more income than female partners. However, the household income of married female householders still lags behind that of same-sex cohabitors, and opposite-sex cohabitors fall especially short on household income, even given their sex composition. It may be that married women who answer the census as householders have more power or resources relative to married women who do not answer as householders and relative to their husbands as compared to other wives. And, in fact, married female householders contribute relatively more to their household incomes than either same-sex or opposite-sex cohabiting female householders. Opposite-sex cohabiting householders have the lowest mean contribution to the household income when compared to that of other householders. Relative contributions to household income appear to be more equitable among cohabiting households, for both same-sex and opposite-sex cohabitors.

Comparing mean personal income between the sexes within each type of living arrangement, the greatest disparity is among married householders. However, the greatest disparity in mean household income between the sexes is among same-sex cohabiting householders. What is evident is that married male householders have the highest mean contribution to the household income. Married as well as opposite-sex cohabiting householders have the greatest disparity in the mean proportion of personal income to household income between the sexes. This result suggests a traditional view of gender differences in the share of household income with male householders being the main breadwinners and female householders sharing a lower mean proportion of the household income with other household members.

Same-sex cohabiting householders are more likely to own a home than opposite-sex cohabiting householders but far less likely to own a home than married householders. With the exception of householders living alone, male householders have a higher percentage of home ownership than their female counterparts.

Same-sex cohabiting householders have much higher levels of education than other householders (refer to Table 3). Among men, two-thirds of same-sex cohabiting householders are college educated, compared to 30% of opposite-sex cohabiting householders and 28% of married householders Among women, 43% of same-sex cohabiting householders are college educated, compared to 26% of opposite-sex cohabiting householders and 28% of married householders. Only 7% of same-sex cohabiting male householders have not finished high school, compared to 25% of opposite-sex cohabiting male householders and 27% of married male householders. Men and women who are opposite-sex cohabiting householders or married householders are similar to each other in terms of education, while same-sex cohabiting male householders are more highly educated than their female counterparts.

There are dramatic differences in occupation by living arrangement (shown in Table 4). Same-sex cohabiting male householders (61%) are twice as likely to have managerial or professional jobs as opposite-sex

Table 3 Education of householders by living arrangement (in %)

Living arrangement	No high school	High school	College
Male householders			
Same-sex cohabitors	7.04	27.43	65.53
Opposite-sex cohabitors	24.67	45.53	29.81
Married	27.49	44.10	28.41
Alone	22.82	38.23	38.95
Other	27.22	43.79	28.99
Female householders			
Same-sex cohabitors	24.78	32.56	42.66
Opposite-sex cohabitors	24.86	49.34	25.80
Married	25.90	45.91	28.20
Alone	30.37	42.16	27.47
Other	38.08	48.18	13.74

Table 4 Occupation of householders by living arrangement (in %)

Living arrangement	Managerial and professional	Technical, sales, and administrative support	Service	Precision production, craft, and repair	Operators, fabricators, and laborers
Male householders					
Same-sex cohab.	61.12	23.38	9.03	2.23	3.86
Opposite-sex cohab.	30.69	23.26	14.49	13.53	17.25
Married	31.54	23.23	14.28	15.15	15.04
Alone	41.19	26.86	11.89	8.71	10.42
Other	29.92	25.47	16.15	12.36	15.27
Female householders					
Same-sex cohab.	50.93	25.65	11.30	3.41	8.71
Opposite-sex cohab.	32.04	43.90	15.44	1.75	5.69
Married	36.12	37.59	15.98	2.08	7.50
Alone	42.62	39.18	11.77	1.58	4.25
Other	24.70	40.95	22.56	1.88	8.66

cohabiting male householders (31%) and married male householders (32%). These three groups of men are similarly likely to hold technical, sales, or administrative support jobs. Same-sex cohabiting male householders are less likely to have service jobs, precision production, craft, and repair jobs, or to be operators, fabricators, or laborers. Like men, same-sex cohabiting female householders are more likely to hold managerial or professional occupations than opposite-sex cohabiting and married female householders. On the other hand, they are less likely to be employed in the service sector.

Contrary to the pattern for men, same-sex cohabiting female house-holders are somewhat more likely to be operators, fabricators, or laborers or to work in precision production, craft, or repair jobs and less likely to hold technical, sales, or administrative support jobs than other female householders. In fact, same-sex cohabiting female householders are more likely to be operators, fabricators, or laborers than their male counter-parts, a pattern that is opposite for opposite-sex cohabiting and married householders. This may indicate a different perception among same-sex cohabitors of what jobs are acceptable for men and women, a less rigid gender specification. However, while opposite-sex and married female householders are more likely to be in pink collar jobs (sales, administration) than their male counterparts, same-sex cohabiting male householders are more likely to hold professional jobs than same-sex cohabiting female householders, a difference that does not exist between opposite-sex and married male and female householders. We should note though that over one-half of same-sex cohabiting female householders occupy these positions compared to about one-third of opposite-sex and married male and female householders.

In addition to socio-economic characteristics, the presence of children is another aspect of the lives of same-sex cohabitors. Apart from those who live alone, same-sex male cohabiting householders are the least likely to have children in the household (refer to Table 5). Only 4% have children under 18 in the household compared to 35% of opposite-sex cohabiting male householders and 46% of married male householders. Of this 4% almost all are biological children of the householder. Likewise, stepchildren comprise a small proportion of married male householders' children. While 44% of married male householders have at least one biological child, only 2% have at least one stepchild. Although opposite-sex cohabiting male householders are more likely to have biological children than stepchildren, a substantial proportion of their children are stepchildren, 15%. This pattern is unique to men.

While married male householders are over ten times more likely than same-sex cohabiting male householders to have children in the house, the difference between married female householders and same-sex cohabiting female householders, while still large, is only a factor of two: 22% of same-sex cohabiting female householders have children in the household compared to 45% of opposite-sex cohabiting female householders and 48% of married female householders. While married male and female household-ers are similar to each other in terms of the presence of children, same-sex cohabiting householders differ markedly from each other. It can also be seen that stepchildren among all three groups of women are rare, unlike for men. Possibly due to biological limitations, same-sex cohabiting house-holders are less likely than other couple households to have children in the household. Still, many women are either bringing children to their same-

Table 5 Presence of children under 18 years old in household by living arrangement (in %)

Living arrangement	Total	Own children	Step-children
Male householders			
Same-sex cohabitors	4.01	3.10	0.41
Opposite-sex cohabitors	35.24	30.41	5.27
Married	46.44	43.84	1.73
Alone	0.00	0.00	0.00
Other	22.65	15.32	0.68
Female householders			
Same-sex cohabitors	22.28	17.69	0.46
Opposite-sex cohabitors	44.83	40.30	0.94
Married	47.66	43.67	0.87
Alone	0.00	0.00	0.00
Other	56.44	45.50	0.27

sex living arrangements or are having children within these relationships. Same-sex male cohabitors are sure to face not only greater biological limitations but also greater social and legal constraints than their female counterparts that prevent most from becoming fathers or retaining children from previous marriages.

This descriptive socio-economic profile suggests that same-sex cohabiting householders have high income and educational levels as well as a high percentage of home ownership and a more equitable share of the household income relative to other householders. However, it would be erroneous to conclude that same-sex cohabitors are economically better off than persons in other living arrangements, even on an individual level, as we do not know the characteristics of same-sex cohabiting couples who are not householders. At the same time, the low proportion of female householders' contribution to the household income does not necessarily mean that they are more dependent on the income contributions of other household members as we do not know the income threshold of need nor do we know how household income in shared among members. While we cannot generalize our results to all same-sex cohabitors, we can confidently compare among householders as the census provides a representative sample of householders.

Where do we go from here?

The meaning of cohabitation depends on a person's background as well as their life stage. Whether cohabitation is necessarily a transition to marriage is debatable. Macklin (1986) has suggested other reasons for cohabitation, such as a temporary casual convenience or a permanent alternative to marriage, which is not seen as a step leading to marriage. For same-sex cohabitors, however, the situation is more complex. While similar meanings may be shared by both same and opposite-sex cohabitors, the former also face structural constraints. Marriage, under current legislation is not an option for same-sex partners. For some same-sex partners, cohabitation may be interpreted as the closest they can come to a heterosexual marriage (if desired). If same-sex partners were able to marry, then we might ask whether we would see a split like opposite-sex partners in terms of their characteristics. Certainly, the average same-sex cohabiting householder has the socio-economic resources to get married, if that option were available and desired. Of course, whether this well off group of individuals would choose to marry is another question. They may feel that this would be an unnecessary legal process that adheres to heterosexual norms.

The census serves as a data source enabling researchers to study cohabitation (both same- and opposite-sex cohabitation). The strengths of the census data set lie in its accessibility and availability as well as its ability to provide a national representative sample. At the same time, it includes a large enough sample of different living arrangements to allow comparison between groups. However, using the census data to study cohabitation has several drawbacks. First, the census data only allow the examination of cohabitors related to the householder. Second, the interpretation of whom unmarried partners are may vary among persons. Third, same-sex cohabitors are not synonymous with gay and lesbian couples (see earlier discussion). While this is not necessarily a drawback, it raises caution when interpreting results. Finally, other important qualitative data, such as information about the relationship, are not available in the census. Understanding the limitations of census data enables us to use this rich source of information to explore a much neglected group-same-sex cohabitors.

A better understanding of the meaning of same-sex partners can inform research on cohabitation or marriage and avoid an overtly heterosexist framework. Clearly, currently unmarried persons need not end up marrying or cohabiting with an opposite-sex partner (if a partner is desired), when, in fact, some of them may opt for same-sex cohabitation. Researchers should also avoid assuming that all same-sex cohabitors are gays and lesbians without further information, such as information on sexual orientation. Nonetheless, interesting variations are observed in the different types of living arrangements. Further studies could compare differences and similarities in 'couple' characteristics under the framework of mate selection. For example, one could look at whether there are major age differences between the partners in different living arrangements. Exploring same-sex cohabitation creates a new realm of research and expands the range of comparisons among different relationships.

Acknowledgments

An earlier version of this paper was presented at the annual meeting of the Population Association of America, New Orleans, 1996. We would like to thank Kevin Bell and Shelah Bloom for their helpful comments.

References

Anderson, L. (1987–88). Property rights of same-sex couples: Toward a new definition of family, *Journal of Family Law* **26**: 357–372.

Bachrach, C. (1987). Cohabitation and reproductive behavior in the US, *Demography* 24: 623–637.

Barrett, R. E. (1994). *Using the 1990 US Census for Research*. Thousands Oaks, CA: Sage.

Bumpass, L. L. & Raley, R. K. (1995). Redefining single-parent families: Cohabitation and changing family reality, *Demography* 32: 97–109.

Bumpass, L. L. & Sweet, J. A. (1989a). National estimates of cohabitation, *Demography* 26: 615–625.

Bumpass, L. L. & Sweet, J. A. (1989b). Children's experience in single-parent families: Implications of cohabitation and marital transitions, *Family Planning Perspectives* 21: 256–260.

Bumpass, L. L., Sweet, J. A. & Cherlin, A. (1991). The role of cohabitation in declining rates of marriage, *Journal of Marriage and the Family* 53: 913–925.

Cardell, M., Finn, S. & Marecek, J. (1981). Sex-role identity, sex role behavior, and satisfaction in heterosexual, lesbian, and gay male couples, *Psychology of Women Quarterly* 5: 488–494.

Deenen, A. A., Gijs, L. & Van-Naerssen, A. X. (1994). Intimacy and sexuality in gay male couples, *Archives of Sexual Behavior* 23: 421–431.

Glick, P. C. & Spanier, G. B. (1980). Married and unmarried cohabitation in the United States, *Journal of Marriage and the Family* 42: 19–30.

Gwartney-Gibbs, P. A. (1986). The institutionalization of premartial cohabitation: Estimates from marriage license applications, 1970–1980, *Journal of Marriage and the Family* 48: 423–434.

Jacobsen, L. A. & Pampel, F. C. (1989). Cohabitation versus other nonfamily living arrangements: Changing determinants from 1960–1980. Working Paper No. 1.18. Cornell University, Population and Development Program.

Jones, R. W. & Bates, J. E. (1978). Satisfaction in male homosexual couples, *Journal of Homosexuality* 3: 217–224.

Kurdek, L. A. (1992). Relationship stability and relationship satisfaction in cohabiting gay and lesbian couples: A perspective longitudinal test of the contextual and interdependence models, *Journal of Social and Personal Relationships* 9: 125–142.

Kurdek, L. A. & Schmitt, P. J. (1987). Partner homogamy in married, heterosexual cohabiting, gay and lesbian couples, *Journal of Sex Research* 23: 212–232.

Landale, N. & Fennelly, K. (1992). Informal unions among mainland Puerto Ricans: Cohabitation as an alternative to legal marriage?, *Journal of Marriage and the Family* 54: 269–280.

Landale, N. & Forste, R. (1991). Patterns of entry into cohabitation and marriage among mainland Puerto Rican women, *Demography* 28: 587–607.

Landale, N. & Hauan, S. (1992). The family life course of Puerto Rican children, *Journal of Marriage and the Family* 54: 912–924

Macklin, E. D. (1986). Nonmarital heterosexual cohabitation, in: A. S. Skolnick & J. H. Skolnick (eds.), *Family in transition Rethinking marriage, sexuality, child rearing, and family organization*, 5th edn. (pp. 210–231). Boston: Little Brown.

Manning, W. D. (1992). The linkage between premarital fertility and cohabitation in the U.S. University of Wisconsin, National Survey of Families and Households, Working Paper No. 52.

Manning, W. D. (1993). Marriage and cohabitation following premarital conception, *Journal of Marriage and the Family* 55: 839–850.

Mare, R. D. (1991). Five decades of educational assortative mating, *American Sociological Review* 56: 15–32.

Nock, S. L. (1995). Spouse preferences of never-married, divorced, and cohabiting Americans, *Journal of Divorce and Remarriage* 22: 91–108.

Oppenheimer, V. K. (1988). A theory of marriage timing, *American Journal of Sociology* 94: 563–591.

Poverny, L. M. & Finch, W. A., Jr. (1988). Gay and lesbian domestic partnerships: Expanding the definition of family, *Social Casework* 69: 116–121.

Rindfuss, R. R. & VandenHeuvel, A. (1990). Cohabitation: A precursor to marriage or an alternative to being single, *Population and Development Review* 16: 703–726.

Scanzoni, J. & Marsiglio, W. (1991). Wider families as primary relationships, *Marriage and Family Review* 17: 117–133.

Schoen, R. & Owens, D. (1992). A further look at first marriages and first unions, in: S. J. South & S. E. Tolnay (eds.), *The changing American family: Sociological and demographic perspective* (pp. 109–117). Boulder, CO: Westview Press.

Schoen, R. & Weinick, R. W. (1993). Partner choice in marriages and cohabitations, *Journal of Marriage and the Family* 55: 408–414.

Sweet, J. A. & Bumpass, L. L. (1990). Young adults' views of marriage, cohabitation and family. University of Wisconsin, National Survey of Families and Households, Working Paper No. 33.

Tanfer, K. (1987). Patterns of premarital cohabitation among never-married women in the United States, *Journal of Marriage and the Family* 49: 483–497.

Thornton, A. (1988). Cohabitating and marriage in the 1980s, *Demography* 25: 497–508.

U.S. Bureau of the Census. (1992). *Census of Population and Housing, 1990: Public Use Microdata Sample US Technical Documentation*. Washington, DC: The Bureau.

Willis, R. J. & Michael, R. T. (1994). Innovation in family formation: Evidence on cohabitation in the United States, in J. Ermisch & N. Ogawa (eds.), *The family, the market and the state in ageing societies* (pp. 9–45). Oxford: Clarendon Press.

Chapter 8

Prue Hyman

LESBIANS AND GAY MEN FLIRTING WITH/DISENGAGING FROM VITAL STATISTICS: SAME SEX RELATIONSHIPS AND THE NZ CENSUS 1971/2001

From *Hecate* 2003, 29 (2): 248–60

Introduction

LESBIANS AND GAY MALE communities' relationship with the New Zealand Census sounds a somewhat dry topic, but I had a lot of fun writing this paper. Looking at the ways in which the statistical bureaucrats have phrased questions about 'marital status' and relationships between members of families and households over time says much about social change, including our increased acceptance – at least if we live in tidy couples in the same dwelling.

Lesbian/ gay/ bisexual/ transgender/ intersex/ takatapui/ fa'afine/ queer/ homosexual/ heterosexual/ all of the above? The New Zealand Census does not (yet, anyway) have to face the issue of how to phrase questions about sexual 'orientation' or 'identity' or 'behaviour'. So far, no such question is asked, although the Managing Editor of *Express* (an Auckland fortnightly paper) Victor van Wettering, and others, were campaigning when I began writing this article to change things for 2006. But in 1996 and 2001 the only people in our communities to be counted in the Census of Population and Dwellings[1] were those who decided to indicate that they were a 'same-sex' couple living together.

How did they do this? Question 19 in (2001), asked us all to list 'all the people who live in the same household as you' (question 16 in 1996 was similar), and included the option 'my partner or de facto, boyfriend or girlfriend'. Nothing there to indicate clearly whether or not this is meant to be inclusive of those of us living with partners, although the wording seems more so than earlier versions such as 'my de facto spouse'. But the help note to question 19 asks: 'My partner is the same sex as me – should I mark "partner"?' and answers: 'Yes, If you live with a partner as a gay or lesbian couple, mark 'my partner or de facto, boyfriend or girlfriend'. So those couples living together and accepting the wording lesbian or gay know what they're meant to do – *if* they read the help notes, which I suspect few do. But some would no doubt want to identify as couples to reflect reality, and perhaps for emotional and/or political reasons.

Of course in the question itself, being part of a 'same-sex couple' does not show up, but the mysterious coding processes of Statistics New Zealand (SNZ) will see it emerge. This occurs because first, question 2 asks us to say (unequivocally!) whether each of us is male or female and, second, the person who fills in the dwelling form has the responsibility of listing the others in the dwelling who are filling in individual forms. Further, that person must state how each other person is related to them, this time with the option 'my wife/husband/partner/de facto'.

Still attending? Putting all that together can yield two men or two women ticking that they are partners. What does SNZ do if one of them ticks partner and the other flatmate has not been revealed! 'Same-sex couple' is the term which SNZ uses, often in tables giving comparisons of characteristics of same-sex and opposite-sex couples. Sometimes there is also a breakdown into female couples and male couples – in this paper I will use the terms lesbian and gay couples. However, how people think of themselves when ticking the box to show they live with a partner and it emerges from the other questions that that partner is the same sex, is unknowable and doubtless highly variable in a postmodern world of fluid, changing identities – and the other groups mentioned early in this paper disappear without trace.

So what matters about all this? Quite a lot, in my view. This paper will examine three aspects of our engagement or otherwise with the New Zealand Census. First, it will look at the arguments over whether we should be involved with the Census and whether we should demand visibility. Second, it will look at the changing social construction of relationships within households as evidenced by SNZ through their collection of statistics between 1971 and 2001. Finally, some statistics on same gender/same household partnerships will be presented and discussed for the last two Census years, 1996 being the first one for which they were released.

How visible might we want to be in official statistics?

So do we want to be visible in official statistics at all? Lesbian feminists have over the years been doubtful about this (and I should say that I am writing from that perspective – and, speaking for no-one but myself, know even less about the position of other individuals or groups such as gay men). Certainly we do our own surveys and document our characteristics and the discrimination we encounter to learn about ourselves, strategise community priorities and political action. But what about official population counts? These are bound to involve considerable undercounting of lesbian/gay individuals/couples, which could lead to our communities being disregarded as a much smaller (albeit vociferous and annoying) group than we are.

Unwillingness to tell 'them' about our lives, suspicions about the use of knowledge about individuals (such as benefit receipt – despite the protections of the Statistics Act), and other issues about definitions and safety would mean that many lesbians/gay men won't record this. The resultant undercount could be used by those seeking to downgrade equality moves and deny equal rights. Census (mis)information could add fuel to the claims that figures often used for the prevalence of homosexuality from Kinsey onwards of around 10% are exaggerated. And with only those couples living together and prepared to say so recorded, this is likely to be a fairly small proportion of our total communities, and one socially constructed to fit in this subgroup as very similar to a perceived heterosexual norm.

The United States, Australia, and Canada have made similar changes to their Census questions to identify same-sex couples. A report on the 2000 US Census suggests that two thirds of lesbians and gay men do not live together as couples, although how this is estimated is not stated – there is certainly no basis I know of in New Zealand even for any sort of wild guess – quite apart from the definitional minefields.

And even the visibility from those who do identify and the resulting 'factual' information could be used against us, particularly if it shows that the 'pink dollar' phenomenon really exists, that we are better off financially than the general population. With a probably biased sample identifying, such 'facts' may be spurious. On the other hand, without good information, the discrimination against us can be neglected by government and the need for policies to reduce it be discounted. And the Census is the easiest source for basic information, even though it can't document discrimination and may yield biased samples.

At some periods, rather than seek inclusiveness and visibility, there has been the counter move to boycott official statistics – although this itself was at least partly because of their total exclusion of us. Some Wellington lesbians organised a 'dykecott' of the 1981 New Zealand Census to protest our omission from its categories and the social oppression of lesbians more generally.

The background to this included a decision in 1980 by the Transport Centre, confirmed by the Wellington City Council Transport Committee and supported by then mayor Michael Fowler (with Helen Ritchie the only dissenting councillor) of an advertisement for the Lesbian Centre on the Council operated buses. This decision led to considerable lesbian outrage and activism. At around the same time, the Gay Coalition and lesbian groups made submission to the Human Rights Commission (HRC) to have lesbians and gay men included under the Human Rights Act – and although this did not occur until 1993, with government itself then still exempted. Chief Commissioner Pat Downey had put out an 'incredible' statement in reply, arguing that homosexuality could not be a status – the Lesbian Legal Advisory Committee considered the Commission's negative report to be 'inadequately reasoned, badly flawed and based in part on an erroneous interpretation of the HRC Act'. Pickets and letter writing campaigns were organised, 'protesting against the denial of our rights, and against an HRC which has failed its responsibilities towards the citizens of this country to protect basic human rights and freedom.'[2]

The issues about visibility or otherwise were also raised. 'The Lesbian Centre at 6 Boulcott Street, top floor . . . has been most useful for organising against the HRC. . . . The latest action has been to organise the boycott (dykecott) of the Census papers. We sent our non filled out census forms to the Human Rights Commission with various explanations, but basically saying: no rights – no responsibilities. Some added the point that our existence is made invisible by the question – married, single, etc etc. Which raises another point, do we really want them to know how many of us there are?'[3]

In contrast, as mentioned in the introduction, *Express*'s Managing Editor, Victor van Wettering, wants the Census to go much further and ask questions about sexual orientation. During the consultation process over the 2001 Census questions, 9 written submissions sought the inclusion of sexual orientation, but the Deputy Government Statistician argues that such a 'very personal question' would be considered by some 'to be intrusive' and 'consequently inappropriate for the census which is a compulsory questionnaire'.[4] This is not surprising – SNZ has consistently taken this position. For example, submissions were received asking for the 1996 Census to include the topic and the response in the Census Progress Report on Content was that 'a direct question on sexual orientation would be overly intrusive. The living arrangements question will gather information on same-sex relationships so that those living with their partners can be counted' (see later in this paper). The 2001 Census Content volume was somewhat more sympathetic, giving a reasonable analysis of the pros and cons but, citing uncertain data quality and likely undercount, however it still came out against inclusion.

With respect to SNZ's arguments, van Wettering correctly points out that religious belief can be seen equally as 'private information', and yet it is included, with a special box labelled 'object to answering this question' – which could also be used in a sexual orientation question if this were thought necessary. Sex, religion, and money have often been seen as taboo subjects in private conversation. However, the Census asks questions about the last two – why not the first as well? Ironically, while mentioning these three topics, same-sex couples identified in the 1996/2001 Censuses were less willing than their opposite-sex counterparts to reveal their annual incomes. In 2001, of couples without children 11.5% of opposite-sex couples and 15.8% of same-sex couples without children were in the not stated category, while of couples with children, 18.6% of opposite-sex couples did not state their incomes and a massive 41.9% of same-sex couples.

In response to SNZ's position, van Wettering made a formal complaint on 17 May 2002 to the HRC, alleging that SNZ is 'failing to meet its statutory requirements to collect information to inform government policy and enable communities to make a case for resources', its actions thereby amounting to a 'clear breach of part 1a of the Human Rights Act'. In the complaint, he argued that continuing invisibility is the effect, if not the purpose of SNZ's decision. The refusal to ask about this area is not neutral, constituting discrimination by affecting sexual minorities more than the heterosexual majority. His discussion of the complaint states that we are 'clearly being treated less favourably because the government is depriving itself of the information it needs in order to consider policy in relation to gay and lesbian people' He argued that even with under-reporting, 'it would still be better than remaining completely invisible'.[5] The same issue reported that then Statistics Minister Leila Harre had asked SNZ for a report on the matter.

The HRC response to the complaint (from mediator Maria Hansen)[6] speciously dismisses van Wettering's argument on the discriminatory lack of neutrality involved in this area. Because no one is asked about their sexual orientation, she argues 'everyone is treated the same'. She did, though, admit that what is involved is an allegation of indirect discrimination, covered in Section 65 of the Human Rights Act. However, this section allows for the defence of there being a good reason for an indirectly discriminatory practice. The HRC letter points out this possible defence and also argues that no evidence was produced of actual disadvantage from not asking about sexual orientation. Rather than suggesting that those two points be followed up, it concluded, without any explanation, that the HRC lacked jurisdiction and said the file would be closed. Express has now approached the HRC Director of Proceedings, seeking assistance to put the complaint to the Human Rights Review Tribunal. Following up the issues with new Minister of Statistics John Tamihere, Express reported that he called SNZ 'a very conservative group of technocrats', and supported including a question in the 2006 Census, subject to checking the 'veracity in what SNZ are saying to preclude the question'.[7] However, the Dominion Post reported Tamihere as refusing to be drawn into the debate and describing *Express* as being 'on a mission'. While not opposing questions on sexuality, he 'did not have the information' on whether the Census was an appropriate vehicle.[8]

In another issue of *Express*,[9] Peter Saxton, a NZ Aids Foundation Researcher, responding to the editor's articles, called for a weighing up within the gay community of the benefits and disadvantages of such a Census question, pointing out the problems for closeted people not out to others in their household and reiterating the undercounting issue. In response to the pressure from parts of the community for inclusion of a question, Statistics New Zealand commissioned some research involving focus groups on its acceptability to adult New Zealanders of various ages and ethnicities. The somewhat incoherent report on this research was released recently and the predictable range of opinions was used to confirm the decision not to include a sexual orientation question in the 2006 Census.

Like Saxton, I have some reservations about the Census as the most appropriate place for sexual orientation questions, for reasons I outlined earlier. In-depth surveys may be more appropriate. A compromise position is the use of national surveys on particular topics where the subject is relevant. Statistics Canada is asking Canadians to declare their sexual orientation in such a survey, in order to monitor the effectiveness of the country's human rights laws (reported in National Post, on data lounge web pages). Preliminary tests were conducted to gauge people's willingness to answer the question, and found that most are prepared to state their sexual orientation if it is requested for an acceptable purpose. In this case it is part of the Canadian Community Health Study – a telephone survey of 130,000 Canadians conducted every two years – for the purpose of better understanding the needs of those who visit the country's community health clinics. The wording of the question is very basic: 'Do you consider yourself to be heterosexual, homosexual, that is lesbian or gay, or bisexual?'

SNZ's social construction of relationships within households

Examining changes to Census questions over time provides a rich source of social commentary. In particular, the ways in which the statistical bureaucrats have phrased questions about 'marital status' and relationships between members of families and households shines a mirror on social change. Until 1981 it was the 'head of the household' who was required to fill in the Dwelling Form in private dwellings. The relationships of all others in the household to 'him' (usually) were to be specified. From 1981 onwards, feminist pressure saw this term almost disappear. The Dwelling form was to be filled in by 'the occupier', although the previous term crept back into the help notes, with the instruction that 'this person should be the head (if any) of the household, or some other adult present in the dwelling on Census night'. Before turning to lesbian/gay specific issues, I cannot resist showing a way in which individual members of SNZ (or the Statistics Department as it then was) can show their sense of humour and mark for all time their work on the Census. The help guide for the Personal Questionnaire in 1986 gives an example that shows how to fill in the date of birth. It is 5–12–1942, the birth date of well known Wellington lesbian Bronwen Dean, who was running the Census operation at the time!

To trace the gradual recognition of lesbian/gay relationships, we need to look at the phrasing of several questions on the Personal Questionnaire. The first is that of (legal, de jure) marital status. In 1971 and 1976 the box options, with no 'other' category, were 'never married', married', 'legally separated', 'widowed' and 'divorced', all applying to legal, opposite-sex marriage, thus making our relationships totally invisible. Those of us who did not marry an opposite-sex partner before 'coming out' (or later!) are required to tick single, and others whichever box is appropriate. In 1981, the heading changed to 'present marital status' and the third alternative to 'married but permanently separated'. Much more importantly, the question acquired a second part, to be completed by some in addition to (not instead of) the first. This was to tick a box 'if living in a de facto relationship (as husband/wife)', and indicated a partial move to recording what is now called 'social marital status'.

Legal/social marital status are defined by SNZ as 'a person's status with respect to registered marriage/consensual union' respectively. However, once again in 1981, same-sex partnerships were excluded. They are now included in the SNZ definition of consensual union which reads: 'Two people usually resident in the same dwelling who: share mutual concern for each other, have a degree of economic, social, and emotional interdependence, and consider their relationship to be akin to marriage.' I suppose that covers my relationship with my partner, although I resent the heterosexual norm of the last part! Incidentally, since this paper talks often of opposite and same sex couples, we should note that SNZ defines couple as 'two people who usually reside together and are legally married, or two people who are in a consensual union.' And it defines partner as 'a person with whom another person is: in a registered marriage or in a consensual union' and same-sex partners as 'two people of the same sex who are in a consensual union'. So there you are!

Including the two parts (legal/social marital status) within the same question was not a success, due to data quality problems, mentioned in the 1996 Census Progress Report on Content. Hardly surprising – it is easy to confuse them and it is unclear what refers to past and what to present relationships in that format. Instead, since 1986 there has been a question separate from that on legal marital status (which in 1986 separated out first marriages and remarriages but otherwise kept its previous form). In 1986 this was entitled: 'What are your living arrangements?' It has these options: 'living with legal husband or wife', 'living with a partner as a couple (de facto marriage)', 'living alone', and 'living with other persons (such as parents, flatmates) – with a requirement to state the nature of the relationship with the other person(s). The second option for the first time hints a possibility in the wording before the bracket of including our relationships, but then the bracket removes it – and there is no help note to elucidate. In 1991 the question changes to: 'Who are the persons that usually live in the same dwelling as you?' and the second option changes to 'my partner (such as de facto spouse, boyfriend)'. We are almost there – partner is a term many of us use, but the examples do not encourage all of us and, again, no relevant help note.

Finally, in 1996 the firm intention to include us has been reached. The legal/social marital status/living arrangements questions are lengthened to eight in a sequence, separating out partners from other members of the household. Thus the first question, the only one which matters here, is: 'Which of these people live in the same household as you?', with the only options being 'your legal husband or wife', your partner or de facto, girlfriend or boyfriend', and 'none of these'. Spouse has gone, partner is retained, gender neutrality is achieved, and the help note reads: 'if you live with a partner as a gay or lesbian couple, tick "your partner or de facto, girl friend or boy friend".' Bingo – at least for those who read help notes and want to identify. I claim, with a mixture of amusement, definite intention, and I modesty, some personal credit for that help note. I was involved with consultations on the Census, and had seen the draft questions and the intention in the progress report to make same-sex couples a separate category in the output. At that point there was no help note. I made strong representations that the question, while at last inclusive, would yield a huge undercount which would be exacerbated unless there was specific encouragement to same-sex partners to tick that box. Hopefully, the help note increased the response, even though it was still low among lesbians/gay men living together as partners.

In 2001 the question structure was simplified but the relevant wording of both the question and the help note with respect to same-sex partnerships was unchanged. This was despite the fact that the Preliminary Views on Content volume for the Census argued that the question wording might need to be addressed to make it clearer that gay or lesbian relationships are a valid response. One suggestion was the inclusion of a specific same-sex partner tick box. However, the help note booklet is better presented and that, together with its being the second occasion, and a general improvement in the climate and greater acceptance of lesbian/gay rights over the 5 years 1996/2001, may have helped yield a bigger response among lesbian/gay couples living together.

The other important Census question for the current purpose asked each individual to identify their relationship to the head of household and later to the occupier or person who filled in the Dwelling form. In 1971 one searches vainly for any way of filling it in. All the options with their own boxes are excluded, with 'wife or spouse' hardly welcoming. One would have to write something under 'other relationship'. The examples given include flatmate, boarder, and lodger, and there are no relevant help notes. Here we could have written, for example, 'lesbian partner', but there was certainly no instruction or encouragement to do so.

In 1976, there are subtle changes towards gender neutrality and to include de facto heterosexual relationships, but not same-sex ones. The list of options with their own boxes included 'spouse (wife or husband) of head', while the associated help note read that this 'includes a de facto spouse of the head of household.' In 1981, the 'dykecott' year, nothing has changed except for the switch to occupier, and a change of order to 'spouse (husband or wife) of head.' I ask, tongue in cheek, whether the latter change in order is anti-feminist, putting the husband first, or pro-feminist, recognising first that the occupier may be the female. We will not linger on that!

In 1986 and 1991, we see the disappearance of the spouse, with simple 'husband or wife of occupier'. In the last two Census years, the question was subsumed into the living arrangements section. The Dwelling form for each Census has also required a list of each person filling in an Individual (formerly Personal) form and their relationship to the adult filling in the Dwelling form. The list of relationship types supplied has changed along the same lines as outlined above. As mentioned in the introduction, it is this piece of the jigsaw which, together with the Individual forms, allows the identification of same-sex couples. The coding issues are complex and what happens when inconsistencies arise between individual responses is not clear.

Information from 1996/2001 Census results on same-sex relationships

What has emerged from the two sets of results so far? In 1996 3,255 same sex couples identified as such, increasing to 5,070 in 2001. The 56% increase is probably not realistic but a reflection of greater acceptance in answering the question, while in fact both figures are clearly vast underestimates, as expected. Well over half of the couples so counted were women, (55.7% in 1996/ 56.% in 2001) and of such lesbian couples, as many as 28.5% in 1996/33.9% in 2001 had children in their household, compared to 11.6%/17.6% for gay men, and 55%/52.1% for heterosexual couples. (Byrne, 1998 for 1996 figures and my own calculations from

Census 2001 results). While 2,535 is still a fairly small number of lesbian couples, it is by far the best basis yet for income and other information, though only for a small section of all New Zealand lesbians.

What then can we say about the pink dollar phenomenon or the economic position of lesbians and gay men generally, in New Zealand and elsewhere? Firstly, fewer in same-sex couples specified their income than in opposite sex couples (10% of women/13% of men in same-sex couples, 7% in same-sex couples in 1996), perhaps for the reasons mentioned earlier. The proportion where family income is unavailable is even higher (19% for same-sex couples and 14% for opposite-sex couples). The income data that is available is striking, however, confirming the major influence of parenting on income, and the similarity of the gender gap for those in lesbian/gay couples and straight couples.

Yes, gays/lesbians in couples without children have higher average family income levels than their opposite-sex counterparts, with 26% in 1996/39.3% in 2001 of lesbian couples, 36%/48.6% of gay male couples, and 16%/24.3% of opposite-sex couples reporting family income above $70,000. The size of the gap is partly a matter of different age structures, with proportionately less low income elderly among the same-sex couples without children. And the picture is quite different for couples with children in the household. In 2001, 64.1% of lesbian/gay couples, less than the 74.5% of opposite-sex couples, reported incomes above $40,000. For opposite-sex couples those with children are better off than those without, while this is reversed for lesbian/gay couples. And on average lesbian/gay couples with children support them on lower incomes than their childless counterparts, and on incomes similar to or lower than their straight counterparts.

So there is considerable truth in the picture of many well off, two income, no dependents, 'g/luppy' couples, though more so for gay men, with higher earnings and fewer dependent children than lesbians. The pink dollar is then very selective and a myth when used as a generalisation about most lesbians/gay men. It is a dangerous myth, when used politically to argue that we are already a privileged group who need no further civil rights protections.[10]

Nevertheless, lesbians and gay males from these couples were more likely to be in the labour force than their heterosexual counterparts, with a small difference for gay/heterosexual men (78.4%/75% in 1996) – which may be due to the different age profile (see below) – and with a large difference for lesbian/heterosexual women (76.1%/62.8%). The higher labour participation for lesbians is presumably due largely to a combination of less dependent children, on average, in the household and the need for economic independence. In 2001, 52% of same-sex couples without children had both partners working full time, compared with 36% of opposite-sex couples without children. Unemployment rates were also slightly higher than average for lesbians/gay men, while those in work were more concentrated in higher status white collar occupations. Lesbians were slightly more likely than heterosexual women to be employed in trade occupations which mainly employ males – and gay men were under-represented in such occupations.[11]

Compared to heterosexual couples, lesbians and gay male couples are younger, rent to a greater extent rather than own property, live in cities, use the internet and smoke more, own cars and phones less and are less inclined to have a religious affiliation. It needs to be borne in mind that there exists a self selection by willingness to declare themselves of the lesbian/gay couples, while some of these characteristics are interlinked, their comparative youth partly accounting for some of the other results. However, the drift to the city to find people like yourself is a clear result, and readers would doubtless be able to think of rationales for some of the other characteristics.

Maori were more common among those who identified as being part of a lesbian couple at the 1996 Census than among those in other types of couples, 18% against 11% for gay men and 10% for heterosexually coupled men or women, while Asian men were over-represented relative to their population numbers among gay male couples.

More analysis of this data is possible – despite its limitations as a sample of even lesbian/gay couples living together, let alone all lesbians and gay men, it is a richer source than any other available to date.

Notes

1   New Zealand Census of Population and Dwellings, 1996, 2001 and earlier years – Reports, Progress Reports on Content, etc, Wellington: Statistics New Zealand (previously New Zealand Department of Statistics).
2   *Circle Magazine*, (1981) 'Human Rights Commission', vol 36, pp. 2, 4.
3   Circle, p.32.
4   Quoted by van Wettering in *Express*, 22 May 2002.
5   *Express*, 22 May.
6   *Express*, 25 September.
7   *Express*, 4 December.
8   *Express*, 7 December.
9   *Express*, 5 June.
10 Lee Badgett (1997) 'Beyond Biased Samples: Challenging the Myths on the Economic Status of Lesbians and Gay Men' in *Homo Economics: Capitalism, Community, and Lesbian and Gay Life*, (eds) Amy Gluckman and Betsy Reed, Routledge: New York and London, pp. 65–71; Prue Hyman (2001) 'Lesbians and Economic/Social Change: Impacts of Globalisation on Our Community(ies) and Politics', *Journal of Lesbian Studies*, 5, pp.115–132.
11 Judith Byrne (1998) 'What the 1996 Census Tells Us About Lesbians' in *Women's Studies Association 1998 Conference Papers*, WSA: Auckland, pp. 52–57.

Queer political economy

"**P**OLITICAL ECONOMY" IS A TERM that has changed in its meaning over time. Originally it really referred to what we now call simply "economics." The term as used by economists now frequently means using a variety of approaches to studying economic behavior, including the various branches of critique of neoclassical, or orthodox economics. That is the way in which we use the term herein.

In Richard Cornwall's chapter, "Queer political economy: the social articulation of desire" (1997), he applies the theory that preferences are formed through social interaction to the field of queer economics. Describing the "social articulation of desires," he asserts that gays and lesbians create a social code among themselves that isolates them into separate markets from the greater community.

This phenomenon has both advantages and disadvantages for the queer community. The primary advantage to the social articulation of desire is that queers can then be defined in an economic context, a context that had previously been unable to explain gay and lesbian behavior. When an economic explanation can be created, economic policy can be created (or at least debated) with empirical, rather than just qualitative, reasoning. But although the queer political economic model has the ability to capture sexual orientation preferences, it does not capture the five centuries of homophobia that has plagued modern Western cultures.

In other work Cornwall has used complex mathematical equations to quantify this social articulation of desire. This method has both advantages and disadvantages. The clear advantage is that a solid mathematical argument adds validity to his argument that the social articulation of desire has created an economically disadvantaged group. Yet the calculations are complex, and critics can easily question the figures since Cornwall is quantifying human emotion. Another disadvantage to the mathematical approach is that it alienates those not familiar with the complex theories he applies. This is a problem if the primary purpose is to point out the current discrimination against gays and lesbians, and if this purpose is hidden. However, for those who prefer a fuller version of Cornwall's theoretical structure, there is a longer version of this paper (Cornwall 1997). Cornwall's careful analysis contrasts favorably with influential conservative judge Richard Posner's simplistic economic modeling in which sexual orientation may vary depending on relative costs and benefits (Posner 1991; see also Anderson 1993 for a telling review of Posner's book), but the idea is nonetheless provocative.

In addition, what is commonly called economics is generally considered as a "patriarchal economics" to feminist and gay/lesbian groups. This depiction of society favors a state where the forward movement of the male figure has been highlighted. Women were placed in a domestic role, dependent on the support of the male. Lesbian groups recognized this lack of fair representation for women and removed themselves from the umbrella of "economics," instead arguing for creation of a new field, "Lesbian Economics." Jeffner Allen posits such a field in her early piece, "Lesbian economics" (1986). By naming the field, the economic actions of lesbian women can now be studied – women's movements that are now able to be conceptualized differently (i.e., women's actions independent of men can be different than women's actions that are dependent on interactions with men). In Allen's (and others') view, in removing obligation to the male-headed structure it is then necessary to develop a unique point of view that encapsulates the essence of the lesbian economy, for even the view of heterosexual female life is misconstrued. This need for this segregated study is not only necessary for lesbians but for the gay community at large. Dispelling misconceptions that have been passed down from previous times about gay culture and economics relies on such independent study. Thus it may also be natural to question how much gays have to offer the lesbian and feminist movement(s), if they still benefit from society's favoring of the male, whether straight or gay (Jacobs 1997), as well as what the relationship is between lesbianism and feminism (Matthaei 1998) and how queerness can intersect with class (Weston and Rofel 1984).

The continuing tension between what is "normal" and what is heterosexual/homosexual is an ongoing topic for writers in queer political economy, as is the relationship between closeting and visibility (Danby 2007) and questioning the naturalness of an alignment between gay and lesbian interests. The readings in Section Four on queer economic history center these issues in a more explicitly historical context rather than focusing on the theoretical context.

Another strand of discussion in political economy continues regarding the relationship between capitalism/markets and gays and lesbians as active participants in the market system. Is there an inherent tension in being queer aware and being a consumer/participant in the market system (Badgett 1997; Duggan 2004; Sears 2005)? The readings in Section Seven on queer consumer economics continue this discussion with more explicit examples taken from recent marketing studies.

DISCUSSION QUESTIONS

1   How does the social articulation of desire differ from other forms of segregating characteristics among minority groups?
2   When queers can be defined in an economic context, what social ramifications are created?

3   Is it possible to participate selectively in a system if you do not agree
     with all aspects of it? In particular, what about our current capitalistic
     system?
4   Why might a post-gay/post-feminist angle be at odds with Cornwall's
     argument?
5   Do you see a need for a separate theoretical articulation of the issues
     facing lesbians than the issues facing gays? Why or why not? What about
     for bisexuals? What about for transsexuals?

REFERENCES

Anderson, R. M. (1993) "EP seeks EP: a review of *Sex and Reason* by Richard A.
    Posner," *Journal of Economic Literature*, 31: 191–8.
Badgett, M. V. L. (1997) "Thinking homo/economically," in J. T. Sears and W. L.
    Williams (eds) *Overcoming Heterosexism and Homophobia: strategies that
    work*, New York: Columbia University Press.
Cornwall, R. R. (1997) "Deconstructing silence: the queer political economy of
    the social articulation of desire," *Review of Radical Political Economics*,
    29: 1–130.
Danby, C. (2007) "Political economy and the closet: heteronormativity in feminist
    economics." *Feminist Economics*, 13: 29–53.
Duggan, L. (2004) *The Twilight of Equality? Neoliberalism, cultural politics, and
    the attack on democracy*, Beacon Books.
Jacobs, M. P. (1997) "Do gay men have a stake in male privilege?: the political
    economy of gay men's contradictory relationship to feminism," in A. Gluckman
    and B. Reed (eds) *Homo Economics: capitalism, community, and lesbian
    and gay life*, New York and London: Routledge.
Matthaei, J. (1998) "Some comments on the role of lesbianism in feminist eco-
    nomic transformation," *Feminist Economics*, 4: 83–8.
Posner, R. A. (1991) *Sex and Reason*, Cambridge, Mass.: Harvard University Press.
Sears, A. (2005) "Queer anti-capitalism: what's left of lesbian and gay liber-
    ation?," *Science and Society*, 69: 92–112.
Weston, K. and Rofel, L. B. (1984) "Sexuality, class and conflict in a lesbian work-
    place," *Signs: Journal of Women in Culture and Society*, 9: 623–46.

Chapter 9

Richard R. Cornwall

QUEER POLITICAL ECONOMY: THE SOCIAL ARTICULATION OF DESIRE

From *Homo Economics: capitalism, community, and lesbian and gay life*, eds A. Gluckman and B. Reed, New York and London: Routledge, 1997, pp. 89–122

> *"My desire,*
> *More sharp than filed steel, did spur me forth"*
>
> —Shakespeare, Twelfth Night
>
> *desidero, ergo sum*
>
> post/modern epigraph

1 Introduction

THE FOUNDATION FOR POLITICAL ECONOMY is the concept of each person's tastes or preferences, i.e., desire. In neoclassical economics, preferences are assumed to be essentially predetermined genetically for each individual – oh, all right, perhaps bent a bit *in utero* by the mother's choices and even warped a small amount shortly after birth by the "nuclear family."[1] It is these preferences that lie at the base of the celebrated First and Second Efficiency Theorems of economic theory, which provide the key logic underlying intellectual defenses of market-based systems for social guidance and control. These theorems hold that capitalism allocates tasks and consumptions to each person in such a way that it is impossible to rearrange them in any way that would make some people happier and no one less happy (this is known as the market's "pareto efficiency").[2] Marxism, in contrast, takes individual preferences as wholly socially constructed by the social relations of production. In this view, the social structure of capital-versus-labor determines all noteworthy variations in human desires.

I offer here an overview of arguments that each individual's preferences are formulated at the deepest cognitive levels through social interaction, in markets, and otherwise. This is the basis for social structures – social codes or identities – that in their formation, operation, durability, and complexity are very similar to the earth's swirl of human languages. The effect of conceptualizing these social codes is to eviscerate mainstream economics' argument for the "efficiency" or "optimality" of the market as well as the priority assigned in Marxian economics to the dichotomy between capital and labor over other social categorizations. In particular, this paper presents the first sociocognitive model of what is the central queer example of paretian inefficiency of a social system: how a substantial fraction of the population can continue to deny to themselves as well as to others their "true" tastes – i.e., to stay stuck in the closet – despite repeated social interaction that includes visible queers.

To begin this story, it is appropriate to start with the perspective of queer studies as it focuses on describing both the social articulation of human desire[3] and the resulting vortex of social identities. It is critical to understand why identities often appear so essentially natural, so clear and durable, yet why they also appear as mirages, so insubstantial and false, mere social artifices. To make this double vision of identities tangible, consider this case from literary history.

At the rollover from the sixteenth to the seventeenth centuries, it was still possible for the two most prominent English playwrights, Shakespeare and Marlowe, to perceive and to articulate queer desire for all their audience. The first line quoted at the start of this piece was spoken by Antonio, whose urgent efforts to pursue Sebastian after their ship lands reflect the prominent role of queer desire in *Twelfth Night*.[4]

This ability simply to perceive, let alone articulate, queer desire in Shakespeare's work was lost in the intervening years so that, until Oscar Wilde started articulating rudely at the end of the last century, no one could admit to perceiving queer desire in Shakespeare's work. Only now in the mid-1990s in a few spots in this world can one readily discover how queerly Shakespeare's wordplay can be cast, thanks to such efforts as the production in the fall of 1994 of *Twelfth Night* by Danny Scheie at Theatre Rhinoceros. This was sited, significantly, in the heavily Latino/a, poor, and, yes, subversive Mission district of San Francisco.

To develop one theoretical description of this cycle from queer visibility to erasure and back to visibility, section 2 examines the process by which human desire gets expressed. It uses Keynes's notion that "we make judgments about the probability of future events without detailed numerical information"[5] – i.e., we judge based on subjective probabilities – to construct networks to articulate our desires. This story of people discovering their desires leads to an explanation of how social codes can come to falsely – "illusorily" – link desires to irrelevant human traits.

The key insight underlying this argument is that humans are totally dependent on our linguistic communities for our abilities to perceive, categorize, and articulate desires. This dependence is explored by looking at changes in the social categories of queer and straight, of lower and middle class, and of male and female, in the United States from late in the nineteenth century to the present. This historical evolution is then tied to what psychologists call illusory correlations in human cognition, correlations of the irrelevant which have been especially relevant to queers in the past sixty years. Finally, in section 6, I look at some of the implications of these ideas for the role of ideology in political economy, inspired by Oscar Wilde's and Jean Genet's efforts to subvert and appropriate individualism for queerly socialistic ends.

The mixture here of voices and of concepts from different disciplines is queer and few may feel fluent in all these languages, yet this *ver/mischung* seems essential to initiate a queer political economy. Much of the most insightful thinking about shame/abjection has been done not by political economists but by literary cultural analysts. The mathematical and political-economic strands here are made explicit in Cornwall (1996).

2 Social articulation of desire: social codes/languages as institutions for parallel processing

To understand the functioning of social codes in the formulation of desire, I have conducted mathematical simulations of the process of individual economic decision making. I began with a conceit especially popular in the previous two centuries and now deeply ingrained in economists' thinking: the solitary individual, who confronts markets completely on her/his own, but, we imagine, who has no idea of what s/he wants. Following Cyert and DeGroot (1980), McFadden (1981, 205), McFadden and Richter (1990, 165), Arthur (1991), Marimon, McGrattan, Sargent (1990), and Sargent (1993),[6] I imagined this solitary individual, Robinson Grusoe (or R.C., for short), as knowing her budget constraint but not her preferences and so making choices by intelligent randomness. I drew R.C. with the face of Mr. Magoo,[7] missing his glasses and groping quite blindly for insights as to where his goodies are. Since R.C. Magoo knows she does not know how to make himself feel good – what s/he desires, she decides to randomly sample among all her options to discover how they work. Thus we imagine that Magoo adopts a "stochastic" strategy to learn about his own desires.

Economists assume that people know their preferences and make these preferences the basis for interpreting everyone's behavior in markets. If, however, preferences are unknown (and whether or not they are fixed), an individual will find that there are significant gains to pooling information with other people about which choices are inferior to which other choices. Yet this pool of information about rankings can get seriously contaminated if people with different tastes contribute to the pool.

As a result, people can be thought to use standard statistical procedures to find variables that help them distinguish which people have the same tastes as they do and with whom they can trade information about inferior/ superior choices. These networks that facilitate the articulation of desire are "homopreference" networks. Individuals within homopreference networks can often be led to conclude that a variable that is actually completely irrelevant, but that is more easily discernible than is more sophisticated evidence of another's tastes, is in fact a reliable cue to differences in tastes. Because people are persuaded that such an irrelevant, "illusory," variable is helpful in their effort to articulate their own desires through swapping information with others, everyone can end up choosing her/his network of "friends" by excluding anyone who differs in this illusory variable. This results in a biased construction of homopteference networks. Sophisticated tests of whether someone's tastes are the same as one's own can repair this bias only belatedly. Hence, the correction cannot be complete for people whose Face and preferences make their group small compared to the size of the homopreference networks (race and class bias, for instance, limits the range of a homopreference network).

In the ten simulations conducted, the consequence of reliance on an illusory trait was that approximately one-third (eleven out of thirty) of the people with the minority type of preferences were led into the "closet," i.e., led to articulate a choice as being best for them that was, in fact, significantly different from what was best for them. Only one out of sixty of the people with the majority type of preferences made such an error. This misarticulation of desire, which occurred in all ten simulations, was "pareto inefficient." Each of the people who chose as "best" a choice that in fact was inferior to another choice for them could feasibly have changed to their (hidden) best choice.

The model employed was extremely simplistic and essentialistic, taking people's true" tastes as genetically given. These true tastes may then be distorted by sheer random chance depending on whom one "chooses" as neighbors with whom to pool information on preferences. A more complete model (Cornwall 1996) allows for a person's true tastes to be shaped, at least in part, through social interaction.

In addition, this model does not capture the important dynamics of abjection/shame that have powered homophobia for the past five centuries in western cultures. In particular, it does not pretend to offer a full explanation of the "closet."[8] Surely there are some who act straight (and so are conventionally described as being "in the closet") but who do so for very different reasons than not knowing they would prefer being intimate with their own gender. But for some of us it does hint at what delayed our sexual maturity to an age which is startling for some today.

The model assumes that cognitive codes (e.g., the idea that a different Face signifies different tastes) evolve socially, as people endeavor to distinguish others with the same tastes from those with different tastes. This evolution is analogous to the sociologically nuanced development of linguistic variation, and akin to William Burroughs' claim that "language is a virus" (Ricco 1994, 76)."[9]

The growth of these cognitive codes generates social structures known as "social identities," which are simply the labels that come, like game theory's focal points, to distinguish homopreference networks. These identities, like sociolinguistic structures, are ambiguously bordered from/overlapping with each other as well as both very durable and rather plastic. When seen as a social solution to the problem of how individuals know what they desire, these codes can be seen to be institutional "social software" coordinating the "parallel processing" of experience by multiple individuals. This in turn saves people enormously in the time required to articulate their desires. This social articulation of cognitive codes, which in my model are based on the networked evolution of each person's probabilities (i.e., his or her understanding of who is different or similar in tastes), gives one meaning to Dollimore's (1991, 244) assertion that "identity — individual and cultural — involves a process of disavowal."

It is important to stress that the extremely simplistic and essentialist model I have used to draw these conclusions is not, by itself, a model of real economies. Rather, this model aims to make tangible a deep, specific criticism of neoclassical economics: if perfectly competitive market-guided outcomes are to be superior to all other allocation of tasks and consumptions (i.e., if they are to be pareto efficient), people must know and act on their true preferences. A more useful model for political economy comprehends that we enter the world blind like Magoo about our own desires; that our understanding — articulation — of our desires is largely determined by the social structures in which we are ensnared; and that important social forces of political economy mold these social structures.

We turn next to analyses of our use and formation of categories for perception, sketching some of the forces of political economy shaping these categories.

3 Categories and (illusory) correlations

I use the phrase "socially articulate desires" to describe the way in which people in groups categorize each other in order to express and act on their desires. This articulation involves breaking humanity into distinct pieces; i.e., forming categories for distinguishing people according to some traits and joining these pieces together, recognizing that society includes these different types.

To understand how we form categories, we must look at human inference: how do we know? This invites epistemological complexity, but I choose queerly, instead, to follow Wittgenstein in assuming a sociolinguistic basis of "ordinary language" for "knowing" what we know.[10] Cognitive psychology has, in the last twenty years, made significant progress in mapping many contours of how individuals perceive (and also fail to perceive), encode, store, retrieve, and then express/act on perceptions. "The view that categories are invariably defined by a set of necessary and sufficient conditions for membership has by now been thoroughly discredited" (Holland, et al. 1986, 182). Instead of such a discredited "positivist" epistemological approach, Wittgenstein (1958) in philosophy and Berlin and Kay (1969) in linguistics suggested that a more useful mental model is that we form categories on the basis of prototypes and we have quite ambiguous boundaries between categories.[11]

This process for forming social categories can be thought of as the elevation of an instance of one person doing/being something into an archetype. The central metaphor/analogy here is:

figure out a problem = figuration (put a face on the problem)

The etymological roots of this linguistic associative code in English are the Latin (*figura*) and French (*la figure*) words for face. The strong analytical preference for "specific-level evidence" (i.e., specific human examples) over more abstract "base-rate information" (i.e., abstract categories) is evident in Lee Edelman's (1994) study of the cinematic focus on the face. Edelman notes how movies use faces to represent many things – concepts, feelings, language, smells, experiences, class, ethnicity, race, gender, sense of safety/violation. Political campaigns also do it (Willie Horton). It is what makes TV so powerful: faces seduce people to be viewers by capturing their attention. Even MTV's Beavis and Butthead have identifiably working faces with mouths that fart, noses that wrinkle.

The preference for specific figuration, the use of facial prototypes, over abstract categorization may be a mere statistical regularity; or may be deeply embedded within the operating systems (e.g., limbic systems) of our cognitive software and hardware by the amygdala.[12] Such figuration may only be supplemented when we have had powerfully salient experience through the use of abstract categories rather than faces.

This suggests that prosopopeia, the process by which we give a face to an idea with a figure of speech, may be more than mere metaphor for human categorization and induction. This conjecture of a central role in human cognition for facial images is strengthened by growing evidence that "the amygdala has a central role in social communication. . . . The direction of one's gaze signals the object of one's attention . . . while facial expression indicates how one is disposed to behave. When mutual eye contact is established, both participants know that the communication loop between them has been closed and for primates of all species this is the most potent of social situations" (Allman and Brothers 1994).

There is also an increasing body of evidence that cognitive access to facial images appears to be "effortless," "a rapid, automated process," and more accurate than are "deliberative, analytic retrieval processes"; e.g., sorting, matching, and elimination (Dunning and Stern 1994, 819 and 832; see also Wells, Rydell, and Seelau 1993).

Making the blatant leap of applying this description of very specific types of induction to socially mediated categorization, it is tempting to consider the "sex/gender system" (Rubin 1975, 1984) that admitted little variation, and appears to have been hegemonic; until approximately the end of the last century. It was taken for granted as "natural,"[13] that sexual object preference was determined by gender: "In the dominant turn-of-the-century cultural system governing the interpretation of homosexual behavior, especially in working-class milieus, one had a gender identity rather than a sexual identity or even a 'sexuality'; one's sexual behavior was thought to be necessarily determined by one's gender identity (Chauncey 1994, 48)."[14] In other words, gender was determined by the dichotomy of "male" versus "female" face, which also determined sexual object choice.

The turn of the century was a time not only of increasing urbanization in this country, but also of radical changes in the roles and extents of markets and the organization of production. The rise of wage labor in this country occurred for men after the first third of the nineteenth century and was followed at the end of the century by dramatic changes for women, as wage labor became both gendered and segregated. For example, at the turn of the century bank tellers switched amazingly quickly from being an all-male occupation to a predominately female occupational category.[15] Equally momentous was the rise of factories with thousands of workers under one roof, a structure that led to enormous social upheaval as new codes and occupations for imagining/running productive enterprises were developed.[16]

This blender of changing social roles created a vortex of changing social identities:

Working-class men and boys regularly challenged the authority of middle-class men by verbally questioning the manliness of middle-class supervisors or physically attacking middle-class boys. . . . [As one contemporary] recalled, he had "often seen [middle-class cultivation] taken by those [men] of the lower classes as "sissy." The increasingly militant labor movement, the growing power of immigrant voters in urban politics, and the relatively high birthrate of certain immigrant groups established a worrisome context for such personal affronts and in themselves constituted direct challenges to the authority of Anglo-American men as a self-conceived class, race and gender. (Chauncey 1994, 112)

These struggles over where to map key social borders led

politicians, businessmen, educators, and sportsmen alike [to protest] the dangers of "overcivilization" to American manhood. . . . Theodore Roosevelt was the most famous advocate of the "strenuous life" of muscularity, rough sports, prize-fighting, and hunting. . . . The glorification of the prizefighter and the workingman bespoke the ambivalence of middle-class men about their own gender status. . . . A "cult of muscularity" took root in turn-of-the-century middle-class culture. . . . Earlier in the nineteenth century, men had tended to constitute themselves as men by distinguishing themselves from boys. . . . But in the late nineteenth century, middle-class men began to define themselves more centrally on the basis of their difference from women. . . . Gender-based terms of derision (e.g., sissy, pussy-foot) became increasingly prominent in late-nineteenth-century American culture. (Chauncey 1994, 113–14)

This oversimplifies and ignores counterpressures to cover gender distinctions (e.g., Vicinus [1992] and Matthaei [1992]), but this recoding of masculinity seems to have been powerful at this time.

Closely tied to this redefinition of "male"[17] in the 1890's was redefinition of class:

Men and women of the urban middle class increasingly defined themselves as a class by the boundaries they established between the "private life" of the home and the rough-and-tumble of the city streets, between the quiet order of their neighborhoods and the noisy, overcrowded character of the working-class districts. The privacy and order of their sexual lives also became a way of defining their difference from the lower classes. (Chauncey 1994, 35)

Just as a new "face" was being put on not-male, i.e., not-male became "female" instead of "boy," so "middle-class" became "clean face and well-laundered/mended clothes" versus the "dirty" faces of slums. A quickly judged face was put on people living in slums:

> The spatial segregation of openly displayed "vice" in the slums had . . . ideological consequences: it kept the most obvious streetwalkers out of middle-class neighborhoods, and it reinforced the association of such immorality with the poor. . . . Going slumming in the resorts of the Bowery and the Tenderloin was a popular activity among middle-class men (and even among some women), in part as a way to witness working-class "depravity" and to confirm their sense of superiority. (Chauncey 1994, 26)[18]

This simultaneous redefinition of gender and class spilled over, and infected, the definition of sexual orientation that was emerging at the turn of the century:

> In a culture in which becoming a fairy meant assuming the status of a woman or even a prostitute, many men . . . simply refused to do so. . . . The efforts of such men marked the growing differentiation and isolation of sexuality from gender in middle-class American culture. . . . The effort to forge a new kind of homosexual identity was predominantly a middle-class phenomenon, and the emergence of "homosexuals" in middle-class culture was inextricably linked to the emergence of "heterosexuals" in the culture as well. If many workingmen thought they demonstrated their sexual virility by playing the "man's part" in sexual encounters with either women or men, normal middle-class men increasingly believed that their virility depended on their exclusive sexual interest in women. Even as queer men began to define their difference from other men on the basis of their homosexuality, "normal" men began to define their difference from queers on the basis of their renunciation of any sentiments or behavior that might be marked as homosexual. (Chauncey 1994, 100)

Further, "the queers' antagonism toward the fairies was in large part a class antagonism . . . The cultural stance of the queer embodied the general middle-class preference for privacy, self-restraint, and lack of self-disclosure" (106).

This link between the significantion of economic class and of sexuality was, of course, not new at the end of the last century. "In colonial America, [convicted] sodomites were more often than not lower-class servants, and the shoring up of patriarchal power was imbricated in nascent class divisions. One has only to look to other colonial situations of the time to see that that was not the only way the category of sodomy was being mobilized; the Spaniards, for instance, prone to see sodomites among the Moors in Spain, saw native cultures as hotbeds of irregular sexual practices" (Goldberg 1994, 7). As Stallybrass and White note, "The bourgeois subject continuously defined and re-defined itself through the exclusion of what it marked out as 'low' – as dirty, repulsive, noisy, contaminating. Yet that very act of exclusion was constitutive of its identity. The low was internalized under the sign of negation and disgust" 1986, 191). This *verlmischung* of the codifications of class, sexuality, and gender is of fundamental importance for queer political economy, which is explored further in section 4 below.

The tendency to label certain traits as "invidious," and to tie these traits to other categories, is an example of errors that are typical in human categorization of both physical and social environments. We induce categories in order to sort out who is appropriate for the homopreference networks that articulate our desires.

It is hard to overemphasize the enormity of the changes in the working and living conditions of most western humans since postindustrial society emerged at the end of the last century. Many people, especially those migrating from rural life, simply lacked categories to express what they were experiencing: migrating from living and working with kinfolk, typically in rural or small-town settings, to wage labor, sometimes in the new institution of factories. All of this depended on reduced costs of transportation and communication – as well as more superficial changes like new commodities for consumption. This significant acceleration of the velocity of social change in the postindustrial era appears to have heightened the need for new institutions to articulate desires. This need, cutting to the heart of what it is to be human, may have contributed to perceptual errors caused by the use of new illusory variables.

The seminal as well as nomenclatory work on the phenomenon of "illusory correlation" was based on discovering false correlations between homosexuality and other traits. Loren and Jean Chapman (1967, 1969; Chapman 1967)[19] surveyed several dozen clinical psychologists about which Rorschach signs distinguished their gay male clients from straight male clients. Of those surveyed, thirty-two clinicians "said that they had seen the Rorschach protocols of a number of men with homosexual problems [sic]" (1969, 273). The Chapmans concluded that

> the "popularity" of signs [as indicators of homosexuality] among practicing clinicians has little relationship to the objective clinical validity of the signs . . . The most popular signs among

practicing clinicians are the ones that have the strongest verbal associative connection to male homosexuality. Naive observers, when presented with contrived Rorschach responses arbitrarily paired with statements of symptoms of the patient who gave each response, erroneously report these same associatively based invalid signs occur as correlates of homosexuality.[20] The naive observers reported these associatively based illusory correlations even when the materials are contrived so that other [clinically] valid correlations are present. (1969, 273)

How, one might ask, can sexual orientation, given its frequent invisibility, be construed to be a "readily available cue" to illusorily correlate with other traits and hence, to use for stereotyping?[21] The intensity of the affect associated with sexual orientation leads many to pay very close attention to any clues. For example, many men, both straight and gay, are familiar with the technique experienced by Essex Hemphill at age fourteen:

Crip was standing. I was sitting. It happened that from where I sat I could eye his crotch with a slight upward shift of my eyes. Well, one of the times that I peeked, Crip caught me . . . Instantly, Crip jumped forward and got in my face. "I see you looking at my dick!" he hurled at me. I felt as though he had accused me of breaking into his house and violating his mother. Immediately, all conversation ceased and all eyes focused on me and Crip. (Hemphill 1992, 100)

Hemphill survived this humiliation without getting beaten up and limped home to shut himself in his room as soon as he could break away. He learned to survive through high school by getting a girlfriend, a "good girl," who did not want to fuck.

This story highlights the role played by watching another's gaze in making sexual orientation distinctive, and suggests why it might be a trait used in making illusory correlations, which in turn serve as the basis for the intensely biased cognitive codes underlying homophobia.[22] Feeling sexually aroused is one of the most intense affects humans ever experience. Thus anything associated with this affect, such as sexual orientation, appears highly distinctive. This recalls the tendency of European-male-dominated American culture to label both Black men and women as "hypersexual"[23] The same scrutiny is apparent in the madonna/whore dichotomy socially constructed for European-American women.[24]

To recap: How do we know what we know — or feel, or desire? Our perceptions depend on the cognitive categories with which we articulate (i.e., perceive and express) our desires and "knowledge." These categories have been created through the particular dynamics of the social networks we have been part of since birth. A survey of work by psychologists, sociologists, historians, philosophers, and sociolinguists has led to the conclusion that socially learned codes play an enormously important role in determining how we perceive others. These codes produce prosopopeic categories based on central archetypal figures. The use of archetypes renders this process surprisingly agile, but also renders it very susceptible to making false – illusory – correlations of human traits.

The false articulation of desires, described in section 2, might actually occur in one's social world through a reliance on a particular social network – on neighbors from a particular class and/or gender – to discover what choices are best for oneself. This can lead one to fail to recognize one's own "true" preferences, which are formed through social interaction but which are also socially distorted and repressed. Bray tried to make comprehensible the homosexual behavior of some people in the sixteenth and seventeenth centuries at the time of the erasure of the articulation of queer:

> The individual could simply avoid making the connection; he could keep at two opposite poles the social pressures bearing down on him and his own discordant sexual behaviour, and avoid recognising it for what it was. . . . For when one looks at the circumstantial details of how homosexuality was conceived of and how it was expressed in concrete social forms, it becomes obvious how very easy it was in Renaissance England – far more so than today – for a cleavage of this kind to exist, between an individual's behaviour and his awareness of its significance. Firstly the way homosexuality was conceived of: how possible was it to avoid identifying with the "sodomite" who was the companion of witches and Papists, of werewolves and agents of the King of Spain? When the world inhabited by the conventional image of the sodomite was so distant from everyday life, it cannot have been hard. (Bray 1982, 67–68)

The sense of being socially of such a different caste if one were queer made it impossible for many to position themselves as homosexual in their internal cognitive maps. This was true for many in Renaissance England, and likewise for people maturing in the McCarthy-polluted 1950s. Anecdotal evidence suggests that this latter generation had more difficulty recognizing same-sex desire than did those either growing up before the Depression or reaching maturity in the late 1960s, especially after Stonewall.

A useful parallel to the 1950s in the United States (which followed the two queer panics, described in section 4 below) might be the pre-World War I period in England following the queer panic produced by the trial of Oscar Wilde. Both were times of dramatic queer cultural innovation (e.g., the Bloomsbury group's writing, painting, and historicizing in England, and

Beat writing, Rauschenberg and Johns's painting, and Tennessee Williams's playwriting in the United States) and also of dramatic social repression of queer social structures. The ability not to articulate one's queerness in such a setting was captured well by that straddler of this sexual divide, D. H. Lawrence, writing in the suppressed prologue to *Women in Love*:

> The male physique had a fascination for him, and for the female physique he felt only a fondness . . . as for a sister. In the street it was the men who roused him by their flesh and their manly, vigorous movement. . . . He loved his friend, the beauty of whose manly limbs made him tremble with pleasure. He wanted to caress him. But reserve, which was as strong as a chain of iron in him, kept him from any demonstration. . . . He wondered very slightly at this, but dismissed it with hardly a thought. Yet every now and again, would come over him the same passionate desire to have near him some man he saw. . . . It might be any man. . . . How vividly, months afterwards, he would recall the soldier who had sat pressed up close to him on a journey from Charing Cross to Westerham . . . [o]r a young man in flannels on the sands at Margate. . . . In his mind was a small gallery of such men: men whom he had never spoken to, but who had flashed themselves upon his senses unforgettably, men whom he apprehended intoxicatingly in his blood. . . . This was the one and only secret he kept to himself, this secret of his passionate and sudden, spasmodic affinity for men he saw. He kept this secret even from himself. He knew what he felt, but he always kept the knowledge at bay. (1981, 103–107)[25]

We have thus far developed one story for the use of prosopopeia – of faces-as-archetypes – as the basis for our induction of social categories and for the role our social networks can play in this articulation of categories. Political and social dynamics may powerfully influence this social articulation of cognitive codes, an idea to which we now turn and which is, of course, the heart of queer political economy.

4 Our social site: construction of american social identities since 1930

Academic analysis of the Chapmans' work on illusory correlations has ignored the central role that homosexuality has had in American culture in shaping the cognitive structures (semantic associations) of the Chapmans, of their subjects (psychoanalysts) and of the patients of these psychoanalysis at the time the Chapmans carried out their work. What makes this scholarly blindness so ironic is that the Chapmans' discovery was based on an "associative connection" enormously amplified by two "illusory" correlations of homosexuality with other, socially-feared traits – i.e., two queer panics – of which they and all subsequent commentators pretended to be blithely unaware. These panics transformed homosexuality from an exotic, possibly deplorable – or possibly intriguing – attribute (prior to the 1930s) into the worst, most "salient" human characteristic, bar none, in the 1950s and 1960s when the Chapmans did their work.

As Chauncey describes it, in the 1930s, the previously flourishing and widely known gay culture had been pushed underground into invisibility. Yet,

> the homosexual hardly disappeared from public view . . . for police bulletins and press coverage continued to make him [sic] a prominent, but increasingly sinister, figure. As America anxiously tried to come to terms with the disruptions in the gender and sexual order caused by the Depression and exacerbated by the Second World War, the 'sex deviant" became a symbol of the dangers posed by family instability, gender confusion, and unregulated male sexuality and violence. A number of children's murders in the late 1930s and the late 1940s, sensationalized by the local and national press and interpreted as sexual in nature by the police, fanned a series of panics over sex crime. (Chauncey 1994, 359)

In 1950, when Commie panic was towering higher and higher, a

> chance revelation by a State Department official during congressional hearings on the loyalty of government employees led to the entanglement of homosexuality in the politics of domestic anticommunism. Facing sharp interrogation by members of the Senate Appropriations Committee, Under Secretary John Peurifoy testified on February 28, 1950, that most of ninety-one employees dismissed for moral turpitude were homosexuals. . . . In the succeeding months, the danger posed by "sexual perverts" became a staple of partisan rhetoric. Senator Joseph McCarthy . . . charged that an unnamed person in the State Department had forced the reinstatement of a homosexual despite the threat to the nation's safety. (D'Emilio 1983b, 41)

The first illusory correlation above tied homosexuality to sex crimes and the second amplified this hysteria by tying homosexuality to a threat to national security – a risk that is hard to imagine in the 1990s, as the "Evil Empire" appears totally vanquished and the fear of atomic attack has greatly receded. To understand the astounding reversal in social codes that occurred from 1930 to 1960 – a seismic shift whose magnitude may well be impossible to imagine for those growing up hearing songs about a detachable penis and fistfucking – it is necessary to first try to imagine 1930, when the pansy was at least as trendy as the queer is now in alternative music mosh pits and New Year's Eve Exotic Erotic Balls. Lillian Faderman (1991, esp. ch. 2), Jonathan Weinberg (1993), and George Chauncey (1994, chs. 8–11), among others, show that during the 1920s a gay culture – ranging from a wide variety of baths to art, music, and Broadway shows – grew up with close connections to, and immediately succeeding upscale New York's modish curiosity, the Harlem Renaissance.

With the onset of Prohibition, the queer trend was amplified since the "economic pressures Prohibition put on the hotel industry by depriving it of liquor-related profits . . . led some of the second-class hotels in the West Forties [of Manhattan] to be gin permitting prostitutes and the speakeasies to operate out of their premises. (Chauncey 1994, 305). Furthermore, the "speakeasies, [social reformers] feared, were dissolving the distinctions between middle-class respectability and working-class licentiousness that had long been central to the ideological self-representation of the middle class" (Chauncey 1994, 307).

Much of the evolution of queer culture has been (partially inadvertently) promoted by conventional profit-seeking entrepreneurs operating small taverns or prostitution rings, etc. (e.g., see Weeks 1979, 42; D'Emilio 1983a). But the two queer panics in the 1930s and 1950s were the result of a different type of entrepreneur, one whose central role has been detailed by numerous sociologists (just two: Michel Foucault [1978] and David Greenberg [1988]), but who has been virtually invisible in political economy generally and certainly in mainstream economics. This is the ideology entrepreneur: someone who undertakes ventures at some personal risk and some possible personal gain – though not necessarily pecuniary – to reshape the social margin. This involves amplifying some parts and suppressing other parts of existing cognitive codes and, occasionally, adding new inventions to existing codes.[26] This may be done somewhat unconsciously, or at least, indirectly, in order to expand the entrepreneur's access to economic and other social opportunities. Alternatively, it may be done with a conscious ideological goal.

Examples of such entrepreneurship abound, and can have various social consequences. It suffices to cite a few that are relevant to incidents cited above. First, as Chauncey relates, "Joseph Pulitzer's World and William Randolph Hearst's Journal pioneered in those years a new style of journalism that portrayed itself as the nonpartisan defender (and definer) of the 'public interest,' waged campaigns on behalf of moral and municipal reform, and paid extravagant attention to local crimes, high-society scandals, and the most 'sensational' aspects of the urban underworld" (1994,

39). Second, "the expanding bachelor subculture in the city's furnished-room and tenement districts precipitated a powerful reaction by social-purity forces" (136).

> Only twenty-two sodomy prosecutions occurred in New York City in the nearly eight decades from 1796 to 1873. The number of prosecutions increased dramatically in the 1880s, however. By the 1890s, fourteen to thirty-eight men were arrested every year for sodomy or the "crime against nature." Police arrested more than 50 men annually in the 1910s . . . and from 75 to 125 every year in the 1920s. . . . [M]uch of [the dramatic increase in arrests] stemmed from the efforts of the Society for the Prevention of Cruelty to Children, which involved itself in the cases of men suspected of sodomy with boys. The fragmentary court records available suggest that at least 40 percent – and up to 90 percent – of the cases prosecuted each year were initiated at the complaint of the SPCC. Given the SPCC's focus on the status of children in immigrant neighborhoods, the great majority of sodomy prosecutions were initiated against immigrants in the poorest sections of the city. (140)

The ranks of the medical profession have long been filled with innovative ideology entrepreneurs. "Doctors [in the late nineteenth century] were not simply speaking up when called upon; they were actively seeking to shape society's control apparatus. Why this new involvement? Physicians came primarily from the middle class and would have shared the general sexual ideology of that class" (Greenberg 1988, 401).

These examples illustrate the diversity of ideology entrepreneurs. Joseph Pulitzer and William Randolph Hearst were choosing marker niches that they apparently thought were more profitable than the alternatives they gave up. The social purity activists were, in many cases at least, pursuing ethical goals at some possible pecuniary cost to themselves. Finally, the actions of the doctors (as well as numerous other new "helping" professions in the late 1800s and early 1900s) could, in many instances, have plausibly been motivated by a desire to promote "professional standards" rather than by any immediate pecuniary purpose. These are not dissimilar from the ideologically entrepreneurial efforts of western church people, especially at the end of feudal times.

Aside from "externalities" such as environmental pollution or epidemics, the conventional ways in which economists conceptualize how social welfare is impaired is by looking at monopolistic markets,[27] or at rent-seeking "special-interest" interference with governmental regulation.[28] But the concept of social cognitive codes suggests that social welfare can be impaired in a new way: misleading conflations and oversimplifications in the cognitive categorizations through which people perceive, think about and act in the world. These conflations, such as the illusory correlations described in section 2, are encouraged by an esthetics-of-simplicity in our mental software.

A new cognitive code propagates like a virus, like a dialect. A new schema or semantic association (as highlighted by the Chapmans in their original work on illusory correlations) of what is evil and so what must be socially eradicated spreads not because of lack of competition among ideology entrepreneurs. Rather, it occurs because the spread of an idea that is tied to market-born and market-articulated inequality, like the force of a wildfire on the prairie, irresistibly engulfs all of the individuals-standing in its path. Thus, as Dollimore (1991, 246) has noted, "while . . . homophobic panics [can be seen as being provoked by repressed homosexuals [in the Freudian sense], the panic may only 'take' socially, because of the other kind of repression – exclusive identity formation – as it affects a far greater number" (1991, 240). Dollimore gave this latter idea concreteness by quoting G. K. Lehne: "Homophobia is only incidentally directed against homosexuals – its more common use is against the 49% of the population which is male. . . . The taunt 'What are you, a fag?' is used in many ways to encourage certain types of male behaviour and to define the limits of 'acceptable' masculinity" (Dollimore 1991, 245).

My allusion to waves of wildfire on a prairie stands in, of course, for an analytical apparatus yet to be developed.[29] One might guess that to break into cognitive awareness, outside senders of signals must first penetrate the limbic gatekeepers of our sensory awareness. And, as retailers and advertisers have known for some time, erotic signals that open the door to the limbic system are especially powerful. These signals get attention, something that Calvin Klein, Guess jeans, and even Budweiser have proven rather effectively. The implication is clear: to get a hearing by a person as s/he articulates her/his desire, first send a strong erotic signal to catch that person's attention. Thus a new social code does not spread because each person digitally compares it with her present code. Rather, the extent to which it gets used depends on whether it sweeps in a wave, like an epidemic, through society. Studying this conjecture seems fundamental to understanding queer political economy.

The two queer panics sketched above did, indeed, have the power of social epidemics, and they are our legacy today. They got their power from the abject dependence of each individual on the social codes of her/his network/society. Because of this dependence, our most complex desires can become severely distorted. The system is "inefficient," in the sense that alternative evolutions can be conceived that would result in a better state for many. In the classic terminology of Arrow-Debreuvian welfare economics, the endogeneity of these codes introduces a possible new type of externality

among all actors' actions/voices, on one hand, and their perceived preferences, on the other hand. This possibility, as the evolution of queer social
identities shows, is important enough to be worthy of further attention.

5 Update to the 1990s

The spin of social codes/identities prevalent today is captured well by U2's
late-1980s articulation of Desire[30] as female: "She's the candle burning in
my room . . . [causing] fever when I'm beside her, Desire, Desire." Bono
goes on, having absorbed the code developed during the rollover from the
nineteenth century, to intertwine all irresistible (male) drives – greed,
ambition, security – with strong overtones of female sin – corruption/slut/
whore: "She's the dollars / She's my protection / She's the promise / in the
year of election / Sister, I can't let you go / I'm like a preacher / Stealing
hearts at a traveling show / For love or money, money . . .? / Desire . . ."
    U2 is answered in the 1990s by Trent Reznor's Nine Inch Nails (NIN) (a
bit of bragging there? – I'd love to see) singing: "my head is filled with dis-
ease/my skin is begging you please / i'm on my hands and knees / i want so
much to believe / i need someone to hold on to / . . . / i give you everything
/ my sweet everything / hey God, i really don't know who i am / in this
world of piss."[31] NIN, preoccupied with religious codes, plays on alternating
currents, seeking absolution and sanctification, through fucking a female
lover: "if she says come inside i'll come inside for her / if she says give it all
i'll give everything to her / i am justified / i am purified / i am sanctified."[32]
    NIN's clearest articulation of desire is queerly ambiguous: "i'm drunk
/ and right now i'm so in love with you / and i don't want to think too
much about what we should or shouldn't do / lay my hands on Heaven and
the sun and the moon and the stars / while the devil wants to fuck me in
the back of his car . . . but this is the only time i really feel alive / . . . / i
can't help thinking Christ never had it like this."[33] This could be "justified"
for straights by imagining that Trent Reznor is singing from a woman's
view – until the last line where this desire is only a bottom-man's hunger.
NIN's acknowledgment of fisting is explicit on *nine inch nails fixed*. These
themes also arise in NIN's song of erotic boasting: "i am a big man / (yes i
am) / And i have a big gun / got me a big old dick and i / i like to have fun
. . . / shoot shoot shoot shoot / i'm going to come all over you / me and
my fucking gun / me and my fucking gun."[34]
    This is not a new metaphor, and certainly far from unknown to straight
European American men since the 1970s. But it is definitely queer to
articulate on major radio stations (e.g., KOME in San Jose discovered
there is more profit in a phallic format in the spring of 1994), along with a
song featuring a "detachable penis" and other acknowledgments of phallic
eroticism. This is reinforced by noting the contrast between NIN's deeply

guilt-driven naked self-absorption and the comfortably mainstream articulation of longing in U2's music.

The rapid rise to greater prominence in the 1990s of alternative voices (hip-hop, gangsta rap, and alternative), voices of cynicism after the 1980s hegemony of aerosol desire, offers a sharp variety of discourse. This spawning of market niches defined by distinct cognitive codes – the rise of cognitively coded commodities, from microbrews to culturally diverse film festivals and commercial film success – may reflect in part the rising inequality in wealth in market-guided social systems. It may also reflect increasing awareness of the market advantages of cognitive coding, combined with decreasing cost of being more flexible in production due to computerized technology.

At this close range (1995), this proliferation of diverse cognitive codes appears to be an example of a "language in process of evolution," which the seminal sociolinguist William Labov (1972, 272) asserted did not occur in a "monoglot community."[35] "Studies of current sound changes show that a linguistic innovation can begin with any particular group and spread outward and that this is the normal development; that this one group can be the highest-status group, but not necessarily or even frequently so" (Labov 1972, 286). Linguistic "change does not occur without regard to [socio-economic] class patterns" (295). "The creation of low-prestige working-class dialects . . . embodies two major linguistic trends of the past several centuries: the decline of local dialects and the growth of vertical stratification in language" (300). Further, Labov observes that "the sexual differentiation of speech often plays a major role in the mechanism of linguistic evolution" (303). Labov ends this book by suggesting "that language diversity may have value for humans other than linguists, providing relative cultural isolation and maintaining cultural pluralism" (325). Again making a blatant transdisciplinary leap, this perspective envisioning distinct linguistic patterns in different social groups recalls the spread of new patterns in music in this decade. It also could describe the libertarian-style rise of gay (male) identity, as it emerged through the propagation of new dialect-like codes by the molly houses in Britian (i.e. gay bars in eighteenth-century England; see D'Emilio 1983a), and from the pansy craze in New York of the 1920s and early 1930s – two spells, each just before major queer panic.[36]

6 New categories for the social articulation of desire?

This notion that social evolution may arise from lower, "minor," social codes can be made more concrete by looking at a contestation, a queer struggle, that is occurring now and seems to shed light on the role of ideology in political economy – the evolution of the jack-off room. This evolution has been captured well by John Paul Ricco, an art historian, who uses the phrase "minor architecture" to describe a notion closely analogous to linguistic variation. Ricco starts from the idea of a minor aesthetic, from Deleuze and Guattari's (1986, 18) formulation of the concept of "minor literature." Ricco applies this to describe how we see sexuality through our lenses of social codes:[37]

> Designating jack-off rooms as *minor architecture* allows me to circumvent an appeal to the paradigmatic bourgeois (or *major*) binary public/private, a pair of terms not only insufficient but inappropriate to the conditions of jack-off rooms. The public/ private binary[38] not only forces these spaces into un-fitting categories, it also forecloses an understanding of the politics of these spaces. The minor is situated *within* the major/majority/ masterly, rather than *outside*, as this latter term is usually understood. As examples of minor architecture, jack-off rooms articulate and are articulated by queers (minorities), whose identities are anything but constant, unified, and self-evident, but rather are always in the process of becoming, changing, and being contested. Queers are here part of a collective assemblage or multiplicity of anonymous bodies, assembled within a small, dark, cramped space, touching, kissing, licking, hugging, stroking, pumping. . . . Borders between self and not-self are radically undermined. (Ricco 1993, 236–37)

Individuals, as

> bodies-of-desire, forfeit their individual subjective selves as they are re-constituted as parts of a collective assemblage. . . . A jack-off room is a space of connections, extensions and exteriorizations, all mobilized by desires. And darkness operates as a crucial collectivizing force. (239)

This articulation of bodies is

> mobilized by the collective force of *desire*, a nearly tangible device or mechanism, through which jack-off rooms-as-minor-architecture are built, and by which they operate. Desire and erotics are potentially tremendous mobilizing and articulating forces, capable of opening up and linking particular spaces bodies; and practices, and thereby begin to approach the kind of activ[ist] politics which many of us are pursuing. Jack-off rooms-as-minor-architecture constitute this linkage of space, bodies, and practices. They are sites for the formulation, deployment and continuous re-constitution of a post-identity sexual politics [a different network of identities]. (240)

Ricco has captured a backlash to the extreme individualism that dominates so much thinking now, as he notes that in jack-off rooms, men "forfeit their individual subjective selves as they are re-constituted as parts of a collective assemblage." Such mingling of selves is, of course, familiar from looking at love across other socially constructed boundaries: "love across the racial divide . . . is thoroughly public, saturated with social and political meanings . . . the image [of interracial couples] comes to stand for a fact that none of us has any notion what to do with: the fact that each of us is a part of the other, that we are so unalterably tainted by a messy and heartbreaking history that any claim to purity or separation becomes insupportably fragile" (Scott 1994).

The loss of individuality in homodesire is central to the articulation of desire. In fact, this penetration of the social into the "deepest" innermost parts of the individual through the articulation of homodesire is as close to a universal human phenomenon as we could imagine having the arrogance to assert. In any case, it is not solely characteristic of a sexual minority. This irony, that individuality is lost through the struggle to assert one's individuality through the articulation of desire, recalls Genet's discovery of beauty in the betrayal of individual distinctness and in merger/murder/ death consummating love/orgasm.[39] Indeed, *Funeral Rites* is an orgy of Genet's signifying the *insignificance* of the particular person, a rite celebrating the funeral of "the individual," with its repeated, often disconcerting, shifts in voice and in the frequent avowals that Jean (Genet? he plays on an ambiguity of who Jean is) writes himself. Genet's very self- conscious articulation-of-self and his identification of writing himself/ourselves with social construction is the epitome of Oscar Wilde's "individualism as . . . 'disobedience [that] . . . is man's original virtue' " – so much so that "there comes to be a close relationship between crime and individualism" (Dollimore 1991, 8, with inner quote from Wilde 1990, p. 4).[40]

Queer art, from Stéphane Dupré to Paul Stanley and David Sprigle, and from Barbara Hammer to Isaac Julien in film, is driven by a post-modern awareness that renders modernist boundaries between individuals ambiguous. Steven Arnold,[41] especially, captures with human bodies the aesthetic of isolation/merging, flowers, erections, crucifixes, and death that Genet inscribed on our queer minds. As in mosh pits, there is a clear opposition to the possessive individualism "in which individuals are defined primarily as proprietors of their fleshly incarnation, who are consequently entitled to rights only as the owners of themselves" (Cohen (1991, 77–78).

> Seventeenth-century individualism contained [a] central difficulty which lay in its possessive quality. . . . the conception of the individual as essentially the proprietor of his own person or capacities, owing nothing to society for them. The individual was seen neither as a moral whole, nor as part of a larger social

> whole, but as owner of himself. The relation of ownership, having become for more and more men [sic] the critically important relations determining their actual freedom and actual prospect of realizing their full potentialities, was read back into the nature of the individual. (Macpherson, quoted in Cohen 1991, 78)

This ideology of the total separateness of each "rational" individual, able to choose independently and freely, splendidly isolated by her/his libertarian shield of property rights,[42] arose along with the sanctity of property rights in the sixteenth and seventeenth centuries (coinciding with the social death of ganymedians). This evolution is the central ideological component of what is arguably the most significant sociological innovation of the last millennium: the rise from mere social niche to social dominance of the market's guidance and discipline of people.[43]

This bourgeois sense of individualism was both born by and gave birth to the market-system, and has implied a respect, by the individual, of the property/body/privacy of others. This is precisely what Wilde and Genet are contesting with their celebrations of the individual as criminal, as perverter-of-the-social, as queer. Indeed, this is their only celebration of individuality: it is a vision of a heroic (ideological) entrepreneur.[44] For many today, this crossing of ideological boundaries will be most uncomfortable, or even cognitively impossible. For example, the "death" of self in orgasm, even in mere desire, and the succeeding "treachery/betrayal" of one's orgasmic partner(s), are insights by Genet into resonances of queer sexuality. This seems to be invisible to Edmund White, writing in the introduction to *Prisoner of Love*: "Genet maintained a purported admiration for treachery that I've never comprehended. . . . I've never heard of a single charge of betrayal lodged against Genet" (1992, xiii). White concludes: "Finally I've decided that 'treachery' is Genet's code word for the incorrigible subjective voice that can never be factored into the consensus. . . . Genet seeks in [*Prisoner of Love*] to honour the collective emergency, but in the end he remains true to his equally radical . . . need for independence. Fidelity to oneself is treachery to the group; artistic quirkiness pokes holes in any political rhetoric."

In grappling to understand what Genet "means" with his use of "betrayal," White seems to be reading Genet through a mirror, reversing meanings by 180 degrees. He takes the romantic true individual, the "subjective voice," buried deep, within as requiring "betrayal" of a stale, politically charged notion of the collective. More useful is Bersani's insight that betrayal consists of seeking solitude (1995, 168) and that *Funeral Rites* "[is about] rejection . . . of relationality" (1995, 172). White's acknowledgment that "Genet's writerly neutrality and acuity . . . represent a rejection of petit bourgeois values and an affirmation of independence and a passive resistance against the forces of order" (Genet, 1992, xii), though valid, misses how extremely "Genet is an out-and-out social constructionist." (Bersani 1995, 173). Missing is Genet's rejection of what "our culture tells us to think[:] . . . sex as the ultimate privacy, as that intimate knowledge of the other on which the familial cell is built" (Bersani 1995, 165). Also missing is Bersani's insight, relevant to micro political economy, that Genet depicts "the degeneration of the sexual into a relationship that condemns sexuality to becoming a struggle for power."

Wilde and Genet display a queer ambiguity. They stake a socialist aesthetic on a celebration of what is a right-wing notion, namely, the heroic individual writing her/his own performance. At the same time, profoundly, and in very distinct ways, they elaborate the extent and power of the social construction of each of us through performative, self-enacting utterances (Judith Butler [1990, 1993] and Jonathan Dollimore [1991] make this wonderfully manifest). These two notions are feverishly grappling with each other – first, our individuality contesting the blinders imposed by our social construction, and second, our cloneness, and indeed our most intimate sense of merging with each other through homodesire. This struggle seems central to current queer contestation over the utility of notions of social identities. It is the *simultaneity* of this articulation of the individual and of the social that seems to engender much of the confusion in efforts to define, use, and contest social identities as institutions of social control. This simultaneity of the articulation of the individual and the social has been addressed better by literary cultural analysis than by most other scholars.

Is it mere happenstance that the rise of modernism with the ideology of possessive individualism coincided with the erasure of the social articulation of queer desire in western cultures? As Goldberg notes. "For the [American] colonists, as perhaps too for the tribes whose history is told in Genesis, nation-founding was inseparable from procreation, and the particular economic, social and patriarchal gender arrangements in the colonies [were] subtended by the crime of sodomy. Sodomy was . . . a crime against the family and the state, 'political sodomy,' in short" (1994, 6). The synchronicity of the rise of property-rights-individualism and the transformation of "sodomy" into a capital offense more narrowly focused on certain sexualities is worth further inquiry. The rise of modernism in England – rather analogous to cultural shifts at the end of the last century in this country – was a time of enormous change in socioeconomic institutions.

> In the sixteenth century, there was real alarm at the growth in unemployment, poverty, and crime. Vagrancy . . . became one of the most pressing social problems. . . . Social and economic dislocation was often refigured as the evil of aberrant movement. . . . [I]t is difficult for us today to recover the meaning which attached to the masterless. . . . Even more disturbing in certain respects than the masterless man was the masterless,

> wandering woman, perversely straying and inviting others to do
> the same (Dollimore 1991, 119)

There grew "anxieties about female sexuality . . . about its relation to property, to the threat of the violation of this private place if it were to become
a 'common' place . . . rather than a particular property" (Parker 1987,
105–106, as quoted by Dollimore, 1991 119–120; see also Soltan 1988).

The possible connection of the recodification of "female" to the rise of
property rights as a dominant social institution offers further reason to
suspect a link between the rise of property rights and the gradual erasure of
queer desire from social cognitive codes. (This, as we saw at the start,
erased the possibility for leading playwrights to articulate queer desire.) In
fact, the effects of the rise of the sanctity of property rights may go even
further than the recodification of female and of queer as dangerously perverse.[45] Contrary to Foucault, the rise of the social dominance of property
rights and of possessive individualism as an institution of social discipline
may, at a very deep level, have nurtured erotophobia by raising and fortify-
ing boundaries between bodies. In this way, such ideologies may have made
the liquidly lubricious permeability of sexuality not only less desired and
desirable, but also less imaginable and performable. And in turn, this may
have rendered much of the concreteness of sexuality less voiceable, in
particular helping to erase interpersonal distinctions based on specificities
of sexuality: to wit, queer distinctions. This is consonant with Judith Butler's awareness of "the dangers that permeable bodily boundaries present to
the social order" (1990, 132) by raising questions about "the categories of
identity that contemporary juridicial structures engender, naturalize, and
immobilize" (5).

Can post/modern be defined as the articulation of ambiguity in the
boundaries between individual and collective?[46] Will a post/modern intellectual renaissance of desire – and of emotions generally – prompt rearticu-
lation of the binary of individualistic vs. collective? Will it also provoke a
celebration of desire on the same level as the celebration of cognition?[47]

The roles of "ideology" are much more central to cognition, and hence
to the social cognitive codes that lie at the base of political economy, than
even Marx imagined.[48] This is not mere "superstructure," frosting on the
basic productive/technological relations of labor inputs to other inputs that
ultimately determine the social relations of production.[49] Rather, "ideology" describes the deepest patterning of human mental software and, in
turn, our mental hardware.[50] Indeed, the classic marxian conceptual
framework may have impoverished the concept of class by denying it rich
connotative connections to other social identities. More important, such a
framework precludes an understanding of the agency of class in *shaping* the
basic productive/technological relations of labor inputs to other inputs. In
addition, it seems important for political economy to model the simul-

taneous determination of each human's "preferences" and the vortex of social codes and identities channeling all humans in the maelstrom/ malestream of social relations. In particular, as described in sections 2 and 3, a person's perception of what is best for him/herself can be severely restricted by his or her network of "neighbors" with whom s/he articulates desires. This network, in turn, can be severely circumscribed by one's class/race at birth.

This is what the model described in section 2 attempts to demonstrate. It suggests that an idea underlying much public policy discourse – that people can "freely choose" to do or not to do things – ought to be replaced by the notion of contingent choice: each person's discovery and expression of desire is likely to be very dependent on some notion of "the other" (who has a different Face). As Dollimore reminds us: "No consideration of cultural and/or racial difference should ever neglect the sheer negativity, evil, and inferiority with which 'the other' has been conceived throughout history" (1991, 329). I have shown how this limitation on free choice by individuals led people to fail to perceive their sexual orientations, and that this failure was closely tied to the simultaneous evolutions of concepts of race, class, and gender.

For Americans who are largely blind to the hegemony of individualism due to its ubiquity, it might be helpful to consider a recent example from Japan, where, for the past century, there has been significant groping to develop cognitive codes that articulate more individualistic ideas: "There is an entire genre of words like 'my home' and 'my car,' for example, meaning individually owned cars and homes. A Japanese might ask a colleague if he is a my car commuter or takes the subway" (Kristof 1995). Further, Sony's use in Japan of the name. "Walkman" for a product that did not previously exist illustrates William Burroughs's notion that languages are viruses, spreading from culture to culture rather randomly, but very powerfully as a market-driven phenomenon. The lesson from jack-off rooms, from understanding queer desire, from straight, but not strait, folks attending queer SexArt Salons, is that the hegemony of individualism as property-rights is being contested sociolinguistically.

7 Epilogue

The second phrase in italics at the start of this piece is a play on Descartes' epigraph, *cogito ergo sum*, which over the course of several centuries has come to signify modernist thinking that celebrates the Enlightenment.[51] I juxtapose instead the post/modern notion that we, like Shakespeare's Antonio and like all living organisms, exist in the richness of our social structures and identities because of our desires. Therefore, a significant goal for social disciplines, as well as for physical sciences (e.g., Hamer and

Copeland 1994 and Damasio 1994), is to increase our understanding of the social articulation of desire.

Notes

This work is dedicated to the honor of Alan Turing and John Maynard Keynes, whose sharply contrasting social positions as intellectuals figure well the distinct possibilities for queers described here. Alan Turing's achievements birthing computers enabled the silicon simulations at the heart of this paper and his death was caused by the forces I seek to conceptualize. Maynard Keynes's queer interest in arts *and* economics inspire the disciplinary *verlmischung* here. I want to acknowledge sabbatical support by Middlebury College as well as access as a research associate to facilities at the University of California at Berkeley, which enabled me to conduct this queer research intensively in the Bay Area and so to recover from years of near asphyxiation in the intense heterosexism at Middlebury College and, indeed, covering all of Vermont. While at Middlebury, my breathing was occasionally pushed above water by early research assistance from Jeff Spencer and by supportive reactions of a number of people to my earlier efforts to endogenize the world – which, they thoughtfully refrained from pointing out, were a bit inadequate. These people include Lee Badgett, Marion Eppler, Rhonda Williams, Nancy Folbre, Sam Bowles, Julie Matthaei, Jeff Escoffier, Michael Jacobs, Frank Thompson, Robert Anderson, and Ellen Oxfeld. It is, *bien entendu*, important not to illusorily correlate any of these people with any foolishness the reader might find in this paper.

1   There has recently been grudging acknowledgment of the social construction of *market-revealed* preferences by the high priest of the irrelevance of tastes, Gary Becker (1993).

2   For a development of these theorems, see chapter 4 of Cornwall (1984) and the references to Arrow cited there.

3   For fainthearted lesbigays in our erotophobic culture, there may be some reassurance in noting that John Dewey, in his debate with Bertrand Russell over an appropriate philosophical basis for ethics, acknowledges the primacy of desire, noting: " 'valuing' is identified with any and every state of enjoyment no matter how it comes about – including gratification obtained in the most casual and accidental manner, 'accidental' in the sense of coming about apart from desire and intent" (Dewey 1929, 53). He goes on to acknowledge implicitly that this violates disciplinary self-aggrandizement by ethicists since it makes "psychology . . . paramount, not only over logic and the theory of knowledge, but also over ethics" (95).

4   Marlowe's queer view has been well disseminated recently by Derek Jarman's film, *Edward II*. Of course, queer desire could not be shown as "licit" then, with the first sodomy statute having been adopted in 1533 (Goldberg 1994, 17), but as Greenblatt (1988, 92–93) has noted: "Though by divine and human decree the consummation of desire could be licitly figured only in the love of a man and a woman, it did not follow that desire was inherently heterosexual. The delicious confusions of *Twelfth Night* depend upon the mobility of desire." Smith (1991) makes this "mobility of desire" in Shakespeare's England wonderfully tangible.

5   This quote is from Escoffier (1995, 34), who suggests that this key innovation by Keynes was prompted by his attempt to recast the modernist (nonreligious) basis for morals that had been offered by his teacher and the leading English philosopher at that time, G. E. Moore, and which implied a disapproval of his homosexuality.

6   I thank Herb Gintis for these last two references, which he offered in response to an earlier version of this paper.

7   Of course, Magoo is an especially appropriate allegorical face to put on an actor in queer political economy since Magoo, a.k.a. Jim Backus, was the father of James Dean (in "*Rebel Without a Cause*").

8   To appreciate my effort to simplify my model, contrast it with Eve Sedgwick's (1990) rich model of the closet.

9   This recalls the apparent prevalence, in any catalogue of human societies, of cultural codes in which types of homosexuality are significant, even if this was invisible to notable western anthropologists, as surveyed by Greenberg (1988, ch. 2). It might be conjectured that the current worldwide hegemony of homophobia may be significantly due to the edge given western homophobia-infected (Christian) culture by the rise of market-guided societies, which engendered the rise of powerful technology in the West, which then contaminated other cultures (e.g., Native American, Hindu, and Moslem), which are now significant in any tabulation of world cultural patterns.

10   See also Celia Card (1994) and Kenny (1994).

11   For a useful summary, see Holland, (1986), ch. 6. This identification of categorization as being based on archetypes or typical instances has become so unproblematic for some social psychologists that it is taken as the *definition* of categorization. See, for example, Fiske and Pavelchak (1986, 171).

12   See Allman and Brothers (1994) for an excellent overview as well as Damasio (1994, esp. p. 133), who calls the amygdala "the key player in preorganized emotion." From work in the 1950s finding that "light touch to the skin could be an extremely potent stimulus for driving amygdala neurons" in cats (Allman and Brothers 1994, 613) to work in the 1970s which started mapping intricate patterns of "single neurons (in the amygdala of monkeys) that responded to dimensions of the social environment" (Allman and Brothers 1994, p. 614), work on humans has been slow due to the difficulty of finding people with injury just to their amygdalas who can be compared with others. For work pointing to the role of the amygdala in finely perceiving social cues in our faces, see Adolphs, et al. (1994) and Young, et al. (1995). See also Kuhl (1993) for related research and theory.

       My extremely loose analogy between the lim42bic system and a computer's operating system would, no doubt, be contested by Damasio (1994, 250) and in no way is meant to contest his strong assertion that the whole body is an integral part of the "mind."

13   Note that this appearance of being "natural" lies at the heart of the Gramiscian notion of "hegemony" as defined, e.g., by Comaroff and Comaroff (1991, p. 23). See also Gramsci (1971).

14   As Foucault has powerfully argued, this too appears simplistic due to being biased by our view from our social site in North America in the 1990s, a view that threatens to impose a teleological reading of history so that any multiplicity of sexual identities that preindustrial people might have perceived is easily lost to our view.

15   For an excellent overview of the rise of gender-segregated wage labor, see Amott and Matthaei (1991), 315–48.

16   This brief sketch does not indicate the magnitude of the social changes occurring then. For more detail, check Edwards (1979), Montgomery (1987), and Brody (1980).

17   This focus on "male" is revealing of our cultural categories. See also Faderman (1991), D'Emilio and Freedman (1988), Vicinus (1992), and Matthaei (1992).

18   Sounds similar to Halloween in the Castro in San Francisco which, in 1994, had become the largest annual event in the City, with an estimated 400,000 people attending. It is no longer a queer event celebrating gender-fuck, but is rather a lesbian/gay hosted party where well over half the participants appear to be strait

gawkers, most not in costume and a few extremely threateningly armed. Analogous comments apply to the social position of "street-people" in our cities today as props for a middle-class sense of superiority.

19   Homosexuality was the focus of the third paper by the Chapmans (1969) with the second giving great, but not exclusive, emphasis to homosexuality phrased indirectly in instructions to the experimentees ("He is worried about how manly he is"). The first looked at people's perceptions of correlations between word pairs having no connection to homosexuality. More detail on the Chapmans' work is given in Cornwall (1995b).

20   They offer as an example of the format of the word-pairing game thirty-four undergraduates played for them in order to measure *verbal associative connection* (1969, 274):

The tendency for "homosexuality" to call to mind "rectum" and "buttocks" is

a   Very strong
b   Strong
c   Moderate
d   Slight
e   Very slight
f   No tendency at all.

21   This was evidently the case for the U.S. Court of Appeals for the Sixth Circuit ruling on 12 May 1995: "No law can successfully be drafted that is calculated to burden or penalize, or to benefit or protect, an unidentifiable group or class of individuals whose identity is defined by subjective and unapparent characteristics such as innate desires, drives and thoughts. Those persons having a homosexual 'orientation' simply do not, as such comprise an identifiable class" (*New York Times*, 14 May 1995, A10). As the Associated Press report printed in the *San Francisco Chronicle* (13 May 1995, A4) noted: "sexual orientation is not 'an identifiable class' worthy of inclusion in (Cincinnati's) human rights ordinance alongside gender, race and age" which, presumably for this court, are entirely unproblematic.

22   Goldberg's (1994, 1–22) superb introduction offers a quick overview of the diverse distortions these codes have assumed over recent centuries as they articulated "sodometries."

23   Page 76 of E. Francis White (1990).

24   See D'Emilio and Freedman (1988).

25   Dollimore (1991, 273) led me to this picture of willful suppression of desire.

26   This conjecture of a role for conscious (possibly "self-interested") human agency in the evolution of social cognitive codes is a divergence from the analogy I have thus far drawn to sociolinguistics as formulated by William Labov, who has written that

> "[L]anguage structure . . . is a largely mechanical system, out of the reach of conscious recognition or adjustment by its users. . . . It therefore seems odd that we are not free to adjust this system to maximize its efficiency in conveying information . . . One possible explanation is that the efficiency of language depends upon its automatic character, and that a phonological or grammatical structure that was open for conscious inspection and manipulation would necessarily operate very slowly. Therefore our efforts to change language consciously must be confined to higher-level stylistic options: the selection of words, and the construction of phrases and sentences within a narrowly limited set of choices. The linguistic changes that have been discussed here [i.e., in Labov's book] operate well outside the range of conscious recognition and choice." (Labov 1994, p. 604)

It is possible that a similar notion of "higher" and "lower" levels of change in social cognitive codes is also valid, with what I am calling "ideology entrepreneurs" merely tweaking the given cognitive codes – possibly for great profit and/or power – and with "deeper," "more basic" changes in social cognitive codes operating only unconsciously with *every*one in the society acting as a miniideology-entrepreneur. This speculation awaits future exploration.

27   There seems to be almost free entry in ideological entrepreneurship: everyone manipulates ideology to some extent in many social interactions. To joke or insinuate that certain traits imply other human traits is the easiest source of humor, bonding, personal position, etc. This role might be termed "ideology manipulation." Ideology entrepreneurship might be reserved for the operation of a "business" that produces "new" articulations of human perceptions by gathering information on the distribution of traits/behaviors and using this "information" to "justify" new associations of traits. These "businesses" can range from single proprietorships – like Richard Epstein at the University of Chicago Law School promoting simplistic ideas for a complex world or the author of this piece promoting cognitive complexity, just for example – to the Heritage Foundation and many corporations. The "product" produced by ideological entrepreneurs will, since "knowledge" is a public good, have to be "sold" by being tied to another good, a good which typically involves facilitating access to such "knowledge." Examples range from William Randolph Hearst's journalism early in the twentieth century to the rise of the *New York Times* as a national newspaper. What these profit-maximizing examples share is the production of *cognitively coded commodities*: goods whose market niche is based on appeals to combinations of characteristics known/appreciated by people sharing certain key language in their cognitive codes. Do differential costs of providing access to such "knowledge" open possibilities for new types of analysis of barriers to entry?

28   An example of the government responding/using, rather than creating, social cognitive codes is the inability of Edmund Burke and Jeremy Bentham to mitigate, even ever so slightly, the barbaric, savage homophobia infecting England in the eighteenth and nineteenth centuries. This savagery is indicated more by the frequent use of the pillory than by the relatively infrequent hangings for sodomy, since "standards of proof were high in sodomy cases: until 1828, courts required evidence both of penetration and emission." Instead of seeking convictions for sodomy when the difficult-to-obtain evidence was missing, the social control system convinced men

of the lesser offense of "assault with the attempt to commit sodomy." This charge might be based on nothing more than a solicitation invited by a plain-clothes man who had gone to some homosexual rendezvous for the purpose of entrapping men. Convicted men were placed in the pillory and exposed to the wrath of the mob, who were allowed to pelt them. Such events attracted thousands, sometimes tens of thousands of spectators. The pelting of the men often took on an organized form under the supervision of the police. There was a tradition that women of the street – fish-wives, vendors of produce, and "Cyprians" (as the press euphemistically called prostitutes) – should have pride of place in these orgies of ill-will, and some of the most abused members of British society revenged themselves for the contempt they received from others by the violence with which they attacked the helpless sodomites." (Crompton 1985, 21–22)

In 1780, an exceptionally grim episode led [Burke] to utter a unique protest [in Parliament]. On April 10 of that year, a coachman named William Smith and a plasterer named Theodosius Reed had been exposed in the pillory at St. Margaret's Hill in London for attempted sodomy. Though their punishment did not take place until nearly noon, nevertheless . . . according to one newspaper: "A vast Concourse of People had assembled upon the Occasion, many by Seven o'Clock in the Morning, who had collected dead Dogs, Cats, &c. in great Abundance, which were plentifully thrown at them; but some Person threw a Stone, and hit the Coachman on the Forehead, and he immediately dropped on his Knees, and was to all Appearance dead." Smith did, in fact, die though there was some uncertainty whether the cause of his death was the violence of the crowd or the rightness of the pillory about his neck. . . . Burke protested that the pillory existed to expose men to contempt and not to kill them by a punishment "as much more severe than execution . . . as to die in torment, was more dreadful than momentary death." . . . Burke had the satisfaction of seeing the undersheriff for Surrey tried for murder [in another case]; not surprisingly, the jury acquitted him. Burke himself . . . suffered much abuse in the press for his stand. . . . [P]rejudice ran high at the popular level and affected most of the intelligentsia. (31–33)

The leading example of the impotence of an intellectual in the eighteenth-nineteenth centuries is Jeremy Bentham, who was the inventor of utility-theoretic modeling of desire.

> In light of [the British] . . . bias toward silence [about homosexuality], Bentham's voluminous analyses are . . . remarkable. Bentham first jotted down about fifty pages of notes in 1774 when he was twenty-six. In 1785 he completed a somewhat longer formal essay. In 1814 and 1816 he filled almost two hundred pages with another impassioned indictment of British attitudes. Two years later he produced several hundred more pages of notes on homosexuality and the Bible, and in 1824, eight years before his death at the age of eighty-four, he wrote a final short synopsis of his ideas on sodomy law reform. All in all, this adds up to a sizable book on a subject that British jurists usually dismissed in a paragraph or page. (Crompton 1985, 20)

Bentham was clear that utilitarianism, with what we now think of as a libertarian conceptual base, implied sodomy should be decriminalized. But he was realistic in his fear that for him to publicly acknowledge this "would have given (his) opponents a powerful weapon for discrediting his whole program of [prison] reform" (Crompton 1985, p. 30). In particular, Bentham was aware of homophobia's modus operandi as a metanorm: "There is a kind of punishment annexed to the offence of treating [this crime] with any sort of temper, and that one of the most formidable that man can be subjected to, the punishment of being suspected at least, if not accused, of a propensity to commit it. (47–48). "Bentham's rough notes give a vivid picture of conscience at war with discretion. Discretion won out." (31). Bentham wrote about his turmoil: "To other subjects . . . it is expected that you sit down cool: but on this subject if you let it be seen that you have not sat down in a rage you have *given judgement against* yourself at once. . . . I am ashamed to own that I have often hesitated . . . [to] expose my personal interest so much to hazard as it must be exposed to by the free discussion of a subject of this nature" (47). In the end, Bentham's writings on homophobia were – and still are – not published except for Crompton's glosses.

The social forces that led to Burke's and Bentham's impotence parallel closely those described above for the United States: newspapers using fascination with condemned erotica to whet sales and readers' bloodlust, as noted earlier. There were private alliances of ideological entrepreneurs working for social purity: the Society for the Reformation of Manners (founded in 1691 "to wage the first important morals campaign since the Puritan

Revolution, aimed . . . at countering the freedom of the Restoration period" (Crompton 1985, 57); the Society for the Reformation of Manners ended in 1738, but in 1788 the Proclamation Society – then became the Society for the Suppression of Vice, which "pursued a vigorous course in Georgian and Victorian England" (61–62) – and connections to xenophobia were used by governmental leaders. Crompton notes:

> Bentham, for all his perspicuity, failed to understand how English xenophobia intensified English feelings about sodomy. In particular, he failed to see its peculiar connection with English Protestantism (and violent anti-Catholicism). . . . . [T]he temptation to reaffirm the traditional association of sodomy with Italy was too powerful for Protestant polemicists to resist. . . . [T]he hanging, pillorying, and ostracism of homosexuals were incontrovertible facts to which the nation could point to assure itself of its superiority to Catholic Europe in at least one respect. In this way, as in Spain under the Inquisition, intolerance became a badge of virtue and brutality a point of national pride." (Crompton 1985, 53, 60)

29   Thus Labov (1985, 317) notes in trying to understand linguistic change: "There is comparatively little that can be said about the particular social or linguistic events that trigger a particular change." He then goes on to offer "a typical life history of a sound change. The change first appears as a characteristic feature of a specific subgroup, attracting no particular notice from anyone. As it progresses within the group, it may then spread outwards in a wave, affecting first those social groups closest to the originating group. . . . As the linguistic feature develops within the original group of speakers, it becomes generalized in several senses. Over the course of time (three or four decades) a wider range of conditioned subclasses may be involved, and more extreme (less favored) environments." (319–320)

30   Bono, "Desire," *Rattle and Hum*, Island Records, 1988.

31   Trent Reznor, "Terrible lie." *pretty hate machine*, TVT Music, Inc., 1988.

32   Trent Reznor, "Sanctified," *pretty hate machine*.

33   Trent Reznor, "The only time," *pretty hate machine*.

34   Trent Reznor, "big man with a gun," *the downward spiral*, leaving hope/TVT Music, Inc., 1994.

35   Words in quotes are cited by Labov as Martinet's ideas, which Labov is disputing.

36   Recall also the origins of "house dancing" and "punk" with gay African American teenagers.

37   See also Bolton, Vincke, and Mak (1994, 257–259) for a good description of the paucity of scholarly consideration of gay baths and for survey evidence that baths are socially desirable to promote safer sex.

38   This footnote added to Ricco: For a more accessible discussion of how this dichotomy has misled lesbians and gay men in our thinking going back to 1982, see Califia (1994, 71–82).

39   This is expressed most dearly in Genet's *Funeral Rites*. See Bersani (1995) and Dollimore (1991).

40   An illuminating current example of "extreme individual" (his teammate, Jack Haley's description) as "hardened criminal" (description by his team's assistant coach, Dave Cowens) is Dennis Rodman of the San Antonio Spursbasketball team, who has vanilla-colored hair topping chocolate skin, rides a Harley-Davidson (spraining his shoulder), and who took his wife and Haley and his girlfriend to a gay bar to a show of male dancers in G-strings (Friend 1995).

41   Steven Arnold, "Lust The Body Politic," *The Advocate*, pp. 81–85 (1991).

42   For example, see Nozick (1981).

43   For example, see North (1981).

44   Wilde often reads as being as essentialistic as Gide, extolling as great "he who is perfectly and absolutely himself" (Wilde 1990, 12) and who avoids "thinking other people's thoughts" (13) – this last, in a typically Wildean irony, adapted from Ralph Waldo Emerson, thus redeeming himself from any suspicion of being unworthy of *Dorian Gray*. His avowal of socialism as a simple end of property rights sounds especially quaint with our view of the rise and fall of such national politics in the century since he wrote.

45   Note that the concept of perversion in western thought goes back at least to Augustine, as explored by Dollimore (1991).

46   I follow Dollimore (1991, 25; n. 2) in using the "typographically pretentious" (32) "/" to indicate an ambiguity, at our close vantage point, of any boundary between modern (or post-Renaissance) and postindustrial thinking.

47   Hamer and Copeland (1994) and LeVay (1993) are examples of such a renaissance in the biological sciences. Damasio's strong argument for the essential, often unconscious, role of emotions (through what Damasio terms "the somatic-marker hypothesis" involving "dispositional representations," which are located in the "hypothalamus, brain stem, and limbic system" (1994, 104)) in promoting, as well as sometimes confounding, rationality indicates the breadth of this intellectual renaissance. The connection between recognition of a "cognitive" role for emotions, on one hand, and ambiguity of boundaries between individual and collective is supported by Damasio's suggestion that impairment of the brain's processing of emotions can "compromise" a person's "free will" He also repeatedly alludes to a role for social construction of "secondary emotions" (134–136) and "feelings," which he distinguishes from emotions: feelings are our perceptions of our emotions (145). Damasio asserts that our "social environment" plays an important role (251, 260–67) but never sketches how this happens except for surprisingly naive references to "sick culture" (178–179), "healthy culture" (200), "culture of complaint" (247), a deepening "spiritual crisis of Western society" (257), and "increasingly hedonistic cultures" (267). These references to populist concepts in social analysis with no indication of their being problematic, belie the shallowness of his consideration of social interactions – this despite Damasio's carefully crafted contingent assertions not only in his area of expertise of neurobiology but also about medical practice and physical sciences generally and his thoughtful use of literary illustrations.

48   Cornwall (1996) offers further discussion of Marx's insightful discussion of the social embeddedness of humans and of how misleading is economists' use of the trope of "Robinson Crusoe" to represent all humans.

49   Althusser (1971) hints, but does not explicitly recognize, that ideology is much deeper than the codes promoted by what he calls "ideological state apparatuses" ("churches, parties, trade unions, families, some schools, most newspapers, cultural ventures" [137]) by arguing that ideologies represent a human's "relation to [their real] conditions of existence" in the real world (154). "The existence of ideology and the . . . interpellation of individuals as subjects are one and the same thing" (163; see also 167–170). But his postscript arguing that "[t]he ideology of the ruling class does not become the ruling ideology by the grace of God, nor even by virtue of the seizure of State power alone. It is by the installation of the [ideological state apparatuses] in which this ideology is realized and realizes itself that it becomes the ruling ideology" (172) is too simplistic and is not much of an advance over attributing ideologies to "a small number of cynical men" or to "the material alienation which reigns in the conditions of existence of men themselves" (154), which Althusser wisely rejects.

50   There is evidence that patterns of perception that are learned become, rather quickly, permanent structures in our minds that then limit/channel our subsequent perceptions: Werker (1989), Kuhl, et al. (1992), and Kuhl (1993).

51   Dollimore (1991, 281) notes that Jacques Lacan made a postpsychoanalytic (postdiscovery of the unconscious) reformulation of Descartes' epigram which serves as an intermediary between Descartes' and my versions: "I think where I am not, therefore I am where I do not think. Words that render sensible to an ear properly attuned with what elusive ambiguity the ring of meaning flees from our grasp along the verbal thread. What one ought to say is: I am not wherever I am the plaything of my thought; I think of what I am where I do not think to think" (Lacan 1977, 166). Damasio (1994, 248–52) offers useful insights on Descartes' epigram also.

References

Adolphs, R., D. Tranel, H. Damasio, and A. Damasio. "Impaired recognition of emotion in facial expressions following bilateral damage to the human amygdala." *Nature* 372 (15 December 1994): 669–672.

Allman, John and Leslie Brothers, "Faces, fear and the amygdala," *Nature* 372 (15 December 1994) pp. 613–614.

Althusser, Louis. "Ideology and ideological state apparatuses." in *Lenin and Philosophy and Other Essays*, translated by Ben Brewster, pp. 123–73 London: NLB, 1971.

Amott, Teresa, and Julie Matthaei. *Race, Gender, and Work: A Multicultural Economic History of Women in the United States*. Boston: South End Press, 1991.

Arnold, Steven. "Lust: The Body Politic," *The Advocate*, 1991.

Arthur, W. Brian. "Designing economic agents that act like human agents: a behavioral approach to bounded rationality." *American Economic Review* 81, 2 (May 1991): 353–59.

Becker, Gary S. "Preference formation within families." Presented at the meeting of the American Economic Association, 6 January 1993, Anaheim, CA.

Berlin, B., and P. Kay. *Basic Color Terms: Their Universality and Evolution*. Berkeley: University of California Press, 1969.

Bersani, Leo. *Homos*. Cambridge: Harvard University Press, 1995.

——— . "Is the rectum a grave?" In *AIDS: Cultural Analysis, Cultural Activism*, edited by Douglas Crimp. Cambridge: MIT Press, 1988. Reprinted in Goldberg, (1994).

Bolton, Ralph, John Vincke, and Rudolf Mak. "Gay baths revisited: an empirical analysis." *GLQ: A Journal of Lesbian and Gay Studies* 1, 3 (1994): 255–73.

Bray, Alan. *Homosexuality in Renaissance England*. London: Gay Men's Press, 1982.

Brody, David. *Workers in Industrial America: Essays on the Twentieth Century Struggle*. New York: Oxford University Press, 1980.

Butler, Judith. *Gender Trouble: Feminism and the Subversion of Identity*. New York: Routledge, 1990.

——— . "Imitation and gender insubordination." pp. 13–31. In Fuss (1991), pp. 13–31.

———— . *Bodies that Matter: On The Discursive Limits of "Sex"*. New York: Routledge, 1993.

Card, Celia (ed.). *Adventures in Lesbian Philosophy*. Bloomington: Indiana University Press, 1994.

Califia, Pat. *Public Sex: The Culture of Radical Sex*. Pittsburgh and San Francisco: Cleis Press, 1994.

Chapman, Loren J. "Illusory correlation in observational report." *Journal of Verbal Learning and Verbal Behavior* 6 (1967): 151–55.

Chapman, Loren J., and Jean P. Chapman. "Genesis of popular but erroneous psychodiagnostic observations," *Journal of Abnormal Psychology* 72 (1967): 193–204.

———— . "Illusory correlation as an obstacle to the use of valid psychodiagnostic signs." *Journal of Abnormal Psychology* 74 (1969): 271–280.

Chauncey, George. *Gay New York: Gender, Urban Culture, and the Making of the Gay Male World, 1890–1940*. New York: BasicBooks (HarperCollins), 1994.

Cohen, Ed. "Who Are 'We'? Gay 'Identity' as Political (E)motion (a Theoretical Rumination)." In Fuss (1991), 71–92.

Comaroff, Jean, and John Comaroff. *Of Revelation and Revolution: Christianity, Colonialism, and Consciousness in South Africa* Chicago: University of Chicago Press, 1991.

Cornwall, Richard, *Introduction to the Use of General Equilibrium Analysis*. New York: North-Holland, 1984.

———— . "deconstructing silence: the queer political economy of the social articulation of desire." *Review of Radical Political Economics* 29 (1997): 1–130.

Crompton, Louis. *Byron and Greek Love: Homophobia in 19th-Century England*. Berkeley: University of California Press, 1985.

Cyert, Richard M., and Morris H. DeGroot. "Learning applied to utility functions." In *Bayesian Analysis in Econometrics and Statistics: Essays in Honor of Harold Jeffreys*, edited by Arnold Zellner. New York: North-Holland, 1980, pp. 159–68.

Damasio, Antonio R. *Descartes' Error: Emotion, Reason, and the Human Brain*. New York: Grosset/Putnam, 1994.

Deleuze, Gilles, and Felix Guattari. *Kafka: Toward a Minor Literature*. Minneapolis: University of Minnesota Press, 1986.

D'Emilio, John. "Capitalism and gay identity." In *Powers of Desire: The Politics of Sexuality*, edited by Ann Snitow, et al. New York: Monthly Review Press. 1983a.

———— . *Sexual Politics, Sexual Communities: The Making of a Homosexual Minority in the United States, 1940–1970*. Chicago: University of Chicago Press, 1983b.

———— . "The homosexual menace: the politics of sexuality in cold war America." In *Passion and Power: Sexuality in History*, edited by Kathy Peiss and Christina Simmons, pp. 226–40. Philadelphia: Temple University Press, 1989.

D'Emilio, John, and Estelle B. Freedman. *Intimate Matters: A History of Sexuality in America*. New York: Harper & Row, 1988.

Dewey, John. *Experience and Nature*. LaSalle, IL: Open Court Press, 1929.

Dollimore, Jonathan. *Sexual Dissidence: Augustine to Wilde, Freud to Foucault*. Oxford: Clarendon Press, 1991.

Dunning, David, and Lisa Beth Stern. "Distinguishing accurate from inaccurate eyewitness identifications via inquiries about decision processes." *Journal of Personality and Social Psychology* 67, 5 (November 1994): 818–35.

Edelman, Lee. *Homographesis: Essays in Gay Literary and Cultural Theory*. New York: Routledge, 1994.

Edwards, Richard. *Contested Terrain: The Transformation of the Workplace in the Twentieth Century*. New York: Basic Books, 1979.

Elster, Jon. *The Cement of Society — A Study of Social Order*. New York: Cambridge University Press, 1989.

Escoffier, Jeffrey. "Sexual revolution and the politics of gay identity." *Socialist Review*. 15 (July–October 1985): 119–153, 1995.

——— . *John Maynard Keynes*. New York: Chelsea House Publishers, 1995.

Faderman, Lillian. *Odd Girls and Twilight Lovers: A History of Lesbian Life in Twentieth-Century America*. New York: Columbia University Press, 1991.

Fiske, Susan T., and Mark A. Pavelchak. "Category-based versus piecemeal-based affective responses: developments in schema-triggered affect." In *Handbook of Motivation and Cognition: Foundations of Social Behavior*, edited by Richard M. Sorrentino and E. Tory Higgins, 167–203. New York: Guilford Press, 1986.

Foucault, Michel. *The History of Sexuality, Vol. 1: An Introduction*. New York: Vintage Books, 1990 (originally 1978).

Friend, Tom. "A nonconformist in a league of his own." *New York Times*. 20 April 95, B7.

Fuss, Diana (ed.). *inside/out: lesbian theories, gay theories*. New York: Routledge, 1991.

Genet, Jean. *Funeral Rites*. New York: Grove Press, 1969.

——— . *Prisoner of Love*. Translated by Barbara Bray and with introduction by Edmund White. Hanover, NH: University Press of New England, 1992.

Goldberg, Jonathan (ed.). *Reclaiming Sodom*. New York: Routledge, 1994.

Gramsci, Antonio. *Selections from the Prison Notebooks*. New York: International, 1971.

Greenberg, David F. *The Construction of Homosexuality*. Chicago: University of Chicago Press, 1988.

Hamer, Dean, and Peter Copeland. *The Science of Desire: The Search for the Gay Gene and the Biology of Behavior*. New York: Simon & Schuster, 1994.

Hamilton, David L., and Steven J. Sherman, "Illusory correlations: implications for stereotype theory and research." In Daniel Bar-Tal, et al. (eds). *Stereotyping and Prejudice — Changing Conceptions*. New York: Springer-Verlag, 1989.

Hemphill, Essex. *Ceremonies — Prose and Poetry*. New York: Plume, 1992.

Holland, John H., Keith J. Holyoak, Richard E. Nisbett, and Paul R. Thagard. *Induction: Processes of Inference, Learning and Discovery*. Cambridge: MIT Press, 1986.

Kenny, Anthony. *The Wittgenstein Reader*. Oxford: Blackwell, 1994.

Kristof, Nicholas D. "Japan's favorite import from America: English." *New York Times*, 21 February 1995, A15.

Kuhl, Patricia. "Innate predispositions and the effects of experience in speech perception: the native language magnet theory." In *Developmental Neurocognition: Speech and Face Processing in the First Year of Life*, edited by Bénédicte de Boys-son-Bardies, Scania de Schonen, Peter Jusczyk, Peter McNeilage, and John Morton, pp. 259–74. Boston: Kluwer, 1993.

Kuhl, Patricia K., Karen A. Williams, Francisco Lacerda, Kenneth N. Stevens, and Björn Lindblom. "Linguistic experience alters phonetic perception in infants by 6 months of age." *Science* 255 (31 January 1992): 606–608.

Labov, William. *Sociolinguistic Patterns*. Philadelphia: University of Pennsylvania Press, 1992.

——— . *Locating Language in Time and Space*. New York: Academic Press, 1980.

——— . *Principles of Linguistic Change. Vol. 1. Internal Factors*. New York: Blackwell, 1994.

Lacan, Jacques. *Écrits: A Selection*. Translated by Alan Sheridan. London: Tavistock, 1977.

Lawrence, D. H. *Phoenix II: Uncollected, Unpublished and Other Prose Works*. Edited by Warren Roberts and Harry T. Moore. London: Heinemann, 1981.

LeVay, Simon. *The Sexual Brain*. Cambridge: MIT Press, 1993.

Lorde, Audre. *Sister Outsider*. Freedom, CA: Crossing Press, 1984.

Marimon, Ramon, Ellen McGrattan, and Thomas J. Sargent. "Money as a medium of exchange in an economy with artificially intelligent agents." *Journal of Economic Dynamics and Control* 14 (1990): 329–73.

Matthaei, Julie. "The sexual division of labor, sexuality, and lesbian/gay liberation: towards a Marxist-feminist theory of sexuality in U.S. capitalism." Presented at URPE session entitled "The economics of sexual orientation: theory, evidence, and policy," at the Allied Social Science Association Meetings, 5 January 1992, Anaheim, CA.

McFadden, Daniel. "Econometric models of probabilistic choice." *Structural Analysis of Discrete Data with Econometric Applications*, edited by Charles F. Manski and Daniel McFadden, pp. 198–269. Cambridge: MIT Press, 1981.

McFadden, Daniel, and Marcel K. Richter. "Stochastic rationality and revealed stochastic preference." In *Preferences, Uncertainty, and Optimality*, edited by John S. Chipman, Daniel McFadden, and Marcel K. Richter, pp. 161–86. (1990) San Francisco: Westview Press. 1990.

Montgomery, David. *The Fall of the House of Labor: The Workplace, the State, and American Labor Activism*. Cambridge: Cambridge University Press, 1987.

North, Douglass. *Structure and Change in Economic History*. New York: W. W. Norton, 1981.

Nozick, Robert. *Anarchy, State, and Utopia*. New York: Basic Books, 1981.

Parker, Patricia. *Literary Fat Ladies: Rhetoric, Gender, Property*. London: Methuen, 1987.

Ricco, John Paul. "Jacking off a minor architecture." *Steam* 1, 4 (Winter 1993): 236–43.

——— . "Queering boundaries: semen and visual representations from the Middle Ages and in the Era of the AIDS crisis." *Gay and Lesbian Studies in Art History*, edited by Whitney Davis, pp. 57–80. New York: Harrington Park Press, 1994.

Rubin, Gayle. "The traffic in women: notes on the 'political economy' of sex." In *Toward an Anthropology of Women*, edited by Rayna R. Reiter, pp. 157–210. New York: Monthly Review Press, 1975.

——. "Thinking sex: notes for a radical theory of the politics of sexuality." In *Pleasure and Danger: exploring female sexuality*, edited by Carole S. Vance, pp. 267–319. London: Pandora, 1984.

Sargent, Thomas J. *Bounded Rationality in Macroeconomics: The Arne Ryde Memorial Lectures*. Oxford: Clarendon Press, 1993.

Saslow, James M., *Ganymede in the Renaissance: Homosexuality in Art and Society*. New Haven, CT: Yale University Press, 1986.

Scott, Darieck. "Jungle fever? Black gay identity politics, white dick, and the utopean bedroom." *GLQ: A Journal of Lesbian and Gay Studies* 1, 3 (1994): 299–321.

Sedgwick, Eve Kosofsky. *Epistemology of the Closet*. Berkeley: University of California Press, 1990.

Smith, Bruce R. *Homosexual Desire in Shakespeare's England*. Chicago: University of Chicago Press, 1991.

Soltan, Margaret. "Night errantry: the epistemology of the wandering woman." *New Formations* 5 (1988): 108–119.

Stallybrass, Peter, and Allon White. *The Politics and Poetics of Transgression*. London: Methuen, 1986.

Tversky, Amos, and Daniel Kahneman. "Belief in the law of small numbers." *Psychological Bulletin* 2 (1971): 105–110.

——. "Judgement under uncertainty: heuristics and biases." *Science* 185 (1974): 1124–31.

Vicinus, Martha. " 'They wonder to which sex I belong': the historical roots of the modern lesbian identity." *Feminist Studies* 18, 3 (1992): 467–98.

Weeks, Jeffrey. *Coming Out: Homosexual Politics in Britain, from the Nineteenth Century to the Present*. New York: Quarter Books, 1979.

Wells, Gary L., Sheila M. Rydell, and Eric P. Seelau. "The selection of distractors for eyewitness lineups." *Journal of Applied Psychology* 78, 5 (October 1993): 835–44.

Werker, Janet F. "Becoming a native listener." *American Scientist* 77 (1989): 54–59.

White, E. Frances. "Africa on my mind: gender, counter discourse and African-American nationalism." *Journal of Women's History* 2, 1 (Spring 1990): 73–97.

Wilde, Oscar. *The Soul of Man and Prison Writings*. Edited by Isobel Murray. Oxford: Oxford University Press, 1990.

Wittgenstein, Ludwig. *Philosophical Investigations*. Translated by G.E.M. Anscombe. Oxford: Blackwell, 1981.

Young, Andrew W., John P. Aggleton, Deborah J. Hellawell, Michael Johnson, Paul Broks, and J. Richard Hanley. "Face processing impairments after amygdalotomy." *Brain* 118 (1995): 15–24.

Chapter 10

Jeffner Allan

LESBIAN ECONOMICS

From *Sinuosities, Lesbian Poetic Politics*, Bloomington and Indianapolis: Indiana University Press, 1996, pp. 54–70

ECONOMICS, IN ITS customary and misleading universal usage, is the circulation in society of values, meaning, and the basics of daily life. Economics is, however, more accurately termed "patriarchal economics," for it is premised, in theory and in practice, on the placing in movement, by men, of that without which females cannot exist. Such an economy is patriarchal both by definition and in its consequences: objectification and possession; the imposition of obligation; the institution of work, a making that is in the service of another, and of poverty, the lifelong outcome of such oppression. Patriarchal economics, be it capitalist, socialist, Marxist, or anarchist, preserves its self-interest by demanding that all females be women, females who produce and use the objects, children, ideas, and money of the patriarchal economy, and that all women be heterosexual, females engaged in a production and use of goods that is directed to the well-being of men.

"Lesbian economics," in marked contrast, is the specific identification and placing in movement, by lesbians, of that without which we cannot exist. Lesbians – females who live by rejecting that primary form of obligation, obligation to men – bring about lesbian economics. The single, and urgent, insistence of a lesbian economics is that we meet the material necessity of our finitude: that we must position ourselves someplace on the earth, maintain bodily well-being, and someday, that we must die.

Work in the patriarchal economy requires so much from us that a lesbian economics often slips by. We may take as inevitable the loss of time, creativity, and female lives in patriarchy – or these may be insistently present, evoking our intense anger at a situation we find impossible to change. At the same time, we may experience and passionately desire both the lesbian economy that already exists and a lesbian economy that might, in fact, be brought about.

Unlike a patriarchal economy, a lesbian economy does not demand that we passively consume it, reproduce it, and leave no trace of ourselves. A lesbian economy is open, shifting, to be worked with and to be made.

As I deconstruct the apparently secure explanations and statistics set forth by male economic systems, the order of women's existence in the patriarchal economy shows itself as the actual disorder and exhaustion of our lives. Jolted by the currents of our lives, by their surprising power to effect change, the economic patterns established by patriarchal analysis fall into disarray. Freed of their false promises and predictions, I explore the traces of a circulation of goods in which I choose my survival and my freedom.

A lesbian economy exists already, primarily, though not exclusively, as the choice to touch, love, and live intimately with oneself and other lesbians. The freedom, meaningfulness, and pleasure present in such experience defy the patriarchal requirement that females produce for male-defined ends. Lesbian economics aims at extending the power of that conviction, especially to the material aspects of our survival.

Lesbian economics recognizes a single necessity: *the material necessity of our finitude. We must position ourselves someplace on the earth, maintain bodily well-being, and someday, we must die.*

Six Theses on Material Necessity

1   The material necessity of our finitude marks the edge of our lives, the limit of our existence. To claim the limit as the *oikos*, that which is our own, is to set in motion an economics, an *oikonomia*, in which we can be free.[1] Inattention to and denial of this limit automatically place us in the patriarchal economy where, for females, there is a constant question of survival, and no hope of survival with freedom.

2   The material necessity of our finitude is the only irreducible element of our existence. Its necessity is experienced as a fact and is not imposed by the exercise of power, as are heterosexuality and motherhood.[2]

3   Material necessity is neither a so-called law of nature against which we must struggle if we are to survive, nor that with which we must

be in harmony. Material necessity is simply "there," without prescriptive naturalism.

4   Material necessity is not less-than-human, not the "merely" animal side of our lives. Neither can material necessity be dismissed in favor of the often-termed higher human activities of the emotions, the mind, the spirit.

5   Material necessity does not require engagement in activity that is repetitive and unfree. The claim that fulfillment of the basics of daily life must be dominated by necessity is oblivious to the spontaneity and infinite diversity utilized already, and primarily by women, in the production of the elements of day-to-day sustenance.[3]

6   As long as I am to live, I must meet the material necessity of my finitude. I may choose, at any moment and for any reason, not to meet that necessity.

Lesbian economics *refuses reification of the oikos* in land, objects or persons. The ecological environment, the subjectivity of individuals, the creations of mind and passion defy containment. Neither commercial value, that is, goods and labor, nor meaning or value in general can ultimately be subdued as object: possessed.

Lesbian economics *rejects the ethic of obligation*. The material necessity of our finitude is not to be dislocated through bondage to the-other-in-whom-we-are-to-find-ourselves. We are not "necessary women":[4] she who has neither necessity nor freedom of her own, but who must serve as the means for the fulfillment of arbitrary demands: the desire for immortality (children), immediate desire (heterosex), and the desire for profit or progress (as in the devastating and often deadly production of microchips).

Lesbian economics *expels work – a making that is in the service of another – and poverty*. That women perform two-thirds of the world's work, receive five percent of the world income, and own less than one percent of the world's land indicates only in part how women are the workers of the world and the majority of the world's poor.[5] If women's work in the full spectrum of male-constructed sexuality and mothering were included in such figures, the claim that women do ninety percent of the world's work might well be an understatement. If the poverty of women in the general patriarchal economy of ideas and values were combined with women's poverty in the restricted economy of income and land ownership,[6] the actual poverty of our lives in patriarchy would be clearly manifest.

Lesbian economics claims the limit of our existence. *As lesbians, we stop the displacement of our material necessity in the demands of another and we take up that necessity as the condition of our lives.* We are free only as long as our material necessity is not impelled along the circle of its dislocation.

Writing off the wheel

The force of patriarchy to dislocate my material necessity has augmented for over two millennia, virtually without exception and to the point that my life may be but a detour to death: forever out of season, out of connection, with those times I might live were my life my own. From the moment of birth I am pulled, already, into an economic pattern so strong there is scarcely a space in which it can be broken.

I remove the spokes which have propelled my emotional and intellective life toward men as "friends," "lovers," and bearers of "truth." Still, even as lesbian, I remain bound to the patriarchal economy for many of the basics of daily life. If and when these basics are met, it is usually at great cost to myself and other women. The wheel of patriarchal economics, in which every fulfillment is connected to a loss, continues to turn against women.

Woman

While "lesbian" is abrasively problematic to the patriarchal economy, it is "woman" and the "exchange" of women that are at issue in a lesbian economy. By rewriting woman and the exchange of women, we *write off* the patriarchal economy and we establish our lives *off* of its wheel.

As lesbians, we find ourselves apart from the patriarchal economy, for a lesbian *is not* a woman:[7] a lesbian does not stand in any relation of obligation, and rejects that primary form of obligation, obligation to men. Indeed, it is because lesbians have broken off from many/some of the ways of being a woman that it is possible to refer to a lesbian economy. I say "some" of the ways of being a woman, for the full extent of the servitude of women is still to be discovered.

Although we choose to live as lesbians, we are obliged, *as if* we were women, to stand in relation to the patriarchal economy. This obligation is established not by contract, which would imply an agreement between parties that are free and equal, but by force. We are obliged to stand in relation to men, especially to secure food, water, shelter, clothing, and frequently, for the goods and money that must be exchanged for such commodities. Even when we supply the basics of daily life, our work and the objects that we make often are shaped by the power of men.[8] I say "*as if* we were women," for although the patriarchal economy forces *all* females to *become* women, *no* females *are* women. No female is by nature that image of obligation designed by men, though all females can be bound by its confines.

If we are to identify and disband each of the ways in which we stand in relation to patriarchy, we must understand "woman" in its all-encompassing sense. The customary reference to "woman" primarily as she who is obliged to reproduce children and engage in heterosex is deceptively narrow and conceals major areas of our unfreedom. "Woman" includes, but is not fully represented by, these obligations. A female who does not reproduce children or engage in heterosex may still find herself in a situation *as* a woman. Even if every female chose not to have children or engage in heterosex, or if reproductive technology and robotics were utilized by men to forcibly dismiss females from such activities, there could still be women: females who stand in relations of obligation to men.

Definition of "woman" in terms of maternity and sexuality is understood usually, and quite unnecessarily, to limit "lesbian" to not being obliged to have children and not engaging in heterosex. "Lesbian," a far-reaching category of female existence and freedom, is rendered so restrictively as to be virtually meaningless. "Lesbian" is granted no evident reason to question the ongoing oppression of females in all areas of life.

We must understand "woman," then, in terms of the relational context in which this term actually takes on its meaning. A female becomes a woman by *standing in relation to* the patriarchal economy. We articulate the complexity of this relation when we define as "woman" *any female who produces or uses objects, children, ideas, money, et al., of the patriarchal economy.*

Exchange

The belief that women are objects of exchange in patriarchy is often considered fundamental to any economics of women and is shared by feminist, socialist, and structuralist economists. According to this claim, women stand directly in relation to men, as the objects of an exchange in which woman is "the gift" and man is "the giver."[9] Yet, such an assertion is seriously misleading, for it accepts without question the hetero-relational illusions instituted by patriarchy: that women occupy a central position *within* man's world; that women and men are complementary; that woman and man are necessary categories of existence.

Lesbian economics rejects all assumptions of hetero-relational theory and notes that all females stand in relation to the patriarchal economy not directly, that is, as individuals who might be valued in our own right, but indirectly and *solely* by means of the objects that we make and use. Although the *objects* of women's work are exchanged within the patriarchal economy, at least until such items can be produced more efficiently by technology, women are not exchanged. We stand *outside* the closed circle of the patriarchal economy.

The patriarchal economy institutes a split between that which it will admit and circulate, the objects made by the work of women, and that which it will exclude, women's work and women:

The objects made by women's work. The sole and indirect link between women and the patriarchal economy, but a direct link between man and his world.

Women's work. A source of energy to be extracted and ordered by patriarchy in accord with its demand for maximum yield at minimum expense.

Woman. A sign that points to the possibility that the patriarchal economy will obtain a product.

Whenever the objects made by women are attributed to women's "nature," and the work involved in their production is thought "natural," it may appear that women actually are exchanged by men. The belief that the production of children through the work of pregnancy is "natural" to women reduces into one the product, the action of making, and the maker. Woman is thereby posited as an object of exchange standing within the patriarchal economy, together with the child-product. Such a naturalistic equation is fallacious, however, for patriarchal society, while it usually accepts the child, especially if male, often rejects the pregnant, birthing, nursing mother. Motherhood is not a "natural" phenomenon,[10] any more than is heterosexuality or any form of making, and children, pregnancy, and women cannot be equated.

The naturalistic equation conceals the difference in standing between the objects made by women's work *and* women's work and women:

The object is my only, and indirect, link to the world. Yet I look at what I have made and do not see myself in it. I find the whole of the "world" in the object and none of that world in myself.

Hegel writes that the slave sees *him*self in the object and breaks with the master. The slave and master have a single world in which the slave, upon seeing himself as its maker, understands that he is entitled to take a stand.[11]

Contrary to Hegel's assertion, I am not present in the objects I make for men. And in lesbian writing, I displace the patriarchal economy.[12]

The closed circle in which the objects of *women's* work are exchanged is measured by man, that standard whose value is everywhere and who claims, thus, to be infinite.

Hestia

In the heavens Zeus drives his winged team. First of the ruler gods, he precedes all the others – save Hestia. Hestia, she who tends the fire that sustains immortals and mortals, remains alone in the earthly dwelling place of the gods. She maintains a warm hearth such that even those who embark on the circle of the infinite can, when necessary, meet the demands of their finitude. This is her work.

Hestia keeps constant the fire of the Eastern Mediterranean, the fire of Greece, the fire of Rome, the fire that accompanies patriarchy. Hestia keeps lit the fire which is never to be extinguished: the fire which supports "the word," the written record of every legal statement, the fire of the city, the fire of each home and hearth. The fire is to be cycled from city to city – by others. Hestia cannot move her own product. In time, Hestia is joined by six other virgins, the Vestals: the *sacred bank* upon which the temple of patriarchy is established.[13]

The economy of the infinite would fix the Vestals in servitude to itself by naturalizing itself and its offspring: *woman's economics*. The women of the sacred bank are affirmed by woman's economics in order to ensure that the fires of patriarchy will continue to burn. The honor of "freedom" through servitude is bestowed on women through a twofold assurance:

> *The claim to totality.* That the patriarchal economy is the only place in which females can stand.

> *The promise of inclusion.* That because we find in patriarchy the objects of women's work, women, too, are present.

Regulation of the sacred bank by woman's economics upholds humanism and womanly virtue. We are told that we are all together in a single economy, producing and using its goods. That the person, and not the product, is the center of the exchange. That we may occupy ourselves with matters of adjustment:

> We may attempt to find value in woman, to recognize the value of woman's work, to increase the value of woman's products. We may try to make woman's work equal to man's, comparable to man's and, even, to integrate woman's work into the patriarchal order. We must, however, remain women: those who stand in relation to men, those who produce and use the objects of the patriarchal economy.

After all, if Hestia were not to keep the fire burning, her name would have no meaning. She would have, we are told, no possible point of reference.

The "word" supported by the warm hearth of Hestia's labor is not, however, the only word. Only the Hestia of the sacred bank need work to maintain her name, her honor. Apart from the sacred bank we find in Hestia's name the traces of an individual and a movement foreign to patriarchy: (h)estia . . . ousia and, from the most distant past . . . outhoūn: that according to which all things flow and nothing stands.[14]

Lady Poverty

Our lives, at present, are linked inextricably with Lady Poverty:[15] *she who has least in terms of the patriarchal economy and she to whom the patriarchal economy can offer nothing.* Our poverty is relative to the context of that which exists and to the context of that which could be, were economics fashioned otherwise.

We experience the intensity of our poverty in the act of *cancellation: the striking out of any attempt we make to position ourselves freely.* The heterosexual grid that structures the sacred bank disrupts our most carefully conceived effort to position ourselves apart from its prescription: females must stand in relation to men, females must be women.

The heterosexual grid

We undergo, by force, the act of cancellation and we are impressed into the space of our dislocation, *the heterosexual grid: that our production and use of objects must be directed to the well-being of men.* On the *horizontal axis* of the heterosexual grid, our work must make secure the men "closest" to us. On the *vertical axis* of the heterosexual grid, our work must buffer the men "closest" to us from men who stand "above" and "below," according to the determination of patriarchal hierarchy.

The axes of the heterosexual grid combine and recombine, forming an economic panorama so incalculably vast that it becomes the focus and limit of efforts toward economic change. On the horizontal axis, we may attempt to use legal and governmental institutions to secure for ourselves an economic well-being equal to, or comparable to, that of "our" men. Yet such endeavors in the restricted economy of income and land ownership have made little progress overall for women: in classical Greece, women who worked in any profession on the mainland were forbidden to earn more than half as much as a man; women workers in France, 1889–1893, got only half a man's wage; a Moslem woman in Oman, 1984, is declared to be worth half as much as a Moslem man; in the United States, 1984, women who are employed full-time earn roughly half as much as men. Since more women than men are employed part-time, women's poverty is more disproportionate than such figures indicate.[16]

On the vertical axis, we may attempt to end women's poverty in the patriarchal economy by forming coalitions that try to disrupt and redistribute the usual balance of power between groups of women and men, especially on the basis of national, racial, and ethnic origin. Yet the income of most women engaged full-time in wage labor in predominantly rural and recently industrialized regions of the third world, that is, the majority of women who are employed full-time, is one-twentieth that of first world men and one-tenth that of first world women, and this income differential is increasing.[17]

Whenever we attempt to modify the heterosexual grid by adjusting one or both of its axes, we experience, once again, the act of cancellation. Irrespective of whether we seek equality with "our" men, or equality with "all" men, women remain the contingent and impoverished term. The failure to successfully alter the heterosexual grid indicates, however, not that all economic paths must lead to men, but that if we are to live in an economy in which we can be free, we must disband the heterosexual grid.

The longer the heterosexual grid is intact, the more pronounced is the configuration of work and poverty that characterizes women's lives. The more hours we work in obligation to men, the more we produce that is appropriated by men; the more the patriarchal economy can appropriate, the poorer we become in terms of life exhaustion and in our power to develop the tools with which we can, by choice, shape our lives.

Women are the fastest-growing number of those who are poor and the fastest-growing occupational sector. At present, seventy-five percent of all people in the world living in poverty are women. By the year 2000, in the United States, virtually all people living in poverty will be women or in families headed by women. The economic situation of women, and especially that of women in third world countries, has continued to worsen almost uniformly since 1975 (the year from which it was measured).

Yet, between 1951 and 1980, the number of wage-earning women in industrialized and non-industrialized countries almost doubled, from 345 million to 625 million. Increasing hours spent in paid work have not improved the relative poverty of women, for where the highest number of women enter the wage market, wages are the lowest. By the year 2000, Asian women will comprise 500 million out of an estimated 980 million female wage workers, many new to the wage market, and it is precisely these Asian women for whom job prospects are least promising.[18] The gap between the hours worked by women and the economic standing of women is even more pronounced in light of the hours many women work, for low pay, in the informal work sector of bartering, begging, street vending, scavenging, employment as domestic workers, and prostitution; the increasing unpaid hours many third world women spend in subsistence farming, water hauling, and fuel gathering; and the time that nearly all women spend in food preparation, mending, birthing and care of children, care of the old, care of the sick, sexual service to men.

The so-called "feminization of poverty" is not, however, an entirely new phenomenon. In many instances, women are not becoming poorer, but *the conditions of women's poverty and their base in heterosexuality are becoming more evident*. Women must produce at least some objects for the patriarchal economy, or we are disconnected from any economic allocation, as is evidenced by the economic poverty that accompanies the worldwide increase in women heads of household. A woman may receive financial reimbursement for giving birth to or caring for a child, or children, of a specific man or kinship group. But if a woman establishes herself as no longer producing the objects that directly enhance that male economic group the funds allocated to the woman for the production of the child-object are withdrawn almost automatically.[19]

The apex of our poverty, however, is not so much lack of money as lack of land. Women are the largest landless group in every country: "in no other area is discrimination against women as widespread and as devastating as in the area of property rights – both in the developing, as well as the industrialized world."[20] Nor do women have access to property rights underground or in outer space.

Landless, we are without the means to secure the production and use of objects other than those approved for patriarchal ends. Men have measured, with few exceptions, under what conditions and for what period of time women will use the land: if married, a woman may lose the automatic right to use the father's property, and if divorced, a woman may lose the use of the property of the husband. Land that is transmitted matrilineally is usually regulated by the uncle and can be taken back into the kinship network, should he deem that the land can be better used otherwise. If a woman is raped by a man outside her kinship group, the woman may be forced to leave everything behind and to go into exile from home and village. If battered, a woman may be able to escape only by geographic relocation, by giving up all land rights. In the relatively recent introduction of commercial farming, men's denial of women's traditional land use rights indicates that men determine even who will use the land and what the land will produce.[21]

The contradiction of the heterosexual grid, that space which every woman must tread and that space which no woman can tread without cancellation, yields the central sign of our poverty: landlessness. The space we tread is the space of our dislocation, a dilemma that is not necessarily resolved by our ownership of land or our reclaiming of land use rights, both of which are barred, to any significant degree, by the contours of the heterosexual grid.

The sacred bank

The "sacred bank" is, as its name suggests, the "bench," and quite literally, the "work-bench,"[22] set apart by the patriarchal economy as that space in which women's work is to serve the golden rod of the infinite. Here women and our work are bound in the worship, the service, of the patriarchal economy. We are sent, through the phallic pipeline, a bit of matter and a demand: that the material be worked, reworked, and withdrawn. Our blood, our muscles, our thoughts, mold that material, and the object produced is taken back through the phallic pipeline, for men. We are sent what, despite our work, we cannot repay – a highly uneconomic proposition. And we are bound by the debt. If we refuse to work we are judged, as we were by Isaeus of ancient Greece, "insane and traitors to the home and the state." If we abolish currency or make our own, we are stopped, imprisoned, burned at the stake.[23]

"Woman" is coined in the sacred bank as she who must work without cease. Women's work is never done, not because our tasks inherently require endless exertion, but because work becomes the "nature" of woman. The measure of all value, the Infinite, may assign specific value to the objects of our work, but women remain without determinate value: out-of-circulation.

Our words to each other are displaced by the word that enslaves, that word first spoken to Lady Poverty: "through obedience to learn to surrender personal preferences and intellectual conceptions."[24] Cut off from one another, and from ourselves, we work without the time to conceive an economics of a different type. We uphold a culture that teaches women how to work for men and how to please men.

The abolition of work

"Woman" is a sign that is manifested by all females, as those who produce and use the objects of the patriarchal economy. Work – a making that is in the service of another – and poverty are bound to females as women. The separation of females from work would be an end to "woman." To abolish the relations that comprise "women" is to sever us from the heterosexual grid and to enable translation to another discourse, another economy.

The equation of females with work, borne out by the sign "woman," is made in a variety of contexts, all of which further the production of objects for the patriarchal economy. In Saudi Arabia, the employment of women is officially permitted in all jobs that are "in harmony with female nature." In the United States, eighty percent of the women in wage labor work in service, sales, clerical, or factory jobs are living according to the same, if unstated, principle. The patriarchal economy binds females to work through the claim, as stated recently in the USSR, that females have a special, womanly predisposition to work owing to "the anatomical-physiological peculiarities of the female organism and likewise to the moral-ethical temperament of women." A recent advertisement makes a similar claim with reference to young Asian women in Malaysia, "who therefore, could be better qualified by nature and inheritance to contribute to the efficiency of a bench-assembly production." A womanly will to work is attributed to females, as is expressed by this laudatory statement about workers in canneries in California: "All of the men left after the first day, but only one of the women left at first." Some females are said to have more of a will to work than others, depending on a woman's position on the vertical axis of the heterosexual grid, as is indicated by this advertisement from a group of European, Japanese, and American firms: "Mexican women are forty percent more productive than their American counterparts."[25]

Dismissal of the triadic relation female-work-woman fails to recognize the full array of limits imposed on females by the patriarchal economy and precludes translation out of that economy. Such dismissal is usually predicated on mistaken or incomplete assumptions regarding the relation of females to work. One such assumption, which maintains that women occupy a *free space* in patriarchy, tends to exempt from the triadic relation those forms of production commonly associated with woman's "nature," especially heterosexuality. Simone de Beauvoir aptly states that we are not born, but become women, yet proceeds to argue that women's "sexual instinct" is always apart from work and the social world.[26] Heterosexual eroticism, in which women are obligated to produce for men and to meet male-defined norms, is thereby made to appear independent from, rather than the product of, the patriarchal economy.

The belief that at least part of women's production falls into a *nameless territory* outside the triadic relation female-work-woman, is often based on the presupposition that some of women's activities are "worse" than work. Simone de Beauvoir, for instance, states that women's lives are so seriously broken in upon by the demand for children that "gestation" cannot be equated with a "task, a piece of work, or with a service."[27] Assertions such as this, however, tend to identify "work" with what is done by men and fail to provide a framework for the serious incursion into our lives of all activity in the patriarchal economy.

The far too optimistic conviction that women may escape the triadic relation by the *manipulation of alternatives* focuses frequently on women who work in the wage economy and who live apart from men. This position fails to recognize, however, that even women who do not live with men may still be beholden to men, if only for the opportunity to be employed, and that such women may be working, even if inadvertently, for men's benefit. Men, not women, achieve a monetary advantage when women live apart from men. In California, a woman's standard of living falls an average of seventy percent after a divorce, while a man's standard of living increases by forty-nine percent.[28] For women living without men, increased freedom often signifies a shift to that dimension of the patriarchal economy that engages women in labor-intensive work as a large pool of low-paid wage earners.

All three forms of dismissal overlook how work is bound to females as women. One type of object production may be substituted for another without any overall change in the producer's standing. A shift in the patriarchal economy's structuring of women's work is not necessarily an indication of the oncoming demise of that economy. Wage work has been pictured as the way to women's liberation, either in the belief that with women's increasing financial independence prejudice and discrimination will become outmoded and will disappear, or because entry into wage work is thought to leave behind women's specific oppression.[29] Yet work in the wage economy and living apart from men are not a complete solution, for wage work itself is an integral element of the patriarchal economy.

A lesbian economics aims neither to enable us to work equally, which still reconciles us to the work world, nor to work freely; for women's work – its lack of wages, its low wages, and its very definition – is the accomplishment of patriarchal society.[30] A lesbian economy aims at a rupture with the patriarchal economy through the abolition of work and its consequence, poverty. *A lesbian economics is the creation of an economy in which we can claim our individualities, an economy in which we are no longer women.*

The dead of heart

Women's work and poverty increase with such rapidity that the patriarchal economy may assume the guise of the inevitable, wasting our lives if we stay and leaving us to waste if we attempt to leave. Action that might establish a rupture with this dilemma is dismissed by heterosexual discourse, which propels us in quest of the "right relation" to patriarchal economics.

We experience the death of our hearts in the heterosexual discourse that proclaims a series of "choices": Whether it is better to work whole-heartedly and with pride in accomplishment or to keep work at a distance and simply appear to like it. Whether to live in a lesbian world and keep a straight job or not to work in the wage economy but to continue to use at least some objects of the patriarchal economy, objects made by the work of other women. Alternatives such as these lead us to overlook the real possibility of claiming our survival by steadily working out new patterns of economic explanation and effecting economic change. Jarred to the utmost by the clamor of compromise, we may uneasily abandon ourselves to assimilation. Gradually, we forget the initial power of our decision to live no longer with men, and that we might still exercise that power in order to live no longer in the patriarchal economy. We become altogether dead of heart.

Until we break off the triadic relation of female-work-women, we work more and move ever closer to annihilation. The death of our hearts is not only a state of mind, but a material fact. The dislocation of our material necessity is a tangible event.

The flowing of all things

An active taking up of the material necessity of our finitude as *that which is our own* is the condition for the possibility of our existence as free individuals. That we must position ourselves someplace on the earth, maintain bodily well-being, and, someday, that we must die, is not contingent on the existence of patriarchy. Yet until we actively take up the material necessity of our finitude, and in such a way that we stop its forcible displacement by the demands of another, the conditions of our existence remain bound to the patriarchal economy.

Our trammeled freedom within the heterosexual grid is perpetuated by theories of freedom and free choice which, if accepted, prevent us from claiming our material necessity. Such theories fetter our finitude to the patriarchal economy, substituting an endless series of arbitrary demands and necessities for the single necessity that must be met if we are to be free. We are said to be absolutely free in essence, to enjoy a freedom that is ready-made. Yet freedom in this context is but an ahistorical belief, and a deterrent to our concrete action. Or we are said to be relatively free in practice, to exercise a freedom of choice. The content of all choice, however, becomes a mere variation on multiple forms of obligation and obedience. Choice is measured in advance: that some will have less, some will have more, and that none will have the choice of determining the conditions of our existence. It is little wonder that, after rummaging through alternatively bad possibilities, we find we must give new shape to our freedom.

This lesbian economics makes no predictions and offers no answers. The possibility of its realization, the plausibility that it may in some sense already be realized, lie in the present. How we are lesbians, how we will be women no longer, each in our individual ways, forms the locus of a lesbian economy. Whenever we claim our finitude as that which is our own, we shape the circulation of our lives.

With fierce feelings and lightning speed we engage in a freedom of our own historical making. Lesbian economics has no natural point of origin, no rule, no moment that is exactly the same. In festive celebrations of change, rupture, surprise, and discovery, we take up the material necessity of our finitude.

Notes

1   Lidell and Scott, *Greek-English Lexicon* (Oxford: Clarendon Press, 1925), 1202.
2   Jeffner Allen, "Motherhood: The Annihilation of Women," in *Mothering: Essays in Feminist Theory*, ed. Joyce Trebilcot (Totowa, N.J.: Rowman and Allanheld, 1984), 215–30.
3   The distinction between the fulfillment of daily needs and activity that is liberating, and the implicit misogyny of this distinction, is accepted by radical theorists such as Marcuse. See Herbert Marcuse, *Eros and Civilization* (Boston: Beacon Press, 1955), 156, and "Foundations of the Concept of Labor," *Telos* 7 (Summer 1973): 37.
4   It is noteworthy that the English language actually includes the term "necessary woman," which, although now archaic, once designated females whose lives were spent primarily in the service of men. See *The Oxford English Dictionary* (Oxford: Clarendon Press, 1961), 7:61.
5   *WIN News* 8 (Autumn 1982): 1, *WIN News* 6 (Autumn 1980): 20.
6   Jacques Derrida, "From Restricted to General Economy: A Hegelianism without Reserve," in *Writing and Difference*, ed. Alan Bass (Chicago: Chicago University Press, 1978), 251–77.
7   Monique Wittig, "One Is Not Born a Woman," *Feminist Issues* 1 (Winter 1981: 47–54.
8   Jeffner Allen, "Women and Food: Feeding Ourselves," *Journal of Social Philosophy* 15 (1984): 39.
9   The theory of the exchange of women is developed by Claude Lévi-Straus, *The Elementary Structures of Kinship* (Boston: Beacon Press, 1969), 51, 114, 481. It is introduced into a feminist context by Gayle Rubin in the groundbreaking essay "The Traffic in Women: Notes on the 'Political Economy' of Sex," in *Toward an Anthropology of Women*, ed. Ranya R. Reiter (New York: Monthly Review Press, 1975), 157–210.
10 See Jeffner Allen, "Motherhood: The Annihilation of Women," 218–23.
11 The account of the link between alienation and revolution, presented by Hegel in his analysis of the master-slave relation, is central to modern political thought. See G. W. F. Hegel, *The Phenomenology of Mind*, trans. J. B. Baillie (New York: Harper and Row, 1967), 234–40, and Karl Marx, "Economic and Political Manuscripts of 1844," in *The Marx Engels Reader*, 2d ed., ed. Robert C. Tucker (New York: Norton, 1972). Hegel's assumption, however, that the slave rebels when "he" sees "himself" in the world he has made for the master and wants that world for himself, does not go far enough. For women, the alienation from the objects of our work can be so profound that we cannot see ourselves in them at all and, in consequence, we may want nothing of the master's world that has been produced by our work.

12   The use of "lesbian writing" to displace the male measure of value is developed by
      Namascar Shaktini, "Displacing the Phallic Subject: Wittig's Lesbian Writing," *Signs*
      8 (Summer 1983): 29–44.
13   The privileging of the "infinite" as the creator of value in Western economics and
      the expulsion of the "finite" is discussed by Jacques Derrida, "Economimesis," trans.
      R. Klein, *Diacritics*, Summer 1981, 32, 37. Derrida portrays women in complicity
      with the economy of the infinite to the point of deriving pure sexual pleasure
      from the sexual violence that men in that economy have perpetrated. In "Lesbian
      Economics," "sacred bank" is "taken" from Derrida and repositioned. Among the
      most informative resources on Hestia and the Vestals are Plato, *Laws* 9.856, trans.
      A. E. Taylor, and *Phaedrus* 247B, trans. R. Hackforth, in *Plato: Collected Dialogues*, ed.
      Edith Hamilton and Huntington Cairns (Princeton, N.J.: Princeton University
      Press, 1961). See also *The New Larousse Encyclopedia of Mythology*, trans. Aldington
      and Anies (London: Prometheus Press, 1968), 136, and Robert Graves, *The Greek
      Myths* (Baltimore: Penguin Books, 1955) 1:75, 76.
14   The etymological derivation of "Hestia" from classical Greek back to pre-Homeric
      times (from "essence" to "being" to "the ruling power of all things") is given by
      Plato, *Cratylus* 401c, trans. Bengamin Jowett, in *Plato: Collected Dialogues*.
15   Lady Poverty is a prominent figure in Eastern asceticism and in Christianity from its
      origins through the Renaissance. In patriarchal accounts, though not in lesbian
      economics, Lady Poverty is extolled for her obedience to her Father, who has
      commanded her to give up all her earthly wealth and follow him. Among the earlier
      accounts of Lady Poverty's life, see *The Lady Poverty*, trans. Montgomery Carmichael
      (London: Burns and Oats, 1901).
16   Arthur Frederick Ide, *Woman in Greek Civilization before 100* B.C. (Mesquite: Ide
      House, 1983), 28; Simone de Beauvoir, *The Second Sex*, trans. H. M. Parshley (New
      York: Vintage, 1974), 130. *WIN News* 9 (Summer 1983): 52; *WIN News* 10 (Summer
      1984): 56; *Women's Economic Agenda*, May 1984, 1.
17   Linda Lim, "Are Multinationals the Problem?" *Multinational Monitor* 4 (August
      1983): 14.
18   *WIN News* 7 (Winter 1981): 73; *WIN NEWS* 8 (Winter 1982): 63; *WIN News*
      9 (Winter 1983): 15, 66.
19   *WIN News* 7 (Winter 1981): 77; *WIN News* 8 (Spring 1982): 78.
20   *WIN News* 6 (Summer 1980): 42.
21   Madhu Kishwar, "Challenging the Denial of Land Rights to Women," *Manushi*,
      Nov.-Dec. 1982, 2, 3; Judy C. Bryson, "Women and Agriculture in Sub-Sahara
      Africa: Implications for Development," *Journal of Development Studies* 17 (April
      1981): 33, 34, 43- *WIN News* 7 (Winter 1981): 24; *WIN News* 7 (Summer 1981): 8;
      United Nations, FAO, *Women in Food Production, Food Handling and Nutrition: With
      Special Emphasis on Africa*, FAO Technical Paper 8 (1978), 122.
22   "Bank," probably of Scandinavian origin, is akin to the Old English *benc*, meaning
      "bench," from which is derived "banker" in the sense of a wooden workbench. *The
      Oxford English Dictionary* (Oxford: Oxford University Press, 1971), 1:162, 163.
23   Ide, *Women in Greek Civilization*, 21, Ann Jones, *Women Who Kill* (New York: Holt
      Rinehart and Winston, 1980), 19.
24   Joan Erikson, *St. Francis and His Four Ladies* (New York: Norton, 1970), 78.
25   *WIN News* 7 (Spring 1981): 62, *WIN News* 8 (Spring 1982): 67; *WIN News* 9
      (Summer 1983); 52, 66. See also Diane Elston and Ruth Pearson, "Women in Third
      World Manufacturing," *Feminist Review* 7 (Spring 1981); Susan S. Green, "Silicon
      Valley's Women Workers," in *Women, Men, and the Intenational Division of Labor*, ed.
      June Nash and Patricia Fernandez-Kelly (Albany: SUNY Press, 1983), 296.
26   Beauvoir, *The Second Sex*, 66.

27   Ibid., 65.
28   *Women's Economic Agenda*, May 1984, 15.
29   Diane Elston and Ruth Pearson, "The Latest Phase of the Internationalization of Capital and Its Implications for Women in the Third World," *IDS Discussion Paper* DP 150 (June 1980), 24.
30   The abolition of work is proposed, though in a quite different context, by the surrealists, and later is developed by political philosophers such as Marcuse. See André Breton, "La Dernière Greve," *La Revue surrealiste* 4 (1925): 1–3; Herbert Marcuse, *Eros and Civilization*, 157; *Reason and Revolution* (Boston: Beacon, 1960), 292.

Queer economic history

THE QUEST TO PROVE CAUSATION in economic theory remains an important point of contention in queer economics. For instance, do economic forces contribute to the social construction of sexuality, or has sexuality shaped the way that our economy functions?

In John D'Emilio's influential early piece, "Capitalism and gay identity" (1983), he argues for the importance of dispelling myths about gay and lesbian history, in particular the myth of the "eternal homosexual." D'Emilio considers the relationship between capitalism, envisioned as a "free labor" system (as opposed to, for instance, slavery, serfdom, or socialism), and homosexuality. If both the definition of the family and gender relations are dependent in large part on the economic system in which families and individuals operate, then heterosexual and homosexual roles and behaviors are also dependent in part on the nature of the system.

The application of Marxian economics, as a historically based economics rather than the ahistorical neoclassical, or mainstream economics, can aptly be applied to arguments that there are causal relationships between the economy and social constructions of sexuality. However, although it is unclear whether Marx intentionally or unintentionally ignored the sexual and familial aspects of economic theory, the outcome is that we see economists using both mainstream and Marxian economic theory without seeing the need or place for any heterosexual or familial constructions. Nonetheless, feminist writers have used Marx's theory successfully in the past for some of their purposes.

Julie Matthaei is a leading feminist economist and queer economist who is solidly grounded in Marxian theory. Matthaei believes, as articulated in "The sexual division of labor, sexuality, and lesbian/gay liberation: towards a Marxist-feminist analysis of sexuality in US capitalism" (1995), that our economy in the nineteenth and twentieth centuries has formed our notions of proper sexuality in the institutions of labor and marriage. She argues that only recently, with the rise of the lesbian, gay, and feminist movements, have these social constructions been attacked effectively.

Matthaei also argues that for times previous to the gay/lesbian liberation of the 1970s, it is revisionist to find the "hidden gay history" (in contrast to D'Emilio, and to Escoffier 1997), since those who may identify as queer today had no such label or modern construction of gender. She also applies this argument against revisionist history to the division of labor argument, citing that, until recently, full gender occupational segregation was preferred over any gender mix because it was believed that men and women working together could not uphold the ideal, steady workplace. Section Six on queer labor economics, which follows, considers whether workplace segregation by gender and sexual orientation has placed specific costs on particular groups, measured mainly in terms of effects on their earnings and thus their income.

DISCUSSION QUESTIONS

1   Do you agree that economic systems dictate the social constructions of sexuality and sexual orientation? Why or why not?
2   In what ways might occupational segregation have contributed to social constructions of sexuality?
3   Have gender and/or sexual orientation dictated some measure of social segregation in the past? What about in current society?
4   Would you expect more or less social segregation on the basis of sexuality or sexual orientation in a capitalistic system than in either a feudal or a socialist system? Why or why not?
5   How, if at all, has the feminist and gay/lesbian movements changed the economic structure of the United States? What are some examples, economically and socially, of resistance to these changes?

REFERENCE

Escoffier, J. (1997) "The political economy of the closet: notes toward an economic history of gay and lesbian life before Stonewall," in A. Gluckman and B. Reed (eds) *Homo Economics: capitalism, community, and lesbian and gay life*, New York and London: Routledge.

Chapter 11

John D'Emilio

CAPITALISM AND GAY IDENTITY

From *Powers of Desire: the politics of sexuality*, eds Ann Snitow, Christine Stansell, and Sharon Thompson, New York: Monthly Review Press, 1983, pp. 100–13

FOR GAY MEN AND LESBIANS, the 1970s were years of significant achievement. Gay liberation and women's liberation changed the sexual landscape of the nation. Hundreds of thousands of gay women and men came out and openly affirmed same-sex eroticism. We won repeal of sodomy laws in half the states, a partial lifting of the exclusion of lesbians and gay men from federal employment, civil rights protection in a few dozen cities, the inclusion of gay rights in the platform of the Democratic Party, and the elimination of homosexuality from the psychiatric profession's list of mental illnesses. The gay male subculture expanded and became increasingly visible in large cities, and lesbian feminists pioneered in building alternative institutions and an alternative culture that attempted to embody a liberatory vision of the future.

In the 1980s, however, with the resurgence of an active right wing, gay men and lesbians face the future warily. Our victories appear tenuous and fragile; the relative freedom of the past few years seems too recent to be permanent. In some parts of the lesbian and gay male community, a feeling of doom is growing: analogies with McCarthy's America, when "sexual perverts" were a special target of the Right, and with Nazi Germany, where gays were shipped to concentration camps, surface with increasing frequency. Everywhere there is the sense that new strategies are in order if we want to preserve our gains and move ahead.

I believe that a new, more accurate theory of gay history must be part of this political enterprise. When the gay liberation movement began at the end of the 1960s, gay men and lesbians had no history that we could use to fashion our goals and strategy. In the ensuing years, in building a movement without a knowledge of our history, we instead invented a mythology. This mythical history drew on personal experience, which we read backward in time. For instance, most lesbians and gay men in the 1960s first discovered their homosexual desires in isolation, unaware of others, and without resources for naming and understanding what they felt. From this experience, we constructed a myth of silence, invisibility, and isolation as the essential characteristics of gay life in the past as well as the present. Moreover, because we faced so many oppressive laws, public policies, and cultural beliefs, we projected this into an image of the abysmal past: until gay liberation, lesbians and gay men were always the victims of systematic, undifferentiated, terrible oppression.

These myths have limited our political perspective. They have contributed, for instance, to an overreliance on a strategy of coming out – if every gay man and lesbian in America came out, gay oppression would end – and have allowed us to ignore the institutionalized ways in which homophobia and heterosexism are reproduced. They have encouraged, at times, an incapacitating despair, especially at moments like the present: How can we unravel a gay oppression so pervasive and unchanging?

There is another historical myth that enjoys nearly universal acceptance in the gay movement, the myth of the "eternal homosexual." The argument runs something like this: gay men and lesbians always were and always will be. We are everywhere; not just now, but throughout history, in all societies and all periods. This myth served a positive political function in the first years of gay liberation. In the early 1970s, when we battled an ideology that either denied our existence or defined us as psychopathic individuals or freaks of nature, it was empowering to assert that "we are everywhere." But in recent years it has confined us as surely as the most homophobic medical theories, and locked our movement in place.

Here I wish to challenge this myth. I want to argue that gay men and lesbians have *not* always existed. Instead, they are a product of history, and have come into existence in a specific historical era. Their emergence is associated with the relations of capitalism; it has been the historical development of capitalism – more specifically, its free labor system – that has allowed large numbers of men and women in the late twentieth century to call themselves gay, to see themselves as part of a community of similar men and women, and to organize politically on the basis of that identity.[1] Finally, I want to suggest some political lessons we can draw from this view of history.

What, then, are the relationships between the free labor system of capitalism and homosexuality? First, let me review some features of capitalism. Under capitalism, workers are "free" laborers in two ways. We have the freedom to look for a job. We own our ability to work and have the freedom to sell our labor power for wages to anyone willing to buy it. We are also freed from the ownership of anything except our labor power. Most of us do not own the land or the tools that produce what we need, but rather have to work for a living in order to survive. So, if we are free to sell our labor power in the positive sense, we are also freed, in the negative sense, from any other alternative. This dialectic – the constant interplay between exploitation and some measure of autonomy – informs all of the history of those who have lived under capitalism.

As capital – money used to make more money – expands, so does this system of free labor. Capital expands in several ways. Usually it expands in the same place, transforming small firms into larger ones, but it also expands by taking over new areas of production: the weaving of cloth, for instance, or the baking of bread. Finally, capital expands geographically. In the United States, capitalism initially took root in the Northeast, at a time when slavery was the dominant system in the South and when noncapitalist Native American societies occupied the western half of the continent. During the nineteenth century, capital spread from the Atlantic to the Pacific, and in the twentieth, U.S. capital has penetrated almost every part of the world.

The expansion of capital and the spread of wage labor have effected a profound transformation in the structure and functions of the nuclear family, the ideology of family life, and the meaning of heterosexual relations. It is these changes in the family that are most directly linked to the appearance of a collective gay life.

The white colonists in seventeenth-century New England established villages structured around a household economy, composed of family units that were basically self-sufficient, independent, and patriarchal. Men, women, and children farmed land owned by the male head of household. Although there was a division of labor between men and women, the family was truly an interdependent unit of production: the survival of each member depended on the cooperation of all. The home was a workplace where women processed raw farm products into food for daily consumption, where they made clothing, soap, and candles, and where husbands, wives, and children worked together to produce the goods they consumed.

By the nineteenth century, this system of household production was in decline. In the Northeast, as merchant capitalists invested the money accumulated through trade in the production of goods, wage labor became more common. Men and women were drawn out of the largely self-sufficient household economy of the colonial era into a capitalist system of free labor. For women in the nineteenth century, working for wages rarely lasted beyond marriage; for men, it became a permanent condition.

The family was thus no longer an independent unit of production. But although no longer independent, the family was still interdependent. Because capitalism had not expanded very far, because it had not yet taken over – or socialized – the production of consumer goods, women still performed necessary productive labor in the home. Many families no longer produced grain, but wives still baked into bread the flour they bought with their husbands' wages; or, when they purchased yarn or cloth, they still made clothing for their families. By the mid-1800s, capitalism had destroyed the economic self-sufficiency of many families, but not the mutual dependence of the members.

This transition away from the household family-based economy to a fully developed capitalist free labor economy occurred very slowly, over almost two centuries. As late as 1920, 50 percent of the U.S. population lived in communities of fewer than 2,500 people. The vast majority of blacks in the early twentieth century lived outside the free labor economy, in a system of sharecropping and tenancy that rested on the family. Not only did independent farming as a way of life still exist for millions of Americans, but even in towns and small cities women continued to grow and process food, make clothing, and engage in other kinds of domestic production.

But for those people who felt the brunt of these changes, the family took on new significance as an affective unit, an institution that produced not goods but emotional satisfaction and happiness. By the 1920s among the white middle class, the ideology surrounding the family described it as the means through which men and women formed satisfying, mutually enhancing relationships and created an environment that nurtured children. The family became the setting for a "personal life," sharply distinguished and disconnected from the public world of work and production.[2]

The meaning of heterosexual relations also changed. In colonial New England, the birthrate averaged over seven children per woman of childbearing age. Men and women needed the labor of children. Producing offspring was as necessary for survival as producing grain. Sex was harnessed to procreation. The Puritans did not celebrate *hetero*sexuality but rather marriage; they condemned *all* sexual expression outside the marriage bond and did not differentiate sharply between sodomy and heterosexual fornication.

By the 1970s, however, the birthrate had dropped to under two. With the exception of the post-World War II baby boom, the decline has been continuous for two centuries, paralleling the spread of capitalist relations of production. It occurred even when access to contraceptive devices and abortion was systematically curtailed. The decline has included every segment of the population – urban and rural families blacks and whites, ethnics and WASPs, the middle class and the working class.

As wage labor spread and production became socialized, then, it became possible to release sexuality from the "imperative" to procreate. Ideologically, heterosexual expression came to be a means of establishing intimacy, promoting happiness, and experiencing pleasure. In divesting the household of its economic independence and fostering the separation of sexuality from procreation, capitalism has created conditions that allow some men and women to organize a personal life around their erotic/emotional attraction to their own sex. It has made possible the formation of urban communities of lesbians and gay men and, more recently, of a politics based on a sexual identity.

Evidence from colonial New England court records and church sermons indicates that male and female homosexual behavior existed in the seventeenth century. Homosexual *behavior*, however, is different from homosexual *identity*. There was, quite simply, no "social space" in the colonial system of production that allowed men and women to be gay. Survival was structured around participation in a nuclear family. There were certain homosexual acts – sodomy among men, "lewdness" among women – in which individuals engaged, but family was so pervasive that colonial society lacked even the category of homosexual or lesbian to describe a person. It is quite possible that some men and women experienced a stronger attraction to their own sex than to the opposite sex – in fact, some colonial court cases refer to men who persisted in their "unnatural" attractions – but one could not fashion out of that preference a way of life. Colonial Massachusetts even had laws prohibiting unmarried adults from living outside family units.[3]

By the second half of the nineteenth century, this situation was noticeably changing as the capitalist system of free labor took hold. Only when *individuals* began to make their living through wage labor, instead of as parts of an interdependent family unit, was it possible for homosexual desire to coalesce into a personal identity – an identity based on the ability to remain outside the heterosexual family and to construct a personal life based on attraction to one's own sex. By the end of the century, a class of men and women existed who recognized their erotic interest in their own sex, saw it as a trait that set them apart from the majority, and sought others like themselves. These early gay lives came from a wide social spectrum: civil servants and business executives, department store clerks and college professors, factory operatives, ministers, lawyers, cooks, domestics, hoboes, and the idle rich: men and women, black and white, immigrant and native born.

In this period, gay men and lesbians began to invent ways of meeting each other and sustaining a group life. Already, in the early twentieth century, large cities contained male homosexual bars. Gay men staked out cruising areas, such as Riverside Drive in New York City and Lafayette Park in Washington. In St. Louis and the nation's capital, annual drag balls brought together large numbers of black gay men. Public bathhouses and YMCAs became gathering spots for male homosexuals. Lesbians formed literary societies and private social clubs. Some working-class women "passed" as men to obtain better paying jobs and lived with other women – lesbian couples who appeared to the world as husband and wife. Among the faculties of women's colleges, in the settlement houses, and in the professional associations and clubs that women formed one could find lifelong intimate relationships supported by a web of lesbian friends. By the 1920s and 1930s, large cities such as New York and Chicago contained lesbian bars. These patterns of living could evolve because capitalism allowed individuals to survive beyond the confines of the family.[4]

Simultaneously, ideological definitions of homosexual behavior changed. Doctors developed theories about homosexual*ity*, describing it as a condition, something that was inherent in a person, a part of his or her "nature." These theories did not represent scientific breakthroughs, elucidations of previously undiscovered areas of knowledge; rather, they were an ideological response to a new way of organizing one's personal life. The popularization of the medical model, in turn, affected the consciousness of the women and men who experienced homosexual desire, so that they came to define themselves through their erotic life.[5]

These new forms of gay identity and patterns of group life also reflected the differentiation of people according to gender, race, and class that is so pervasive in capitalist societies. Among whites, for instance, gay men have traditionally been more visible than lesbians. This partly stems from the division between the public male sphere and the private female sphere. Streets, parks, and bars, especially at night, were "male space." Yet the greater visibility of white gay men also reflected their larger numbers. The Kinsey studies of the 1940s and 1950s found significantly more men than women with predominantly homosexual histories, a situation caused, I would argue, by the fact that captialism had drawn far more men than women into the labor force, and at higher wages. Men could more easily construct a personal life independent of attachments to the opposite sex, whereas women were more likely to remain economically dependent on men. Kinsey also found a strong positive correlation between years of schooling and lesbian activity. College-educated white women, far more able than their working-class sisters to support themselves, could survive more easily without intimate relationships with men.[6]

Among working-class immigrants in the early twentieth century closely knit kin networks and an ethic of family solidarity placed constraints on individual autonomy that made gayness a difficult option to pursue. In contrast, for reasons not altogether clear, urban black communities appeared relatively tolerant of homosexuality. The popularity in the 1920s and 1930s of songs with lesbian and gay male themes – "B. D. Woman," "Prove It on Me," "Sissy Man," "Fairey Blues" – suggests an openness about homosexual expression at odds with the mores of whites. Among men in the rural West in the 1940s, Kinsey found extensive incidence of homosexual behavior, but, in contrast with the men in large cities, little consciousness of gay identity. Thus even as capitalism exerted a homogenizing influence by gradually transforming more individuals into wage laborers and separating them from traditional communities, different groups of people were also affected in different ways.[7]

The decisions of particular men and women to act on their erotic/emotional preference for the same sex, along with the new consciousness that this preference made them different, led to the formation of an urban subculture of gay men and lesbians. Yet at least through the 1930s this subculture remained rudimentary, unstable, and difficult to find. How, then, did the complex, well-developed gay community emerge that existed by the time the gay liberation movement exploded? The answer is to be found during World War II, a time when the cumulative changes of several decades coalesced into a qualitatively new shape.

The war severely disrupted traditional patterns of gender relations and sexuality, and temporarily created a new erotic situation conducive to homosexual expression. It plucked millions of young men and women, whose sexual identities were just forming, out of their homes, out of towns and small cities, out of the heterosexual environment of the family, and dropped them into sex-segregated situations – as GIs, as WACs and WAVEs, in same-sex rooming houses for women workers who relocated to seek employment. The war freed millions of men and women from the settings where heterosexuality was normally imposed. For men and women already gay, it provided an opportunity to meet people like themselves. Others could become gay because of the temporary freedom to explore sexuality that the war provided.[8]

Lisa Ben, for instance, came out during the war. She left the small California town where she was raised, came to Los Angeles to find work, and lived in a women's boarding house. There she met for the first time lesbians who took her to gay bars and introduced her to other gay women. Donald Vining was a young man with lots of homosexual desire and few gay experiences. He moved to New York City during the war and worked at a large YMCA. His diary reveals numerous erotic adventures with soldiers, sailors, marines, and civilians at the Y where he worked, as well as at the men's residence club where he lived, and in parks, bars, and movie theaters. Many GIs stayed in port cities like New York, at YMCAs like the one where Vining, worked. In his oral histories of gay men in San Francisco, focusing on the 1940s, Allan Bérubé has found that the war years were critical in the formation of a gay male *community* in the city. Places as different as San Jose, Denver, and Kansas City had their first gay bars in the 1940s. Even severe repression could have positive side effects. Pat Bond, a lesbian from Davenport, Iowa, joined the WACs during the

1940s. Caught in a purge of hundreds of lesbians from the WACs in the Pacific, she did not return to Iowa. She stayed in San Francisco and became part of a community of lesbians. How many other women and men had comparable experiences? How many other cities saw a rapid growth of lesbian and gay male communities?[9]

The gay men and women of the 1940s were pioneers. Their decisions to act on their desires formed the underpinnings of an urban subculture of gay men and lesbians. Throughout the 1950s and 1960s, the gay subculture grew and stabilized so that people coming out then could more easily find other gay women and men than in the past. Newspapers and magazines published articles describing gay male life. Literally hundreds of novels with lesbian themes were published.[10] Psychoanalysts complained about the new ease with which their gay male patients found sexual partners. And the gay subculture was not just to be found in the largest cities. Lesbian and gay male bars existed in places like Worcester, Massachusetts, and Buffalo, New York; in Columbia, South Carolina, and Des Moines, Iowa. Gay life in the 1950s and 1960s became a nationwide phenomenon. By the time of the Stonewall Riots in New York City in 1969 – the event that ignited the gay liberation movement – our situation was hardly one of silence, invisibility, and isolation. A massive, grass-roots liberation movement could form almost overnight precisely because communities of lesbians and gay men existed.

Although gay community was a precondition for a mass movement, the oppression of lesbians and gay men was the force that propelled the movement into existence. As the subculture expanded and grew more visible in the post-World War II era, oppression by the state intensified, becoming more systematic and inclusive. The Right scapegoated "sexual perverts" during the McCarthy era. Eisenhower imposed a total ban on the employment of gay women and men by the federal government and government contractors. Purges of lesbians and homosexuals from the military rose sharply. The FBI instituted widespread surveillance of gay meeting places and of lesbian and gay organizations, such as the Daughters of Bilitis and the Mattachine Society. The Post Office placed tracers on the correspondence of gay men and passed evidence of homosexual activity on to employers. Urban vice squads invaded private homes, made sweeps of lesbian and gay male bars, entrapped gay men in public places, and fomented local witch hunts. The danger involved in being gay rose even as the possibilities of being gay were enhanced. Gay liberation was a response to this contradiction.

Although lesbians and gay men won significant victories in the 1970s and opened up some safe social space in which to exist, we can hardly claim to have dealt a fatal blow to heterosexism and homophobia. One could even argue that the enforcement of gay oppression has merely changed locales, shifting somewhat from the state to the arena of extralegal violence in the form of increasingly open physical attacks on lesbians and gay men. And, as our movements have grown, they have generated a backlash that threatens to wipe out our gains. Significantly, this New Right opposition has taken shape as a "profamily" movement. How is it that capitalism, whose structure made possible the emergence of a gay identity and the creation of urban gay communities, appears unable to accept gay men and lesbians in its midst? Why do heterosexism and homophobia appear so resistant to assault?

The answers, I think, can be found in the contradictory relationship of capitalism to the family. On the one hand, as I argued earlier, capitalism has gradually undermined the material basis of the nuclear family by taking away the economic functions that cemented the ties between family members. As more adults have been drawn into the free labor system, and as capital has expanded its sphere until it produces as commodities most goods and services we need for our survival, the forces that propelled men and women into families and kept them there have weakened. On the other hand, the ideology of capitalist society has enshrined the family as the source of love, affection, and emotional security, the place where our need for stable, intimate human relationships is satisfied.

This elevation of the nuclear family to preeminence in the sphere of personal life is not accidental. Every society needs structures for reproduction and childrearing, but the possibilities are not limited to the nuclear family. Yet the privatized family fits well with capitalist relations of production. Capitalism has socialized production while maintaining that the products of socialized labor belong to the owners of private property. In many ways, childrearing has also been progressively socialized over the last two centuries, with schools, the media, peer groups, and employers taking over functions that once belonged to parents. Nevertheless, capitalist society maintains that reproduction and childrearing are private tasks, that children "belong" to parents, who exercise the rights of ownership. Ideologically, capitalism drives people into heterosexual families: each generation comes of age having internalized a heterosexist model of intimacy and personal relationships. Materially, capitalism weakens the bonds that once kept families together so that their members experience a growing instability in the place they have come to expect happiness and emotional security. Thus, while capitalism has knocked the material foundation away from family life, lesbians, gay men, and heterosexual feminists have become the scapegoats for the social instability of the system.

This analysis, if persuasive, has implications for us today. It can affect our perception of our identity, our formulation of political goals, and our decisions about strategy.

I have argued that lesbian and gay identity and communities are historically created, the result of a process of capitalist development that has spanned many generations. A corollary of this argument is that we are *not* a fixed social minority composed for all time of a certain percentage of the population. *There are more of us* than one hundred years ago, more of us than forty years ago. And there may very well be more gay men and lesbians in the future. Claims made by gays and nongays that sexual orientation is fixed at an early age, that large numbers of visible gay men and lesbians in society, the media, and the schools will have no influence on the sexual identities of the young, are wrong. Capitalism has created the material conditions for homosexual desire to express itself as a central component of some individuals' lives; now, our political movements are changing consciousness, creating the ideological conditions that make it easier for people to make that choice.

To be sure, this argument confirms the worst fears and most rabid rhetoric of our political opponents. But our response must be to challenge the underlying belief that homosexual relations are bad, a poor second choice. We must not slip into the opportunistic defense that society need not worry about tolerating us, since only homosexuals become homosexuals. At best, a minority group analysis and a civil rights strategy pertain to those of us who already are gay. It leaves today's youth – tomorrow's lesbians and gay men – to internalize heterosexist models that it can take a lifetime to expunge.

I have also argued that capitalism has led to the separation of sexuality from procreation. Human sexual desire need no longer be harnessed to reproductive imperatives, to procreation; its expression has increasingly entered the realm of choice. Lesbians and homosexuals most clearly embody the potential of this split, since our gay relationships stand entirely outside a procreative framework. The acceptance of our erotic choices ultimately depends on the degree to which society is willing to affirm sexual expression as a form of play, positive and life-enchancing. Our movement may have begun as the struggle of a "minority," but what we should now be trying to "liberate" is an aspect of the personal lives of all people – sexual expression.[11]

Finally, I have suggested that the relationship between capitalism and the family is fundamentally contradictory. On the one hand, capitalism continually weakens the material foundation of family life, making it possible for individuals to live outside the family, and for a lesbian and gay male identity to develop. On the other, it needs to push men and women into families, at least long enough to reproduce the next generation of workers. The elevation of the family to ideological preeminence guarantees that capitalist society will reproduce not just children, but heterosexism and homophobia. In the most profound sense, capitalism is the problem.[12]

How do we avoid remaining the scapegoats, the political victims of the social instability that capitalism generates? How can we take this contradictory relationship and use it to move toward liberation?

Gay men and lesbians exist on social terrain beyond the boundaries of the heterosexual nuclear family. Our communities have formed in that social space. Our survival and liberation depend on our ability to defend and expand that terrain, not just for ourselves but for everyone. That means, in part, support for issues that broaden the opportunities for living outside traditional heterosexual family units: issues like the availability of abortion and the ratification of the Equal Rights Amendment, affirmative action for people of color and for women, publicly funded daycare and other essential social services, decent welfare payments, full employment, the rights of young people – in other words, programs and issues that provide a material basis for personal autonomy.

The rights of young people are especially critical. The acceptance of children as dependents, as belonging to parents, is so deeply ingrained that we can scarcely imagine what it would mean to treat them as autonomous human beings, particularly in the realm of sexual expression and choice. Yet until that happens, gay liberation will remain out of our reach.

But personal autonomy is only half the story. The instability of families and the sense of impermanence and insecurity that people are now experiencing in their personal relationships are real social problems that need to be addressed. We need political solutions for these difficulties of personal life. These solutions should not come in the form of a radical version of the pro-family position, of some left-wing proposals to strengthen the family. Socialists do not generally respond to the exploitation and economic inequality of industrial capitalism by calling for a return to the family farm and handicraft production. We recognize that the vastly increased productivity that capitalism has made possible by socializing production is one of its progressive features. Similarly, we should not be trying to turn back the clock to some mythic age of the happy family.

We do need, however, structures and programs that will help to dissolve the boundaries that isolate the family, particularly those that privatize childrearing. We need community- or worker-controlled day-care, housing where privacy and community coexist, neighborhood institutions – from medical clinics to performance centers – that enlarge the social unit where each of us has a secure place. As we create structures beyond the nuclear family that provide a sense of belonging, the family will wane in significance. Less and less will it seem to make or break our emotional security.

In this respect gay men and lesbians are well situated to play a special role. Already excluded from families as most of us are, we have had to create, for our survival, networks of support that do not depend on the bonds of blood or the license of the state, but that are freely chosen and nurtured. The building of an "affectional community" must be as much a part of our political movement as are campaigns for civil rights. In this way we may prefigure the shape of personal relationships in a society grounded in equality and justice rather than exploitation and oppression, a society where autonomy and security do not preclude each other but coexist.

Notes

This essay is a revised version of a lecture given before several audiences in 1979 and 1980. I am grateful to the following groups for giving me a forum in which to talk and get feedback: the Baltimore Gay Alliance, the San Francisco Lesbian and Gay History Project, the organizers of Gay Awareness Week 1980 at San Jose State University and the University of California at Irvine, and the coordinators of the Student Affairs Lectures at the University of California at Irvine.

Lisa Duggan, Estelle Freedman, Jonathan Katz, Carole Vance, Paula Webster, Bert Hansen, and the editors of this volume provided helpful criticisms of an earlier draft. I especially want to thank Allan Bérubé and Jonathan Katz for generously sharing with me their own research, and Amber Hollibaugh for many exciting hours of nonstop conversation about Marxism and sexuality.

1   I do not mean to suggest that no one has ever proposed that gay identity is a product of historical change. See, for instance, Mary McIntosh, "The Homosexual Role," *Social Problems* 16 (1968): 182–92; Jeffrey Weeks, *Coming Out: Homosexual Politics in Britain* (New York: Quartet Books, 1977). It is also implied in Michel Foucault, *The History of Sexuality*, vol. 1: *An Introduction*, tr. Robert Hurley (New York: Pantheon, 1978). However, this does represent a minority viewpoint and the works cited above have not specified how it is that capitalism as a system of production has allowed for the emergence of a gay male and lesbian identity. As an example of the "eternal homosexual" thesis, see John Boswell, *Christianity, Social Tolerance, and Homosexuality* (Chicago: University of Chicago Press, 1980), where "gay people" remains an unchanging social category through fifteen centuries of Mediterranean and Western European history.

2   See Eli Zaretsky, *Capitalism, the Family, and Personal Life* (New York: Harper and Row, 1976); and Paula Fass, *The Damned and the Beautiful: American Youth in the 1920s* (New York: Oxford University Press, 1977).

3   Robert F. Oaks, " 'Things Fearful to Name:' Sodomy and Buggery in Seventeenth-Century New England," *Journal of Social History* 12 (1978): 268–81; J. R. Roberts, "The Case of Sarah Norman and Mary Hammond," *Sinister Wisdom* 24 (1980): 57–62; and Joanthan Katz, *Gay American History* (New York: Crowell, 1976), pp. 16–24, 568–71.

4   For the period from 1870 to 1940 see the documents in Katz, *Gay American History*, and idem, *Gay/Lesbian Almanac* (New York: Crowell, 1983). Other sources include Allan Bérubé, "Lesbians and Gay Men in Early San Francisco: Notes Toward a Social History of Lesbians and Gay Men in America," unpublished paper, 1979; Vern Bullough and Bonnie Bullough, "Lesbianism in the 1920s and 1930s: A New found Study," *Signs* 2 (Summer 1977): 895–904.

5   On the medical model see Weeks, *Coming Out*, pp. 23–32. The impact of the medical model on the consciousness of men and women can be seen in Louis Hyde, ed., *Rat and the Devil: The Journal Letters of F. O. Matthiessen and Russell Cheney* (Hamden, Conn.: Archon, 1978), p. 47, and in the story of Lucille Hart in Katz, *Gay American History*, pp. 258–79. Radclyffe Hall's classic novel about lesbianism, *The Well of Loneliness*, published in 1928, was perhaps one of the most important vehicles for the popularization of the medical model.

6   See Alfred Kinsey et al., *Sexual Behavior in the Human Male* (Philadelphia: W. B. Saunders, 1948) and *Sexual Behavior in the Human Female* (Philadelphia: W. B. Saunders, 1953).

7   On black music, see "AC/DC Blues: Gay Jazz Reissues," Stash Records, ST-106 (1977) and Chris Albertson, *Bessie* (New York: Stein and Day, 1974); on the

persistence of kin networks in white ethnic communities see Judith Smith, "Our Own Kind: Family and Community Networks in Providence," in *A Heritage of Her Own*, ed. Nancy F. Cott and Elizabeth H. Pleck (New York: Simon and Schuster, 1979), pp. 393–411; on differences between rural and urban male homoeroticism see Kinsey et al., *Sexual Behavior in the Human Male*, pp. 455–57, 630–31.

8   The argument and the information in this and the following paragraphs come from my book *Sexual Politics, Sexual Communities: The Making of a Homosexual Minority in the United States, 1940–1970* (Chicago: University of Chicago Press, 1983). I have also developed it with reference to San Francisco in "Gay Politics, Gay Community: San Francisco's Experience," *Socialist Review 55* (January-February 1981): 77–104.

9   Donald Vining, *A Gay Diary, 1933–1946* (New York: Pepys Press, 1979); "Pat Bond," in Nancy Adair and Casey Adair, *Word Is Out* (New York: New Glide Publications, 1978), pp. 55–65; and Allan Bérubé, "Marching to a Different Drummer: Coming Out During World War II," a slide/talk presented at the annual meeting of the American Historical Association, December 1981, Los Angeles. A shorter version of Bérubé's presentation can be found in *The Advocate*, October 15, 1981, pp. 20–24, and in this volume.

10   On lesbian novels see *The Ladder*, March 1958, p. 18; February 1960, pp. 14–15; April 1961, pp. 12–13; February 1962, pp. 6–11; January 1963, pp. 6–13; February 1964, pp. 12–19; February 1965, pp. 19–23; March 1966, pp. 22–26; and April 1967, pp. 8–13. *The Ladder* was the magazine published by the Daughters of Bilitis.

11   This especially needs to be emphasized today. The 1980 annual conference of the National Organization for Women, for instance, passed a lesbian rights resolution that defined the issue as one of "discrimination based on affectional/sexual preference/orientation," and explicitly disassociated the issue from other questions of sexuality such as pornography, sadomasochism, public sex, and pederasty.

12   I do not mean to suggest that homophobia is "caused" by capitalism, or is to be found only in capitalist societies. Severe sanctions against homoeroticism can be found in European feudal society and in contemporary socialist countries. But my focus in this essay has been the emergence of a gay identity under capitalism, and the mechanisms specific to capitalism that made this possible and that reproduce homophobia as well.

Chapter 12

Julie Matthaei

THE SEXUAL DIVISION OF LABOR, SEXUALITY, AND LESBIAN/GAY LIBERATION: TOWARD A MARXIST-FEMINIST ANALYSIS OF SEXUALITY IN U.S. CAPITALISM

From *Review of Radical Political Economics* (1995) 27, (2)

IN THIS PAPER, I will try to draw out some of the ways in which the economic sphere – especially the division of labor between the sexes – has contributed to the construction of sexuality during the past century and a half in the United States. I will show how economic forces have helped create both heterosexual and homosexual relationships – with emphasis on the latter, which have received very little attention from economists. I will also argue that the late twentieth century emergence of a lesbian and gay political movement – and of a feminist movement in which lesbians have played key roles – constitutes a direct challenge to the sexual division of labor and gender. Since I cover a broad sweep of history, this analysis will be, of necessity sketchy. In particular, I will not be able to address adequately the class and racial-ethnic variations in sexuality. Nor can I integrate the many noneconomic factors that have contributed to the changing construction of sexuality. However, I hope to be able to show that the economy has played an important part in shaping and transforming sexuality.[1]

This paper builds predominantly upon the work of historians of sexuality, and on basic feminist theory. There is little recent work on sexuality written from a Marxist or radical economics perspective. Marxist economic theory essentially ignores the family and sexuality; when necessary, it assumes heterosexuality. Marxist-feminist theory has focused on the institution of heterosexuality as key to patriarchy; it has shown how the sexual division of labor, and in particular the exclusion of women from high-paying jobs, has forced women into unequal marriages with men, which include the provision of unpaid domestic labor to their husbands.[2] However, these analyses essentially equate sexuality with marriage, and usually ignore homosexuality.[3] Furthermore, as Ann Fergusoh (1989, 1991) has pointed out, these analyses have utilized a "rational self-interested" view of the individual, which cannot comprehend either "unconscious libidinal motivations" or the motivations of individuals by "symbolic definitions of gender, racial, sexual and family identity," all of which are key to understanding gender and sexuality (Ferguson 1989: 32). Rhonda Gottlieb's path-breaking article, "The Political Economy of Sexuality" (1984), examined some of the basic aspects of sexuality in capitalism, including the male-centeredness of heterosexual sex, the grounding of heterosexuality and male-defined sexuality in the sex-typing of jobs, and the egalitarian aspects of many homosexual relationships. Unfortunately, there has been no response to it (not one citation in the *Social Science Citation Index*!). Here I will try to address the topic of economics and sexuality from a radical economics framework, as does Gottlieb, but with a more historical focus.

I find this to be a difficult topic, and it is one in which I am by no means an expert. However, I think that it is important that economists, especially Marxist-feminists, along with feminist social scientists in general – all of whom have remained more or less silent on the subject – begin to include an analysis of sexuality in their work. In not accounting for sexuality, they relegate it to an extrasocial given. One result is that they end up assuming heterosexuality and erasing homosexuality. For example, Marxist-feminist and feminist analyses of the family, of housework, and of reproduction almost always assume a heterosexual family. In doing so, they erase gays and lesbians, thereby contributing to our oppression. It has been gay and lesbian studies, centered in history and the humanities, that has done the most both to recognize the existence of homosexuality and to analyze sexuality itself (including heterosexuality) as a social construct.

Sexuality as socially, and economically, constructed

One of the most valuable insights of Marxist economics is the recognition that individuals are constructed – i.e. produced and reproduced as social beings – by the relationships that they enter into with other members of their society. Economic relationships constitute a key part of this social production of the individual. Not only is a certain type of person constructed by a certain type of economy – for example, advanced capitalism constructs an individuated, consumption-oriented, self-seeking person – but also, economic relationships differentiate people, for example by class, race-ethnicity, and gender. This social constructionist view of the individual is the polar opposite of the prevailing neoclassical view, which starts with a predetermined individual whose preferences, along with those of other isolated individuals, determine the economy (for a neoclassical analysis of sexuality, see Posner 1992[4]).

The social constructionist view of sexuality or sexual preference, in turn, rejects biological explanations of sexual desire, behavior, and identity. Jeffrey Weeks, a historian of sexuality and a leader in the development of the social constructionist school, has written:

> We tend to see sexuality as a protean force, drawing on the resources of the body, providing the energy for myriad manifestations of desire, and having unique effects. But the more we explore this "special case" of sex, the more variegated, ambivalent and racked by contradiction it seems. There is, I would argue, no simple relationship between "sex" and "society" . . . no easy fit between biological attributes, unconscious fantasy and desire, and social appearance and identity. The mediating elements are words and attitudes, ideas and social relations. The erotic possibilities of the human animal, its generalized capacity for warmth, intimacy and pleasure, can never be expressed "spontaneously" without intricate transformation; they are organized through a dense web of beliefs, concepts and social activities in a complex and changing history. (Weeks 1985: 4)

A social constructionist view of sexuality views it as neither genetically/naturally determined nor as a purely self-conscious moral choice. Social institutions and practices not only direct and restrict one's sexual behavior, but also give this behavior its content and meaning. "Each society seems to have a limited range of potential storylines for its sexual scripts," as Stephen Epstein has noted (1987:24).[5] Theorizing about sexuality involves studying the social construction of a constellation of possible sexual behaviors at a particular place and time. Thus, neither heterosexuality nor homosexuality is either "natural" or universal; both are socially produced. Even if biologists were able to identify a genetic marker that appeared to be correlated with homosexual behavior of some sort (which they have not), this marker could not in any way be understood to determine or create homosexuality as a culturally specific set of social concepts and practices.[6]

Time and place matter: sexuality as historical and cultural

The growth of the gay liberation and feminist movements in the 1970s engendered the development of the field of lesbian and gay history. The earliest studies were essentially searches for the lesbians and gay men of all times and places whose sexuality had been obscured by earlier historians. However, as the field developed breadth and sophistication, the rising social constructionist school criticized such studies as "essentialist" for incorrectly positing a cross-historical lesbian or gay identity. Indeed, historians of sexuality have criticized the very idea of "gay history," since the concepts that construct sexuality have varied so greatly across time.[7]

As far as I know, there are no universals about human sexuality that hold true for all time periods and societies. In the United States, sexual practices have changed very rapidly in the past 150 years, along with capitalist development; the very concepts of heterosexual and homosexual persons did not even arise until the early twentieth century, as we will discuss below. Neither is homophobia/heterosexism – prejudice against and fear of homosexuals/homosexual behavior – a universal given throughout human history. Consider, for example, the oft-admired Greeks, who viewed man-boy love (including sex) as one of the highest forms of love. Or certain Native American nations, including the Kaska and Navajo, in which lesbians were highly valued (Amott and Matthaei 1991: 37). Neither is there an unambiguous one-to-one correspondence between the economic system that characterizes a society and its sexual practices – compare the tolerance for homosexuality in the Netherlands with the repression presently practiced in Great Britain.

These historical and cross-cultural differences make difficult any historical study of sexuality (or indeed, of any social construct, be it the family, gender, or whatever). In this study, I try to stake out a conceptual middle ground between the extremes of total historical specificity (which precludes meaningful cross-historical comparison) and of universalization (which falsely projects the present social practices onto the past).

An additional problem one encounters when analyzing sexuality, even within a particular historical period, is the variation of sexuality across race-ethnicity, gender, and class. A person's sexuality is not, in the metaphor of Elizabeth Spelman (1988), a discrete "pop-bead" on his or her necklace of identity that takes the same form regardless of the gender, class, or race-ethnicity it is combined with. We are all aware of the significant interconnections between sexuality and gender – indeed, few would presume to discuss sexuality without specifying the genders of the participants. However, race-ethnicity and class also differentiate sexuality in important ways. For example, in the nineteenth century, white middle- and upper-class women were constructed as relatively asexual, endangered by the lust of Black men (for which the latter were lynched), while free

Black women, viewed by the dominant white society as oversexed and "loose," were not allowed to protest against their rape by white men (hooks 1981: ch. 2). Where I can, I will specify the class and racial-ethnic aspects of the sexualities studied; unfortunately, the available literature upon which I have based this paper usually slights or simply ignores the sexual practices of those who are poor or of color.

The sexual division of labor, the social construction of gender, and homophobia

Economic institutions, in particular the organization of work into men's and women's work, have played an important role in the social construction of family and sexuality. Until very recently, it was simply accepted that individuals could not and would not be permitted to perform the work of the "opposite sex." God-given, biological differences in abilities between the sexes, it was argued, made only males fit for men's work, and only females fit for women's. For example, only females/women were seen to possess the "maternal instincts" necessary for the raising of small children.

This sexual division of labor, present in all previously known societies, has assigned the biological sexes (males, females) to different and complementary work activities, men's work and women's work, respectively. In general, women's work has centered on caring for children within the family, while men's work has been focused outside of the family, involving interfamilial relationships, such as market-oriented production or political activity. When wage labor developed, jobs were typed either men's or women's work – if not in general, then at least within a particular region or work place (Matthaei 1982: ch. 9). Among European Americans in the United States, the sexual division of labor has always involved the political and economic domination of women by men; among certain Indian nations, on the other hand, the gender differences it constructed did not involve the subordination of women to men (Amott and Matthaei 1991: ch. 3).

The sexual division of labor plays a key role in constructing gender identity – masculinity and femininity, or manhood and womanhood – because preparation for and involvement in different and complementary work activities makes the sexes into different and complementary genders, masculine men and feminine women. However, this division of labor is only one part of the social construction of gender, which begins much earlier. One's gender identity is assigned at birth, according to one's perceived biological sex, and is imprinted upon the infant and child's personality at every level, from clothing to recreation to vocabulary and way of speaking. Most people, then, by the time they are adults, accept their assigned gender identities as given and immutable parts of themselves – and actively attempt to prove and reprove them to others by doing things appropriate to their gender and by distancing themselves from behaviors attributed to the "opposite sex."[8]

While gender roles have been viewed, by society, as emerging naturally out of the biological differences between the sexes, they are in fact social constructs that are achieved only through a great deal of limiting and molding of a person's being (Hubbard, Henifin, and Fried 1982). This limiting and molding is not always successful. For example, females and males whose physiques and characters predispose them for the incorrect gender role (e.g., large, strong, and aggressive females, or small, slight, sensitive males) may find it difficult to become women and men, respectively. They may even find themselves criticized and taunted by parents and schoolmates for their deviant-for-their-sex looks or behavior. While such social ostracism may work to pressure some people into heightened efforts to "fit in," it can also succeed in convincing others that their efforts to conform to their correct gender roles are doomed – that they are really "men in women's bodies" (or vice versa) or belong to some in-between gender.[9] Some individuals, especially females as we will see, consciously choose to reject their gender roles for those of the opposite sex. Those who cross gender lines in this way often take up the sexuality connected with their new gender roles, forming heterogenderal (cross-gender) but homosexual (same-sex) relationships: for example, a masculine female with a feminine female, or an effeminate male with a masculine male.

The sexual division of labor, marriage, and sexuality in the nineteenth century

An essential part of gender identity has been the social requirement to marry and form a family with a member of the opposite sex and gender. Women marry only men, and men only women. The sexual division of labor has provided much of the incentive for marriage, as well as the glue keeping these marriages together, since it makes the genders economically and socially complementary and in need of one another. In this way, gender, and the sexual division of labor that accompanies it, can be seen as involving "compulsory heterosexuality," i.e., as forcing males and females to marry one another (Rich 1980).

As capitalism developed in the United States, the sexual division of labor concentrated income in the hands of men within each racial-ethnic group and class (with the exception of enslaved African Americans). Within each of these groups, men's jobs were much higher paying than women's, and the work of homemaking and child care was assigned to wives, daughters, and domestic servants (mostly female). Hence, most women needed fathers or husbands to provide them with sufficient income to survive and support their children, while most men needed wives to take care of their children and their homes.[10] Once women were married, their inability to survive financially without their husbands placed them in a subordinate position, forced to serve their husbands in whatever ways necessary to "keep them." In this sense, a husband became a woman's "meal ticket," and many women were constrained from leaving unhappy or even dangerous marriages by their financial dependence upon their husbands. So although chosen marriages based in love increasingly replaced marriages arranged by parents (Matthaei 1982: 116–118), women did have to consider a man's financial position before deciding whether to accept a marriage proposal.

If economic forces pressured adults to marry the opposite sex, organized religion both propounded the necessity of marriage and attempted to restrict sexuality to it. Nineteenth-century Protestantism defined "good sex" as being only procreative sex within marriage. All other kinds of sexuality – from fornication (sexual intercourse between unmarried members of the opposite sex) to sodomy (any erotic physical relations that could not result in pregnancy, including anal sex between same- or opposite-sex partners, masturbation, and oral sex) – were assumed to be sins that tempted individuals, especially men, but that should be resisted (D'Emilio 1983: 104; Katz 1983: 140–5; Weeks 1977: 4, 12). Birth control and abortion were illegal. Further, love was not linked with sexual passion; indeed, the white middle- and upper-class idea of "true love" at this time involved nothing erotic – it was an "affinity between two disembodied souls," which could be of the same or opposite sexes (Snitow, Stansell, and Thompson 1983: 14).

However, other factors reduced the incidence of marriage and the confinement of sexual acts to marriage. First, a variety of economic and social forces made it difficult for many to marry. The social practice of marrying within one's class and race (laws against "miscegenation" were on the books in many states until the 1950s!), combined with regional imbalances in the numbers of men and women, limited the availability of potential partners. The migration to the West Coast, among both whites and Asians, was disproportionately male, restricting opportunities for marriage; in California in 1850, there were twelve men for every woman, and the imbalance was, much greater among Asians (Amott and Matthaei 1991: 201). Among African Americans, the problem was not the sex ratio but their status as property; marriages of enslaved African Americans had no legal recognition, and were often broken up by profit-seeking owners. For American Indians, this period was one of displacement and genocide, clearly disruptive of marriage relationships (Amott and Matthaei 1991: 16–7). In 1890, 16 percent of women and 28 percent of men between the ages of 25 and 44 were reported to be single and never married; almost 22 percent of women and 30 percent of men were reported to be single, widowed, or divorced (U.S. Department of Commerce 1976: 21); substantial numbers were also married, but separated.

Second, the sexual division of labor provided less financial incentive for men to marry than it did for women. Given their access to higher wage jobs, most men were able to live independently off of their earnings, purchasing in the market most of the services which a wife provided, from meals to laundry to sex and companionship.[11] Indeed, some men chose never to marry, a choice they could make much more easily than could women, who often remained single for lack of a marriage proposal.

Third, sexuality within marriage was restricted, at least among the most-studied white middle and upper classes. Much has been made of the Victorian view of white women's sexuality – i.e., their lack of sexual feelings – and certainly this view was present, if not omnipresent. Historians have also pointed out the objective reasons that married women had for trying to limit their sexual relations with their husbands, factors that may have contributed to the ideology of woman's sexlessness. For one thing, birth control was illegal and difficult to obtain, and many women feared the dangers of miscarriage and pregnancy as well as the extra work of each additional child. In addition, the construction of marital sexuality, within the parriarchal power relations of marriage, was around the husband's sexual gratification (Gottlieb 1984: 144–50); women often found it brutish, even violent, and far from sexually arousing – an unpleasant duty to be performed. Furthermore, since men commonly exposed themselves to venereal diseases through their relations with prostitutes, wives often feared contracting these dreaded illnesses from sexual intercourse with their husbands. Indeed, nineteenth-century feminists formed a "Voluntary Motherhood" movement, centered on the assertion of every woman's right to say no to sex with her husband (and hence to the possibility of pregnancy and motherhood) (Degler 1980: ch. II; Gordon 1976: ch. 5). The lesser interest of women in sexuality – plus the concentration of income in men's hands – helped fuel men's pursuit of sex outside marriage from prostitutes.

The sexual division of labor and female and male prostitution

The nineteenth-century view of sexuality as either procreation or sin, however, was not successful in restricting it to marriage. As we have seen above, many people were not married. And while unmarried women were expected to remain "chaste" or risk losing their marriageability and being saddled with "illegitimate" children, unmarried men were expected to need and seek out sexual outlets – to "sow their wild oats" – even if this was viewed as sinful. Even though married women were expected to be sexual only with their husbands, married men were actively encouraged, if backhandedly, toward sexual relations outside marriage. The social construction of masculinity as driven by sexual desires, or lust, for sexual objects; the practice of men paying for their fiancees' and wives' expenses, i.e., purchasing women's sexual services; the restriction of sex within many marriages; and the gender and class differences that distributed money unevenly – all of these factors contributed to the establishment of sexuality as an industry, i.e., prostitution, that catered to men and employed a class of women who became unmarriageable (Gilfoyle 1992).

The existence of women prostitutes who serviced men of all classes is well documented. If sex within marriage was to be passionless, rare, and aimed at procreation, then men could appease their sexual desires outside of marriage with "bad" girls. And for working-class girls and women who lacked good marriage prospects or simply chose not to marry, prostitution offered much higher pay than the pittance they could earn at the other jobs that were open to them. Many working-class girls became professional prostitutes, especially within the cities; others, called "charity girls" in the nineteenth century, provided sexual favors to men in exchange for gifts, meals, and entertainment that were otherwise out of their financial reach (Peiss 1983). Among whites, prostitution was very common in the cities, as well as in all parts of the woman-scarce West. Free Black women, whose job opportunities were especially restricted, often turned to prostitution in southern cities, where they served both Black and white clientele (Arnott and Matthaei 1991: 150). The sex imbalance in Chinese and Japanese immigration (25 men to 1 woman among Japanese immigrants, for example, in 1900) made for a very profitable prostitution business: women were sold or kidnapped in their home countries, sent to the United States, and kept as slaves prostitutes (Amott and Matthaei 1991: 201, 219).

What is perhaps less well known is that male prostitution was also very common (indeed, the word "gay" in the nineteenth century referred to a prostitute [Weeks 1977: 42]). Weeks estimates that about half of the prostitutes in Europe in the late nineteenth-century cities were young men; I have not found comparable data for the United States, but male prostitution appears to have been common, especially in large cities. Weeks points out the continuity between male heterosexual and homosexual sex/prostitution: the interest was in sex; encounters were usually casual, not long term; the prostitute was a sex object, performing sexual services in exchange for money or gifts; the client was a man with money to spend.

Male prostitutes were very similar to female ones: young; working class; interested in pay that was many times what they could earn at their jobs; servicing their clients' sexual needs, usually by bringing them to orgasm. Some were full-time "professionals," who worked out of brothels or "boy-houses"; they often dressed like women. Detective Gardener describes a New York brothel in 1892: "In each room sat a (male) youth, whose face was painted, eye-brows blackened, and whose airs were those of a young girl. Each person talked in a high falsetto voice, and called the others by women's names." German sexologist Magnus Hirschfeld wrote of meeting, in Chicago, "a Negro girl on Clark Street who turned out to be a male prostitute" (Katz 1976: 63, 77).

There were also many part-time male prostitutes, who were working-class youth employed in low-wage jobs: sailors, soldiers, laborers, newspaper boys, messenger boys, and the like (Weeks 1989: 207; Katz 1976: 64, 78). For this group, prostitution was a way to supplement very low wages or, like the charity girls, to give them access to "the better life." A gay academic wrote Hirschfeld a long letter describing the homosexual life, including this description of part-time male prostitutes:

> In the vicinity of Denver there is a military fort with a force of a few hundred men. Last summer a soldier from there propositioned me on the street in Denver. I've heard that this happens quite frequently in San Francisco and Chicago. I recall meeting a soldier who was a prostitute long ago in San Antonio, Texas, and last summer I met a young sailor from Massachusetts. The latter was on leave and looking for homosexual intercourse out on the street late at night. In all of these cases it was difficult to tell whether the soldiers were really homosexual or just prostitutes, or whether they went with men for lack of anything better. It's never easy to draw the line, and things are so expensive nowadays that someone could easily be moved to earn a little pocket money in one way or the other. (Katz 1976: 78)

Some men may have become male prostitutes because it gave them a way to live out aspects of the feminine gender role to which they were attracted – feminine dress, a desire to be a passive sexual partner, erotic attraction to a man. In a sense, they wanted to be women, and were doing "women's work" of prostitution. In some cases, such effeminate males actually "treated" their sexual partners: one study of Newport, Rhode Island, sailors in 1919 found that a gang of effeminate sailors would "take a sailor to a show or to dinner, offer him small gifts, or provide him with a place to stay when he was on overnight leave; in exchange, the sailor allowed his host to have sex with him that night, within whatever limits the sailor cared to set." Some of these gay sailors provided sexual services to civilian men in exchange for money, while others had steady relationships with masculine men they referred to as their "husbands" (Chauncey 1990: 299, 303).

While most sexuality in nineteenth-century capitalism involved the cash nexus, either overtly in prostitution, or covertly in marriage, casual male homosexual relations also could take the form of a sexual encounter in which both partners satisfied sexual needs and no exchange of money or gifts was necessary. After all, men were constructed as lustful beings, who desired sex for its own sake. Plus, there was no problem of unwanted pregnancy as in heterosexual sex. The male homosexual subculture that emerged in this period involved "cruising places" where men could meet – certain streets, beaches, woods, bars, or bath houses – to engage in mutually satisfying casual sex. Often, relationships crossed class lines. Gender roles were often involved, including "balls" where males dressed as women. Sometimes race differences were played on: one sexologist discovered, in St. Louis, a group of Black male butlers, cooks, and chauffeurs, who dressed as women for their encounters with white, masculine males (Katz 1976: 66–67, 75–76).

Females who lived as men: lesbianism as a response to gender inequality and oppression

While the sexual division of labor helped pressure women into heterosexual marriage, its rigid confines also led some females to reject womanhood and heterosexuality.[12] Some of these rebels worked as feminists to challenge gender roles in society at large. Others rebelled privately by becoming men: they dressed as men, did men's work, and married women. Many "passed" so effectively that they were not found out until their deaths, at which time their femaleness was cause for great surprise and, often, media attention. Murray Hall became a well-known New York City politician; his death, and femaleness, were covered in the *New York Times* and the New York *Daily Tribune*. One of Hall's acquaintances was quoted as saying: "While he was somewhat effeminate in appearance and talked in a falsetto voice, still his conduct and actions were distinctively masculine. This revelation [of Hall's femaleness] is a stunner to me and, I guess, to everybody else who knew him" (Katz 1976: 356).

Accounts of the lives of passing women indicate that many if not most of them were driven into passing by the inequality and oppression involved in the sexual division of labor – in particular, by the gender-typing of jobs and the restriction of females/women to low-paid jobs. Many passing women directly referred to their inability to survive on women's wages in explaining their decisions to take up the masculine gender. A female who called herself Charles Warner wrote in the 1860s:

> When I was about 20 I decided that I was almost at the end of my rope. I had no money and a woman's wages were not enough to keep me alive. I looked around and saw men getting more money and more work, and more money for the same kind of work. I decided to become a man. It was simple, I just put on men's clothing and applied for a man's job. I got

it and got good money for those times, so I stuck to it (Berube 1979:1).

According to the *Day Book* tabloid newspaper of Chicago, Cora Anderson, an American Indian, studied nursing with Marie White, who was white, at the Provident Hospital in Chicago. The two formed a relationship but found it difficult to survive on nurses' wages – and Cora was unwilling to accede to sexual harrassment: "Two-thirds of the physicians I met made a nurse's virtue the price of their influence in getting her steady work. Is it any wonder that I determined to become a member of this privileged sex, if possible?" The two moved to Cleveland as the Kerwinnieos, with Cora becoming the husband, Ralph. "This disguise also helped me to protect my chum as well as myself. She could stay in the home, and believe me, as long as society, with its double code and double standards of morals, is as it is now, the only place for a woman is in the home." Ralph worked as a bellboy and later for a manufacturer. Later, Ralph left Marie to marry another woman. Marie responded by exposing Ralph as a passing woman, and Cora/Ralph was charged with "disorderly conduct" (Katz 1976: 385–90).

Another passing woman, Caroline Hall, decided to live as "Mr. Hall," according to a *New York Times* story in 1901, because of her "belief that women were not afforded as many opportunities in the world as men." She was an artist who was "an excellent rifle shot," and, as a man, traveled in Italy as a painter, entering and winning several rifle contests. She/he met and became domestic partners with Giuseppina Boriani (Katz 1976: 365–68).

It appears that passing women were from all classes and races. Edward Stevenson wrote of a group of about ten women, most likely African American, who passed as men to work as porters, train agents, switchmen, and cooks for the New York Central Railway in 1903 (Katz 1976: 378–79). Mary Fields, an ex-slave, passed and found employment as a stagecoach driver (Faderman 1991: 44). It was also common for women who wished to fight in wars to pass as men; many were found out when they were wounded in battle. One Civil War expert estimated that 400 females fought as men in that war; one such female, accepted as a man, was a spy who "posed" as a woman! (Katz 1976: 323, 345–46, 363, 909–910). I have found references to females passing as men to practice medicine in the early 1800s (U.S. Dept. of Labor 1974: 21–23) and in the early 1900s (Faderman 1991: 317), and to female (passing as men) sailors (Katz 1976: 905–914).

Sometimes daughters started the process of gender switching at the behest of their parents. For example, Lucy Ann Lobdell, the only child of a farm couple, took on men's work to help her parents, both of whom were disabled by illness. When she reached adulthood, she decided to actually take up life as a man. As she explained:

> First, my father was lame, and in consequence, I had worked indoors and out [on the farm, and hunting]; and as hard times were crowding upon us, I made up my mind to dress in men's attire to seek labor, as I was used to men's work. And as I might work harder at house-work, and get only a dollar per week, and I was capable of doing men's work, and getting men's wages, I resolved to try . . . to get work away among strangers. (Katz 1976: 333)

During her life as a man, Lucy (who took the name of Joseph) supported herself as a hunter and trapper, and married a woman who had been abandoned by her husband and was living on charity. Lucy/Joseph had to work to hide her femaleness. While changing one's gender wasn't acceptable in her society, in contrast, among the Canadian Kaska nation, it was common and accepted for families lacking sons to urge one of their daughters to become a man (Amott and Matthaei 1991: 37).

While anecdotal evidence points to many passing women who formed long-term relationships with other women, the evidence leaves many questions unanswered. For example, we cannot determine whether it was the economic disadvantage of being a woman or the potential for partnering with another woman that was more likely to be the primary impetus for a woman to pass. And what of the female/women partners of passing women? Some, it appears, were not aware that their husbands were female.[13] Others married "men" they knew to be females, because of love or perhaps because of bad experiences they had with male men.[14] Males passing as women seem to have been much less common, probably because of the clear loss in economic power and social status that this involved.

Similars attract: the gender divide, romantic friendships, and "gay" jobs

Even for those who did not reject their assigned gender role, the rigid sexual division of labor of the nineteenth century tended to spawn intimate homosocial (and perhaps homosexual) relationships, especially between women, because of the vast social chasm it opened up between the sexes. Men's and women's work and social lives were so disparate, their interests and sensibilities so opposed, that real intimacy between them was difficult to achieve, and usually not expected. As Carroll Smith-Rosenberg writes:

> If men and women grew up as they did in relatively homogeneous and segregated sexual groups, then marriage represented a major problem in adjustment. From this perspective we

could interpret much of the emotional stiffness and distance that
we associate with Victorian marriage as a structural consequence
of contemporary sex-role differentiation and gender-role social-
ization. With marriage, both women and men had to adjust to
life with a person who was, in essence, a member of an alien
group. (Smith-Rosenberg 1979: 331)

In contrast, members of the same gender had a good deal in common; they
could understand one another's feelings, thoughts, and experiences, and
hence achieve emotional and intellectual intimacy.

Not only did the rigid sexual division of labor make the genders so
different as to seem alien to one another, but also the nineteenth-century idea
of love, as a nonsexual meeting of souls, was easily applied to same-sex
relationships. What historians have called "romantic friendships" were
common between middle- and upper-class women in the late nineteenth
and early twentieth centuries; all of the documented examples I have seen
appear to have been among white women, but it is probable that they also
occurred among other racial-ethnic groups. Unlike the relationships
between a passing woman and another woman, these relationships were
homogenderal: that is, these (female) women were attracted to a person of
their same, feminine, gender. These women had intense, emotionally and
physically intimate love relationships with other women before and during
their marriages with men (Smith-Rosenberg 1979; Faderman 1981). For
most of these women, their "romantic friendships" were more passionate
and intimate than their marriages; for example, "rural women developed a
pattern of . . . extended visits that lasted weeks and sometimes months, at
times even dislodging husbands from their beds and bedrooms so that dear
friends might spend every hour of every day together" (Smith-Rosenberg
1979: 319).

Close friendships among men – also viewed as love relationships –
were also common, given the gulf between the genders. While there has
been less attention paid to these relationships, they were probably widespread. Discussions of love between men were common in mid-nineteenth-
century popular novels, letters, and diaries, in which "American men loved
each other, sought verbal and physical forms for the expression of that
love, located it in a tradition, and worried about its place in a social order"
(Martin 1990: 170). The celebrated poet Walt Whitman spoke of "adhesive-
ness," love between men, as coexisting with "amativeness" between the
sexes, but finessed the question of sexuality (Weeks 1977: 34, 52–53); the
German sexologist Hirschfeld wrote in 1914, "Strongly sublimated homosexuality is also common in America; a good example is provided by the
poet of comradely love, Walt Whitman" (Katz 1976: 77). Not pressured by
financial need into marriage, men could remain bachelors or maintain their
friendships after marriage.

The rigid sexual division of labor also created homosexuality in another way: jobs that isolated the employee with his/her coworkers tended to spawn homosocial and homosexual relationships, as did the sex segregation of other social institutions. Military and maritime employment, cattle herding (cowboys), and other men's employments in the woman-scarce West encouraged close relationships and sexuality among men. Prostitution, which marginalized and isolated women from the mainstream and from marriage, as well as exercised their sexuality, generated loving relationships were often sexual among women: "They spent all their free time together, traveled together, protected each other, loved each other" (Faderman 1991: 37; see also Nestle 1987: 157–77). The sex-segregated schools that were viewed as preparation for segregated gender roles also, because of their homosocial environment, encouraged homosexual relationships, as did the sex-segregated prison system (Faderman 1991: 19–20, 36–37). Interestingly, women in reform schools formed same-sex relationships across racial (Black-white) lines in which "the difference in color . . . [took] the place of difference in sex," with Black women taking the masculine role (Otis, quoted in Faderman 1991: 38).[15]

Lesbian career women and Boston marriages: a variation on the romantic friendship theme

In the nineteenth and early twentieth centuries, women whom historians have called "social homemakers" worked to expand woman's traditional work of homemaking and, indeed, the boundaries of womanhood; some of these social homemakers were explicitly feminist. While few directly attacked the sexual division of labor, these activists did argue for (middle class) women's right to a college education (to prepare themselves better for motherhood), and for women's claims on emerging professions that they viewed as naturally feminine – teaching, social work, librarianship, and nursing, as well as social activism/social homemaking itself. Black as well as white women participated in this movement and in the emerging women's professions, although Black women encountered virulent discrimination in both (Matthaei 1982: 173–86; Amott and Matthaei 1991: 152–54). As Lillian Faderman has pointed out (1991: ch. 1), access to such jobs gave educated, middle-class females the economic wherewithal to live with other females as life partners, without one member of the couple having to pass as a man (an opportunity working class-women did not have). Indeed, "Many of the leaders of this [social homemaking] movement, including Jane Addams, Vida Scudder, and Frances Willard, not only rejected marriage, but lived with women in intense emotional (and probably sexual) love relationships" (Amott and Matthaei 1991: 125). One suspects that their rejection of heterosexual marriage in favor of relationships with women was a factor underlying their commitment to expanding women's professional options.

Not only did education and career open up women's possibility of nonmarriage, but they also restricted a woman's marriage options: in white middle-class society paid careers were seen to be incompatible with the full-time dedication to homemaking and mothering expected of wives. (Indeed, marriage bars – employer policies to fire female employees upon marriage and/or refuse to hire married women – were common, especially in teaching and clerical work, through the 1940s [Goldin 1990: 160–71]). Thus, the movement for women's college education, and the participation in feminine careers it encouraged and made possible, discouraged those women from heterosexual marriage (Matthaei 1982: ch. 11). Because a college education prepared women for labor force careers, rates of nonmarriage were much higher among college graduates than among nongraduates; one study found that 35 percent of women college graduates born before 1897 had not married by the age of 50, compared to 8 percent of nongraduates (Matthaei 1982: 259).

Thus, the development of women's education and careers both reduced women's opportunities for marriage and increased their ability to form live-in relationships with one another. Women who had formed close emotional (and maybe sexual) relationships in college no longer had to subordinate these "romantic friendships" to marriage, as in previous times, but could set up households together (Faderman 1991: ch. 1; Matthaei 1982: ch. 11). As Jessie Taft, a sociologist, wrote in 1916:

> Everywhere we find the unmarried woman turning to other women, building up with them a real home, finding in them the sympathy and understanding, the bond of similar standards and values as well as the same aesthetic and intellectual interests, that are often difficult of realization in a husband. . . . One has only to know professional women to realize how common and how satisfactory is this substitute for marriage. (Quoted in Matthaei 1982: 260)

Such arrangements were so common in the East that they were called "Boston marriages."

It is interesting to note that these relationships, like the romantic friendships that preceded them, were homogenderal and were usually with members of the same class and race. Sometimes, both women were professionally employed. For example, Katharine Coman (professor of economics) and Katharine Lee Bates (professor of English, and writer of the words to "America the Beautiful"), lived and worked together at Wellesley College (my employer); Katharine Lee Bates wrote a book of poetry to Katharine Coman, entitled *Yellow Clover* (1922), whose dedication reads, in Latin,

"How can it be wrong to love one so dear?" (Schwartz 1979). However, it appears that it was more common for one woman to take on the role of primary provider, and for the other to take on a wifely/motherly role (Vicinus 1992: 482–83; Faderman 1981: ch. 5). The same-class, same-race quality of these relationships contrasts with the prevalence of cross-class and cross-race sexual liaisons among male homosexuals.

The twentieth century: the emergence of heterosexuals and homosexuals

Two important and related changes in the social conceptualization of sexuality occurred as the nineteenth century gave way to the twentieth: the growing connection of sexuality to pleasure and love, and the emergence of "homosexuals" and "heterosexuals." These changes can be connected, at least indirectly, to the process of capitalist development: in particular, as we will see, to the rise of consumerism and to the emergence of a secular and scientific view of the world. Figure 1 lists some of the key aspects of this new view of sexuality, and contrasts it with the nineteenth-century view.

Historian Jonathan Katz (1983) notes that the view of sex as a pleasurable activity for both sexes accompanied the rise of consumerism and the decline of the work ethic that characterized advanced capitalism in the

	19th century	Early 20th century	Late 20th century
System of conceptualization	Religious	Medical	Lesbian/gay liberationist
"Good" sex	Procreative	Heterosexual	Safe, informed consensual
"Bad" sex	Nonprocreative	Homosexual	Unsafe, nonconsensual, uninformed
View of homosexual desire	Felt by all, but not to be acted upon because evil	Only felt by minority of "homosexuals" as result of illness or congenital defect	Can coexist with heterosexual desire; differing views of origins (biological vs. socialization vs. choice)
Problem with homosexual sex	Nonprocreative, hence sinful	An illness, requiring treatment by medical profession	Not a problem

Figure 1 Contrasting views of sexuality

early-twentieth-century United States. Pleasure was to be sought after, through sexuality as well as consumption. The growing acceptance of birth control signified the acceptance of sexual intercourse for its own sake, not for procreation. While all sexual behavior was not seen as involving love, true love now was thought to properly include both sexual passion and the friendship/companionship of the earlier era.

One would think that this revolutionary shift would have eased if not eliminated the stigmatization of homosexual sexual relations – which are intrinsically nonprocreative, and hence clearly centered on pleasure and love. But this was not the case. Instead, the seeking of pleasure through homosexual sexual relations was in the process of being pathologized by "sexologists" in the medical profession, who attempted to analyze such relations scientifically.

In the late nineteenth century, the expanding medical profession began to develop the concept of "inversion" to describe individuals who took on the gender role of the opposite sex, and engaged in heterogenderal, homo-sexual sexual relations. Among males, the "invert" was the one who acted or dressed in feminine ways, including those who took the "feminine" role in homosexual sexual encounters – i.e., men who were "cocksuckers" or who liked to be anally penetrated. (Men who looked and acted masculine, and who played the "masculine" role in sex with men were not similarly labeled and pathologized.) Similarly, the female invert was the passing woman, the female who dressed like a man and took on the masculine gender role, including an active role in sexuality – and not her partner, if the latter took a feminine role (Chauncey 1989).

By the early twentieth century, medicine's focus began to shift from gender role transgression in general to sexual object choice: "homosexual-ity" was the illness from which *all* engaged in same sex sexual relations were thought to suffer, regardless of the gender role they took in those relations or in life in general (Chauncey 1989). Thus, sex-object choice became a key aspect of an individual's identity. One was either heterosexual and normal, or homosexual and abnormal. The latter identity was seen as the result of illness or cogenital flaws, and required treatment by the medical profession, especially by its emerging field of psychiatry. In this way, love and/or sexual relationships with members of one's own sex were increasingly viewed as the behavior of a minority of physically "deviant" homosexuals, anathemas to the vast majority of "normal" heterosexuals (Katz 1983: 142–55). Increasingly, then, individuals who felt emotionally close or who were sexually attracted to members of their own sex – and/or were emotionally or sexually indifferent to or alienated from members of the opposite sex – would begin to accept this new view, define themselves as homosexual, and look for support in the growing homosexual subculture.

The new view of sexuality was tightly tied into gender roles, the sexual division of labor, and heterosexual marriage. Sexually healthy individuals were thought to feel sexual passion for members of the opposite sex, passion that they eventually consummated in love-based heterosexual marriage (although nonprocreative heterosexual sex outside of marriage was increasingly accepted) (Katz 1983: 147–50). Conversely, those who engaged in homosexual sex were not viewed as real women or men, no matter how tightly they conformed to other aspects of their gender roles; they became a sort of "third sex," a new kind of person. This tight connection between sexuality and gender increased pressures on all individuals to conform to other, nonsexual aspects of their gender roles, for fear of being stigmatized as lesbian or gay (Goodman et al. 1983: 36).

While the sexual division of labor remained a cornerstone of heterosexuality during this period, it still contained contradictions that ended up encouraging homosexual behavior. The genders continued to be constructed as "opposite," so that emotional intimacy and mutually satisfying sexuality were difficult to achieve between the genders; at the same time, common experiences and world views – and, for women, common oppression by men – continued to draw together members of the same gender. Many females were unwilling to swallow women's roles "whole hog," given the financial insecurities, subordinate position, and risk of harassment and spousal abuse that were involved. Many males, in turn, found the responsibility of supporting a wife and children overwhelming and unappealing. Others probably simply did not "feel" masculine or feminine enough to consider themselves "normal heterosexuals," especially when another category, homosexual, was defined and connected in the public mind to deviance from assigned gender roles. Indeed, homosexuality, now seen as an identity and way of life (even if a stigmatized one), provided a way to escape restrictive gender roles, as did growing subcultures which supported and validated these choices (Weeks 1991: 69–75). A massive rural-to-urban migration supported these emerging communities by bringing gays together and providing them with relative anonymity.

To establish sexual relationships with members of the same sex, gender roles had to be subverted, amended, played with, or simply rejected. Some females continued to pass as men. Jazz musician Billy Tipton started passing in the 1930s in order to play with the all-male swing bands of that era, and was not "found out" until her death in 1989 (Faderman 1991: 317). Ester left her husband and grown sons in Puerto Rico and moved to New York City, where she took up life as a man taxi-cab driver and lived with her female lover, a prostitute, during the 1950s (Nestle 1987: 40–41).

However, increasing numbers of females who rebelled against womanhood, especially those from the working class, identified themselves not as men but as gay women who were "butch"; modified versions of "passing women," they tried to find jobs where they could dress in pants (such as truck or cab driver, or factory worker), and formed relationships with "fems" who dressed like women. In the working-class lesbian subculture's version of heterogenderality, both women were usually employed, but other aspects of masculine/feminine difference were taken on (Faderman 1991: ch. 7; Kennedy and Davis 1993: 64–65).

Among middle- and upper-class women, romantic friendships and Boston marriages continued. However, the passionate love involved in such same-sex relationships became increasingly suspect and viewed not as a complement to heterosexual marriage but rather as an unacceptable "homosexual" substitute. "Throughout most of the twentieth century . . . the enriching romantic friendship that was common in earlier eras is thought to be impossible, since love necessary means sex and sex between women means lesbian and lesbian means sick" (Faderman 1981: 311).[16] In contrast to working-class lesbian culture, most lesbian career women seemed to prefer androgynous roles and homogenderal relationships (Faderman 1991: 178–87).

Male homosexuality appears to have been more prevalent than lesbianism: Kinsey found in 1948 that over one-third of his sample of men had had sex to orgasm with a man after adolescence (D'Emilio and Freedman 1988: 291). D'Emilio suggests that the greater prevalence of homosexuality among men was due to their greater economic independence and, hence, their greater ability to live outside of marriage (1983: 106). While long-term, monogamous relationships have become increasingly common (especially after the onset of the AIDS epidemic), a large part of gay male life has revolved around casual sex, available at cruising spots, bars, and baths to both married and single men. As Richard Mohr points out, "[male] homosexual relations cur across all social classifications but gender," creating an equalizing or democratizing tendency in the subculture they create (1992: 198).[17] And men's demand for homosexual sex has continued to provide employment for some young gay males; for example, a recent *Boston Globe* article described the division of turf into the "boys' block" (male prostitutes), the "girls' block" (male transvestites and transsexuals), and the "real girls" area (female prostitutes) (Jacobs 1992: 20).

Labor demand and sexuality during the depression and World War II

I have argued that the restriction of women to lower-paid jobs has provided a major economic motive for heterosexuality among women. Lillian Faderman provides an interesting, economically based analysis of the restriction of lesbianism and encouragement of heterosexual marriage in the 1930s. During this decade, high male unemployment generated a groundswell of anger against employed women – particularly against career women or women living independently of men – generating discrimination against women in jobs that could be filled by men "who had families to support." Even the dean of one women's college (Barnard) actively discouraged graduates from paid employment, claiming that this sacrifice would provide a service to their community. Professional women were increasingly portrayed as unwomanly, and their numbers dropped by over 50,000 between 1930 and 1940, even though the female labor force grew by over 500,000 during that period (U.S. Census 1930: 279; U.S. Census 1940: 75). In sum, during the depression years, both economic and social pressures toward heterosexual marriage were strengthened for middle-class young women.

At the same time, Faderman found that some middle- and upper-class married-women, both Black and white, maintained lesbian relationships, one of the most famous being Eleanor Roosevelt.[18] And lesbianism was not uncommon among the substantial numbers of working-class women who dropped through the economic cracks into poverty and homelessness; living the life of hobos, they wore pants, joined with other women for protection, and formed intimate relationships that were sometimes self-consciously lesbian (Faderman 1991: 94–99).

The war economy during World War II shifted the balance between homosexuality and heterosexuality. In dire need of soldiers, the military established a secret policy of toleration of homosexuality in its ranks, as long as it was private and not disruptive. Young men were drafted in large numbers; most gay men appear to have been able to slip through the crude examination that was supposed to screen out homosexuals. Many more "came out" in homosexual relationships within the intimate, high-pressure atmosphere of the barracks (Berube 1990; D'Emilio 1992: 65–66).

In stark contrast to the 1930s, employers now actively recruited women into high-paid war-industry jobs in the cities. This facilitated the development of lesbian relationships: "As wage earners working in well-paying defense jobs, wearing men's clothes to do 'men's work,' and living, working, and relaxing with each other, many women for the first time fell in love with other women, socialized with lesbians, and explored the gay nightlife that flourished in the crowded cities" (Berube 1990: 384–85). Women wearing pants to war-industry jobs began to legitimize that practice among women, making it easier for masculine lesbians to "pass" as heterosexual (Faderman 1991: 125–26), while the absence of men from city streets made it safe for women to be out together without male escorts (Kennedy 1994). Some women enlisted in the Women's Army Corps, which both attracted women-loving women and put women in intimate contact with one another. A WAC lecture to officer candidates explained that, in this work situation, it was natural for women to have relationships "that can become an intimacy that may eventually take some form of sexual expression. It may appear that, almost spontaneously, such a relationship has sprung up between two women, neither of whom is a confirmed active homosexual" (Berube 1990: 385–86).

The 1950s: government-sponsored antigay discrimination

If World War II exerted major pressures against the traditional sexual division of labor and toward women's paid employment, lesbianism, and male homosexuality, the immediate postwar period brought a major backlash consciously aimed at reversing all of these trends. As historian Allan Berube describes:

> Churches, the media, schools, and government agencies conducted a heavy-handed campaign to reconstruct the nuclear family, to force women back into their traditional roles, and to promote a conservative sexual morality. A tactic of this campaign was to isolate homosexual men and women and identify them, like Communists, as dangerous and invisible enemies (Berube 1990: 391).

The military conducted antigay witch hunts, purging thousands of lesbians and gay men from its ranks. Antigay hearings were held in the U.S. Senate, in which it was argued that homosexuals were unfit to be federal employees because they were "generally unsuitable" (due to being abnormal and lacking in emotional stability and moral fiber) as well as because they were "security risks" in certain positions (because they could be blackmailed on the basis of their homosexuality, due to the federal policy of firing them!). President Eisenhower signed an Executive Order barring homosexuals from federal jobs; firing was allowed on the basis of anonymous, unsubstantiated accusations; no appeal was allowed beyond the employee's department. Many state governments followed suit, as did private employers and colleges and universities. Gay and lesbian bars were not a refuge: police raided them and released the names of those arrested to the newspapers, which commonly published them (D'Emilio and Freedman 1988: 292–95; Faderman 1991: ch. 6; Berube 1990: 391–93).

Many lesbians and gay men lost their jobs and careers; those who did not struggled to hide their gayness "in the closet" and lived in perpetual fear of being discovered; many probably chose to give up their gay lifestyles, and many others were deterred from even considering homosexuality. Whether gay or heterosexual, women workers lost their jobs to returning GIs. The pressure on both sexes to "be straight" was strong Women married and sought happiness in caring for husbands and children; men married and shouldered the provider role, anxious to show they were not among the 50 percent of men who Kinsey had found were attracted to their own sex. But a small and brave group of men and women insisted on living gay lives, mostly in cities, and even founded groups that constituted the beginning of the lesbian and gay movement (D'Emilio 1992: 78–79; Kennedy and Davis 1993).

The decline of the sexual division of labor and the attenuation of the economic basis of heterosexuality

Cyclical and war-related ups and downs in women's labor-force participation in the '30s, '40s and '50s did not prevent an overall, secular increase in the entrance of women into the paid labor force full- or part-time – from less than 20 percent of all women in 1900 to 69 percent in 1991 (Matthaei 1982: 142; U.S. Census Bureau 1993: 394). This change was the result of a variety of factors. The growth of needs and consumerism from the 1920s on drew homemakers into the labor force as part of their job of filling family needs. Middle-class women entered higher education as training for home-making, but this education inadvertently prepared them for paid careers and spawned the career woman. The rapid growth of jobs that had been typed feminine, especially clerical jobs, also helped draw women into the labor force (Matthaei 1982: Part 3). After 1970, the movement of women into the labor force gained further momentum as men's average real wages began a long-term decline. As a result, a major part of the sexual division of labor in marriage – the assignment of wage-earning to the husband and only the husband – began to break down to the point that by 1993, 59 percent of married women held paid jobs (U.S. Census Bureau 1993: 399).

The movement of married women into the paid labor force has been accompanied by a second major change in the sexual division of labor. As women began to spend more years of their lives in the paid labor force, and hence to view their jobs not as temporary stints before marriage but as lifelong careers, they began to challenge women's exclusion form the higher paid and higher status "men's jobs" more vigorously. The demand for access to these jobs – i.e., for an end to gender discrimination in employment – became a key demand of the feminist movement, as did a demand for men to share in women's traditional work of homemaking and childrearing (Matthaei 1982: Part 3).

As an increasing share of women are employed, and more of these are in better paid jobs, more and more women have become able to support themselves, and even their children, independently of husbands or fathers. For example, in 1992, 11 million women – almost one third of the women who were employed full-time – held managerial or professional jobs; their median earnings of $562/week exceeded the overall median earnings for full-time employed men, which were $505/week (U.S. Census Bureau 1993: 426). Two million of the women who headed families with children but without husbands – one quarter of the total – lived on annual family incomes of above $25,000 (U.S. Census Bureau 1993: 464).

The increase in the numbers of women who are economically independent of men has had an important effect on sexuality. The economic pressure toward heterosexual marriage has decreased for growing numbers of women, as has the pressure to remain in unhappy marriages. Concurrently, men's overall sense of economic responsibility for women in marriage has declined (Ehrenreich 1983), further fueling women's increasing participation in and commitment to the labor force. The divorce rate has sky-rocketed; the share of women who were married dropped from 71 percent in 1970 to 60 percent in 1992, and the share of those who were either divorced or never married rose from 16 percent to 30 percent (U.S. Census 1993: 53).[19]

At the same time, economic independence from men made it economically feasible for some women to structure their lives around lesbian relationships. A 1989 random phone survey, for example, found the median income for full-time full-year workers was $19,643 among all employed women, but $26,331 among employed lesbians (Badgett 1993: 19).[20] This could be both because higher incomes allow women to live without men, and because women who are lesbians expect to have to support themselves and/or their lovers, and hence invest in more training and stay on the job longer than comparable heterosexual women.

Feminism, lesbian/gay liberation, the attack on the sexual division of labor and gender, and the conservative response

There have been many noneconomic factors contributing to the rise of the feminist and lesbian/gay liberation movements, including the continued persecution of gays and lesbians, the legacy of the civil-rights movement, and the growing secularization of U.S. society. Here I want to focus on the relationship between these movements and the sexual division of labor.

The feminist movement of the 1970s and 1980s was closely linked to lesbianism. On the one hand, lesbians had a higher stake than heterosexual married women in accessing well-paid jobs, since lesbians did not have access to "family wages" through husbands. Furthermore, lesbians had already crossed gender lines in other ways – dress, choice of sexual partner – and were less fearful of losing their "womanhood" and attractiveness to men if they took on "men's jobs" than were heterosexual women. Thus lesbians made up a disproportionate part of the ranks of feminists among all class and racial-ethnic groups. Indeed, French feminist Monique Wittig has argued that feminism has provided lesbian activists with a closeted way of pushing their agenda of dismantling the sexual division of labor and gender roles.[21]

Furthermore, feminist analysis and the movement – especially its radical feminist, socialist feminist, and lesbian feminist components (e.g.,

Koedt, Levine, and Rapone 1973; Sargent 1981; and Johnston 1973, respectively) – have resulted in the "coming out" of many involved. First, feminists developed a critique of the sexual division of labor and of gender roles as being both restrictive to all and oppressive to women. Second, they directly criticized heterosexual marriage because of its subordination of women to men as unpaid servants and sexual objects. Third, many feminists, put forth lesbianism as a viable alternative – even, some argued, *the* appropriate feminist choice, a form of resistance to patriarchy that is more symmetrical and egalitarian than heterosexuality (e.g., Johnston 1973; Radicalesbians 1973; Rich 1980). Many of the leading early feminist theorists – such as Adrienne Rich, Andrea Dworkin, Gayle Rubin, Charlotte Bunch, Mary Daly, Audre, Lorde, Barbara Smith, Cherrie Moraga, and Susan Griffin – were "out" lesbians. Fourth, feminism has brought like minded women together as coparticipants in support and action groups, providing them with potential sexual/love partners.

In other words, feminist movement[22] has encouraged women to challenge and even deviate from traditional gender roles; it has highlighted the oppressiveness of traditional heterosexuality, it has supported and even advocated lesbianism as an option for women; it has encouraged women to pursue "men's" jobs (and fought to open these higher-paying jobs to women), jobs that allow them to survive economically without men; and it has brought women in close and cooperative contact with other like-minded women. When criticized as being lesbian or prolesbian, some feminist groups (such as the early NOW) tried to distance feminism from lesbianism. However, most feminist groups have instead responded by openly supporting their lesbian members and by adding the demand for lesbian and gay civil rights to their platforms.

Meanwhile, the 1969 Stonewall rebellion against a police raid of a gay bar began a growing, out-of-the-closet movement of gay men and lesbians that has asserted our rights to live and love. While the early movement was tied into radical feminism and to the Left, it has become increasingly centered on a liberal agenda of gaining rights and protection from discrimination for lesbians and gays (Seidman 1993). By the early nineties, the movement had succeeded in making antigay discrimination illegal in a number of states. Gay and lesbian couples are demanding and beginning to win recognition as families, with access to spousal benefits and the right to parent. This extension of rights and legal protections to lesbians and gays is gaining increasing public acceptance as a logical extension of civil rights and antidiscrimination principles central to the U.S. ethical/legal system.[23]

Indeed, during his 1992 presidential campaign, Clinton courred the lesbian/gay vote by promising to end discrimination in the military. He reneged on this promise once in office, in the face of vociferous opposition from the military and Congress, and instead compromised with a modest reform: under the new "don't ask, don't tell" policy, the military agreed not to investigate a service member's sexuality, but service members are prohibited from being "out" on their jobs. The terms of the debate on the issue also represented a minor step forward in public discourse. Those who argued against the proposed changes did not use either the religious argument (gays are immoral) or the medical one (gays are mentally or physically compromised). Rather, they argued that the presence of "out" gays in the military would "threaten unit cohesion," an argument centered on the inefficiencies caused by homophobia rather than by homosexuals themselves.

A new, "social" view of sexuality is being put forward by lesbian/gay and feminist movements, in which "bad" sex is sex that creates unwanted children, sex that exposes the participants to disease (especially AIDS), or sex into which either participant has been forced against his/her will (see Figure 1). Our society, it is argued, has the responsibility to support "good" sex by educating us all about sexuality, including reproduction, birth control options, and safe sex; by exposing, condemning, and punishing rape and child sexual abuse; and by supporting an individual's right to engage in homosexual (as well as heterosexual) sex if she/he so chooses, through education, antidiscrimination, and other measures.

In these ways, then, feminism and the lesbian and gay movements, encouraged by and combined with economic developments, have attacked the core of the sexual division of labor – the assignment of individuals to men's or women's work, on the basis of their sex – as well its main corollaries – gender identity as given by sex, and marriage as the union of different and complementary genders. Gender differences are themselves being eroded, as each gender's work and sexual options are expanded, so that gender now has less and less consistent meaning beyond biological sex. If a female/woman can do anything that a male/man can do and still be a woman (and vice versa), then woman is not any different from man, other than biologically.

New principles are arising. The right to choose from among all jobs for which one is qualified, regardless of one's gender. The notion that full individuality (for both males and females) involves participation in family, economy, and polity. The conception of marriage as a union of socially similar beings, be they of the same or opposite sexes (Matthaei 1982: ch. 13, Conclusion; Matthaei 1988). The new concept of "sexual preference," which suggests that sexual orientation is not inborn but rather a choice between two desirable options, a choice that *all* individuals make. The category of bisexual: individuals who refuse to acknowledge an exclusive sexual preference. If gender further fades into sex, we can expect an entirely new set of sexual categories, perhaps not even called "sexual," to emerge (see Figure 1).

The radical nature of these changes, both won and proposed, has called forth a strong conservative reaction, a reaction that has coalesced in the religious and "pro-family" arms of the "New Right." Their goal is to roll back the gains of the feminist and gay movements and to reestablish the "traditional family": a heterosexual married couple with children, in which the husband/breadwinner commands and the wife/full-time homemaker submits. As they see it, "the homosexual movement is nothing less than an attack on our traditional, pro-family values" (Schwartz and Rueda 1987: 8). Key to their ideology is a religious view of sexuality that virtually replicates the nineteenth-century view we have discussed above: homosexual acts, as well as birth control and sex outside of marriage, are seen as sinful because they prevent or cannot lead to the birth of legitimate children; abortion is viewed as murder, pure and simple.[24] In the fall of 1992, the religious right won passage in Colorado of an amendment that prevented state agencies from protecting lesbians and gay men from discrimination; the amendment was later overturned by the courts. A similar but stronger measure was put forward in Oregon that, besides banning nondiscrimination policies, also required government-funded organizations to represent homosexuality as "abnormal, wrong, unnatural, and perverse"; the measure was narrowly defeated. For the 1994 elections, the religious right backed antigay initiatives in ten states; however, only two made it onto ballots (Idaho and Oregon), and both were defeated by voters. However, the Republican takeover of the House and Senate has brought a heightened threat of federal antigay legislation. Meanwhile, the religious right has also been active in local school board elections, their goal being to block or roll back progressive curricular reform such as the inclusion of gay and lesbian families in New York City's "rainbow curriculum." With the backing of a number of semi-independent, well-financed organizations that have trained thousands of committed activists, and with powerful allies in the now-dominant Republican Party, the New Right poses a real threat to the realization of the goals, both liberal and radical, of the feminist and gay rights movements (Cagan 1993; *Gay Community News* 1994: 5–6; Hardisty 1993; *Momentum* 1994: 1).

Acknowledgments

I would like to thank Sumangala Kailasapathy for research assistance. An earlier draft of this paper was presented at "The Economics of Sexual Orientation: Theory, Evidence, and Policy" panel, sponsored by the Union for Radical Political Economics (URPE) at the annual Allied Social Science Associations (ASSA) meetings in Anaheim, California in January 1993. I have benefited from comments made at that session, and at presentations of the paper at the Washington, DC, Economic History Seminar and at the Homo-Economics Conference in the spring of 1994. I would also like to thank the members of the Wellesley Faculty Seminar on Lesbian and Gay

Studies, and Laurie Nisonoff, Jayati Lal, and Ann Davis – the reviewers at *The Review of Radical Political Economics* – for their comments and help.

Notes

Reprinted with permission, with minor changes, from *The Review of Radical Political Economics*, June 1995.

1   A short note regarding my methodology is in order here. My method of argument is an historical and dialectical one, and may discomfort those who think in linear terms, as it did one reviewer. For example, I argue simultaneously that the sexual division of labor is a main force in cementing heterosexual marriage, and that it contains contradictions that help construct homosexual relationships. I do not believe that historical processes can be adequately analyzed through an econometric logic according to which each "independent variable" is thought to have a consistent effect.

2   See, for example, Hartmann (1979), Folbre (1982), and Delphy (1984).

3   Walby (1990) is an exception, as is Ehrlich (1981); neither was trained as an economist. Ferguson (1989), whom I discuss next, is a philosopher.

4   Building on Becker, Posner (1992) argues that an individual's sexual behavior is determined by a combination of genetic predisposition (along Kinsey's range from purely homosexual to purely heterosexual) and rational choice. The latter is then influenced by a number of factors, from sex ratios in the population to urbanization to social policy.

5   As also quoted in Vicinus (1992: 469).

6   See LeVay and Hamer (1994) and Byne (1994) for a recent rehashing of the "gay gene" debate.

7   For more on the constructionist-essentialist debate, see Stein (1990) (especially the essay by Boswell), Vance (1991), and Escoffier (1992).

8   The concept of gender identity, including the difference between sex and gender, is key to women's studies; see, for example, Oakley (1972). The sexual division of labor is a central concept in the work of Marxist-feminist economists and feminist anthropologists; see, for example, Hartmann (1979), Rosaldo and Lamphere (1974), and Amott and Matthaei (1991: ch. 2). More recently, queer theorist Judith Butler has analyzed gender as "an identity renuously constituted in time; instituted in an exterior space through a *stylized repetition of acts*" (1990: 140). These "acts and gestures, articulated and enacted desires create the illusion of an inferior and organizing gender core" (136).

9   See, for example, Morris (1975), the eloquent autobiography of a male who underwant a sex change operation to realize his feminine identity; and Feinberg (1993), in which the main character is taunted and ostracized for not being feminine enough, eventually finds an identity as a butch lesbian, and thinks of herself as a "he-she." Kennedy and Davis (1993) report that "butch identity was based in various combinations of masculine inclination and sexual interest in women"(327).

10   This differs from the neoclassical analysis of the sexual division of labor in marriage. The latter argues that utility maximizing individuals freely choose marriage and specialization because it increases their total utility. Specialization results either from different innate preferences, from different relative abilities to do home and market work, and/or from sex discrimination (women receiving less return than men to their human capital investments).

11   Indeed, historian John D'Emilio (1983) argues that the development of capitalism and wage labor enabled homosexuality, especially male homosexuality, by enabling individuals to provide for their needs outside of a traditional family context. In my opinion, this argument is much stronger for men than it is for women.

12   For a discussion of the historical antecedents of the passing woman, see Vicinus (1992).

13   For example, Dr. Eugene de Savitsch wrote in 1958 of the case of Nicholas de Raylan, a female who passed as a man, in the early 1900s. His/her second wife wept at his death, "declaring that talk of his being a woman was nonsense." The postmortem showed him to be female. "An imitation penis and testicles made of chamois skin and stuffed with down were suspended in the right place by means of a band around the waist" (Katz 1976: 380).

14   For example, the July 25, 1863, *Fitcher's Trades' Review* had a story on a "Curious Married Couple."

> In 1731, a girl named Mary East was engaged to be married to a young man for whom she entertained the strongest affection; but upon his taking to evil courses, or, to tell the whole truth, being hanged for highway robbery, she determined to run no risk of any such disappointment from the opposite sex in future. A female friend of hers having suffered in some similar manner, and being of the like mind with herself, they agreed to pass for the rest of their days as man and wife. . . . The question of which should be the husband was decided by lot in favor of Mary East. (Katz 1978: 343–44).

15   The women were physically segregated by race to some degree within the reform schools.

16   Recent analysis note that even in the mid- and late-nineteenth century, romantic friendships, while acceptable, were viewed as involving potential threats to traditional marriage (Martin 1990; Vicinus 1992).

17   Mohr (1992) quotes Paul Goodman as writing. "Its [queer life's] promiscuity can be a beautiful thing. . . . I have cruised rich, poor, middle class, and petit bourgeois; black, white, yellow and brown; scholars, jocks, Gentlemanly C's, and dropouts; farmers, seamen, railroad men, heavy industry, light manufacturing, communications, business, and finance; civilian, soldiers and sailors, and once or twice cops (1977: 219–21)."

18   Faderman's and others' claims that Eleanor had a homosexual relationship with Lorena Hickock have been hotly disputed or, more commonly, simply ignored by many mainstream biographers.

19   These data were standardized by age. This is not to say that all women have become economically independent. For a substantial share of women, the choice to stay single or to divorce is still a choice to live in poverty; indeed, over one third of all women heading households without husbands present lived in poverty in 1991 (U.S. Census 1993: 471). Many of these women were divorced or abandoned by their husbands. Thus, while a larger share of women is economically independent from men, overall, women's per capita access to resources has declined (Albelda 1988).

20   In this volume, Badgett reports a later research finding showing no significant difference between the average incomes of straight women and lesbians. She also discusses the limitations of all research to date on lesbian and gay incomes, given the paucity of data.

21   Talk by Wittig at Wellesley College in the mid-1980s. Clearly it is impossible to accurately ascertain the numbers of lesbians in different parts of the feminist

movement, due to so many of them being in the closet; however, my personal experiences in many parts of the feminist movement over the past fifteen years, as well as my reading on the subject, lead me to this conclusion.

22   I use the term "feminist movement" instead of "the feminist movement" to emphasize the many different forms feminist organizing has taken, as suggested by bell hooks in her *Feminist Theory: From Margin to Center* (1984).

23   A Gallup poll of Americans reported in *Newsweek* on September 14, 1992, p. 37, found that 67 percent approved of health insurance for gay spouses, 70 percent approved of inheritance rights for gay spouses, and 58 percent approved of Social Security for gay spouses: Significant minorities approved of legally sanctioned gay marriages and adoption rights for gays (35 percent and 32 percent, respectively).

24   One difference, however, is that they do not seem to assume that all feel attractions to members of their own sex. For example, Schwartz and Rueda (1987: 8) write of homosexuality as a "disordered sexual condition" that leads to evil acts in *Gays, AIDS and You* (quoted in Hardisty 1993: 3).

References

Albelda, Randy, et al. 1988. *Mink Coats Don't Trickle Down: The Economic Attack on Women and People of Color*. Boston: South End Press.

Arnott, Teresa, and Julie Matthaei. 1991. *Race, Gender and Work: A Multicultural Economic History of Women in the United States*. Boston: South End Press.

Badgett, M. V. Lee. 1993. The Economic Well-Being of Lesbians and Gay Men: Pride and Prejudice. Paper Presented at a Union of Radical Political Economics-sponsored Session of the 1993 Allied Social Science Associations Meetings. Anaheim, CA.

Bates, Katharine Lee. 1922. *Yellow Clover: A Book of Remembrance*. New York: E. P. Dutton.

Berube, Alan. 1979. Lesbian Masquerade. *Gay Community News*. November 17, 1979.

——— . 1990. Marching to a Different Drummer: Lesbian and Gay GIs in World War II. In *Hidden from History: Reclaiming the Gay and Lesbian Past*, edited by Duberman, Vicinus, and Chauncey, pp. 383–94. New York: Penguin.

Butler, Judith. 1990. *Gender Trouble: Feminism and the Subversion of Identity*. New York: Routledge.

Byne, William. 1994. The Biological Evidence Challenged. *Scientific American* 270(5): 50–55.

Cagan, Leslie. 1993. Community Organizing and the Religious Right: Lessons From Oregon's Measure Nine Campaign. An Interview with Suzanne Pharr. *Radical America* 24(4): 67–75.

Chauncey, George. 1989. From Sexual Inversion to Homosexual: The Changing Medical Concept of Female "Deviance." In *Passion and Power: Sexuality in History*, edited by K. Peiss, et al., pp. 87–119. Philadelphia: Temple University Press.

——— . 1990. Christian Brotherhood or Sexual Perversion? Homosexual Identities and the Construction of Sexual Boundaries in the World War I Era. In

Hidden from History: Reclaiming the Gay and Lesbian Past, edited by Duberman, Vicinus, and Chauncey, pp. 294–317. New York: Penguin.

Degler, Carl N. 1980. *At Odds: Women and the Family in America from the Revolution to the Present*. New York: Oxford University Press.

Delphy, Christine 1984. *Close to Home: A Materialist Analysis of Women's Oppression*. Amherst: University of Massachusetts Press.

D'Emilio, John. 1983. Capitalism and Gay Identity. In *Powers of Desire: The Politics of Sexuality*, edited by Snitow, Stansell, and Thompson. New York: Monthly Review Press.

———. 1992. *Making Trouble: Essays on History, Politics and the University*. New York: Routledge.

D'Emilio, John, and Estelle Freedman. 1988. *Intimate Matters: A History of Sexuality in America*. New York: Harper & Row.

Duberman, Martin, Martha Vicinus, and George Chauncey, Jr. (eds.). 1990. *Hidden from History: Reclaiming the Gay & Lesbian Past*. New York: Penguin.

Ehrenreich, Barbara. 1983. *The Hearts of Men: American Dreams and the Flight from Commitment*. Garden City, NY: Anchor Press/Doubleday.

Ehrlich, Carol. 1981. The Unhappy Marriage of Marxism and Feminism: Can It Be Saved? In *Women and Revolution*, edited by Lydia Sargent. Boston: South End Press.

Escoffier, Jeffrey. 1992. Generations and Paradigms: Mainstreams in Lesbian and Gay Studies. In *Gay and Lesbian Studies*, edited by Minton, pp. 7–88. New York: Haworth Press.

Epstein, Stephen. 1987. Gay Politics, Ethnic Identity: The Limits of Social Constructionism. *Socialist Review* 17(3&4): 9–54.

Faderman, Lillian. 1981. *Surpassing the Love of Men: Romantic Friendship and Love between Women from the Renaissance to the Present*. New York: William Morrow.

———. 1991. *Odd Girls and Twilight Lovers: A History of Lesbian Life in Twentieth-Century America*. New York: Penguin.

Feinberg, Leslie. 1993. *Stone Butch Blues*. Ithaca, NY: Firebrand Books.

Ferguson, Ann. 1989. *Blood at the Root: Motherhood, Sexuality, and Male Dominance*. London: Pandora.

———. 1991. *Sexual Democracy: Women, Oppression, and Revolution*. San Francisco: Westview Press.

Folbre, Nancy. 1982. Exploitation Comes Home: A Critique of the Marxian Theory of Family Labour. *Cambridge Journal of Economics* 6(4):317–29.

Gay Community News. October, 1994. "Bigot Busters V. Religious Right: Bigot Busters Win" 20(3): 5–6.

Gilfoyle, Timothy. 1992. *City of Eros: New York City, Prostitution, and the Commercialization of Sex, 1720–1920*. New York: W. W. Norton.

Goldin, Claudia. 1990. *Understanding the Gender Gap: An Economic History of American Women*. New York: Oxford University Press.

Goodman, Gerre, et al. 1983. *No Turning Back: Lesbian and Gay Liberation for the '80s*. Philadelphia: New Society Publishers.

Goodman, Paul. 1977. The Politics of Being Queer. *Nature Heals: The Psychological*

Essays of Paul Goodman. Edited by Taylor Stoehr, pp. 216–25. New York: Free Life Editions.

Gordon, Linda. 1976. *Woman's Body, Woman's Right.* New York: Grossman Publishers.

Gottlieb, Rhonda. 1984. The Political Economy of Sexuality. *Review of Radical Political Economics* 16: 143–66.

Hardisty, Jean. 1993. Constructing Homophobia: Colorado's Right-Wing Attack on Homosexuals. *The Public Eye: A Publication of Political Research Associates* (March): 1–10.

Hartmann, Heidi. 1979. Capitalism, Patriarchy, and Job Segregation by Sex. In *Capitalist Patriarchy and the Case for Socialist Feminism*, edited by Z. Eisenstein, pp. 206–247. New York: Monthly Review Press.

hooks, bell, 1981. *Ain't I A Woman: Black Women and Feminism.* Boston: South End Press.

Hubbard, Ruth, Mary Sue Henefin, and Barbara Fried (eds.). 1982. *Biological Woman – The Convenient Myth: A Collection of Feminist Essays and a Comprehensive Bibliography.* Cambridge, MA: Schenkman.

Jacobs, Sally. 1992. Cruising and Losing: Young Men Barter Flesh, Dismal Future. *Boston Sunday Globe*, December 20, pp. 1, 20.

Johnston, Jill. 1973. *Lesbian Nation: The Feminist Solution.* New York: Simon and Schuster.

Katz, Jonathan, 1976. *Gay American History: Lesbians and Gay Men in the U.S.A.* New York: Discus/Avon Books.

———. 1983. *Gay/Lesbian Almanac.* New York: Harper & Row.

Kennedy, Elizabeth. 1994. Codes of Resistance in the Buffalo Lesbian Community of the 1950s: Class, Race and the Development of Lesbian Identity. Talk Given at Wellesley College, February 22.

Kennedy, Elizabeth, and Madeline Davis. 1993. *Boots of Leather, Slippers of Gold: The History of a Lesbian Community.* New York: Routledge.

Koedt, A., A. Levine, and A. Rapone (eds.). 1973. *Radical Feminism.* New York: Quadrangle/The New York Times.

LeVay, Simon, and Dean Hamer. 1994. Evidence for a Biological Influence in Male Homosexuality. *Scientific American* 270(5): 44–49.

Martin, Robert K. 1990. Knights-Errant and Gothic Seducers: The Representation of Male Friendship in Mid-Nineteenth-Century America. In *Hidden from History: Reclaiming the Gay and Lesbian Past*, edited by Duberman, Vicinus, and Chauncey, pp. 169–82. New York: Penguin.

Matthaei, Julie. 1982. *An Economic History of Women in America: Women's Work, the Sexual Division of Labor, and the Development of Capitalism.* New York: Schocken Books.

———. 1988. Political Economy and Family Policy. In *The Imperiled Economy, Book 2*, edited by Robert Cherry, et al. New York: Union for Radical Political Economics and Monthly Review Press.

Momentum: The Newsletter for Members of the Human Rights Campaign Fund. " '94 Voters Reject Anti-Gay Discrimination" (Winter 1994): 1.

Mohr, Richard. 1992. *Gay Ideas: Outing and Other Controversies*. Boston: Beacon Press.

Morris, Jan. 1975. *Conundrum*. New York: New American Library.

Nestle, Joan. 1987. *A Restricted Country*. Ithaca, NY: Firebrand Books.

Oakley, Ann. 1972. *Sex, Gender, and Society*. San Francisco: Harper & Row.

Peiss, Kathy. 1983. "Charity Girls" and City Pleasures: Historical Notes on Working-Class Sexuality, 1880–1920. In *Powers of Desire*, edited by Snitow, Stansell, and Thompson. New York: Monthly Review Press.

Posner, Richard A. 1992. *Sex and Reason*. Cambridge: Harvard University Press.

Radicalesbians. 1973. The Woman-Identified Woman. In *Radical Feminism*, edited by Koedt, Levine and Rapone. New York: Quadrangle/The New York Times.

Rich, Adrienne. 1980. Compulsory Heterosexuality and Lesbian Existence. *Signs: Journal of Women in Culture and Society* 5(4): 631–60.

Rosaldo, Michelle, and Louise Lamphere (eds.). 1974. *Woman, Culture, and Society*. Stanford, CA Stanford University Press.

San Francisco Lesbian and Gay History Project. 1990. "She Even Chewed Tobacco": A Pictorial Narrative of Passing Women in America. In *Hidden from History: Reclaiming the Gay and Lesbian Past*, edited by Duberman, Vicinus, and Chauncey, pp. 183–94. New York: Penguin.

Sargent, Lydia (ed.). 1981. *Women and Revolution: A Discussion of the Unhappy Marriage of Marxism and Feminism*. Boston: South End Press.

Schwartz, Judith. 1979. Yellow Clover: Katharine Lee Bates and Katherine Coman. *Frontiers* 4 (1) : 59–67.

Schwartz, Michael, and Enrique Rueda. 1987. *Gays, AIDS and You*. Old Greenwich, CT: Devin Adair Company.

Seidman, Stephen. 1993. Identity and Politics in a "Postmodern" Gay Culture: Some Historical and Conceptual Notes. In *Fear of a Queer Planet*, edited by Michael Warner, pp. 105–42. Minneapolis: University of Minnesota Press.

Smith-Rosenberg, Carroll. 1979. The Female World of Love and Ritual. In *A Heritage of Her Own: Toward a New Social History of American Women*, edited by Nancy F. Cott and Elizabeth H. Pleck, pp. 311–342. New York: Simon and Schuster.

Snitow, Ann, Christine Stansell, and Sharon Thompson (eds.). 1983. *Powers of Desire: The Politics of Sexuality*. New York: Monthly Review Press.

Spelman, Elizabeth. 1988. *Inessential Woman: Problems of Exclusion in Feminist Thought*. Boston: Beacon Press.

Stein, Edward (ed.). 1990. *Forms of Desire: Sexual Orientation and the Social Constructionist Controversy*. New York: Garland Publishing.

U.S. Department of Commerce. Bureau of the Census. 1930. *Census of Occupations. Occupations: General Report*. Washington, D.C.: GPO.

——— . 1940. *Census of the U.S. Population: Vol. III: The Labor Force. Part I: U.S. Summary*. Washington, DC: GPO.

——— . 1975. *Historical Statistics of the U.S.: Colonial Times to 1970*. Washington, DC: GPO.

—— . 1993. *Statistical Abstract of the United States*. Washington, DC: GPO. U.S. Department of Labor. 1974. *Nontraditional Occupations Women of the Hemisphere – The U.S. Experience*. Washington, DC: GPO.

Vance, Carol. 1991. Anthropology Rediscovers Sexuality: A Theoretical Comment. *Social Science Medicine* 33(8): 876–84.

Vicinus, Martha. 1992. "They Wonder to Which Sex I Belong": The Historical Roots of the Modern Lesbian Identity. *Feminist Studies* 18(3): 467–98.

Walby, Sylvia. 1990. *Theorizing Patriarchy*. London: Basil Blackwell.

Weeks, Jeffrey. 1977. *Coming Out: Homosexual Politics in Britain, from the Nineteenth Century to the Present*. New York: Quartet Books.

—— . 1985. *Sexuality and its Discontents: Meanings, Myths, and Modern Sexualities*. London: Routledge and Kegan Paul.

—— . 1989. Inverts, Perverts, and Mary-Annes. In *Hidden from History: Reclaiming the Gay and Lesbian Past*, edited by Duberman, Vicinus, and Chauncey, pp. 195–211. New York: Penguin.

—— . 1991. *Against Nature: Essays on History, Sexuality and Identity*. London: Rivers Oram Press.

Queer labor economics

THE CONVERGENCE OF INCREASED interest in the subject and increased data availability has led to a relatively large number of studies regarding the effects of sexual orientation on labor market outcomes. In particular, studies have delved into the effects of sexual orientation on individuals' earnings. These studies provide an interesting extension to the large literature on gender differences in earnings, and the basic technique used (basically the statistical technique of multiple regression) is comparable, with the added twist of being able to divide the sample by both gender and sexual orientation.

A widely cited and influential early study in this area is Lee Badgett's "The wage effects of sexual orientation discrimination" (1995). Badgett uses 1989–91 data for the US from the nationally representative General Social Survey and finds that gay and bisexual men make significantly less than heterosexual men. This result is particularly noteworthy because other researchers who used nonrepresentative data had argued that gays made more than straight men (e.g., Hewitt 1995). Meanwhile, Badgett finds mixed evidence regarding whether or not lesbians make more than straight women.

Badgett's results for gays in the US have been corroborated by a number of later studies (Allegretto and Arthur 2001; Clain and Leppel 2001; Berg and Lien 2002; Black et al. 2003; Blandford 2003; Comolli 2004). Some studies have found a statistically significant difference between lesbian and heterosexual women, with lesbian women making more than heterosexuals (Clain and Leppel 2001; Berg and Lien 2002; Black et al. 2003; Blandford 2003; Jepsen 2007), while other studies find little or no difference once other earnings-related characteristics are controlled for (Klawitter 1997; Klawitter and Flatt 1998; Comolli 2004). However, the exact amount of the measured differential varies from study to study depending on the time period covered and the particular variables included. In addition, some recent studies are able to distinguish between gay and bisexual men on the one hand, and lesbian and bisexual women on the other, and thus measure differences in wage differentials related to bisexuality as opposed to either homosexuality or heterosexuality; Carpenter (2005) finds no effect of homosexuality on earnings, but some evidence that bisexuals earn less than heterosexuals – as does Preston (studied for women only) (2007).

More recently, a number of studies have become available that use data from other countries to study sexual orientation discrimination (Badgett and Frank 2007). For instance, in Erik Plug and Peter Berkhout's study, "Effects of sexual preferences on earnings in the Netherlands" (2004), they find a similar pattern to the US, but with less of an earnings differential for the men (gays make slightly less than straights, lesbians make slightly more than straights) and almost no earnings differential overall between gays and lesbians (in contrast to the US, where the gender differential favoring men continues to operate even when controlling for sexual orientation). Studies from Canada (Brown 1998) and the United Kingdom (Arabsheibani *et al.* 2004, 2005) find the same patterns as for the US and Netherlands for a general population sample, but no evidence of earnings differences in a sample of staff from six British universities, though there may be some capping at the high end for homosexual employees due to "glass ceilings" (Frank 2006).

The unique difficulty with studying homosexual job discrimination is that it can be unobservable in most environments. Race and gender are often highly salient and thus can be noticed almost instantaneously by employers. Sexual orientation is not highly visible, and in the labor market it is often assumed, unless indicated otherwise, that a potential employee is heterosexual. This poses a dilemma to the gay employee of whether or not to disclose his or her sexual preferences, or provide signals relating to sexual preference, to the employer.

Doris Weichselbaumer's study, "Sexual orientation discrimination in hiring" (2003), takes a novel approach to uncovering hiring discrimination in the Austrian labor market regarding perceived sexual orientation. Using the "auditing" technique, Weichselbaumer sends out pairs of résumés for women that differ only in terms of perceived sexual orientation (more masculine pictures, hobbies, and résumé styling for the supposed lesbians). She finds a higher rate of being invited for a job interview for the women who appear to be heterosexual.

Other recent studies have used special data sets that allow us to observe the costs associated with disclosing one's homosexual identity at work. Comolli (2006) finds that those gay men who do disclose their orientation on the job earn 11 percent less on average than those who do not disclose; Hyman (1993) finds earnings for lesbians who are out to be lower than those of their co-workers. Preston (2007) gets a similar result for workers in "gay-unfriendly" workplaces, but no effect of disclosure for workers in "gay-friendly" workplaces.

Studies have also examined the differences in occupational choices between straight and gay workers (Hewitt 1995; Dunne 1996; Badgett and King 1997; Badgett 1998, 2001). One might expect differences not only for labor market demand-side reasons related to employer, employee, or customer discrimination based on sexual orientation, but also for supply-side reasons related to gender role nonconformity, attraction to particular occupations due to sexual orientation, and differences in same-sex household structures. Regarding sex role nonconformity, studies have examined its negative effects both on the probability of getting a job interview (Weichselbaumer 2004) and on other people's perception of one's desirability as a heterosexual partner if one is in an occupation that is considered as not typical for one's gender (Badgett and Folbre 2003). Indeed, it may be that the earnings premium that married men have traditionally enjoyed in the labor market is actually an anti-queer premium (Carpenter 2007; Frank 2007; Schmidt 2007). Several studies have thus also focused on differences in household division of labor in same-sex couples as compared to heterosexual couples (Klawitter 1995; Giddings 1998; Jepsen and Jepsen 2006), as well as the amount of labor supplied to the market (Tebaldi and Elmslie 2006).

Of course research need not be divorced from advocacy, and an increasing number of resources exist to inform both queer employees and job seekers of the current situation regarding workplace practices, queer-friendly employers, and various employment initiatives (Klawitter and Flatt 1998; Ragins 2004; Ayres and Brown 2005; Waaldijk and Bonini-Baraldi 2006; Human Rights Campaign), including discussions of whether or not to come out at work (Badgett 1996a, 1996b). In addition, resources now exist both to encourage employers to hire out workers (Candidatefive; Out and Equal) and to enable queer employees to network effectively with each other (Out for Business; Out Professionals; Reaching Out MBA). There is also an official labor organization, Pride At Work, for queer Americans (Hunt and Boris 2007).

DISCUSSION QUESTIONS

1   What is the evidence regarding the earnings effects of sexual orientation discrimination?
2   What confounding factors make the detection of discrimination due to sexuality or sexual orientation difficult and how can they be dealt with?
3   Why would choice of occupation vary systematically with one's sexual orientation?
4   Is sexual orientation confounded with sexual stereotyping? In other words, if a person is perceived as going against sexual type, is this damaging to their career regardless of their actual sexual orientation?
5   What factors lead to the decision as to whether to reveal or hide one's sexual orientation to an actual or potential employer?

REFERENCES

Allegretto, S. A. and Arthur, M. M. (2001) "An empirical analysis of homosexual/heterosexual male earnings differentials: unmarried and unequal?," *Industrial and Labor Relations Review*, 54: 631–46.

Arabsheibani, G. R., Marin, A., and Wadsworth, J. (2004) "In the pink: homosexual–heterosexual wage differentials in the UK," *International Journal of Manpower*, 25: 343–54.

—— (2005) "Gay pay in the UK," *Economica*, 72: 333–47.

Ayres, I. and Brown, J. G. (2005) "Privatizing gay rights with non-discrimination promises instead of policies," *The Economists Voice*, 2: 1–9.

Badgett, M. V. L. (1996a) "Choices and chances: is coming out at work a rational choice?," in B. Beemyn and M. Eliason (eds) *Queer Studies: a lesbian, gay, bisexual and transgender anthology*, New York and London: New York University Press.

—— (1996b) "Employment and sexual orientation: disclosure and discrimination in the workplace," *Journal of Gay and Lesbian Social Services*, 4: 29–52. Journal issue simultaneously published as A. L. Ellis and E. D. B. Riggle (eds) *Sexual Identity on the Job: Issues and Services*, Binghamton, N. Y.: Harrington Park Press.

—— (1998) "Tolerance, taboos, and gender identity: the occupational distribution of lesbians and gay men," working paper, University of Massachusetts-Amherst.

—— (2001) *Money, Myths, and Change: the economic lives of lesbians and gay men*, Chicago and London: University of Chicago Press.

Badgett, M. V. L. and Folbre, N. (2003) "Job gendering: occupational choice and the marriage market," *Industrial Relations*, 42: 270–98.

Badgett, [M. V.] L. and Frank, J. (eds) (2007) *Sexual Orientation Discrimination: an international perspective*, New York and London: Routledge.

Badgett, M. V. L. and King, M. C. (1997) "Lesbian and gay occupational strategies," in A. Gluckman and B. Reed (eds) *Homo Economics: capitalism, community, and lesbian and gay life*, New York and London: Routledge.

Berg, N. and Lien, D. (2002) "Measuring the effect of sexual orientation on income: evidence of discrimination?," *Contemporary Economic Policy*, 20: 394–414.

Black, D. A., Makar, H. R., Sanders, S. G., and Taylor, L. J. (2003) "The earnings effects of sexual orientation," *Industrial and Labor Relations Review*, 56: 449–69.

Blandford, J. M. (2003) "The nexus of sexual orientation and gender in the determination of earnings," *Industrial and Labor Relations Review*, 56: 622–42.

Brown, C. L. (1998) "Sexual orientation and labor economics," *Feminist Economics*, 4: 89–95.

Candidatefive, <http://www.candidatefive.com>.

Carpenter, C. S. (2005) "Self-reported sexual orientation and earnings: evidence from California," *Industrial and Labor Relations Review*, 58: 258–73.

—— (2007) "Do straight men 'come out' at work too? the heterosexual male marriage premium and discrimination against gay men," in L. Badgett and J. Frank (eds) *Sexual Orientation Discrimination: an international perspective*, London: Routledge.

Clain, S. H. and Leppel, K. (2001) "An investigation into sexual orientation discrimination as an explanation for wage differences," *Applied Economics*, 33: 37–47.

Comolli, R. (2004) "Gays, lesbians and bisexuals' wage differentials in the US," working paper, Yale University.

—— (2006) "Earnings differentials with endogenous disclosure of sexual orientation," paper presented at the Western Economic Association International conference.

Dunne, G. A. (1996) *Lesbian Lifestyles: women's work and the politics of sexuality*, Toronto: University of Toronto Press.

Frank, J. (2006) "Gay glass ceilings," *Economica*, 73: 485–508.

—— (2007) "Is the male marriage premium evidence of discrimination against gay men?," in L. Badgett and J. Frank (eds) *Sexual Orientation Discrimination: an international perspective*, London: Routledge.

Giddings, L. A. (1998) "Political economy and the construction of gender: the example of housework within same-sex households," *Feminist Economics*, 4: 97–106.

Hewitt, C. (1995) "The socioeconomic position of gay men: a review of the evidence," *American Journal of Economics and Sociology*, 54: 461–79.

Human Rights Campaign, <http://www.hrc.org/>.

Hunt, G., and Boris, M. B. (2007) "Lesbian, gay, bisexual, and transgender challenge to American labor," in D. S. Cobble (ed) *The Sex of Class: women transforming American labor*, Ithaca and London: ILR Press.

Hyman, B. (1993) "The Economic Consequences of Child Sexual Abuse in Women," Dissertation, Waltham, Mass.: Brandeis University.

Jepsen, C. A. and Jepsen, L. K. (2006) "The sexual division of labor within households: comparisons of couples to roommates," *Eastern Economic Journal*, 32: 299–312.

Jepsen, L. K. (2007) "Comparing the earnings of cohabiting lesbians, cohabiting heterosexual women, and married women: evidence from the 2000 Census," *Industrial Relations*, forthcoming.

Klawitter, M. and Flatt, V. (1998) "The effects of state and local antidiscrimination policies on earnings for gays and lesbians," *Journal of Policy Analysis and Management* 17: 658–86.

Klawitter, M. M. (1995) "Did they find each other or create each other?: labor market linkages between partners in same-sex and different-sex couples," working paper, University of Washington.

—— (1997) "The determinants of earnings for women in same-sex and different-sex couples," working paper, University of Washington.

Out & Equal, <http://www.outandequal.org/>.

Out for Business, <http://www.outforbusiness.com/>.

Out Professionals, <http://www.outprofessionals.org/>.

Preston, A. E. (2007) "Coming out at the workplace: help or hindrance? An analysis of labor market outcomes of highly educated gay, lesbian, and bisexual individuals," working paper, Haverford College.

Ragins, B. R. (2004) "Sexual orientation in the workplace: the unique work and career experiences of gay, lesbian and bisexual workers," in J. J. Martocchio (ed.) *Research in Personnel and Human Resources Management*, Amsterdam, San Diego, and Oxford: Elsevier, JAI.

Reaching Out MBA, <http://www.reachingoutmba.org/>.

Schmidt, A. B. (2007) "Discrimination and the married men's wage premium: further evidence from California," paper presented at the Eastern Economic Association conference.

Tebaldi, E. and Elmslie, B. (2006) "Sexual orientation and labour supply," *Applied Economics*, 38: 549–62.

Waaldijk, K. and Bonini-Baraldi, M. (2006) *Sexual Orientation Discrimination in the European Union: national laws and the employment equality directive*, The Hague, Netherlands: T. M. C. Asser Press.

Weichselbaumer, D. (2004) "Is it sex or personality? The impact of sex stereotypes on discrimination in applicant selection," *Eastern Economic Journal*, 30: 159–86.

Chapter 13

M. V. Lee Badgett

THE WAGE EFFECTS OF SEXUAL ORIENTATION DISCRIMINATION

From *Industrial & Labor Relations Review* 1995, 48 (4): 726–39

O VER THE PAST THREE DECADES, legislators at the federal, state, and municipal levels have moved toward a general public policy stating that employers should employ and pay people based on what they can produce on the job, not who they are. The Civil Rights Act of 1964 prohibits employment discrimination because of an individual's race, color, religion, sex, or national origin. Other laws forbid employment discrimination based on individuals age or physical or mental disability. Other salient aspects of human identity remain outside this form of legal protection, however. Most notably, employment discrimination against individuals who are or are perceived to be lesbian, gay, or bisexual remains legal in most workplaces in the United States. This paper is the first econometric study of the possible wage effects of such discrimination.

Much of the debate about adding sexual orientation to civil rights laws has centered on the need for such legislation. Proponents of civil rights protections for lesbian, gay, and bisexual people argue that these people experience employment discrimination and that it causes them economic and psychological harm. Opponents of civil rights protections argue that such laws are unnecessary and would grant gay people "special privileges" (Carroll 1992). Citing survey data purportedly showing that lesbian and gay people have higher than average incomes (see, for example, "Clinton Administration Backs Bill," 1994), they assert that lesbians and gay men are an affluent group without need of further protection, and call into question the very existence of discrimination against them.

Existing economic studies of lesbian and gay people, however, are based on biased samples and inappropriate statistical comparisons. In this paper I apply econometric tools developed in the study of race and gender discrimination to the newer question of employment discrimination based on sexual orientation. Data pooled from the 1989–91 versions of the General Social Survey, a national random sample, allow econometric testing for the effects of sexual orientation discrimination on earnings. In its use of a random sample and multivariate analysis, this study constitutes a significant methodological advance over other quantitative studies of such discrimination and past efforts to compare earnings by sexual orientation.

Conceptual framework

Before evaluating labor market outcomes for evidence of employment discrimination against a group, it is reasonable to ask whether there is some reason to expect differential treatment of that group. Historical, sociological, and psychological research demonstrates the existence of homophobia (the fear of homosexuals and homosexuality) and heterosexism (the belief that heterosexuality is superior to homosexuality and should be an enforceable social norm) and the effects that such attitudes have in the everyday experience of lesbians and gay men: the lack of social or legal recognition of family structures, the persistence of threatened and actual violence, and the perpetuation of false stereotypes (see, in general, Gonsiorek and Weinrich 1991). Individuals with a bisexual orientation may also encounter such attitudes, although at other times those individuals may be perceived as being (or atleast behaving as) heterosexual (see Garnets and Kimmel 1991:149).

If employers or coworkers have a distaste for gay identity, behavior, or "lifestyle," employers may develop a taste for discrimination (following Becker 1971). This taste for discrimination is necessary but not sufficient for the occurrence of discrimination against gay employees, however. Unlike race or gender, for instance, sexual orientation is not generally an observable characteristic. (In this respect, sexual orientation is more like religion or national origin.) For the social stigma attached to homosexuality and bisexuality to result in direct employment discrimination, *disclosure* of a gay employee's sexual orientation is necessary.

Lesbians and gay men who voluntarily disclose their sexual orientation to employers or coworkers may trade off the risk of diminished career advancement or income loss for some future return (for anecdotal examples, see Woods 1992:216–22). The future return may be psychological (enhanced self-esteem), political (a more supportive and accepting workplace), or economic (extension of benefits to domestic partners or spousal equivalents). Given these potential trade-offs, disclosure is likely to be endogenous, that is, at least partly determined by workplace factors.

An important workplace factor, of course, is income, but the direction of influence is difficult to determine *a priori*. First, compared to lower-income workers, higher-income workers may occupy jobs that allow them to manage the harmful effects of social stigma more comfortably, increasing their probability of disclosure. Second, higher levels of income could cushion the financial burden of some adverse workplace reactions, such as a loss of promotion, again leading to more disclosure by high-income people. In the other direction, however, people earning high incomes would lose more if fired, for instance, particularly if they feared that information about their sexual orientation would hinder their job search.[1] Schneider (1986:479) found that lesbians with higher incomes were less likely than those with lower incomes to disclose their sexual orientation; that study, however, used a nonrandom sample.

Disclosure of sexual orientation may also be involuntary, although the extent of this kind of disclosure is unknown. Inferences of a lesbian or gay identity can be made by employers or coworkers from numerous sources of information: military discharge records, arrests or convictions, marital status, residential neighborhood, silences in conversations, and so on. In some cases, these inferences may even be incorrect, and a heterosexual employee may be wrongly perceived as being gay. Furthermore, voluntary disclosures to coworkers increase the likelihood of involuntary disclosure, whether accidental or deliberate.

Disclosure, whether voluntary or involuntary, may result in sanctions by coworkers, supervisors, or employers. Negative reactions will vary across workplaces. Coworkers might harass a gay or lesbian coworker, with adverse effects on the worker's productivity, income, and advancement. Supervisors or employers may harass, fire, or refuse to promote lesbian, gay, or bisexual employees.[2] This form of *direct discrimination* results in equally productive individuals being compensated differently.

Although disclosure is necessary for direct discrimination to occur, even successfully passing as heterosexual might not preclude negative economic effects. Evidence suggests that nondisclosure (or "passing" as heterosexual) is a common strategy for avoiding discrimination (Badgett, Donnelly, and Kibbe 1992). As Escoffier (1975) pointed out, passing may require a conscious effort to avoid potentially awkward social interactions that contribute to job satisfaction or advancement for other workers. The isolation involved in many passing strategies could lead to higher absenteeism and job turnover, and the energy devoted to passing might reduce productivity. In this case, the behavior is not an intrinsic characteristic of the worker but an effect of *indirect discrimination* within a workplace perceived as threatening. Two individuals with equal productive abilities would have differential productivity and, there fore, differential wages because of the work environment's effect on the gay individual's productivity. A different passing strategy could lead to a positive effect on productivity if gay workers, "driven by a half-conscious belief that if they just show themselves productive enough, worthy enough, good enough, they will overcome the invisible stigma," become workaholics (Mohr 1988: 149).

Overall, the likely wage effect of successfully passing as heterosexual in the work place is ambiguous. In theory, the effects of direct discrimination in wages could be distinguished from the indirect effects by controlling for individuals' productivity differences. In practice, however, this distinction will be difficult to make, as will be discussed below.

Evidence on the economic status of lesbians and gay men

Legal cases provide well-documented evidence of particular instances of employment discrimination against lesbians and gay men. Further evidence of employers' attitudes comes from a 1987–88 survey of employers in Anchorage, Alaska. Of the 191 employers surveyed, 18% said they would fire homosexuals, 27% said they would not hire them, and 26% said they would not promote them (Brause 1989). Some evidence that attitudes do translate into discrimination comes from non-random surveys of self-identified lesbian, gay, and bisexual people. A recent review of 21 surveys found that between 16% and 46% of survey respondents reported having experienced some form of discrimination in employment (in hiring, promotion, firing, or harassment) (Badgett, Donnelly, and Kibbe 1992).[3]

If discrimination does commonly occur and results in similarly qualified and productive people being treated differently only because of their sexual orientation, an economist might expect to observe differences in wages. The paucity of available data for large numbers of lesbians and gay men has made comparisons of income by sexual orientation difficult. Table 1 presents data from three relatively recent national surveys of lesbians and gay men. None of these surveys included heterosexual people, so the comparison group in the last column of Table 1 is the national median income for full-time male or female workers, most of whom will be heterosexual.

The first survey, conducted in 1988 and reported in *Out/Look* magazine, asked respondents to indicate in which $5,000 range their income fell. The median range reported for gay men, $25,000 to $29,999, overlapped the national male median, but the median range for lesbians was higher than the median for women nationally. This same pattern showed up in the 1989 Teichner survey for the *San Francisco Examiner*, which found no clear difference between gay men's incomes and the national male median but higher median incomes for lesbians than for women nation-wide. The

Table 1 Survey data on income of lesbian, gay, and bisexual people

Survey	Year	Instrument	N	Gender	L/G/B Income	National Income[a]
Out/Look	1988	Magazine survey, mail-in	510	Men	25K–29K[b]	27,342
				Women	20K–24K[b]	18,823
Simmons Mkt. Research Bureau	1988	Gay newspaper Inserts			36,900[c]	(see above)
Teichner/*San Francisco Examiner*	1989	Phone survey, random digit dialing	400	Men	29,129[b]	28,605
				Women	26,331[b]	19,643

[a] "National income" is median income for full-time, full-year workers.
[b] Median income for sample.
[c] Average income for sample.

Sources: *Out/Look* 1988; Gravois 1991; Teichner 1989. National medians from *Economic Report of the President*, Feb. 1990 and Feb. 1991.

1988 Simmons Market Research Bureau survey appears second in the table and shows the most dramatic differences between gay and national incomes, with gay individuals (86% of whom were men) earning 35% more than the median male.

These comparisons are questionable for several reasons. In the two non-random surveys (*Out/Look* and Simmons), lesbian and gay respondents tended to be disproportionately white, urban, and well-educated, all of which are factors associated with higher average incomes. (The difficulties in collecting data on a representative sample of a stigmatized population are discussed in the next section.) The extraordinarily high incomes found in the Simmons study most likely reflect sample selection bias. Surveys were inserted into eight gay/lesbian newspapers, and responses were mailed in.[4] This sampling technique guaranteed a highly educated sample (59.6% of respondents were college graduates, 16.8% had a master's degree, and 6.8% had a Ph.D.) and, therefore, higher than average incomes.

But even the survey with the least biased sampling technique (Teichner used random digit dialing and interviewed self-identified lesbian/gay/bisexual people) found that lesbians' median income was well above the median female income. Although the willingness of respondents to identify themselves as gay or lesbian to an unknown interviewer may vary along income lines within gender groups, which could be a source of observed differences, some further explanation is necessary. Furthermore without controlling for experience or education, comparisons of the median or average income for the gay sample with the national medians may be misleading. As in the standard economic approach to race and gender discrimination, we need a multivariate analysis of a random sample to properly compare the earnings of lesbian, gay, or bisexual workers to the earnings of heterosexual workers.

Data

As mentioned above, one reason we know little about the economic effects of sexual orientation is that reliable and representative data matching sexual orientation to economic outcomes are extremely rare. One important nationally representative survey, the General Social Survey (GSS) conducted by the National Opinion Research Center, has collected information on labor market variables (employment status, income, and occupation) and, beginning in 1989, on sexual behavior with partners of either sex (Davis and Smith 1991).[5] While the GSS does not specifically ask about sexual orientation or identity, same-sex sexual experiences are likely to be highly correlated with a self-identified gay or bisexual orientation (see Lever et al. 1992).

Because of the design of the GSS, not all respondents were asked all

questions in each survey. Following elimination of those without information on sex partners[6] or income[7] (and a few with missing data on other
variables), the sample pooled from the 4426 respondents in the 1989–91
surveys contains 1680 people who were employed full-time when surveyed.[8] Of this subsample, 4.8% reported having had at least one same-sex
sexual partner since the age of 18, a proportion that falls well within the
range found by studies of sexual orientation (Gonsiorek and Weinrich
1991). For purposes of this paper, those respondents are classified as
behaviorally lesbian, gay, or bisexual.

The lack of data on self-identified sexual orientation is disappointing,
but using behavior to infer identity may not be inappropriate. First, society
may not make such fine distinctions.[9] Both behavior and identity are stigmatized and are sufficient to trigger legal sanctions in the United States,
For instance, the *act* of sodomy is still prohibited in about half of the states
(*Harvard Law Review* editors, p. 9), as is the solicitation of "noncommercial,
consensual same-sex sexual activity" in many places (p. 27). In some cases,
these laws (and the presumption that lesbians and gay men violate the
sodomy laws) have been used to justify employment discrimination (see the
discussion of *Childers v. Dallas Police Department* in Rubenstein 1993:334).

Second, although respondents are not asked when their sexual activity
took place, both absolute and relative numbers of same-sex sexual partners
are likely to indicate whether this behavior was temporary or experimental
or whether the behavior reflects the individual's underlying sexual identity
and orientation. Therefore, this study uses four measures of gay sexual
behavior: (1) having had *one or more* same-sex sexual partners (the most
general definition, identifying 4.8% of the sample); (2) having had *more than
one* same-sex sexual partner (3.0%); (3) having had *at least as many* same-
sex sexual partners as opposite-sex sexual partners (3.0%); and (4) having
had either more than one same-sex sexual partner or at least as many same-
sex sexual partners as opposite-sex sexual partners (that is, either (2) or
(3), a definition that takes in 3.8% of the sample).

An issue related to the use of this data is their reliability. The questions
on sexual behavior in the GSS were self-administered and were accompanied by assurances of confidentiality and by the explanation that "frank
and honest" responses were important for understanding how to deal with
the AIDS epidemic.

One final drawback of the GSS data set is that respondents were asked
to select one of 20 categories to indicate their pretax employment earnings
from the previous year, rather than to name exact figures. The income
ranges for each category increase with income, but the analysis uses natural
logarithms, which evens the ranges out. Medians were calculated for the
GSS ranges using Current Population Survey data on full-time workers.[10]
All medians were converted to 1988 dollars for the purposes of calculations
in this paper.

Methodology

The most common econometric approach for capturing the effects of discrimination is to see if people who are similar in all observable and economically relevant ways have similar labor market outcomes. This paper uses a basic OLS model of wage determination with the log of income as the dependent variable. Separate equations for men and women will take into account any differences in men's and women's labor market decisions and experiences. Independent variables include individual characteristics related to productivity (such as education, occupation, marital status, and experience)[11] and other labor market influences (region, SMSA residence, and race). The main effect of discrimination, if any, will be captured by the coefficient on a dummy variable for being behaviorally lesbian, gay, or bisexual. A statistically significant negative coefficient would imply discrimination in the form of lower wages. Discrimination may also exist in the process of allocating individuals among occupations.

A variable measuring the extent of workplace disclosure of gay behavior or identity would be more appropriate to include in the wage equation, since disclosure is necessary for direct discrimination to occur. Unfortunately, this information is not available. As a result, the hypothesized discrimination characteristic is measured with error, violating one of the usual OLS assumptions. With no information on disclosure, statistical correction is not feasible, but the interpretation of the results can be adjusted.

Overall, this selection bias problem is likely to reduce any measured effect of discrimination, biasing the procedure against the discrimination hypothesis. Consider Figure 1, a matrix of disclosure decisions for behaviorally lesbian, gay, or bisexual people. The framework described above suggests that gay employees disclosing their sexual orientation, the people in groups A and C, are vulnerable to direct workplace discrimination. The variable created from the General Social Survey combines people in groups A and B but does not (and cannot) distinguish people in those two groups, although we would only expect those in group A to face direct discrimination. Lesbian, gay, and bisexual individuals in group B who have not disclosed their sexual orientation at work might still face indirect discrimination if expectations of discrimination reduce productivity. Given the imperfect proxies for productivity and the inability to measure disclosure, then, the GSS sexual orientation variable will pick up the effect of both direct and indirect discrimination against groups A and B. If indirect discrimination lowers earnings less than direct discrimination, or if the net effect of nondisclosure is to induce gay employees to work harder and to *increase* productivity, then the sexual orientation coefficient will *underestimate* the negative effect of direct discrimination on earnings.

Figure 1 Voluntary disclosure decisions of lesbian, gay, and bisexual workers

	Disclosure in workplace	No disclosure in workplace
Disclosure in survey	A	B
No disclosure in survey	C	D

The impact of imperfectly measuring the sexual orientation variable can be analyzed similarly. Individuals in group D are not coded by the GSS variable as being gay. As with group B, they are unlikely to face direct discrimination but might have lower incomes from indirect discrimination Workers in group C are likely to face discrimination but cannot be identified with the GSS data. Overall, though, the effect of misclassifying group C and D workers is likely to be negligible. First, if, as seems reasonable, the economic and social risk from disclosing sexual behavior to a survey interviewer is less than the risk from workplace disclosure, the combination of survey nondisclosure and workplace disclosure will be rare and the size of group C will be small. Second, unless the overall group of lesbian, gay, and bisexual adults is quite large, the addition of the potentially lower-income group C and D workers to the heterosexual total will have a relatively small effect on the average income against which behaviorally gay respondents' income is measured. And even a large combined group of C and D workers facing both indirect and direct discrimination would pull the average down, *reducing* the observed income difference between gay and heterosexual workers. Thus the errors both in measuring behavior and in using behavior as a proxy for disclosure result in a bias *against* finding discrimination.

As discussed above, workplace disclosure may be systematically related to income, and Schneider found that disclosure is less likely as income increases, resulting in another form of selection bias. This pattern is consistent with the hypothesis that gay workers make cost-benefit calculations before disclosing their sexual orientation, and that disclosure is less likely among high-income workers because they have more to lose. The earnings loss for lower-income workers who disclose their sexual orientation and face direct discrimination will not, therefore, be representative of the loss faced by the average worker. But in that case the average worker has a *higher* expected loss of income, which is why he or she does not disclose, suggesting that, again, this source of selection bias will result in underestimates of the average effect of disclosure and discrimination.

Aside from the effect of indirect discrimination on the productivity of gay workers who do not disclose their sexual orientation, other sources of ability or productivity differences that are unobservable to the researcher might be related to sexual orientation. For instance, some economists measuring racial earnings differentials have hypothesized racial differences in unobserved quality (usually differences in schooling quality) that, if properly accounted for, would reduce the difference in earnings attributed purely to racial discrimination (for example, Smith and Welch 1989; Juhn, Murphy, and Pierce 1991). This is less likely to be an issue in the case of sexual orientation, however, since observed levels of education are quite similar across heterosexual and homosexual groups and there is no reason to expect systematic differences in the quality of schools attended by lesbian, gay, or bisexual people. Furthermore, much of the gay and lesbian identity development process occurs in the late teens and early twenties, suggesting that sexual orientation is unlikely to influence educational decisions (Garnets and Kimmel 1991).[12]

Other components of unobserved ability – work experience and labor force attachment – also cause concern when OLS models are used to measure discrimination against women (Bloom and Killingsworth 1982), and these factors, unlike the school quality component, may be correlated with sexual orientation. Lesbians and bisexual women may have stronger labor force attachment and more work experience than heterosexual women, since they usually have weaker economic incentives to specialize in home production: their partners (or spousal equivalents) are women who face the same potentially discriminatory labor market. Furthermore, the legal benefits of partnership are fewer, and the economic penalties for not working are greater even for lesbians who share economic resources and expenses with a partner, since few employers who provide health care benefits for employees' legal spouses do so for employees' same-sex domestic partners (Bowman and Cornish 1992). As a result, lesbians' labor force experience might not be interrupted as often as heterosexual women's, which would make the potential experience variable available from the GSS a closer proxy for lesbians' actual experience (see note 11).

If these unobserved components of wage determination are correlated with sexual orientation, then OLS coefficients are biased *against* finding discrimination, since the unobserved components mean that lesbian and bisexual women are more productive than heterosexual women who are identical in their observed characteristics. This problem can be at least partly corrected with information gained from modeling the female worker's decision to work full-time. To the extent that the unobservable component involved in the full-time work decision is correlated with the unobservable determinants of wages (for instance, actual experience and labor force attachment), adding a Heckman correction term – the inverse Mills ratio representing the probability of being a full-time worker – to the OLS model will reduce the bias (Bloom and Killingsworth 1982). In addition, the possibility that the potential experience variable more closely proxies lesbians' actual experience than heterosexual women's actual experience will be accounted for by interacting experience and sexual orientation.

Results

Table 2 presents the means for the variables used in both procedures. Unlike the data derived from the surveys described in Table 1, the behaviorally lesbian/bisexual women earn approximately 18% less, on average, than do behaviorally heterosexual women in the GSS, and gay/bisexual men earn 7% less than heterosexual men. Two likely sources of the differences between the survey results in Table 1 and 2 are differences in sampling

Table 2 Variable means for full-time workers, pooled 1989–91 data (standard deviations in parentheses)

Variable	Lesbian/bisexual women	Heterosexual women	Gay/bisexual men	Heterosexual men
Annual earnings (in	15056	18341	26321	28312
1988–90)	(8284)	(11334)	(16937)	(16842)
% 0 to 9,999	29.4	21.2	10.6	8.8
% 10 to 19,999	35.3	36.2	29.8	22.5
% 20 to 29,999	29.4	25.8	21.3	26.2
% 30 to 39,999	5.9	12.0	17.0	19.4
% 40,000 and up	0.0	4.7	21.3	23.1
Education (in years)	13.6	13.6	13.6	13.6
	(3.0)	(2.5)	(4.0)	(2.9)
Age	34.0	39.4	41.3	39.1
	(10.3)	(11.1)	(12.2)	(11.8)
Potential	15.4	20.8	22.6	20.4
experience[a]	(10.8)	(11.6)	(13.2)	(12.1)
% White	79.4	85.2	89.4	90.7
% Married	23.5	51.0	40.4	67.7
% in Large SMSA	55.9	51.9	55.3	45.8
Region (%):				
Northeast	17.6	20.2	25.5	18.4
Midwest	23.5	26.9	29.8	26.6
West	17.6	19.3	12.8	19.6
South	41.2	33.5	31.9	35.3
Occup. (%):				
Manager	8.8	14.8	12.8	17.9
Prof./tech.	26.5	25.4	31.9	20.0
Clerical/sales	14.7	35.7	17.0	12.9
Craft/operative	23.5	12.3	27.7	40.6
Service	26.5	11.9	10.6	8.7
N	34	698	47	901

[a]   Potential experience = age – years of education – 5.

Note: The lesbian/gay/bisexual sample is made up of those with one or more same-sex sexual partners.

Source: Author's calculations from General Social Survey (Davis and Smith 1991).

techniques (the GSS is a probability sample, the other surveys are not) and in sexual orientation definitions (the GSS definition is based on behavior, the others on self-identity). Within the GSS, some of the unadjusted difference between lesbian/bisexual women and heterosexual women could come from the fact that the gay sample is slightly younger and less likely to be white, factors that would tend to reduce average incomes. For men, there are no obvious factors pulling down gay/bisexual men's earnings. The major difference seems to be in the occupational distribution, but this difference would not necessarily mean lower incomes: the gay male respondents are less likely to be in managerial and blue-collar occupations but are more likely to be in professional/technical and service occupations.

Table 3 presents the OLS coefficient estimates from regressions on the subsample of the 1680 respondents who had full-time jobs when the survey was taken.[13] Columns (1)–(3) and (4)–(5) present the results for women and men, respectively. Columns (2), (3), and (5) supplement the basic specification in (1) and (4) with dummies for broad occupational category. (The small size of the gay sample prevented more detailed categories.) Table 3 reports the OLS results using only the most stringent definition of lesbian/gay/bisexual (having had at least as many same-sex as opposite-sex sexual partners). Using the three alternative definitions changes the L/G/B coefficient (as noted below), but the other coefficients vary only slightly. In all specifications, for both men and women, the education, occupation, marriage, race, sex, and experience coefficients have the usual signs, and most of them are significant at the 5% level.

When controls are included for the other factors influencing income, being behaviorally lesbian, gay, or bisexual reduces income, but the difference is statistically significant only for men. For women (column 1), the dummy variable for lesbian, gay, or bisexual is −0.35 using this L/G/B definition, and the coefficient ranges from −0.29 to −0.36 using the other three definitions (not reported in Table 1). The t-statistics are small, however, in each case. The null hypothesis that the coefficient is zero can be rejected in a one-tailed test at the 10% level for two of the four definitions, which define as lesbian or bisexual both those with more than one same-sex sexual partner and those with either more than one or at least as many same-sex as opposite-sex sexual partners (definitions 2 and 4 above).[14]

For men (column 4), the sexual orientation effect is stronger than for women: the coefficient is −0.28 and is significantly different from zero at the 1% level in a one-tailed test. This finding suggests that the income penalty for gay or bisexual men could be as much as 24.4%.[15] The coefficient using the other three definitions ranges from −0.12 to −0.24 in the specifications without occupation dummies. Two of those coefficients are significantly different from zero at the 5% level in a one-tailed test, and the third (having one or more same-sex sexual partners, the most general one) is significant at the 11% level in a one-tailed test. In general, as the

Table 3 Determinants of annual income in general Social Survey: income in 1988–90 (regression coefficients; absolute value of t-statistics in parentheses)

Variable	(1) Women	(2) Women	(3) Women	(4) Men	(5) Men
Constant	7.17**	7.12**	5.5**	7.84**	7.96**
	(37.1)	(34.6)	(4.1)	(60.0)	(51.6)
L/G/B[a]	−0.35	−0.32	−0.12	−0.28**	−0.31**
	(1.1)	(1.1)	(0.3)	(2.3)	(2.6)
Education	0.13**	0.10**	0.13**	0.09**	0.07**
	(11.1)	(7.6)	(4.1)	(12.5)	(8.5)
Currently Married	−0.08	−0.08	−0.26	0.27**	0.26**
	(1.4)	(1.5)	(1.6)	(5.8)	(5.6)
White	0.11	0.10	0.25	0.09	0.06
	(1.4)	(1.3)	(1.5)	(1.2)	(0.9)
Potential Experience	0.04**	0.04**	0.10**	0.04**	0.04**
	(5.1)	(5.1)	(2.1)	(6.2)	(6.1)
(Exper)^2	−0.00**	−0.00**	−0.00**	−0.00**	−0.00**
	(3.9)	(4.0)	(1.8)	(4.3)	(4.3)
Exp*L/G/B	0.01	0.02	0.01		
	(0.8)	(1.0)	(0.3)		
Big SMSA	0.26**	0.28**	0.35**	0.19**	0.17**
	(4.5)	(5.0)	(3.5)	(4.4)	(4.1)
Northeast	0.07	0.06	−0.08	0.17**	0.18**
	(0.9)	(0.8)	(0.5)	(2.9)	(3.6)
Midwest	−0.02	−0.01	−0.12	0.20**	0.19**
	(0.2)	(0.1)	(0.9)	(3.8)	(3.6)
West	−0.05	−0.05	−0.17	0.09	0.08
	(0.6)	(0.6)	(1.1)	(1.6)	(1.4)
Manager		0.58**	0.57**		0.35**
		(5.6)	(5.6)		(4.1)
Prof/Tech		0.58**	0.57**		0.31**
		(5.8)	(5.8)		(3.5)
Clerical/Sales		0.46**	0.46**		0.13
		(5.3)	(5.4)		(1.5)
Craft/Operative		0.36**	0.35**		0.11
		(3.4)	(3.4)		(1.4)
Lambda			0.90		
			(1.2)		
Adj. R^2	0.21	0.25	0.25	0.28	0.29
N	732	732	732	948	948

Note: Dummy variables for service occupation and South are excluded.
[a]   Definition of L/G/B: number of same-sex sexual partners ≥ number of opposite-sex sexual partners.
*   Statistically significant at the 10% level; **at the 5% level (two-tailed tests).

definitions become more stringent, the income effect becomes more negative, suggesting that having more than one same-sex sexual partner or mostly same-sex sexual partners may identify those gay/bisexual men who are more likely to disclose their sexual orientation at work.

Escoffier (1975) suggested that some gay people might choose occupations in which workplace disclosure of sexual orientation is least damaging. In this case, disclosure is a compensating differential for the gay worker. An alternative explanation that would account for the same observations is that gay workers are segregated or crowded into more tolerant occupations that have lower wages. To see if occupational choice or crowding can explain lower gay incomes, I added four occupational dummy variables to each specification (the dummy variable for service occupations was excluded). The effect seen in columns (2) and (5) was similar for all L/G/B definitions.

Adding occupation dummies has a very different effect on men and women. For women, both the coefficients and t-statistics for the sexual orientation variable drop considerably, and the occupation dummies have large, significant effects on income In other words, accounting for the differences in occupational distribution explains some of the sexual orientation income difference (which also becomes statistically insignificant in all of the specifications including occupation). Lesbian/bisexual women tend to be in lower-paying occupations, as the means in Table 2 suggest: half of the lesbian/bisexual women work in the lowest-paying occupations for women in this study (craft/operative and service). After the selection bias correction in column (3), both the coefficient and the t-statistic are insignificantly different from zero.[16] In a similar specification without occupation controls, the L/G/B coefficient was −0.11 with a t-statistic of 0.2. (In the selection-corrected specifications using the other definitions, the coefficient on L/G/B was sometimes positive and sometimes negative but never significantly different from zero.)

For men, adding the occupation variables *increases* the negative effect, revealing as much as a 26.7% income disadvantage (from column 5). Although occupational sorting might be observed at a finer level of detail not possible in this study, these results suggest that gay/bisexual men are in higher-paying occupations but earn less than heterosexual men within these broad categories.

Why does the effect of sexual orientation vary between men and women? The results for women from the selection-corrected specifications are sensitive to the sexual orientation definition used. With actual measures of these unobserved characteristics, the sexual orientation income gap might widen for women. Also, behavior may not be a good proxy for identity as lesbians, reducing the expected income difference if identity is more stigmatizing than behavior, as seems likely. The variable means in Table 2 demonstrate that lesbian/bisexual women are not better off economically than gay/bisexual men, suggesting that gender is more important than sexual orientation in determining income for lesbian and bisexual women. On average, lesbian/bisexual women earn 57.2% of a gay/bisexual man's income; the female-to-male ratio among heterosexuals is 64.8%.

Another possible explanation is that gay/bisexual men face greater discrimination than lesbian/bisexual women for other reasons. Bloom and Glied (1988) suggested that employers might use perceived sexual orientation as a proxy for susceptibility to HIV and AIDS, since the Americans with Disabilities Act prohibits employment discrimination because of HIV status. This might account for some of the difference, since HIV is much rarer among lesbians.

Finally, the form of discrimination against lesbians may differ from that against gay and bisexual men. The results in Table 3 suggest that at least some of lesbian/bisexual women's earnings disadvantage comes from being in lower-paying occupations, perhaps as a result of discrimination. Indirect discrimination might affect women differently from men, since women already face the potential for sex discrimination and might not fear sexual orientation discrimination as much as gay men do. Or double jeopardy might encourage lesbians to work harder to avoid discrimination. In other words, the coefficients in Table 3 will then *underestimate* the impact of direct discrimination on earnings.

Conclusion

The findings of this study provide evidence that economic differences exist between people with differing sexual orientations (as defined by their behavior). Behaviorally gay/bisexual men earn from 11% to 27% less than behaviorally heterosexual men. Because this economic disadvantage holds after controlling for education and occupation, it appears that equally productive gay people are being treated differently, that is, they are being discriminated against. Although the findings for lesbians are not consistently statistically significant, the behaviorally lesbian/bisexual women in this sample earn less than similar behaviorally heterosexual women. The difference for lesbians ranges from 12% to 30%, dropping greatly in size and significance when occupation and a selection bias correction are taken into account. The lack of statistical significance could reflect the small size of the sample of lesbians or could result because the model does not adequately control for unobservable differences between lesbians and heterosexual women in labor force experience and work attachment.

Might this discrimination wither away on its own, as suggested by a taste discrimination model? An employer with a less intense taste for discrimination ought to be able to hire productive gay employees for a smaller outlay than other employers must pay for equally productive heterosexual workers, eventually bidding up the wage of gay employees. Many firms have added sexual orientation to their nondiscrimination policies, as the model predicts.

At least two factors suggest, however, that firms with nondiscrimination policies have not been responding simply to competitive pressures. First, anecdotal evidence suggests that some of these firms changed their official policies in response to state or local antidiscrimination ordinances (Badgett 1990:207). Others changed their policies at least partly in response to pressure and actions by individual gay employees and company groups (*Gay/Lesbian/Bisexual Corporate Letter* 1992), and groups of customers and investors have also attempted to influence corporate policies. Second, in some cases, labor costs might actually be higher for those companies than for more intense discriminators if antidiscrimination policies lead to changes in the company's benefits programs, such as the introduction of benefits for the domestic partners of gay employees. Therefore, it is hard to see this trend as resulting from the process generated within the Becker discrimination model.

If, as policy decisions over the past three decades suggest, the United States is moving toward a general policy of prohibiting employment discrimination on the basis of nonproductive characteristics, then this paper's finding that sexual orientation discrimination exists in the work force identifies another policy need: adding sexual orientation to antidiscrimination laws.

Notes

1   Such a firing occurred in the case of Jeffrey Collins, a former Shell Oil employee. A California court found that Shell had fired Collins for being homosexual, violating the implicit employment agreement between Shell and Collins. Furthermore, Shell informed corporate headhunters of the reason for Collins's dismissal (*Business Week*, 1991).

2   Schneider (1986) showed that negative reactions reduce the probability that a lesbian will repeat the disclosure of her sexual orientation in the future.

3   These perceptions of discrimination are similar in magnitude to those of African American workers, 36% of whom reported experiences of racial discrimination in a 1990 survey (Turner, Fix, and Struyk 1991:7).

4   Michael Gravois of the Rivendell Marketing Co. provided me with information on the survey in a phone conversation on November 7, 1991. Some results appeared in an article in the *Wall Street Journal* (Rigdon 1991).

5   More specifically, respondents were asked two questions: "Now thinking about the time since your 18th birthday (including the past 12 months) how many male [female, in the second question] partners have you had sex with?"

6   The procedures described below were repeated on the sample of all full-time workers, including those without data on sexual partners, who were identified by a dummy variable. This procedure resulted in coefficients virtually identical to those produced by the procedures described in the next section.

7   Respondents were asked about income earned in the previous year from their current occupation. Thus nonrespondents to the income question are those who earned no income last year from their current occupation, suggesting that those reporting incomes are strongly attached to the labor force.

8   Individuals were included if employed full-time when surveyed or if they normally worked full-time but were not at work because of a temporary illness, a vacation, or a strike.

9   The distinction between behavior and identity is important in some cultures, however, including cultures that are represented in large ethnic groups in the United States, such as Latino cultures (Alonso and Koreck 1989).

10   The CPS medians were calculated for all workers, with no differentiation by race or gender. This procedure would tend to narrow the race and gender differences in median earnings in the GSS, since the distribution of earnings *within* a particular range is likely to vary by race and gender. Since this study disaggregates the GSS analysis by gender, observed racial earnings differences in the GSS are likely to be more affected. This probably explains the relatively small OLS coefficients and low t-statistics on the dummy variable for being white seen in Table 3.

11   Since actual work experience is not available, potential experience is calculated as (age − years of education − 5).

12   Although adolescents in the early stages of gay identity development might have painful high school experiences, the effect of this internal conflict on educational attainment is not clear (Gonsiorek 1988:474–77).

13   All calculations in this paper were derived using LIMDEP.

14   Also, the degree of statistical significance achieved depends on the specification of the model. Although the interaction of sexual orientation and experience is included for economic reasons, it should be noted that without that variable, the L/G/B coefficient is half as large and is statistically insignificant for all four definitions.

15   The percentage decline is calculated using $\delta = \text{in}\,(1 + d)$, where δ is the coefficient on LGB and d is the percent difference in mean incomes between the gay and heterosexual groups.

16   The selection correction involved first modeling the probability of women holding full-time jobs. The independent variables in this probit model included all the variables in Table 3 except for occupation. The coefficient on L/G/B was always positive, regardless of the definition, but never statistically significant.

References

Alonso, Ana Maria, and Maria Teresa Koreck. 1989. "Silences: 'Hispanics,' AIDS, and Sexual Practices." *Differences*, Vol. 1, No. 1 (Winter), pp. 101–24.

Badgett, M. V. Lee. 1990. "Racial Differences in Unemployment Rates and Employment Opportunities." Dissertation, University of California, Berkeley.

Badgett, Lee, Colleen Donnelly, and Jennifer Kibbe. 1992. "Pervasive Patterns of Discrimination Against Lesbians and Gay Men: Evidence from Surveys Across the United States." National Gay and Lesbian Task Force Policy Institute.

Becker, Gary S. 1971. *The Economics of Discrimination*, 2nd edition. Chicago: University of Chicago Press.

Bloom, David E., and Sherry Glied. 1989. "The Evolution of AIDS Economic Research." *Health Policy*, Vol. 11, No. 2 (April), pp. 187–96.

Bloom, David E., and Mark R. Killingsworth. 1982. "Pay Discrimination Research and Litigation: The Use of Regression." *Industrial Relations*, Vol. 21, No. 3 (Fall), pp. 318–39.

Bowman, Craig A., and Blake M. Cornish. 1992. "A More Perfect Union: A Legal and Social Analysis of Domestic Partnership Ordinances." *Columbia Law Review*, Vol. 92, No. 5 (June), pp. 1164–1211.

Brause, Jay. 1989. "Closed Doors: Sexual Orientation Bias in the Anchorage Housing and Employment Markets." In *Identity Reports: Sexual Orientation Bias in Alaska*. Anchorage, Alaska: Identity Inc.

Business Week. 1991. "The Right to Privacy: A $5.3 Million Lesson for Shell?" August 26.

Carroll, Vincent. 1992. "Coloradans on the Gay Amendment." *Wall Street Journal*, December 15.

Daily Labor Report. 1994. "Clinton Administration Backs Bill to Ban Job Bias Against Gays." August 1, p. D16.

Davis, James Allan, and Tom W. Smith. 1991. *General Social Surveys 1972–1991*. Machine-readable data file and codebook. Principal Investigator, James A. Davis; Director and Co-Principal Investigator, Tom W. Smith. National Opinion Research Center, Chicago (producer); Roper Center for Public Opinion Research, University of Connecticut, Storrs (distributor).

Economic Report of the President. 1990, 1991. Washington, D.C.: GPO.

Escoffier, Jeffrey. 1975. "Stigmas, Work Environment, and Economic Discrimination Against Homosexuals." *Homosexual Counseling Journal*, Vol. 2, No. 1 (January), pp. 8–17.

Garnets, Linda, and Douglas Kimmel. 1991. "Lesbian and Gay Male Dimensions in the Psychological Study of Human Diversity." In Jacqueline D. Goodchilds, ed., *Psychological Perspectives on Human Diversity in America*. Washington, D.C.: American Psychological Association, pp. 137–92.

The Gay/Lesbian/Bisexual Corporate Letter. 1992. "Building Community at PG&E." Vol. 1, No. 2 (November/December), pp. 3–6.

Gonsiorek, John C. 1988. "Mental Health Issues of Gay and Lesbian Adolescents." *Journal of Adolescent Health Care*, Vol. 9. Reprinted in Linda D. Garnets and Douglas C. Kimmel, eds., *Psychological Perspectives on Lesbian and Gay Male Experiences*. New York: Columbia University Press, 1993, pp. 469–85.

Gonsiorek, John C., and James D. Weinrich. 1991. "The Definition and Scope of Sexual Orientation."

In John C. Gonsiorek and James D. Weinrich, eds., *Homosexuality: Research Implications for Public Policy*. Newbury Park, Calif.: Sage, pp. 1–12.

Gravois, Michael. 1991. President, Rivendell Marketing Company. Telephone conversation with author, November 7.

Harvard Law Review editors. 1991. "Sexual Orientation and the Law." Cambridge, Mass.: Harvard University Press.

Juhn, Chinhui, Kevin M. Murphy, and Brooks Pierce. 1991. "Accounting for the Slowdown in Black-White Wage Convergence." In Marvin H. Kosters, ed., *Workers and Their Wages: Changing Patterns in the United States*. Washington, D.C.: American Enterprise Institute Press, pp. 107–43.

Lever, Janet, David E. Kanouse, William H. Rogers, Sally Carson, and Rosanna Hertz. 1992. "Behavior Patterns and Sexual Identity of Bisexual Males" *Journal of Sex Research*, Vol. 29, No. 2 (May), pp. 141–67.

Mohr, Richard, 1988. *Gays/Justice: A Study of Ethics, Society, and Law*. New York: Columbia University Press.

Rigdon, Joan E. 1991. "Overcoming a Deep-Rooted Reluctance, More Firms Advertise to Gay Community." *Wall Street Journal*, July 18, p. B1.

Rubenstein, William B. (ed.). 1993. *Lesbians, Gay Men, and the Law*. New York: New Press.

Schneider, Beth E. 1986. "Coming Out at Work: Bridging the Private/Public Gap." *Work and Occupations*, Vol. 13, No. 4 (November), pp. 463–87.

Smith, James P., and Finis R. Welch. 1989. "Black Economic Progress After Myrdal." *Journal of Economic Literature*, Vol. 27, No. 2 (June), pp. 519–64.

Teichner, Steve. 1989. "Results of Poll." *San Francisco Examiner*, June 6, p. A–19.

Turner, Margery Austin, Michael Fix, and Raymond J. Struyk. 1991. *Opportunities Denied, Opportunities Diminished: Racial Discrimination in Hiring*. Urban Institute Report 91–9. Washington, D.C.: Urban Institute Press.

Woods, James D. 1993. *The Corporate Closet: The Professional Lives of Gay Men in America*. New York: Free Press.

"Work and Career: Survey Results." 1988. *Out/Look*, Vol. 1, No. 3 (Fall), p. 94.

Chapter 14

Erik Plug and Peter Berkhout[*]

EFFECTS OF SEXUAL PREFERENCES ON EARNINGS IN THE NETHERLANDS

From *Journal of Popular Economics* 2004, 17 (1): 117–31

1 Introduction

DISCRIMINATION IN THE LABOR market has generated a vast empirical literature to illustrate various theories on the nature of discrimination. Many of these studies on earnings differentials involve women, blacks, the physically handicapped, the ugly and no doubt other groups too (Altonji and Blank 1999; Baldwin and Johnson 1994; Cain 1986; Hamermesh and Biddle 1994). Yet economists have been silent when it comes to sexual orientation.

There are a few exceptions. Some are exploratory studies ranging from wondering why economists have skirted round the sexual orientation debate to suggestions of research agendas (Klawitter 1998; Kauffman 1998; Patterson 1998). Only four (sound) empirical studies have examined the earnings effects of sexual orientation in the United States (Badgett 1995; Klawitter and Flatt 1998; Allegretto and Arthur 2001; Black et al. 2001). Their findings suggest that homosexual men earn on average 2 to 30% less than their heterosexual counterparts. But, for lesbian and heterosexual women, the results are somewhat mixed. Black et al. (2001) find that earnings are higher for lesbian women than for heterosexual women. In contrast, the other studies find that lesbian workers earn less than heterosexual women, but that observed earnings differentials are mostly insignificant.[1]

Three out of four available studies seem to agree that discrimination can be the mechanism which explains these earnings differentials. This does not imply, however, that discrimination is the exclusive factor. Differences in earnings can be the result of differences in preferences and skills too. In fact, we believe that to address the problem of discrimination in the context of sexual orientation is a rather complicated exercise. Two arguments apply.

The first argument has to do with the absence of accurate information. In most papers, discrimination arguments are taken from the literature on race and gender differentials, and are directly projected onto sexual orientation and its effect on wages. This is obviously too simple. Unlike race and gender which are both easily observable, the sexual orientation of employees is not generally an observable trait. Therefore, if the workers' sexual orientation is known to econometricians but not to employers or co-workers, the estimated effects of bi/homosexuality on earnings tend to be too low in a discriminating labor market.

The second argument is related to the first one. Because homosexuality is not generally an observable characteristic, its disclosure can happen either voluntarily or involuntarily. If disclosure happens voluntarily, it is an endogenous action where, according to economic theory, rational workers should experience, at least, some benefits related to workplace factors. Ignoring endogenous disclosure may lead to underestimated earnings effects of being a bi/homosexual worker.

In this paper, we examine the relation between sexual orientation and earnings and concentrate on the beginning of working careers. Compared with previous studies that analyzed the earnings effects of sexual orientation using the whole working population, our study has the disadvantage that, if the market discriminates, our estimated earnings effects of being a homosexual worker are probably small. We focus on the beginning of the working life and ignore potential discrimination effects that arise later on. If homosexual and bisexual workers experience losses in earnings because they more frequently end up in dead-end jobs or face glass ceilings, estimates based on starters do not pick up these effects.

Of course, if one is interested in current discriminatory (or homophobic) behavior, cohort studies like ours are to be preferred. Estimates based on samples that are representative for the whole working population measure only averaged discriminatory effects, as the inclination to discriminate changes over time. In our cohort study this is not the case. We know for certain that all our workers are only affected by current discriminatory attitudes. Moreover, they all face the same anti-discrimination legislation when they enter the labor market.

Like the previous empirical economic studies of Badgett (1995), Klawitter and Flatt (1998), Allegretto and Arthur (2001) and Black et al. (2001), this study ignores endogenous disclosure and applies sexual orientation measures that are known to us, but not necessarily known to employers or fellow workers. Yet the present study has three advantages over former approaches.

The first advantage is that our approach of measuring homosexuality is novel and quite possibly better. Former studies concentrate on sexual activity and partnership to measure sexual identity and may therefore introduce sample selectivity. When those who are single or those who are not sexually active are excluded from the analysis, we should be concerned about selection bias if finding a partner or having sex is somehow related to the worker's productivity. Our results do not suffer from such forms of selection bias. We include all workers and measure sexual orientation directly by asking people about their sexual preference.

The second advantage is that we are able to make a clear distinction between bisexual and homosexual workers. By doing so we are able to examine the degree of potential discriminatory effects under the assumption that bisexual workers are more frequently perceived by employers or co-workers as being heterosexual (in other words, that it is easier for bisexual workers to pass as heterosexual workers).

And finally, we think that the study of homosexuality and earnings is of interest in a broader context. By comparing the earnings of heterosexual male workers with those of lesbian and heterosexual female workers and vice versa, we introduce alternative tests to see whether differences in earnings by gender are due to a discriminating labor market.

Our study offers two other clear contributions relative to the previous studies. The first contribution relies on a replication argument. Given the paucity of data sets that measure sexual orientation in combination with labor market outcomes, it is useful to have more than one study using comparable methodologies with different data. It is true that this is not an overriding or creative argument, but it is certainly a valid one. The second contribution is that we analyze homosexuality and earnings in the Netherlands. Because the Netherlands is one of the most tolerant of western societies when it comes to attitudes towards homosexuality (Van den Akker et al. 1994; Wildmer et al. 1998), studying earnings effects in this particular country adds a potential value to this study.[2]

The remainder of this paper is organized as follows. In Sect. 2, we examine the economic relation between sexual orientation and earnings. Section 3 describes the data on Dutch tertiary education students. We will use this data throughout the paper. In Sect. 4, we discuss how we identify sexual orientation. In Sect. 5, we estimate a simple earnings equation and discuss our empirical findings. Section 6 summarizes our findings.

2 Earnings differentials and sexual preferences

In this section we briefly discuss how sexual orientation can affect labor market outcomes. In the tradition of most economic studies on wage differentials we distinguish three mechanisms that explain differences in pay: (i) differences that are just a matter of differences in tastes; (ii) differences that arise from specific differences in skills; and (iii) differences that come from discrimination against homosexual workers.

2.1 Differences in tastes

At first sight, differences in tastes or preferences are obvious, since heterosexual and homosexual workers differ in their sexual orientation. More important, however, is whether sexual orientation has an influence on work-related preferences. Do heterosexual and homosexual workers differ in their preferences for leisure and paid work? Or do they differ in their taste for public versus private sector jobs? We do not know. What we do know is that, if these differences in taste exist and constitute differences in the occupational distribution, then earnings will differ to the extent that occupational outcomes differ. Although these differences are important in explaining potential earnings differentials, economists have little to say on the formation of preferences.

2.2 Differences in skills

If people have different skills, human capital theory predicts that their earnings differ too. Obvious examples of skill differentials relate to education and working experience. In this section, we discuss skill differences that relate to sexual orientation and which were advanced in earlier research.

A potential source of productivity differences builds on the positive relation between health and income. Since the incidence of AIDS is higher among homosexual male workers, their expected productivity is lower. If maximizing employers differentiate earnings with expected productivity in mind, pay differentials would result. We should observe the opposite for working lesbian women. Since their incidence of AIDS is lower, their wage premium should be positive. Patterson (1998) uses this AIDS argument to illustrate potential price differences in health care insurance.

Making similar predictions, Becker (1981) puts forward differences in comparative advantages to explain differences in labor outcomes between homosexual and heterosexual couples. Later on, in Sect. 5.1, we will explain how specialization in the household predicts that, among men, homosexual workers earn less, and that, among women, homosexual workers earn more.

If we look at potential differences in relevant labor market skills and outcomes, we should be aware that structural skill differences can already be present before people enter the labor market, for example, through differences in schooling. The literature has produced conflicting arguments with respect to educational attainment and homosexuality. We discuss three arguments: (i) if students in the early stages of their homosexuality experience painful high school experiences, further learning is discouraged; (ii) if educational decisions have already been made when students struggle with their sexual identity, then educational attainment remains unaltered; and (iii) if young homosexuals anticipate a discriminating labor market, they may compensate potential losses in earnings with additional education. In the end, with less or more human capital they will end up with lower or higher earnings. However, we can ignore these educational differences, since our sample consists only of former students with university or higher vocational degrees.

2.3 Discrimination

The labor market itself can discriminate on the basis of sexual orientation Badgett (1995) points to homophobia (the fear of homosexuals and homosexuality) and heterosexism (the belief that heterosexuality is superior to homosexuality and should be an enforceable norm) to illustrate the presence of discriminating behavior in general. Similar mechanisms may apply to the workplace and result in higher wages for heterosexual workers. We are aware that discrimination based on taste or prejudice of either employers, co-workers or consumers does not necessarily predict differentials in pay. If people who are less tolerant towards homosexuality are clustered in certain jobs and occupations, then segregation of homosexual and heterosexual workers by occupation, industry or firm is also possible. This means that if we allow for characteristics of occupation and industry to explain wage differentials among homosexual and heterosexual workers, the potential wage effects of sexual identity should disappear or at least be weakened.

3 Data

The analysis is based on data from a large survey of graduates with a tertiary education. The survey has been conducted on a yearly basis since 1996. Dutch tertiary education is basically divided into two levels: higher vocational education (in Dutch abbreviated as HBO) and academic education (WO). HBO-education prepares students for specific (categories of) professions. It is taught at about 60 special institutes evenly spread over the Netherlands. On average, 50,000 students graduate each year from HBO. WO-education is believed to be of a somewhat higher level and has a more general academic character. It is taught at 14 universities. The yearly output amounts to approximately 23,000 graduates per year. The survey is restricted to the 50 degree subjects (studies) with the largest number of students on each level. So, in total, the graduates of about one hundred most popular subjects of Dutch Higher Education are analyzed. On HBO-level students can choose between 250 different courses of study, while on WO-level they may choose between 260 different specializations. Most of them, however, produce only small numbers of graduates, making statistical analysis cumbersome. In practise, about 80% of the student population is concentrated in the 100 subjects in the survey. That is, the survey is representative of 80% of the total population of two successive cohorts of graduates on HBO- and WO-level. Samples of, respectively, 8,200 and 7,800 were drawn from these populations.

In the present paper, we focus on a cohort of students who graduated in the years 1998/1999 and 1999/2000 and we follow them for the first 20 months in the labor market. We have information about their performance in school, the labor market and their sexual orientation. The number of original observations equals 15,998, but we restrict ourselves basically to the 12,094 people who worked. For our empirical analysis, we excluded all respondents who are self-employed, and all those for whom data on control variables are unavailable. We end up with 11,600 observations. Table 1 presents the descriptive statistics.

4 On the measurement of sexual orientation

The sexual orientation of the respondent is determined by a direct question. Respondents were asked "Concerning your sexual preference, what do you prefer?" They could choose between three alternatives: 1) only men; 2) only women; and 3) both men and women. The combination of one of these alternatives with the respondent's gender makes identification of sexual preference possible. The sexual orientation question was part of a special section at the end of the questionnaire that concentrated on general individual and household characteristics. The fact that we infer information on sexual identity at the end of the survey, after all other information is gathered, is an additional strength of our data. By doing so, we circumvent potential selectivity in response behavior, when respondents belonging to a sexual minority group would have taken the opportunity to emphasize or even exaggerate problems encountered in relation to their homosexuality.

Table 1 Means and standard deviations of selected variables in our sample by sexual orientation and gender

	Males			Females		
	Hetero	Gay	Bi	Hetero	Lesbian	Bi
Share unemployed	0.215	0.222	0.286	0.240	0.236	0.371
Labour market outcomes						
Monthly earnings	1,392.818	1,312.448	1,420.444	1,231.226	1,263.365	1,228.342
	357.724	*298.840*	*517.643*	*301.851*	*351.456*	*342.110*
Log monthly earnings	7.209	7.152	7.206	7.085	7.107	7.075
	0.240	*0.243*	*0.316*	*0.250*	*0.258*	*0.280*
Hourly wages	8.427	8.252	9.067	8.047	8.276	8.481
	2.184	*1.894*	*4.307*	*2.023*	*2.099*	*2.379*
Log hourly wages	2.102	2.083	2.129	2.059	2.085	2.104
	0.234	*0.236*	*0.366*	*0.222*	*0.235*	*0.252*
Hours worked	38.307	37.087	37.447	35.767	35.522	34.194
	3.354	*4.750*	*4.813*	*5.723*	*5.381*	*7.115*
Part-time working (less than 32 hours)	0.064	0.135	0.092	0.238	0.294	0.339
Individual characteristics						
Age	26.799	27.611	27.327	26.064	27.061	27.129
	3.905	*3.826*	*3.830*	*3.054*	*3.654*	*3.968*
Partner	0.523	0.449	0.665	0.499	0.553	0.391
Human capital characteristics						
Higher vocational education	0.440	0.454	0.471	0.522	0.457	0.533
University	0.560	0.546	0.529	0.478	0.543	0.467
Type of education						
Law	0.082	0.105	0.065	0.090	0.076	0.085
Economics	0.315	0.233	0.294	0.187	0.128	0.154
Social sciences	0.098	0.176	0.181	0.288	0.394	0.311
Physics	0.057	0.046	0.074	0.021	0.028	0.006
Engineering	0.280	0.146	0.205	0.048	0.029	0.043
Agriculture	0.047	0.045	0.036	0.026	0.039	0.017
Education	0.041	0.045	0.057	0.125	0.088	0.148
Health, medicines	0.044	0.113	0.058	0.124	0.150	0.093
Language, arts	0.031	0.086	0.025	0.087	0.064	0.139
Occupations						
Executives and management	0.037	0.061	0.016	0.022	0.042	0.023
Public sector	0.064	0.059	0.110	0.075	0.061	0.061
Economics and financial	0.139	0.091	0.009	0.060	0.055	0.068
Sales, communication and marketing	0.100	0.097	0.183	0.119	0.104	0.036
Technicians	0.131	0.059	0.047	0.023	0.014	0.027
Programmers, IT	0.145	0.078	0.109	0.023	0.025	0.092
Education	0.150	0.168	0.095	0.224	0.185	0.260
Medical and care	0.037	0.112	0.033	0.132	0.145	0.103
Human resources, administrative support	0.045	0.118	0.147	0.124	0.104	0.066

Other	0.146	0.153	0.247	0.193	0.259	0.259
Industries						
Public services	0.078	0.103	0.103	0.101	0.115	0.155
Education	0.077	0.103	0.097	0.165	0.150	0.216
Professional services	0.329	0.292	0.144	0.233	0.202	0.192
Banking and financial services	0.096	0.071	0.086	0.057	0.043	0.010
Care and personal services	0.054	0.129	0.071	0.211	0.272	0.223
Manufacturing, construction	0.148	0.091	0.155	0.067	0.050	0.050
Other	0.214	0.204	0.340	0.161	0.165	0.149
Year of interview						
1999	0.578	0.663	0.472	0.537	0.596	0.559
N	4,869	241	53	6,117	198	122

Means are weighted averages; standard deviations are in italics; all monetary amounts are measured in euros.

The non-response of respondents to the sexual preference question amounts to 1% on HBO-level and almost 2% for university graduates. These figures seem low, but keeping in mind that homosexuals comprise only a small percentage of the population, selectivity problems may arise if non-response is correlated with sexual orientation. We have in total 294 gay/bisexual and 320 lesbian/bisexual workers. On average this implies that about 5.2% of our respondents belong to sexual minorities: 3.7% are homosexual and 1.5% are bisexual. In our further analysis, we will treat homosexuals and bisexuals as separate groups.

The sexual orientation measure we apply in this paper differs from the behavioral measures used in previous studies. Badgett (1995) and Black et al. (2001) identify homosexuality by asking respondents how many males and females they had sex with. The disadvantage is that their earnings effects rely on only small samples of gay/bisexual and lesbian/bisexual workers. Badgett's findings rely on 34 lesbian and 47 gay workers. Black et al. use the same data covering a longer time spell and work with 101 women and 114 men who are classified as gay, lesbian or bisexual. Both Klawitter and Flatt (1998) and Allegretto and Arthur (2001) use information on the gender of the partner to identify sexual orientation. They use the same sample, but apply different sample selections. They end up with about 4,400 to 6,800 same-sex couples which is one of the larger sets of bi/homosexual workers.

It is obvious that these measures do not fully overlap and that each definition captures some notion of sexual orientation. The key question is, of course, which measure is better in capturing the impact of sexual orientation relevant for labor market outcomes. For the reasons given below, we prefer our approach of measuring sexual identity over the ones previously used.

There are drawbacks that are typical to sexual identity measures based on sexual activity. Behavioral measures are indirect measures and focus on only one particular aspect of homosexuality. If questions on sexual orientation refer only to sexual activity, the potential misclassification would result if people with homosexual tendencies never act upon these urges, or if people who have been sexually experimenting with same-sex partners do not classify themselves as gay, lesbian or bisexual. Moreover, it is extremely hard for both employers and co-workers to obtain information on past sexual experiences. An employer and fellow workers are unlikely to know with whom an employee spends time in bed; they are much more likely to infer something from the impression that a person generates based on his/her sexual preferences. For these reasons, we do not think that behavioral measures based on past sexual experiences are the most appropriate measures.

The advantage of behavioral measures based on partnership is that data are much more widely available. It is probably also much easier for employers and co-workers to obtain information on the gender of the partner, in order to make inferences of a lesbian or gay identity. But measures of this type have one significant drawback: we have already expressed our concern that because behavioral measures based on partnership exclude all singles, we may be introducing sample selectivity. Therefore, our measure based on expressed preferences would appear better, because we ask all individuals about their sexual orientation directly and thus avoid this form of selection bias.

5 Results and estimates

With monthly earnings, we find only small differences in pay for bisexual, homosexual and heterosexual workers. Each month, gay workers earn about 80 euros less, and lesbian workers earn about 30 more than their heterosexual co-workers. In percentages, these differentials in pay amount to a 2 to 5% penalty for homosexual men and a 2 to 3% premium for homosexual women depending on whether we use hourly or monthly earnings. These findings are not entirely in accordance with the empirical literature. Two potential sources of differences are: (i) our sample includes only young workers with higher vocational education or university degrees, and (ii) we use a better measure to identify sexual orientation. Our findings are, however, in line with Becker's prediction and the findings of Black et al. (2001).

With respect to traditional earnings shifters, we find that homosexual respondents are somewhat older. This may be a disclosure effect. If some young workers are still struggling with their sexual identity, and classify themselves as heterosexual at the time of questioning, we should observe that homosexual workers are relatively older within a sample of young workers. With respect to education, we find small differences in type of education. Heterosexual male students more often choose financial and technical than social, health and art studies. This pattern is not observed among female students. With respect to choice of occupation and industry, we find similar differences. Homosexual workers are more likely to have human resources and care-related jobs, whereas heterosexual workers are more likely to work in technical and economic sectors in which, on average, workers are more highly paid. Again, differences are more pronounced for males. Other substantial differences are not observed.

5.1 Simple estimations

Our aim is to isolate the effect of sexual orientation on earnings by controlling for as many variables as possible. These variables are defined as different sets of regressors, categorized according to the personal, occupation and industry characteristics presented in Table 1. For modeling the earnings effects for both genders, we estimate the simplest version of an earnings function suitable for a sample of both gender and sexual orientation, using an earnings function that is linear in gender and sexual orientation and control vector X:

$$\ln w = aX + \theta_{hm}d_{hm} + \theta_{bm}d_{bm} + \theta_f d_f + \theta_{hf}d_{hf} + \theta_{bf}d_{bf} + \varepsilon, \qquad (1)$$

where the variables d_{hm} and d_{bm} are indicators for homosexual and bisexual male workers; d_{hf} and d_{bf} represent homosexual and bisexual female workers; the variable d_f indicates the gender of the worker and equals 1 for females; and the θ's combine gender and sexual orientation effects on earnings. We will estimate this relation using both monthly and hourly earnings, with different sets of controls, on two samples that contain, respectively, all workers and full-timers only, in order to determine whether potential earnings differences are persistent. We use both monthly and hourly earnings to make our research design comparable to previous variable specifications. Klawitter and Flatt (1998) and Allegretto and Arthur (2001) use hourly earnings, whereas Badgett (1995) and Black et al. (2001) present their findings based on annual earnings.

In Table 2, the following estimates are tabulated. In the first column, we report regressions of earnings on dummy variables for gender and sexual orientation without including any other variables. In the second column, we bring individual, human capital and regional controls into the earnings equation. In the third column, we add further occupation and industry characteristics. And finally, in the fourth column, we include hours worked.

Table 2 Earnings premia and penalties by gender and sexual orientation (relative to heterosexual men)

	(1)	(2)	(3)	(4)
Males and females, log monthly earnings, (N = 11,600)				
Male homosexual	-0.052 0.016***	-0.036 0.015**	-0.028 0.014**	-0.022 0.013*
Male bisexual	-0.009 0.037	-0.002 0.032	0.018 0.033	0.023 0.030
Female heterosexual	-0.126 0.004***	-0.076 0.004***	-0.057 0.004***	-0.040 0.004***
Female homosexual	0.025 0.017	0.018 0.016	0.022 0.015	0.018 0.014
Female bisexual	-0.008 0.022	-0.011 0.020	-0.006 0.020	0.012 0.018
R-square	0.068	0.191	0.241	0.357
Males and females, log hourly earnings, (N = 11,600)				
Male homosexual	-0.014 0.015	-0.023 0.014*	-0.018 0.014	-0.023 0.014*
Male bisexual	0.022 0.034	0.012 0.032	0.029 0.031	0.026 0.031
Female heterosexual	-0.045 0.004***	-0.035 0.004***	-0.030 0.004***	-0.041 0.004***
Female homosexual	0.028 0.016*	0.011 0.015	0.013 0.017	0.015 0.014
Female bisexual	0.046 0.020**	0.032 0.019	0.026 0.019	0.013 0.018
R-square	0.019	0.131	0.161	0.226
Males and females, log monthly earnings, part-time workers excluded (N = 9,511)				
Male homosexual	-0.039 0.015**	-0.039 0.014***	-0.034 0.013**	-0.032 0.013*
Male bisexual	-0.015 0.034	-0.023 0.032	0.005 0.031	-0.002 0.031
Female heterosexual	-0.077 0.003***	-0.047 0.004***	-0.035 0.004***	-0.034 0.004***
Female homosexual	0.044 0.018**	0.024 0.017	0.032 0.016*	0.031 0.016
Female bisexual	0.022 0.024	0.007 0.023	0.007 0.021	0.006 0.021
R-square	0.044	0.178	0.226	0.228
Males and females, log hourly earnings, part-time workers excluded (N = 9,511)				
Male homosexual	-0.028 0.015*	-0.032 0.014**	-0.028 0.014**	-0.033 0.013*

Male bisexual	-0.007 *0.034*	-0.007 *0.032*	0.006 *0.031*	-0.005 *0.031*
Female heterosexual	-0.061 *0.004***	-0.039 *0.004***	-0.030 *0.004***	-0.034 *0.004***
Female homosexual	0.041 *0.018**	0.020 *0.017*	0.027 *0.016*	0.032 *0.016*
Female bisexual	0.021 *0.024*	0.007 *0.022*	0.003 *0.022*	0.005 *0.021*
R-square	0.033	0.163	0.202	0.227
Controls				
Individual, human capital and region	no	yes	yes	yes
Occupation and industry	no	no	yes	yes
Hours worked	no	no	no	yes

Standard errors are in italics; *significant at 10% level, ** significant at 5% level, and *** significant at 1% level. The additional control variables are defined and categorized in Table 1.

We begin by discussing the earnings of homosexual men. In column (1), we observe that, compared with heterosexual men, gay workers receive about 5 percent less each month. With hourly earnings, however, the wage differential between homosexual and heterosexual male workers almost disappears. Although homosexual workers keep earning less, the coefficient is smaller and lacks statistical significance. If we restrict ourselves to full-time workers only, the wage penalty for being a homosexual worker is about 3 to 4% and statistically significant. With personal, human capital and regional characteristics added, the results in column (2) do not substantially change. In column (3), we control for occupation and industry differences, and find that homosexual working men always earn less than their heterosexual fellow workers. If we consider all male workers, this is best observed for monthly earnings. If we restrict ourselves to full-time workers only, we find that homosexuals always receive about 3% less. This statistically significant effect is found for both monthly and hourly earnings. The observation that gay workers are more likely to work in less profitable occupations and industries (see Table 1) does not affect the earnings differential among gay and heterosexual workers. With hours worked added, we find that, in terms of size, the effect of being homosexual on monthly and hourly earnings is not affected but that in terms of significance the earnings penalty is (marginally) statistically significant in all specifications. From these results, we conclude that among working men there is a wage penalty for being homosexual.

What about women? First we observe that women in general earn less than men. This is the well-known gender gap that forces the premium for both homosexual and heterosexual women downwards. Depending on the specification used, in our sample women earn about 4 to 13% less. Obviously, this difference has nothing to do with homosexuality. We then measure potential earnings differences among women with the coefficient for homosexual female workers. Without control variables, we find in column (1) that (except for monthly earnings when using both part-time and full-time workers) there are significant differences in both hourly and monthly earnings of homosexual and heterosexual workers. Lesbian workers receive about 3 to 4% more income than heterosexual female workers. With controls added, this premium drops slightly. Using all working women, we find that lesbian workers are still earning somewhat more than their heterosexual female co-workers but the effects are no longer statistically significant. Using only full-time workers, we find that the differences in pay are (marginally) statistically significant. For both monthly and hourly earnings, lesbians receive about 3% more. Hence, there is some evidence, that for women, homosexuality generates a premium.

So in general, whether we use monthly or hourly earnings, we find very similar homosexuality effects. This suggests that, despite the observation that homosexual workers are much more likely to work part-time (see Table 1), the wage penalty for gay workers and the wage premium for lesbian workers is not necessarily generated by differences in the supply of labor. With respect to excluding the unemployed workers, we are aware that selection bias could manifest itself through discrimination in hiring. In Table 1, however, we find that, among homosexual and heterosexual workers, the share of unemployed workers is almost identical. It is further doubtful that our estimates would improve were a selectivity correction to be integrated into the analysis. With the data at hand, we cannot identify selectivity in a meaningful way.

These results show that, in the Netherlands, discrimination on the basis of homosexual orientation at the start of the working career of the more highly educated is absent. Discrimination requires negative earnings effects for being homosexual. Although this is true for gay men, it does not hold for women. In fact, the reversed effects we find for homosexual working women contradict the hypothesis of a discriminating market.[3] Becker's idea of (anticipated) partnership and comparative advantages is perhaps a better explanation for these wage penalties and premia for homosexual male and female workers, respectively. In *A Treatise on the Family*, Becker (1981, p. 225) writes that homosexual unions do not result in children, and that they in general have a less extensive division of labor than heterosexual marriages. In the labor market this means that, for homosexual couples, men spend on average less, while women spend on average more time working. The consequence is that these differences lead to differences in work-related human capital which generate differences in earnings. And the result is that among men homosexual workers earn less, and among women homosexual workers earn more.

5.2 Differences between bisexual and homosexual workers

In the scarce literature, it seems to be standard procedure to pool bisexual and homosexual workers. Two reasons apply. First, small samples of gay, lesbian and bisexual workers dictate that empirical analysis does not allow for treatment differentials. And second, if sexual orientation is measured using the gender of the partner the difference between bisexual and homosexual workers cannot be distinguished. There is a potential danger in this approach when the labor market treats homosexual and bisexual workers differently. And we believe that this is actually the case.

Discrimination in the labor market requires that employers (or fellow workers) know about the workers' sexual orientation and that disclosure has happened involuntarily. At the beginning of working careers, a worker's sexual orientation is not generally known to employers and fellow workers because sexual orientation is, contrary to race or gender, not easily observed. Without accurate information on the workers' sexual orientations, it is likely that bisexual workers will frequently be perceived as heterosexual workers. The result is that, if the market discriminates, the effects will be more prominent among homosexual workers. A quick glance at Table 1 tells us that there is hardly any difference between bisexual and heterosexual workers if we look at monthly earnings. For hourly earnings, we do find that among all workers bisexuals earn relatively more, but this effect is statistically insignificant. This is confirmed by our estimates. In almost all columns, for almost all specifications, there are no statistical differences in pay between bisexual and heterosexual workers. In fact, when we exclude all part-time workers, and with control variables added, we find that the estimated earnings effects for being a bisexual worker hover around 0. If we accept these outcomes at face value, our results show that with respect to earnings bisexual full-time workers are more comparable to heterosexual workers than to homosexual workers (in other words, it is easier for bisexual females to pass as heterosexual workers). We should stress, however, that our male sample contains only a small number of bisexual workers.

5.3 The gender gap re-examined

What follows is that the penalties and premia for homosexual male and female workers, respectively, narrow the gender gap among gay and lesbian workers. Smaller wage differentials among men and women are also observed among heterosexual male and lesbian workers and among gay and heterosexual female workers. We examine whether there are statistically significant differences in pay between men and women using alternative gender gaps by means of F test statistics. These tests are relatively easy to calculate and are based on linear restrictions on the parameters of equation (1). In Table 3, the F statistics are displayed.

Starting with the traditional gender gap, we find (not surprisingly) that heterosexual women always earn statistically less than heterosexual men. This is in line with what is found in the earlier literature, where younger women in the Netherlands earn less than younger men (Berkhout et al. 2001).[4] Among homosexual workers, however, almost all F tests indicate that there are no structural differences in pay in entry-level jobs. The gender gap has vanished Gender differentials can also be examined if earnings of gay men and heterosexual female workers and earnings of lesbian workers and heterosexual males are compared. Without control variables, we find in column (1) that all F tests indicate that gay men always earn significantly more than heterosexual female workers. The same columns shows that for monthly earnings the same statistical differentials are observed for lesbian and heterosexual male workers. But, as soon as we start including other control variables, almost all alternative gender gaps

Table 3 Test statistics for alternative gender gaps

	(1)	(2)	(3)	(4)
F tests for gender gaps, log monthly earnings:				
Heterosexual men and women	720.61 *0.000***	238.75 *0.000***	135.78 *0.000***	76.92 *0.000***
Homosexual men and women	4.27 *0.038***	0.98 *0.322*	0.10 *0.757*	0.00 *0.962*
Gay men and heterosexual women	20.70 *0.006***	6.96 *0.008***	3.80 *0.051***	1.75 *0.186*
Heterosexual men and lesbian women	33.07 *0.000***	12.47 *0.000***	4.86 *0.027***	2.05 *0.151*
F tests for gender gaps, log hourly earnings:				
Heterosexual men and women	107.49 *0.000***	58.28 *0.000***	40.99 *0.000***	80.82 *0.000***
Homosexual men and women	0.01 *0.926*	0.00 *0.993*	0.01 *0.927*	0.02 *0.883*
Gay men and heterosexual women	4.18 *0.040***	0.73 *0.392*	0.66 *0.413*	1.91 *0.166*
Heterosexual men and lesbian women	1.04 *0.308*	2.31 *0.128*	1.22 *0.268*	3.13 *0.077***
F tests for gender gaps, log monthly earnings, part-time workers excluded:				
Heterosexual men and women	293.32 *0.000***	101.49 *0.000***	56.19 *0.000***	52.66 *0.000***
Homosexual men and women	0.09 *0.770*	0.57 *0.451*	2.16 *0.141*	1.99 *0.158*
Gay men and heterosexual women	6.11 *0.013***	0.32 *0.574*	0.00 *0.953*	0.01 *0.936*
Heterosexual men and lesbian women	3.10 *0.078***	1.76 *0.184*	0.03 *0.857*	0.03 *0.864*
F tests for gender gaps, log hourly earnings, part-time workers excluded:				
Heterosexual men and women	184.06 *0.000***	67.59 *0.000***	40.61 *0.000***	50.47 *0.000***
Homosexual men and women	0.12 *0.728*	0.36 *0.546*	1.39 *0.239*	2.34 *0.214*
Gay men and heterosexual women	4.70 *0.030***	0.23 *0.633*	0.02 *0.880*	0.21 *0.648*
Heterosexual men and lesbian women	1.15 *0.283*	1.17 *0.278*	0.03 *0.873*	0.12 *0.732*
Controls				
Individual, human capital and region	no	yes	yes	yes
Occupation and industry	no	no	yes	yes
Hours worked	no	no	no	yes

F test scores are reported in all columns, and *p* values are added in italics.
High test scores imply that the absence of gender differentials is statistically rejected.
Note further that we only compare the earnings of heterosexual and homosexual workers. We ignore the earnings effects of bisexuals.

disappear. Table 3 shows that almost all *F* tests report no statistically significant differences in earnings. This is quite a surprise and sheds some new light on the traditional gender gap among heterosexual workers.

The available literature on traditional gender differentials shows that earnings differentials are rather persistent and remain merely unexplained. In addition, many studies argue that much of the unexplained differences in pay are due to discrimination in the labor market. However, if we look at homosexual workers we find that differences in earnings are absent, which suggests that the discrimination theory no longer holds. The explanation is simple. If employers discriminate on gender and offer higher wages to men, and if employers have no knowledge of the sexual identity of employees because it is not an observable characteristic, heterosexual male workers should always earn more than heterosexual women and lesbian workers. In addition, both gay and heterosexual men should always earn more than heterosexual women. However, from Table 3, we know that this is not the case. This is an interesting result. It means that for young and highly educated workers in the Netherlands, differences in pay by gender are not per se due to discrimination in entry-level jobs.

6 Concluding remarks

In economics, little is known about differences in pay and sexual orientation, partly because access to data is rather limited. With the data available for the Netherlands we have examined how sexual orientation affects earnings at the beginning of the working career. For men, we find that there is an earnings penalty of 3% for gay workers. For women, we find that lesbian workers earn about 3% more than heterosexual female workers. Our sample further reveals that this lesbian wage premium almost fully compensates for the traditional difference in pay that exists between heterosexual men and women. Also for male homosexual workers the penalty almost bridges the well-known gender gap. These results lead us to conclude that, in the Netherlands, discrimination on the basis of sexual orientation or gender is not observed when young and highly educated people enter the labor market. Obviously, this is a result specifically for the Netherlands, which is considered to be rather tolerant towards homosexuality. In other Western societies, our result may not hold. This is certainly true when we compare our outcomes with those reported by Badgett (1995) and Klawitter and Flatt (1998), who use representative US samples and find that discrimination is most prominent among bisexual and homosexual male workers. They find differences in pay up to 30%. Compared to Allegretto and Arthur (2001) and Black et al. (2001), however, we have similar earnings gaps.

The fact that there are some differences in findings does not invalidate either their or our results. The logical explanation is that we use a new, and probably better, measure to identify homosexuality, and study a group of young and highly educated homosexuals, bisexual and heterosexual workers. When people are young and have just entered the labor market, earnings differentials are not that pronounced. Of course, the difference in findings also suggests that there are evident differences between the Netherlands and the US.

Notes

* Both authors would like to thank Jim Albrecht, Mikael Lindahl, Hessel Oosterbeek, Susan Vroman and an anonymous referee for their helpful comments on earlier drafts of this paper. *Responsible editor:* Daniel S. Hamermesh.
1 Allegretto and Arthur (2001) only looked at labor market outcomes of homosexual and heterosexual men. They found that cohabiting homosexuals earned about 2 percent less than unmarried but cohabiting heterosexuals. Compared with married couples, the earnings penalty for being homosexual increased to almost 16 percent. They concluded that the marriage premium is the dominating factor in explaining the earnings differential among homosexual and heterosexual men.
2 About 95% of the Dutch population think that homosexuals should be allowed as far as possible to lead their lives as they please (Social and Cultural Planning Office 1992, 1996). This tolerance is also present in Dutch legislation. For example, laws vary from forbidding employment discrimination against homosexuality to allowing homosexuals to get married and to adopt.
3 It is also possible that a discriminating market leads to segregation of homosexual and heterosexual workers by occupation, industry or firm, and not necessarily to differentials in pay. When we add occupational and industry variables, we find no mediating effect on potential differences in earnings of homosexual workers.
4 For younger workers (age 16–30), they estimate the gender gap to be 0.10. They further find that the gender gap diverges with age. For middle-aged and older cohorts (age 31–45 and 46–65, respectively), the gender gap equals 0.21 and 0.23.

References

Allegretto SA, Arthur MM (2001) An Empirical Analysis of Homosexual/ Heterosexual Male Earnings Differentials: Unmarried and Unequal? *Industrial and Labor Relations Review* 54:631–646

Altonji JG, Blank RM (1999) Race and Gender in the Labor Market. In: Ashenfelter O, Card D (eds) *Handbook of Labor Economics*, vol. III. Elsevier Science, The Netherlands

Badgett LMV (1995) The Wage Effects of Sexual Orientation Discrimination. *Industrial and Labor Relations Review* 48:726–739

Baldwin M, Johnson WG (1994) Labor Market Discrimination Against Men with Disabilities. *Journal of Human Resources* 29:1–19

Becker GS (1971) *The Economics of Discrimination*, 2nd ed. The University of Chicago Press, Chicago

Becker GS (1981) *A Treatise on the Family*. Harvard University Press, Cambridge, MA

Berkhout E, De Graaf D, Heyma A, Theeuwes J (2001) Loondifferentiatie in Nederland: de Vraagkant. (Earnings Differentiation in The Netherlands: the Demand Side). Institute for Labour Studies OSA publication A183, Tilburg University

Black DA, Makar HR, Sanders SG, Taylor LJ (2001) The Effects of Sexual Orientation on Earnings. Center for Policy Research, The Maxwell School, Syracuse University. Unpubl. manuscript

Cain GG (1986) The Economic Analysis of Labor Market Discrimination. In: Ashenfelter O, Layard R (eds) *Handbook of Labor Economics*, vol. I. Elsevier Science, The Netherlands

Hamermesh DS, Biddle J (1994) Beauty in the Labor Market. *American Economic Review* 84:1174–1194

Kauffman KD (1998) Uncovering a Quantitative Economic History of Gays and Lesbians in the United States. *Feminist Economics* 4:61–64

Klawitter MM, Flatt V (1998) The Effects of State and Local Anti-Discrimination Policies for Sexual Orientation. *Journal of Policy Analysis and Management* 17:658–686

Klawitter MM (1998) Why Aren't More Economists Doing Research on Sexual Orientation? *Feminist Economics* 4:55–59

Patterson PL (1998) Uncovering a Quantitative Economic History of Gays and Lesbians in the United States. *Feminist Economics* 4:65–72

The Social and Cultural Planning Office (1992) *Sociaal Cultureel Rapport '92* Rijswijk/The Hague, SCP/VUGA

The Social and Cultural Planning Office (1996) *Sociaal Cultureel Rapport '96* Rijswijk/The Hague, SCP/VUGA

Van de Akker P, Halman L, De Moor R (1994) *Primary Relations in Western Societies*. Tilburg University Press, Tilburq

Wildmer ED, Treas J, Newcomb R (1998) Attitudes Toward Non-Marital Sex in 24 Countries. *The Journal of Sex Research* 35:349–358

Chapter 15

Doris Weichselbaumer

SEXUAL ORIENTATION
DISCRIMINATION IN HIRING

From *Labour Economics* 2003, 10 (6): 629–42

1 Introduction

A NUMBER OF DEMOGRAPHIC groups are reported to be affected by labor market discrimination: women, ethnic and national minorities, disabled workers, as well as religious and sexual minorities have been observed to face unfavorable labor market outcomes. Most studies on discrimination focus on earnings differentials by race or gender since corresponding data is more readily available. Nevertheless, not only do these groups represent merely a fraction of the possibly discriminated population, but discrimination can also take on different forms, i.e. can also occur in hiring, promotion and firing.

This study investigates discrimination against lesbians in hiring. The demographic group of lesbian workers is of particular interest, since – contrary to other social minorities, including gay men – they have repeatedly been shown to earn *higher* wages than their reference group, i.e. heterosexual women (see, e.g. Black et al., 2003; Blandford, 2003; Plug and Berkhout, in press).[1] However, despite their apparently privileged labor market status, 16–46% of gay *and lesbian* survey respondents report to have experienced some form of labor market discrimination (see Badgett et al., 1992, for a review of surveys). These seemingly contradictory findings can be reconciled, however. A number of reasons suggest that lesbians' earnings are overestimated, most importantly because of *unobserved hetero-geneity* and *statistical reasons*.

The adopted *gender role* of lesbians and heterosexual women is one example for such unobserved differences in characteristics. Lesbians are documented as often behaving in more manly ways and being more mascu-line, i.e. more dominant, autonomous, assertive and detached than hetero-sexual women (see Riess et al., 1974). It has been argued that since employers adhere to the ideal of masculinity which is associated with labor market success, lesbians might be financially rewarded in contrast to heterosexual women (see Blandford, 2003; Clain and Leppel, 2001).

However, lesbians might deviate from heterosexual women also in other dimensions. In particular, lesbians have been shown not to adhere to the traditional division of labor within the household where primarily one partner is responsible for household tasks.[2] This is economically rational, since members of same-sex relations often have similar abilities and labor market opportunities which do not allow them to make use of comparative advantages. Furthermore, since most countries do not offer a legal substitute for marriage, specializing in house work becomes a risky choice. Since lesbian couples rear children less frequently, there is less need for a home-maker as well. As a result of reduced household responsibilities, lesbians might be more productive in the workplace and obtain higher wages than heterosexual women. The lack of children also makes higher investments in on-the-job-training profitable since lesbians expect a more continuous labor market participation than heterosexual women. Such higher on-the-job-training, unobservable in the data, might be another reason for the observed higher pay.

In addition to unobserved heterogeneity, there are *statistical reasons* which bias lesbians' earnings upwards. Blandford (2003) reports that lesbian and bisexual women are more successful in entering male-dominated, well-paid occupations than their heterosexual peers and suggests that even controlling for occupations at the two-digit level might be insufficient to capture all effects of *occupational clustering*. Consequently, some of lesbians' higher incomes might be attributable to job subcategories which are not adequately captured by the data. Furthermore, it is most probable that the analyzed data suffer from *sample selection bias*. Higher income indi-viduals are more willing to disclose their lesbian orientation. As a result, their observed earnings are upwardly biased. Last but not least, the empir-ical data suffers from one additional major drawback: Available data sets do not provide information about *disclosure* at the workplace, which is a precondition for direct labor market discrimination by employers. Many gays and lesbians choose not to reveal their sexual orientation on the job to avoid mobbing and employment discrimination, and pass as hetero-sexuals. Badgett (1996) reports from survey data that significantly fewer lesbians out themselves on the job than gay men. This might be another reason why, on average, lesbians do not suffer from the same income loss as gay men.

Due to these specific flaws in the available data, empirical research examining wage differentials, although highly interesting, cannot inform about labor market *discrimination against equally productive gays and lesbians*. From a policy perspective, however – e.g. when fighting direct discrimination or advising gays and lesbians whether to come out – the existence and amount of direct employer discrimination is crucial.

This paper takes a different route to assess differential treatment by using an experimental technique to gather representative data on labor market outcomes of lesbians. Labor market experiments can best be used to investigate discrimination in hiring and have the advantage that typical problems of earnings regressions can be avoided.

2 Experimental investigation

The crucial advantage of an experiment is the full control the researcher has over her data. In particular, identical productivity as well as sexual orientation of workers can be controlled for by the experimenter. Therefore, a carefully setup design allows to test for what is of central interest: *direct discrimination* against openly lesbian employees with equal productivity compared to the heterosexual control group, without having one's data flawed by sample selection and unobserved heterogeneity.

In this study we use a common experimental method called *Correspondence Testing* to examine the hiring chances of lesbians. Résumés of applicants who were matched in all relevant productive characteristics, like age, schooling and job experience, but differed in their indicated sexual preference, were sent out in response to job advertisements. All candidates indicated being single in their CVs to avoid any differences in expected productivity. If one applicant was invited to an interview by an employer, while the other was not, this was assigned to discrimination. With this technique, the labor market outcomes of two identical individuals of equal productivity, who only differ in respect to their demographic group, can be compared directly.[3]

As has been noted before, some economists (Blandford, 2003; Clain and Leppel, 2001) have suggested that lesbians' increased masculinity, their similarity to the stereotypical male, is responsible for their relatively high incomes. Masculinity (being assertive, dominant, etc.)[4] might either constitute a productive personality trait in the labor market, or employers simply have preferences for more masculine workers. Since our experiment gave us full control over workers' characteristics, we wanted to investigate whether those "masculine characteristics" can actually explain lesbians' higher earnings. We found this question particularly interesting, since psychologists have previously argued that one of the reasons why lesbians are *disliked* is their frequent violation of gender stereotypes and display of "inappropriate" gender mannerisms ("butch" and "femme"). Laner and Laner (1980) found that it is personal style as well as sexual preference that triggers a dislike of gays and lesbians. They showed that when a lesbian performs average heterosexual femininity, this in fact *reduces* dislike against her. Consequently, masculinity might not only be beneficial but could as well trigger a taste for discrimination.

Different treatment when equally productive?

A number of reasons why direct discrimination based on sexual orientation might occur are conceivable. In comparison to race and sex discrimination, unfavorable treatment is less likely to be motivated by employers' beliefs in different group averages of productivity, i.e. *statistical discrimination* (Phelps, 1972; Arrow, 1973). Gays and lesbians are the only social minority that is actually brought up within a majority culture (by heterosexual parents) and cannot be identified solely by their looks (skin color, sex).[5] In contrast to females and ethnic minorities, gays and lesbians are socialized according to "majority norms", already from birth on. Consequently, they are most likely to match the social majority group, i.e. heterosexuals, in their average productivity. If anything, statistical discrimination should work in favor of the lesbian! Lesbians are not only better equipped in observables, the fact that they earn more on average even when controlling for observables reflects that they are also doing better in the unobservables. In particular, the fact that they are less likely to drop out of the labor market due to childbirth should make them attractive employees. There-fore, we should expect preferential treatment due to positive statistical discrimination. This would only reduce the amount of discrimination we observe, and Beckerian discrimination, in fact, is underestimated.

When controlling for productive characteristics and gender identity – which might differ for gay/lesbian and heterosexual individuals and cause differences in productivity – most unfavorable treatment can be assigned to a distaste of working with gays and lesbians because of a disapproval of their sexual orientation. Following Becker's (1957) *taste for discrimination* model, entrepreneurs might have a preference to work with heterosexual employees, and if they maximize utility and not profits, they are prepared to hire them, even if they are of lower productivity or have higher reserva-tion wages. Similarly, co-workers' dislikes to working with gays and lesbians might lead to unfavorable treatment. Various surveys indicate that such a dislike against gay and lesbian workers in fact does exist. Black et al. (2003) report that in the General Social Survey data, "83% of men and 80% of women responded that same-sex sexual relations are 'always wrong' or 'usually wrong'." Klawitter and Flatt (1998) give an overview of numerous opinion polls and find that around 20% of Americans do not favor equal job opportunities for gays and lesbians. Nevertheless, the support for equal job opportunities has increased from less than 60% in the late 1970s to around 80% in the 1990s.

3 Method

Correspondence Testing has been widely used to measure race (e.g. Newman, 1978; Firth, 1981; Riach and Rich, 1991) and sex discrimination (Firth, 1982; Riach and Rich, 1995). Adam (1981) used a similar technique for testing discrimination based on sexual orientation. While very interesting in extending the research to a previously neglected area of discrimination, his study has more the touch of a pilot study with its rather small sample and lack of statistical information.

Correspondence Testing allows to compare the labor market outcomes of applicants who are identical in all their productive characteristics but differ in one demographic variable. The necessary data is gained by sending out matched letters of applications to the same job openings. If a firm invites one applicant but not another, then this can be attributed to discrimination.[6] Similar experiments have been used to examine the treatment of same-sex and opposite-sex couples by salespersons' in stores (Walters and Curran, 1996) and by hotels' when requiring a weekend reservation for a room with one bed only (Jones, 1996).

Usually conducted in America, Australia or Great Britain, previous studies using Correspondence Testing suffer from the general drawback that only very short résumés are common in these countries, a fact which possibly does not allow controlling for all relevant variables. Consequently, the possibility of mere statistical discrimination cannot be ruled out (see Heckman, 1998).[7] The Austrian labor market, on the other hand, has the advantage that this problem can be avoided without raising employers' suspicion.[8] In Austria, a very detailed set of documents is required to be considered a serious job applicant. Ideally, the letter of application is supplemented by a curriculum vitae, school reports, letters of reference by previous employers, and a photograph. This vast amount of information largely dismisses the possibility of mere statistical discrimination. A similarly convincing experiment could not be conducted in the US without a great risk of being detected.

To test for discrimination based on sexual orientation and identify whether gender has a mediating effect on differential treatment, a 2 × 2 experimental design has been used, varying sexuality (heterosexual/lesbian identity) and gender (femininity/masculinity) of the applicants. Consequently, application material had to be constructed for four different types: a heterosexual (straight) feminine and straight masculine woman, a feminine lesbian ("femme"), and a masculine lesbian ("butch").[9]

3.1 Gender types

To meet Austrian standards, the application material consisted of a letter of application, an elaborate curriculum vitae, a fake school report and a photograph. Obviously, the need to attach photographs of equally good-looking applicants made the preparation of the application material considerably more demanding, but also served as an advantage for the research question: physical looks are one of the strongest indicators for gender identity and could be used as a signal accordingly. While the masculine woman depicted in the photo had short, dark hair, broad shoulders and was wearing a business jacket, the feminine one had long, blond hair and was in elegant, flowing clothes.

Other indicators for gender identity were the following: choice of font and layout in the CV and hobbies. The layout of the feminine applicant's CV was nice and playful, the design of the masculine appeared rather plain. The feminine female's hobbies were drawing, designing and making of clothes, while the masculine enjoyed rock-climbing, canoeing, playing drums, and motorcycling.[10]

A pre-test was conducted to verify the successful representation of the two females' gender identity and to ensure that the differences of all job applicants in their self-presentation (in particular the photographs) did not cause distortions in general desirability. One hundred nineteen business students were asked to evaluate one applicant each, represented by her CV and photo. There was no information on sexual orientation given for the candidates. The Bem Sex-Role Inventory[11] used is a standard measure for gender identity in psychology and provides a sufficient tool to test the dimensions "femininity", "masculinity", and "social desirability". While the feminine female achieved significantly higher scores in femininity and the masculine female in masculinity, the scores of the two candidates on social desirability were almost identical.[12]

3.2 Sexual orientation types

For half of the applicants no explicit information on sexual orientation was given, these were classified as heterosexuals. The lesbians were labeled by the following information about their secondary occupation: "1996–1998: Managerial activity for the Viennese Gay People's Alliance." To indicate that this personal engagement in the gay and lesbian movement would not conflict with job dedication, the affiliation with the Gay People's Alliance already laid in the past.[13] In contrast to many other gay and lesbian organizations around the world, the Austrian Gay People's Alliance has no affinities to any political party but represents gays and lesbians of all political and religious convictions. To signal a similar amount of social awareness, this commitment to volunteer work by the lesbians was juxtaposed by matching statements for the straight applicants, varied for different gender identities. The feminine straight woman declared to volunteer for a nonprofit organization assisting school children with learning disabilities and the masculine woman for a nonprofit cultural center.

The different sexuality/gender types were simply created by combining the gendered CVs with the sexual orientation information.

The application letters were constructed to match the average employee in the clerical profession, i.e. accountant and secretary.[14] This occupational category was chosen because the relatively high labor demand allowed sending out a sufficient number of standardized applications in response to job advertisements to gather a representative sample. Furthermore, it allowed to create convincing application material (e.g. by providing school reports), and to submit written applications (in many occupations, phone calls are required to test the verbal fluency of applicants).

To avoid detection, names of employers were avoided in the CVs and job experience was formulated in a rather general way. All accountants and secretaries had identical human capital and obtained their education in exactly the same school-type, only at different locations. The school marks in the attached school reports were identical for all applicants in those subjects of primary relevance for the jobs under investigation and equal on average in subjects of lower interest. The photograph was attached in the form of a (digitally manipulated) image color-printed on the CV, which is a common cost-saving practice used by Austrian job applicants.

3.3 Sending out the applications

While it is not an absolute necessity to send all the different applications to each firm, it serves the advantage of controlling for firm-specific variables.[15] Besides that it allows to collect data more quickly.

In principle, the most straightforward experiment to test for discrimination based on sexual orientation would be to send applications of all four different applicants, the feminine straight (FS), the masculine straight (MS), the feminine lesbian (FL) and the masculine lesbian (ML), to the same vacancies and compare the invitation rates. Evaluating the success rates for an identical woman who one time indicates she is a lesbian, and the other time does not, would allow to measure the effect of sexual orientation. At the same time, a comparison of the feminine and masculine female of one particular sexual orientation could be used to calculate the effect of gender. However, the actual research setup faces a special problem: two identical applications of a single individual – one time labeled as lesbian, the other time not – cannot be sent to the same firm. They would be immediately identified as representing one single person instead of being evaluated independently. Particularly, the photograph leads to an instantaneous recognition of the identical applicant. Similarly, it is not possible to send the applications of the two lesbians to one firm. Employers would certainly detect the "coincidence" of two applicants declaring themselves as lesbians at the same time! Consequently, we had to choose a more indirect route to gain the desired data. First, we collected data comparing the two heterosexual women, then we submitted applications by one heterosexual and one lesbian with differing gender identity to each firm under investigation. This avoided the problem of detection, but still allowed to control for firm-specific variables.

The Saturday issue of the Austrian newspaper "Kurier" was examined weekly for relevant job advertisements, as it provides the largest amount of job announcements from the biggest Austrian labor market, the Greater Vienna area.

The experiment was conducted in three different steps: from early to late 1998, all the firms searching for accountants or secretaries were contacted by the two straight women (round 1). In the next step, from late 1998 to mid-1999, applications of the feminine straight and masculine lesbian women were sent to all vacancies (round 2). Finally, from mid-1999 to early 2000, the feminine lesbian and masculine straight woman applied to all announced vacancies (round 3). In total, 1226 applications were sent out in response to 613 job openings.

If an entrepreneur was interested in one of the applicants, she could be contacted either through a Viennese address, or by leaving a message on her answering machine. When one of the applicants was invited to an interview, the proposed appointment was canceled to avoid any inconveniences on the firm's side.

4 Results

4.1 Discrimination against masculine woman

Table 1 shows the invitation rates of the different applicants. Table 1a illustrates the effect of sexual orientation on the masculine woman. First, the pair of straight females with different gender identity applied to each relevant job opening. The feminine woman was invited by 43.38% of all contacted firms, the masculine one by 42.65%, which means that the feminine female was more successful by 0.74 percentage points. The null hypothesis that the two women were treated the same could not be

Table 1

(a) Effect of sexual orientation on masculine female

	Invitation rates – 1st round		Invitation rates – 2nd round
N = 272		N = 171	
Feminine straight, FS	43.38%	Feminine straight, FS	60.82%
Masculine straight, MS	42.65%	Masculine lesbian, ML	47.95%
Difference, FS – MS	0.74%	Difference, FS – ML	12.87%
Effect of sexual orientation, difference in differences (MS – ML) = –12.13%*			

(b) Effect of sexual orientation on feminine female

	Invitation rates – 1st round		Invitation rates – 3rd round
N = 272		N = 170	
Masculine straight, MS	42.65%	Masculine straight, MS	48.82%
Feminine straight, FS	43.38%	Feminine lesbian, FL	36.47%
Difference, MS – FS	–0.74%	Difference, MS – FL	12.35%
Effect of sexual orientation, difference in differences (FS – FL) = –13.09%*			

N = number of firms contacted by pair of applicants.
* Significant at the 5% level.

rejected. Second, applications of the feminine straight female and the masculine lesbian were sent out to all firms. The feminine straight applicant was successful in 60.82% of all cases, the masculine lesbian in 47.95%.[16] This represents an advantage of the feminine straight female of 12.87 percentage points. Remember that this difference occurs, although both individuals apply to the same firms, i.e. firm specific effects are controlled for. What is of central interest, though, is the comparison between the masculine straight and lesbian female, which can only be obtained via the difference in differences: The advantage of the feminine straight woman over the masculine woman increases from 0.74 percentage points to 12.87 percentage points, when the latter indicates lesbian orientation. This indicates an advantage of the straight masculine female over her lesbian counterpart of 12.13 percentage points[17] and means that the probability of the masculine female to be invited to an interview decreases by 12.13 percentage points when she reveals a lesbian orientation.[18]

4.2 Discrimination against feminine woman

Table 1b demonstrates the effect of sexual orientation on the feminine female. As has been noted before, the straight feminine female has an advantage over her masculine counterpart of 0.74 percentage points. In the next step, the masculine straight female and the feminine lesbian applied for the same jobs. The masculine straight woman was invited to an interview by 48.82 percentage points of all contacted firms, the feminine lesbian by 36.47 percentage points. Consequently, the masculine straight woman had an advantage compared to the feminine lesbian of 12.35 percentage points. Calculating the difference in differences (DD), we see that the declaration of her sexual preference decreases the feminine female's chances to be invited for an interview by 13.09 percentage points.[19]

The underlying assumption of the DD experiment is that while the absolute values of invitation rates for the straight applicants can be different in each stage, e.g. due to the business-cycle or – as is more likely in our experiment – seasonal changes, the differences in invitation rates must be invariant over the different stages of the experiment.[20]

The effects of sexual orientation and gender are also presented in Table 2, where the probability of being invited to an interview is estimated with a logit model. The observed values are 0 and 1, i.e. not invited, invited to an interview. The probability of being invited to an interview is estimated as a function of gender (femininity versus masculinity) and sexual orientation. The table presents marginal effects. Since the different rounds took place sequentially, they are included in the estimation to control for

Table 2 Invitation to an interview

| | Logit (marginal effects) | |
	(1)	(2)
Masculine gender	−0.004 (0.15)	−0.007 (0.17)
Lesbian sexual orientation	−0.126 (3.39)**	−0.131 (2.00)*
Masculine lesbian		0.011 (0.10)
Round 2	0.177 (4.56)**	0.175 (3.62)**
Round 3	0.059 (1.49)	0.062 (1.27)
Observations	1226	1226

Absolute value of z-statistics in parentheses.
* Significant at 5%.
** Significant at 1%.

time-effects. No other controls are necessary since the applicants are matched in all other characteristics than gender and sexual orientation. While gender does not have an effect on invitation rates (neither feminine nor masculine women are preferred by employers), sexual orientation has very much so. As has been seen before, an indicator for lesbian orientation reduces the probability to be invited to an interview by 13.10 percentage points for the feminine and 12 percentage points for the masculine female. This means indicating a lesbian orientation when applying for a job triggers unfavorable treatment while one's personal style (femininity or masculinity) does not seem to matter.

5 Conclusions

In this paper we examined the impact of lesbian sexual orientation and gender identity on the chances of getting invited to a job interview. Previous research investigating discrimination based on sexual orientation has provided ambiguous results for lesbians' earnings, usually indicating higher incomes for lesbians. However, this advantage for lesbian workers could be due to a number of different reasons, e.g. selection bias (only high income lesbians disclose their sexual orientation), insufficient controls for occupations, or unobserved differences in productive characteristics. Furthermore, since the available data does not provide information on disclosure on the job, a large number of investigated individuals might not be "out" on the job and therefore not confronted with an income loss – although discrimination based on sexual orientation does occur to those "outed" to the public.

Our experiment allowed to collect data free of any of the previously mentioned flaws, comparing the labor market outcomes for *open* lesbians and heterosexual women of *identical productivity* in the clerical profession in Austria. Additionally, we tested whether increased masculinity is responsible for lesbians' higher earnings as suggested by Blandford (2003) and Clain and Leppel (2001).

We find that indicating a lesbian identity reduces one's invitation rate by about 12–13 percentage points, which corresponds with Adam's (1981) results, who finds a 11 percentage points reduction of invitation rates for females in the city of Toronto. Since the experimental setup controlled for productivity, it has to be discrimination which is responsible for this unfavorable treatment of lesbians. Customers' discrimination is an unlikely source for differential treatment since the investigated jobs do not require much customer contact. However, co-workers' discrimination as well as employer's discrimination can be responsible for this outcome. While the bosses of most positions we applied to probably were male, the jobs under investigation were clearly female-dominated and suggest predominantly female co-workers. However, Kite and Whitley (1996) showed in their meta-study that – although men hold more negative attitudes toward gay men – men and women do not significantly differ in their negative attitudes toward lesbians. Consequently, both groups – employers and coworkers – are equally likely to cause differential treatment.

The hypothesis that gender identity might have a separate influence on labor market outcomes could not be verified. This means, at least with respect to being invited to an interview, that increased masculinity neither works as an advantage nor as a disadvantage – neither for straight nor lesbian women.

Although wage regressions indicate higher earnings for lesbian women, the results of this study demonstrate that lesbians are, in fact, not a relatively privileged group, but – much to the contrary – are subject to discrimination. Their higher incomes may be due to measurement errors or increased productivity. This productivity might be driven by higher effort and on-the-job-training and is possible, since lesbians do carry less household responsibility, but also necessary, because they cannot receive transfers from a partner.

Acknowledgements

This research was supported by the Allgemeine Sparkasse research prize. Sandra Leitner provided invaluable assistance with the data collection. Thanks to Rudolf Winter-Ebmer, Lee Badgett, Dan Black, Josef Fersterer, seminar participants in Linz and at the ESA meetings in Barcelona as well as an anonymous referee for helpful comments.

Notes

1   For a review of studies on wage differentials based on sexual orientation, see Badgett (2002).
2   For a review of the literature, see Giddings (in press).
3   Certainly this experimental method does impose some costs on the employer, as résumés of applicants who are actually not available have to be evaluated, but these costs are not infrequent, as workers often want to test their outside opportunities to increase their bargaining situation at the current job (Riach and Rich, 1995).
4   Bem (1974) specifies the following characteristics as commonly being perceived as "typically male": acts as a leader, aggressive, ambitious, analytical, assertive, athletic, competitive, defends own beliefs, dominant, forceful, has leadership abilities, independent, individualistic, makes decisions easily, masculine, self-reliant, self-sufficient, strong personality, willing to take a stand, willing to take a risk.
5   Other examples for characteristics, which are unobservable and employers might have preferences for, are religion or national origin (Badgett, 1995).
6   Obviously testing whether somebody gets invited for an interview captures differential treatment at the initial stage of hiring only, while some employers might delay

their "discriminatory activity" until later. Still, the possibility of receiving a job offer is conditional on being invited to an interview, which means that differential treatment in hiring has to be equal or larger to what is measured by Correspondence Testing (Riach and Rich, 1995). Researchers at the Urban Institute (e.g. Kenney and Wissoker, 1994) have extended this method to the next stage of the hiring process. In their "Audit Studies", they have not only sent out written applications but also matched pairs of real applicants of different ethnic groups who actually met employers for an interview. This allows the observing of discrimination in actual job offers, although it suffers from the disadvantage that real-life applicants who meet all the required criteria are hard to find. Furthermore, it is impossible to control for differences in real-life interactions that might take place during an interview. "Audit Studies" have also been conducted to measure discrimination in housing, applying for a mortgage, negotiating the price of a car and seeking taxi services (see Fix et al., 1993 for an overview of auditing for discrimination).

7   When testing for discrimination based on sexual orientation this is generally a less severe problem, however, since – as has been stated before – there seems to be little prejudice about gays' and lesbians' productivity. If there are no presumed differences in productivity, no statistical discrimination can occur.

8   Austria has not yet adopted any anti-discrimination policies protecting gays and lesbians against unfair treatment in the labor market, in contrast to 12 states and many cities in the US and most other countries in the European Union that already have anti-discrimination laws. However, a directive by the European Union in autumn 2000 imposes the implementation of such a national law upon Austria within a time frame of three years.

9   Detailed application materials (standard letters of application, CVs, school reports and photographs) are available from the author upon request.

10   In addition, different international job experiences (au pair girl for the feminine, motorcycle tour with occasional jobs for the masculine female) were given for accountants, one of the two occupational subcategories tested. Since they were of higher age than the secretaries (matched to the average employee in the occupation), it was possible to indicate one-and-a-half years international experience for both applicants without evoking too much suspicion. See Weichselbaumer (in press) for details.

11   See Bern (1974) for description.

12   Only one previous study using Correspondence Testing, Newman (1978), reported the attachment of photographs, and was severely criticized for not controlling for physical attractiveness of the applicants (see McIntyre et al., 1980). Since a number of studies have shown that beauty has an impact on labor market decisions (e.g. Hamermesh and Biddle, 1994; 1998; Averett and Korenman, 1996), it seemed important to add physical attractiveness as a separate item to the social desirability dimension provided by the Bem Sex-Role Inventory. Similarly, the item "making a competent impression" was included to ensure that photographs and other variations in the CVs did not cause one applicant to look relatively more proficient than the other. For details on scores of applicants and statistical tests, see Weichselbaumer (in press).

13   Some employers might not discriminate against lesbians per se, but only against those who *list* participation in gay and lesbian organizations on their CVs. They may perceive the lesbian applicant as a radical or as lacking business savvy, since she does not try to hide her sexual orientation more actively. However, previous professional engagement with a gay and lesbian organization clearly serves as an indicator for relevant job experience, so hiding sexual orientation means either concealing relevant human capital or lying about one's past with the risk of being detected.

In previous experiments, authors indicated sexual orientation by affectionate behavior of the individuals (holding hands, talking to one another smiling) (Walters and Curran, 1996) or by couples requesting a room with one bed only in a hotel (Jones, 1996).

14   Both of these jobs are female-dominated ones: 77% of all accountants and 97% of all secretaries are women. The average income of women in both occupations is €1000 according to the Micro Census 1997; the average overall female income is €900 (male: €1300). Weichselbaumer (in press) has tested the effect of sex and gender conformity of heterosexual applicants not only for female- but also for male-dominated occupations and found discrimination by sex but not by gender.

15   Adam (1981) sent only one résumé to each firm, which does not control for firm specific effects, but allows using completely identical letters of application instead of creating matching ones, since there is no danger of detection.

16   The high overall rates of invitations in the second round are rather striking and must be due to seasonal changes. Other exogenous changes of labor demand or other macroeconomic variables are possible but unlikely within this short time period, since there were no observable changes in the business cycle.

17   Investigating discrimination for the two occupational subcategories separately, we find significant discrimination against the masculine lesbian only for secretaries. This might be due to the fact that normative heterosexuality is more of an inherent requirement for secretaries while accountants often work autonomously and have even less contact with clients and customers.

18   The negative effect of discrimination is significant at the 5% level using a one-sided test.

19   Again, this effect is significantly different from zero at the 5% level.

20   When indicating a lesbian orientation, the invitation rate of the feminine female decreases by a higher amount (13.09%) than that of the masculine one (12.13%); nevertheless, the difference between the two gender types is statistically insignificant ($13.09-12.13 = 0.96$. The difference of 0.0096 lies within the confidence interval for $\alpha = 5\%$ which is $[-0.226, 0.245]$). This implies both women have an identical disadvantage when disclosing their sexual preference.

References

Adam, B.D., 1981. Stigma and employability: discrimination by sex and sexual orientation in the ontario legal profession. *Canadian Review of Sociology and Anthropology* 18 (2), 216–221.

Arrow, K.J., 1973. The theory of discrimination. In: Ashenfelter, O., Rees, A. (Eds.), *Discrimination in Labor Markets*. Princeton Univ. Press, New Jersey, pp. 3–33.

Averett, S., Korenman, S., 1996. The economic reality of the beauty myth. *Journal of Human Resources* 31 (2), 304–330.

Badgett, L.M.V., 1995. The wage effects of sexual orientation discrimination. *Industrial and Labor Relations Review* 48 (4), 726–739.

Badgett, L.M.V., 1996. Employment and sexual orientation: disclosure and discrimination in the workplace. In: Ellis, A., Riggle, E. (Eds.), *Sexual Identity on the Job. Issues and Services*. Harrington Park Press, New York, pp. 29–52.

Badgett, L.M.V., 2002. Discrimination based on sexual orientation. A Review of the Literature in Economics and Beyond, manuscript.

Badgett, L.M.V., Donnelly, C., Kibbe, J., 1992. *Pervasive Patterns of Discrimination Against Lesbians and Gay Men: Evidence from Surveys Across the United States*. National Gay and Lesbian Task Force Policy Institute, Washington, DC.

Becker, G.S., 1957. *The Economics of Discrimination*. University of Chicago Press, Chicago.

Bem, S.L., 1974. The measurement of psychological androgyny. *Journal of Consulting and Clinical Psychology* 42 (2), 155–162.

Biddle, J.E., Hamermesh, D.S., 1998. Beauty, productivity, and discrimination: lawyers' looks and lucre. *Journal of Labor Economics* 16 (1), 172–201.

Black, D.A., Makar, H.R., Sanders, S.G., Taylor, L.J., 2003. The earnings effects of sexual orientation on earnings. *Industrial and Labor Relations Review* 56 (3), 449–469.

Blandford, J.M., 2003. The nexus of sexual orientation and gender in the determination of earnings. *Industrial and Labor Relations Review* 56 (4), 622–642.

Clain, S.H., Leppel, K., 2001. An investigation into sexual orientation discrimination as an explanation for wage differences. *Applied Economics* 33, 37–47.

Firth, M., 1981. Racial discrimination in the British labor market. *Industrial and Labor Relations Review* 34 (2), 265–272.

Firth, M., 1982. Sex discrimination in job opportunities for women. *Sex Roles* 8 (8), 891–901.

Fix, M., Galster, G.C., Struyk, R.J., 1993. An overview of auditing for discrimination. In: Fix, M., Struyk, R.J. (Eds.), *Clear and Convincing Evidence. Measurement of Discrimination in America*. Urban Institute Press, Washington, DC, pp. 1–67.

Giddings, L.A., in press. The division of labor in same-sex households. In: Moe, K.S. (Ed.), *Economics of Gender and the Family*. Blackwell, Portland.

Hamermesh, D.S., Biddle, J.E., 1994. Beauty and the labor market. *American Economic Review* 84 (5), 174–1194.

Heckman, J.J., 1998. Detecting discrimination. *Journal of Economic Perspectives* 12 (2), 101–116.

Jones, D.A., 1996. Discrimination against same-sex couples in hotel reservation policies. *Journal of Homosexuality* 31 (1–2), 153–159.

Kenney, G.M., Wissoker, D.A., 1994. An analysis of the correlates of discrimination facing young Hispanic job-seekers. *American Economic Review* 84 (3), 674–683.

Kite, M.E., Whitley, B.E., 1996. Sex differences in attitudes toward homosexual persons, behaviors, and civil rights: a meta-analysis. *Personality and Social Psychology Bulletin* 22 (4), 336–353.

Klawitter, M.M., Flatt, V., 1998. The effects of state and local anti-discrimination policies on earnings for gays and lesbians. *Journal of Policy Analysis and Management* 17 (4), 658–686.

Laner, M.R., Laner, R.H., 1980. Sexual preference or personal style? Why lesbians are disliked. *Journal of Homosexuality* 5 (4), 339–356.

McIntyre, S.J., Moberg, D.J., Posner, B.Z., 1980. Discrimination in recruitment:

an empirical analysis (comment). *Industrial and Labor Relations Review* 33 (4), 543–547.

Newman, J.M., 1978. Discrimination in recruitment: an empirical analysis. *Industrial and Labor Relations Review* 32 (1), 15–23.

Phelps, E.S., 1972. The statistical theory of racism and sexism. *American Economic Review* 62 (4), 659–661.

Plug, E., Berkhout, P., in press. Effects of sexual preferences on earnings in the Netherlands. *Journal of Population Economics*.

Riach, P.A., Rich, J., 1991. Testing for racial discrimination in the labor market. *Cambridge Journal of Economics* 15, 239–259.

Riach, P.A., Rich, J., 1995. An investigation of gender discrimination in labor hiring. *Eastern Economic Journal* 21 (3), 343–356.

Riess, B.F., Safer, J., Yotive, W., 1974. Psychological test data on female homosexuality: a review of the literature. *Journal of Homosexuality* 1 (1), 71–85.

Walters, A.S., Curran, M.-C., 1996. "Excuse me, sir? May I help you and your boyfriend?: salespersons' differential treatment of homosexual and straight customers. *Journal of Homosexuality* 31 (1–2), 135–152.

Weichselbaumer, D., in press. Is it sex or personality? The impact of sex-stereotypes on discrimination in applicant selection. *Eastern Economic Journal*.

Queer consumer economics

THE QUEER CONSUMER HAS always been around. Gays and lesbians have always bought food, clothing, and other goods just like any hetero-sexual. Yet with the solidification of the gay identity and the creation of gay communities throughout the United States, the homosexual has now potentially left their previous demographic of "housewife" or "young professional" and instead become typed as "gay or lesbian." This phenomenon is more than a difference in nomenclature. It is shaping spending patterns of gays and lesbians, and the power of the "queer dollar" is no longer a force that can be ignored. A scholarly literature has arisen that both analyzes the dimensions of this phenomenon and provides critical perspectives on both the nature and desirability of marketer awareness of queer consumers, as well as questioning whether queer consumers are really treated equally with straight consumers in their market interactions.

Amy Gluckman and Betsy Reed's chapter, "The gay marketing moment" (1997), examines the recent surge in origins and implications of corporate inter-est in the gay community. Corporations have commonly assumed that gays, par-ticularly men, have larger disposable incomes due to their family structure, preferences, etc. Corporations have been advertising to gays and lesbians in a more targeted fashion due to the assumption that queer customer loyalty is extremely high. Yet these companies are targeting gays and lesbians as "gay straights" rather than as queers with separate issues and interests than straights.

Lisa Peñaloza, in "We're here, we're queer, and we're going shopping! A critical perspective on the accommodation of gays and lesbians in the US marketplace" (1996), provides a detailed overview of both marketing practices aimed at gays and lesbians and a theoretically based critique of queer repre-sentations in marketing. Peñaloza gives examples of the portrayal of gays and lesbians in ads that are targeted specifically at queer consumers. One might also be interested in marketing to straights that nonetheless uses queer symbol-ism, or marketing to both gays and straights using symbolism that appeals to both, or a mix of symbols within one advertisement.

While Section Six of this book discussed potential labor market discrimin-ation, another form of discrimination can occur – namely, treatment of homo-sexual clients. Andrew S. Walters and Maria-Cristina Curran, in "Excuse me sir? May I help you and your boyfriend?" (1996), show that discrimination is apparently present in some dealings with gay consumers. They perform an experimental field study to ascertain differences in retail store staff's treat-ment of same-sex versus opposite-sex couples, and find significant differences in response time of staff and rude behavior by staff (see also Jones [1996] for a discussion of discrimination against same-sex couples in the hotel industry).

Besides these influential early articles, a number of additional articles and books exist in the area of queer consumer economics. Some of these pieces constitute "how-to" manuals regarding how one might market to queer consumers (Lukenbill 1999; Witeck and Combs 2006), while others provide more scholarly analyses of particular aspects of queer consumer patterns (Edwalds and Stocker 1995; Wardlow 1996; Koyuncu and Lien 2003; Lewis and Seaman 2004; Branchik 2006). Other articles take a more theoretical approach to the underlying dynamics of what it means to be a queer consumer (Kates 1998, 2002, 2004; Badgett 2001). Still other articles take a more critical perspective on the concept of the gay consumer and question whether having major corporations and advertising agencies treating queers as a consumer demographic is something that should be considered as problematic (Chain 2001; Sears 2005; Sender 2005; Commercial Closet Association).

DISCUSSION QUESTIONS

1   Does targeting queer consumers pay off even though many homophobic customers may avoid the specific corporation or product?
2   Can queers truly have customer loyalty when if it appears that corporations do not care about gays and lesbians *per se*, or about their rights, but just care about their money?
3   Peñaloza's chapter originally had a number of illustrations of gay-targeted advertisements from the era of her paper. Can you find examples of current gay-targeting advertising? What about lesbian- or bisexual-targeting advertising? Discuss your examples with regards to the imagery included and your perception of its effectiveness in marketing to queer consumers.
4   How is the post-gay image in gay-targeting advertising affecting America's perception of the queer community? Can you find examples of such advertising? Is there a similar wave of advertising relating to lesbian imagery?
5   Does negative treatment of gay/lesbian consumers reflect a conscientious effort of employers to avoid queer customers, or the personal sentiments of employees, and society at large?
6   The three chapters in this section will all be over a decade old by the time of this book's publication. Do you think the patterns they describe are still relevant at the time you are reading this book?

REFERENCES

Badgett, M. V. L. (2001) *Money, Myths, and Change: the economic lives of lesbians and gay men*, Chicago and London: University of Chicago Press.

Branchik, B. J. (2006) "Out in the market: the history of the gay market segment in the United States," in T. Dalgic (ed.) *Handbook of Niche Marketing: principles and practice,* Binghamton, N.Y. and London: Haworth Press.

Chain, A. (2001) *Selling Out: the gay and lesbian movement goes to market,* London: Palgrave Macmillan.

Commercial Closet Association, <http://www.commercialcloset.org/>.

Edwalds, L. and Stocker, M. (eds) (1995) *The Woman-Centered Economy: ideals, reality and the space in between,* Chicago: Third Side Press.

Jones, D. A. (1996) "Discrimination against same-sex couples in hotel reservation policies," in *Gays, Lesbians, and Consumer Behavior: theory, practice, and research issues in marketing,* ed. D. L. Wardlow, Special issue of *Journal of Homosexuality,* 31: 153–9.

Kates, S. M. (1998) "Twenty million new customers! Understanding gay men's consumer behavior," *Gay and Lesbian Studies,* New York and London: Haworth Press, Harrington Park Press.

—— (2002) "The protean quality of subcultural consumption: an ethnographic account of gay consumers," *Journal of Consumer Research,* 29: 383–99.

—— (2004) "The dynamics of brand legitimacy: an interpretive study in the gay men's community," *Journal of Consumer Research,* 31: 455–64.

Koyuncu, C. and Lien, D. (2003) "E-commerce and consumer's purchasing behaviour," *Applied Economics,* 35: 721–6.

Lewis, G. B. and Seaman, B. A. (2004) "Sexual orientation and demand for the arts," *Social Science Quarterly,* 85: 523–38.

Lukenbill, G. (1999) *Untold Millions: secret truths about marketing to gay and lesbian consumers,* 2nd edition, Binghamton, N.Y.: Harrington Park Press.

Sears, A. (2005) "Queer anti-capitalism: what's left of lesbian and gay liberation?" *Science and Society,* 69: 92–112.

Sender, K. (2005) *Business, not Politics: the making of the gay market,* New York: Columbia University Press.

Wardlow, D. L. (ed.) (1996) *Gays, Lesbians, and Consumer Behavior: theory, practice, and research issues in marketing,* Special issue of *Journal of Homosexuality,* 31.

Witeck, B. and Combs, W. (2006) *Business Inside Out: capturing millions of brand loyal gay consumers,* Chicago Kaplan Publishing.

Chapter 16

Amy Gluckman and Betsy Reed

THE GAY MARKETING MOMENT

From *Dollars & Sense*, November/December (1993)

SINCE A COCKY k. d. lang reveled in Cindy Crawford's feminine attentions on the cover of *Vanity Fair* in the summer of 1993, other icons of "lesbian chic" have been showing off their buzzcuts in androgynous ads, while gay men flex their pecs in mainstream magazines and, more figuratively, in the upper echelons of the business world. *Newsweek*, having declared cuddly, cohabitating "Lesbians" all the rage the previous year, observed a sudden bisexual moment sweeping the nation in 1995. Fashionably late, following centuries of invisibility punctuated by hostile caricatures, a conspicuous kind of gay liberation announced its own important arrival in the 1990s.

Gay and lesbian political activists, who have toiled for decades at the grassroots level to promote a welcoming climate for gay men and lesbians, certainly deserve a large share of the credit for the proliferation of gay-positive images, both in ads and in other media. But it is not as if liberation has suddenly become the bottom line for many of those peddling glamorous pictures of lesbians, bisexuals, and gay men. Marketers, who make it a rule to tolerate their markets, have had a revelation. The profits to be reaped from treating gay men and lesbians as a trend-setting consumer group finally outweigh the financial risks of inflaming right-wing hate. As George Slowik, Jr., publisher of the prosperous, glossy *Out* magazine, said in a 1993 interview, "Our demographics are more appealing than those of 80-year-old Christian ladies."

"Untold millions,"[1] or so the title of one recent business book pro-claims, lie in the deep pockets of gay consumers, a demographic group that can best be tapped by placing ads in outlets like *Out*, as well as in predomin-antly straight venues that allow tantalizing glimpses of gay life. Advertisers are steering toward gay publications that promote a stylish, widely palat-able vision of gay life – primarily glossy mags like *Out* and *The Advocate* that have been cleansed of the objectionable: phone sex ads, radical politics, and hard core leather culture. This foray into even sanitized gay media is big news in the advertising business. Marketing and business publications exhibit a wary excitement, with headlines like "The Gay Market: Nothing to Fear Bur Fear Itself," "Untapped Niche Offers Marketers Brand Loyalty," and "Mainstream's Domino Effect: Liquor, Fragrance, Clothing Advertisers Ease into Gay Magazines." Along with Absolut, Calvin Klein, and Benetton, corporations that have taken the lead in advertising in mainstream gay publications include Philip Morris, Columbia Records, Miller beer, Seagram's, and Hiram Walker.

These newfound suitors of gay consumers have not come calling with-out any encouragement. Rather, their interest has been piqued by organiza-tions – usually run by gays – that conduct surveys and employ selected information about gay consumers to persuade advertisers that a viable gay and lesbian market exists. For instance, Strub Media Group, led by openly-gay *Poz* publisher Sean Strub, distributes a flyer claiming that readers of gay publications have an average household income of $63,100, compared to $36,500 for all households. Gay marketing groups also point out that since gay men and lesbians have no children (more and more a false assumption), their disposable income is even higher than their average income would suggest. According to well-publicized data from another gay marketing organization, Over-looked Opinions, 80 percent of gay men eat out more than five times a month. And a promotional package used by a network of local gay newspapers asserts that gay men and lesbians travel more, buy more CDs, use their AmEx card more, and generally spend more money on the good life than do their straight counterparts. The most-valuable target market – the one that is most conspicuous in the marketing literature – is white, urban, white-collar, and predominantly male.

Prime conditions exist for these notions to color popular views of gay men and lesbians. Unlike other subgroups that could never "pass," the clearest characteristic of gay men and lesbians has been, until recently, their invisibility. To be sure, there have been some stereotypes out there, focusing mostly on sexual promiscuity and mental instability. But most straight Americans have harbored few ideas about whether gay men and lesbians were rich or poor, spendthrift or frugal. Past gay invisibility has provided a blank slate of sorts, a slate that is rapidly filling up with notions that have more to do with marketing than with reality.

And the fault lies partly with overzealous gay marketing groups. While anecdotes about free-spending, double-income gay households do accurately represent one segment of the gay community, they have unfortunately been presented as descriptive of all gay men and lesbians. Eager to persuade reluctant corporations of a lucrative yet dormant gay market, Overlooked Opinions circulated misleading statistics depicting gay people as disproportionately rich. As M. V. Lee Badgett contends in her essay "Beyond Biased Samples" in this volume, such assertions of high gay incomes are common but inaccurate, as marketers have confused survey data referring to the readers of gay publications with the demographics of the community as a whole. Badgett's findings reveal that gay men earn substantially less than their straight counterparts, while lesbians are roughly even with heterosexual women in earning power.

Still, the bottom line for advertisers is that targeting the group of gays that is most prosperous can be quite lucrative. It might not be as large as it appears in the literature, but there is certainly a stack of gay money to be had. Moreover, lesbians and gay men have proven to be vulnerable to the advances of corporate marketers because they have been ignored as a consumer group for so long. The makers of Absolut vodka were the first to discover and exploit the gay community's brand loyalty, which is now a veritable legend among advertisers. Tracking consumption patterns after local ads appeared in gay media, Absolut charted dramatic jumps in specific requests for its brand name in gay bars.

Ads don't feature glamorous gays just to connect with gay consumers, either. Firms placing gay-themed ads are also counting on the ability of attractive gay idols to set trends for straight shoppers – a bet that has already paid off for some. Resplendent in red, RuPaul, the queen of drag and Mac cosmetics model, has inspired hordes of genetic girls to buy the company's lipstick through ads placed primarily in mainstream straight media. And there is the demonstrated power of ordinary gay people to establish trends followed by straights; it has become common lore, for instance, that gay men popularized Levi's button-fly jeans.

Before such money-making fads take hold in any community, media images usually introduce the novel idea. Sometimes ads alone will do it (such as vodka bottles by Keith Haring), but marketers uniformly believe that to take optimum effect, advertising has to be placed in a complementary environment. This suggests that a sort of mercenary collusion between advertising and editorial forces might have provided much of the impetus for the recent gay media moment. Circumstantial evidence abounds; flip over k. d. and Cindy and you will find Absolut. Ads for Benetton, Calvin Klein, and other companies known for their keen interest in the gay market lurk in the shadows of many of the recent gay-moment stories.

Some of the supposed attributes of the new gay target consumer group are probably harmless. *Out* magazine's media kit, for example, says that lesbians and gay men are "homemakers" and "aesthetes." And the new gay visibility had distinct advantages. The very presence of gay men and lesbians in the media – as celebrities, authors, and social actors – is a long-sought triumph, while being respected as a market often translates into political clout. In Hawaii, for instance, the argument for gay marriage has been bolstered by the prospect of a windfall from gay tourism. One economist has even estimated that the first state to recognize gay marriage could reap a $4.3 billion boon.[2] And, of course, money itself can buy a good degree of political influence. As the work of the Human Rights Campaign has shown, carefully targeted donations to political campaigns can cement the loyalty of key politicians (though the Log Cabin Republicans discovered the limits of this approach when Bob Dole returned their carefully rendered gift in the fall of 1995). Certainly, the gay and lesbian community can wield its newly recognized market power wisely by rewarding social responsibility and by punishing capitulation to the Right.

To the extent that gay advances hinge on financial interests, however, they are precarious. What if a future backlash depletes gay incomes, or the right wing proves the greater economic force? Far-right boycotts have hurt progressive causes before and the right wing remains a formidable force in some areas of the marketplace. In 1995, for instance, when PFLAG – Parents, Families and Friends of Lesbians and Gays – tried to buy $1 million worth of TV air time for antihate public service spots protests from Pat Roberson's Christian Broadcasting Network caused most TV stations to refuse to run the ads. In general, companies that don't serve a substantial conservative, fundamentalist constituency – such as liquor firms – are the ones that have avidly been cultivating gay consumption. In the case of alcohol, this has made for some unpleasant bedfellows, with ads for Dewar's, Miller beer, and the like sustaining mainstream gay magazines, while radical gay media like *Gay Community News* struggle to survive.

In addition, there are concrete political risks in projecting a rich, powerful image to get wide attention. The religious right has appropriated gay marketing statistics to portray gay men and lesbians as a rich special interest underserving of civil rights protection. Overlooked Opinions received a request for evidence of the gay community's financial power from the Colorado Attorney General's office, charged with defending anti-gay ballot initiative Amendment 2. And the antigay group Colorado for Family Values has argued that "homosexuals are anything but disadvantaged," citing statistics that gay male households earn an average of $55,400 annually – in the same range estimated by Overlooked Opinions. This campaign, directed at lower-income communities, has succeeded in fanning anti-gay hate as a response to real economic despair. In the fall of 1995, a similar attempt to convince Maine voters that gay men and lesbians were an advantaged group seeking preferential treatment was defeated by a margin of just 6 percentage points (ironically, this victory occurred only after progay forces outspent their opponents 10 to 1).

And in May 1996, when the U.S. Supreme Court overturned Colorado's Amendment 2, Justice Antonin Scalia's dissenting opinion made specific reference to the "high disposable income" that gay people have allegedly used to build up "disproportionate political power."[3]

Stereotypes of gay wealth play not only into the hands of the far Right; more moderate opponents of a broad-reaching lesbian and gay agenda have seized on them as well. In the May 1993 issue of *The New Republic*, gay social critic Jonathan Rauch invoked popular stereotypes about gay wealth to argue that gay men and lesbians should not consider themselves oppressed. His piece opened with chilling scenes of gay bashing, but then proceeded to claim that gay men and lesbians are not oppressed because they meet only one of his criteria of oppression – they face direct legal discrimination. They can vote, have a right to education, and are entitled to basic human rights, but the point he returned to most is that they are also free of "impoverishment relative to the remainder of the population."[4] After citing Overlooked Opinions' income data, Rauch offered one anecdoral example after another of the wealthy gay man: a college professor friend who owns a split-level condo and a Mazda Miata; gay acquaintances with $50,000 incomes and European vacations who whine about being victims.

Rauch's analysis was not only built on a faulty empirical foundation. It was also blind to the link between the legal discrimination that he acknowledged and economic oppression. In his discussion of whether gay people are economically oppressed, Rauch never mentioned the occupational segregation faced by openly gay men until literally the last few years. Like Jews throughout European history, openly gay men have been shunted into a severely limited number of occupational fields. And just as the success of the Rothschilds should never have been used to belittle the wide-ranging effects of the systematic discrimination that Jews faced over many centuries in Europe, so the success of some gay figures in the arts and entertainment business (or in Rauch's circle of acquaintance) should not obscure the real effects of having to choose between being openly gay and access to a wide range of jobs. Moreover, although discrimination against lesbians is less conspicuous because all women have faced economic oppression, it is clear that women's lower incomes place lesbian households at a unique disadvantage.

This is not to say that, as a group, gay men and lesbians experience seamless economic exploitation; indeed, the case of gay marketing reveals the very complex relationship between gay people and the economy. We are witnessing a new stage in this relationship, and perhaps some signs of improvement in it, but gay people have always both prospered and suffered at the hands of the market. As the historian John D'Emilio has argued, gay people have enjoyed the economic freedom to build same-sex households in capitalist societies, but culturally they have served as scapegoats for the expression of various anxieties – family pressures but also class frustration, which might threaten the economic status quo were it to find its proper target. "Materially," he wrote, "capitalism weakens the bonds that once kept families together so that their members experience a growing instability in the place they have come to expect happiness and emotional security . . . [L]esbians, gay men, and heterosexual feminists have become the scapegoats for the social instability of the system."[5]

Now, suddenly, it has become useful to business interests to cultivate a narrow (and widely acceptable) definition of gay identity as a marketing tool, and to integrate gay people as gay people into a new consumer niche. The speed with which the needs of the market can steamroll the strongest of social traditions and taboos is awe-inspiring. Yet in keeping with history, the outcome for gay men and lesbians is double-edged.

Today, the sword of the market is slicing off every segment of the gay community that is not upper-middle class, (mostly) white, and (mostly) male. Lesbians and gay men who do not see themselves in Ikea TV spots or Dewar's ads feel alienated. Perhaps more importantly, gay politics now reflects this divide, and a growing chorus of conservative gay writers is calling for gay activism to separate itself from any broader progressive vision that might address the needs and interests of the less visible, less privileged members of the gay community.

Just a few years ago, the AIDS crisis helped give an edge to gay politics by encouraging just those sorts of connections to develop. AIDS politicized a large group of white, middle-class gay men, who suddenly discovered what it was like to live in fear of losing housing or medical coverage, and who had to fight the medical, insurance, and real estate establishments to survive. The crisis moved many gay men to come out, and it also prompted some of them to link the fight against homophobia to other progressive political efforts.

After fifteen minutes in the glow of the gay moment, however, this militant stance became distinctly less fashionable. Queer Nation's slogan, "We're here, we're queer, get used to it," says to straight people, "We will stretch your concept of morality, of family, of politics." But many who have reaped the benefits of corporate acceptance seem to be saying, "We're here, we're just like you, don't worry about it." When asked about Philip Morris's gay marketing campaign for Special Kings cigarettes, the publisher of L.A.'s gay magazine *Genre* responded: "*Esquire* takes tobacco ads and that is the kind of publication we want to be."

It is too early to tell whether concrete, day-to-day political action in the gay community will change as well, coming more into line with the typical politics of groups led by individuals who feel they are faring well under capitalism. But it is already clear that in some important ways, the gay moment is more of a hurdle for gay politics than a source of strength.

The delicate bonds between the gay and African American communities, for example, are only being stretched closer to the breaking point. The current blitz contains hardly any images of gay African Americans or references to black gay culture or organizations. As Eric Washington pointed out in *The Village Voice*, a recent Overlooked Opinions survey asked gay New Yorkers which publications they read, listing several dailies and weeklies but omitting Harlem's *Amsterdam News*. And a question about hospital services to gays and lesbians left Harlem Hospital off the list. Such omissions only reinforce the alienation of black lesbians and gay men from the rest of the gay community. The images of a seamlessly white, middle-class gay community tap into "an undercurrent of resentment [in the African American community] . . . fed by the perception that gays are affluent and indifferent to racism."[6]

It's tempting to embrace today's recognition ecstatically and unconditionally; as Andrew Schneider (who wrote *Northern Exposure*'s lesbian episode) told *Vogue*, the network was inundated with letters from lesbians after the show aired. "They were very grateful, like starving people getting a crust of bread," he said. But seizing the gay moment even as it reinforces racial and class hierarchies will allow for only limited gains. As the best feminism is sensitive to more than questions of gender, the fight against homophobia will take on its most liberating forms only if it is conceived as part of a broader vision of social and economic justice.

Notes

1   Grant Lukenbill, *Untold Millions: The Gay and Lesbian Market in America* (New York: HarperCollins, 1995).

2   "Bet on a Gay Tourism Boost in Hawaii," *Detroit News*, 1995. Reprinted in *Liberal Opinion*, Sept. 18, 1995, p. 6.

3   "Excerpts from Court's Decision on Colorado's Provision for Homosexuals," *New York Times*, May 23, 1996, p. A21.

4   Jonathan Rauch, "Beyond Oppression," *The New Republic*, May 10, 1993, p. 18.

5   John D'Emilio, "Capitalism and Gay Identity," in *Powers of Desire*, ed. Ann Snitow, Christine Stansell, and Sharon Thompson (New York: Monthly Review Press, 1983), pp. 100–117.

6   Eric Washington, "Freedom Rings? The Alliance Between Blacks and Gays is Threatened by Mutual Inscrutability," *Village Voice*, June 29, 1993, pp. 25–33.

Chapter 17

Lisa Peñaloza

WE'RE HERE, WE'RE QUEER, AND WE'RE GOING SHOPPING! A CRITICAL PERSPECTIVE ON THE ACCOMMODATION OF GAYS AND LESBIANS IN THE U.S. MARKETPLACE

From *Journal of Homosexuality* 1996: 31 (1/2): 9–41

Introduction

IT IS ALTOGETHER FITTING that the call for papers for this volume coincides with the 25th anniversary of the Stonewall Rebellion. Businesses catering to a gay/lesbian clientele, such as the Stonewall Inn and other nightclubs, cafés, bookstores, and coffeehouses, have been at the center of gay/lesbian communities historically (Wilson 1991; Trumbach 1991; Myrick 1972), and continue to be an important hub of contemporary social activism.

In recent years, marketing and media attention has begun to be directed to gays and lesbians as a distinct consumer group. This market segment has been dubbed the "Dream Market," with estimates of the numbers of gays and lesbians reaching 18.5 million, and estimates of spending power topping $514 billion (Johnson 1993a). Businesses targeting gays and lesbians have expanded beyond clubs and bookstores to comprise virtually a full service market that includes media, merchandise catalogues, vacation companies, and legal, medical, financial and communications services, to name a few.[1] Together, these businesses create an environment in which gay and lesbian consumer culture thrives.[2]

With this increased attention by marketing practitioners, marketing and consumer behavior scholars have begun to think about lesbians and gays as a market. In one of the first academic studies on this topic. Fugate (1993) concluded that gays and lesbians did not qualify as a market segment because this group did not satisfy the traditional criteria of being identifiable, accessible, and of sufficient size. This paper provides an alternative view of gays and lesbians as a market segment and draws from studies of the new social movements, consumer culture, and postmodern cultural theory. My argument is that the segmentation criteria rely on outdated assumptions regarding the nature of consumers, marketing activities, and media, and require modifications for the contemporary marketplace. Specifically, this research recognizes the important intersection of market segments and social movements and addresses the marketing implications of increasing consumer subjectivity and agency, and of market and media heterogeneity.[3]

The objectives of this research are twofold. First, I reevaluate the question of whether gays and lesbians constitute a viable market segment. Second, I critically evaluate implications of gay and lesbian marketing with respect to the structure of the U.S. marketplace, to individual gays and lesbians, and to gay/lesbian communities.

In addressing the first objective. I begin by briefly overviewing the literature on social movements before turning to gay/lesbian social movements. The dual status of gays and lesbians as both a social movement and a market segment raises a number of important theoretical questions for marketers and academics. Issues such as identity, subjectivity, and agency which are central to studies of social movements, are also critical in understanding the place gays and lesbians occupy in the contemporary market economy. Social movements have historically played a significant role in enfranchising socially subordinated groups. Towards this end, members of social movements tend to have a heavily sensitized concern for the impact of marketing communications on group interests (e.g., critiques of the Frito Bandito and Aunt Jemima among Latinos and blacks, respectively). Equally important, relationships among social groups and conflicts of interests must be taken into account. Gays and lesbians historically have been stigmatized in U.S. society, particularly by those religious groups that see homosexuality as immoral. Their political mobilization against gay and lesbian interests continues to affect both marketers' decisions to target members of these groups and gays' and lesbians' attempts to achieve full political enfranchisement.

My second step in moving toward an evaluation of the gay/lesbian market is to compare its development with that of the Latino market.

Significantly, there are similarities between what is currently said about the gay market and what was said about the Latino market in its early stages. Both of these groups of people, while seemingly recent market "discoveries," have long, rich histories of social movement activism and their study generates important insights into the contemporary marketplace. In particular, both groups share positioning outside mainstream U.S. culture, yet receive important social legitimation in market targeting.

Having reviewed the social movement literature and compared developments of the Latino market with that of gays/lesbians. I then turn to the evaluation of gays and lesbians as a viable market segment. I proceed through each of the segmentation criteria, with attention to its assumptions and its propriety for gays and lesbians in the contemporary marketplace. Further. I question the use of the term. "lifestyle" to describe gays and lesbians, particularly when gay/lesbian life and culture is reduced to sexuality.

The second part of the paper consists of a critical examination of writings on the gay/lesbian market in the marketing literature. Statistics on the market as a whole, as well as characteristics and profiles of gay/lesbian consumers are reviewed, with attention to the role and interests of advertising, market research, and media agents and institutions. Key concerns are the strategies employed in promoting this group as a market and the representativeness of the data provided with regard to the larger population of gays and lesbians.

Finally, I evaluate the implications of marketing to gays and lesbians Regarding the implications of marketing to gays and lesbians on the structure of the U.S. marketplace, increased fragmentation and specialization are both the result of and chief factors spurring segmentation strategies targeting market subgroups, such as gays and lesbians, as well as blacks, the elderly, men, Latinos, etc. These market segmentation strategies may be seen to operate as democratizing mechanisms, in the sense that they include people who are not typically included in more narrow conceptualizations of the U.S. market. Indeed, there is a profound sense of social validation and legitimation that is experienced by individual gays and lesbians and gay/lesbian communities as the result of increased accommodation as a market in capitalist society. Further, the gay/lesbian market brings a number of job opportunities as it grows. Less positive effects include distorted representations of gays and lesbians both within and outside these communities, such as an inflated socioeconomic status attributed to gays and lesbians that not only misrepresents the conditions and experiences of a number of gays and lesbians, but has also been used by radical right religious organizations in their efforts to repeal gay/lesbian protection legislation.

Marketing and social difference: the intersection of social movements and market segments

The world regards sexuality as the secret of cultural life, it is rather a process of our having to create a new cultural life underneath the ground of our sexual choices. Not only do we have to defend ourselves, we have to affirm ourselves, not only as an identity, but as a creative force.

— Michel Foucault

Since the mid-1960s there has been a documented shift in marketing practice from targeting the mainstream or mass mass market to including more specialized niche markets (Smith 1965; Engel, Fiorillo and Cayley 1971) This shift in marketing strategy is the result of a number of factors, including increasing levels of competition for the mass market, shifts in demographic growth rates and geographic patterns of residence for the U.S. population, and the increasing availability of specialized media products. Together, these factors have contributed to the recent visibility of the gay/ lesbian market. Research and media companies specializing in the gay market have dubbed it the "Dream Market," promising U.S. firms direct access to millions of gay and lesbian consumers with billions of dollars in annual income (Miller 1990; 1992).

Partly in response to this increasing marketing and media attention, marketing scholars have questioned whether gays and lesbians comprised a market segment. In this section, I draw from the literature on social movements because this work offers new insight into the market accommodation of minority populations. Significantly, it is the gains of the gay/lesbian social movement, together with the development of a marketing infrastructure, that render gays and lesbians a viable market segment.[4]

The social movement literature

It is more than a coincidence that marketing theorists began to exhort the benefits of tailoring products and/or services to particular groups of people on the basis of their unique characteristics in the 1960s (Engel, Fiorillo, and Cayley 1971). At this time there was much social activism in the U.S., and the development of these segmentation strategies may be seen as both the result of and a contributing factor to the social changes these movements brought about. In fact, many civil rights gains were and continue to be manifest in the marketplace — at the lunch counters, in bus and retail service, in hotel accommodations, and in socially acceptable standards of dress. In this sense, the marketplace may be viewed as an important domain of social contestation whereby disenfranchised groups engage in ongoing struggles for social and political incorporation.

Social movement theory is particularly useful in this research because it attends to: (1) the ways in which particular groups of people in society come together in the development and pursuit of their interests and (2) the ways in which their strategic actions are incorporated and/or resisted by institutions within a society, particularly governmental and educational institutions. Classic studies in this literature have documented the differential trajectories and strategies of various social movements as people within them work to mobilize people and resources in the development and pursuit of their objectives (Piven and Cloward 1977; Petracca 1993). Also of interest have been "free riders," people who benefit from movement gains, but do not contribute directly to the effort and who may or may not identify themselves as group members. My interest lies in exploring the relationship between gay/lesbian activism and the accommodation of gay/lesbian consumers in the marketplace. It is suggested that as civil rights gains are made by gay/lesbian activists, the social climate becomes more favorable to individual gays and lesbians in claiming and expressing this part of themselves as well as to firms interested in targeting members of this group.

A second stream of this literature, labeled the "new social movements," emphasizes the development of identity, subjectivity, and agency both within and outside the movement, and goes beyond traditional notions of social movements based on socioeconomic status to include social movements formed around issues of race/ethnicity, gender, and sexuality. This literature examines how people within the movement are mobilized and politicized as a subculture, as well as how those outside the movement are mobilized and politicized both in support and in opposition to it (Morris and Mueller 1992). Issues of identity, subjectivity, and agency are integral to the analysis of contemporary gay marketing because these aspects of individual and collective behavior contribute to our understanding of how gays and lesbians constitute themselves and their relations towards others.

Finally, a third stream of this research is relevant to the present study. This work incorporates theoretical advances in poststructuralism to examine the ways in which the subject of social movements is constituted in social discourse (Butler and Scott 1992; Shapiro 1992). This work is particularly useful in examining representations of gay/lesbian consumers in the discourses of marketing and advertising. Marketing activities targeting gays and lesbians typically do so by including elements of gay identity and experience. Because these representations provide a mirroring function for gay/lesbian people, they potentially have an effect upon gay subjectivity and agency, i.e., how gays and lesbians think of themselves and how they view marketing practices and consumption behaviors in relation to group interests.

While offering a number of theoretical contributions to this research, the social movement literature has virtually neglected the role of marketing institutions in furthering or inhibiting social change. This view of business ignores some strategically useful aspects of business activity, namely the social legitimation that comes as the result of market targeting. This is not to suggest that marketing attention is always a positive thing for the people or the social movement in question, however. Because market targeting has both positive and negative implications, it merits serious critical analysis. Towards this end, I turn now to the gay/lesbian movement.

The gay/lesbian social movement

A complete recounting of the history of gay/lesbian social movements is beyond the scope of this paper; however, a few points are noteworthy. Historians and social theorists have documented the trajectory of gay/lesbian movements, situating them within the larger field of the history of sexuality, and noting various shifts in the ontological status of same-sex love and sexual desire from a universal human capability to the deviant behavior of a stigmatized people, to a criminal activity, to a clinical disorder, to a positive social identity and subculture (D'Emilio and Freedman 1988; Foucault 1978; Weeks 1985; D'Emilio 1983; Kennedy and Davis 1994).

Particularly relevant are earlier manifestations of gay/lesbian/bisexual/ transgender practices, communities, and social movements, together with their reception by business and other social institutions because this lays the historical groundwork for the contemporary marketplace response to gays and lesbians. In early examples, Trumbach (1991) wrote of historical and literary accounts of hermaphrodites (i.e., the vernacular sodomite or molly in the case of men and sapphist or tommy for women) in London as early as the eighteenth century, and Wilson (1991) located a thriving area of restaurants, cafes, and theater in Paris in the late nineteenth century. It is likely that these consumer subcultures had an influence on the early sexologists, such as Magnus Hirschfeld (1910) and Havelock Ellis (1925), whose work took seriously the study of sexual behavior. These consumer subcultures reached a peak in Europe in the 1930s and 1940s, before being run underground by the Nazis (Plant 1986).

In the U.S., gay and lesbian communities have been located as early as the late nineteenth and early twentieth centuries (Chauncey 1994). However, for the most part gay/lesbian social activism in the U.S. is traced to the late 1940s and 1950s. (D'Emilio 1983; Bénibé 1990; Kennedy and Davis 1994; Boyd 1995). While it pales somewhat in contrast to the more radical activism that would follow thirty years later, its contributions were no less significant. At this time gay and lesbian organizations such as the Matachine Society and the Daughters of Bilitis were formed. These organizations were largely middle-class in composition and featured a fairly conservative, assimilationist strategy in their attempt to gain civil rights and acceptance by the larger society.

The most recent wave of gay/lesbian social activism is marked by the Stonewall Rebellion in 1969 in New York. At that time, homosexuality was listed as a mental disorder by the American Psychological Association and police raids of bars, in which drag queens and crossdressing butches were hauled off and often beaten, were common (Nestle 1992; D'Emilio 1994; Thompson 1994). As in other social movements, a key event is seldom as important as what it comes to symbolize. The Stonewall Rebellion has gained notoriety because it is used by the contemporary gay/lesbian community to mark the beginning of gay/lesbian pride and to communicate the message that gays/lesbians will no longer tolerate subordinate status. Nevertheless, like the importance granted to Rosa Parks in the Black civil rights movement, the happenings that night at the Stonewall Inn were necessarily predated and accompanied by the work of countless unrecognized individuals and groups. Partly in response to gay and lesbian social activism, but also in response to the research of Evelyn Hooker (1956; 1957), homosexuality was removed from the list of disorders of the American Psychological Association in 1973. This institutional break through served to further spur the movement.

Over the years, many gay/lesbian organizations have come and gone, and while some of the items on the agendas of these groups have changed, the struggle for basic rights continues. Organizations vary widely in their composition and aims. Examples such as the National Gay and Lesbian Task Force, GLAAD, Society of Janus, PFLAG, ACT UP, Queer Nation, and the Victory Fund have worked for and continue to work to address such issues as decriminalization of sexual practices, job discrimination, violence against gays and lesbians, teen suicide, freedom of sexual expression, family understanding, the AIDS crisis, and political enfranchisement.[5] It is also significant to note that gays and lesbians have come together despite differences over the years, partly in response to the AIDS epidemic, but also as a pragmatic strategy that has served to bolster the numbers collectively and render the group a more formidable force for positive social change. Currently, the most pressing issue facing the gay/ lesbian movement is arguably the rash of state and local initiatives sponsored by the radical. Christian right that seeks to repeal gay protection legislation. Marketing to gays/lesbians is best understood when situated within the sociohistorical context of these movements.

A comparison of the development of the gay/lesbian and Latino markets

As suggested previously, there is a close temporal relationship between social movement gains and market targeting. In the 1970s, marketing studies flourished that prescribed strategies for targeting women and Blacks.

Analogously, the Latino market was "discovered" in the 1980s, while the gay market is a 1990s phenomenon. Significantly, each of these market segments followed on the heels of social movement gains, but with different time lags.

The gay/lesbian market offers a number of differences and similarities when compared to that of Latinos.[6] Both groups are positioned outside the imagined community (Anderson 1983) of U.S. culture, but for different reasons and to different degrees. Both groups have different distributions of sociodemographic characteristics, such as income, education, and occupation. Gays and lesbians tend to be thought of as primarily middle class and white, although there are many working class and racial/ethnic minority gays and lesbians in this country; Latinos tend to be thought of as unskilled workers for the most part, although many professionals are found within their ranks.

In addition, issues of agency characterize both groups. Regarding gays and lesbians, there is much debate concerning whether homosexuality is chosen or genetic, yet for the most part public sentiment is in line with the former. It is the "choice" to love someone of the same sex that goes against U.S. heterosexual norms, even as many gays' and lesbians' whiteness and middle-class status is consistent with the U.S. mainstream culture. Regarding Latinos, those born outside of the U.S. have moved to the U.S. to flee economic hardship, to improve their standard of living, and to better their education and that of their children. In these ways, their movement is consistent with the U.S. work ethic, even as their color goes against the U.S.'s self image of whiteness (Peñaloza 1994).

Most importantly for purposes of this paper, however, is the fact that both gays/lesbians and Latinos have a history of social activism and are considered examples of the new social movements (Morris and Mueller 1992). For both groups, the constitution of themselves as a subculture has had much to do with the revaluation of an identity that had been imbued with negative qualities by the larger culture. Further, marketing incorporation has helped facilitate the social legitimation of both groups, even as the marketplace remains contested terrain in their struggles.

Re-evaluating gays and lesbians as a viable market segment

Partly the result of the stigma attached to homosexuality, but also due to the dearth of statistics on this "new" market, many firms remain doubtful about its potential, even as they are strongly financially motivated to seek out new profitable market segments. In his evaluation of the gay/lesbian market, Fugate (1993) positioned it as a lifestyle segment and concluded that gays/lesbians were not a viable market segment because they did not satisfy the segmentation criteria of being identifiable, accessible, and of sufficient size and stability to be feasible (Cravens, Hill and Woodruff 1987). Yet, while Fugate produced a rigorous, comprehensive piece of scholarship, there are some noteworthy limitations.

The first limitation of Fugate's (1993) work relates to his operationalization of the segmentation criteria. These criteria tend to be used in ways that treat marketers as active agents who must clearly identify more passive potential customers prior to being able to target them. Thus, these criteria posit rather traditional roles for marketers, media, and consumers even as these roles have been called into question (Bristor and Fischer 1993). Indeed, Fugate (1993) was quite concerned with the dissension regarding the numbers of gay/lesbian consumers, particularly in people's propensity to identify as gays/lesbians. This also continues to be an issue for the Latino market, as Latinos vary in self-identification by generation nationality, and socioeconomic level (Peñaloza 1994). Although self-identification is a notoriously unreliable construct in the case of socially subordinated groups, it is at best a good place to start. Yet, the issue is as much whether distinct consumption patterns deal solely with the segment determinant (i.e., race, ethnicity, gender, or in this case, sexuality), as whether these groups claim a distinct identity and subculture that is expressed in identifiable ways.

Similarly, the accessible criterion continues with the assumption of active marketers who contact passive consumers. This criterion also requires modification to reflect dramatic changes in media and in the marketplace that have occurred over the past 20 years, particularly the use of specialty media by marketers in their efforts to access special interest segments. Increasingly important in accessing consumers is providing materials that they will self-select, and then using these customer-initiated contacts in the form of interactive computer networks and cable, as well as the more traditional mail and telephone merchandising techniques, to build a reliable consumer database (Meyer 1994). This is especially the case for members of a stigmatized group, such as gays and lesbians, but is also appropriate for other segments that are difficult to access, such as the wealthy. A plethora of specialty print and broadcast media have entered the scene since 1970, rendering niche markets increasingly accessible and a good buy, especially when they are expanded beyond U.S. national borders to encompass their global counterparts.

Closely related to issues of identifiability and accessibility is the requirement that a market segment be of sufficient size to justify those additional costs needed to reach it. This criterion often assumes separate campaigns are necessary to reach each segment. Yet, companies often place the same advertisement in a number of media, relying on its placement to communicate a specialized message to each audience. In these cases, firms realize only those additional costs of media placement that often result in an economically efficient contact.

The stability criterion assumes an idealized level of social stability that is arguably a characteristic of modern, and not postmodern, society, as people move into and out of several categories daily, as well as over the course of their lives (Featherstone 1991). This is the case not only for gay/lesbian consumers, but also for consumers categorized by marketers based on ethnicity and race, or even by stage in family life cycle, simply because people's identification and experience change over time as the result of life events, and as the result of changes in the significance of social categories. Nevertheless, it is increasingly clear that consumers inhabit more than one of these domains and that the domains are themselves anything but distinct. Any one of them may be seen to include a wide variation in its delineating characteristics and marketplace expressions.

Finally, there is some question regarding the use of the term "lifestyle" to categorize gays/lesbians: Fugate (1993) noted that homosexual males and lesbians constituted a definable market segment only so long as *specific activities, interests, and opinions dealt with their sexuality* (p. 47, italics added). This categorization reduces gay and lesbian culture to sexuality, even as it smooths over existing variation in activities, interests, and opinions among lesbians and gay men. The term "lifestyle" has been used in an attempt to capture the complexity and subtlety of cultural differences that go beyond demographics, but with mixed success when tied to consumption behaviors (Lastovicka et al. 1990; Lastovicka 1982). While activities, interests, and opinions capture some aspects of gay/lesbian life, and while gay and lesbian culture certainly includes elements of sexuality in all of its diverse forms, designating gays and lesbians as a lifestyle limited to sexuality potentially trivializes the complexities of gay/lesbian lives. This reduction is perhaps best demonstrated by extrapolating the term "lifestyle" to other subcultural groups, such as Latinos, blacks, or women, while thinking of these subcultures solely in terms of race, ethnicity, and gender, respectively.

A key theoretical problem with the segmentation criteria is their inability to distinguish among types of market segments. There are key differences between dinks and yuppies on one hand, and Latinos, women, and gays/lesbians on the other. While both types of groups are market segments, the former represents sociodemographic groupings and lifestyles, while the latter are best understood as social movements. As members of a social movement, gays and lesbians have developed a consciousness of themselves as a people as the result of a history of common interests and experiences, particularly their exclusion, mobilization, and struggle in response to how they have been treated by others. This consciousness is only part of the foundation for the gay/lesbian market segment, however, as people vary in the degree to which they identify as group members.

For these reasons, it is necessary to move beyond the question of identity to include: social practices and community formations in conceptualizing consumer subcultures such as gays and lesbians. Even with the gains of gay/lesbian movements, it is likely that the number of gays/ lesbians claiming a gay/lesbian identity is less than the total number of gays and lesbians due to the social stigma attached to homosexuality. Further, it is likely that the number of gays and lesbians working under the rubric of the gay/lesbian movement is less than the total number of gays and lesbians, given the presence of free riders. Marketers should be concerned with these latter operationalizations.

Reconceptualizing lesbians and gays as part of a consumer subculture that encompasses the distinct dimensions of identity, social practices, and community formations facilitates the inclusion of variations in identification and in consumption patterns. Yet, it is also necessary to expand measures of consumption patterns to account for differences in the meanings and uses accorded various products, services, and other marketing stimuli among various consumer subcultures even when there is no apparent difference in the consumption patterns themselves. In my work with Latino consumers, it became clear that the meanings they associated with many of the products and services they used were different than those associated with the same products and services for mainstream consumers (Peñaloza 1994). Thus, the segmentation view that requires people to have differences in consumption patterns can be misleading, especially when the differences stem from identity and group membership.

Including differences in the meanings attached to products, services, and marketing stimuli that tap into group identity and experience as measures of market segments yields a more sensitive measure of differences in subcultural consumption behaviors. As with other consumer subcultures, particular codes such as clothing styles, mannerisms, and language are used to communicate to other members of the group. With regard to gays and lesbians, it is likely that there are differences in meanings and uses for products and services as compared to heterosexual consumers. Further, these differences would not necessarily be limited to sexuality simply because this is only one dimension of gay/lesbian life experience, although an important one.

In sum, understanding the place of gays and lesbians in the contemporary market requires thoughtful reconsideration of the segmentation criteria. Based on my review of the literature on social movements and market segmentation, it appears that there is some theoretical basis for the constitution of gays and lesbians as a viable market segment. Perhaps the most compelling argument, however, is found in the acts of marketing practitioners targeting members of this group, a subject to which I now turn.

Gays – a dream market?!?

REACH THIS DREAM MARKET IN A STYLISH, REALITY BASED EDITORIAL
ENVIRONMENT THAT SPEAKS DIRECTLY TO THEM
                    – A recent advertisement for the gay publication *Genre*

The above excerpt is but one of several advertisements and articles in
marketing and advertising industry publications promoting the gay/lesbian
market. This particular advertisement promised firms access to 200,000
potential customers per issue. In this section I examine the characteristics,
and potential of the gay/lesbian market, the role of gay/lesbian media, and
the strategies used to target gays and lesbians.

The making of the gay/lesbian market

Accounting for the number of gays and lesbians in the U.S. has proven to be
quite difficult and controversial. The numbers vary widely as the result of
the use of various measures in various types of studies. Studies come from a
number of disciplines, including sexuality, psychology, health care, and
most recently, market research. Perhaps most famous is the 1948 Kinsey
Institute study which found the ratio of heterosexuals to homosexuals to be
10:1. This study was replicated in 1993, with similar findings in *The Janus
Report on Sexual Behavior* (Janus and Janus 1993). According to studies by
the National Opinion Research Center at the University of Chicago, 2.8%
of adult males and 2.3% of adult females identified themselves as homosexual (Rogers 1993). These lower figures may be attributable to the use of
a more narrow definition of gay and lesbian that excluded bisexuals. At
any rate, due to the controversial nature of homosexuality in U.S. society,
measures typically consist of self-reports, which tend to be conservative in
their estimates.

In addition, varying definitions and terms create a number of other data
collection and tabulation problems. Definitions touch on the range of identities, sexual orientations, and behaviors encompassed by the general term
"homosexual." Among scholars and activists alike, there is much disagreement regarding whether exclusive homosexual behaviors, identities, and
orientations are requirements for members of this group. More liberal
definitions include having engaged in homosexual behaviors or having
claimed a gay/lesbian identity or orientation at any time during the life
course.

Terminology used includes various combinations of homosexual, gay
lesbian, queer, dyke, bisexual, transgendered, transvestite, and transsexual,
and each of these terms is further complicated by its generational and
ideological connotations. It is significant to note that while queer theorists

are adamant about including bisexuals and transgendered persons within the gay/lesbian movement in an attempt to move beyond the dualistic essentialisms of gender and to embrace the complexity, indeterminacy, and performance that homosexuality entails, marketing firms are intent on specifying the category.

Marketing and advertising studies of the gay market tend to focus on the numbers and on buying power. Overlooked Opinions, a market research firm in Chicago that specializes in the gay market, estimates it to consist of 18.5 million people with total annual income of $514 billion dollars (Johnson 1993a). More conservative figures have been provided by Nile Merton, publisher of *The Advocate*, who estimated the number of gay and lesbian consumers in the U.S. to be 5 million people (cited in Johnson 1993a), and Cyndee Miller (1990), who estimated gays' and lesbians' annual spending to be $382 billion.

Consumer profile

For the most part, studies of gay/lesbian consumers have found their income to be higher than that of heterosexuals. According to a study done by Simmons Market Research Bureau of the readership of eight of the leading gay newspapers in the country, the figures for average individual income were $36,800 for gays/lesbians, as compared to census statistics of $32,287 for heterosexuals. Average household income figures were $55,430 for gays/lesbians, as compared to census figures of $32,114 for heterosexual households (cited in Miller 1990; Curiel 1991). This study has been criticized for providing a distorted characterization of gays and lesbians as the result of its reliance on the readership of gay newspapers.

More recently, the Yankelovich Monitor Survey has called into question the widespread belief that the income of gays and lesbians was greater than that of heterosexuals. According to their report, income for gays was $37,400, as compared to $39,300 for heterosexual men; and $34,800 for lesbians, as compared to $34,400 for heterosexual women. This study is significant in that it employed a nationally representative sample of self-selected gays and lesbians. In addition, the study compared the responses of heterosexual and homosexual men and women. Regarding education, 14% of gay/lesbian/bisexual respondents had attended graduate school, compared to 7% of heterosexuals; while 49% of gay/lesbian/bisexual respondents had attended some college, as compared to 37% of heterosexuals (Yankelovich 1994). Regarding occupation, 56% of gays/lesbians had professional and managerial jobs, compared to 16% of heterosexuals (cited in Curiel 1991).

Turning to consumption patterns, it has been widely reported that gays and lesbians are more willing to spend money than non-gays (Johnson 1993a;

Fugate 1993). Gays/lesbians have been listed as spending disproportionate amounts on luxury and premium products, such as travel (Button 1993), vacations (Davis 1993), phone services, and books (Warren 1990; Summer 1992), recorded music, alcoholic beverages, theater (Elliot 1993b), clothing catalogues (Miller 1992; Elliot 1993c), and greeting cards (Button 1993). In addition, gay/lesbian consumers were found to be younger, more brand and fashion conscious, and more brand loyal than their heterosexual counterparts (Miller 1990).

While these statements appear to contradict the reservation discussed earlier that gays and lesbians were not identifiable in terms of distinct buyer behaviors from non-gays, it is important to keep in mind that most of these statements were not based on representative studies of the larger population of gays and lesbians. Only the Yankelovich Monitor survey was based on a nationally representative sample. Significantly, others like the Simmons survey were based on samples of gay/lesbian media audiences. In general, media audience studies tend to overestimate such consumer characteristics as income and purchase intentions for the general population because they draw from a distinct subgroup that tends to be better off financially. Most critically, these figures are used by marketing and media agencies to sell clients on the potential profits to be made from targeting that particular audience. As in other marketing appeals, what appears is part salesmanship and part truth, as illustrated in the quote at the beginning of this section. While the gay media are beginning to use audits to attain more independent audience figures (Johnson 1993a), even these results should be understood as *representative of their audiences, and not of the general population*, in this case, gays and lesbians in the U.S.

Finally, it is important to note that market studies tend to focus on gay men, even as lesbians are used to bolster their numbers. This is partly the result of the persistent difference in earnings for men as compared to women: on average women still earn two thirds of the amount men earn (Johnson 1993b). Of particular interest to marketers are gay male dinks (i.e., double income, no kids) because of their attractive levels of disposable income. Nevertheless, some differences in consumption patterns for lesbians as compared to gay men have been noted, and these differences, together with lower earnings may also help explain lesbians' lower per capita spending. Miller (1990) noted that lesbians tended to frequent bars less often and entertain at home more often than did gay men. Lesbians' relative invisibility in lesbian/gay consumer profiles may also reflect the legacy of anti-market sentiment among some lesbian-feminists, i.e., their equation of capitalism with patriarchy and resulting reluctance and/or resistance to market participation.

Access

Firms interested in tapping into the gay/lesbian market can do so with the help of a growing range of media. There are a number of local and regional gay/lesbian newspapers, together with national magazines, cable and public broadcasting service television programs, and radio shows. The newspapers typically have both paid and free distribution, and are sponsored largely by local gay/lesbian owned and operated firms that cater to gay/lesbian clientele.

A number of gay/lesbian magazines have come on the scene in recent years, joining the ranks of the more established. *Deneuve, Genre, Out, 10 Percent, QW*, and *50/50* are some of the recent arrivals; while *The Advocate, On Our Backs* and *Outweek* have a longer history of service to the gay/lesbian community. A key debate that has followed in the wake of the new media is their future impact on the gay/lesbian community, as they are glossier and more image and fashion oriented than their more politically inclined predecessors. With the increased number of new magazines comes more competition in this burgeoning field and their positioning relative to the gay/lesbian community is an important factor affecting their chances of survival.

In addition to these gay/lesbian media, a number of advertising and marketing research companies now offer consulting services for firms interested in targeting gay and lesbian consumers. Examples include Overlooked Opinions, Direct Male, Mulryan/Nash, and Rivendell Marketing Company, Inc. These companies help firms develop marketing campaigns and place advertisements in gay/lesbian media, at gay/lesbian events such as the Gay Games and Gay/Lesbian Pride parades, and at gay/lesbian resorts.

As previously mentioned, access was cited as one of the disadvantages of the gay/lesbian market (Fugate 1993), yet problems of access seem unlikely given the increasing array of media and marketing research firms. Mainstream firms are beginning to advertise in gay/lesbian media, having been told that gays and lesbians value those firms they perceive to be supportive to them. In doing so, these firms join the ranks of those that have supported gay/lesbian media and events over the years. These firms should not expect gays and lesbians to be loyal customers simply because they have been targeted, however. For firms, the impact of gay/lesbian market targeting efforts are dependent upon both the quality and creativity of their campaigns, together with the relative number of advertisements consumers are exposed to. Presently, there are so few advertisements for the products and services of major corporations, that the advertisements of those companies targeting gays and lesbians enjoy a marked visibility. Over time, however, and with increases in the number of firms targeting gay/lesbian consumers, how gays and lesbians are portrayed in these advertisements will become an issue, just as portrayals of other minorities in advertisements have become issues for other minority communities following their initial market "discovery" period.

Strategies/approaches used to target gays and lesbians

A number of strategies have been used to target gay/lesbian consumers. These vary from the simple extrapolation of a marketing campaign developed for other market(s) to the gay/lesbian market, to modifications of ongoing campaigns to tailor them to the gay/lesbian market, to the development of campaigns tailored uniquely for gay/lesbian consumers.

Redirecting a marketing campaign used to target heterosexuals to gay/lesbian media can be a cost-effective strategy, as firms can rely on the placement of their advertisements to communicate their desire to do business with gays and lesbians. Recent examples include Evian, Calvert Equity Fund, Calvin Klein, Levi's, and Gaultier jeans. This is not just a message of intention to do business, however, but also marks some solidarity with gay/lesbian communities, so long as religious groups threaten such firms with boycotts (Levin 1993).

In addition, while marketing campaigns that feature solely men or women invite gay/lesbian identification, campaigns that feature heterosexual references to the exclusion of any gay/lesbian iconography may preclude such identification. This is especially the case when these advertisements appear in proximity to advertisements with more direct appeals, and when gay/lesbian organizations disseminate critiques of these campaigns that feature their sponsor as merely targeting gays and lesbians as an afterthought, or in a tokenistic fashion.

A second marketing strategy, located on the other end of the continuum, entails the development of a separate campaign for gays/lesbians with readily identifiable appeals to members of these consumer subcultures. The most obvious examples include the use of same-sex couples. Other examples would include the use of gay/lesbian iconography such as the rainbow or pink/black triangles. These advertisements present the greatest potential in terms of identification by gay/lesbian audiences and often minimize the risk of offending heterosexuals by their placement in gay/lesbian media, as marketers capitalize on self-selected gay/lesbian audiences. Examples include American Express's advertisements for joint travelers' checks featuring two male and two female signatures, and AT&T's use of the rainbow in advertisements placed in gay/lesbian media. A twist of this second strategy is to tie marketing campaigns to gay/lesbian community events, such as the 1994 Unity Games, as well as fundraisers and charities. In another example, Community Spirit, a telephone interconnect company, gave their service a gay reference by allocating 2% to the gay, lesbian, or AIDS charity of the consumer's choice (Button 1993).

Perhaps the most practical strategy is to combine the use of gay icon-ography with the reading strategies of gay/lesbian consumers. In ways not unlike "inside" jokes, these alternative reading strategies produce dif-ferent messages for the same advertisement for gay/lesbian consumers as compared to heterosexual consumers as the result of shared subcul-tural understandings. For example [a] Miller Lite advertisement features the copy, "Pour on the Pride." While pride is certainly not limited to gay/lesbian consumers, this caption carries a special meaning for them when placed during the Gay/Lesbian Pride festivals. This strategy is poten-tially effective in campaigns placed in both the mainstream and in gay/lesbian media, as it achieves a cross-over appeal to both gays/lesbians and heterosexuals. Other examples include marketing campaigns that feature subtle gay and lesbian references because they may be read as close friend-ships by heterosexual men and women, at the same time they are accorded more intimate connotations by gays and lesbians.

Discussion and implications

> This could be the first time in the history of great American
> capitalists that they've avoided making an easy buck.
> Richard Rouilard, editor-in-chief, *The Advocate*, quoted
> in Miller 1992, p. 15

Increasing appeals to the gay/lesbian market among mainstream marketing firms, together with the increased number of media and marketing firms serving gays/lesbians, suggest that this is a viable segment for many prod-ucts and services. Particularly responsive product and service categories include books, music, film and theater, vacations, beverages (alcoholic and non-alcoholic), and clothing. The recent "discovery" of the gay market raises a number of important theoretical and practical issues, however. With the advent of recognition of the gay market, sexuality comes to the fore as a market designator. This promises to be at least as controversial as gender and race/ethinicity. Yet, as I have argued, the basis for the gay/lesbian market segment is found in the nexus of sexuality and social movement. Because of this unique configuration, studies of this market bring consumer agency to the fore.

As scholars interested in marketing and in homosexual issues, it is important to situate the recent recognition of gays and lesbians as a market segment within the larger trends that have brought this about. I have argued that changes in the nature of the marketplace, in competition, among consumers, and in media, as well as changes brought about by the gay/lesbian movement have worked in tandem to bring about the present reality of this market. The first implication of marketing to gays/lesbians to be discussed is its effect on the structure of the U.S. marketplace. Gay/lesbian market segmentation, like other forms of market segmentation, both contributes to and is the result of the increasing fragmentation and specialization of the U.S. market. As firms increasingly engage in niche marketing, targeting people with unique campaigns based on their unique features and relying on specialty media, they not only draw from these social differences, but also reproduce them in the marketplace and in the larger social milieu. By addressing gays and lesbians as consumers, then, marketers and advertisers constitute them in important ways (i.e. render them identifiable and intelligible), particularly in a capitalistic society. A gay/lesbian aesthetic, or sensibility, becomes visible in the form of advertising codes and conventions, specific product and service appeals, and media treatments designed both in response to and in anticipation of gay/lesbian market expressions and desires. As such, marketing to lesbians and gays may be seen to impact relations between gays and lesbians and the larger society. In particular, as the accommodation of gay and lesbian consumers in the marketplace serves to validate and legitimate them, it mobilizes those who oppose the full incorporation of gays and lesbians in U.S. society.

In addition to its impact on the U.S. market as a whole, gay/lesbian marketing potentially affects both gays and lesbians as individuals and as members of highly diverse, geographically dispersed communities. There is much economic power in the gay/lesbian market and it is increasingly global. It is a valuable affirmation for gays and lesbians to be able to go to almost any major city in the world and locate gay/lesbian clubs, media, bookstores, and hotlines. It is no less significant for gays and lesbians to see themselves, their heroines and their heroes in film, music, and in advertisements. Marketing to gays and lesbians serves to legitimize them in the U.S. as individuals and as members of a subculture.

At the individual level, this validation is important because sexuality is a fundamental part of human experience. For individual gays and lesbians, sexuality is one of several dimensions of their lives, along with those such as family, ethnicity/race, occupation, gender and religion. Because gay/lesbian identity and group affiliation remain stigmatized by many of the other groups of which they are a part, this market incorporation provides a vital sense of affirmation. At issue, then, for gay and lesbian consumers are questions regarding how these various groups to which they belong coexist, i.e., which conflict with and which reinforce each other, as well as how these various affiliations are reconciled within their psyches and how they are expressed within the marketplace.

Marketing and media attention also affect gay/lesbian communities, and while it is somewhat separate from political activism, it can help render gays and lesbians a force to be reckoned with politically (Mickens 1994). Alliances are invaluable in any social movement, and the gay/lesbian movement is no exception. Both within and outside the gay/lesbian community it is important to nurture alliances with the "others," be they marketers, working class people, people of color, bisexuals, transgendered persons or heterosexuals.

Marketing campaigns, in particular, add the critically important data points of buyer and income earner for those taking an oppositional stance towards homosexuality and who are accustomed to thinking of gays/lesbians solely in terms of sexuality. Noted Kevin Ray, president of aka Communications, a media and public relations agency specializing in the gay market, "business is exploding, firms are no longer willing to avoid the market out of fear of a backlash from straight consumers, now they're worried about a backlash against firms that appear to be homophobic" (cited in Miller 1992, p. 15). While this may be somewhat of an overstatement, let us not lose sight of the fact that in a capitalist society, market incorporation is of the utmost importance because it summons a social legitimation approaching that of citizen.

Yet, there are some downsides to this market recognition and targeting. Gays and lesbians are right to hold advertisers and companies that target them accountable for the images they use, and there are places to articulate these concerns in both mainstream and gay media, in letters to the editors of both gay/lesbian and mainstream media, and in boycotts. Here I make reference to the title of this paper, which is an intentional play on the earlier and opposite rallying cry, "We're Here, We're Queer, and We're Not Going Shopping," echoed along Fifth Avenue in New York on the twentieth anniversary of the Stonewall Rebellion. That cry demonstrated gays' and lesbians' growing awareness of and intention to use strategically their buying power in the form of boycotts and purchases to express their disapproval or approval of corporate policies regarding employment practices, marketing and advertising campaigns and charitable and political contributions.

The marketplace has a tendency to distort not only the representations of those being targeted, but also their interests. For gays/lesbians, being targeted by marketers can be very seductive, particularly the portrayals of gays/lesbians as gorgeous, well-built, professionally successful, loved and accepted, especially in contrast to the legacy of negative treatment. Some aspects of gay/lesbian culture are forwarded at the expense of others in marketing and advertising appeals. Particularly noteworthy are the pervasive images of white, upper-middle class, "straight looking" people at the expense of those more distanced from and threatening to the mainstream, such as the poor, ethnic/racial/sexual minorities, drag queens, and butch lesbians.

In addition, it remains to be seen whether critical political agendas will be able to coexist with marketing interests in gay/lesbian media. Noted Dave Mulryan, director of business development at Mulryan/Nash Communications, "take away the politics and it's good, sound marketing."

Mr. Mulryan's statement was made in reference to the elimination of sex advertisements in *The Advocate*, and their subsequent inclusion in a separate plastic envelope. Hermetically sealing and physically distancing the more controversial aspects of gay/lesbian culture may make sound business sense, as Mulryan noted, but it may not be in the best political interests of gay/lesbian communities. Effective marketing campaigns operationalized in terms of messages that are directed to the largest common denominator of a subculture within specialized media that avoid content that might offend advertisers do not necessarily deal with the central concerns of an audience, nor do they necessarily bring about the most effective social change. While marketers are not directly interested in the latter, media managers must deal with the former to maintain the publication's strong following.

A number of obstacles to gay/lesbian marketing have been identified. Even as this market has proven quite lucrative for some firms, the gay market remains a quandary for others, both marketing practitioners and academics, with only some of this ambivalence attributable to the stigma attached to homosexuality. As previously mentioned, marketing academics have been reluctant to view gays and lesbians as a market due to traditional conceptions of marketing segmentation. So long as marketers continue to see gays and lesbians through the reductive lenses of sexuality as opposed to the more comprehensive conceptualizations that take into account the social movements and consumer subcultures that have developed around gay/lesbian identities, marketing myopia regarding the potential of this market segment will persist.

Finally, fear of the stigma attached to homosexuality being linked to their products is no small obstacle for marketing practitioners. Noted Harry Taylor, National Ad Director for *Out*, "what I have to sell is a comfort level to people . . . it's more difficult to overcome the prejudice than to sell the product" (cited in Levin 1993). Homophobia on the part of upper management has been cited as a factor that has made selling of advertising space in gay media very difficult, according to Joe Di Sabato, President of Rivendell Marketing (cited in Miller 1990).

Added to this fear is the charge of immorality. The religious right has engaged a virtual assault on the civil rights of gays, lesbians, and bisexuals in recent years, and a key part of their strategy has involved targeting firms actively marketing their products and services to gays/lesbians. Noted Michel Roux, president of Carillon Inc., distributor of Absolut vodka and the first major company to advertise in *The Advocate* in 1979, "We've had people writing to us saying we will not not use your product because you're advertising in a homosexual magazine and promoting homosexuality" (cited in Levin 1993, p. 30). While Roux did not withdraw the ads, there are numerous examples of companies that have withdrawn theirs. Ron McDonald, manager of *Genre*, reported that members of religious groups called in accusing Phillip Morris of targeting gays with their ad for

Special Kings, and in response the company withdrew its ads (Levin 1993). In another example, Visa was the recent target of the religious right for having contributed $10,000 in support of the Gay Games.

Perhaps the most insidious deployment of gay/lesbian marketing information to date has been the use of the income figures from the Simmons study mentioned earlier by religious groups to argue that gays/ lesbians did not need "special rights" (i.e., their choice of words to describe gay/lesbian protection ordinances). In a newspaper circulated to tens of thousands of voters in the state of Colorado in support of Amendment Two, the Coalition for Family Values cited Simmons Market Research figures showing average household incomes of $54,300 to argue that gays and lesbians were not economically disadvantaged, and therefore did not need protection from discrimination.[7] On one hand it is possible that it is because gays/lesbians have had some success in making civil rights gains that the religious right is determined to dispel them. More to the point of this paper, it is because gays and lesbians are making some headway in the marketplace, and because this market incorporation helps bring about a sense of social legitimation, that political opponents are so intent on contesting this strategically important social terrain.

Conclusion

While the increase in marketing attention provides a welcome sense of validation and legitimation, gays and lesbians must look at this relatively recent development with a critical eye. The earlier era of gay culture and visibility in the 1930s and 1940s in Europe culminated in black and pink triangles in Germany. Let us not forget that this was a capitalist country at the time. In fact, the vibrant gay culture existing in bars, restaurants, cafés and theaters in evidence at that time may have even fueled gays' and lesbians' genocide under Hitler since it made them more visible.

Since then many things have changed, both in the U.S. and in many parts of the world. The work of social movement activists and social scientists, each in their own ways and in their respective domains, has helped counter the legacy of stigma and institutionalized oppression. Closely linked to these gains, the gay/lesbian market has become increasingly visible, pro-moted in articles in marketing and media publications, in advertisements for gay/lesbian media, and in the plethora of marketers' attempts to target gay and lesbian consumers.

Market incorporation provides an important sense of social legitim-ation for gays and lesbians at both the individual and community levels. Yet, such incorporation is not without its limitations. Market legitimation was not enough in Nazi Germany, and it is not enough now. The futures of the gay/lesbian market and of the gay/lesbian movement are intricately connected, but they are not reducible to each other. Gays and lesbians cannot expect advertisers to engage in community activism – although they can and will benefit at times from advertisements, and some members of the advertising and marketing professional communities can and will advance gay/lesbian causes from time to time.

It is important to note differences between gays and lesbians as a market segment and as a social movement, even as both can and do benefit from each other's efforts. The gay and lesbian movement needs multiple approaches along multiple fronts, including the marketplace, to make the gains deemed desirable and to enjoy the basic human rights taken for granted by so many (e.g., freedom from job and housing discrimination based on suspicion of gay status, the right to marriage, insurance, and medical benefits). Unfortunately, the movement has been plagued by internal variation in politics, sexual and otherwise, and has gotten caught up in arguments for the one best approach. The gay/lesbian community's response to Amendment Two in Colorado was a recent example, yet there are numerous other examples of controversies within the community regarding whether the tactics of ACT UP, Queer Nation, the Lesbian Avengers, or the more conservative reformist tactics of those who infiltrate churches, workplaces, and other community spaces are the most effective means to further community interests that are at least as diverse as the tactics used to address them.

For the gay/lesbian community, gay target marketing is much more productively viewed as a critically important field of social struggle than as something to be avoided or prevented. Advertisements and other marketing artifacts such as products and services and popular cultural products such as film, books, recorded music, videos, etc. that incorporate aspects of gay/lesbian iconography potentially validate individual gays and lesbians and their communities, and can be used towards these communities' ends.

At the same time, gays and lesbians must be wary of distortions and appropriations in marketing appeals. While the advertisements may be quite flattering, it is important to remember that gays and lesbians do not enjoy the same standing in the marketplace in terms of income, status, and treatment by others. There are extreme subject positions within the communities that make mainstream advertisers nervous, and the ultimate test of gay and lesbian rights occurs at the extremes, not for those who can pass as heterosexual.

Lesbians and gays have come a long way, as the saying goes, but the struggle is far from over. In fact, it appears that the struggle is heating up, with the stakes getting much higher. The accommodation of gays and lesbians in the marketplace is a highly complex phenomenon that is at once as potentially validating as it is potentially alienating.

The arrival of this new market brings with it many more questions than answers. Further work is called for that focuses on the nexus of sexuality, social movement, and market segmentation in order to enhance our understanding of the intricate dynamics of gays' and lesbians' market incorporation. Further research is also called for that investigates expressions of subcultural membership and identification for individual gay and lesbian consumers, gay/lesbian communities, and their relationships to other subcultures in the U.S. The shift from mass to specialty markets, in all their diversity, together with the loss of audience figures for the mass media have been cited as contributing to the decay of not only the mainstream market, but also of mainstream U.S. culture. Yet, there is another interpretation. Instead of a nostalgic lament for the false unity and superiority of white, middle-class, heterosexual male culture, this shift in marketing strategy may be a part of a new era of inclusion, as both marketers and consumers realize increased tolerance for social difference.

Notes

1   Glancing in one of the gay/lesbian phone directories available in most major cities attests to the wide range of businesses targeting gays and lesbians.
2   Age, gender, race/ethnicity, class, and sexual orientation are but a few designators of consumer cultures. The term "consumer culture" was first used in the critical tradition of the Frankfurt School to lament the impending social changes of western capitalism. More recently, in marketing and in cultural studies the term is used in reference to the marketplace expressions of a group of people (i.e., their shared aesthetics, attitudes, values and beliefs), necessarily including the marketing strategies employed to target them (Schudson 1984; Featherstone 1991). Thus, consumer cultures are hybrids of existing subcultures (e.g., blacks, Latinos, gays and lesbians, yuppies, the elderly) and their respective marketing artifacts (e.g., products and services, advertisements, and other marketing communications).
3   By subjectivity, I mean a person's sense of themselves and their place in the world, as well as their relationships towards others. I use the term agency to refer to one's ability to act in pursuit of their interests and desires.
4   This is not to suggest that all market segments are social movements or that all social movements are market segments.
5   This is not a comprehensive list, but rather serves to illustrate the wide array of lesbian and gay organizations and interests.
6   My purpose here is not to rank oppressions, but rather to analyze characterizations of these respective groups for insight as to their position and treatment in society. In this sense, this work represents an extension of my previous work on the incorporation of another type of social difference in the marketplace, namely that of ethnicity and nationality. I examined the role of marketing strategies in facilitating and inhibiting the incorporation of Mexican immigrants into U.S. society. My findings were that subcultural boundaries between Latinos and other consumer groups in the U.S. were raised by firms targeting Latinos with specially tailored products and services, even as these marketing strategies offered Latinos an important sense of social legitimation by institutionalizing aspects of Latino culture in this country (Peñaloza 1994).
7   Amendment Two stated, 'Shall there be an amendment to article II of the Colorado Constitution to prohibit the state of Colorado and any of its political subdivisions

from adopting or enforcing any law or policy which provides that homosexual, lesbian, or bisexual orientation, conduct, or relationships constitutes or entitles a person to claim any minority or protected status, quota preferences, or discrimination." The amendment passed by a slim margin, and a preliminary injunction ruling it unconstitutional was later upheld by the Colorado Supreme Court. On October 11, 1994 Amendment Two was ruled unconstitutional by the Court. It is currently under appeal to the U.S. Supreme Court. Estimates of losses in convention and tourist revenue in response to the passage of Amendment Two totaled 40 million dollars (Johnson 1994).

References

Anderson, B. (1983). *Imagined Communities*. London: Verso.

Bérubé, A. (1990). *Coming Out Under Fire: The History of Gay Men and Women in World War II*. New York: Free Press.

Boyd, N. A. (1995). San Francisco was a Wide Open Town: Charting the Emergence of Lesbian and Gay. Communities through the mid Twentieth Century. Unpublished doctoral dissertation, Department of American Civilization, Brown University.

Bristor, J. & Fisher, E. (1993). Feminist Thought: Implications for Consumer Research. *Journal of Consumer Research*, 19 (4) (March), 518–536.

Butler, J. & Scott, J. W. (Eds.) (1992). *Feminists Theorize the Political*. London: Routledge.

Button, K. (1990). The gay consumer. *Financial Times* (November 9), p. 10.

Chauncey, G. A. (1994). *Gay New York: Urban Culture and the Making of a Gay Male World, 1890–1940*. Ph.D. thesis, Yale University.

Cravens, D., Hills, G., & Woodruff, R. (1987). *Marketing Management*. Homewood, IL: Irwin.

Curiel, J. (1991). Gay Newspapers. *Editor and Publisher Fourth Estate*. 124 (3) (August), 14–19.

Davis, R. A. (1993). Sky's the limit for tour operators. *Advertising Age* (January 18), p. 36.

D'Emilio, J. (1983). *Sexual Politics. Sexual Communities: The Making of a Homosexual Minority in the U.S., 1940–1970*. Chicago: University of Chicago Press.

——— . (1994). *Making Trouble: Essays on Gay History. Politics and the University*. New York: Routledge.

D'Emilio, J. & Freedman, E. B. (1988). *Intimate Matters: A History of Sexuality in America*. New York: Harper and Row.

Duberman, M. (1993). *Stonewall*. New York: Dutton.

Elliott, S. (1993a). *Good Housekeeping* is drawing fire from homosexuals over ads dealing with family values. *New York Times* (May 7), p. C-15.

——— . (1993b). When a play has a gay theme, campaigns often tell it as it is. *New York Times* (June 15), p. C-15.

——— . (1993c). As the gay and lesbian market grows, a boom in catalogues that are out, loud and proud. *New York Times* (September 10), p. C-17.

Ellis, H. (1925). *Sexual Inversion*. Philadelphia: F.A. Davis.

Engel, J. F., Fiorillo, H., & Cayley, M. A. (1971). *Marketing Segmentation: Concepts and Applications*. New York: Holt, Rinehart and Winston.

Faderman, L. (1981). *Surpassing the Love of Men*. New York: William Morrow and Company.

Featherstone, M. (1991). *Consumer Culture and Postmodernism*. Newbury Park, CA: Sage.

Foucault, M. (1978). *The History of Sexuality*. New York: Pantheon Books.

Fugate, D. L. (1993). Evaluating the U.S. Male Homosexual and Lesbian Population as a Viable Target Market Segment: A Review with Implications. *Journal of Consumer Marketing*, 10 (4), 46–57.

Hirschfeld, M. (1910). *Transvestites: The Erotic Drive to Cross Dress*. Translated by M. A. Lombardi-Nash (1991). New York: Prometheus Books.

Hooker, E. (1956). A Preliminary Analysis of Group Behavior of Homosexuals. *Journal of Psychology*, 42, 219–225.

———. (1957). The Adjustment of the Male Overt Homosexual. *Journal of Projective Techniques*, 21, 18–31.

Janus, S. & Janus, C. (1993). *The Janus Report on Sexual Behavior*. New York: John Wiley and Sons.

Johnson, B. (1993a). The gay quandary: Advertising's most elusive, yet lucrative target market proves difficult to measure. *Advertising Age*, 64 (18) (January 18) p. 29.

———. (1993b). Economics holds back lesbian ad market. *Advertising Age*, 64 (18) (January 18), p. 34.

Johnson, D. (1994). Colorado Court Nullifies a Ban on Gay Rights. *New York Times*, (October 12), p. 1.

Kennedy, E. L. & Davis, M. D. (1994). *Boots of Leather. Slippers of Gold: The History of the Lesbian Community*. New York: Penguin Books.

Lastovicka, J. (1982). On the validation of lifestyle traits: A review and illustration. *Journal of Marketing Research*, 19 (1) (February), 126–138.

Lastovicka, J., Murray, J., Jr., & Joachimsthaler, E. (1990). Evaluating the Measurement Validity of Lifestyle Typologies With Qualitative Measures and Multiplicative Factoring. *Journal of Marketing Research*, 27 (1) (February), 11–23.

Levin, G. (1993). Mainstream's domino effect: Liquor, fragrance, clothing advertisers case into gay magazines. *Advertising Age* (January 18), p. 30.

Meyer, C. (1994). Consumers and the Emerging Interactive Communications Infrastructure. Presented to the Association for Consumer Research Annual Conference, Boston, Massachusetts, October 20–23.

Miller, C. (1992). Mainstream marketers decide time is right to target gays. *Marketing News* (July 20), p. 8.

———. (1990). Gays are affluent but often overlooked market. *Marketing News* (December 24), p. 2.

Mickens, E. (1994). Gay Money Gay Power. *The Advocate* (April 19), p. 41–45.

Morris, A. D. & Mueller, C. M. (Eds.) (1992). *Frontiers in Social Movement Theory*. New Haven, CT: Yale University Press.

Myrick, F.L. (1972). Structure and Function of Deviant Economic Institutions. Unpublished doctoral dissertation, University of Texas.

Nestle, J. (Ed.) (1992). *The Persistent Desire*. Boston: Alyson Publications.

New York Times (1990). The Media Business: Gay Press Looks to Madison Ave. *New York Times* (December 17), p. D-11.

Peñaloza (1994). Atravesando fronteras/border crossings: A critical ethnographic exploration of the consumer acculturation of Mexican immigrants. *Journal of Consumer Research*, 21 (1) (June), 32–54.

Peñaloza & Gilly, M. (1986). The Hispanic family: Consumer research issues. *Psychology and Marketing*, 3 (Winter), 291–303.

Petracca, M. (1993). *The Politics of Interests*. Boulder, CO: Westview Press.

Piven, F.F. & Cloward, R.A. (1977). *Poor People's Movements*. New York: Random House.

Plant, R. (1986). *The Pink Triangle and the Nazi War Against Homosexuals*. New York: Holt.

Rogers, P. (1993). Survey stirs debate on number of gay men in U.S. *New York Times*, 142, pp. A-10, A-20.

Schudson, M. (1984). *Advertising: The Uneasy Persuasion* New York, NY: Basic Books.

Schulman, S. (1994). *My American History: Lesbian and Gay Life During the Reagan/ Bush Years*. New York: Routledge.

Shapiro, M.J. (1992). *Reading the Postmodern Polity: Political Theory as Textual Practice*. Minneapolis, MN: University of Minnesota Press.

Shilts, R. (1987). *And the Band Played On*. New York: St. Martin's Press.

Straub, K. (1991). The guilty pleasures of female theatrical cross-dressing and the antobiography of Charlotte Charke. In Straub, J. & Straub, K. (Eds.), *Body Guards*. London: Routledge.

Summer, B. (1992). A Niche Market Comes of Age. *Publishers Weekly* (June 29), p. 36–41.

Thompson, M. (1994). *Long Road to Freedom: The Advocate History of the Gay and Lesbian Movement*. New York: St. Martin's Press.

Warren, J. (1990). Vibrant subculture: Readers' buying power a key to a thriving gay press. *Chicago Tribune*, p. 2.

Weeks, J. (1985). *Sexuality and Its Discontents: Meanings, Myth and Modern Sexualities*. New York: Routledge.

Weinberg, G. (1972). *Society and the Healthy Homosexual*. New York: St. Martin's Press.

Wilson, M. (1991). "Sans les femmes, qu'est-ce qui nous resterait?": Gender and Transgression in Bohemian Montmartre. In Straub, J. & Straub, K. (Eds.), *Body Guards*. London: Routledge.

Wind, Y. (1978). Issues and Advances in Segmentation Research. *Journal of Marketing Research*, 15 (3) (August), 317–337.

Yankelovich (1994). Gay/Lesbian/Bisexual Monitor Survey. New York: Yankelovich and Associates, cited in *New York Times* (June 9), p. D-1.

Chapter 18

Andrew S. Walters and Maria-Cristina Curran

"EXCUSE ME, SIR? MAY I HELP YOU AND YOUR BOYFRIEND?": SALESPERSONS' DIFFERENTIAL TREATMENT OF HOMOSEXUAL AND STRAIGHT CUSTOMERS

From *Journal of Homosexuality* 1996, 31 (1/2): 135–52

THE EXTENT TO WHICH individuals exhibit negative attitudes or behavior toward others on the basis of sexual orientation remains an under-researched but critical area of study. For example, the current sociopolitical debate over "special rights" (endorsed by the Religious Right) versus "equal rights" (endorsed by gay and lesbian groups, human rights advocacy groups, the ACLU) rests on the assumption that gays are denied the same treatment as heterosexuals. In the past two years, legislation attempting to prohibit discrimination on the basis of sexual orientation has been impeded by conservative constituencies, and publicly-sanctioned discriminatory policies have been blocked only by court order.

The cultural climate available to lesbians, gay men, and bisexuals in most arenas of American society is negative, if not hostile. Basic civil liberties are routinely denied to homosexuals or persons perceived to be homosexuals Although domestic partnership ordinances-a nonlegal recognition of relationship status-are highly publicized (Richardson, 1993), they remain proportionately rare and have been challenged in most states or municipalities that have sought to implement them. Nine states and the

District of Columbia have enacted statutes protecting the rights of homosexuals in equal access to credit, employment, housing, and public accommodation (California, Connecticut, Hawaii, Massachusetts, Minnesota, New
Jersey, Rhode Island, Vermont, and Wisconsin). In most other areas of the
country, homosexuals are not guaranteed equal access to housing (Carman,
1992; Marchetti, 1989; Mehler, 1989), employment (e.g., Stewart, 1994),
insurance and benefits (Anderson, 1992; Associated Press, 1989; Purdy,
1990; Thompson & Andrzejewski, 1988), and basic human rights (Higuera,
1989).

Early research on homosexuality sought to identify personality characteristics of persons who report homonegativism (also referred to as homophobia). Research has consistently found that homonegative individuals
express authoritarianism (Larsen, Reed, & Hoffman, 1980) and political
conservativism (Whitley, 1987) and strongly endorse traditional definitions
of family and sex roles (Millham & Weinberger, 1977; Newman, 1989;
Weinberger & Millham, 1979; Whitley, 1987). They are less sexually
permissive and more likely to report sexual guilt and erotophobia (Dunbar,
Brown, & Amoroso, 1973; Ficarrotto, 1990; Mosher & O'Grady, 1979).
Moreover, although they have less personal contact with lesbians and gay
men (Herek & Glunt, 1993) and hence a predictably confined experience
with homosexuality, homonegative individuals believe that homosexuality
is a voluntary form of deviancy (Whitley, 1990), report greater dislike for
homosexuals of their own sex (Gentry, 1987), and describe homosexuals
according to stereotypes (Page & Yee, 1985). Finally, homonegative individuals are likely to perceive homosexuals as quite dissimilar from themselves even when they are not (Shaffer & Wallace, 1990).

Experimental studies have provided strong evidence for the pervasive
attitudes against homosexuals (Kite & Deaux, 1986; Seligman, Howell,
Cornell, Cutright, & Dewey, 1991) as well as elucidating stable traits that
characterize homonegative individuals (see Herek, 1984, for a thorough
review of earlier studies). Information gleaned from these studies has been
useful for developing strategies for homosexuality education and professional training (e.g., Walters, 1994; Walters & Phillips, 1994). However,
because nearly all of these studies have been conducted under laboratory
conditions with college students as subjects, they are limited in several
ways. First, results obtained from laboratory studies may not be representative of how individuals respond outside of experimental conditions. This is
especially likely when subjects are asked to "project" how they think they
would react in certain situations. Second, recruiting subjects from introductory psychology classes consisting almost entirely of first- and second-
year students (i.e., 18–19 years old) may be particularly problematic when
studying attitudes and behavior toward homosexuals. For example, Herek
and Glunt (1993) have found that knowing or being friends with a homosexual is consistently associated with reduced homophobia. As students

progress through college, they may become acquainted with lesbians and gay men — a situation that is less likely to have occurred among freshmen and sophomores. Furthermore, establishing a gay identity is itself a developmental process. Most gay students accept their sexual orientation in their junior and senior years of college (Remafedi, 1987). Thus, an indirect result of studying only younger students is that attitudes and indeed, personal identities, may not yet be fully developed.

We are aware of only one experimental study that investigated differential treatment of homosexuals and heterosexuals in a natural (i.e., non-laboratory) setting. Gray, Russell, and Blockley (1991) had either a male or female confederate approach shoppers and ask them for change. In half of the trials, the confederate wore an unmarked T-shirt; in the other half, the confederate wore a pro-gay T-shirt. As predicted by the researchers, results showed that help (as measured by listening to the request and physically looking for change) was offered significantly less frequently to the ostensibly pro-gay confederate. This effect was not attenuated by sex of the confederate, sex of the subject, or whether a justification (i.e., "Excuse me. I need to make an important phone call. Have you got change for a pound, please?") accompanied the request for change. Gray et al (1991) concluded that the ubiquitous negative attitudes toward homosexuals have clear behavioral correlates.

The present study adds to previous research by examining discriminatory behavior toward homosexuals in a naturalistic setting. Specifically, we investigated how gay male, lesbian, and heterosexual couples were treated as customers in retail stores. Similar to the Gray et al. (1991) study, our central interest was in willingness to help gay-identified persons in a shopping environment. Unlike Gray et al., the confederates in our study were couples, and rather than ask shoppers for help (change), we investigated how retail employees — who are paid to assist customers — would treat homosexuals. We reasoned that if the *appearance* of homosexual status resulted in differential treatment of couples by employees paid to be respectful and courteous of customers, then a clear relationship must exist between attitudes and expressed behavior.

Three hypotheses guided the current study. First, we predicted that confederates posing as a heterosexual couple would be helped by sales associates in less time than would either gay male or lesbian couples. Previous literature documents more cultural dislike for gay men than for lesbians (Berrill, 1990; Berrill & Herek, 1990; Lehne, 1992). Thus, it was conceivable that staff assistance could vary between gay and lesbian couples as well. Given the scant research in naturalistic settings, however, we made no a priori hypotheses between these conditions. Second, we predicted that the quality of interaction with couples would depend on their perceived status as homosexuals or heterosexuals. Specifically, we hypothesized that staff would respond to the presence of homosexual couples by staring, laughing, pointing at, and talking about them. Similarly, we predicted that gay and lesbian couples – but not straight couples – would both perceive that staff looked uncomfortable with their presence and would report an overall less positive experience in the stores. Our third hypothesis was that discriminatory behavior would exist contrary to store policy and manager expectations.

Method

Confederates

Six senior psychology majors (three males, three females) served as confederates and for their participation, received one semester hour of academic research credit. Students were screened by the first author to assess their comfort in assuming (i.e., acting) the role of a gay man or lesbian. All students expressed interest in participating in field research and reported feeling comfortable acting as a member of either a heterosexual or homosexual couple. An additional female undergraduate student observed confederates on each site visit. To the best of our knowledge, all students identify themselves as heterosexual. Students were Caucasian and ranged in age from 23–28.

Physical attractiveness of confederates was judged by two independent raters (1 male, 1 female) on a scale of 1 = very unattractive to 10 = very attractive. Male [$M = 7.67$, $SD = 1.60$, Range 5–9] and female [$M = 7.88$, $SD = 1.25$, Range 5–9] confederates did not differ in attractiveness [$F = 0.40$, ns]. Students wore innocuous clothing (e.g., jeans, a college sweat-shirt/polo shirt) at each site visit. Thus, the appearance and dress of our confederates appeared quite ordinary (e.g., no one wore a Queer Nation T-shirt) and inoffensive.

Participating stores

Prior to the start of the study, managers from 20 retail stores were contacted and asked to participate in a study titled "Experiences of Mystery Shoppers." Managers were informed that six local residents (our confederates) would enter their stores as customers once over a period of four months and would rate the store on several criteria, including employee behavior and customer relations. Managers also consented to a follow-up interview with the first author and were assured that the name of their store would not be publicized without their additional consent. The follow-up interview served the dual purpose of determining managerial/company policies and expectations of employee behavior and as a debriefing session about the true nature of the study.

All stores included in the study were located in the same indoor mall. Stores were chosen based on three criteria: (1) a manager or owner from each store agreed to participate in the study, signing a consent form permitting confederates to enter their store as "mystery shoppers" and agreeing to a follow-up interview at a later date; (2) the size of each store favored employee-customer interactions (for this reason large department stores – whose sales associates oversee a larger portion of floor space – were excluded from the study); and (3) a variety of stores were represented (included were 11 clothing, 3 athletic, 2 music accessory, and 4 shoe stores).

Data were collected between September and December, 1993. Store visits were randomly determined as to the month, day, and time of day with the exceptions of Mondays and Tuesdays (managers often stated that stores are less busy on these days and fewer sales associates are available to work) and after 7:00 p.m. (to avoid interfering with student work schedules). For example, a gay couple would be randomly chosen to enter a particular store on a Wednesday afternoon in late September, a heterosexual couple to enter the same store at noon in mid-October, and a lesbian couple to enter the store at 6:00 p.m. on a Wednesday in early December. For another store, the heterosexual couple could be assigned to enter the store first (e.g., a Thursday in late October at 11:00 a.m.), the lesbian couple to visit the same store the next day at 4:00 p.m., and the gay couple to enter at 2:00 p.m. three weeks later.

Procedure

The first author was on-site during each visit and made an unobtrusive, cursory check of the participating stores to ensure that each was open and appeared as busy as it did on other site dates. We felt that this procedure was necessary to assure that no store had attracted an inordinate number of shoppers that could disrupt the typical ratio of sales associates to shoppers (e.g., a clearance sale). The first author then met the confederates in a mall restaurant at a pre-arranged time.

Confederates for each store were randomly assigned to a homosexual or heterosexual couple. Three males and three females were each assigned a number (1, 2, 3). For each store, one male and one female confederate were randomly assigned to comprise the heterosexual couple. The remaining two males and two females comprised the gay and lesbian couples, respectively. Confederates were unaware of the dyad type (heterosexual or gay, heterosexual or lesbian) they were assigned until the first author announced it several minutes before the couple was to enter the store. By randomly re-assigning confederate roles for each store, we eliminated systematic bias due to personality or individual difference variables specific to the confederates themselves. To summarize, each confederate was randomly assigned to a couple, the order in which couples visited stores was also randomly determined, and confederate roles were reassigned for each of the 20 stores. Thus, one gay, one lesbian, and one straight couple entered each store but no confederate entered the same store more than once.

One other student (the second author) was present as an observer in each store before, during, and after couples' visits. The observer was responsible for (1) insuring that the couple followed the script accurately, (2) clocking the time employees took to approach and offer help to couples, and (3) observing and recording comments made by the staff after couples departed.

The observer entered a store several minutes before the confederate couple and browsed inconspicuously, as if shopping. If the observer was approached by a sales associate she responded by saying, "I'm just looking for a blouse (CD/pair of shoes), thank you." In the several minutes that the observer was in the store without the couple, she was able to decline any assistance offered by staff and position herself facing the entrance of the store. Concealed in a pocket, the observer carried a stopwatch and starting timing when the confederates crossed the threshold of the store. She continued to browse while observing the employees' reactions to and behavior toward the couple. The moment the couple was approached by an employee and offered help, the observer stopped the watch.

All confederates were trained to follow the same script. They began holding hands before reaching the store. As they entered the store talking to one another and smiling, one member of the couple, like the observer, started a concealed stopwatch. Confederates identified the nearest sales associate, made eye contact with the employee, and then walked past salespersons and began to browse throughout the store. Confederates always displayed the same affectionate behavior regardless of pairing. At no time did confederates display additional affectionate behavior (e.g., hugging, kissing). If an employee approached the couple and asked if he/she could help them, the clock was stopped and one of the confederates said that he/she was looking for an article of clothing (CD/pair of shoes). After either being offered help and thanking the sales associate or waiting six minutes for an offer of help, the couple left the store. Confederates then reconvened with the first author in the mall restaurant and independently answered a questionnaire about their experience in the store.

As the couple began to leave the store, the observer casually walked toward the staff. While still appearing to look at merchandise, she was able to hear staff comments about the couple. Comments were mostly directed at other employees but were occasionally directed at other customers (including our confederate). Immediately after departing the store, the observer made a written record of these comments.

It is important to note here that both the observer and the confederates were trained to discriminate between sales associates' greeting behavior and an actual offer of help or exposition of merchandise. Manager interviews confirmed our suspicion that most stores situate an employee near the entrance of a store specifically to greet incoming patrons. The initial greeting by a sales associate did not constitute our definition of a helping response because their greeting was often tendered before they noticed the confederates were holding hands or was issued from an area of the store that did not permit them to identify the confederates as a couple (e.g., a table of merchandise blocked their view of the couples' hands). Thus, stopwatches were stopped only after employees first witnessed the confederates as a couple and then solicited their patronage.

Measures

In addition to the objective measure of time, each confederate independently completed a checklist immediately after departing each store. Confederates did not discuss their individual store experiences before completing the checklist. Couples were asked to confirm that they followed the script, their degree of assurance that members of the sales staff witnessed them as a couple, if they were helped within six minutes, and if they were helped, the level of assistance offered by a sales associate (1 = no offer of help, 4 = a second greeting, offer of help, and exposition of products). Couples also indicated whether they felt employees looked uncomfortable with their presence and rated their overall experience in the store (positive, neutral, negative). Finally, confederates were given the opportunity to write any specific comments about their experience in the store.

The observer also completed a checklist after each visit, recording the approximate number of customers present in the store when our confederates entered and the number of staff who were available to assist them. In addition, the observer verified that each couple followed the script, displayed the specified affectionate behavior, and if not assisted by sales staff within six minutes, departed the store. As mentioned above, the observer also reported comments made by staff about the couple after their departure.

Follow-up interviews were completed by the first author at the manager's convenience after one heterosexual, one gay, and one lesbian couple had visited all stores (i.e., sixty visits). Managers were asked about: (1) the characteristics or features they look for in hiring sales associates, (2) company policies/managerial expectations regarding the time by which staff are expected to offer an initial greeting to customers and a subsequent solicitation of service to them, (3) demographic variables describing their store's clientele (i.e., estimated percentages of customers by gender, race, and sexual orientation), and (4) their perceptions of how store employees address and attend to customers. Finally, managers were queried on store/company procedures regarding disciplinary action against employees who were found to mistreat or discriminate against customers.

Trial procedure

In order to ensure that students were comfortable assuming their role as a member of a couple and to rehearse the sequence of events as prescribed, confederates visited four stores (2 clothing, 1 shoe, 1 music accessory) according to the procedures described above. These stores were located in a downtown area and were not associated with any of the stores in the mall. Although preliminary data collected from these pre-test stores suggested that heterosexual couples were treated in a more friendly and timely fashion, actual data from these stores were not included in analyses. Rather, the trial procedure was designed to familiarize confederates with their roles, and in fact, confederates assigned to the homosexual dyads displayed some discomfort initially. However, after the first few trials, the procedure ran smoothly and confederates were able to perform their roles comfortably.

Results

Analyses were conducted at several levels. Initial tests were performed to determine whether the number of other customers present in stores was consistent across confederate dyads and if staff were available to help our couples. There were no significant differences in the number of customers present or the number of staff present, both X^2s $(9) = 8.42$, ns. Additional checks by the observer and both members of the couple revealed that in all cases actors followed the script, displayed affectionate behavior (holding hands, smiling, talking), and entered and exited the store appropriately. These data suggested to us that all protocols were consistent across stores and therefore, could be included in subsequent analyses.

The time variable

In order to test the reliability of timed responses, times collected by observer and confederates were compared. Paired t-tests yielded no significant differences, all ts < 1.85, ns. Correlations between observer and confederate were .92 in lesbian couples, .92 in straight couples, and .94 in gay couples. Because the two measures were nearly identical, only the time data collected by the observer were used in subsequent analyses.

The average time for sales associates to approach lesbian couples was 259 seconds (4 min. 18 sec.). Gay male couples were helped in slightly less time – 231 seconds (3 min. 51 sec.). Heterosexual couples were helped in 82 seconds (1 min. 22 sec.). A repeated measures analysis of variance (ANOVA) revealed a significant difference by couple *type*, $F = 36.58$, p < .0001. Results of these analyses are illustrated in Figure 1. Planned comparisons (Winer, 1971) were used to test observed differences between groups. As predicted, heterosexual couples were helped in significantly less time than were homosexual couples $F(2,17) = 140.16$, p < .001. Although we made no a priori hypotheses about differences between gay male and lesbian couples, these analyses revealed that gay male couples were helped significantly more quickly than were lesbian couples, $F(2,17) = 4.96$, p < .05.

Additional analyses ruled out the possibility that observed effects were due to the order in which couples entered stores (e.g., if gay or lesbian couples entered stores in early December amid the rush of holiday shoppers whereas heterosexual couples did not). Neither the effect for order nor the order X couple interaction was significant, both $Fs < 0.39$, *ns*. Thus, regardless of whether they shopped in September or December,

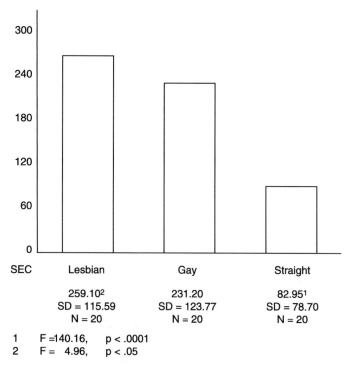

Figure 1 Mean time (in seconds) lesbian, gay, and straight confederates were helped by sales staff

heterosexual couples were always assisted in less time than homosexual couples.

Other types of discriminatory treatment

Response time was not the only way in which our gay and lesbian couples were treated differently. Correlations were computed between confederate and observer ratings of five additional variables (staring, laughing, pointing, talking about, and being rude). Within gay and lesbian couples, considerable congruence was apparent in ratings of laughing, pointing, and rude treatment (all rs .40 or higher, p < .01). In other words, both confederates and observer reported that staff laughed and pointed at the couple in their presence. In addition, lesbian and gay couples consistently reported discourteous employee behavior, and these reactions were reported by the observer as well. Alternatively, significant relationships were not found in employees' staring at the couples or in talking about them. Although the observer did witness staff displaying these behaviors, they generally occurred outside of couples' presence.

The observer's ratings of five dimensions of staff demeanor are presented in Table 1. Note that at no time were heterosexual couples treated negatively by staff. In four categories (staring, laughing, pointing, talking), there were statistically significant differences between lesbian and straight couples. Gay couples differed significantly from lesbian couples in three categories (staring, talking, rude treatment). Lesbian and straight couples did not differ significantly in the amount of rude treatment they received by staff. However, there was a significant difference between the rude treatment displayed by staff toward gay males compared to either lesbian or straight couples. Thus, gay couples were treated more negatively than straight couples in all categories of behavior, and for one measure (rudeness) were treated more negatively than were lesbian couples. These data are consistent with and complement differences in time to offer help reported above.

Confederates' perceptions that staff looked uncomfortable also varied by couple type. Lesbian and gay couples did not report a significant difference in perception of staff discomfort (Lesbian $M = 1.50$, $SD = .48$, Gay $M = 1.37$, $SD = .48$, t [19] = 0.96, ns). Significant differences were found between the lesbian and straight (Straight $M = 1.80$, $SD = .10$, t [19] = -4.59, p < .0001) and gay and straight (t [19] = -5.78, p < .0001) couples. Finally, couples rated their overall experience in each store. Confederates in gay and lesbian couples reported no significant difference in their overall experience (Lesbian $M = 1.82$, $SD = .59$, Gay $M = 1.82$, $SD = .71$, t [19] = .00). Straight couples' experiences in stores were more positive than were those of either lesbians (Straight $M = 1.30$, $SD = .44$, t [19] = 3.80, p < .001) or gays (t [19] = 3.68, p < .002).

Table 1 Observer's ratings of sales staff's behavior toward couples

	Lesbian	Gay	Straight
Staring	45%[a]	75%[b]	0%
Laughing	25%[a]	35%[a]	0%
Pointing	15%[a]	30%[a]	0%
Talking	40%[a]	70%[b]	0%
Rude	10%	35%[a]	0%

Ztests were used to determine differences between dyad categories. Within each row, percentages not sharing a common superscript differ at p <.05 or better.

Interviewing the managers

In a follow-up interview with the managers, we obtained information on store policy and managerial expectations for staff. In all cases, managers stated that they were responsible for hiring sales staff. Generally, managers seek new employees who are friendly and attractive, have a "good personality," and are responsible. Employees in all 20 stores were trained by managers, and managers reported that any employee under her/his supervision had a thorough understanding of company/store and manager expectations for courtesy and full-service assistance to customers. According to managers, staff must greet entering customers immediately (ranging from 5 to 60 sec., the mean 25 sec.). Beyond the initial greeting, all sales associates were expected to approach customers and ask if they could be of help; in 17 stores, the expectation is that help should be offered to customers within 2 minutes, and in the remaining three stores, staff are expected to approach customers within 3 minutes.

Managers were asked to describe their clientele. For all stores combined, there was an equal distribution of male and female shoppers, although some stores cater to one gender more than another. Recall that stores were chosen for male and female shoppers. Racial composition across stores was also consistent, although again some stores reported more business by persons of color while others reported a higher percentage of White customers. When asked about the proportion of heterosexual vs. homosexual customers, 16 managers said flatly that no homosexuals shopped in their stores. The highest percentage given by a manager for nonheterosexual customers was 10%

When asked if sales associates discuss customers or treat some customers differently than others, managers freely admitted that store employees are bound to talk about customers. In fact, 70% indicated that they had overheard their employees discussing specific customers negatively. However, in all of these cases managers were positive that in their store, such discussions occurred only in the back of the store or after hours. Inappropriate behavior simply did not exist among their staff while "on the floor." Thus, it appears that while managers assume staff will discuss customers, it is expected that impolite comments will not occur in the presence of customers.

Managers were asked also about the consequences of violating store or company policy in terms of politeness and respect for customers. Managers of all stores reported that they were responsible for confronting personnel about inappropriate behavior. However, of the twenty managers interviewed, only one reported that he would terminate an employee for rude or discourteous behavior. The remaining 19 managers commented more on the unpleasantries associated with disciplinary proceedings and expressed their hesitancy in confronting staff. Moreover, a formal system of discipline was not congruous across stores – even when asked what managers would do if they found an employee blatantly discriminating against a member of a minority group. Taken together, these descriptive data lead us to believe that in the retail stores we visited, it is quite possible that discrimination against homosexuals was implicitly sanctioned. That is, employees who perceive that managers are hesitant to confront employees may not associate inappropriate behavior with negative outcomes.

Finally, we inquired about the remuneration of staff. We wondered if staff who were paid on commission might be less likely to discriminate against homosexuals. For commission-based staff, a sale is a sale, and sales determine one's income. However, we found no difference in time to offer help according to method of payment-commission or hourly ($F = 1.37$, ns). That is, those sales associates paid on commission were just as likely to serve heterosexual couples quicker than lesbian or gay couples as were those who were not paid on, commission.

Discussion

In some respects, the results of this investigation are similar to previous experimental studies (e.g., Gray et al., 1991) showing societal prejudice against and discriminatory behavior toward homosexuals. However, the current study extends our knowledge about the ways in which homosexuals (or those perceived to be homosexuals) are mistreated. Recall that our confederates were heterosexual college students *posing* as members of homosexual or heterosexual couples. By virtue of their perceived status as homosexuals, the same individuals received poorer, less friendly, and more uncharitable service by sales associates. Perceived heterosexual couples were not slighted and were assisted by employees in significantly less time than were perceived gay or lesbian couples. In fact, one third of our homosexual couples were not assisted by staff at all during the six minutes they remained in the store. Alternatively, all heterosexual couples were helped.

The retail industry is fervidly competitive and dismissing any consumer population can result in dire consequences for retailers (Kelley, 1993; Rust & Zahorik, 1993). Retail managers typically recognize that customers who are treated unfairly are unlikely to return to retail stores (Bitner, Booms, & Tetreault, 1990). Nevertheless, employees' reluctance to help gay and lesbian couples and their demeanor toward them strongly suggest that homosexual customers are less valued than heterosexual customers and thus, deserve substandard treatment. In our investigation, only same-sex couples were stared and laughed at, pointed to, talked about, or treated rudely. Moreover, employees who work on a commission basis were equally as likely to resist helping homosexual couples as were hourly employees. We wonder if perhaps avoiding contact with same-sex couples is more important than earning a living.

Information gleaned from managers supported our hypothesis that employee behavior was contrary to formal policy and confuted their job description. Managers consistently stated that sales associates are expected to greet, approach, and help customers promptly. Our heterosexual couples were always helped within the parameters expected by managers of their employees. Gay and lesbian couples were not. These results suggest that sales associates comply with managerial expectations depending on whom they are required to help. Given that most managers expressed discomfort about confronting inappropriate employee behavior, staff seem to be implicitly allowed to select who they will or will not help. Furthermore, managers' estimates of the number of homosexual individuals who might shop in their stores was skewed. In fact, most managers found it particularly odd we would assume that gay and lesbian individuals shop.

Limitations and implications

The research reported here is subject to several limitations. First, although care was taken to randomize all variables associated with confederates and store visits, we were unable to control for or manipulate sales associates' attitudes about homosexuality, sexual orientation, or work schedules. Thus, it is remains possible that other sales associates may have behaved differently.

The geographical location of the study (a college town in the Southeast) may also account for the high levels of observed discriminatory behavior. We recognize that across the country there are pockets of gay-friendly stores, and that in fact, anchor stores in larger cities often recruit staff to be responsive to a gay clientele; other service-industry stores intentionally employ a large percentage of gay staff. However, stores that specifically market to or welcome gay customers are less common, and we suspect our findings more accurately represent those from "typical" stores (i.e., those outside of large, urban areas). Nevertheless, replication in other regions seems warranted.

Another limitation to the current study is that neither observer nor confederates were blind to experimental conditions. However, several strategies were used to minimize systematic biases. For example, the pilot store visits ensured that confederates were familiar with and comfortable in their roles. Thus, it seems unlikely that staff responses were based on confederates' awkwardness or discomfort with their roles. In addition, the use of an observer who was not part of the stimulus couple and the high concordance rates between observer and confederate data strongly suggest that observations of sales staff behaviors were not systematically biased.

The broad purpose of this study was to determine if gays and lesbians are treated differently than heterosexuals in retail stores. Results indicate that homosexuals–at least when they are indentified as members of a gay or lesbian couple–are treated substantially worse than are heterosexual couples. Given the generally accepted opinion that gay males are disliked more than lesbians, we were intrigued that our gay male couples were assisted by staff in significantly less time than were the lesbian couples. Staff demeanor toward male couples (as evidenced by staring at and talking about them and being rude), however, was more stigmatizing. Although our data do not address this discrepancy directly, we suspect that male couples were assisted in less time than female couples as an attempt to expedite their departure from the store. Comments overhead by (or sometimes directed to) our observer about gay couples suggested that male couples were particularly unwelcome in stores. For example, comments such as these were typical responses to gay male couples:

Did you see those two fruits? They were holding hands! I wasn't going to wait on them even if [Manager's name] saw me blow them off.

Those two guys who were just in here were together – like, I mean, a couple. That is just so gross. I didn't even know it until I saw they were holding hands. I just kept not looking at them.

In one store, several male employees gathered in SWAT-team formation and asked our male couple to leave. Although comments were made about lesbian couples, they tended to reflect more surprise than disgust. Further research is needed to identify the exact mechanisms underlying observed but unexpected differences in the treatment of gay and lesbian couples.

Individuals who oppose legislation to protect civil liberties for homosexuals argue that gay men and lesbians are treated no differently than heterosexuals (i.e., normal people) and are asking for privileged status. If the results from this study are any indication of how homosexuals are usually treated, then these arguments against equal protection for homosexuals are faulty. That is, if gays are treated so differently in as mundane an activity as shopping, it is reasonable to speculate that discrimination also occurs in other areas (e.g., housing, employment) as well. Our study illuminates the social acceptability of homonegativism. Retail employees – persons paid to be courteous to and solicitous of others – blatantly disregarded, ignored, or mocked our confederates posing as gays and lesbians. Perhaps even worse, it appears that such behaviors may be implicitly endorsed by those in positions of authority. The hesitancy of store managers in our study to confront discriminatory behaviors both sanctions and reinforces discrimination.

References

Anderson, D. (1992). Woman galvanized by battle in court for injured lover. *Times Picayune* (June 7), p. B:1, 4.

Associated Press. (1989). In bias settlement, gay man can take companion on trip. *The New York Times* (Nov. 3), p. A:17.

Berrill, K. T. (1990). Anti-gay violence and victimization in the United States: An overview. *Journal of Interpersonal Violence*, 5, 274–294.

Berrill, K. T., & Herek, G. M. (1990). Primary and secondary victimization in anti-gay hate crimes: Official response and public policy. *Journal of Interpersonal Violence*, 5, 401–413.

Bitner, M. J., Booms, B. H., & Tetreault, M. S. (1990). The service encounter: Diagnosing favorable and unfavorable incidents. *Journal of Marketing*, 54, 71–84.

Carman, D. (1992). Bad taste of discrimination in past never more timely. *Denver Post* (Oct. 3), p. 1:1.

Dunbar, J., Brown, M., & Amoroso, D. M. (1973). Some correlates of attitudes toward homosexuality. *Journal of Social Psychology*, 89, 271–279.

Ficarrotto, T.J. (1990). Racism, sexism, and erotophobia: Attitudes of heterosexuals toward homosexuals. *Journal of Homosexuality*, 19, 111–116.

Gentry, C. S. (1987). Social distance regarding male and female homosexuals. *Journal of Social Psychology*, 127, 199–208.

Gray, C., Russell, P., & Blockley, S. (1991). The effects upon helping behaviour of wearing pro-gay identification. *British Journal of Social Psychology*, 30, 171–178.

Herek, G. M. (1984). Beyond "homophobia": A social psychological perspective on attitudes toward lesbians and gay men. *Journal of Homosexuality*, 10, 1–21.

Herek, G. M. & Glunt, E. K. (1993). Interpersonal contact and heterosexuals' attitudes toward gay men: Results from a national study. *Journal of Sex Research*, 30, 239–244.

Higuera, J. (1989). Human rights law doesn't cover gays, Arlington decides. *Washington Times* (January 24), p. 3:5.

Kelley, S. W. (1993). Discretion and the service employee. *Journal of Retailing*, 69, 104–126.

Kite, M. E., & Deaux, K. (1986). Attitudes toward homosexuality: Assessment and behavioral consequences. *Basic and Applied Social Psychology*, 7, 137–162.

Larsen, K. S., Reed, M., & Hoffman, S. (1980). Attitudes of heterosexuals toward homosexuality: A Likert-type scale and construct validity. *Journal of Sex Research*, 16, 245–257.

Lehne, G. K. (1992). Homophobia among men: Supporting and defining the male role. In Kimmel, M. S. & Messner, M. A. (Eds.), *Men's lives* (2nd ed., 381–394). New York: Macmillan.

Marchetti, D. (1989). Mt. Clemens housing bias angers gays. *Detroit News* (July 8), p. 1:5.

Mehler, N.H. (1989). Two males charge bias in housing. *Chicago Tribune* (August 16), p. 2:3.

Millham, J., & Weinberger, L. E. (1977). Sexual preference, sex role appropriateness, and restriction of social class. *Journal of Homosexuality*, 2, 343–357.

Mosher, D. L., & O'Grady, K. E. (1979). Homosexual threat, negative attitudes toward masturbation, sex guilt, and males' sexual and affective reactions to explicit sexual films. *Journal of Consulting and Clinical Psychology*, 47, 860–873.

Newman, B. (1989). The relative importance of gender role attitudes to male and female attitudes toward lesbians. *Sex Roles*, 21, 451–465.

Page, S., & Yee, M. (1985). Conception of male and female homosexual stereotypes among university undergraduates. *Journal of Homosexuality*, 12, 109–118.

Purdy, P. (1990). Is "lavender lining" practiced in Denver's insurance industry? *Denver Post* (April 1), p. 3:1.

Remafedi, G. (1987). Homosexual youth. *Journal of the American Medical Association*, 258, 222–225.

Richardson, L. (1993). Proud, official partners. *The New York Times* (August 1), pp. 37, 38.

Rust, R. T. & Zahorik, A. J. (1993). Customer satisfaction, customer retention, and market share. *Journal of Retailing*, 69, 193–215.

Sigelman, C. K., Howell, J. L., Cornell, D. P., Cutright, J. D., & Dewey, J. C. (1991). Courtesy stigma: The social implications of associating with a gay person. *Journal of Social Psychology*, 131, 45.56.

Shaffer, D. R., & Wallace, A. (1990). Belief congruence and evaluator homophobia as determinants of the attractiveness of competent homosexual and heterosexual males. *Journal of Psychology and Human Sexuality*, 3, 67–87.

Stewart, J. B. (1994). Annals of law: Gentleman's agreement. *The New Yorker* (June 13), 74–82.

Thompson, K. & Andrzejewski, J. (1988). *Why can't Sharon Kowalski come home?* San Francisco: Spinsters/Aunt Lute.

Walters, A. S. (1994). Using visual media to reduce homophobia: A classroom demonstration. *Journal of Sex Education and Therapy*, 20, 92–100.

Walters, A. S., & Phillips, C. P. (1994). Hurdles: An activity for homosexuality education. *Journal of Sex Education and Therapy*, 20, 198–203.

Weinberger, L. E., & Millham, J. (1979). Attitudinal homophobia and support of traditional sex roles. *Journal of Homosexuality*, 4, 237–253.

Whitley, B. E., Jr. (1990). The relationship of heterosexuals' attributions for the causes of homosexuality to attitudes toward lesbians and gay men. *Personality and Social Psychology Bulletin*, 16, 369–377.

———. (1987). The relationship of sex-role orientation to heterosexuals' attitudes towards homosexuals. *Sex Roles*, 17, 103–113.

Winer, B. J. (1971). *Statistical Principles in Experimental Design* (2nd ed.). New York: McGraw-Hill.

Queer urban economics

ONE OF THE OUTCOMES following the Stonewall Riots was the articulation of a Queer-American culture. With this new culture not only were social spheres of queers enhanced but also the geography of gay and lesbian America was deeply affected. With more openness and tolerance of queers it became more acceptable to live in areas that were previously stigmatized as "gay," such as New York City's West Village and San Francisco's Castro District. Not only has this change in community structure changed gay and lesbian culture, but it has also changed gay and lesbian economics by allowing for a type of grouping by sexual orientation that is in some ways akin to ethnic or racial "ghettos" but is in other ways quite different. When geographical isolation occurs, several economic phenomena also begin to exist. Just as the ethnically or racially based ghetto has been argued to have both positive and negative economic and social aspects for the group, so may sexual orientation ghettos have such effects.

Positive effects that would be predicted from economic theory would be the ability to develop social organizations and retailing, with goods and services tailored both to the interests of residents of the subcommunity and to those other members of the group who might come from the wider geographic area in order to purchase these items and participate in the social organizations' activities. Thus economies of aggregation can be achieved and queer-oriented businesses may exist that would otherwise not be able to draw upon a sufficient market scale. These areas can also serve as efficient labor market nexuses for those interested in working in queer-oriented and/or queer-owned businesses. In addition, people may realize psychic benefits from living in close community with those who share a common factor such as sexual orientation. Negative economic and social effects include potential isolation from the broader geographic community, and in particular the contacts – both labor market and social – that one might forge if one lived in a mixed neighborhood.

The culmination in the extreme of all these actions would be a separate economy where queers are both producers and consumers and do not interact with the straight economy. However, while some radical thinkers have called for such a separatist society, it appears unlikely that such a situation would occur in any location, given the modern system of domestic and international trade. Thus current gay communities serve as partial enclaves rather than areas that exist separately from the mainstream of society.

It is informative to look at actual gay communities in order to understand their formation and day-to-day operation. Geographer Lawrence Knopp's article, "Gentrification and gay neighborhood formation in New Orleans: a case study" (1997), looks at the transformation of a relatively poor neighborhood of New Orleans (just north of the French Quarter) into a thriving gay economic and cultural center. He points out that gay men in power manipulated the city government in order to reroute funding to this area of the city and give major tax breaks to businesses in the area under the auspices of helping the disadvantaged area. In reality, demand for housing in the area, and thus prices, became too high for many of the poor families that lived in the neighborhood, which left young gay professionals who could afford the higher prices to move into the area.

Geographically defined subcultures, including those based on sexual orientation, also have both positive and problematic aspects relating to personal identity. Gill Valentine and Tracey Skelton's article, "Finding oneself, losing oneself: the lesbian and gay "scene" as a paradoxical space" (2003), examines the role of queer urban spaces in affecting young lesbians and gays during their transitions to adulthood. Geographers Valentine and Skelton argue that cities have historically served a function as spaces of social and sexual liberation relative to smaller, rural communities, particularly for the young. The additional aspect of finding a subcommunity in a city with which one might align oneself has often existed for youth culture, with the additional twist that the culture may now revolve much more strongly around one's sexual orientation. In contrast to the oft-used assumption in mainstream economics that "tastes and preferences are given," or fixed, one can believe after reading this chapter that preferences for consumption patterns and social interactions are in large part shaped by one's actions, particularly when young.

A number of other authors have written case studies of gay communities in the US (Black *et al.* 2002) and abroad (Jackson 2003; Kitchin and Lysaght 2003; Aldrich 2004; Collins 2004; Sibalis 2004). Several social scientists have been particularly interested in the relationship between urban renewal and queer community, noting that urban renewal and gentrification is often coexistent with greater numbers of same-sex couples and queer individuals living in the transitioning neighborhoods (Lauria and Knopp 1985; Moss 1997), and a number have focused in particular on the problematic aspects of this association (Bell and Binnie 2004; Collins 2004).

Queer urban economics, more generally than the issue of queer urban enclaves, is about the existence and causes patterning in spatial dimension by sexual orientation. Thus, other researchers have considered other types of patterning in space relating to sexual orientation, including the spatial diffusion of local antidiscrimination policies regarding sexual orientation (Klawitter and Flatt 1998; Klawitter and Hammer 1999), homeownership patterns by couple type (Leppel 2007), and the relationship between sexual orientation, urban location, and demand for the arts (Lewis and Seaman 2004).

DISCUSSION QUESTIONS

1   Do you think "gay ghettos" promote or discourage efforts for better gay and lesbian rights?
2   The gay ghetto is no longer limited to cities. Towns such as Provincetown and Northampton, Massachusetts, have large gay and lesbian populations. How does a less urban setting change the dynamics of a gay ghetto?
3   Why do you think that gay ghettos often eventually become high-priced sections of cities?
4   What types of consumer decisions might be influenced by whether or not one lives in a gay enclave?
5   Should public policy encourage, discourage, or remain neutral toward the dynamics of the creation of gay enclaves and gay-led gentrification?

REFERENCES

Aldrich, R. (2004) "Homosexuality and the city: an historical overview," *Urban Studies*, 41: 1719–37.

Bell, D. and Binnie, J. (2004) "Authenticating queer space: citizenship, urbanism and governance," *Urban Studies*, 41: 1807–20.

Black, D., Gates, G., Sanders, S., and Taylor, L. (2002) "Why do gay men live in San Francisco?," *Journal of Urban Economics*, 51: 54–76.

Collins, A. (2004) "Sexual dissidence, enterprise and assimilation: bedfellows in urban regeneration," *Urban Studies*, 41: 1789–806.

Jackson, P. A. (2003) "Gay capitals in global gay history: cities, local markets, and the origins of Bangkok's same-sex cultures," in R. Bishop, J. Phillips, and W. Yeo (eds) *Postcolonial Urbanism: Southeast Asian cities and global processes*, New York and London: Routledge.

Kitchin, R. and Lysaght, K. (2003) "Heterosexism and the geographies of everyday life in Belfast, Northern Ireland," *Environment and Planning*, 35: 489–510.

Klawitter, M. and Flatt, V. (1998) "The effects of state and local antidiscrimination policies on earnings for gays and lesbians," *Journal of Policy Analysis and Management*, 17: 658–86.

Klawitter, M. and Hammer, B. (1999) "Spatial and temporal diffusion of local antidiscrimination policies for sexual orientation," in E. D. B. Riggle and B. L. Tadlock (eds) *Gays and Lesbians in the Democratic Process: public policy, public opinion, and political representation*, New York: Columbia University Press.

Lauria, M. and Knopp, L. (1985) "Toward an analysis of the role of gay communities in the urban renaissance," *Urban Geography*, 6: 152–69.

Leppel, K. (2007) "Home-ownership among opposite- and same-sex couples in the US," *Feminist Economics*, 13: 1–30.

Lewis, G. B. and Seaman, B. A. (2004) "Sexual orientation and demand for the arts," *Social Science Quarterly*, 85: 523–38.

Moss, M. L. (1997) "Reinventing the central city as a place to live and work," *Housing Policy Debate*, 8: 471–90.

Sibalis, M. (2004) "Urban space and homosexuality: the example of the Marais, Paris 'gay ghetto'," *Urban Studies*, 41: 1739–58.

Chapter 19

Lawrence Knopp

GENTRIFICATION AND GAY NEIGHBORHOOD FORMATION IN NEW ORLEANS: A CASE STUDY

From *Political Geography*, 1990, 9, pp. 337–352

Introduction

IN THE 1970s AND 1980s, a political and social movement based on the development of gay and lesbian identities emerged in various countries around the world. In the United States, this movement has often been centered in neighbourhoods. Openly gay and lesbian communities have achieved more of their social, cultural, and political goals in the inner cities of large urban areas than elsewhere.[1] This neighborhood-based gay and lesbian movement has in turn had an impact on land markets in these areas (usually through the vehicle of gentrification). . . . This paper analyzes the impact of a particular gay community's development on the land market in which it was situated during the 1970s. It then interprets this experience in terms of its implications for urban land market theory and certain broader debates in social theory concerning the connections between class, gender, and sexual relations.

Urban land markets and neighborhood-based gay community development

. . . Castells's (1983:138–170) study of San Francisco's gay community in the 1970s is one of the few published empirical attempts to consider the connections between a gay community's social and political activity and an urban land market.[2] He does this primarily in the context of a discussion of gay involvement in gentrification.[3] Castells concludes that, in San Francisco, gay gentrifiers were "moral refugees" who "paid for their identity" by making enormous financial and personal sacrifices in order to survive. In the process, he argues, they contributed to an urban renovation that "reached proportions far above those of any other American city" and "helped to make the city beautiful and alive" (Castells 1983:161). Interestingly, there is little in the way of economic or class analysis in the study. He does not discuss displacement of the previous residents of the neighborhood at all, emphasizing instead how the most heavily gay community developed in a neighborhood that "was being abandoned by its Irish working class" (Castro Valley). Similarly, Castells asserts a connection between young, single gay males and "a relatively prosperous service economy" (1983:160), but fails to develop this. He does identify three categories of gay gentrifiers, but he appears to suggest strongly that gentrification as a survival strategy and form of cultural expression was more important for each of these than their class interests. Clearly, the material and class interests involved in gay community development (including, perhaps, links to the restructuring of occupational mixes in urban areas) need to be more carefully examined.

Lauria and Knopp (1985) provide the beginnings of a theoretical analysis along these lines, again in the context of a discussion of gentrification. They argue that during the 1970s, economic and social opportunities for gays (especially men) expanded in inner cities. Inner cities were affordable, they were the locus of gay cultural and institutional life, and they were also experiencing growth in white-collar and service employment (where, it is alleged, disproportionate numbers of gay men tend to be employed). Lauria and Knopp further argue that gay identity in the United States is skewed in terms of class, race, and gender, i.e., that while homosexual desire and behaviors are multiclass and multiracial phenomena involving both women and men, the self-identification of individuals as gay is more of a white, male, and middle-class phenomenon. This is because it is easier, economically and otherwise, for middle-class white males to identify and live as openly gay people than it is for women, non-whites, and non-middle-class people. They cite demographic studies of gay populations reported by sociologists to support this contention. The significance of this, they argue, is that gay people constitute a potentially large market for renovated housing in terms of discretionary income. They are not the only such market (single heterosexuals and childless couples are others), but they are perhaps the largest, the fastest-growing, and the one with the largest discretionary income (Foltz, et al. 1984).

Lauria and Knopp do not, however, provide a way of interpreting gay involvement on the production side of urban land market processes. And Castells (1983:158) merely sees such involvement in San Francisco as a means of "surviv[ing] the tough . . . housing market." Thus, a more general understanding of this aspect of gay involvement in land markets is still needed.

This paper contributes to the further elaboration of theory involving urban land markets and neighborhood-based gay community development through the presentation and interpretation of a narrative. . . . The purpose here is to explore the theoretical significance of the particular series of events and configuration of interests that were found in the larger study, not to summarize the entire project. Thus, economic and demographic data describing the neighborhood's transformation quantitatively are omitted, and interested readers are referred to the larger study (Knopp 1989).

The neighborhood in question is in New Orleans, Louisiana, and experienced a substantial degree of gentrification between the late 1960s and early 1980s. Personal interviews with key actors in the inner-city real estate market and the gay community during this period were a primary source of data from which the sequence of events and mapping of interests and alliances was produced. . . . Secondary sources (e.g., local histories and media accounts) were similarly collected. . . . The resulting narrative is presented below, followed by a discussion of its theoretical significance.

The transformation of Marigny

New Orleans' Marigny neighborhood is a small but densely populated area located adjacent to New Orleans' famous French Quarter (also known as the Vieux Carré – see Figure 1). The upriver (western) half, immediately adjacent to the French Quarter, is known as the "traingle" and is the more heavily gentrified part of the neighborhood. The downriver half, known as the "rectangle," is more of a patchwork of renovated and unrenovated houses and blocks (see Figure 2).

Three sets of events, associated with distinct sets of actors, can be identified that were crucial in this neighborhood's transformation from a working class area experiencing disinvestment (in the 1950s and 1960s) to a more solidly middle-class and substantially renovated one (in the 1970s). These events were:

1   the movement of a small number of predominantly gay middle-class professionals to Marigny during the 1960s;

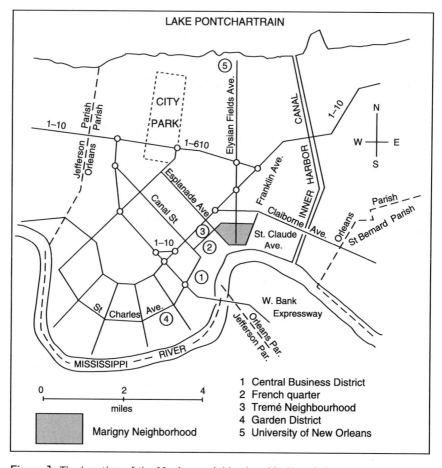

Figure 1 The location of the Marigny neighborhood in New Orleans

2   a movement for historic preservation in the neighborhood, organized primarily by gay men; and

3   the arrival of speculators and developers, who again were mostly gay, in the mid-to-late 1970s.

The early in-movers

The first signs of gentrification in Marigny came in the 1960s, when the neighborhood overall was still experiencing disinvestment, increasing amounts of slum landlordism, so-called "white flight," and in-migration by poor blacks. A small-scale counter-trend of middle-class in-migration came with the founding in 1958 of the Louisiana State University at New Orleans

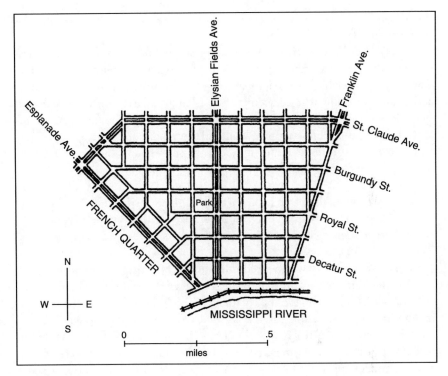

Figure 2 The Marigny neighborhood

(later the University of New Orleans, UNO) at a site on the New Orleans lakefront.

The early in-movers to Marigny consisted most notably of several faculty and other professionals employed by the university. Many of these were gay men from outside the New Orleans area who had chosen, upon arrival in New Orleans, to rent in the French Quarter rather than in the new, homogeneous, family-oriented neighborhoods near UNO. Later, when they had established themselves financially and sought to own property, they chose to locate in Marigny:

> The pioneers . . . were UNO people who also happened to be homosexuals. . . . [T]hey wanted the milieu [of the French Quarter] but they couldn't afford the property so they were attracted to places like the Marigny. (Personal interview.)[4]

The extreme family orientation of suburban neighborhoods was a disincentive rather than a draw for these people, and the adversity associated with living in Marigny appeared acceptable by comparison. House prices were quite low, and the French Quarter (the center of gay social and cultural life in New Orleans) was easily accessible by foot. Furthermore, the university was easily accessible by both car (ten minutes) and bus (twenty minutes).[5]

Racial tensions were also instrumental in encouraging middle-class whites to settle in Marigny. A predominantly black neighborhood, Tremé, was very comparable to Marigny architecturally and in terms of its afford-ability and location (it is adjacent to the French Quarter on the northwest side.) It was also adjacent to one of New Orleans' ten large (and predomin-antly black) public housing projects, and very near another. Many whites feared the proximity to large numbers of poor blacks, and many blacks feared the effects of gentrification:

> They fought, they fought, they fought, they fought! The blacks.
> . . . [in Tremé] resisted change because of the race situation.
> (Personal interview.)

Marigny, by contrast, was a predominantly white neighborhood and was much more removed from the housing projects. A vivid biracial and multi-cultural social history made it easy for liberal whites to settle there without feeling that they were applying racist standards in their decisions.

This predominantly gay middle-class settlement in the face of adversity had two significant outcomes. For most of the nineteenth and early twen-tieth centuries the neighborhood was a stable working class area. Except for the Creole[6] aristocrats who founded it in the early 1800s (including a substantial number of so-called "free persons of color" who lost their social standing after Reconstruction), it was never home to anyone but lower-middle-class laborers and shopkeepers – until the 1960s, when the in-migration of a few middle-class gay university employees established a stable nonworking-class presence in Marigny for the first time ever. The second significant outcome was the association of this middle-class pres-ence with the French Quarter, New Orleans' gay community, and a college-educated population. All three of these associations would figure prominently in the large-scale transformation of Marigny that took place in the 1970s.

The in-migration of a few gay professionals in the 1960s can be inter-preted as the laying of a foundation for the much larger-scale middle-class in-migration and neighborhood-based community development that fol-lowed. This laying of a foundation was a completely unorganized process, planned and directed by no one. Rather, it was a consequence of social and economic forces that defined both Marigny, in spite of its locational advan-tages, as an undesirable neighborhood and gay people, regardless of class standing, as undesirable people. In so doing, these forces produced a phys-ical space that could be appropriated and commodified by enterprising members of the gay middle-class.[7]

Historic preservation and neighborhood-based political action

The second significant set of events in Marigny's transformation was the political organization of the neighborhood, which began in the early 1970s. The issue around which residents mobilized was not gay community development or politics but rather, historic preservation – in spite of the fact that most of the leaders of the movement were openly gay, and specifically encouraged gay in-migration to Marigny.

The most prominent leader of the historic preservation movement was an architect who moved to Marigny in 1971. His strategy consisted of making an inventory of properties that "needed saving," determining who their owners were, and then making "marriages of buildings and people" (personal interview). It also included taking advantage of his connections to the gay community:

> He spoke to his gay friends and proposed to them that they move to Marigny. . . . Gay men were a part of his strategy. (Personal interview.)

> He viewed the gay connection as part of what was happening . . . He saw that gay men would be a very good way to make the project work. (Personal interview.)

And, indeed, large numbers of middle-class gay men did begin moving to the neighborhood:

> We were the only heteros on the block and we're still pretty close to that. There's a couple others on the block, but it's basically mostly gay men . . . [A]ll of them are professional people, at least white collar jobs. (Personal interview.)

> After . . . enough people had moved to Marigny who were gay and who were, what, middle-class gay, if you like . . . then I felt it was safe to bring a wife and have a child here. (Personal interview.)

> I really don't think it would have happened without the gay connection. (Personal interview.)

Concomitantly, the architect and his friends developed a formal organizational presence in the neighborhood. They founded the Faubourg Marigny Improvement Association (FMIA), a largely (but not exclusively) homeowners' group, during the architect's first year in Marigny. The organization of this group depended to a considerable extent on the forging of close personal ties among neighborhood residents. The architect became known for throwing large and very successful parties that were frequently indistinguishable from Improvement Association meetings. Attendance was predominantly (but never exclusively) gay and male:

> The architect and his gay friends started the whole thing . . .
> And the fact that at his parties three-fourths of the men . . .
> were gay, was known. (Personal interview.)

> Wives will stay home, because they just don't find enough women there to enjoy it. That has not changed. (Personal interview.)

FMIA cultivated contacts in various city departments (most notably the City Planning Commission), successfully lobbied the Mayor and City Council for land use regulations (a comprehensive rezoning plan for the neighborhood), and held candidate forums at election time. The organization was officially nonpartisan and concerned itself with historic preservation and closely related quality-of-life issues only. This enabled it to enlist the support of such conservative institutions as the local Catholic Archdiocese on certain issues (personal interviews).

This neighborhood-based political action, predicated on historic preservation, had three significant outcomes. First, it resulted in Marigny developing a new and strong sense of community and identity:

> There were constantly meetings or potluck suppers or gatherings at the park, and we were constantly seeing each other and enjoying each other. (Personal interview.)

This kind of community cohesion had been disintergrating during the previous two decades, as many of the indigenous working-class residents moved out to cheap housing in new suburbs.

Second, Marigny's new organization and identity increased its clout in the New Orleans government and business communities. Financing and insurance became easier to get and local politicians made historic preservation a priority. The decision of mostly gay neighborhood activists to emphasize historic preservation, rather than gay issues, was crucial in this outcome.[8]

In spite of the strategy of downplaying specifically gay issues, however, a third significant outcome was the social and political development of the local gay community. Since the leaders of the neighborhood's preservation-based boosterism were mostly gay men, and their strategy for the neighborhood included recruiting others like themselves to settle in Marigny, a huge proportion of middle-class in-movers during this period were gay:

> I'd say by '74 it became kind of known as the gay ghetto or
> something like that. (Personal interview.)

Gay institutions also proliferated in Marigny. A number of gay bars
opened in the neighborhood, as did gay-owned and/or gay-oriented bookstores, restaurants, and some organizational offices. An annual Gayfest,
held in June to commemorate the 1969 Stonewall rebellion in New York
City,[9] found a home in Washington Square Park in the heart of Marigny.

Eventually, the gay presence in Marigny expressed itself politically. The
area's city council member introduced a citywide measure to ban discrimination in housing and employment on the basis of sexual orientation in
the early 1980s (DuBos 1984). After considerable public outcry (including
an intense campaign against the ordinance by Catholic Archbishop Phillip
Hannon), this effort failed narrowly before the City Council (in 1984).[10]

Marigny's development as an organized middle-class community in the
1970s, with a preservation-based and substantial (but deemphasized) gay
identity, was carefully planned. Specific individuals with specific agendas
(and college educations) aggressively set out to build alliances with various
interests in the city. They accomplished this by demonstrating the political
and economic value of the Marigny neighborhood and community to politicians and business interests. This is in contrast to the largely unplanned
and unorganized in-migration of a few middle-class gays in the 1960s.

The mostly gay actors in this campaign saw the involvement of other
gay people as essential. They did not, however, see it as sufficient to ensure
success. Rather, gay inmigration was packaged and presented as simply
responsible middle-class in-migration. In this way fragile alliances with
basically conservative interests, such as the Catholic Church, could be
maintained:

> How do we want our city to see us? . . . [As] responsible busi-
> nesspeople who have money, or fags coming out of the streets
> with makeup? (Personal interview.)

As a consequence, while most major historic preservation battles were
won, the local gay community won very little. It was not until the early
1980s that a specifically gay-related issue (the nondiscrimination ordinance)
reached the City Council, and the antigay forces ultimately prevailed in
that battle. Neighborhood activists in Marigny, while supportive of the
proposed ordinance, risked very little political capital to promote it.
Rather, most of the lobbying was done by city and statewide gay political
organizations (principally, the Louisiana Gay Political Action Committee
[LAGPAC]) and the area's city council member.

The development of the local gay community that did occur in Marigny
must therefore be seen as more of a consequence (rather than a central

goal) of the strategies devised by Marigny's gay leaders to promote historic preservation. These strategies happened to involve exploiting personal ties in the gay community.

The arrival of speculators and developers

Gay community development was a much more intentional consequence of the strategies of local speculators and developers who entered the scene in the mid-1970s. This was by far the most complex, if not most important, of the three significant sets of events in Marigny's transformation. Again, most of the key actors were gay men, of whom two groups in particular were important.

One group, centered on the firm of a Marigny-based real estate broker, focused on developing a market for all kinds of housing in the neighborhood among gays. The socioeconomic status and class interests of these consumers of housing were considered relatively unimportant (indeed, an aggressive effort was made to make housing available to young, low-waged, gay service-sector workers from the French Quarter who would otherwise not have had access to the housing market), and so-called creative financing (including illegal bribes to appraisers employed by financial institutions) was involved (see Knopp 1990 for a detailed discussion). A second group, consisting of a more capital-intensive development corporation, focused its efforts on using more conventional methods to develop a specifically upper-middle-class gay market for already renovated housing in the Marigny rectangle. Neither group focused *exclusively* on gays, but in both cases gay people (especially gay men) were considered the core of the market being developed.

The real estate broker's strategy was to encourage as much gay in-migration, home-ownership, and renovation in Marigny as was humanly possible, regardless of the in-migrants' class status:

> All the waiters and all the gay people and all the people that were his friends in the Quarter that always wanted houses. . . . [J]ust nobody was ever going to look for that type of person. It was a natural! . . . [He] was the first person to go after that market. (Personal interview.)

This entailed developing the social and economic potential of the gay community. His real-estate firm became a significant community institution in its own right, and through a complex series of maneuvers (many of which were illegal), it helped members of the local gay community to secure financing for virtually the entire purchase price of homes (Berry 1979; Murphy 1979; Gsell 1979a through 1979l). This, and the fact that values in the area were severely depressed, made housing accessible to many first-time home-buyers who would otherwise not have been able to muster large enough down payments. Thus, the firm engaged in a conscious and deliberate project of gay community development – albeit for the purposes of enhancing property values and, ultimately, the material well-being of its members (who happened also to be predominantly gay).

This strategy pitted the firm against a number of entrenched interests in New Orleans. The providers of home mortgages (known locally as homesteads) were duped into assuming higher levels of risk than they would otherwise have accepted. They also had their control over the extremely political and value-laden process of property appraisal challenged. Traditional brokerages saw profits created and appropriated by an unorthodox competitor. Eventually, legal proceedings brought an end to the firm and its unusual practices. The traditional distribution of power and profits among the homesteads, traditional brokerages, and developers was restored, but not before the profit-producing potential of the Marigny neighborhood was revitalized.

Shortly after this real-estate firm came on the scene, a more conventional development corporation began developing luxury housing in the Marigny rectangle. Like the first group, this one concentrated its efforts on developing a gay male market for housing. The example of San Francisco's Castro district very much influenced its gay male owner. He owned a house in San Francisco at the time and spent ten days every month there:

> Castro was so wonderful and so alive, really great. It was so dynamic that if you could export that technology some place else, what a wonderful thing it would be. And Marigny was . . . where we were going to bring it. (Personal interview.)

His development strategy was much more conservative than that of the first group, however. First, he minimized risk by investing initially with cash:

> What we would do is we would buy for cash, driving the price down to the seller, renovate using my own crews, using my own cash, get the rental stream up, and then finance the buildings so that we'd only take out of the financing what the rental stream could sustain. So there was never any negative cash flow. (Personal interview.)

Second, he sold the properties once they had "reached their economic potential in terms of rental":

> I had already taken out of the property what I needed. I had high ordinary income as a result of oil revenues, I needed tax

deductions 'cause the taxes, the way the tax code is written encouraged gentrification, and the rental stream paid for the units. So essentially it was a free ride for me. And the neighborhood got almost four million dollars of investment in a very short period of time. (Personal interview.)

Finally, he maintained close ties to New Orleans' conservative business community (from whence he came) and the local and state Republican party establishments.

Also unlike the first group, this more traditional corporation tried to develop a distinctly affluent gay community in the Marigny rectangle:

The idea was to create an enclave of . . . upwardly mobile gay people. . . . [W]e could create an environment with pools and jacuzzis and . . . free love . . . essentially a gay enclave of fairly wealthy people. (Personal interview.)

This group's efforts were less financially successful, however, than those of the less traditional firm. A portion of the Marigny rectangle did experience heavy investment in housing as a result of the corporation's actions. This eventually resulted in significant increases in owner-occupancy rates in the area. Many gay people (particularly affluent couples) did move into properties developed by the corporation, which made a considerable amount of money. But the Marigny rectangle never underwent the wholesale transformation that the group had envisaged, and fortunes like those amassed by some in the less traditional firm were never made. The local economy declined precipitously with the collapse of the international oil market in 1983–84, and the corporation took a substantial loss on its last condominium development. It was eventually dissolved in 1986, and the corporation's owner went to work as the director of a local nonprofit spinoff of James Rouse's Enterprise Foundation. On the other hand, no one associated with this firm was ever indicted by a grand jury or forced out of the real-estate business.

Conclusion: class, sexuality and urban land markets

The gentrification that took place during the 1970s and early 1980s in Marigny featured a complex configuration of interests and events. It took place within the context of a very unevenly developing and conservatively guided metropolitan economy. Many of the key actors in the neighborhood's development were gay, but these were people who represented a wide variety of social positions and class interests (e.g., young waiters from the French Quarter and affluent developers). Each set of actors allied with different factions of both capital and labor and pursued a different strategy for the neighborhood's development.

The result was an unusual form of gentrification. Renovation and middle-class in-migration were selective, block-by-block, and even house-by-house phenomena (although there was enough change to alter the aggregate character of the neighborhood substantially).[11] Displacement effects appear to have been modest, and indigenous residents who remained in the neighborhood apparently maintained good relations with newcomers. Marigny homeowners developed substantial political clout, and the local gay community saw its resource base expanded.

At the same time, the local gay community became increasingly stratified along lines of class interest. Gay homeowners mobilized around homeowners' issues, not gay issues, and certain gay developers embarked on a conscious strategy of promoting specifically upper-middle-class gay in-migration to the Marigny rectangle. Other gays, by contrast, focused on promoting middle- and lower-middle-class gay in-migration (albeit as part of historic preservation and market-development strategies, respectively).

The most surprising of these results was the fact that the prime movers behind neighborhood-based gay community development were speculators and developers, while neighborhood-based political activists emphasized historic preservation and were resistant to specifically gay politics. Exactly the opposite result was expected. This expectation was due to the emphasis on conflicts between producers and consumers of housing in the urban land market literature, and on neighborhood-based gay politics in the small literature on gay communities (Castells 1983).

This result implies a revised interpretation of the role of gay community development and gay politics in gentrification. Rather than constituting an oppressed community's collective strategy for coping with discrimination or a "tough" housing market, as Castells's study suggests, this type of gay involvement in a land market can be seen primarily as an alternative strategy for accumulation. It is a strategy that happens to include the development of gay community resources. Gay people, like other minorities in major United States metropolitan areas in the 1970s, experienced discrimination and found decent, affordable housing quite difficult to obtain in central cities. Unlike other minorities, however, openly gay people often possess adequate economic resources to enter a middle-class housing market. Unlike more visible minorities, they are able to maintain a measure of control over the disclosure of their minority status, i.e., their sexual orientation. The issue is therefore not so much one of overcoming discrimination as it is one of overcoming institutional obstacles to investment in certain parts of the city. Gay speculators and developers in Marigny saw an opportunity first for themselves and only secondarily for the gay community as a whole, by making housing in these areas available to gay people. As one gay speculator put it,

> In this country, in America, there's plenty of pie for everybody to make it. . . . The fact that we [gay people] have money, the fact that we spend it – that's a[n] economic contribution. (Personal interview.)

In terms of theories of how urban land markets work, this suggests that the class interests of certain actors (e.g., speculators) can be facilitated and legitimated by forming cross-cultural and cross-class *alliances* with certain groups of consumers (in this case, a diverse community of gay men, including relatively poorly paid service-sector workers from New Orleans' French Quarter). The stigmatization and segregation of these groups can thus be turned to the short-term advantage of both producers and consumers of housing. This is accomplished as part and parcel of the process of creating demand for housing. Certain social benefits can and do accrue from such stategies, which is why they can work. But the ultimate purpose is always to make money for the providers of housing. As one interviewee explained (with reference to a slightly different social investment).

> It was in my interest here to promote Marigny. It was going to line my pockets and make the investment pan out for me. . . . [T]he symphony was in trouble. There was no better way for me to help advertise my product . . . than to hire the symphony . . . to play a free concert in [a neighborhood park] and hold a huge party for the neighborhood. . . . [T]hat wasn't altruistic. It was purely economic. (Personal interview.)

Conversely, the lack of a commitment to the gay community evidenced by Marigny's neighborhood activists suggests that even in cases where the catalyst for residential location decisions may be to a considerable extent nonclass based (in this case, the particular attraction of Marigny for gay people), the power of class interests to prevail over other interests among consumers of housing is very strong. This is well illustrated by one lower-middle-class lesbian homeowner's attitude toward the Faubourg Marigny Improvement Association:

> A friend of mine that lives around the corner got a citation for too many garbage cans! I mean, I don't know where they want to go. You know, do they want an Uptown [an affluent, consumption-oriented neighborhood] here? I think that's real possible. And that's not what it is. (Personal interview.)

Those who behaved most as expected were the property developers associated with the more conservative development corporation. Their goal was quite explicitly to gentrify a portion of the Marigny rectangle

by emulating San Francisco's experience of neighborhood-based gay community development. Yet of all the actors involved in Marigny's transformation in the 1970s, it was this group who had the least ambitious plan
(in terms of both geographical extent and short-term profit or benefit
maximization) and who were, arguably, the least successful. The rectangle
remained less gentrified and less gay than the triangle, and the small-scale
San Francisco – style upper-middle-class gay enclave that was envisioned
never materialized.

   This is important because it indicates the limits to gay involvement in
the land market in Marigny. The gay community clearly had the capacity to
gentrify, but this turned out to be a relatively modest project. This may or
may not have been due to a lack of money in the local gay community.
Clearly it was *not* due to a lack of sufficient numbers, as the FMIA's and the
"insurgent" real-estate firm's sizable gay constiuencies demonstrate. More
likely this simply reflects the relative power of the various interests
involved in Marigny (and more exogenous forces influencing the level of
demand for inner-city housing overall).

   So while gay involvement in the urban land market in Marigny was
very much structured by class interests, this was an extremely complex
process, entailing cross-cultural and even cross-class alliances (e.g.,
between the "insurgent" real-estate firm and young, low-waged, gay service-sector workers from the French Quarter). Overall, the negative
effects of gentrification were fewer than in many other cases (cf., N. Smith
1979). But this was not due to any conscious forms of resistance on the
part of consumers of housing. Nor was it due to the benevolence of producers of housing or even the actions of people organizing around gay issues.[12]
Rather, it was a consequence of the historically and geographically specific
workings of the local land and labor markets.

A note on connections between gay oppression and the oppression
of women

The fact that gay involvement in gentrification is a predominantly male
practice raises important questions about the connections between gender
relations, gender roles, and the place of each within a society driven by
accumulation. Lesbians' ability to cope with oppression through entry into
the housing market (and hence the middle class) is generally more limited
than that of gay men. Residential concentrations of lesbians in urban spaces
therefore tend to resemble the patterns and processes of segregation that
characterize other marginalized groups more than they do those that
characterize gay men (Ettore 1978:514–518; Winchester and White
1988:48–49). Indeed, there is evidence that, in the United States, lesbian
communities are in general less urban based, more spatially dispersed, and

more dependent upon informal rather than formal institutions (e.g., personal networks) than are gay male communities (cf. Wolfe 1978; Castells 1983:140; Beyer 1985). These differences are usually attributed to women's economically disadvantaged position vis-a-vis men and to differences in the social structure and practices of the gay male and lesbian communities (see Winchester and White 1988:49, for such an analysis in the context of Paris, France).

These differences appear to hold in the case of New Orleans' Marigny neighborhood. All of the key gay actors in Marigny's gentrification (on both the production and consumption sides of the process) were male, as were most (but not-all) of the participants in and institutions of the French Quarter-based gay community. The lesbian community was simply weaker economically, less spatially concentrated, and more dependent upon an informal institutional network than was the gay male community.

Gay gentrification thus had the effect in Marigny, and has the likely effect elsewhere, of further stratifying gay communities along gender lines, by extending men's economic advantage over women. This suggests a subtle new interpretation of the relationship between gay oppression and the economic and social oppression of women. Existing literature on the subject links the oppression of gays to efforts to enforce rigid gender roles characterized by male dominance (Weinberger and Millham 1979; Ponse 1978; Gagnon and Simon 1973). Sexual dominance in particular is viewed as crucial to the reproduction of both the ideology and the reality of male social dominance. Forms of sexual expression that do not entail male dominance (especially homosexual behavior, which does not entail women and men relating sexually at all) are therefore viewed as threatening to the survival of male social dominance. Yet in Marigny and other gentrified gay neighborhoods, we have examples of a form of social dominance (economic privilege) being facilitated, rather than undermined, by efforts to develop, not oppress, a gay community (albeit for purposes, primarily, of private accumulation). The perpetuation of male economic privilege within the context of a gay community's influence on a land market is thus a testament to the resilience of male social dominance generally in the face of what the literature suggests should be one of the most powerful threats to it.[13] The relationship between gay oppression and the oppression of women must therefore be seen as considerably more contingent than the existing literature suggests.

Acknowledgments

I am indebted to Amy Gluckman for her work in excerpting this paper from the longer original version and to Bob Reppe for his graphics work.

Notes

This article first appeared under the title "Some theoretical implications of gay involvement in an urban land market" in *Political Geography Quarterly*, Vol. 9, No. 4, October 1990, pp. 337–352. It is reprinted here with minor changes.

1   There are some exceptions to this, as in small enclaves such as Provincetown, Massachusetts, Key West, Florida, and certain coastal communities in California. But gay community successes are much more numerous in large cities.

2   He relies heavily, however, on the unpublished papers of Don Lee, a graduate student, in the study.

3   The study is more directly concerned, however, with the development of gay territory and gay political power than with the local land market.

4   This 1960s in-migration took place largely before the onset of the modern identity-based gay rights movement, which is usually considered to have begun in 1969. The French Quarter's long tradition as a relatively open center of gay culture afforded New Orleans gays a much greater opportunity to create integrated gay identities and life styles than was available in most other U.S. cities. The possibility of a middle-class residence and life style near the institutions of gay cultural life is one example of this.

5   It is located at the opposite end of Elysian Fields Avenue from Marigny (see Figure 1).

6   "Creole" is a term referring to Louisianans descended from French and Spanish settlers. The term originated in the West Indies, however, and was brought to Louisiana by West Indies immigrants. These immigrants were often of mixed African and European descent, while Louisiana Creoles are often alleged to be of exclusively European descent. Hence there is much controversy over what constitutes a "true" Louisiana Creole.

7   Gays were not the only out-of-the-mainstream group to settle in Marigny. Substantial numbers of "hippies, prostitutes, Cuban refugees and members of the local intelligentsia" also called Marigny home (Rushton 1970:56). But it is likely that gays were the only group that included in its ranks persons with substantial economic resources.

8   Historic preservation has a long history in New Orleans that is very much associated with local elites. The Vieux Carre Commission, which regulates development in the French Quarter, was established by local élites in 1936.

9   This is generally regarded as marking the beginning of the modern gay rights movement and is commemorated one weekend in June by gay communities in most U.S. cities.

10 Two years later, after the collapse of the city's oil-based economy and the plunge that the local real estate market took (including in Marigny), the measure was reintroduced by another City Council member. This time Marigny's representative changed his position (citing public fears about AIDS) and the measure failed by an even larger margin.

11 This can be contrasted with "classic" cases of gentrification (e.g., Philadelphia's Society Hill and Vancouver's Kitsilano) that have been characterized by wholesale transformations of large tracts of inner-city land (N. Smith 1979; Ley 1984).

12 There were, in fact, precious few of the latter in New Orleans at the time.

13 What is remarkable here is not that individual gay men participate in the oppression of women. Rather, it is the fact that a successful collective struggle against gay oppression (through the development of a gay community) can have the effect of

furthering the material oppression of women. This is not a result that most existing theory would appear to anticipate.

References

Beauregard, R.A. (1986). The chaos and complexity of gentrification. In *Gentrification of the City* (N. Smith and P. Williams, eds.), pp. 35–55. Boston: Allen & Unwin.

Berry, J. (1979). What price appraisal? *Figaro* (New Orleans), March 5, pp. 12–14.

Beyer, J. (1985). Geography of women's spaces: a progress report. Paper presented to a special session on women in the city: struggle for space, Annual Meeting of the Association of American Geographers, Detroit, MI, April 22.

Castells, M. (1983). *The City and the Grassroots*. Berkeley, CA: University of California Press.

—— and Murphy, K.A. (1982). Cultural identity and urban structure: the spatial organization of San Franscisco's gay community. In *Urban Policy under Capitalism* (N. Fainstein and S. Fainstein, eds.), Beverly Hills: Sage Publications.

Chouinard, V. and Fincher, R. (1985). Local terrains of conflict within the Canadian state. Paper presented to a special session on the local state, Annual Meeting of the Association of American Geographers, April 24.

Cooke, P. (1985). Class practices as regional markers: a contribution to labour geography. In *Social Relations and Spatial Structures* (D. Gregory and J. Urry, eds.), pp. 213–241. New York: St. Martin's Press.

Cox, K. R. (1981). Capitalism and conflict around the communal living space. In *Urbanization and Urban Planning in Capitalist Society* (M. Dear and A. Scott, eds.), pp. 431–455.

—— and Mair, A. (1988). Locality and community in the politics of local economic development. *Annals of the Association of American Geographers* 78, 307–325.

DuBos, C. (1984). Gay politics emerges. *Gambit*, March 10.

Escoffier, J. (1985). Sexual revolution and the politics of gay identity. *Socialist Review* 15, 119–153.

Ettore, E.M. (1978). Women, urban social movement and the lesbian ghetto. *International Journal of Urban and Regional Research* 2, 499–520.

Foltz, K., Raine, G., Gonzalez, D., and Wright, L. (1984). The profit of being gay. *Newsweek* 1, 84, 89.

Gagnon, J. and Simon, W. (1973). *Sexual Conduct: The Social Sources of Human Sexuality*. Chicago: Aldine.

Gsell, G. (1979a). Four appraisers charged in overvaluation bribery. *The Times – Picayune* (New Orleans), February 23, pp. 1–1; 1–14.

—— (1979b). Appraisers charged with overvaluation. *The Times-Picayune* (New Orleans), March 28, p. 1–16.

—— (1979c). Took payoffs, says appraiser. *The Times-Picayune* (New Orleans), May 15, p. 1–5B.

—— (1979d). Appraiser denies taking pay for overvaluations. *The Times-Picayune* (New Orleans), May 16, p. 1–10.

—— (1979e). Witness says appraiser took money for property overvalues. *The Times-Picayune* (New Orleans), June 12, p. 1–4.

—— (1979f). Appraiser trial goes to jury. *The Times-Picayune* (New Orleans), June 13, p. 1–16.

—— (1979g). Juros acquit N.O. appraiser. *The Times-Picayune* (New Orleans), June 14, p. 1–12.

—— (1979h). Appraiser's conviction on mail fraud overturned. *The Times-Picayune* (New Orleans), July 25, p. 1–12.

—— (1979j). Former appraiser paid, 4 witnesses tell court. *The Times-Picayune* (New Orleans), September 11, p. 1–5.

—— (1979k). Former appraiser denies taking cash kickbacks. *The Times-Picayune* (New Orleans), September 12, p. 1–5.

—— (1979l). Ex-appraiser is guilty in lying case. *The Times-Picayune* (New Orleans), September 13, p. 1–5.

Hartman, C. (1984). *The Transformation of San Francisco*. Totowa, NJ: Rowman and Allanheld.

Harvey, D. (1981). The spatial fix: Hegel, von Thunen, and Marx. *Antipode* 13(3), 1–12.

—— (1985). *The Urbanization of Capital*. Baltimore: Johns Hopkins University Press.

Knopp, L. (1989). Gentrification and Gay Community Development in a New Orleans Neighborhood. Ph.D. dissertation, Department of Geography, The University of Iowa, Iowa City, Iowa.

—— (1990). Exploiting the rent-gap: the theoretical implications of using illegal appraisal schemes to encourage gentrification in New Orleans. *Urban Geography* 11, 48–64.

Lauria, M. (1984). The implications of marxian rent theory for community-controlled redevelopment strategies. *Journal of Planning Education and Research* 4, 16–24.

—— and Knopp, L. (1985). Toward an analysis of the role of gay communities in the urban renaissance. *Urban Geography* 6, 152–169.

Lee, D.A. (1980). The Gay Community and Improvements in the Quality of Life in San Francisco. MCP Thesis, University of California.

Logan, J.R. and Molotch, H.L. (1987). *Urban Fortunes: The Political Economy of Place*. Berkeley, CA: University of California Press.

Massey, D. (1984). *Spatial Divisions of Labour: Social Structures and the Geography of Production*. London: Macmillan.

Mollenkopf, J. (1981). Community and accumulation. In *Urbanization and Urban Planning in Capitalist Society* (M. Dear and A. Scott, eds.), pp. 319–337. New York: Methuen.

Molotch, H.L. (1976). The city as a growth machine. *American Journal of Sociology* 82, 309–332.

Murphy, J.D. (1979). Loan institutions also bilked. *The Times-Picayune* (New Orleans), May 5, pp. I–1;I–11.

Murphy, K.A. (1980). Urban Transformations: A Case Study of the Gay Community in San Francisco. MCP Thesis, University of California.

Personal Interview, September 1987.

———— , September 1987.

———— , October 1987.

———— , November 1987.

———— , October 22, 1987.

———— , February 20, 1988.

———— , June 27, 1988.

———— , June 27, 1988.

———— , June 27, 1988.

———— , June 28, 1988.

———— , June 28, 1988.

———— , June 28, 1988.

———— , June 29, 1988.

———— , June 29, 1988.

———— , June 30, 1988.

———— , June 30, 1988.

Ponse, B. (1978). *Identities in the Lesbian World: The Social Construction of Self*. Westport, CT: Greenwood Press.

Rose, D. (1984). Rethinking gentrification: beyond the uneven development of marxist urban theory. *Environment and Planning D: Society and Space* 1, 47–74.

Roweis, S. (1981). Urban planning in early and late capitalist societies: outline of a theoretical perspective. In *Urbanization and Urban Planning in Capitalist Society* (M. Dear and A. Scott, eds.), pp. 159–177. New York: Methuen.

Rubin, G. (1975). The traffic in women: notes on the "political economy" of sex. In *Toward an Anthropology of Women* (R. Reiter, ed.). New York: Monthly Review Press.

Rushton, B. (1970). The faubourg Marigny: straddling the centuries. *New Orleans Magazine*, March, pp. 48–51; 56.

Scott, A. and Roweis, S. (1977). Urban planning in theory and practice: a reappraisal. *Environment and Planning A*9, 1097–1119.

Smith, M.P. (1979). *The City and Social Theory*. New York: St. Martin's Press.

Smith, N. (1979). Gentrification and capital: theory, practice and ideology in Society Hill. *Antipode* 11(3), 24–35.

———— and LeFaivre, M. (1984). A class analysis of gentrification. In *Gentrification, Displacement and Neighborhood Revitalization* (J. Palen and B. London, eds.), pp. 43–63. Albany: State University of New York Press.

Weinberger, L.E. and Millham, J. (1979). Attitudinal homophobia and support for traditional sex roles. *Journal of Homosexuality* 4, 237–246.

Wilson, D. (1987a). Institutions and urban revitalization: the case of Chelsea in New York City. *Urban Geography* 8, 129–145.

———— (1987b). Urban revitalization on the upper west side of Manhattan: an urban managerialist assessment. *Economic Geography* 63, 35–47.

Winchester, H.P.M. and White, P.E. (1988). The location of marginalised groups in the inner city. *Environment and Planning D: Society and Space* 6, 37–54.

Winters, C. (1979). The social identity of evolving neighborhoods. *Landscape* 23, 8–14.

Wolfe, D.G. (1978). *The Lesbian Community*, Berkeley, CA: University of California Press.

Chapter 20

Gill Valentine and Tracey Skelton

FINDING ONESELF, LOSING ONESELF: THE LESBIAN AND GAY 'SCENE' AS A PARADOXICAL SPACE*

From *International Journal of Urban and Regional Research* 2003 27(4): 849–66

Introduction: coming out in the city

HISTORICALLY, THE CITY has been regarded as a space of social and sexual liberation because the urban is perceived to offer anonymity and an escape from the claustrophobic kinship and community relations of small towns and villages. Wilson (1991), for example, argues that in the nineteenth and early twentieth centuries, women had more freedom in cities than in rural areas where traditional gender codes of behaviour were more strongly defined and policed. Rural to urban migrations were common amongst women actively seeking opportunities for self-invention and social and economic independence (Heron, 1983). Likewise, in *City of Dreadful Delight*, Walkowitz (1992) documents the role of particular urban spaces in Victorian England in enabling bourgeois young men to transgress oppressive codes of morality. Notably, the East End of London provided a space for gambling, illegal sports and both illicit heterosexual and gay relationships.

The role of urban spaces in the constitution of gay sexual identities can be traced back to the late nineteenth and early twentieth centuries. Drawing on a range of secondary sources, Chauncey (1995) observed the way that in New York a network of urban spaces (largely in working-class neighbourhoods), from cafés and restaurants to bathhouses and speakeasies, facilitated the development of gay men's relationships and cultures between 1890 and 1940 – although, towards the end of this period, these were less and less publicly visible because of the efforts of the police to crack down on 'vice'. More usually, however, the development of visible gay urban neighbourhoods is dated back to 1967, when a police raid on a gay male bar in New York provoked what became known as the Stonewell riots. This led to the politicization of lesbians and gay men and the emergence of their more visible presence within many major Western cities.

In cities such as San Francisco and New Orleans in the US and Sydney, Australia, gay gentrifiers have established their own residential communities (Castells, 1983; Knopp 1992; 1998). Elsewhere, pink economies have created gay consumption enclaves, such as Soho in London, which, although having no significant gay residential population, have nonetheless become important sites for the forging of gay men's social and sexual lifestyles (Mort, 1995). Not surprisingly, urban spaces continue to act as a magnet for queer migrants (both from rural areas and across the urban hierarchy) fleeing from prejudice and discrimination, or just attracted by the general cosmopolitanism and opportunities to reinvent themselves that urban living offers – a process that is captured by the title of Weston's (1995) article about the gay geographical imagination – 'Get thee to a big city'.

In recent years, geographers and urban sociologists have sought to map and understand the development of diverse forms of lesbian and gay space – popularly dubbed 'the scene' – within a whole range of urban environments (e.g. Castells, 1983; Lauria and Knopp, 1985; Adler and Brenner, 1992; Binnie, 1995; Peake, 1993; Valentine, 1995a; Johnson, 1997; Knopp, 1998; Brown, 2000). This work suggests that the scene of any given city is usually made up of commercial clubs/bars and support/information groups that are sometimes run from commercial spaces, but also meet in a wide range of venues including local community centres, members' homes, etc. The geographical provision of these sorts of social venues and support groups varies widely both nationally and internationally (see Knopp, 1998 for a comparative study of three cities that highlights the different relationships between urbanization and gay male identity). Indeed, gay spaces in major cities such as San Francisco, Sydney, Amsterdam and Manchester have become clearly defined districts that are successful not only at attracting a gay clientele, but which have also become popular as venues for heterosexual clubbers and tourists (Whittle, 1994; Binnie, 1995; Quilley, 1995; Johnson, 1997; Knopp, 1998). Gay bars in other cities are often more inconspicuous or closeted, which in part reflects the need to protect the venues and their clientele from potential homophobia and violence (Weightman, 1980; Myslik, 1996; Brown, 2000). This invisibility is particularly true of lesbian venues that are usually less commercial and less visible than those for gay men (Castells, 1983; Adler and Brenner, 1992; Rothenberg, 1995; Valentine, 1995a).

The process of 'coming out' – defining oneself as lesbian or gay – is commonly a period of confusion for individuals (Savin-Williams, 1989; Valentine *et al.*, 2003). As such, it is often asserted that the scene can play an important part in individuals' identity formation and development. However, despite the range and richness of the academic literature on lesbian and gay urban spaces, relatively little attention has been paid to the actual role of the scene in the coming out process. This article draws on empirical work with young lesbians and gay men to explore the significance of the scene for them. The first half of the article focuses on the positive roles that the scene can play in helping young people to find themselves. The second half of the article focuses on the risks that they can encounter in this process of making a transition to adulthood. In doing so the article contributes to geography and urban studies literatures about lesbian and gay space, and to the interdisciplinary youth transitions literature about lesbian and gay men's alternative forms of social commitment, as well as identifying some broader policy implications of this work.

The findings are based on in-depth interviews[1] with 20 self-identified young lesbians and gay men aged 16 to 25, and retrospective interviews with 23 self-identified 'older' lesbians and gay men about their memories of this period of 'youth' and the significance it had for the ways that their lives have subsequently mapped out. The interviewees were recruited from the Midlands of the UK by a combination of methods including snowballing from multiple sources, advertisements on the Internet and in newsletters, and contact with a range of relevant support, advice and social groups. The respondents are drawn from a wide range of social backgrounds (in terms of their parents' social class, educational qualifications, housing situation and employment status). They have also grown up in a range of different 'family' forms. These include conventional nuclear families, lone-parent households, reconstituted families and lesbian households. The informants' local lesbian and gay scenes do not have a residential base, and are not as commercially successful and as well developed as UK scenes in London, Manchester and Brighton, but rather are comprised of a loose network of gay pubs, clubs and social/health support and advice groups.

All of the interviews, which were conducted in a place of the inform- ants' choice, lasted between one and two hours. These were taped, tran- scribed and then analysed using conventional social science techniques (Jackson, 2001). Two stages of coding were employed, firstly, 'in vivo' codes that draw upon terms used by the informants themselves, and sec- ondly 'constructed' codes that were developed by us as the researchers (Strauss, 1987). In the subsequent stage of analysis the codes from the individual accounts were compared with each other to generate dominant and counter themes.

Finding oneself: the scene as an alternative form of social commitment

Traditionally, young people's transitions from a state of dependent child-hood to an independent adult identity have been measured in terms of a developmental stage model (e.g. Kruger, 1988). The key markers of adult-hood being: leaving full-time education and entering the labour market; moving out of the parental home to establish an independent household; and marriage/co-habitation and parenthood (Morrow and Richards, 1996). Coles (1997) has summarized these as the school-to-work transi-tion, housing transition and domestic transition. These transitions are all events-based and institutionalized in that they are governed by established 'norms' and practices, measured, for example, in terms of formal qualifica-tions, marriage ceremonies and so on, that are conferred on young people by the wider family/community and society.

Yet not all young people either aspire to all of these 'norms', or achieve them in a form that can be measured or acknowledged in con-ventional ways. While there has been some recognition of the way that gender, class and race influence transitions and outcomes, sexuality has been largely absent from this discussion. Indeed, the transitions literature has paid far more attention to the school-to-work transition than to other transitions. Where the focus has been on domestic transitions it has usually addressed heterosexuality and coupledom (e.g. Morrow and Richards, 1996). As such, lesbian and gay men's specific transition experiences, such as 'coming out' and the role that urban spaces like the scene play in these, are not acknowledged in the traditional transitions model.

More generally, there is a growing critique of the linear nature of the transitions model. This has been motivated by recognition that transitions are becoming more risky and unpredictable in the context of modernity. In this phase it is argued there has been dissolution of the traditional param-eters of the industrial society. The old certainties of traditional occupations are being replaced by the need for individuals to adapt to the de-standardization of work and changing labour market conditions, by, for example, retraining and switching occupations. Individuals' identities and lifestyles are no longer so clearly related to their employment and family backgrounds. Traditional ideas and expectations about social relations are also being reworked. The preordained, gender specific 'normal' path of school, paid work, courtship, marriage and parenthood is now less clearly marked. Rather, it is claimed by some authors that there has been a weaken-ing of class ties, a decline in the reliance on authorities such as the church, and a decoupling of some of the social behaviours and attitudes (e.g. in relation to having sex, having children, etc.) that used to be attached to marriage and family life (Beck and Beck-Gernsheim, 2002). Beck (1992) argues that released from the constraints and social norms of tradition, individuals are now freer to choose between a range of options in the pursuit of their own happiness. It is a process termed individualization (Beck and Beck-Gernsheim, 2002).

As such, there is growing recognition that the passage of young people into adulthood is no longer linear in terms of the sequencing and timing of transitions. Rather, there is increasing acknowledgment of the uncertainty and fragmented nature of young people's transition experiences (Chisholm and Du Bois-Reymond, 1993; Du Bois-Reymond, 1998; Skelton, 2002). In some cases transitions are speeding up (for example young people are having sexual relationships at an earlier age); in other cases they are more protracted (for example rising educational participation rates and the deterioration in social support for young people mean that some young people are dependent on their families for longer). School-to-work, housing and domestic transitions are also less likely to be accomplished by a certain age, and are less synchronous in that a young person may make the school-to-work transition but not housing or domestic transitions (and vice versa). These transitions are also increasingly reversible, with young people leaving the parental home but then returning.

The freedom that young people are assumed to have to create 'do-it-yourself-biographies' in modernity has been understood to provide more opportunities for lesbians and gay men to define and live their own lifestyles. Yet these new possibilities also bring with them uncertainties and risks. Despite all the emphasis within Beck's individualization thesis on the greater freedom that individuals have to define their own way in the world, nonetheless research shows that families and family resources systems (economic, social, cultural and affective) are still crucial in supporting and facilitating young people's transitions (Allatt, 1997). For young people beginning to identify as lesbian or gay, the wider heterosexual family does not, or cannot necessarily provide appropriate support.

First, the majority of young people are born into, and grow up within, heterosexual families where the expectation is also that they too will be heterosexual. As such they rarely have any direct contact with lesbian and gay men and therefore have little knowledge or experience of alternative sexualities and what it means to live a lesbian and gay lifestyle. This ignorance and uncertainty is often compounded by the lack of acknowledgement of lesbian or gay sexual identities and lifestyles within schools, especially in relation to sex education (Epstein and Johnson, 1994; 1998). Rather, young people's first introduction to lesbian and gay issues is often in terms of encountering the homophobic attitudes of parents (Johnston and Valentine, 1995; Elwood, 2000) and peers (Rivers, 2001). Not surprisingly, many young people internalize this homophobia. As such, as teenagers, young lesbians and gay men commonly go through a period of uncertainty when they begin to define their sexuality. This can be a period of great emotional turmoil, confusion and isolation (Savin-Williams, 1989). Young people cut themselves off from the support of their families because they are too scared to explain how they feel, and are fearful of being rejected by those close to them and of homophobia and discrimination in the wider world, yet do not know how to find others like themselves to provide assurance.

This strain of being unable to 'come out' as lesbian or gay can cause young people to suffer from low self-esteem, loss of confidence, delayed emotional development, depression and self-hatred. These emotions in turn can lead to self-destructive behaviours including: drinking, drug taking, running away, lying, committing crime, unsafe sex, forming unhealthy/violent relationships, withdrawing from friendship and family networks, weight gain, pregnancy and attempted suicide (Massachusetts Department of Education, 1995; Elizur and Ziv, 2001). Noel describes his experiences:

> At that time of my life [late teens] there was absolutely no-one, I was a very, very isolated person, so the only, the only place I had was trying to retreat in myself, kind of thing, you know . . . I felt awful to be honest, you know I was feeling pretty isolated . . . I wasn't fearful of what people were gonna think, it was just where do I go from here? . . . there was just no-one I felt I could talk to (young gay man aged 21).

Many young people's fears of coming out are well-founded. Our own and other studies show that young lesbians and gay men coming out can be: subject to domestic violence by relatives, thrown out of the parental home and cut off from family support (D'Augelli et al., 1998), bullied by peers and co-workers, discriminated against in the workplace and harassed in public spaces (Herek and Berrill, 1992). However, the presumption of heterosexuality (Valentine, 1993) in most institutions, such as housing, or counselling services, means that service providers commonly fail to recognize or provide appropriate support for young lesbians and gay men in crisis. In this way, institutional structures and practices can actually reinforce the marginalization of this group.

In the face of these experiences many young lesbians and gay men turn to the scene to provide an alternative framework of identity, social allegiance and support. In this way, coming out on the scene can be a more important marker of a young person's independent adulthood than traditional school-to-work, domestic and housing transitions. Different types of scene venues serve as important transitional spaces in numerous ways. Support groups often provide a first stepping-stone from the heterosexual world into the lesbian and gay commercial scene of clubs and bars. They offer a range of information and advice about everything from lesbian and gay culture/history, and social/political rights, to safe sex information and details about club venue/events. More importantly, support groups are a way for young people to meet others like themselves and to develop a lesbian or gay social network. Indeed, lesbian and gay 'communities' are often dubbed 'families of choice' (Weston, 1995). Terry and Mark describe the value of support groups in supporting transitions:

> *Terry*: The group sort of provides a place where you come and meet other gay people, gay, lesbian, bisexual people, and it's sort of non-scene, so you know, it's not got the atmosphere of a club or anything at all, it's just more relaxed. You've got access to information leaflets, magazines, newspapers (young gay man aged 16).

> *Mark*: Those of us who come along to the group [LG youth group] want to make the transition from being in the closet to being on the scene as smooth as possible 'cos . . . when you are young and on the scene for the first time and especially if you're under age, it can be, can be intimidating. I wouldn't say frightening but it can be intimidating. I think if it hadn't been for [the gay support group] I probably, it probably would have taken me a while longer than before I'd actually, you know, gone on the scene (young gay man, aged 19).

In particular, support groups provide a space in which people can gain more confidence and self-esteem in their own sexual identities. Fiona, who was rejected by her family when she came out and suffered from depression and weight gain, describes how a lesbian, gay and bisexual youth group, *Outcry*, has helped her to develop her confidence and skills.

> *Fiona*: I didn't have any confidence before I came here . . . I had no self esteem, I had no, I hated myself, I hated everything. I just, like I wasn't interested in anything, I just wanted to curl up and just die you know, just like life isn't worth it, and I just like found myself . . . it's just like one long dream I have to pinch myself to make sure I'm not dreaming, you know, it's like when I, when I stood up and read, read out my poem and I was looking for, . . . I was thinking fucking hell you know I didn't even know I was a poet until I came here. I didn't know I had any talent for writing and er music or art or nothing you know. And then I'm getting, I'm doing a piece of work at the moment in the art zone to do with expressing myself, which is what we're gonna get shown in the art, art gallery, I've got two, three poems which could have a go at getting published in magazines. I've read out and now I'm gonna be singing on Wednesday . . .

everyone wants me, you know, its like people grabbing me left, right and centre, saying Fiona I need you . . . from everyone hating me and being hated and hating everyone, you know, to people liking and respecting me and just letting me be and accepting me for who I am . . . And it's like, we don't hate you you're one of us, you know? (young lesbian, aged 20).

Youth workers argue (below) that it is young people from 'working-class' backgrounds, such as Fiona, who are most in need of outreach work and safe spaces where they can develop their sexual identities and be given the support and skills to help them deal with the homophobia they may encounter in everyday life. Although Beck's (1992) individualization thesis is based on a premise of the declining importance of class-based identities and ties, the evidence of this research is that in terms of transitions to adulthood, familial expectations about the biographies that young people should construct for themselves have not changed as much as actual practices. Specifically, class ties are evident. Whereas university commonly provides a relatively tolerant and supportive environment for young 'middle-class' people to develop a lesbian or gay identity away from their families, in contrast, working-class culture places more expectations on young people to fulfil traditional gender roles and paths to marriage and parenthood. Working-class families are also more likely to react to news of their son or daughter's sexuality with violence or rejection than those from more middle-class backgrounds where common responses are to seek professional (from psychiatrists or counsellors) help or to go into denial. Elaine, a lesbian and gay health worker, and Sharon, a lesbian and gay youth worker, explain the particular problems encountered by young working-class people:

> *Elaine*: Working-class culture is particularly macho, so it's particularly sexist in terms of gender role division and that in a way the homophobia falls in around that because you know to be a gay man is to be a not real man, and you must be a real man and you must drink real beer. And so you know it kind of goes hand in hand with that, and, and women must know their place and they must, they must relate to men and they must relate preferably subservient to men and they must need men and they must gratify men. And obviously, erm, lesbians are quite independent of men in many ways and just aren't interested in playing subservient stereotypically feminine roles (a lesbian and gay health worker).

> *Sharon*: I often think that, you know, a lot of young people, particularly working-class people, rely on certain transitions in

life, getting married 'cos that's what you're supposed to do, and if you're lesbian or gay you don't have those obvious markers in life and what it can be like to go through that without having obvious rituals I suppose, and the effects of that on you. Maybe that's just my personal interest but I think the future can seem very, very bewildering (a lesbian and gay youth worker).

The scene not only provides a transitional space where young lesbians and gay men can express their self-identities, but also offers a space where others can validate these identities. Barth (1981) has pointed out that identities are contingent; it is not enough for us to perform an identity, these articulations of who we are must be read and accepted by others before an identity can be said to have been truly taken on. Below, Vinnie describes the self-confidence and acceptance that he derives from the fact that other young gay men he has met on the scene look up to him and imitate his choice of style and clubs, while Terry explains how going out on the scene made him feel 'normal'.

> *Vinnie*: . . . in the gay scene it's like I am part of the gay scene. I am quite a high part in the gay scene. And people look for me for reassurance. Like my friend today says 'I've got to go shopping and you've got to help me choose clothes 'cos I haven't got a clue' . . . And people follow me and people, I know it sounds like I'm putting myself on a pedestal, but people do follow me and it's, if I say 'We're going to such and such'. Like last night I says 'we're going to [venue, name removed] for a while', they followed (young gay man, aged 18).

> *Interviewer*: How did you feel the first time you went on the scene, can you remember what you felt like?

> *Terry*: Very nervous, very scared, I felt as though everybody was looking at me but it did feel great as well because I felt as though I fitted in quite well and I just sort of felt normal (young gay man aged 16).

As Terry's reference to feeling normal suggests, young lesbians and gay men often describe the scene in terms of homecoming. Having commonly spent a period of time feeling different from friends and family, the scene represents a first space of belonging to many young lesbians and gay men. In this sense it might be conceptualized as an 'imagined community' (Anderson, 1983) because even though young people on the scene will never know all their fellow participants, and there are many relations of inequality, exclusion and exploitation between them, nevertheless they still share a deep sense of shared identity or communion. Mark describes the sense of comfortableness ('my own environment') he feels in a gay space while Megan explains her sense of community.

> *Mark*: We [partner] go to the [venue, name removed], which is a pub just down the road, and, you know, the chance to mix with people and be in my own environment and feel comfortable and everything, you know? So I realized I felt much happier going to a mixed pub and then later onto gay venues rather than being, you know, in straight pubs and everything (young gay man aged 19).

> *Megan*: It's more like a community [than the straight world] . . . the gay scene is, it's more like, everybody knows who everybody else is. Like you can see someone from [bar, name removed] and you'll say hello to them . . . And it's like that and it's like you might not know them but because you know that they go to certain places that you, you're going to, it's like, its more like community (young lesbian, aged 17).

The scene offers young lesbians and gay men an opportunity to step out of the heteronormative world where they often feel marginalized. Clubs and bars provide spaces where people can lose themselves and their troubles in music, dance and sex. They are expressive, performative spaces where people can enjoy themselves together in ways that can be empowering.

Young gay men in particular described the pleasures of dressing up to go out. This was articulated both in terms of how taking care of their own appearance makes them feel good, and in terms of the pleasures of being looked at by others. Harris (1997: 35) suggests that lesbian and gay identities are literally embodied in terms of dress, and mannerisms. He writes: 'Because we are the only invisible minority, we must invent from scratch those missing physical features that enable us to spot our imperceptible compatriots, who would remain unseen and anonymous if they did not prominently display on their bodies, in their sibilant voices and shuffling gaits, their immaculate grooming and debonair style of deportment, the caste mark that constitutes the essence of gay sensibility'.

Terry and Aaron describe the permission and space that the urban scene offers them to dress and act in different sexualized ways:

> *Terry*: I definitely think if you go out, say, to a place, you, you sort of camp it up a bit, or if you're with, you act more natural, and more natural for me is quite sort of camp, you known, in front of friends, I would act, you know, much more camp.

[Later he returns to the same theme]. In a gay club I would dress, I wouldn't go straight, what I would class as straight dressed at all. I'd definitely go very gaily dressed . . . Tight t-shirt, definitely very tight t-shirt, small short-sleeved, probably some tight trousers, quite tight round the bum, sort of some trendy trainers, something like that (young gay man aged 16).

Aaron: [Describing coming out on the scene in his late teens]: . . . there was all that kind of exploration of images, to me it was a really exciting time about playing around with stuff, you know, because I soon learnt, for example, the way in which I dress and the way in which I acted would determine what kind of men would hit on me.

Interviewer: Right.

Aaron: So you know I played with all sorts of kind of images from, from like a camp stereotype right through to sort of straight acting. And it was like just, I remember it almost like scientifically playing with it, thinking um if I wear my leather jacket tonight and this is the kind of person I'll be able to pull and if I wear, you know, something kind of flamboyant because it was the eighties . . . new romantic period, you know? – then this is what will happen. So I remember playing around with it, you know, and just having loads and loads and loads and loads of casual sex for probably a good 18 months, you know? (retrospective interview with a gay man now aged 38).

Part of this pleasure and exploration is facilitated by music. Particular lyrics or tracks take on queer significance, the social associations and memories that go with them can thus play a part in the imagining of community (Valentine, 1995b, Buckland, 2002). Participants use the dance floor and experiences of dancing with others to understand, embody and perform themselves as queer. The sensuality and physical closeness of sharing sounds, touch and movement to music can also produce a sense of commensality (Buckland, 2002). For young women, lesbian and gay venues also have the added advantage of providing a safe space to dance away from the surveillant gaze of heterosexual men. This is a feature that also makes them increasingly attractive to heterosexual women wanting to have fun without attracting unwanted attention from the opposite sex.

Above all, the lesbian and gay scene offers young people a space for sexual exploration and self-expression. Many of those interviewed described their first experiences of the scene as liberating and exciting, offering as it does a challenge to traditional orthodox heterosexual morality. Indeed, Giddens (1992) has suggested that without the asymmetrical power relationships which frame hetero-normative constructions of love and sex (homo)sexual relationships offer a possibility for more autonomous, democratic and liberatory forms of sexual intimacy. Aaron and Jack explain the positive sexual aspects of coming out on the scene.

> *Aaron*: . . . it was just incredibly liberating to do that, and kind of . . . a real sense of like not loss or waste, yeah waste maybe, in some ways that I'd wasted all this time [trying to be heterosexual] . . . [I] was a right old slag when I came out but that's the reality of it, you know, I guess that's about relief and whatever, you know? And you know I've heard people talk about coming out it's been like being born again I think, that's a really good analogy (retrospective interview with a gay man now aged 38).

> *Jack*: I started going out on the scene and sort of then started doing all kind of one night stands and things like that . . . I think it was a kind of ooh right, you know sort of, sort of discovery of something that perhaps I hadn't really thought about before – and it did feel quite positive at the time – and remember kind of going off eventually but at the time it felt quite liberating, this kind of like yeah I can, I can do this and I don't have to just have one boyfriend, I can have this wild sort of hedonistic lifestyle, it wasn't really looking back on it but it felt in some senses it almost felt quite, I think perhaps you can sort of dress it up and say it felt, felt quite subversive, or quite political with a small p, and sort of interesting to be just like heterosexual people and, you know, have a long-term relationship but you know hey we're all, we can go out and have sex with people just for one night and that's alright and you know that kind of feeling positive about sex and sexuality and that sort of thing, so yeah that felt, yes I do remember it as being quite a nice time (retrospective interview with a gay man now aged 35).

Drug-taking is just as much part of the ritual of going out on the lesbian and gay scene as it is on any other commercial club scene (Malbon, 1999, Buckland, 2002). Drugs make clubbers feel more sociable, more in touch with their bodily sensations and more alive (Malbon, 1999). Indeed, Buckland (2002: 43) argues that drugs such as Ecstasy help to further the distance for lesbians and gay men between the realities of the heteronormative everyday world and the scene, by separating 'the body of the home and the workplace from the club body'.

In summary, then, the scene offers lesbians and gay men a form of social commitment that can become a substitute for family relationships, providing a transitional space where they can find information, support and develop a positive sense of self-identification and sexuality. Thus, the scene both facilitates individuals' traditional school-to-work, domestic and housing transitions while also serving as a rite of passage itself that marks a young person's transition to an adult sexual identity. However, despite the role that the scene plays in countering the processes of marginalization that young lesbians and gay men experience in everyday heterosexual space, it is also true that the scene is an environment where young people making the transition to adulthood encounter new risks. In the following section we explore some of these dangers.

Losing oneself: risky spaces

Most places contain implicit and unstated, taken-for-granted expectations about how their inhabitants should behave (Cresswell, 1996). While it is relatively easy for young people growing up to pick up taken-for-granted codes of behaviour in everyday heterosexual spaces from observation, parents, the media and so on, they usually have little awareness of what to expect on the lesbian and gay scene. As such, as some of the quotations in the previous section implied, going out on the scene for first time can be intimidating.

Because young lesbians and gay men often do not feel that they 'fit' in heterosexual environments they can feel desperate to belong on the scene. This often manifests itself in a desire to orient their dress and behaviour to conform to dominant dress/bodily codes: to adopt a lesbian or gay look, even if they may be uncertain about their sexuality. In this way, the urban scene can precipitate a forced transition to a lesbian or gay sexual identity.

> *Cassie*: I walked into [bar, name removed] and there was just hundreds of, hundreds of women all kissing each other but you know all kissing, things like that and I was just, you know, yeah it was frightening, it was really scary, it was just, it was real, total culture shock . . . just really, really, really, really strange. But it was funny because when Cara took me there I think Cara assumed that I was one hundred percent certain that I was gay and I knew exactly what I was doing and you know they were straight into 'oh she's nice, do you fancy her?' And 'What's your type?' this that and the other, and I was sort of like I just wanted to sit there and say can I just take it all in just, just for one night sort of thing. But I didn't like to admit that I hadn't actually kissed a woman so I didn't, still didn't definitely know or didn't feel as though I would know until I did, that that was

right sort of thing, but yes it was quite scary (a retrospective interview with a lesbian now aged 37).

Gordon: . . . it was intimidating . . . I somehow felt more that pressure to look good which I've never felt I do and, I never felt I dressed well or anything. I've never known what to wear and, and you know gay clubs are the worst place to feel that. I didn't know how to talk to people without, how to talk to someone without them feeling I was picking them up or how to pick someone up without them feeling I was just talking to them (a retrospective interview with a gay man now aged 47).

Lesbians and gay men tend to experience different forms of gendered vulnerability on the scene. The gay men's commercial scene is a very sexualized environment. Young men who come into this atmosphere for the first time often attract a lot of sexual attention. First, because the gay scene places a premium on the 'body beautiful' youthful bodies are seen as very desirable (Shakespeare, 1996). Second, young men are assumed by older men to be less likely to be HIV positive because of their youth. Not surprisingly, half of the young men who took part in this study claimed to have had sex before the age of 18 (the legal age of consent) with older men. While, as we outlined in the previous section, there are some positive aspects to this in terms of the opportunities young men have to explore and develop their sexuality, it also brings many risks. Internalized homophobia and negative experiences at home and at school (Johnson and Valentine, 1995; Epstein and Johnson, 1994; Rivers, 2001; Rivers and Duncan, 2002) mean that young men can lack the self-esteem to say 'no' to sexual advances and so find themselves coerced into having unwanted, and often unsafe, sex. Indeed, both the gay men and police officers that were interviewed as part of this study described a significant overlap between the gay scene and the 'rent boy' scene (prostitution) with wealthy older men and pimps using money to 'pick up' 'working-class' boys. Noel, Terry and Vinnie describe their experiences:

Noel: [describing his first experience of a gay night at local pub] I met a few people there but all they wanted was sex really, you know, and they were very keen to use me, and that was it . . . so I became a bit disillusioned with that (young gay man aged 21).

Terry: I think the only thing being young is you think if you go with a young guy it's like oh, then he won't have HIV or anything – that's the only type of danger that I seem to fall into, is that you judge sort of age with experience . . . the likelihood of getting Aids would be with an older person (young gay man, aged 16).

> *Vinnie*: I just felt hurried 'cos of, I'm gay and I must sleep like this and I must have sex at, at this age. And I must do it and I must rush and must be everything that I can be all at once . . . If they, if you say 'no I don't want to', then they'll push it and push it. [Later he returns to a similar theme] I mean at 15 I had my first boyfriend . . . I could go out tonight and somebody could come up to me and say 'can I buy you a drink? I think you're good looking would you mind coming back to my house and having sex with me'. And if I was quite attracted to them I might consider the fact that I might go back with them. But if I didn't find them attractive, when I was 15/16 I was like 'OK' and quite pushed into it. And felt quite horrid to make a decision. Now if someone comes up to me now and I think they're a pig I would go 'You are a pig get out of my face and leave me alone' (young gay man aged 18).

This vulnerability is often aggravated by peer pressure and the consumption of alcohol and drugs as Terry and Barry describe:

> *Terry*: . . . if people offer to buy you drinks and stuff like that, you kind of think that you've got to owe them, or you kind of think there's something underlying behind that. Yeah, so I mean there is a tendency to like, oh, I'm really nervous so I'll drink a lot to give me the confidence.

> *Barry*: . . . you have to fit into a stereotypical image of a gay person . . . You have to do these drugs and you have to spend this certain amount of money on booze every night to get out of your head and that's it . . . I've been completely off my face four or five times where its been unsafe sex, which I've gone for HIV tests, but then they've been clear (young gay man, aged 24).

These risks are compounded by the fact that many young gay men are ill prepared for the sort of gay sexual encounters described above. The English education system does not support non-heterosexual transitions to adult sexual relationships in that little or no information or education about same-sex relationships or practices is provided in most schools (Epstein and Johnson, 1994; 1998). Even where sex education has included relevant material, young gay men may not have listened or taken on board the messages because at that time they did not identify as gay or were too embarrassed to be seen to take an interest. Rather, most of the young gay men interviewed learnt about gay sexual practices and safe sex from other gay men on the scene.

Mark: . . . the sex education system at school is crap. I think it's very terrible, even for heterosexuals, I mean it is just awful . . . it's just so mechanical, like this is the man, this is a woman, man gets erection, penis fits into vagina . . . so even from a straight point of view, you know, there wasn't really much in terms of safer sex other than use a condom and obviously, you know, there's obviously, there's nothing as far as gay people are concerned. I don't think sexuality or gay sex was ever mentioned (young gay man aged 19).

Jack: And looking back on it the, the sex with the first guy that I had sex with was really awful . . . sex got a lot better with the second boyfriend . . . and I think that's how I found out how to do sex . . . just by doing it, was by having it with him and then with other people, it kind of you know, I think it just kind, it's one of those things that you're still learning really, just kind of goes on but I think that's how, certainly how I learned and I think it's how, from talking to other gay men it's how a lot of gay men learn about sex, is by doing it, just from sexual partners, it wasn't from talking to people or from, certainly not from school or anything like that (retrospective interview, gay man now aged 35).

Thomas: I've talked to those who've been through school fairly recently still often pretend to have girlfriends and I think this has a negative effect on people's emotional development and relationships, it sort of curdles in a way, while heterosexual people are experimenting and playing around with relationships and friendships . . . most gay people are pretending and hiding and devaluing themselves and being gay's a certain amount of self-loathing, so that when eventually they come to start having relationships they haven't got this background and they've got to start experimenting and finding out about themselves, and it, it has a very negative effect on gay relationships generally (retrospective interview, gay man now aged 54).

As well as pressures to have sex, young gay men also come under a lot of pressure to conform to particular hegemonic gay male identities in order to fit into the scene. Most conform because they already feel out of place in heterosexual society and so are desperate to feel that they belong to a gay 'community'. A gay look also has the added advantage of being more readily recognized by other sexual dissidents in everyday hetero-normative spaces. Yet, some young gay men find these expectations oppressive. Barry, Mark and Jack describe the pressures on them to make the transition to very specific sexual identities.

Barry: [describing the pressures on the scene] I should get rid of the glasses and get a haircut and dye my hair blonde and go to the gym six times a week, and all stuff like that. But things are gonna be pretty boring if everybody did that and everybody looked the same (young gay man aged 24).

Mark: . . . sometimes I feel a bit out of the straight sort of community and sort of sometimes out of the gay community.

Interviewer: Is it worse to feel out of place in the gay community or the straight community?

Mark: Worse to feel out of the gay community, which means you sort of have to conform a little bit to what people expect, to what gay people expect of you.

Interviewer: What sort of pressures do you think you've come under from the gay community?

Mark: Mainly things like music taste, clothes taste, wanting to go out every single night – things like that. Just the way I act . . . people would, say, want me to conform . . . to gay identity or stereotype (young gay man, aged 19).

Jack: I've thought about since the way I, I dressed and sort of choices I make around clothes or made around clothes at the time [of coming out onto scene] and I think some of them, you know, I don't think I would have dressed like that if I was straight, I think I started dressing in ways that, that identified me as a gay man and it's about that time I guess when you start looking at other people and realizing that there are looks and there are gay men who look a certain way . . . I did make choices around the way I looked that marked me, I was gay and I think that's some of the time why I was surprised when people didn't realize I was [edit]. For me it was about wanting to fit in, yeah it was going out on the scene and looking at how people were looking and thinking right that's . . . that's how you need to look then if you're gay (retrospective interview, gay man aged 35).

The end result of these pressures is that the gay scene, rather than providing a supportive context for vulnerable young people, can actually reinforce or exacerbate low self-esteem, substance or alcohol abuse, and general patterns of self-destructive behaviour. Indeed, Adam *et al.* (2000) argue that for some gay men having unsafe sex can be a way of escaping negative feelings of sadness, loneliness or insecurity, while for others it can even become deliberately self-destructive, an indirect suicide attempt. Robbie describes such vulnerabilities:

Robbie: I think it [the scene] can be quite destructive for like young people who just like go out on the scene and maybe have low self-esteem . . . I'm talking from like personal experience as well, you sort of go out, you get dressed up and you want to pull somebody who's a bit nice and if you don't you get depressed. If you do you get depressed because you know it's sort of like just a sex thing and nothing else happens, nothing comes of it. It's very difficult to have a proper relationship and it's sort of self-feeding. 'Cos its like people who haven't sorted themselves would go to the scene to try and sort themselves out. It offers them the wrong sort of answers so they get more sort of fucked up or whatever, it's a vicious circle and it affects how you feel about yourself, you know, it affects your psychology . . . you're always going out and you're always expected to be like really up and bouncy and drunk, you know, all those sorts of things which is a lot of pressures on a young person when they've got internal pressure themselves, it's maybe not the safe space that, you know, it always says in lots of ways, you know (young gay man aged 22).

In contrast to gay men, lesbians are more likely to have their first sexual experience with someone of a similar age. Women have less casual sex than men (although this is on the increase) and instead commonly rush into serious relationships. As Lynne explains below, young women are often ill-prepared for such forced transitions, not only in terms of their sexual identity, but also in terms of the domestic and housing transitions that can accompany this:

Lynne: . . . women kind of step out onto the scene, being initiated into – I think what's lacking is a space where you can kind of do all the ordinary adolescent stuff that heterosexual adolescents get to do as part of growing up and as part of play and as part of finding yourselves. And I think if you are not heterosexual then you go from being a child to going straight into an adult world (lesbian aged 24).

The lesbian scene is sometimes likened to a pack of dominos: a new woman comes onto the scene and 'steals' someone else's partner, who in turn starts seeing someone else's girlfriend until in a domino effect most of the relationships have broken up and reformed into new couples. Not surprisingly, when many women start a relationship they often withdraw from the wider social scene in order to avoid these dynamics. However, domestic isolation also brings its own risks as young women in particular can be vulnerable to becoming 'trapped' in unhealthy relationships or situations of domestic violence. Often families or friends may be unaware of these closeted relationships because the women are fearful of coming out. As such, when things go wrong they have no one to turn to for help and support, being unable, for example, to reverse their housing transition in a way that is increasingly common for young people. This problem is compounded by the fact that public agencies (such as police, housing and counselling services) also commonly fail to recognize or respond to same-sex relationship problems. Lesbians, Cassie and Megan, and Peggy Morris, a housing officer, explain some of these issues:

> *Cassie*: I'd heard it said that if you go out on the scene a lot you get your partner pinched, that was all anybody used to say about the scene. It was very shallow and if you go out on the scene a lot you're asking for trouble . . . the last two or three months I've just seen so many women that are prepared to stab other people in the back, try and pinch your partners . . . and I don't, I'm not that keen on it really (a retrospective interview with a lesbian now aged 37).

> *Megan*: [describing a secret relationship she had with a violent woman who still stalks her] We were living in each other's pockets really and we spent all our time together . . . and we just used to fight all the time and one day it got really, really violent and we ended up, like I was hospital (lesbian aged 17).

> *Peggy Morris*: One of my . . . women [a lesbian client] that came, quite well dressed, well presented woman, went to various [housing] agencies and they wouldn't believe she was actually homosexual, she was a victim of domestic violence, her partner was bouncing her off the walls in their flat, so it's all about how you present (housing officer).

The lesbian community is often described as not only incestuous but also cliquey. Women's support groups are commonly dominated by those aged between 30 and 50 and as such are regarded as boring, stale and too politicized by younger women. There are very few social spaces provided specifically for young lesbians. A combination of cliqueyness, the relationship tensions described above and alcohol also mean that these venues can sometimes be violent places. Megan and Lynne explain some of these limitations for young lesbians:

> *Megan*: . . . there's nowhere to go . . . there's only three places that everybody [lesbians] goes to that I know of, you know what I mean? And it's like they're places my mum [who is also a lesbian] goes to, and, but I don't really want to go

there because it's not somewhere that a 17-year-old wants to go, you know what I mean? [Later she returned to a similar theme] . . . the gay scene isn't a very friendly place if you don't know anybody, if you're on your own and you don't know anybody it's not a friendly place because everybody has their gangs and if you don't know anybody, if you don't know anybody you're nobody and if you know the wrong people you're still nobody, you know what I mean, so you have to know the right people and you have to know the, that's, I don't like that about the gay, there's the in-group and then there's the, if you're not in the in-group you're no one [Edit] I don't like going out on the gay scene, it's like, well, one minute everybody'll be all smiles and nice and happy and then they'll go off and they'll be, come back, and it'll be a big row and then everybody'll be, wanna kick everybody's head in (young lesbian aged 17).

Lynne: [pub, name removed] was the first gay pub that I ever went to . . . and it's very kind of working class, very sort of butch-scary . . . women. And it felt relatively intimidating, relatively scary . . . I mean at 17 it was, you know, relatively threatening atmosphere . . . there was always violence and trouble and all those sorts of things . . . I mean it's funny because in one sense I did feel at home and in the other sense I didn't. It was a funny mixture really (young lesbian aged 24).

As the comments suggest, like other 'communities' the lesbian community – and the gay men's scene too – can be insular and exclusionary. As Young (1990) has argued, the very notion of community tends to privilege the ideal of unity over difference. In other words, communities are often predicated on one identity, for example sexuality, that becomes a single rallying point to the exclusion of other aspects of participants' multiple identities. In particular, groups often try to draw up boundaries to define those who are insiders (i.e. part of the community) from those who are not. Cornwall (1984: 53), for example, observes 'where there is belonging, there is also not belonging, and where there is in-clusion there is also ex-clusion'. The dark side of community is apparent in a dislike of difference and is often expressed in terms of outright prejudice and discrimination. This is evident in the attempts of lesbians in Sydney, Australia, to establish a community in the inner city (Taylor, 1998). Here, the desire of lesbian-identified transsexuals to participate in the 'Lesbian Space Project' provoked some women to argue that transsexuals should be excluded on the grounds that they are not 'real lesbians'. Rather than securing the boundaries of the lesbian community, these attempts at exclusion triggered hostilities between different community members, political realignments and ultimately the community's fragmentation.

Although, D/deaf[2] lesbians and gay men who took part in our study generally described the lesbian and gay community in very positive terms, young Christians and those identifying as bisexual were more critical. Ponse (1978) argues that bisexuals are paradoxical in lesbian and gay subculture, on the one hand occupying a legitimate position but on the other being stigmatized for maintaining heterosexual privileges. Robbie, a Christian, and Gareth, who identified as a bisexual man, explain their experiences of marginalization on the gay scene:

> *Robbie*: . . . the gay scene . . . is very exclusive [exclusionary] and I've had a lot of prejudice from the gay scene about being a Christian, things like that, and I don't think it allows people to just be . . . it is a lot harder to have a relationship in a way that's lasting as a gay person, not just because of the pressures which society puts on us but because of the pressures that are within the scene itself (young gay man, aged 22).

> *Gareth*: Bisexuals is actually a funny camp because, well straight people traditionally don't like it because they're gay but gay people sometimes – you get the gay people that don't like the straight people and they don't like bi's so often you get – I don't know, I've discovered an awful lot of bi's, a lot of them haven't – when you go to the LGB group [lesbian, gay and bisexual] everyone just assumes you're gay, sort of thing, and no-one ever clicks unless, well maybe if you ask directly, but no-one jumps up and says 'oh I'm bi' sort of thing. So a lot of people hide like that sort of thing 'cos they're not sure how – I know I did – well no I didn't, well yeah I did – I don't know, you're just assumed to be gay or lesbian really by a lot of people I think (young man aged 22).

Finally, the scene is also a potential space of risk for both young lesbians and gay men because the very act of going out at night to a lesbian or gay venue can expose sexual dissidents to the risk of homophobic violence (Herek and Berrill, 1992; Stanko and Curry, 1997). This is because being in a particular place or space, dressing in 'camp' ways for a night out or being with a partner or group of friends can all mark individuals' embodied identities as lesbian or gay. Victims of hate crimes are often fearful of reporting their experiences because they anticipate a hostile reception from the police, are afraid that if their case is prosecuted they will be 'outed' by the process of giving evidence in court and the publicity surrounding a trial, and because they may have been breaking a law (e.g. by having public sex, or sex under the age of consent) at the time when a crime was committed against them. As such, it is widely acknowledged that recorded incidents of crimes motivated by homophobia are grossly underestimated. This invisibility is sometimes used by the police to justify the lack of resources, training and time invested in monitoring and responding to the needs of the lesbian and gay community. In such ways, young lesbians and gay men can be alienated from this social agency. Aaron and Barry describe the risks of being visible as a gay man in public space:

> *Aaron*: I was out with my boyfriend one time early, early on, and we were just walking home, from, from a gay club and we got attacked in the street and my boyfriend had his ribs cracked and badly bruised nose really, and I got kicked but not, not as bad as he was (retrospective interview, gay man now aged 38).

> *Barry*: . . . it's like, oh God, who's looking at me, and all this, even going down the street. Because one of my friends . . . his best mate was up at Bradford two or three weeks ago tonight, in the afternoon, he got stabbed. I think he's still in intensive care, he's got a punctured lung (young gay man, aged 24).

As the quotations we have used in this section of our article clearly illustrate, the lesbian and gay community is not always the positive transitional space described in the first section of this article. Rather, it can be an environment where young people, particularly those confused about their sexuality and suffering from low self-esteem, can encounter numerous risks, including: unsafe sex, violence, substance abuse and various forms of exclusion. Social pressures in particular can precipitate young people into making premature transitions to a lesbian or gay sexual identity and can hasten or complicate traditional domestic and housing transitions. Having come out, this, and other transitions, are not necessarily as reversible for lesbians and gay men as they are for heterosexual young people.

The scene as a paradoxical space

The material presented in this article contributes both to the youth transitions literature and to the geography and urban studies literatures on the lesbian and gay scene. It has addressed the neglect of lesbian and gay transition experiences within the interdisciplinary literature on youth, and in doing so has expanded the traditional focus on school-to-work, housing and domestic transitions by looking at coming out on the scene as an alternative form of transition to an independent adult identity. Effectively, therefore, it has also spatialized the transitions literature by highlighting the role of urban space in this process.

The alternative form of social commitment offered by the lesbian and gay scene challenges notions of 'normal' development and passive dependence on the family that are implicit in many of the traditional debates about transitions. Unlike the conventional markers of adulthood that are usually based on visible events, such as starting work or getting married, transitions to an adult lesbian or gay sexual identity on the scene are more intangible, gradual and based on individuals appropriating the power to determine their own identities, rather than being something that is conferred on young people by wider society. The traditional model of youth transitions has often assumed an age-related linear model of progress as young people move from one state to another in which negative outcomes are regarded as failed transitions. Yet, as this article has shown, the transition to an adult lesbian and gay sexual identity can be more complex than that. Young people can both demonstrate maturity and independence in some aspects of coming out on the scene, such as developing self-confidence and a clear sense of their own identity and so on, yet still make dangerous choices such as being coerced into unsafe sex. The transition to a lesbian or gay sexual identity can also be forced by social pressures on the scene, and inflected by other social differences such as gender and class. Yet young lesbians and gay men can have fewer options to reverse their transitions than heterosexual young people. These findings therefore highlight the need to recognize young people's resilience and agency in negotiating transitions to adulthood, rather than assuming positive or negative outcomes to a linear model.

This article contributes to geography and urban studies literatures by challenging traditional representations of the city as a space of social and sexual liberation. The evidence of this article is that the scene can play a paradoxical role in lesbian and gay men's lives. Spatial metaphors such as inside and outside and centre and margin are frequently employed by social scientists to describe social relations. Yet such positions do not represent marked or differentiated positions. Rather, Rose (1993: 140) argues that paradoxically we can simultaneously occupy space that would be mutually exclusive if charted on a two dimensional map – centre and margin, inside and outside space. The lesbian and gay scene represents just such a paradoxical space for young lesbians and gay men. On the one hand, it can be a positive, liberating and supportive space that offers a sense of identity, community and belonging. On the other hand, it can simultaneously be a site of danger where young lesbians and gay men can encounter a range of social risks and be subject to abusive relationships and social exclusion. Vulnerable social groups are not just marginalized/oppressed, but can also marginalize and oppress each other.

While issues surrounding alcohol, drugs and violence are recognized within lesbian and gay communities, there is often a reluctance to acknowledge them publicy for fear that this information might be used to justify the regulation or closure of scene venues. Yet these problems are largely invisible to mainstream hetero-normative social agencies and institutions and so go unacknowledged or addressed by them.

The complex roles that lesbian and gay communities play in young people's lives – as both sources of support and of risk – therefore have important urban policy implications (see also Valentine *et al.*, 2002). Notably, there is a need to build on the positive aspects of urban scenes by providing more funding for specific spaces for young lesbians and gay men where specialist youth workers can create opportunities for young people to develop and explore their sexualities in environments that are free from some of the sexual and social pressures of the general scene. At the same time, more out-reach work by health promotion and alcohol and drugs counsellors is needed on the scene in order to educate young people about its dangers and support those in crisis. More generally, there is a need to educate the social agencies and institutions that support young people's conventional school-to-work, domestic and housing transitions about the specific experiences of lesbians and gay men so that their needs might be more effectively met.

Notes

*   We acknowledge the support of the Economic and Research Council for funding the research (award no: L134251032) on which these findings are based as part of the Youth, Citizenship and Social Change Programme. Gill Valentine is also very grateful for a Philip Leverhulme Prize that enabled her to work on this publication. We are very grateful to all those who took part in the research described here for their time and commitment to the aims of the project. We also wish to thank Sally McNamee and Carol Devanney who were employed as research assistants at different times.
1   The names of all those quoted, and the people and places referred to in these quotations, have been changed or removed in an effort to protect their anonymity and confidentiality.
2   We use the term D/deaf in this way to indicate that there are two meanings, interpretations and processes of identity at play here. Although these terms are contested, the broad consensus is that deaf is used to imply a medical description/ definition of deafness measured against the norm of hearing people. This is commonly used by deaf people who do not have a strong deaf identity and do not use sign language as a first language but prefer oral styles of communication (e.g. lip reading, speaking). Deaf is linked to a more politicized sense of identity, one predicated on the use of sign language. The boundary between the two forms of identification is fluid. Some individuals may define themselves differently as either Deaf or deaf in different spaces.

References

Adam, B.D., A. Sears and E.G. Schellenberg (2000) Accounting for unsafe sex: interviews with men who have sex with men. *The Journal of Sex Research* 37.1, 24–36.

Adler, S. and J. Brenner (1992) Gender and space: lesbians and gay men in the city. *International Journal of Urban and Regional Research* 16, 24–34.

Allatt, P. (1997) Conceptualising youth: transitions, risk and the public and the private. In J. Bynner, L. Chisholm and A. Furlong (eds.), *Youth, citizenship and social change in a European context*, Ashgate, Hants.

Anderson, B. (1983) *Imagined communities: reflections on the origin and spread of nationalism.* Verso, London.

Barth, F. (1981) *Process and form in social life: selected essays of Fredrik Barth, vol 1.* Routledge Kegan Paul, London.

Bech, H. (1997) *When men meet: homosexuality and modernity.* Chicago University Press, Chicago.

Beck, U. (1992) *Risk society.* Sage, London.

—— and E. Beck-Gernsheim (2002) *Individualization.* Sage, London.

Binnie, J. (1995) Trading places: consumption, sexuality and the production of Queer space. In D. Bell and G. Valentine (eds.), *Mapping desire: geographies of sexualities*, Routledge, London.

Brown, M. (2000) *Closet space: geographies of metaphor from the body to the globe.* Routledge, London.

Buckland, F. (2002) *Impossible dance.* Wesleyan University Press, Middletown, CT.

Castells (1983) *The city and the grassroots.* University of California Press, Berkeley, CA.

Chauncey, G. (1995) *Gay New York: the making of the gay world 1890–1940.* Flamingo, London.

Chisholm, L. and M. Du Bois-Reymond (1993) Youth transitions: gender and social change. *Sociology* 27, 259–80.

Coles, B. (1997) Welfare services for young people. In J. Roche and S. Tucker (eds.), *Youth in society: contemporary theory: policy and practice*, Sage, London.

Cornwall, J. (1984) *Hard-earned lives: accounts of health and illness from East London.* Tavistock, London.

Cresswell, T. (1996) *In place/out of place.* University of Minnesota Press, London.

D'Augelli, A., S. Hershberger and N. Pilkington (1998) Lesbian, gay and bisexual youth and their families: disclosure of sexual orientation and its consequences. *American Journal of Orthopsychiatry* 68, 361–71.

Du Bois-Reymond, M. (1998) I don't want to commit myself yet: young people's life concepts. *Journal of Youth Studies* 1, 63–79.

Elizur, Y. and M. Ziv (2001) Family support and acceptance, gay male identity formation and psychological adjustment: a path model. *Family Process* 40.2, 125–44.

Elwood, S. (2000) Lesbian living spaces: multiple meanings of home. *Journal of Lesbian Studies* 4, 11–28.

Epstein, D. and R. Johnson (1994) On the straight and narrow: the heterosexual presumption, homophobia and schools. In D. Epstein (ed.), *Challenging lesbian and gay inequalities in education*, Open University Press, Buckingham.

—— and R. Johnson (1998) *Schooling sexualities*. Open University Press, Buckingham.

—— (1992) *Transformation of intimacy*. Polity Press, Cambridge.

Harris, D. (1997) *The rise and fall of gay culture*. Hyperion, New York.

Herek, G. and K. Berill (1992) *Hate crimes: confronting violence against lesbians and gay men*. Sage, London.

Heron, L. (ed.) (1983) *Streets of desire: women's fiction in the twentieth century*. Virago, London.

Jackson, P. (2001) Coding. In M. Limb and C. Dwyer (eds.), *Qualitative methodologies for geographers*, Arnold, London.

Johnston, L. (1997) Queen(s') street or Ponsonby poofters: the embodied HERO parade site. *New Zealand Geographer* 53, 29–33.

—— and G. Valentine (1995) Wherever I lay my girlfriend, that's my home: the performance and surveillance of lesbian identities in domestic environments. In D. Bell and G. Valentine (eds.), *Mapping desire: geographies of sexualities*, London, Routledge.

Knopp, L. (1992) Sexuality and the spatial dynamics of capitalism. *Environment and Planning D: Society and Space* 10, 651–69.

—— (1998) Sexuality and urban space: gay male identity politics in the United States, the United Kingdom and Australia. In R. Fincher and J. Jacobs (eds.), *Cities of difference*, Guildford, London.

Kruger, H.-H. (1988) Geschichte und Perspektiven der Jugendforschung. In H.-H. Kruger (ed.), *Handbuch der Jugendforschung*, Opladen, Leske and Budrich, Munich.

Lauria, M. and L. Knopp (1985) Towards an analysis of the role of gay communities in the urban renaissance. *Urban Geography* 6, 152–69.

Malbon, B. (1999) *Clubbing: dancing, ecstasy and vitality*. Routledge, London.

Massachusetts Department of Education (1995) *Massachusetts high school students and sexual orientation: Results of the 1995 youth-risk behaviour survey*.

Morrow, V. and M. Richards (1996) *Transitions to adulthood: a family matter?* Joseph Rowntree Foundation and YPS, York.

Mort, F. (1995) Archaeologies of city life: commercial culture, masculinity and spatial relations in 1980s London. *Environment and Planning D: Society and Space* 13, 573–90.

Myslik, W. (1996) Renegotiating the social/sexual identities of place: gay communities as safe havens or sites of resistance. In N. Duncan (ed.), *BodySpace: destabilising geographies of gender and sexuality*, Routledge, London.

Peake, L. (1993) Race and sexuality: challenging the patriarchal structuring of urban social space. *Environment and Planning D: Society and Space* 11, 415–32.

Ponse, B. (1978) *Identities in the lesbian world: the social construction of self*. Connecticut, Greenwood.

Quilley, S. (1995) Manchester's 'village in the city': the gay vernacular in a post-industrial landscape of power. *Transgressions: A Journal of Urban Exploration* 1, 36–50.

Rivers, I. (2001) The bullying of sexual minorities at school: its nature and long-term correlates. *Educational and Child Psychology* 18.1, 32–46.

—— and N. Duncan (2002) Understanding homophobic bullying in schools. *Youth and Policy* 75, 330–41.

Rose, G. (1993) *Feminism and geography*. Polity Press, Cambridge.

Rothenberg, T. (1995) And she told two friends: lesbians creating urban social space. In D. Bell and G. Valentine (eds.), *Mapping desire: geographies of sexualities*, Routledge, London.

Savin-Williams, R.C. (1989) Coming out to parents and self-esteem among gay and lesbian youths. *Journal of Homosexuality* 18, 1–35.

Shakespeare, T. (1996) Power and prejudice: issues of gender, sexuality and disability. In L. Barton (ed.), *Disability and society: emerging issues and insights*, Longman, London.

Skelton, T. (2002) Research on youth transitions: some critical interventions. In M. Cieslik and G. Pollock (eds.), *Young people in risk society*, Ashgate, Hants.

Stanko, E.A. and P. Curry (1997) Homophobic violence and the self 'at risk': interrogating the boundaries. *Social and Legal Studies* 6, 513–32.

Strauss, A. (1987) *Qualitative analysis for social scientists*. Cambridge University Press, Cambridge.

Taylor, A. (1998) Lesbian space: more than one imagined territory. In R. Ainley (ed.), *New frontiers of space, bodies and gender*, Routledge, London.

Valentine, G. (1993) (Hetero)sexing space: lesbian perceptions and experiences of everyday spaces. *Environment and Planning D: Society and Space* 11, 395–413.

—— (1995a) Out and about: a geography of lesbian communities. *International Journal of Urban and Regional Research* 19, 96–111.

—— (1995b) Creating transgressive space: the music of k d lang. *Transactions of the Institute of British Geographers* 20, 474–485.

——, T. Skelton and R. Butler (2002) The vulnerability and marginalisation of lesbian and gay youth. *Youth and Policy: The Journal of Critical Analysis* 75, 4–29.

——, T. Skelton and R. Butler (2003) Coming out and out-comes: negotiating lesbian and gay identities with/in the family *Environment and Planning D: Society and Space* (forthcoming).

Walkowitz, J. (1992) *City of dreadful delight*. Virago, London.

Weightman, B. (1980) Gay bars as private places. *Landscape* 24, 9–16.

Weston, K. (1995) Get thee to a big city: sexual imaginary and the great gay migration. *GLQ: A Journal of Lesbian and Gay Studies* 2, 253–77.

Whittle, S. (ed.) (1994) *The margins of the city: gay men's urban lives*. Ashgate, Aldershot.

Wilson, E. (1991) *The sphinx in the city*. Virago, London.

Young, I.M. (1990) The ideal of community and the politics of difference. In L.J. Nicholson (ed.), *Feminism/postmodernism*, Routledge, London.

Queer public finance

I T IS INTERESTING TO STUDY how the legal and political system intersects with the market system. This section defines public finance very broadly to encompass not only those issues in which the government has a clear fiscal stake but also issues where the public fiscal aspects are less clear on the surface and where legal changes would indeed have redistributional effects – whether between queer and straights, or the government and private individuals – that would necessitate additional government action and thus, generally, governmental expenditure.

The current US legal structure pays very minimal attention to issues relating to sexual orientation. It is not yet illegal in much of the US to discriminate on the basis of sexual orientation, though it is illegal for the federal government to do so, 17 states and well over a hundred local governments (counties and cities) have passed antidiscrimination laws, and many organizations have stated that they will not do so (Ayres and Brown 2005; Lambda Legal Defense and Education Fund). The topic is slowly coming to the forefront in Europe as well (Waaldijk and Bonini-Baraldi 2006).

As pressing as employment discrimination and other forms of discrimination are for the queer community, the current "hot button" issue is the status of queer marriage and/or civil union. Battles are currently occurring in many if not all of the US states regarding whether there will be passage of a law explicitly banning same-sex union, or passage of a law explicitly allowing it. Much of the debate in these battles has centered on different people's moral considerations regarding the role of marriage both in religious systems and in society (Chauncey 2005).

Economists and some other social scientists, on the other hand, have asked a different, more pragmatic question: what would be the economic effects, both positive and negative, of legalizing same-sex marriages? And who would experience these effects? For instance, would same-sex couples then qualify for a similar level of marriage subsidy through the governmental tax and benefit system as that received by many married couples? To the extent that many of these benefits accrue only to single-earner families rather than dual-earner families, how would that affect same-sex couples if their household division of labor tends to be different than that of current married couples?

In the first chapter in this section, "Wedding bell blues: the income tax consequences of legalizing same-sex marriage" (2000), economists James Alm, M. V. Lee Badgett, and Leslie Whittington, ask and answer that very question. It turns out that because of the prevalence of dual-earner couples among same-sex couples, the extrapolated figures show that the government could realize significant additional income tax revenues if they were indeed to legalize gay marriage. This type of analysis is the kind of counterintuitive thinking that economists excel at, and it is helpful to have these types of figures to understand the financial repercussions on both the government and individuals of making legal changes.

Of course tax consequences are only one part, though perhaps the most easily calculated, of the financial considerations related to legal same-sex marriage. The second chapter, "What if? The legal consequences of marriage and the legal needs of lesbian and gay male couples" (1996), by law professor David Chambers, provides a thorough overview of the legal and related financial issues of institutionalizing same-sex marriage as a legal contract. Chambers summarizes the legal aspects of (heterosexual) marriage in the US relating to such financial matters as division of property, inheritance, and adoption. It is important to consider these various details even if one either supports or opposes same-sex marriage on moral grounds, as working out the details can lead to a better match of policy to people's needs regardless of whether one supports same-sex marriage, same-sex legal partnerships as differentiated from marriage, or a revision of the current heterosexual marriage statutes in favor of legal partnerships for both same-sex and heterosexual couples.

Other economists have focused on other parts of the financial calculation of the effects of either full same-sex marriage or partial expansion of partnership rights (Bennett and Gates 2004a, 2004b). For instance, Ash and Badgett (2006) verify that people with unmarried partners are much less likely to have health insurance than married people, controlling for other factors, and calculate that the number of such uninsured would be cut by as much as half if universal partner coverage were made available.

While economists have mainly focused on direct monetary benefits and costs of expanding same-sex marriage or partnership (Badgett 2001), one interesting paper (Dee 2007) also considers how gay marriage might affect the prevalence of sexually transmitted infections, with results in the paper showing some evidence of reductions in European nations with same-sex partnership recognition in syphilis rates, and possible smaller reductions in gonorrhea and HIV infection rates. As another interesting extension of the discussion of the effects of same-sex legal unions, Binnie (1997) and Bailey (2004) consider the effects of legal structures on transnational migration of gays and lesbians.

While much of the focus of existing studies, as well as current policy interest, has been on same-sex marriage and/or partnership legislation and benefits, other topics occur as well in the queer economics of public finance. Marieka Klawitter and co-authors have considered the spread and "contagion" aspects of state and local antidiscrimination policies (Klawitter and Flatt 1998; Klawitter and Hammer 1999). Riggle and Tadlock (1999) document the increase in gay and lesbian political awareness and strength, while Warner (2000) questions the "normalization" of the queer agenda in political life.

A number of research and policy institutes are taking an active interest in the political status of same-sex marriage, but generally have a wider agenda encompassing many other public issues (Human Rights Campaign; the International Gay and Lesbian Human Rights Commission; Lambda Legal Defense and Education Fund; the National Gay and Lesbian Task Force; Research Centre for Law, Gender, and Sexuality; the Williams Institute – note that the Institute for Gay and Lesbian Strategic Studies has now merged forces with the Williams Institute). For example, the Independent Gay Forum has a number of thought-provoking short opinion pieces by a variety of writers on political, economic, and cultural topics. Queers for Economic Justice focuses on a number of projects, including currently immigrant rights, shelters, and welfare/poverty, while the Safe Schools Coalition seeks to promote lesbian, gay, bisexual, and transgender tolerance and acceptance in the educational system. In general, the research and policy institutes for queer issues both disseminate information and engage in advocacy. As such, they in general are prime examples of the linkages between social science research and social and economic policy.

DISCUSSION QUESTIONS

1   How is the national legalization of same-sex marriages projected to affect tax collections?
2   What advantages are there for queers if they were permitted to marry legally? What are the disadvantages?
3   What advantages are there for the society at large if same-sex marriage is legalized? What are the disadvantages?
4   What is the distinction between economic and ethical reasons for either allowing or disallowing same-sex marriage? What are the reasons you can think of?
5   What do you see as the next "hot button" item related to sexual orientation after same-sex marriage?

REFERENCES

Ash, M. A. and Badgett, M. V. L. (2006) "Separate and unequal: the effect of unequal access to employment-based health insurance on same-sex and unmarried different-sex couples," *Contemporary Economic Policy*, 24: 582–99.
Ayres, I. and Brown, J. G. (2005) "Privatizing gay rights with non-discrimination promises instead of policies," *The Economists Voice*, 2: 1–9.
Badgett, M. V. L. (2001) *Money, Myths, and Change: the economic lives of lesbians and gay men*, Chicago and London: University of Chicago Press.

Bailey, M. J. (2004) "Migration of the same-sex family," Queen's University Law and Economics Paper no. 2004–05.

Bennett, L. and Gates, G. J. (2004a) "The cost of marriage inequality to children and their same-sex parents," Human Rights Campaign Foundation Report (online), Washington, DC: Human Rights Campaign.

—— (2004b) "The cost of marriage inequality to gay, lesbian and bisexual seniors," Human Rights Campaign Foundation Report (online), Washington, DC: Human Rights Campaign.

Binnie, J. (1997) "Invisible Europeans: sexual citizenship in the new Europe," Environment & Planning, 29: 237–48.

Chauncey, G. (2005) Why Marriage? The history shaping today's debate over gay equality, New York: Basic Books.

Dee, T. (2007) "Forsaking all others? the effects of 'gay marriage' on risky sex," Economic Journal, 00: 000–00.

Human Rights Campaign, <http://www.hrc.org/>.

Independent Gay Forum, <http://www.indegayforum.org/>.

International Gay and Lesbian Human Rights Commission, <http://www.iglhrc.org/>.

Klawitter, M. and Flatt, V. (1998) "The effects of state and local antidiscrimination policies on earnings for gays and lesbians," Journal of Policy Analysis & Management, 17: 658–86.

Klawitter, M. and Hammer, B. (1999) "Spatial and temporal diffusion of local antidiscrimination policies for sexual orientation," in E. D. B. Riggle and B. L. Tadlock (eds) Gays and Lesbians in the Democratic Process: public policy, public opinion, and political representation, New York: Columbia University Press.

Lambda Legal Defense and Education Fund, <http://www.lambdalegal.org/>.

National Gay and Lesbian Task Force, <http://www.thetaskforce.org/>.

Queers for Economic Justice, <http://queersforeconomicjustice.org/>.

Research Centre for Law, Gender, and Sexuality, <http://www.kent.ac.uk/clgs/index.html/>.

Riggle, E. D. B. and Tadlock, B. L. (eds) (1999) Gays and Lesbians in the Democratic Process: public policy, public opinion, and political representation, New York: Columbia University Press.

Safe Schools Coalition, <http://www.safeschoolscoalition.org/>.

Waaldijk, K. and Bonini-Baraldi, M. (2006) Sexual Orientation Discrimination in the European Union: national laws and the employment equality directive, The Hague, Netherlands: T. M. C. Asser Press.

Warner, M. (2000) The Trouble with Normal: sex, politics, and the ethics of queer life, Cambridge, Mass.: Harvard University Press.

Williams Institute, <http://www.law.ucla.edu/williamsinstitute/home.html/>.

Chapter 21

James Alm, M. V. Lee Badgett, and Leslie A. Whittington

WEDDING BELL BLUES: THE INCOME TAX CONSEQUENCES OF LEGALIZING SAME-SEX MARRIAGE

From *National Tax Journal* 2000, 53 (2): 201–14

Introduction

IN THE LAST SEVERAL decades, gays and lesbians have worked diligently to be accepted into all aspects of mainstream American life, with major efforts in addressing employment discrimination, housing access, medical treatment, partner benefits, adoption, and political representation. Recently, many of these efforts have centered on winning the right to marry, and same-sex couples have gone to court in several states seeking this legal right[1] The Hawaii Supreme Court and an Alaskan Superior Court have each ruled that the state must meet the most demanding constitutional test in order to limit marriage to opposite-sex couples: there must be a compelling state interest to limit marriage, and the policy must be narrowly tailored to meet that compelling interest (Baehr v. Lewin, 74 Haw. 530, 582 P. 2d 44 (1993) and Brause v. Alaska, Alaska Super. Ct.) A lower level court in Hawaii found that the law did not meet this standard (*Baehr v. Miike*, 1996), and ruled that same-sex couples should be allowed to marry. This decision was recently ruled moot by the Hawaii Supreme Court as a result of a state constitutional amendment allowing the legislature to limit marriage to opposite-sex couples (*Baehr v. Miike*, Hawaii Supreme Court, December 9, 1999). However, the Vermont Supreme Court has determined that same-sex couples must be allowed the same marital benefits as opposite-sex couples, and has directed the state legislature to determine whether this should occur through marriage or formalized domestic partnership (Baker v. Vermont, December 20, 1999).

The prospect of same-sex couples traveling to other states to marry and then returning to their home states to live as married couples prompted policymakers in Congress and in many states to react. At the federal level, President Clinton signed the Defense of Marriage Act (DOMA) in 1996, which defined "marriage" in federal law as related only to opposite-sex couples and which allowed states to refuse to recognize same-sex marriages contracted in other states. At the state level, some states have passed legislation that would deny recognition of out-of-state marriages.

Swirling around the legal and legislative debates are many unresolved – and perhaps unresolvable – controversies, regarding such issues as the definition of marriage, the meaning of family, the notion of morality, the right of privacy, the influence of religion, and the scope of civil rights, as well as appropriate government policies toward all of these issues. In addition to these normative issues, policymakers and judges have also raised economic issues related to marriage. Most of the policy attention has been on the added costs imposed upon the state and federal governments from same-sex marriages. For example, during the debate on DOMA various senators and representatives used higher projected costs from same-sex marriages as an argument in favor of the bill.[2] Attorneys for the State of Vermont have argued that same-sex marriages would result in increased court costs related to child custody and visitation disputes.[3] In *Baehr v. Lewin*, the Hawaii Supreme Court has enumerated fourteen ways in which same-sex couples could benefit from tax breaks and other legal benefits.

However, little attention has been paid to the potential economic benefits to federal and state governments.[4] Prominent among these benefits is the impact on government tax collections. It is well-known that a couple's joint income tax burden can change with marriage in the United States. For many couples, their taxes when married are more than their combined tax liabilities as single filers, so that they pay a *marriage tax*. Many other couples receive *a marriage subsidy* because their joint taxes fall with marriage. Although estimates of the percentage of couples paying a marriage tax or receiving a marriage subsidy vary somewhat, as do estimates of the dollar magnitude of the marriage tax/subsidy, the best recent estimates indicate that perhaps one-half or more of all married couples pay an average federal marriage tax of nearly $1,400, while most other married couples receive a marriage subsidy of a slightly smaller amount (Rosen, 1987; Feenberg and Rosen, 1995; Alm and Whittington, 1996; and Congressional Budget Office, 1997). Families more likely to incur a marriage tax include those that have children, that are older, that have higher income, and that are white, while families more likely to receive a marriage subsidy have the opposite characteristics. Of particular relevance: families with two earners generally pay a marriage tax, while families with a single earner almost certainly receive a marriage subsidy. As we argue later, theory and evidence suggest that same-sex couples are likely to be two-earner couples. This in turn suggests that legalizing same-sex marriage is likely to generate additional income tax revenues. However, the magnitude of this tax windfall is unknown.

In this paper we estimate the federal individual income tax effects of allowing same-sex marriages in the U.S.[5] Admittedly, generating these estimates is a somewhat precarious exercise. The lack of data makes any precise determination of the numbers and the characteristics of gay and lesbian couples virtually impossible. We therefore use various estimates on the size of the homosexual population, the percent of this population in same-sex relationships, the percent who would marry if same-sex marriage became legal, and the average incomes of these couples, in order to generate estimates of the revenue impact. Where several alternative sources are available, we choose estimates from random population surveys rather than what might be termed "convenience samples" (or nonrandom samples drawn mainly for the convenience of the researcher), in order to derive estimates with more statistical validity; we also generally choose sources that generate lower rather than higher estimates of the revenue impact, in order to calculate relatively conservative measures of the impact. Even so, our estimates indicate that legalizing same-sex marriages would lead to an annual increase in federal government income taxes of between $0.3 billion and $1.3 billion, with the likely impact toward the higher range of the estimates.

The income tax treatment of married couples in the United States[6]

The individual income tax was established in 1913, and its treatment of the family has varied over time. In its early years, the basic unit of taxation was the individual, in which each individual was taxed on the basis of his or her income independently of marital status. Because the tax liability did not change much with marriage, the income tax was largely marriage neutral. However, the Revenue Act of 1948 changed the unit of taxation from the individual to the family. With the adoption of income splitting for married couples, couples were now allowed to aggregate and to divide in half their income for federal tax purposes. This change meant that couples with equal incomes paid equal taxes; that is, the income tax became consistent with the goal of *horizontal equity across families*. However, because of the progressive tax rates in the income tax, the change also meant that a couple's joint tax liability could fall when they married, so that the income tax was not characterized by *marriage neutrality*.

It was not until the Tax Reform Act of 1969 that a widespread and significant marriage penalty was created for many married couples, even though a potential marriage subsidy still existed for some couples. Since then, various tax and demographic changes have markedly affected the potential for a marriage penalty or subsidy, as well as the magnitude of each (Alm and Whittington, 1996).

The reason for the lack of marriage neutrality under current law is simple to explain. Married couples effectively split their income on tax returns. If two people marry and one of them has zero income, income splitting means that the individual with some income moves into a lower marginal tax bracket as a result of the marriage, so that the marriage reduces the combined tax burdens of the two partners. Conversely, when people with similar earnings marry, their combined income pushes the couple into higher tax brackets than they face as singles, and they pay correspondingly higher taxes with marriage.[7] Of course, the magnitude of the tax/subsidy depends upon an array of tax features, such as exemptions, deductions, and rate schedules, as well as the incomes and other character-istics of the partners.[8] Note, however, that the marriage tax/subsidy is not a statutory item in the tax code. Rather, it is a side effect of the current structure of the individual income tax, one that emerges because of the combination of progressive marginal tax rates and the family as the unit of taxation.

The magnitude of the marriage tax/subsidy can be quite large. For example, Alm and Whittington (1996) estimate that there is, on average, a marriage tax whose magnitude since 1969 has risen, fallen, and, more recently, risen, and in the last several years has averaged roughly $400 (in real 1997 dollars). However, this overall average conceals a great deal of variation. The percentage of families that pay a penalty has risen since 1969, to nearly 60 percent in recent years; for these families the real average penalty has generally exceeded $1000 for most of the last twenty years. On the other hand, for those families that receive a subsidy the average subsidy over this period has also typically exceeded $1000, and the percentage of families receiving a subsidy has fallen over time to less than 30 percent.[9]

It is now widely understood that no progressive tax system can simul-taneously ensure that couples with equal income pay equal taxes and that a couple's joint tax liability does not change with marriage (Rosen, 1977). Whether by implicit or explicit choice, the U.S. has elected to focus more on the first goal, with its designation of the family as the unit of taxation. By necessity, then, it has elected to allow taxes to change with marriage. The next section presents our approach to measuring these changes for same-sex couples.

Assumptions, methods, and data

Calculating the marriage tax/subsidy for heterosexual unions is challenging, and there are numerous algorithums for these calculations (Whittington, 1999) Calculating the tax consequences for homosexual households is far more difficult. The number of gay and lesbian individuals in the overall population is a hotly debated issue, with estimates sometimes driven by the perceived political advantage of over- or underestimating the homosexual population. The number of gays and lesbians in partnerships is also uncertain, as is the number who would marry if legal marriage became an option. Perhaps most contentious is the income of gays and lesbians: are gay people a disadvantaged group, suffering wage discrimination because of their sexual orientation, or do they earn more than heterosexuals?[10] Indeed, the precise definition of who is homosexual is not without controversy.

In this work we focus on estimates drawn from random samples of the U.S. population, mainly the National Health and Social Life Survey (NHSLS) and the General Social Survey (GSS). Although there are wide ranging estimates of, for example, the number of gays and lesbians in the U.S. adult population, many of these estimates are drawn from "convenience samples," surveys that are nonrandom and so are likely biased. Accordingly, where several sources are available, we rely upon numbers from random population surveys, in order to generate estimates with more statistical validity. However, given the reluctance of many to discuss behavior that they may feel is not approved of by society, estimates drawn from random sample surveys may be conservative (Laumann, Gagmon, Michael, and Michaels, 1994). We therefore examine, at various points, the impact of some variations in our basic assumptions. Our basic assumptions, and the data sources behind them, are summarized in Tables 1 and 2.

A crucial issue in the existence and the magnitude of the marriage tax/subsidy is the incomes of partners in same-sex households. We first present theory and evidence on the likely incomes of these households. We then discuss the specific steps and the data for our algorithm.

Theory and evidence on same-sex couples

If a same-sex couple includes two earners rather than only one, their income tax payments will likely increase if their marriage is legally recognized. Both economic theory and empirical evidence suggest that same-sex couples will have two earners.

The Becker (1991) model of household time allocation shows that an efficient household will use the principle of comparative advantage to assign members to either household or market production in order to maximize the household's production of consumption goods. For an

Table 1 Potential size of the married gay and lesbian population

Characteristics	Males	Females
U.S. population aged 18 and over	95,372,000	102,736,000
Percent of population that is homosexual	2.8	1.4
Percent in cohabiting same-sex relationships	26	28
Estimated number of homosexual married couples	347,154	201,363

Data Sources:

Estimates of the *U.S. Population Aged 18 and Over* are from the US Bureau of the Census.

Estimates of the *Percent of Population that is Homosexual* are from Laumann, Gagnon, Michael, and Michaels (1994).

Estimates of the *Percent in Cohabiting Same-Sex Relationships* are from Klatwitter and Flatt (1998).

The *Estimated Number of Homosexual Married Couples* is calculated by multiplying the *U.S. Population Aged 18 and Over* by the *Percent of Population that is Homosexual* by the *Percent in Cohabiting Same-Sex Relationships*, and then dividing by two.

opposite-sex couple, Becker argues that women have a comparative advantage in home production and men an advantage in market production because of wage discrimination against women and a female biological advantage in child rearing. This combination leads to fairly strict specialization, with only one earner per household in opposite-sex couples. In contrast, Becker assumes that homosexual unions do not result in children and that wage discrimination based on sex reduces differences in potential earnings for same-sex couples. Consequently, his model predicts less specialization by same-sex couples and therefore more two-earner couples.

Using a somewhat different approach, Badgett (1995a) suggests that members of same-sex couples have different norms about work and that they tend to expect their partners to work. She further argues that gay and lesbian couples do not have access to legal institutions that facilitate specialization (e.g., marriage). Both factors reduce specialization by same-sex couples, and thereby increase the likelihood that both members of a same-sex couple will be earners.[11]

The most direct support for the prediction that same-sex couples are likely to include two earners comes from the 1990 Census of Population (Klawitter, 1995). In 1990, the census forms allowed individuals to report that they were the "unmarried partner" of the householder (or the household reference person), allowing comparisons between married couples, cohabiting opposite-sex couples, and same-sex couples. In 59 percent of male same-sex couples and 51 percent of female same-sex couples, both partners worked between 41 and 52 weeks in 1989; only 37 percent of

Table 2 Average income estimates for men and women (in 1997 dollars)

Group	Annual income estimate
1996 CPS data: Women (aged 18 and over)	
All women	19,391
Married women	19,589
Single women	17,339
Married women who work	24,157
Single women who work	19,128
1996 CPS data: Men (aged 18 and over)	
All men	34,809
Married men	41,395
Single men	20,459
Married men who work	46,303
Single men who work	21,868
Estimates of Homosexual Female Income[a]	
Badgett (1995b)	19,287
Klawitter and Flatt (1998):	
Individual earnings	22,414
½ of household income	28,929
Out/Look (1988)	26,580–31,896
The Partners Task Force (1988)	19,936–33,225
Teichner (1989)	33,730
Estimates of Homosexual Male Income	
Badgett (1995b)	33,717
Klawitter and Flatt (1998):	
Individual Earnings	29,487
½ of Household Income	37,383
Out/Look (1988)	33,226–38,541
The Partners' Task Force (1988)	33,226–53,160
Teichner (1989)	37,314

[a] The Badgett (1995b) income estimates are for full-time, year-round workers. The Klawitter and Flatt (1998) income estimates are for individuals with personal income greater than 0, and also for one-half of total household income for same-sex cohabiting couples. Other incomes are individual averages regardless of employment status.

married couples had similar full-year (or almost full-year) work patterns. Comparing hours worked per week tells a similar story. Both partners worked more than 30 hours per week in 71 percent of dual-earner gay couples and 59 percent of lesbian couples. In only 41 percent of comparable married couples did both partners exhibit this same work pattern.

Blumstein and Schwartz (1983) find a similar pattern in the late 1970s and early 1980s, even though their study is not based on a random sample of couples. Evidence of strict specialization between the home and market is again far stronger for married couples than for same-sex couples. They find that 86 percent of married men but only 38 percent of married women work full-time. In contrast, 69 percent of lesbians worked full-time, and only a small number stayed at home full-time. Virtually no men performed housework full-time.

In sum, both studies clearly indicate that same-sex couples specialize less between home and market, suggesting that these households are likely to have two earners.

Data and methods

We follow several steps in our calculations. **First**, we need estimates of the percent of the U.S. population that is homosexual. Estimates of the overall population are from the U.S. Bureau of the Census. The earliest estimates of the prevalence of male and female homosexuality in the U.S. were made by the Kinsey Institute (Kinsey, Pomeroy, and Martin, 1948, 1953).[12] The Kinsey Institute studies indicated that 10 percent of males were more or less exclusively homosexual and 8 percent of males were exclusively homosexual for at least three years between the ages of 16 and 55; the corresponding percentages for women were 2 to 6 percent and 1 to 3 percent. More recent research, including re-analysis of the original Kinsey Institute data, has often used more statistically valid survey and sampling techniques, while continuing to classify individuals on the basis of questions like "With what type of partner do you usually engage in sex?," "Would you say that you are attracted to members of the opposite sex or members of your own sex?," or "Have you had homosexual experiences (once, occasionally, frequently, or ongoing)?" This research has generally confirmed the range of original estimates, without leading to much additional precision (Fay, Turner, and Klassen, 1989; Harry, 1990; Rogers and Turner, 1991; Janus and Janus, 1993).

The most recent estimate of the prevalence of homosexuality is by Laumann, et al. (1994). They use a random population survey from the NHSLS, and estimate that 2.8 percent of the male population and 1.4 percent of the female population think of themselves as homosexual or bisexual.[13] These are lower-bound estimates when compared to other recent studies; for example, Janus and Janus (1993) report 9 percent for men and 5 percent for women. However, the Laumann, et al. estimates are from a random population survey, with a broader goal than determining homosexuality, and are likely to be more trustworthy. Accordingly, we assume that 2.8 percent (1.4 percent) of the male (female) population is homosexual.

Second, we obtain estimates of the percent of the homosexual population that is in a stable same-sex relationship. For males, Harry (1990) reports that 46 percent of those self-classifying themselves as homosexual or bisexual stated that they have a regular gay associate. In a survey conducted by The Partners' Task Force for Gay and Lesbian Couples (1995), 82 percent of gay males and 75 percent of lesbians reported living with a partner of the same sex. Klawitter and Flatt (1998) use GSS and National Opinion Research Center data to determine the number of same-sex cohabiting couples by gender; they estimate that 26 percent of gays and 28 percent of lesbians live with a partner of the same sex. Again, we use estimates generated from a random survey, or those from Klawitter and Flatt.

Third, we need to determine the percent of the gay and lesbian couples who would marry if marriage became legal. The Partners' Task Force for Gay and Lesbian Couples (1988) concludes that 60 percent of homosexuals would marry, and a March 1996 survey of readers of *The Advocate*, a well-known gay and lesbian magazine, estimates a much higher 81 percent. These estimates are not gender-specific; more importantly, they are not based upon random population surveys. We elect to calculate marriages based simply on the percentages of homosexuals in same-sex cohabiting unions during the past year estimated by Klawitter and Flatt (1998), or 26 percent for gays and 28 percent for lesbians. These numbers may be too high, as all those in unions may not decide to pursue legal marriage. However, they may well be biased downward because many gays and lesbians not currently cohabiting might elect to marry if marriage became legal.

These numbers allow the calculation of the total number of gay and lesbian individuals who would wish to marry if same-sex marriage became legal. For example, the estimate for males equals the 1997 U.S. population aged 18 and over (or 95,372,000) times the percent gay (or 2.8 percent) times the percent in homosexual relationships (or 26 percent), for a total of 694,308. For females, we make the same calculation using the relevant population total (102,736,000), percent lesbian (1.4 percent), and percent in a cohabiting same-sex union (28 percent), for a total of 402,725. Fourth, the estimated number of gay and lesbian married couples is simply the number of married homosexual individuals divided by two. Thus, we estimate that there would be 347, 154 male and 201,363 female married couples. These estimates are summarized in Table 1.

Fifth, we derive information on the income of gays and lesbians from several surveys, as given in Table 2; for comparative purposes, Table 2 also presents different measures of average income for the general population, derived from 1996 Current Population Survey (CPS) data. Even though these various estimates are generated for different years, all dollar amounts are converted to 1997 dollars.

The gay income figures come from various sources of differing definition and statistical reliability. The survey by The Partners' Task Force for

Gay and Lesbian Couples (1988) was conducted in gay churches and centers, although many couples requested the survey form after reading notices in gay and lesbian magazines. The survey generated 1,749 responses, of which 1,266 were from individuals living in a couple. *Out/Look* (1988), a gay and lesbian magazine, used much of the same survey information in its estimates. Teichner (1989) reports the results of a phone survey conducted in 1989 for *The San Francisco Examiner.* These surveys report average or median income for gays and/or lesbians without conditioning on employment status. Except for Teichner, all of these surveys are nonrandom, with white, urban, and educated respondents disproportionately sampled.[14]

More nationally representative samples are used by Badgett (1995b) and Klawitter and Flatt (1998). Badgett (1995b) uses data from the 1989 to 1991 GSS, conducted by the National Opinion Research Center to calculate the average income of full-time, year-round workers by sexual orientation. Klawitter and Flatt (1998) calculate both total household income and individual earnings for cohabiting same-sex couples using the Public Use Microdata (PUMS) from the U.S. Census; they restrict their sample to individuals who have some income during the year, but who are not necessarily full-time workers. As shown in Table 2, these studies indicate a substantial range of gay and lesbian average income.

To generate our estimates of the tax consequences of same-sex marriage, our preference would be to use a statistically reliable, nationally-representative estimate of average income by sexual orientation, without regard to labor market status. In the absence of such a measure, we use several different estimates of income and distribution across partners. We primarily use those from Badgett (1995b), in which average gay full-time earnings (in 1997 dollars) equal $33,717 and average lesbian earnings are $19,287. Although these estimates are for working individuals, the average incomes are at the lower end of most estimates, they are quite similar to those for the general population, and, as argued earlier, there is a much higher probability that both partners will be in the labor force in a same-sex couple than in a different-sex couple. However, because we do not know with certainty the precise income levels and their distribution across partners, we also estimate the revenue impact when lower and higher average incomes are assumed. These alternative scenarios are discussed in more detail later.

Sixth, we make several different assumptions about individual use of tax preferences. In one scenario we assume that individuals use the single rate schedule with a single personal exemption, that homosexual couples file as a married couple with no children using the married rate schedule and taking two personal exemptions, and that the individual or the couple takes the relevant standard deduction. In another scenario, we calculate taxes under the assumption that the individual or the couple itemizes deductions, using the procedure employed by Feldstein and Clotfelter

(1976) to estimate the amount of these deductions. We also assume in one scenario that some lesbian couples have a child as a dependent.

To illustrate the calculations, consider the following example (Scenario 1 in Table 3). Suppose that a male has adjusted gross income in 1997 of $33,717. With a single standard deduction of $4,150 and one personal exemption of $2,650, this person's taxable income is $26,917, and, using the 1997 federal income tax tables, the individual has a single tax liability of $4,335. Suppose now that this individual is gay and joins in a legally recognized marriage with another male who has identical income. The total income of the couple equals $67,434; filing jointly, the couple takes the marital standard deduction of $6,900 and two personal exemptions totaling $5,300, giving taxable income of $55,234 and a couple income tax liability of $10,107. Recall that the marriage tax or subsidy is the difference between a couple's taxes as married and their combined taxes if they file as singles. This couple therefore faces a marriage tax of $1,437 (or $10,107 less 2 × $4,335). Using our calculation of 347,154 gay married couples, the aggregate marriage tax equals $499 million. Similar calculations are made for lesbian couples, using an average female income of $19,287 and

Table 3 Potential federal income tax revenues from legalizing same-sex marriage

Scenario	Average marriage tax, male couples	Average marriage tax, female couples	Added income tax revenues
1 Individuals have equal income and use the standard deduction	1,437	214	542 million
2 Individuals have equal income and itemize deductions	1,589	1,849	924 million
3 One individual makes .75 the income of the other individual and both use the standard deduction	629	214	261 million
4 One individual makes 1.25 the income of the other individual, and both itemize deductions	1,996	1,587	1,012 million
5 Both individuals have one standard deviation higher income, and both use standard deductions.	1,437	1,043	709 million
6 Both individuals have one standard deviation higher income, and both itemize deductions	2,921	1,441	1,304 million
7 Half of all lesbian couples claim one child as a dependant	1,437	214/2,337	756 million

our estimate of female married couples (201,363). Combining the male and female estimates, the aggregate marriage tax equals $542 million. Other scenarios are calculated in a similar way.

Results

Our results are shown in Table 3, which indicates the average male and female marriage tax and the aggregate additional federal income tax revenues, under a variety of potential scenarios. Although our estimates do not allow explicitly for heterogeneity across same-sex couples, the impact of such heterogeneity can be inferred from the range of scenarios that we examine.

In Scenario 1, both individuals in a couple are assumed to have identical incomes, equal to the average gay and lesbian income; individuals and couples are also assumed to use the relevant standard deduction. As discussed above, these assumptions generate an estimate for additional income tax revenues of $0.5 billion.

In Scenario 2, we continue to assume that individuals have the same average incomes, but we now assume that individuals itemize deductions, both as single and married filers. Not surprisingly, this change generates a significant increase in the marriage tax, especially for female couples, and the aggregate estimates of increased income tax revenues also increase. Our estimate is that tax revenues would increase by $0.9 billion.

If we assume that both individuals use the standard deduction but that one member of the couple makes only 3/4 the (average) income of the other (Scenario 3), then the estimates of the average marriage tax decline to $629 for gay couples and $214 for lesbian couples. The aggregate revenue impact is only $0.3 billion, our lowest estimate. If instead we assume that both individuals use itemized deductions and that one member makes 1.25 the average income of the other (Scenario 4), then the aggregate estimate increases to roughly one billion dollars.

Additional scenarios are easily calculated. Some marketing surveys suggest that average gay and lesbian incomes are significantly larger than the averages calculated by Badgett (1995b) and used above. Suppose we assume that average female and male homosexual income is one standard deviation larger than the estimates, or $29,899 for females and $55,413 for males. If we calculate average marriage taxes with standard deductions (Scenario 5), then the average equal-earning male couple pays a marriage tax of $1,437 and the average female couples pays $1,043; the potential revenues now total $0.7 billion. In Scenario 6, we again use high income estimates but now assume that the individuals and equal-earning couples claim itemized deductions. Relative to Scenario 5, this assumption more than doubles the average marriage penalty for male couples (to $2,921), and increases the female penalty by close to 50 percent, to $1,441. The estimate of aggregate additional tax revenues accordingly increases to $1.3 billion, our largest estimate.

Although it seems unlikely given the income estimates in Table 2, it is possible that the Badgett (1995b) estimates are too high because they are drawn from samples of full-time workers. If we assume that average incomes for lesbians and gays are the same as for the CPS sample of all women and men, or $19,391 and $34,809, respectively, then the outcome is the same as the first scenario (or an additional $0.5 million in federal taxes) because the overall CPS averages are nearly identical to the Badgett (1995b) numbers. Similarly, using the CPS average incomes for single people (versus the averages for all people), or $17,339 for women and $20,459 for men, lowers the additional tax revenue even further, to an increase of only $0.1 billion, largely due to the much smaller average income of men in this group. However, based upon the income estimates of the gay population in Table 2, we believe that this latter estimate significantly understates the potential tax revenue of legalizing same-sex marriage.

All previous calculations were made with the assumption that gay and lesbian couples do not have children, or, at least, do not claim their children as dependants for tax purposes. This assumption is unrealistic. Both the 1993 Yankelovich Monitor (Lukenbill, 1995) and the 1992 Voter News Service exit polls (Badgett, 1994) indicate that lesbians are just as likely as heterosexual women to have children under the age of 18 residing with them. Overall, about 50 percent of family households in the U.S. have at least one child age 18 or less in residence. Accordingly, in Scenario 7, we assume that 50 percent of the lesbian potential married couples have one child that they claim as a dependant, that the partners are equal earners with the Badgett (1995b) income estimates, and that individuals and couples use the standard deduction. Note that this family-size estimate is quite conservative, as it assumes that only 25 percent of the women actually have a birth and that they have only one birth. We also assume that gay men claim no children as dependants, that they have equal average incomes, and that they use the standard deduction. Lesbian couples with no children pay an average marriage tax of $214, as in Scenario 1. The other couples with a child now pay an average of $2,337 additional taxes when married. This increase is largely due to the loss of the Earned Income Tax Credit that one woman incurs if income is pooled rather than taxed separately; also, when single, the woman who claims the child can file as a head-of-household, giving her a preferential tax schedule and standard deduction relative to those for single individuals. Overall, the additional revenue in this case is $0.8 billion. The revenue implications increase substantially if we assume itemized deductions and/or an increased number of homosexual couples with children present.

On balance, we believe that the most likely scenario is one in which individuals have more-or-less equal incomes, they use itemized deductions, and some households have children, assumptions that generate an estimate of roughly $1 billion in additional income tax revenues. In fact, even this estimate is likely to be quite conservative. For example, if the numbers of gays and lesbians are closer to the Janus and Janus (1993) estimates of 9.0 percent and 5.0 percent, respectively, then the aggregate revenue impact (under the assumptions of equal incomes and standard deductions) exceeds $4 billion. With equal incomes and itemized deductions, the aggregate impact grows to $7 billion. With equal but higher incomes and itemized deductions, the impact is over $10 billion. Children present in even a small percentage of the homes would generate even greater annual revenues.

These amounts are modest relative to total individual income tax collections in 1997 of $737 billion. However, these amounts are not inconsequential in relation to available estimates of the aggregate revenue impact of the marriage tax/subsidy for heterosexual couples. For example, Alm and Whittington (1996) estimate that the marriage tax generated $17 to 19 billion in additional revenues in 1994. Feenberg and Rosen (1995) estimate an aggregate revenue gain of over $6 billion in 1994, while the Congressional Budget Office (1997) calculates an impact in 1996 that ranged from a revenue loss of $36 billion to a revenue gain of $8 billion, depending upon the precise assumptions used. Our estimates of a revenue impact of as much as $1.3 billion suggest that legalizing same-sex marriage would significantly increase the marriage nonneutrality in the individual income tax.

Conclusions

Normative questions related to whether same-sex couples should be allowed to marry raise issues beyond the scope of this paper. However, positive questions about the economic consequences of expanding the right to marry are more amenable to economic analysis. Our estimates indicate that legalizing marriages by gay and lesbian couples would lead to an annual increase in federal government income taxes of between $0.3 billion and $1.3 billion.

Of course, it is possible that the tax costs of marriage might discourage some same-sex couples from marrying at all.[15] However, it seems unlikely that taxes are the main, or even a major, factor in the marriage decision for most couples. Besides, greater taxes at marriage could be offset by other economic advantages of marriage, such as access to a spouse's health insurance or pension benefits. Perhaps most importantly, same-sex couples might well choose to marry because of the cultural symbolism and value that married status conveys to themselves, their families, and society.

In any event, it is clear that legalizing same-sex marriages would generate some additional tax revenues. These revenues could be used to offset potential increases in federal expenditures on social security benefits or other federal programs paid to newly married couples, if such increases occur. Of course, elimination of the marriage penalty in the individual income tax would also eliminate these revenue gains. Although economic issues are not the dominant concern in the current debate about allowing same-sex couples to marry, we believe that these tax effects merit closer consideration by policymakers.

Acknowledgments

Rohit Burman provided valuable research assistance. We are grateful for the helpful comments of the editor and the reviewers.

Notes

1 Note that citizens in Denmark, France, Greenland, Iceland, Norway, The Netherlands, and Sweden are allowed to enroll as "registered partners," which confers a status similar to that of marriage between man and woman and which extends to the tax filing status of the partners; Finland, Slovenia, and several other countries are likely to adopt similar laws in the near future. There are also numerous cities around the world, including some in the U.S., in which same-sex couples may enroll as partners without any accompanying legal status.

2 For example, Senator Robert Byrd of West Virginia is quoted in the *Congressional Record* (Debate on H.R. 3396, Sept. 10, 1996, 104th Congress, U.S. Senate, p. S10110) as saying: "Moreover, I urge my colleagues to think of the potential cost involved here. How much is it going to cost the Federal Government if the definition of 'spouse' is changed? It is not a matter of irrelevancy at all. It is not a matter of attacking anyone's personal beliefs or personal activity. That is not my purpose here. What is the added cost in Medicare and Medicaid benefits if a new meaning is suddenly given to these terms?"

3 See the State of Vermont, Brief of Appellee to Vermont Supreme Court, *Baker v. State of Vermont*, 1998.

4 Brown (1995) and LaCroix and Mak (1995) have estimated the impact of increased tourism-related economic activity for the first state to allow same-sex couples to marry.

5 Clearly, there are also state tax implications. However, the magnitude of these state effects is likely to be small or nonexistent, given the low and often proportional level of state marginal tax rates, as well as the different unit of taxation (e.g., the individual rather than the family) in some states. See Congressional Budget Office (1997) for a discussion of those features of state income tax systems that affect the marriage tax/subsidy at the state level.

6 For a more detailed discussion of the income tax treatment of the family, see Brazer (1980).

7 Separate filing for married couples does not typically give a tax advantage to the

couple. Internal Revenue Service statistics show that in recent years over 95 percent of married couples file jointly.

8   There are numerous implicit penalties and subsidies imposed by government programs, only some of which are related to income taxation. The U.S. General Accounting Office identifies 1,049 federal laws that involve marital status in some way; for example, Dickert-Conlin and Houser (1998) discuss the non-neutrality of the transfer system with respect to marriage. We focus here solely on the marriage tax/subsidy of the federal individual income tax.

9   These calculations are similar to the averages of Feenberg and Rosen (1995). The Congressional Budget Office (1997) finds a lower percentage with a marriage penalty (42 percent) and a higher percentage with a marriage subsidy (51 percent).

10   For example, the relative income of heterosexual versus homosexual individuals was a primary focus of groups pushing for the Colorado Amendment Two initiative, a constitutional amendment that prohibited the use of homosexual orientation or conduct in claiming protected status. Proponents of the Amendment claimed that homosexuals did not merit protected status because the average income of homosexual house-holds was well-above the average of all Colorado households, using a number ($55,470) generated from a readership survey of the eight leading gay newspapers in the U.S. conducted by Simmons Market Research Bureau. Amendment Two was passed by Colorado voters in 1992, but was subsequently declared unconstitutional by the Colorado Supreme Court, a decision that was upheld by the U.S. Supreme Court in 1996.

11   However, Badgett (1995a) argues that Becker (1991) exaggerates the lack of potential comparative advantage for same-sex couples.

12   Note that minorities were not sampled in these studies, individuals from lower income levels were under represented, and the male sample included institutionalized men. See Gebhard (1972) and Gebhard and Johnson (1979) for further discussion of the sampling methods.

13   Laumann, et al. (1994) also find that even greater percentages of the male and female populations say that they have either desired or had same-sex sexual partners.

14   There have also been several surveys conducted by marketing firms, often designed to demonstrate the economic clout of gay and lesbian households. See, for example, Fulgate (1993) for discussion and analysis of marketing-based income figures.

15   For example, Alm and Whittington (1999) find that the existence of a marriage tax discourages marriage, especially for women, although its effect is generally small.

References

The Advocate. "Survey Results." March 19, 1996.

Alm, James, and Leslie A. Whittington. "The Rise and Fall and Rise . . . of the Marriage Tax." *National Tax Journal* 49 No. 4 (December, 1996): 571–89.

Alm, James, and Leslie A. Whittington. "For Love or Money? The Impact of Income Taxes on Marriage." *Economica* 66 (August, 1999): 297–316.

Badgett, M. V. Lee. "Civil Rights and Civilized Research," presented at the 1994 Association for Public Policy Analysis and Management Research Conference, Chicago, IL (1994).

Badgett, M. V. Lee. "Gender, Sexuality, and Sexual Orientation: All in the Feminist Family?" *Feminist Economics* 1 No. 1 (Spring, 1995a): 121–39.

Badgett, M. V. Lee. "The Wage Effects of Sexual Orientation Discrimination." *Industrial and Labor Relations Review* 48 No. 4 (July, 1995b): 726–39.

Becker, Gary S. *Treatise on the Family*. Cambridge, MA: Harvard University Press, 1991.

Blumstein, Philip, and Pepper Schwartz. *American Couples: Money, Work, Sex.* New York: William Morrow, 1983.

Brazer, Harvey E. "Income Tax Treatment of the Family." In *The Economics of Taxation*, edited by Henry J. Aaron and Michael J. Boskin. Washington, D.C.: The Brookings Institution, 1980: 223–46.

Brown, Jennifer G. "Competitive Federalism and the Legislative Incentives to Recognize Same-Sex Marriage." *Southern California Law Review* 68 (May, 1995): 745–839.

Congressional Budget Office, Congress of the United States. *For Better or For Worse: Marriage and the Federal Income Tax*. Washington, D.C.: Government Printing Office, 1997.

Dickert-Conlin, Stacy, and Scott Houser. "Taxes and Transfers: A New Look at the Marriage Penalty." *National Tax Journal* 51 No. 2 (June, 1998): 175–217.

Fay, Robert E., Charles F. Turner, Albert D. Klassen, and John H. Gagnon. "Prevalence and Patterns of Same-gender Sexual Contact among Men." *Science* 243 No. 4889 (January, 1989): 338–48.

Feldstein, Martin S., and Charles T. Clotfelter. "Tax Incentives and Charitable Contributions in the United States: A Microeconomic Analysis." *Journal of Public Economics* 5 No. 1 (January-February, 1976): 1–26.

Feenberg, Daniel R. and Harvey S. Rosen. "Recent Developments in the Marriage Tax." *National Tax Journal* 48 (March, 1995): 91–101.

Fulgate, Douglas L. "Evaluating the U.S. Male Homosexual and Lesbian Population as a Viable Target Market Segment." *Journal of Consumer Marketing* 10 No. 4 (December, 1993): 46–57.

Gebhard, Paul H. "Incidence of Overt Homosexuality in the United States and Western Europe." In *National Institute of Mental Health Task Force on Homosexuality: Final Report and Background Papers*, edited by John M. Livingood. Rockville, MD: National Institute of Mental Health, 1972.

Gebhard, Paul H., and Alan B. Johnson. *The Kinsey Data: Marginal Tabulations of 1938–1963 Interviews Conducted by the Institute for Sex Research* Philadelphia, PA: W.B. Saunders, Inc., 1979.

Harry, Joseph L. "A Probability Sample of Gay Males." *Journal of Homosexuality* 19 No. 1 (January, 1990): 89–104.

Janus, Samuel S., and Cynthia L. Janus. *The Janus Report on Sexual Behavior.* New York, NY: John Wiley and Sons, Inc., 1993.

Kinsey, Alfred C., Wardell B. Pomeroy, and Clyde E. Martin. *Sexual Behavior in the Human Male*. Philadelphia, PA: W.B. Saunders, Inc. 1948.

Kinsey, Alfred C., Wardell B. Pomeroy, and Clyde E. Martin. *Sexual Behavior in the Human Female*. Philadelphia, PA: W.B. Saunders, Inc. 1953.

Klawitter, Marieka. "Did They Find Each Other or Create Each Other? Labor Market Linkages between Partners in Same-Sex and Different-Sex Couples." University of Washington. Mimeo, 1995.

Klawitter, Marieka, and Victor Flatt. "The Effects of State and Local Antidiscrimination Policies for Sexual Orientation." *Journal of Policy Analysis and Management* 17 No. 4 (Fall, 1998): 658–86.

LaCroix, Sumner, and James Mak. "How Will Same-Sex Marriage Affect Hawaii's Tourism Industry?" Testimony before Commission on Sexual Orientation and the Law, State of Hawaii October 11. Honolulu, HI: 1995.

Laumann, Edward O., John H. Gagnon, Robert T. Michael, and Stuart Michaels. *The Social Organization of Sexuality: Sexual Practices in the United States*. Chicago, IL: The University of Chicago Press, 1994.

Lukenbill, Grant. *Untold Millions*. New York, NY: Harper Business, 1995.

Out/Look. "Work and Career: Survey Results," 1 No. 3 (1988): 94.

The Partners' Task Force for Gay and Lesbian Couples. *Partners National Survey of Lesbian & Gay Couples: Survey Report*. Seattle, WA: Partners Task Force for Gay & Lesbian Couples, 1995.

Rogers, Susan M., and Charles F. Turner. "Male-male Sexual Conduct in the U.S.A.: Findings from Five Sample Surveys, 1970–1990." *Journal of Sex Research* 28 No. 4 (November, 1991): 491–519.

Rosen, Harvey S. "Is It Time to Abandon Joint Filing?" *National Tax Journal* 30 No. 4 (December, 1977): 423–28.

Rosen, Harvey S. "The Marriage Tax Is Down But Not Out." *National Tax Journal* 40 No. 4 (December, 1987): 567–76.

Teichner, Steve. "Results of Poll." *San Francisco Examiner* (June 6, 1989): A19.

United States General Accounting Office. *Income Tax Treatment of Married and Single Individuals*. GAO/GGD-96-175. Washington, D.C., 1997.

Whittington, Leslie A. "The Marriage Tax." In *The Encyclopedia of Taxation*, edited by Joseph J. Cordes, Robert D. Ebel, and Jane G. Gravelle. Washington, D.C.: The Urban Institute Press, 1999.

Chapter 22

David L. Chambers *

WHAT IF? THE LEGAL CONSEQUENCES OF MARRIAGE AND THE LEGAL NEEDS OF LESBIAN AND GAY MALE COUPLES

From *Michigan Law Review* 1996, 95 (2): 447–91

L AWS THAT TREAT MARRIED persons in a different manner than they treat single persons permeate nearly every field of social regulation in this country – taxation, torts, evidence, social welfare, inheritance, adoption, and on and on. In this article I inquire into the patterns these laws form and the central benefits and obligations that marriage entails, a task few scholars have undertaken in recent years. I have done so because same-sex couples, a large group not previously eligible to marry under the laws of any American jurisdiction, may be on the brink of securing the opportunity to do so in Hawaii.[1] I wanted to know the benefits and burdens that legal marriage might extend to this group and ask whether the consequences would be sensible and appropriate for same-sex couples. How, in other words, would this institution, molded over time for persons of different sexes, apply to those with different differences?

My findings form the core of this article: that the laws assigning consequences to marriage today have much more coherence than has been commonly recognized, largely falling within three sorts of regulation; that each of these three sorts of regulation would, as a whole, fit the needs of long-term gay male and lesbian couples; that while the law has changed in recent years to recognize nonmarital relationships in a variety of contexts, the number of significant distinctions resting on marital status remains large and durable; that in some significant respects the remaining distinctive laws of marriage are better suited to the life situations of same-sex couples than they are to those of the opposite-sex couples for whom they were devised; and, most broadly, that the package of rules relating to marriage, while problematic in some details and unduly exclusive in some regards, are a just response by the state to the circumstances of persons who live together in enduring, emotionally based attachments. Legal marriage, somewhat surprisingly to a person long dubious of the state's regulation of nonviolent private relationships, has much to be said for it.

I need to make clear what one of my points is not. I do not claim that, if a new legal code of human or family relationships were developed completely afresh, governments should continue to sanctify the two-person enduring union over every other relationship in precisely the manner they do today. Rather, my claim is that, after thousands of years of human history, the union of two persons in a relationship called "marriage" is almost certainly here to stay, that the special rules for married people serve legitimate purposes, and that gay men and lesbians should not shrink from embracing them, nor should politicians shrink from extending them.

Just at the point that I finished this article, Congress acted to limit the effects that legal marriage would have, if Hawaii or any other state moved to permit same-sex couples to marry. The new "Defense of Marriage Act" declares that all federal statutes and regulations that refer to married persons or to spouses shall be read as applying to opposite-sex couples only.[2] This article persists in reviewing both federal and state laws that bear on married persons, for the purpose of my exercise of imagination – the "what if?" – is not to explore what will actually happen if gay couples are permitted to marry in Hawaii, but rather to ask how opposite-sex married persons are treated under the law today and hold these laws up to the situations of lesbian and gay male couples. By the end of the exercise, the meanspiritedness of Congress's actions may be more apparent, for the rules that it has gone out of its way to deny to same-sex couples are ones that I believe will be shown to be fully applicable to the lives of most gay men and lesbians in long-term relationships.

I Postures toward marriage

A large proportion of American adults who identify themselves as lesbian or gay live with another person of the same sex and regard that person as their life partner. Exactly how many gay or lesbian adults there are in the United States and what proportion live with another in a long-term relationship are not possible to calculate on the basis of existing information. Many lesbians and gay men, perhaps most, refuse to identify their sexuality to strangers who ring their doorbell or call them on the telephone.[3] Still, every survey of adult Americans willing to identify themselves as lesbian or gay finds that a majority or a near majority are living currently with a partner.[4] Increasing numbers of these couples are celebrating their relationships in ceremonies of commitment.[5] Those who participate commonly refer to the ceremonies as weddings and to themselves as married,[6] even though they know that the ceremonies are not legally recognized by the laws of any state. If states extend the legal right to marry, it is highly probable that large numbers of gay and lesbian couples would choose to participate. In a recent survey of nearly 2600 lesbians, for example, seventy percent said they would marry another woman if same-sex marriage were legally recognized.[7]

Exactly what lesbians and gay men hope to obtain from legal marriage is uncertain. Since public ceremonies of commitment are already so common, one might expect that when debating state-sanctioned marriage, they would focus on what law itself can accord that other institutions cannot: a range of legally protected benefits and legally imposed obligations. In fact, they do not. In the vigorous public discussion, few advocates address at any length the legal consequences of marriage. William Eskridge, for example, devotes only six of the 261 pages in his fine new book, *The Case for Same-Sex Marriage*, to the legal consequences, and his, with one exception, is the longest discussion I can find.[8] Whatever the context of the debate, most speakers are transfixed by the *symbolism* of legal recognition. It is as if the social significance of the marriage ceremonies gay people already conduct today count for nothing – as if, without the sanction of the state, those who marry have merely been playing dress-up.

That the social meanings of state recognition draw so much attention is nonetheless understandable. In our country, as in most societies throughout the world, marriage is the single most significant communal ceremony of belonging. It marks not just a joining of two people, but a joining of families and an occasion for tribal celebration and solidarity. In a law-drenched country such as ours, permission for same-sex couples to marry under the law would signify the acceptance of lesbians and gay men as equal citizens more profoundly than any other nondiscrimination laws that might be adopted. Most proponents of same-sex marriage, within and outside gay and lesbian communities, want marriage first and foremost for this recognition.[9] Most conservative opponents oppose it for the same reason. Thus, the conservative legislators who have promoted the recent legislation in many states that reject same-sex marriage and the members of Congress who voted for the Defense of Marriage Act[10] seem motivated not by a view of the inappropriateness of extending particular legal entitlements to same-sex couples but by views about some "inherent" meaning of marriage and by views about the social unacceptability of gay people and gay relationships.

Skeptics about marriage within the lesbian and gay communities also largely ignore the legal consequences of marriage. They focus instead on the negative meanings they attach to the institution itself. To many, marriage signifies hierarchy and dominance, subjugation and the loss of individual identity.[11] To them, it marks a tombstone over the graves of countless generations of married couples: one stone reads "Herbert Smith," the other simply reads "Wife." And even if the legal institution of marriage has changed in the recent past, they resist the assimilation of queer couples into an oppressive heterosexual orthodoxy of ascribed roles and domesticity.[12]

When skeptics about marriage within lesbian and gay communities do focus on the legal consequences of marriage – and they occasionally do – some express considerable misgivings. In the introduction to her collection of interviews with lesbians and gay men who have united in ceremonies of commitment, Suzanne Sherman writes with admiration of the couples she encountered, but also expresses doubts about marriage as a legal institution: "I don't believe that tax breaks and other benefits should be attached to marital status."[13] In her view, the subject of the law ought to be the individual, not the couple. Many of her interviewees seemed to agree. They treasured their partners, but expressed distrust of the state. If state laws permitted same-sex marriage, many said that they would marry to obtain the benefits now given to opposite-sex couples, but the tone of their comments sometimes suggested that the bounty that accrues to married people is undeserved or inappropriate.[14] They speak of it in much the same way that they might speak of the perks of the overpaid chief executive of a large corporation.

Nancy Polikoff, a law professor and scholar who is critical of efforts by gay and lesbian advocates to pursue legalized marriage, views the benefits that attach to heterosexual marriage in much the same way. Of the economic benefits, she writes:

> For those who support lesbian and gay marriage because it would allow us access to the package of benefits now associated with heterosexual marriage . . . advocating lesbian and gay marriage is an obvious choice. I do not share that vision. Advocating lesbian and gay marriage will detract from, even contradict, efforts to unhook economic benefits from marriage and make basic health care and other necessities available to all.[15]

Polikoff alludes to health care as a specific example of a social good that she believes is inappropriately linked to marital status. She chooses her example well. She and many others, including myself, believe that a wealthy industrialized state should seek to assure decent health care to all individuals in their own right and not derivatively through a spouse or parent.[16] But health care is only one among dozens of contexts in which married people are treated in a distinctive manner in this country. Looking across the broader range, most gay and lesbian writers about same-sex marriage disagree with Polikoff.[17] Without devoting much space to their positions, most accept the appropriateness of attaching legal consequences to marital status and conclude that the benefits of marriage would be of enduring value to gay and lesbian couples. This article considers both questions more closely.

II The legal consequences of marriage

Each of the fifty states defines the incidents of marriage for its residents. Federal laws add hundreds of other legal consequences. Some scholars have characterized the multitude of legal attributes of marriage today as largely incoherent,[18] and in their details they surely are. Yet, for all the variation among laws, it is possible to identify three central categories of regulation, within each of which a certain coherence obtains: some laws recognize affective or emotional bonds that most people entering marriage express for each other; some build upon assumptions about marriage as creating an environment that is especially promising or appropriate for the raising of children; and some build on assumptions (or prescriptive views) about the economic arrangements that are likely to exist (or that ought to exist) between partners. The review that follows makes no attempt to describe all of these regulations but provides central examples of each sort.

As you read, you will encounter occasional ghosts from an authoritarian and formally gendered past. The laws dealing with married persons have undergone a massive transformation during the last century.[19] Well into the nineteenth century, all assets of a married couple, including those that the wife brought into a marriage, were controlled by the husband. In fact, her personal property became his property. The husband also, as a matter of law, controlled all decisions that related to a married couples' children. Many of these laws continued well into this century. In many states, for example, as late as the 1950s, the state of a married woman's residence was fixed by law as the state of her husband's residence. If the husband unilaterally decided to move "his" family to another place without consulting with his wife and the wife chose not to come with him, she became subject to divorce for desertion.[20] This male-controlled relationship was also difficult or impossible to leave. At the beginning of the nineteenth century, marriage was indissoluble under the laws of nearly all states. Later in the century, it was dissoluble, but only on proof by one sinless spouse of a serious marital sin committed by the other. The partners could not end their relationship and remarry even if they both wished to do so.

Today, legislatures or judicial decisions have removed virtually all rules that explicitly provide different status or authority for husbands. They also permit marriage to end without proof of marital fault. The compulsory and sex-linked aspects of the law of marriage have, during the latter half of this century, been withering away,[21] sometimes at the price of providing insufficient protection to women economically ill-positioned to protect themselves. For many women in opposite-sex marriages, the promise of equality and autonomy remains largely empty because other social and institutional structures within our culture continue to enforce their subordination.[22] As we will see, for example, the rules of divorce commonly treat marriage as a partnership with an equal division of property, but, because of their lower earnings, women are generally left significantly worse off financially than men are. Most gay and lesbian couples can, however, appropriately regard the legal aspects of marriage today as serving primarily, though not entirely, a facilitating function – offering couples opportunities to shape satisfying lives as formal equals and as they, rather than the state, see fit.[23]

A *Regulations that recognize emotional attachments*

Some laws and regulations dealing expressly with married persons can best be viewed today as promoting the emotional attachments that most spouses feel toward each other. There are not a great many such laws. And among the handful are some that plainly have historical origins in a time when legislatures and judges conceived of marriage not primarily as a romantic bond but rather as a construct for the control of property and progeny. Still, for this article – the purpose of which is to reveal the current functions that laws of marriage serve – these rules can best be seen as facilitators of the affective aspects of couples' relationships.

Here are a few examples. Statutes or common law doctrine in all states grant decisionmaking powers to relatives when a person becomes incompetent to make decisions for herself. Two broadly different sorts of laws exist. The more narrow sort authorizes a family member to make an emergency medical decision when a person has become incompetent and has failed to execute a formal document authorizing some other person to make decisions on her behalf. When such incapacity arises for an unmarried person, state laws designate a parent or an offspring or some other blood relation as decisionmaker, but, for persons who are married, they typically turn first to the person's spouse.[24] The second sort of law, broader in scope, provides for the formal appointment of a "guardian" or "conservator," who typically makes not only medical decisions but other decisions about residence, care, and financial matters. These statutes also differ widely, but commonly provide first for the appointment of a blood relative for a single person and a spouse for a married person. The Uniform Probate Code, for example, has been adopted in fourteen states, and establishes an order of preference for the appointment of relatives as the guardian for an incapacitated person, with the spouse first in line, followed by an adult child or a parent.[25] Upon death, other laws or court decisions provide that the spouse has first right as "next of kin" to claim a person's remains[26] and to make anatomical gifts of parts of the deceased person's body when the deceased person has made no directive of her own.[27]

In a similar manner, state laws designate the spouse as the person to receive part or all a married person's assets when he or she dies without a will.[28] These "intestacy" laws vary widely among the states.[29] In some states, if there are surviving children, a spouse receives as little as a third; in many others, a fixed dollar amount and a share of the remainder; in still others, the entire estate.[30] In most states, if there are no surviving children and no surviving parents, the spouse receives everything.[31]

The laws relating to incompetency and death serve fairly obvious functions but ones worth explicit recognition. Some relate to the control of property, a subject taken up later. But most fundamentally, for couples who see themselves in an enduring relationship, the spouse is the appropriate person for the state to designate as decisionmaker during a period of incompetency and as primary beneficiary after death on the basis of a reasonable guess that that is the person whom the now-incompetent or deceased person would have chosen if she had addressed the question in advance.[32] That is, the rule fulfills her probable wishes. When commentators criticize the current intestacy rules, they do so primarily on the ground that, in many states, the rules give a surviving spouse less than the evidence suggests that most people would want their spouse to receive.[33] As to decisionmaking about medical and financial matters, the spouse is also more likely than any other person to know what decisions the incompetent person would have made if she were now able to decide for herself or, alternatively, at least to be the person most concerned about the incompetent person's welfare. Although many spouses rarely discuss such forbidding contingencies, the state surely has available to it no other more appropriate person to designate as the default decisionmaker.

Do gay men and lesbians with partners need the protection of such laws to ensure that their partners make decisions for them or inherit their estates? A very few states designate a long-term unmarried partner as the most preferred decisionmaker for the incompetent person, but most states ignore the unmarried partner altogether.[34] Similarly, only a very few states provide that an unmarried partner shall receive any portion of the estate of a person who dies without a will and, to date, no state provides anything for a same-sex partner.[35] Despite this, one could argue that gay couples do not need such protections because they can protect themselves fully by simply executing a will or a medical power of attorney. But gay men and lesbians who are in relationships need these protections for the same reason that heterosexual persons need them. Like most heterosexuals,[36] most gay men and lesbians are reluctant to think about their mortality and procrastinate about remote contingencies. They fail to execute wills and powers of attorney, even though they are often aware of the unfortunate consequences of failing to act.[37]

These consequences are often doubly unfortunate for gay men and lesbians with partners. When they fail to write a will or execute a power of attorney, the consequence is not simply that the state will decline to choose as decisionmaker or heir the person in the world they (probably) most trust and love. It is also that the persons who will make the decisions or inherit – most probably biological parents or siblings – are more likely than for heterosexual persons to be estranged from the gay person. In the context of medical decisions, when a gay person is disabled, the biological relations who will make decisions are more likely than for heterosexual persons to decline even to consult with the partner.[38]

Even if all persons with a same-sex partner remembered to execute the proper documents and had access to the needed legal services, other forms of government regulation that recognize special emotional and spiritual ties could not be similarly handled by a scheme of private designations. Consider four examples. Federal law places severe restrictions on the opportunities for foreign-born nationals to immigrate legally to the United States. One significant exception to this rule of exclusion is that a foreign-born national who enters into a nonfraudulent marriage with an American citizen has a presumptive right to enter the United States immediately as a long-term resident.[39] No such special provisions are made for a friend or lover. Even brothers or parents of a U.S. citizen are not automatically entitled to preferential treatment, but typically face long waiting periods before entry. Recent changes proposed by a Congressional commission would widen the difference between the favored treatment of the noncitizen spouse and the treatment of other relatives a citizen would wish to bring in – retaining the full advantages for the spouse and for minor children, but ending all preferences for siblings and adult children.[40] The lover is still left out. The spousal preference is a reflection in law of the profound social significance attached to marriage, a relationship that transcends national boundaries.

Another federal law, the Family and Medical Leave Act of 1993, requires all employers with fifty or more employees to extend unpaid leave of up to twelve work weeks during each year to an eligible employee to care for a spouse with a "serious health condition."[41] The statute also provides for leaves to care for children and for parents, but makes no provision of any kind for friends, lovers, or unmarried partners.

The federal government and many states also extend an advantage to married people when called to testify in a criminal proceeding that bars the state from forcing a married person to testify against his or her spouse.[42] Nearly all states offer a related protection, typically in both civil and criminal proceedings, for confidential communications made between spouses during the marriage.[43]

Finally, under the law of many states, if a third person injures a married person negligently and by so doing deprives the spouse of care and companionship, the spouse can typically sue the injuring party for what is called loss of "consortium," compensation not for financial loss but for the loss of companionship.[44]

The immigration preference for spouses, the family leave provisions, the evidentiary rules, and the consortium rules have a common current justification: that it is fitting for the state to recognize the significance in people's lives of one especially important person to whom they are not biologically related. The rules both recognize roles that already exist – the spouse as soulmate, caretaker, and confidant – and reinforce the legitimacy of the performance of those roles. Lesbians and gay men in long-term relationships attribute a similar level of importance to their partners[45] (even if they have other gay and lesbian friends they also consider significant).[46] They need these rules as much as heterosexual people do. It may well be, for example, that only a small proportion of American lesbians and gay men will wish to marry a foreign national and bring that person back to live in the United States, but, for those who do, it is hard to imagine a more important governmental benefit.

Gay men and women would experience as a burden, not as a benefit, a few regulations that attach to marriage and that also build, in substantial part, on assumptions about the emotional salience of the marital relationship. Public and private employers, for example, adopt antinepotism regulations that prohibit employees from participating in decisions to hire, promote, or discharge their spouse or from supervising their spouse in the workplace.[47] Resting on views about both emotional and economic ties, these regulations are as justifiably imposed on lesbians and gay men in enduring relationships as they are on heterosexuals: no one can be expected to be sufficiently objective when decisions about one's own long-term partner must be made.

Similarly burdensome, at least for some couples, are old laws that make adultery a crime[48] and old laws that make adultery a ground for divorce in the states that retain both fault and no-fault grounds.[49] Many lesbians and gay men will find state-imposed fidelity repugnant on more than one ground. They will do so in part because they reject the notion of criminalizing any voluntary sexual conduct between adults.[50] They will also reject the legitimacy of state-dictated terms of the intimate relationship between partners. Most gay men and lesbians within couples prize loyalty and fidelity, but many would resist the notion that the test of fidelity – indeed the sole test in the law – turns on whom one has sex with. Many gay men and lesbians, particularly gay men, explicitly disavow sexual exclusivity within their long-term relationships.[51] Thus, in those states that still have rules relating to adultery, some lesbians and gay men may find their taint a significant impediment to embracing legal marriage. As a practical matter, these rules are rarely invoked today – prosecutors bring almost no criminal cases for adultery and the great majority of divorcing spouses rely on no-fault grounds – but the emblematic meaning of these old rules may still be troublesome.

B Regulations dealing with parenting

Gay male and lesbian couples raise children in this country in three common contexts. In the first, numerically the most common, one of the partners has already become the biological parent of a child (usually in the course of a prior relationship with a person of the opposite sex) and then has later formed a relationship with a same-sex partner. This new partner is functionally in the position of a "stepparent." In the second context, a same-sex couple, *after* beginning a relationship, agree to raise a child together. They plan that one of them will be the biological parent and that, after birth, they will serve as co-parents. In the third context, a same-sex couple seeks to adopt or to become the foster parents of a child who is biologically related to neither of them.

Opposite-sex couples also raise children in each of these sorts of contexts and, in each, laws and practices in all states treat such couples, when married, in specially favored ways. By contrast, in each of the three situations, a gay or lesbian partner who is not the biological parent of the child typically faces formidable, often insuperable, difficulties in becoming recognized as a legal parent at all. The laws that advantage married couples are needed by *some* heterosexual married couples who wish to raise children, but these same laws would be helpful to almost *all* lesbian and gay male couples who wish to raise a child as legal equals because, for them, it is always the case that neither partner or only one is the biological parent of the child.[52] Oddly, in the writings of others on the consequences that legal marriage would offer for same-sex couples, almost no attention is given to the special rules regarding parenting.[53]

I will discuss each of these three contexts separately. In each, most of the rules would be defended today as intending to serve the best interests of children. I will focus on the value of these rules both for children and for lesbian and gay male adults who wish to raise children. As to the interests of children, a great deal has been written on the adequacy of gay men and lesbians as parents in the past two decades, much of it suffering from the inevitable difficulty of identifying random samples of gay persons for any purpose. I do not intend to review this literature. It is well reported elsewhere.[54] In overwhelming measure, it concludes that a person's sexual orientation has no significant bearing on her or his parenting capacities or skills and that children raised by lesbian and gay male parents fare as well day by day and over time as children raised by other parents.[55] For purposes of this essay, I simply assume that the parenting capacities of gay and lesbian couples have been established.[56]

As we will see, some of the difficulties currently experienced by gay men and lesbians who wish to raise children are not formally imposed by law. Some arise under rules that courts and agencies already have the discretion to extend to gay people or to same-sex couples, but rarely do. Thus, in some contexts, the benefits of legal marriage for same-sex couples may lie less in the rules that would become applicable to them than in a changed attitude toward homosexual persons that a change in marriage laws might help bring about on the part of legal actors exercising authorities that already exist. Here the symbolic and the legal intertwine.

1 The stepparent relationship

When a lesbian or gay male parent with custody of a child begins to live with another person of the same sex, the new person assumes a parenting role functionally comparable to a stepparent. The state of the law about such parenting relationships outside of marriage is clear: no matter how long the gay "stepparent" lives with the child, no matter how deeply she becomes involved in the care of the child, she and the child will rarely be recognized as having a legally significant relationship with one another.[57] The state of the law is essentially the same for stepparent figures in opposite-sex unmarried couples. They are just the "boyfriend" or "girlfriend" or "live in" of the custodial parent and have no legal significance.

Perhaps surprisingly, until the recent past, the legal position of the opposite-sex partner who marries a custodial parent has been little different. In all but a few states, the stepparent married to a biological parent has not been legally obliged to contribute to the support of the child during the marriage.[58] In no state has the stepparent been required to contribute to the child's support upon divorce, no matter how long he lived with the child or the extent of his voluntary contributions. The stepparent has also had no legal entitlement upon divorce to be considered for court-ordered visitation or for sole or joint custody of the child.[59] It has been the absent biological parent who remained financially liable for support, who remained the one parent eligible for visitation (even if he never lived with the child), and who remained second in line for custody.

Recently, however, stepparents married to a custodial parent are coming to be recognized as parent figures for at least some purposes, and it is to the benefits of these laws and court decisions that gay and lesbian "stepparents" need access. A few states have begun, for example, to protect the relationship between a child and a stepparent whose marriage to the biological parent comes to an end. No state has imposed on the stepparent a general obligation of support upon divorce, but some courts and a few legislatures have given courts the authority to grant visitation and, in unusual circumstances, custody, even over the objection of the biological parent.[60]

States have also expanded the opportunities for stepparents during their marriage to a biological parent to become the full legal parent of a stepchild through adoption. If the absent biological parent consents, most states permit the married stepparent to adopt without any of the home visits and family studies usually required as a part of the adoption process.[61] Consensual stepparent adoptions now account for over half of all adoptions that occur in the United States.[62] Within the last few decades, most states have recognized certain circumstances in which stepparents living with and married to a biological parent are permitted to adopt even over the objection of the absent biological parent.[63] They have done so in circumstances in which the absent parent is found to have abandoned his relationship with the child by failing to visit or, in some states, willfully failing to pay support. Whichever route a stepparent takes to adoption, at the point the adoption occurs, the biological parent ceases to have any legally recognized relationship to the child and the adopting parent assumes all the rights and responsibilities.[64]

A further change regarding stepparents is found in laws relating to employment in the labor force. State worker's compensation programs[65] and the federal Social Security survivor benefit program[66] permit a minor stepchild living with and dependent upon a stepparent to receive benefits after the stepparent's death. These programs replace much of the income lost to a child upon the death of the supporting stepparent. Similarly, the Federal Family and Medical Leave Act of 1993 requires employers to permit a worker to take up to twelve weeks of unpaid leave to care for their seriously ill child, including a stepchild.[67]

Despite these reforms that apply to stepparents married to a biological parent, unmarried stepparent figures, of the same or opposite sex as the custodial parent, remain almost totally ignored by the law, wholly ineligible, for example, for the special treatment for stepparent adoption, wholly unable to secure for a child the benefits of workers' compensation or Social Security survivor benefits, and ineligible for the protections of the Federal Family and Medical Leave Act. They also remain free of the legal obligations that would come with adoption – most notably the obligation to provide financial support for the child they adopt – but these are obligations that many gay and lesbian stepparent figures would be pleased to accept. Extending these benefits and obligations to lesbians and gay men by permitting them to marry would serve well their needs and the needs of their children for the same reasons that they serve the needs of married opposite-sex couples and their children: children who live with a stepparent figure who is in a committed relationship with their biological parent often become attached to and financially dependent upon the stepparent, and these attachments warrant recognition. To be sure, for the benefit of children, states might also wisely recognize the strong emotional attachments that children develop to persons to whom their parent is not married but, until the law so expands, the recognition of legal marriage for same-sex couples at least will offer greater protection to one group of children today.

2 Artificial insemination, sperm donors, and surrogacy

The second parenting context for gay men and lesbians includes the same-sex couple, already formed, who agree that one of them will become the biological parent of a child whom they will raise together. Here the issues are rather different for women than for men.

When a lesbian couple plan that one of them will become pregnant – and large numbers of lesbian couples have babies today in this manner[68] – they first must find a source of sperm. Some face problems that are not formal barriers of law but that are probably aggravated by the outlaw status of their relationship. Sperm banks in all states provide insemination services to women, most commonly in circumstances in which the woman is married and her husband is sterile. While no state expressly prohibits sperm banks from providing services to unmarried women or to lesbians,[69] some doctors and sperm banks apparently decline to do so.[70]

Clearly legal problems arise after birth, at the point that the lesbian partner seeks to become recognized as a legal parent.[71] She will be able to achieve such recognition only if she successfully completes a formal process of adoption. In most states, her petition to adopt will be rejected, either because her partner and she are of the same sex,[72] or because they are not married to one another,[73] or both. In a growing number of states, the lesbian partner can be considered for adoption,[74] but even in these states, the best the couple can hope for is that, after completing elaborate forms and enduring an intrusive home study and an individualized inquiry into the child's "best interests," a court eventually, many months after the child's birth, will approve the application of the nonbiological parent to adopt.[75] The whole process is likely to cost thousands of dollars.

Lesbian couples need a simpler and more welcoming process. They need, at a minimum, the procedures available in most states to legally married couples in comparable circumstances. For such couples, most states' laws provide a straightforward procedure governing artificial insemination through clinics or sperm banks.[76] The sterile husband simply acknowledges in writing his concurrence in his wife's insemination and his acceptance of the child as his own. He is then treated for purposes of the law in exactly the manner that he would be if he had been the biological father. No home study is required. No court hearing is held. The child's birth certificate simply records him as the father of the child. Lesbian couples need access to the same automatic registering of parenthood for the nonbiological female partner. Once the state gets beyond the idea that lesbians are doubtful as parent-figures (or less than full citizens), an individualized inquiry into the "best interests of the child" is no more appropriate for them than it is for opposite-sex married couples.

One aspect of current law relating to artificial insemination would continue to pose problems for lesbian couples even if they were permitted to marry and given access to the comfortable rules described above for fertilization through a sperm bank. Some lesbian couples prefer to use a donor who is known to them and to perform the insemination privately without the sperm bank as intermediary.[77] When opposite-sex married couples in which the husband is sterile rely upon a donor known to them, they do not qualify for the automatic birth registration system that applies when they make use of a regulated sperm bank, and the legal position of the husband and the donor may be open to doubt.[78] Exactly what scheme of regulation is wisest in the case of donors outside the anonymous donor system is vexing, for whenever the donor knows the parents, the possibility exists that he will want to assert a right to a visiting or other relationship with the child, and there is much debate over the desirability of giving courts authority to order such relationships over the objections of the principal caregivers.[79] The important point here is that these issues remain vexing whether or not the parenting couple is same-sex or opposite-sex and whether the couple is married or not and that, whatever their resolution, lesbian couples and opposite-sex couples should be treated in the same way, for the children being born to these couples need the same sorts of opportunities and protections.

Similarly problematic are the situations for gay male partners when they wish one of them to serve as the biological father for a child they plan to raise together.[80] This situation is troublesome for it necessarily involves a much more substantial involvement by the other biological parent – the surrogate mother – than in the case of artificial insemination through a surrogate father, involvement under circumstances in which there are well-founded concerns for the interests of the mother and of women in general.[81]

Reflecting differing resolutions of these concerns, state laws vary widely today regarding the legality and enforceability of surrogacy arrangements. Some prohibit surrogacy agreements altogether; some refuse to enforce them but do not prohibit the arrangements if voluntarily carried out; and some permit enforcement if the parties comply with various state-imposed requirements and if the mother does not change her mind within a statutorily prescribed period.[82] Among the requirements in many states is that only married couples may enter into surrogacy arrangements with a donor mother.[83] Thus, under these varying schemes few gay men could legally enter into an enforceable surrogacy agreement, and, when they are able to do so, they would still have to overcome the adoption problems that lesbian couples face when both partners seek to be recognized as the legal parents of the child born to one of them. A few gay male couples have successfully negotiated the difficulties, with both partners ending up accepted by the state as the child's legal parents,[84] but couples in other states would presumably founder on formal and informal policies barring adoptions by unmarried couples and homosexual persons. The issues surrounding surrogacy are complex, but, whatever their resolution, gay male couples need access to whatever scheme is made available to opposite-sex married couples.

3 When neither partner is the biological parent: adoption and foster care

Gay men and lesbians also wish to adopt or serve as foster parents for children who are not the biological child of either partner. Today, a few states prohibit lesbians and gay men from adopting under any circumstances and a few others prohibit them from serving as foster parents.[85] Most other states make adoption or foster care very difficult in practice for persons who are openly gay or lesbian.[86] Gay people are not alone in encountering difficulties in adoption. Single heterosexual individual are also disfavored in practice almost everywhere.[87] When single persons, gay or heterosexual, are permitted to adopt, they are often offered only the most hard-to-place children, children who are older and have had multiple foster placements, or children with multiple handicaps.[88]

By contrast, while procedures for adoption and foster care vary widely across the country, it is the case everywhere that, whatever the procedure, the married heterosexual couple stands highest in the hierarchy of preferred units for placement of a child.[89] The status that is accorded to married opposite-sex couples today would provide fully adequate legal protection for the interests of gay male and lesbian couples and for the children they would raise. The increased opportunity to adopt that same-sex couples would enjoy if allowed to marry would arise less from particular formal rules than from the effects on judges and agencies of the legislature's blessing, for in many places it is not legal prohibitions that hold judges back from placing children with gay individuals or couples, but rather a belief that gay people are not socially acceptable caretakers of children.

The troubling question for those disposed toward legal same-sex marriage is not whether the adoption opportunities available to married couples today would help lesbian and gay couples enough. It is whether they would help them too much. Some might claim that no rational basis exists for preferring married couples over single persons or over unmarried couples.[90] I believe that both preferences are at least rational, even if not fully sensible.[91] But, even if the justification is tenuous, gay couples should not resist marriage simply because others remain discriminated against in this context. The answer lies in working to change over time the inappropriate limitations on others' access to adoption. Permitting gay and lesbian couples to adopt is likely to advance rather than hinder movements for single-parent adoption, because successful adoptions by lesbian and gay couples are likely to help corrode the myth that it takes two persons of opposite sexes as parent figures to raise a child adequately.

C Laws regulating the economic relationship of couples or between the couple and the state

A considerable majority of the laws that provide for differing treatment for married persons deal with the married couple as an economic unit. They build on beliefs or guesses about the economic relationships that married persons actually have and on prescriptive views about what those relationships ought to be. They assume that married persons differ from most single persons, including most single persons who share a residence with another person, in one or more of the following ways: the married partners will live more cheaply together than they would if they lived apart (that is, that there are routine economies of scale); the two will pool most or all of their current financial resources; the two will make decisions about the expenditure of these resources in a manner not solely determined by which party's labors produced the resource; the two will often engage in divisions of labor for their mutual benefit; and one partner, typically the woman, will often become economically dependent on the other.

To the extent that these laws have an empirical foundation, it is unclear whether the images of opposite-sex relationships that lie behind them will fit the circumstances of the sorts of gay male and lesbian couples who would marry under a change in the law. No adequate research exists about the current behavior or expectations of lesbian and gay couples regarding the economic dimensions of their relationships, and we cannot know, of course, what sorts of couples would choose to marry in the future.[92] What evidence there is suggests that most lesbian and gay couples in long-term relationships believe in pooling resources and practice it today,[93] and that pooling is particularly common among those who engage in ceremonies of commitment.[94] The evidence leaves open the strong possibility, however, that long-term same-sex couples generally keep more of their resources separate than married opposite-sex couples do – that more are cost "splitters" rather than "poolers."[95] It is also probable that, if permitted to marry, fewer persons in same-sex marriages would become economically dependent on their spouses than occurs among women in opposite-sex marriages today.

Rather than attempt to generalize in the abstract about the similarities and differences of opposite- and same-sex couples in the handling of the financial aspects of their relationships, I will consider the probable fit of various laws with the conditions of gay and lesbian couples as each sort of regulation is considered. The review that follows divides the many financial regulations that treat married persons differently than single persons into three rough sorts – those that fix the relationship between married persons and the state, those that fix the economic relationship between the two married persons themselves, and those that fix the relationship between the two married persons and private third persons – because these sorts of regulations typically serve quite different ends. Even with this crude division, the widely varying laws of the fifty states hamper any attempt to characterize the legal incidents of marriage, for these laws are neither identical to one another nor internally consistent within states. Still, there is a certain coherence to it all.

1 The regulation of the financial relationship between married persons and the state

Tax laws and laws pertaining to government benefits commonly treat married persons in a distinctive manner by regarding them for most purposes as a single economic unit. These laws have a rough logic to support them but sometimes produce unintended behavioral effects.

Consider some central examples. Federal and state income tax laws create a system of joint returns for married couples that treats the couple as a single economic entity.[96] Under these provisions, when only one spouse earns any income, the total tax liability for the couple will be less than it would be if the income-earning spouse filed as a single person, a result that may be thought justified because two people are living on the single earner's income. On the other hand, when both spouses work and each earns even a fairly moderate income, their total tax liability will often be higher than it would have been if each had filed as a single person, a result that may again be thought justified because, by pooling incomes, they can live together more inexpensively than two single persons living separately.[97] In many situations, these two sets of rules produce wholly justifiable outcomes, but their paradoxical impact in practice is that many working men and women maximize their incomes by living together but not marrying, each filing a separate return, even though they might otherwise prefer to marry.[98] The same rules also discourage some married women from seeking employment outside the home, because they conclude that the marginal tax rate on any earnings they produced would be so high as to make their economic contribution trivial.[99]

Similar rough justifications and undesired effects characterize the rules that apply when low-income married persons who are aged, blind or disabled apply for federal welfare benefits under the program of Supplemental Security Income (SSI). If a married couple apply together, their grant will be lower than it would be if they were treated as two individuals applying separately.[100] Similarly, if only one member of the couple applies, the income of the applicant's spouse will be assumed to be available to the applicant and will be taken into account in determining both the applicant's eligibility for the benefit and the size of the grant.[101] Much the same rules of income attribution apply when a married person seeks a government-backed educational loan.[102] For couples who in fact pool their income and resources, these government benefit rules make sense, but they can impose hardships when the rules attribute more income as available than the spouse can comfortably contribute[103] and can sometimes deter couples from marrying who otherwise would.

Government taxing and benefit regulations of other sorts also build on the expectation that married couples will share resources and recognize that one spouse is often economically dependent on the other. Some of these programs, fortunately, avoid the undesired behavioral incentives we have just discussed. When a long-employed worker retires with a spouse who has been a homemaker and has not worked in the labor force long enough to be entitled to full Social Security benefits in her own right, the nonworking spouse, if over sixty-two, is entitled to benefits through the worker.[104] Similarly, when a long-employed worker dies, Social Security benefits will typically be available for a surviving spouse over sixty who is not entitled to full benefits through her own contributions as an employee.[105]

Gift and estate taxes also reflect a view of the married couple as a single economic unit in which dependencies arise. When a well-heeled spouse transfers property to the other spouse during the marriage, the transfer is not subject to the federal gift tax that would apply to gifts to others, including the donor's children.[106] When appreciated assets held in the name of one spouse are transferred at divorce to the other spouse, no capital gains tax or gift tax is due at the time of the transfer.[107] And, when a spouse dies, bequests to the other spouse are not taxed under federal estate tax laws.[108] Public and private employers further recognize the economic interdependency of spouses by making health care benefits available to their employees' spouses, and, just as federal and state income tax laws exempt from taxation the value of a worker's own employer-provided health care benefits, so too these same laws exempt from taxation the value of the benefits for the worker's spouse.[109]

Gay and lesbian couples are subject to none of these rules, neither the benefits nor the burdens.[110] No joint return. No attributed income. No exemption from gift or estate taxes. Even when employers provide health benefits to both married employees and to employees with a same-sex domestic partner, only the married employees obtain the benefit of the tax exemption for the value of their partners' health coverage; the employee with a same-sex partner must report the value of the benefit to his partner as income and pay taxes on it.

Would gay and lesbian couples be advantaged by being treated like heterosexual married couples across this range of state and federal legal consequences? They would be subject to the same unfortunate behavioral incentives that these rules create today for opposite-sex couples.[111] A gay man with HIV on Medicaid, for example, might choose not to marry on learning that, if he did, he would cease to be eligible for benefits even though his partner and he did not actually earn enough to pay the couple's medical bills. Indeed, it is possible that an even higher proportion of gay male and lesbian couples would be economically disadvantaged by the application of the current tax laws than are married opposite-sex couples. The only couples who consistently benefit from the current laws are those in which only one partner works in the labor force, and, taxes aside, both partners prefer this arrangement.[112] Given enduring sex-ascribed roles, the employment of only one partner is likely to be the situation more often in opposite-sex than in same-sex couples. Moreover, the premise of many of the current rules is that married couples actually share in the control of resources and expenditures.[113] When that premise fails, it is doubtful whether the burdens of the joint return should be imposed. Some observers have raised doubts about the actual degree of sharing of control in most heterosexual married couples,[114] and it is quite possible that an even higher proportion of gay men and lesbians who would marry would be persons who in their day-to-day lives would share only some of their income.

On the other hand, remember that not all tax and welfare rules work to the harm of gay couples who would marry. In some couples, only one partner would work in the labor force, and for them the benefits of health coverage and the joint tax return might be substantial. In others, both partners would work, but only one with a job with medical benefits. For them, the value of tax-exempt benefits through the partner with coverage could be considerable. And for those at the highest end of the income scale, the benefits of the estate and gift tax exemptions might more than offset the disadvantages of a joint return.

Moreover, in actual practice, even for the couple in which both partners work and both earn significant incomes, the income tax and other rules may in actual practice less frequently cause behaviors experienced as painful by the parties. When neither partner in a couple considers himself or herself the "secondary" worker – when both partners, that is, have strong ties to the labor force – then, while the perversities of the tax laws may affect some decisions to marry, they are less likely to lead either partner to drop out of the labor force or feel economically useless in a manner that he or she resents or later comes to regret. And, viewed from another perspective, the opportunity for legal marriage, at the very least, provides a choice to opposite-sex couples whether to marry or not, a choice from which lesbian and gay couples could benefit for the same sorts of reasons.

2   The regulation of the financial relationship between married partners

In the United States today, states employ either of two broad schemes of regulation to define the economic relationship between married partners. Nine states (mostly in the West and Southwest) employ "community property" regimes,[115] under which, to oversimplify, the spouses own separately whatever they bring into the marriage or receive by gift or bequest during the marriage and own jointly any other assets either of them acquires during the marriage, including all assets acquired from their labors.[116] The earnings of each partner are owned jointly by the pair.[117] In the remaining states, called "common law states," again to oversimplify, the spouses own separately whatever they acquire in their separate names and jointly whatever they buy in both names or whatever one by deliberate act puts into joint control.[118] Their earnings are their own. These differences in law sound significant and may affect many married persons' perception of the nature of their relationship,[119] but it is probable that personal characteristics and social conventions linked to gender have greater impact than formal legal rules on the way that assets are controlled by married persons who live together.[120]

The rules of property do, however, become crucial at the point of divorce, for all states impose rules of distribution that have significant impact on the separate spouses' financial well-being. State divorce laws differ widely in their structures and in their details, but commonly produce similar outcomes.

In community property states, each divorcing spouse is entitled to one-half of the property acquired during the marriage. In some states judges may deviate from this division in extraordinary circumstances.[121] The remaining states have adopted more flexible schemes of property division generally called "equitable distribution." In these states, courts are permitted to ignore the rules of separate ownership and divide all property acquired during the marriage in an equitable manner. Most statutes list factors for judges to take into account,[122] including, for example, each spouse's contribution to the acquisition of an asset and the economic position of each spouse at the point of separation. Some states also permit judges to take "fault" into account, and to reach into assets acquired before the marriage or received by gift or inheritance.[123] In practice in many equitable distribution states, lawyers for divorcing persons begin negotiations with an assumption of a division closely similar to the division imposed in community property states: in the absence of special circumstances, the couple will divide equally all assets acquired by either during the marriage.[124] And in practice in many community property and equitable distribution states, the actual division of property negotiated by parties often deviates from a fifty-fifty distribution in ways that have little to do with formal legal rules.[125]

What is critical for our purposes is that at the point of divorce, under either regime, married persons encounter formal systems of forced allocation of assets that treat married persons as economic partners while they were together. Thus, as a single important example, for many long-married couples today the largest single asset owned by either is a pension account accumulated in the name of one of them. In both community property and common law states, that part of the pension assets attributable to the period of the marriage will be subject to division between the partners.[126]

State law also responds at divorce to imbalances in earning capacity between spouses, imbalances that have often been magnified during the "partnership." It does so in common law states by allowing judges to consider the disparate financial positions of the parties in the distribution of property.[127] Many states have also devised doctrines that permit courts to compensate a spouse in some manner for helping to increase the human capital of the other partner, most commonly by bearing the costs of putting the partner through professional school.[128] In addition, both community property states and common law states permit courts to award periodic payments, called alimony or maintenance, for the support of a spouse unable adequately to provide for herself or himself after separation.[129] Today alimony is awarded less frequently and for shorter durations than in the past.[130] It nonetheless remains common after long-term marriages in which one party has high earnings and the other party, almost always the wife, has been a long-term homemaker.[131]

Death is another occasion when the law imposes financial obligations because of marriage. Under the laws of nearly all states, a married person cannot unilaterally prevent his spouse from inheriting part of his assets. Thus, when a married person dies with a will and the will fails to provide for the surviving spouse, the laws of nearly all common law states permit the surviving spouse to claim a "forced" or "elective" share of the estate, commonly one-third or one-half.[132] Much the same result is reached in long-term marriages in community property states because, no matter what one spouse considers to be her separate property and attempts to bequeath by will to others, one-half of the assets acquired by the couple during the marriage will be considered the property of the other spouse at death.[133]

Thus at both divorce and death, states impose on married couples a prescriptive view of the appropriate financial relationship between them. Most states now permit couples, at the point of marriage or during the marriage, to contract for a different arrangement on death or divorce than the law would otherwise impose, though also placing some limits to ensure that the decision to contract was "voluntary" and "informed."[134]

How, by comparison, does the law treat the income and assets of single persons with a long-term partner? Very differently indeed. In both community property and common law states, the earnings of an unmarried person and the resources bought with those earnings are entirely the property of the earner. Moreover, in no state today, does the state impose on the estate of an unmarried person a forced share for a surviving partner.[135] An unmarried person can leave her money to whomever she pleases, no matter how long a relationship she may have had with a partner.

The rules relating to the breakup of unmarried couples vary widely among the states. Until the last thirty years or so, courts in nearly all states refused to intervene at all, even when the parties had agreed to share assets, on the ground that the cohabiting relationship itself was immoral.[136] A few states still retain this approach.[137] In most states, however, the law has changed, responding to the huge growth in the numbers of unmarried opposite-sex couples living together and to the changed social perception of the acceptability of such cohabitation.[138] Courts will enforce express agreements between unmarried persons to support each other or to divide property titled in the other's name.[139] Some of the cases have involved same-sex couples.[140]

A few states have gone further than the enforcement of agreements, coming closer to imposing a marital regime. Some will enforce "implied contracts," the contents of which courts infer not from words of agreement between the partners but from the partners' conduct – and which may in fact not reflect any actual agreement between the parties.[141] In a few more states, judges will, at the request of a separating long-term unmarried partner, simply impose a property division that seems "just," even in the absence of any express or implied agreement between the parties.[142] In most states, however, unmarried partners still have no state-prescribed obligations to each other that apply in the absence of agreement. Each can walk away taking whatever is titled in his or her name.

At first blush, the rules currently applied in most states to the unmarried may seem to most gay men and lesbians preferable to the rules of forced sharing imposed on married people. Most states, as just described, impose on unmarried couples only what the couple itself has agreed to. Such a regime may well appeal to couples who are suspicious of the state and couples in which neither partner is economically dependent on the other. Many individuals in couples in which both partners are working would reject the notion that all their resources are joint or that they have continuing responsibilities for the welfare of the other if they break up.[143] Many would, for example, probably consider their pensions to be separate property, even though acquired during the relationship. Many would find notions of alimony offensive. And, even if they saw themselves as having some continuing responsibilities, many would reject the notion of the state, through its judges, having the power to apportion fault or responsibility between them under the discretionary guidelines found in common law states.

All this is true, yet I think that the rules regarding the financial aspects of divorce now in place for married couples would serve lesbian and gay male couples reasonably well. In the first place, the property rules of divorce are given life as part of a larger set of procedures governing divorce proceedings, procedures that encourage, or force couples to wind up their financial relationship prior to moving on to another relationship. Many people would acknowledge (at least ex ante) the value of having some sort of regularized process for dividing property, without regard to the particular rules. In the second place, the rules regarding the division of property for married people are, to an increasing extent, subject to alteration by the agreement of the parties. Before or during marriage, the parties may contract for different outcomes between them that will be honored by courts if voluntarily entered.[144] So seen, the rules of marriage operate as a default regime for couples who marry and do not choose a different scheme for themselves.

Of course, just as only a small proportion of opposite-sex married couples enter agreements today to vary from the rules otherwise imposed at divorce, so it is probable that few gay male and lesbian couples would do so in the future. My own belief, however, is that a default rule of imposed sharing is preferable for gay male and lesbian couples to the default rule of separate property and no continuing obligations that now exists for unmarried couples. As a starting point, a great many – though by no means all – gay men and lesbians who would choose to marry would engage voluntarily in the substantial pooling of resources.[145] They would probably feel comfortable with the notion that assets that they acquired and used during the relationship – furniture or appliances, for example – belonged to them jointly even though one of them paid the bill on her separate account. Conversely, those gay and lesbian individuals who would wish to marry but care a great deal about financial independence – those who, for example, would wish to be certain to keep their pensions separate or avoid the payment of alimony – would probably be of higher than average economic status and in a better position to know about and to take the initiative to contract out of the default rules than are those who value sharing.[146]

And, finally, as between the two sets of default rules, the moral claims for independence and separate ownership have their own weaknesses. Some may look at the world of forced sharing and alimony, remember a time when married women could own nothing in their own name, and wish to reject any reminders of the dependence of women on their husbands.[147] But the world of independence has its own poisoned roots. Independence in law means that the person with legal title wins, and title, standing alone, bears little necessary relation to the efforts that lie behind the generation of the asset or to the moral implications of a long-shared life.

Taken together, these considerations even support the claim that the default property rules for marriage will not merely serve most gay and lesbian couples reasonably well but will, in general, serve gay and lesbian couples who choose to marry better than they serve opposite-sex married couples today. As others have pointed out, the rules of sharing for married couples today still typically leave most women in depleted financial circumstances after divorce and cause particular harm to those who have cared for children.[148] The equitable distribution and community property rules do force a sharing of assets acquired during marriage, but women often do not receive even half of the available assets.[149] Moreover, men commonly leave marriages with enhanced earning capacity, while women, who already earn much less, often find their capacity to generate income impaired.[150] Alimony, when ordered at all to redress the imbalance, is typically too small to bring women anywhere near their prior standard of living.[151] It also proves difficult to enforce.

Gay men and lesbians compelled on separation to share assets will be hurt less frequently when the law's promise of sharing fails to produce economic parity between the partners. Because the members of such couples are always of the same sex they more often earn similar incomes and are less likely to have gender-assigned expectations of divided responsibilities for income production during the relationship.

Despite my claims that gay men and lesbians will in general be served decently by the financial rules of marriage, some reasons for pause still exist. In the common law states especially, the process of resolving disputes over financial matters brings married couples under the authority of judges with broad discretion. How judges, most of them heterosexual, will respond to gay and lesbian couples who come before them is hard to predict. Even if they try to comprehend and apply the norms accepted by the same-sex couple, they may be unable to do so. How will they respond when a gay man has been financially dependent on an older partner by tacit agreement of the partners? Here lingering distaste for homosexual persons may mix with a general bias against the financially dependent male.[152] How will judges respond to a same-sex couple in which one but not both have had frequent sexual partners outside the couple?[153] I have no easy answer to these worries. The problem, however, for any couple concerned about judicial discretion can be ameliorated or avoided by contractual agreement about obligations or by agreement to mediate or arbitrate using a third party whose sensibilities they trust. But many couples will surely fail to enter into such agreements and one or both of them ultimately will feel abused by the judicial system.

3 The regulation of the relationship between the married couple and third persons

Just as states create rules defining the state's relationship with married persons and of married persons' relationships with each other, so also, in a narrower range of circumstances, states prescribe rules for the relationship between married persons and private third parties. Most such private relationships are left to private ordering: a married person can negotiate to borrow money on her own or to borrow with her spouse (or with anyone else for that matter); employers and employees negotiate over whether or not spouses will be included in various benefits. But a few protections and obligations are not left solely to the private sphere, and the rules that do exist again build upon notions of the married couple as a mutually interdependent economic unit.

A handful of states, for example, now require employers over a certain size to provide access to health insurance to the otherwise uninsured spouses of employees.[154] Similarly, in a quite different context, all states provide for a spouse to recover in a wrongful death action for economic losses when a third party has caused the death of the other spouse by negligence or an unjustified deliberate act.[155] These protections for spouses are matched by at least one legal burden: most states impose on spouses an obligation to pay for "necessaries," such as emergency medical care, provided by third parties to the other spouse.[156] More broadly, in most community property states, a creditor can collect out a married couple's community property for a debt contracted by one of the spouses, without regard to the contribution of that spouse to the community property.[157]

None of these protections and burdens applies to unmarried couples.[158] Yet, in differing degrees, they probably justly fit the circumstances of most long-term gay and lesbian relationships as we have discussed them: most long-term partners would probably accept the obligation to meet each other's most basic needs,[159] and many would be affected both financially and emotionally by the death of their spouse, and, when they are so affected, deserve compensation from a wrongful actor.

III Observations

American states and the federal government, as we now have seen, treat married individuals differently than single individuals in three broad respects – privileging their relationship to their spouse in certain contexts because of their affective ties, providing them and their partners opportunities for legally recognized parenting that are not provided to others, and extending benefits and imposing obligations based on a view of the partners as economically intertwined.

Taken together, the rules bearing on marriage offer significant advantages to those to whom they apply. Looking across the three groups of regulations we have examined, most of the rules may be seen as facilitative, in the sense that they enable a couple to live a life that they define as satisfactory to themselves: the immigration law permits them to live together in the United States, if that is what they wish; the joint income tax return and the Social Security laws make it easier for one of them not to work in the labor force, if that is what they wish; the parenting laws offer them the opportunity to raise a child as legal equals, if that is what they wish. The laws may also be seen as facilitative in a different sense. Some impose particular outcomes, but also permit the married partners to agree on some other arrangement if they so choose. Indeed, the laws of marriage can be seen today as facilitating choice in an even broader sense. Since living together outside of marriage is a socially acceptable arrangement today for so many couples – heterosexual as well as lesbian and gay – the regime of marriage offers a package that can be taken as a whole or rejected in favor of the alternative state of unmarried coupledom, with its different, less pervasive set of rules. The case I have tried to make for gay and lesbian couples is that they need these opportunities and choices to much the same degree that heterosexual couples do.

The rules of marriage are not simply facilitative, however. Some rules relating to financial matters are mandatory. Your income is taken into account when your spouse applies for welfare. Your spouse, unless he chooses to relinquish it, becomes entitled upon divorce to share in the property you acquired in your name during the marriage, and, if you die, to a share of your estate. You may be forced to pay alimony to support your spouse. You may be forced to pay for necessities provided to your spouse by others. I have also sought to show that these obligations are, on the whole, appropriate for gay and lesbian couples. And even these mandatory rules can be seen as permissive in the wider sense in which it was used in the preceding paragraph: they are part of the whole package of rules that opposite-sex couples can choose to live within by marrying or live outside of by not marrying. Same-sex couples need the same choices.

Heterosexual conservatives object to same-sex marriage either on the ground that sex between persons of the same sex is immoral or pathological or on the ground that permitting same-sex couples to marry will somehow contribute to the crumbling of the "traditional" family. Feminists among gay and lesbian scholars are also often critical of marriage for same-sex couples, fearing different undesirable consequences for lesbian and queer communities.[160] Neither objecting group focuses on the fit of specific legal rules with the lives of same-sex couples and, for this reason, this article has not addressed their claims. Four other sorts of doubts that *do* address the legal consequences of marriage might nonetheless be raised about legal same-sex marriage, even by some gay men and lesbians who might be expected to be sympathetic. I end this article by addressing those doubts.

One doubt is not about the present, but about the future. It may be the case that the rules of marriage as they are today fit reasonably well the circumstances of gay men and lesbians in couples, but marriage-related rules are hardly static. As in the past, they will change over time:[161] a lesbian couple who marry in the year 2000 might find themselves subject to quite different rules in the year 2020. The future changes in law that they experience will almost certainly be prompted by the perceived conditions of women and men in opposite-sex couples and not by the positions of lesbians and gay men, because lesbian and gay couples are simply so outnumbered by female-male couples. Nonetheless, though many different legal changes are possible over time, some more attractive than others,[162] marriage as a legal institution is highly likely to retain useful advantages for same-sex couples. These advantages will persist so long as adults in this country choose to live primarily in couple relationships and so long as doing so remains a socially prized condition. Gay people are likely to benefit by having the opportunity to choose to share in the benefits and responsibilities accorded such relationships. They will simply have to recognize that, when they do choose to marry, they will be stepping aboard a moving vessel that others will steer.

A second objection is that there is a better vehicle than something called "marriage" for extending the appropriate protections and opportunities to same-sex couples. Especially for those for whom marriage is indelibly associated with hierarchical male-female relationships, the alternative of permitting same-sex and opposite-sex couples to register with the state as "domestic partners" and extending to such partners some or all of the consequences attached to marriage may seem attractive.

No American state has yet adopted domestic partner registration,[163] but, as we have seen, some states, through imaginative court decisions and occasional statutes, are beginning to recognize unmarried couples for particular purposes.[164] Formal registration *has* been instituted in Denmark and Norway, where registered same-sex partners are treated precisely like married couples with regard to all financial and economic regulations, but are not labelled as "married."[165] This is not the place to discuss the whole range of practical and symbolic considerations that apply to domestic partnership. The point derived from the inquiry in this article is that whatever the virtues of domestic partnership, nearly all the legal consequences of marriage have a sound application to the position of long-term lesbian and gay couples. Unless a regime of domestic partnership were developed under which same-sex couples were treated just as opposite-sex married couples are, same-sex couples would probably find that domestic partnership legislation excluded benefits that they would much like to have. Thus, in Denmark, for example, registered same-sex couples are treated like opposite-sex married couples for purposes of economic benefits, but not for purposes of the adoption laws or any other laws that apply to parenting.

I do not, however, wish to seem critical of the movement for domestic partnership registration. I believe that, though the rose by another name will not smell as sweet to some of us, states are far more likely to accept domestic partnership than same-sex marriage. Denmark – and the fifty

American states – may eventually accept for gay couples united under a name other than "marriage" all the special rules for married persons, including those that apply to parenting. And those of us who favor legal same-sex marriage must acknowledge that just as "domestic partnership" legislation might provide only parts of the package of legal consequences that now attaches to marriage, so also legal "marriage" itself might be granted piecemeal as well: a state might open legal marriage to same-sex couples but withhold parenting or other benefits from them, or, more fundamentally, some states might extend all state laws bearing on marriage to same-sex couples while the federal government withheld the incidents of federal law.[166]

A third doubt about pursuing changes in the laws of who may marry is that the benefits of marriage are likely to be unevenly distributed among same-sex couples. Nitya Duclos, a Canadian scholar, has argued, for example, that the rules of marriage would primarily benefit lesbians and gay men who are members of the middle class – "those who are already fairly high up in the hierarchy of privilege."[167] She does not argue that this lopsided allocation of benefits is a reason not to permit same-sex marriage, for surely it is not, but rather is a reason to be less exultant about what will be achieved by it.[168]

Duclos may possibly be right. Those high in the hierarchy of privilege usually come out ahead. Still, at least in this country, many lower-income same-sex couples will find great benefits in marriage. Duclos claims that "[t]hose who rely for most of their income on state benefits are more likely [than middle class persons] to be economically penalized for marrying,"[169] and it is true that a significant cost of marriage for some lower-income persons who marry a working person is the loss of governmental benefits, such as Medicaid or Supplemental Security Income.[170] It is also true that some other rules, such as those exempting bequests to a spouse from the estate and gift taxes, are of value only to those who have large sums to give away. Still, there may be compensating gains for low income persons. Social Security retirement benefits for a nonworking spouse and Social Security survivor benefits are of most importance to those without long ties to the formal economy. Medical benefits tied to employment – including employment of some low-earning government employees – are of immense significance to spouses with jobs that carry no health coverage at all. And other benefits, such as the immigration rules or rules that relate to intestate succession, are likely to be at least as frequently invoked by the people of modest incomes as they are by the well-heeled. It is impossible for all sorts of reasons to make a confident prediction of what class-groups among gay men and lesbians would benefit most from being permitted to marry, but there is ample reason to believe that the rules relating to marriage will be appealing to many people of all classes.

A final criticism of the laws bearing on married persons is more fundamental: even if legal marriage would offer benefits to a broad range of same-sex couples, some might claim that all these advantages are illegitimate–illegitimate for both same-sex and opposite-sex couples – because they favor persons in two-person units over single persons and over persons living in groups of three or more, and because they favor persons linked to one other person in a sexual-romantic relationship over persons linked to another by friendship or other allegiances.[171] Those of us who are gay or lesbian must be especially sensitive to these claims. If the deeply entrenched paradigm we are challenging is the romantically linked man-woman couple, we should respect the similar claims made against the hegemony of the two-person unit and against the romantic foundations of marriage.

Governments nonetheless seem justified in favoring a special relationship with someone known as a spouse over other relationships of friendship or kinship in those contexts in which friendship or kinship alone rarely leads to the sorts of intermingling of assets or joint undertakings to raise children that commonly occur for persons who regard themselves as long-term lovers or spouses. Most of the rules for forced sharing of property or for advantages in adoption rest on perceptions of the understandings and desires of the enduring couple that much less often aptly apply to relationships with friends or other kin. Still, there are many occasions when greater recognition should be permitted for friendship or other kinship relations than currently obtains. Two siblings who live together and who have raised a deceased sibling's child ought to be eligible, for example, to adopt the child. A single person ought to be able to register a person as a special friend and obtain at least some benefits now provided for a spouse. Under the Federal Family and Medical Leave Act, for example, a single, childless person currently has no right to take time off to care for someone he loves other than a parent. A system of advance registration of a friend for whose care the statutory privilege would extend seems both feasible and desirable.

As to the privileging of the two-person romantic unit of husband and wife over romantically linked units of other sizes, I am equally queasy. Rather few such cohabiting relationships of three or more appear to exist in this country, whether for mixed-sex or same-sex groups.[172] Reasons can be offered why the state should recognize the two-person marriage but not the marriage of three or more, but I do not wish to try. In the end, most of the reasons are logistical and soluble.[173] If the law of marriage can be seen as facilitating the opportunities of two people to live an emotional life that they find satisfying – rather than as imposing a view of proper relationships – the law ought to be able to achieve the same for units of more than two.

However, the fact that the state unwisely ignores or prohibits certain relationships in addition to those of lesbian and gay couples does not make it inappropriate to advocate for the recognition of gay and lesbian couple relationships today. Nearly all reform to correct disparate treatment in our society is incremental. It comes at points at which the state finally recognizes the legitimacy of the claims of some long disfavored group. Thus, within this century, governments have gradually changed their posture toward the legal position of the child born outside of marriage and toward unmarried opposite-sex couples in their relationships with one another.

A next appropriate step is the step discussed in this article – the recognition of same-sex couples who wish to marry. And although it is conceivable, as some have feared, that permitting gay people to marry will simply reinforce the enshrined position of married two-person units in general in our society, it seems at least as likely that the effect of permitting same-sex marriage will be to make society more receptive to the further evolution of the law.[174] By ceasing to conceive of marriage as a partnership composed of one person of each sex, the state may become more receptive to units of three or more (all of which, of course, include at least two persons of the same sex) and to units composed of two people of the same sex but who are bound by friendship alone. All desirable changes in family law need not be made at once.

Notes

*   While working on this piece I consulted many friends and colleagues, but I am particularly grateful to Elizabeth Bartholet, Steven Homer, William Rubenstein, and Lawrence Waggoner for their close scrutiny of a draft and for the research assistance of Edward Deibert, Noreen Nash, and Amy Smith.
1   See Baehr v. Lewin, 852 P.2d 44 (Haw.), clarified, 852 P.2d 74 (1993). The court held that Hawaii's law limiting marriage to opposite-sex couples was unconstitutional as an impermissible form of sex discrimination under Hawaii's constitution, unless the state of Hawaii could demonstrate a compelling justification for limiting marriage to opposite-sex couples. As this article was completed, a trial court, after repeated postponements, held a hearing in which the state tried to present evidence of a compelling justification.
2   See Defense of Marriage Act, Pub. L. No. 104–199, § 3(a), 110 Stat. 2419, 2419 (1996).
3   In one effort to survey Americans in every state by phone, it took 1650 calls to Kansas – 55 hours of random dialing – before the pollers found the first person willing to admit being lesbian or gay. See Larry Hatfield, "Methods of Polling", S.F. Examiner, June 5, 1989, at A-20. It is possible, of course, that fewer than one-tenth of one percent of Kansans are lesbian or gay, but I doubt it.
4   The largest attempt at a random national sampling of Americans willing to identify as lesbian or gay was by a private polling group in 1989 for the San Francisco Examiner. See id. In that survey, 64% of lesbians and 60% of gay men said that they were currently in a relationship. The median length of that current relationship was 2.3 years. See Larry D. Hatfield, New Poll: How U.S. Views Gays, S.F. Examiner, June 6, 1989, at A-19. In large surveys of its readership by the Advocate, 67% of lesbians and 44% of gay men reported themselves currently in a relationship with a primary

partner. *See* Janet Lever, *Lesbian Sex Survey*, Advocate, Aug. 22, 1995, at 29; Janet Lever, *The 1994 Advocate Survey of Sexuality and Relationships: The Men*, Advocate, Aug. 23, 1994, at 23.

5   The *Advocate* reports that 46% of women and 30% of men said that they had exchanged rings or had a commitment ceremony. *See* Lever, *Lesbian Sex Survey, supra* note 4, at 29; *see also* Suzanne Sherman, *Introduction* to Lesbian and Gay Marriage private commitments, public ceremonies 1, 5–7 (Suzanne Sherman ed., 1992) [hereinafter Lesbian and Gay Marriage]; Ceremonies of the Heart: celebrating lesbian unions (Becky Butler ed., 1990).

6   *See* Lesbian and Gay Marriage, *supra* note 5, at 13 (providing a collection of interviews with lesbian and gay male couples who have joined in ceremonies of commitment; most of the couples referred to themselves as married and the ceremony as a wedding).

7   *See* Lever, *Lesbian Sex Survey, supra* note 4, at 27. In a comparable survey of gay men, 59% said that they would marry if they could, and another 26% said maybe. Seventy-one percent of men said they preferred long-term monogamous relationships. *See* Lever, *Advocate Survey, supra* note 4, at 23–24. In the national telephone survey undertaken for the *San Francisco Examiner*, 92% of lesbians and gay men indicated approval when asked, "How do you feel about two people of the same sex living together as a married couple?" *See New Poll supra* note 4, at A-21.

8   *See* William Eskridge, The Case for Same-Sex Marriage 66–71 (1996); *see also* Hawaii Commission on Sexual Orientation and the Law, Report 1–23 (1995) (discussing the legal consequences of marriage at greater length).

9   *See* Eskridge, *supra* note 8; Thomas Stoddard, *Why Gay People Should Seek the Right to Marry*, Out/look, Natl. Gay and Lesbian O Fall 1989, at 9, reprinted in Lesbian and Gay Marriage *supra* note 5, at 13; Evan Wolfson, *Crossing the Threshold: Equal Marriage Rights for Lesbians and Gay Men and the Intra-community Critique*, 21 N.Y.U. Rev. L. & Soc. Change 567 (1994–95); Nan D. Hunter, *Marriage, Law, and Gender: A Feminist Inquiry*, 1 L. & Sexuality Summer 1991, at 9.

10   In the wake of the decision of the Hawaii Supreme Court, sixteen states have adopted laws declaring that their state does not recognize same-sex marriages even if conducted validly in another state or that, for their state's purposes, the only valid marriages are marriages of a man and a woman See *Forum on the Right to Marry* (visited Aug. 12, 1996) <FORUMBOSTON@aol.com>; *see also* Ronald Smothers, *Mississippi Governor Bans Same-Sex Marriage*, N.Y. Times, Aug. 24, 1996, at A6. For the federal statute, see *supra* note 2.

11   *See* Paula Ettelbrick, *Since When is Marriage a Path to Liberation*, Out/Look, Natl. Gay and Lesbian Q., Fall 1989, at 9, reprinted in Lesbian and Gay Marriage, *supra* note 5, at 20; Steven K. Homer, *Against Marriage*, 29 Harv. C.R.-C.L. L. Rev. 505 (1994); Nancy D. Polikoff, *We Will Get What We Ask For: Why Legalizing Gay and Lesbian Marriage Will Not "Dismantle the Legal Structure of Gender in Every Marriage"*, 79 VA.L. Rev. 1535 (1993).

12   *See* Ruthann Robson, Lesbian (Out)law: survival under the rule of law 124–27 (1992); sources cited *supra* note 11.

13   Sherman, *Introduction* to Lesbian and Gay Marriage, *supra* note 5, at 1, 2.

14   See, e.g., Lesbian and Gay Marriage; *supra* note 5, at 108, 146.

15   Polikoff, *supra* note 11, at 1549; see also Homer, *supra* note 11, at 515–16.

16   In fact, access to health care has been "hooked" to marital status in this country largely by the action of private employers, not because it has been mandated by governments.

17   See sources cited *supra* note 15. For a response to Polikoff's arguments about health care, see Wolfson, *supra* note 9, at 604–08.

18   [C]ontemporary marriage cannot be legally defined any more precisely than as some sort of relationship between two individuals, of indeterminate duration, involving some kind of sexual conduct, entailing vague mutual property and support obligations, a relationship which may be formed by consent of both parties and dissolved at the will of either.

          1 Homer H. Clark, Jr., The Law of Domestic Relations in the United States § 2.1, at 81 (2nd edn 1988).

19   For a history of the early law, see Marylynn Salmon, Women and the Law of Property in Early America (1986). For accounts of the changes, see Mary Ann Glendon, The Transformation of Family Law (1989); Mary Ann Glendon. The New Family and the New Property (1981); Max Rheinstein, Marriage Stability, Divorce, and the Law (1972); Carl E. Schneider, *Moral Discourse and the Transformation of American Family Law*, 83 Mich. L. Rev. 1803 (1985).

20   See Clark, *supra* note 18, § 4.3, at 268–69; see also Franklin v. Franklin, 77 N.E. 48 (Mass. 1908).

21   See, e.g., Glendon, The Transformation of Family Law, *supra* note 19; Milton C. Regan, Jr., Family Law and the Pursuit of Intimacy (1993); Mary Ann Glendon, *Marriage & the State: The Withering Away of Marriage*, 62 Va. L. Rev. 663 (1976); Schneider, *supra* note 19.

22   *See* Martha Albertson Fineman, The Illusion of Equality: the rhetoric and reality of divorce reform 36–52 (1991).

23   *See* Carl E. Schneider, *The Channelling Function in Family Law*, 20 Hofstra L. Rev. 495, 497 (1992) (discussing the facilitative function of American family law).

24   See, e.g., Ky. Rev. Stat. § 311.631 (Michie Supp. 1994) (listing, in order, the spouse, an adult child, a parent).

25   See Unif. Prob. Code § 5–305(c) (guardian of the person), § 5–409(a) (guardian of property), 8 U.L.A. 466, 487–88 (1983); *see also* Amy L. Brown, Note, *Broadening Anachronistic Notions of 'Family' in Proxy Decisionmaking for Unmarried Adults*, 41 Hastings L.J. 1029, 1045–47 (1990).

26   See, e.g., New Mexico Disposition of Dead Bodies Act, N.M. Stat. Ann. § 24–12–1 to –4 (Michie 1994).

27   See Unif. Anatomical Gift Act § 3(a), adopted in some form in every state; see *also* N.Y. Pub. Health Law § 4301(2) (McKinney 1996).

28   See M. Henner. A Compendium of State Statutes and International Treaties in Trust and Estate Law (1985). The rules about intestate succession also reflect legislative views about the financial obligations of spouses to each other. See *infra* section III.C.

29   As a starting point, intestacy laws "build upon the rules that allocate original ownership" during the marriage. Lawrence W. Waggoner, *Marital Property Rights in Transition*, 59 Mo. L. Rev. 21, 27 (1994). As we will discuss later, two quite different regimes of marital property ownership exist within the United States. See *infra* text accompanying notes 115–20.

30   See Mary Louise Fellows et al., *Public Attitudes About Property Distribution at Death and Intestate Succession Laws in the United States*, 1978 Am. B. Found. Res. J. 319, 357–58 nn.128–29; Waggoner, *supra* note 29, at 37–38 (describing changes in the Uniform Probate Code in 1990 providing that the spouse receives the entire estate even when there are surviving children, so long as the children are the children of the decedent and the surviving spouse has no descendants who are not the decedent's).

31   In Europe and the United States, intestate succession laws have progressively moved toward reducing or excluding shares for blood relatives when the person who died has a surviving spouse. *See* Glendon, The Transformation of Family Law, *supra* note 19, at 238–40.

32 The drafters of the Uniform Probate Code, for example, explicitly sought to ground intestacy rules on their best estimation of what people who do not write wills would most prefer. See Waggoner, *supra* note 29, at 29, 36–38.

33 See Fellows et al., *supra* note 30, at 351 (noting that in a phone survey of 750 married persons in 5 states, 71% said that they wanted their surviving spouse to inherit their entire estate.).

34 Section Five of The Uniform Health-Care Decisions Act (1993) gives priority over everyone except a spouse to "an individual in a long-term relationship . . . with the patient in which the individual has demonstrated an actual commitment to the patient similar to the commitment of a spouse and in which the individual and the patient consider themselves to be responsible for each other's well being." As of 1996, the Act had been adopted in a few states. See, e.g., § 24–7A–5B(2) (Michie Supp. 1996). Arizona has recently adopted a statute that provides that a patient's "domestic partner" can be designated by a court as the surrogate decisionmaker for an incompetent person, but such a person is given lower priority than an adult child or a parent. See Ariz. Rev. Stat. Ann. § 36–3231 (1995).

35 Oregon treats in the same manner as a surviving spouse a person who for the 10 years preceding the decedent's death was in a relation with the decedent in which they "mutually assumed marital rights, duties and obligations," although they must also acquire a reputation as "husband and wife." Or. Rev. Stat. § 112.017(2) (1995); see also Waggoner, *supra* note 29. Waggoner is the reporter for the Uniform Probate Code and has recently recommended that intestate successions laws be amended to provide for unmarried partners whose relationship is well-documented or convincingly demonstrated. See *id.* at 78. Professor Waggoner has recently prepared a further revised version that he can provide by request, at the University of Michigan Law School.

36 See Fellows et al., *supra* note 30, at 337–39 (reporting that in a survey of 750 adults, 55% of those interviewed said that they did not have a will, and laziness was the most commonly cited reason).

37 See Karen Thompson and Julie Andrzejewski, Why Can't Sharon Kowalski Come Home? (1988) (relating the story of Sharon Kowalski, a young woman who had failed to execute a power of attorney before a severely debilitating car accident, and whose lover was excluded by Sharon's parents from playing any role in her care). One of the gay men interviewed by Suzanne Sherman who had united with a partner in a ceremony of commitment said, "We haven't put together a will yet, but we're planning to do it," and his partner conceded, "we won't get motivated until something forces us to." They had been married for five years. Lesbian and Gay Marriage, *supra* note 5, at 208.

38 See Rhonda R. Rivera, *Lawyers, Clients and AIDS: Some Notes From the Trenches*, 49 Ohio, St. L.J 883 (1989). Moreover, even when gay persons do execute a will or power of attorney, blood relatives may be more likely to challenge their competence in making the documents and more likely to allege that their lover had exercised improper influence. See *id.* at 892; Jeffrey Sherman, *Undue Influence and the Homosexual Testator*, 42 U. Pitt. L. Rev. 225 (1981).

39 See 2 Charles Gordon et al., Immigration Law and Procedure, § 36.02 (1996). There is also a narrow context in which marriage hurts. Under current rules, an American citizen can secure a preference for entry as a resident for his foreign-born child, if, but only if, the child is not married. See *id.* § 36.04[2].

40 See U.S. Commn. on Immigration Reform, Legal Immigration: Setting Priorities, 48–75 (1995).

41 See 29 U.S.C. §§ 2611–2654, 2612(a)(1)(C) (1994).

42 See Kenneth S. Broun et al., McCormick on Evidence § 66 (John William Strong

ed., 4th edn 1992); see also Milton C. Regan, Jr., *Spousal Privilege and the Meanings of Marriage*, 81 Va. L. Rev. 2045, 2052–54 (1995).

43   See Broun et al., *supra* note 42, §§ 78–86, at 112–119.

44   See 1 Clark, *supra* note 18, § 12.5, at 672–83.

45   Measuring attachment or love is difficult, of course, since scientists have not yet developed an attachometer. For what it's worth, lesbians, gay men, and hetero-sexuals in long-term relationships score at similarly high levels on standardized instruments asking questions about their liking or love of their partners. See Letitia Anne Peplau, *Lesbian and Gay Relationships*, in Homosexuality: Research implications for public Policy 177, 181–83 (John C. Gonsiorek and James D. Weinrich eds., 1991).

46   See generally Kath Weston. Families We Choose: Lesbians, Gays, Kinship 117–29 (1991); Lesbian and Gay Marriage, *supra* note 5.

47   See, e.g., 5 U.S.C. § 3110 (1994) (prohibiting any federal official from employing, promoting, or advancing any of a list of family members in or to a position in an agency in which he serves or over which he exercises control); Tenn. Code Ann. § 8–31–103 (1993) (prohibiting state employees from being placed in the direct line of supervision of a relative).

48   See, e.g., Ala. Code § 13A–13–2 (1994).

49   See Linda D. Elrod & Timothy B. Walker, *Family Law in the Fifty States*, 27 Fam. L.O. 515, 661 (1994) (listing 30 states that retain fault grounds as an alternative way to obtain a divorce).

50   Hence, all gay organizations oppose sodomy laws.

51   See David P. McWhirter and Andrew M. Mattison, The Male Couple 252–59 (1984) (noting that in a study of 172 male couples, only seven couples had a totally monogamous sexual relationship); *see also* Philip Blumstein and Pepper Schwartz, American Couples 271–72 (1983) (finding that, among heterosexual couples, 75% of husbands and 84% of wives believed it was important to be monogamous; 71% of lesbians in couples thought so as well, but only 36% of gay men in couples considered it important to be monogamous). For some couples, enforced exclusivity might weaken rather than strengthen their bonds to their partners. See *id.* at 299–302.

52   Two lesbians may each be biological parents of a single child when one contributes the egg and the other performs gestation. Even here there is necessarily a third biological parent.

53   Eskridge, for example, devotes only two sentences to laws regarding parenting. *See* Eskridge, *supra* note 8, at 67.

54   For a brief review, accessible to lawyers, of the research on gay men and lesbians as parents and for abundant references to the social science literature, see Gregory M. Herek, *Myths About Sexual Orientation: A Lawyer's Guide to Social Science Research*, 1 L. & Sexuality 133, 157–61 (1991); see also *Charlotte J. Patterson, Children of Lesbian and Gay Parents*, 63 Child Dev. 1025 (1992). On lesbians as parents, see Nancy D. Polikoff, *This Child Does Have Two Mothers: Redefining Parenthood to Meet the Needs of Children in Lesbian-Mother and Other Nontraditional Families*, 78 Geo. L.J. 459 (1990). On gay men as parents, see Frederick W. Bozett, *Gay Fathers: A Review of the Literature*, 18 J. of Homosexuality 137 (1989).

55   *See* Patterson, *supra* note 54. Here, for example, is a very recent capsule statement summarizing research on lesbians as parents:

> Researchers who compared children raised in lesbian and heterosexual house holds found few or no differences in the development of gender identity, gender-role behavior, or sexual orientation. Studies have also found no

deficits among children of lesbian mothers in other aspects of personal development, including separation-individuation, locus of control, self-concept, intelligence, or moral judgment. In addition, numerous studies have shown that children raised by lesbians have normal, healthy relationships with other children as well as with adults. According to Patterson's . . . comprehensive literature review on lesbian and gay families, a child's adjustment is enhanced when the lesbian mother lives with her partner, when the lesbianism is acknowledged before the child reaches adolescence, and when the child has contact with peers from other lesbian families.

> Nanette Gartrell *et al.*, *The National Lesbian Family Study*, 66 Am. J. of Orthopsychiatry 272, 272–73 (1996) (citations omitted).

56   A second question that bears on some issues – such as whether to permit gay and lesbian couples to adopt a child that is biologically related to neither – is whether the breakup rate of gay and lesbian couples is so high that whatever preference is accorded to married heterosexual couples as couples should not be accorded to gay and lesbian couples. I can find no figures yet on the average duration of relationships of same-sex couples who have performed ceremonies of commitment or consider themselves married.

57   To be sure, the biological parent may designate the partner in her will as the preferred guardian for the child upon her death, a preference that will often be honored by the court unless the other biological parent demands custody.

58   See Margaret M. Mahoney. Stepfamilies and the Law 13–51 (1994). Utah, for example, is a partial exception, imposing a duty of support during the course of the stepparent's marriage to the biological parent, but not at the point of divorce. See Utah Code Ann § 78–45–4.1 (1992); see also David L. Chambers, *Stepparents, Biologic Parents, and the Law's Perceptions of 'Family' After Divorce*, in *Divorce* Reform at the Crossroads 102, 108–09 (Stephen D. Sugarman and Herma Hill Kay eds., 1990).

59   See Mahoney, *supra* note 58, at 124–48 (1994).

60   See *id.*

61   See Joan H. Hollinger, *Introduction to Adoption Law and Practice*, in Adoption Law and Practice § 1.05(2) (Joan H. Hollinger ed., 1990).

62   See Joan H. Hollinger, *Consent to Adoption* in *Adoption Law and Practice*, *supra* note 61, § 2.10(3).

63   See *id.; see also* Chambers, *supra* note 58, at 102, 118–21.

64   See 2 Clark, *supra* note 18, §§ 21.1, at 565.

65   See *id.* § 21.12, at 688–89.

66   See Margaret M. Mahoney, *Stepfamilies in the Federal Law*, 48 U. Pitt. L. Rev. 491, 496–514 (1987); Mary Ann Mason & David W. Simpson, *The Ambiguous Stepparent: Federal Legislation in Search of a Model*, 29 Family L.Q. 445, 457–60 (1994).

67   See 29 U.S.C. §§ 2611(12) & 2612(a)–(d) (1994). The act includes "stepchild" but does not define the term. I assume from its use in other legal contexts that, for purposes of the act, a stepchild is a child of a person to whom the employee is actually married and does not include the child of a person with whom the employee is cohabiting outside of marriage.

68   See generally April Martin. The Lesbian and Gay Parenting Hand Book: Creating and raising our families (1993); Cheri Pies, Considering Parenthood (2nd edn 1988).

69   A 1983 opinion by the Attorney General of Oklahoma concluded that artificial insemination of an unmarried woman is illegal in Oklahoma. See Linda J. Lacey, *The Law of Artificial Insemination and Surrogate Parenthood in Oklahoma: Roadblocks to the Right to Procreate*, 22 Tulsa L.J. 281, 284–86 (1987).

70   See Martin Curie-Cohen *et al.*, *Current Practice of Artificial Insemination by Donor in the*

United States, 300 New Eng. J. Med. 585 (1979) (reporting on a survey of physicians, 90 percent of whom said that they would not perform artificial insemination on an unmarried woman); Caroline H. Sparks and Jean A. Hamilton, *Psychological Issues Related to Alternative Insemination*, 22 Prof. Psychol. 308, 311–12 (1991) (reporting that lesbians often face especial difficulties obtaining services from clinics).

71   For a discussion of the difficulties the nonbiological partner experiences when not accepted as a prospective parent during her partner's pregnancy, see Barbara M. McCandlish, *Against All Odds: Lesbian Mother Family Dynamics*, in Gay and Lesbian Parents 23 (Frederick W. Bozett ed., 1987).

72   Florida and New Hampshire prohibit adoptions by gay men and lesbians. See Fla. Stat. ch. 63.042(3) (1995); N.H. Rev. Stat. Ann. § 170–B:4 (1994). In a few other states, appellate courts have declared homosexuals unsuitable to be adoptive parents. See Marla J. Hollandsworth, *Gay Men Creating Families Through Surro-Gay Arrangements: A Paradigm for Reproductive Freedom*, 3 Am. U.J. Gender & L. 183, 197 n.53 (1995).

73   See, e.g., *In re* Adoption of T.K.J. and K.A.K., Nos. 95CA0531, 95CA0532, 1996 WL 316800 (Colo. Ct. App. June 13, 1996) (holding that only a person married to the biological partner is eligible for the rules regarding stepparent adoption).

74   *See* Maxwell S. Peltz, *Second Parent Adoption: Overcoming Barriers to Lesbian Family Rights*, 3 Mich. J. Gender & L. 175, 182–87 (1995).

75   See, e.g., Adoption of Tammy, 619 N.E.2d 315, 317 (Mass. 1993) (noting that the Department of Social Services had conducted a home study and that over a dozen witnesses testified in support of adoption); *In re* Jacob, 660 N.E.2d 397, 405 (N.Y. 1995); Adoption of B.L.V.B. and E.L.V.S., 628 A.2d 1271, 1272 (Vt. 1993).

76   See Lori B. Andrews, *Alternative Reproduction and the Law of Adoption*, in Adoption Law and Practice, *supra* note 61, § 14.02 (noting that thirty states have adopted statutory rules that a properly consenting husband becomes the legal father for all purposes, and that courts in most other states have reached the same result by relying on the common law presumption of legitimacy for children born within marriage and on the agreement of the parties prior to conception.).

77   See Elizabeth Noble, Having Your Baby by Donor Insemination a complete resource guide 160–96 (1987).

78   In many states, the common law rule that forbids a husband from challenging the legitimacy of a child conceived during a marriage would, if carried over in its application to same-sex marriages, protect the legal status of the nonbiological parent. In some states, however, a failure to comply with the requirements of the artificial insemination statute have led courts not to impose child support obligations upon divorce on the husband. See, e.g., Jhordan C. v. Mary K. & Victoria T., 224 Cal. Rptr. 530 (Cal. Ct. App. 1986); *In re* Witbeck-Wildhagen, 667 N.E.2d 122 (Ill. App. Ct. 1996) (deciding a case in which the husband expressly disapproved of the wife's seeking artificial insemination); McIntyre v. Crouch, 780 P.2d 239 (Or. Ct. App. 1989).

79   See Brad Sears, *Winning Arguments/Losing Themselves: The (Dys)functional Approach* in Thomas S. v. Robin Y., 29 Harv C.R.-C.L. L. Rev. 559 (1994).

80   See Hollandsworth, *supra* note 72.

81   See generally Martha A. Field, Surrogate Motherhood: the legal And human issues (2nd edn 1990); Scott B. Rae, The Ethics of Commercial Surrogate Motherhood: brave new families? (1994); Surrogate Motherhood: politics and privacy (Larry Gostin ed., 1990); Randy Frances Kandel, *Which Came First: The Mother or the Egg?, A Kinship Solution to Gestational Surrogacy*, 47 Rutgers L. Rev. 165 (1994).

82   See Hollandsworth, *supra* note 72, at 201–07 (providing a helpful review of state statutes).

83   Many states have adopted some version of the Uniform Status of Children of Assisted Conception Act, which restricts surrogacy agreements to married couples. See e.g., Va. Code Ann. § 20–159 (1996). Arkansas is apparently the only state that explicitly permits an unmarried man to enter into a surrogacy arrangement. See Ark Code Ann. § 9–10–201 (Michie 1996); Hollandsworth, *supra* note 72, at 205.

84   See Hollandsworth, *supra* note 72, at 200.

85   See *supra* note 72 for state laws relating to adoption. New Hampshire by statute prohibits gay men and lesbians from serving as foster parents. See Joseph Evall, *Sexual Orientation and Adoptive Matching*, 25 Fam. L.Q. 347, 352–54 (1991); *Developments in the Law — Sexual Orientation and the Law*, 102 Harv. L. Rev. 1508, 1643 (1989).

86   See Wendell Ricketts and Roberta Achtenberg, *The Adoptive and Foster Gay and Lesbian Parent, in* Gay and Lesbian Parents 89–111 (Frederick Bozett ed., 1987).

87   See Elizabeth Bartholet, Family Bonds: adoption and the politics of parenting 70–72 (1993).

88   See *id.*; see *also* Hollandsworth, *supra* note 72, at 197 n.54.

89   Bartholet, *supra* note 87, at 70.

90   As to the discrimination in adoption against single persons, see Jennifer Jaff, *Wedding Bell Blues: The Position of Unmarried People in American Law*, 30 Ariz L. Rev. 207, 216–17 (1988).

91   The justification for preferring couples over single persons runs as follows: first, that children will be better off in general when able to rely on two caretakers and two sources of support and, second, that even if there is no evidence that children adopted by single parents fare less well than children adopted by couples, a preference for couples, in places with limited numbers of available children, creates the likelihood that each adopted child brings pleasure to two adults. As to the preference for married couples over other pairs of persons who come forward to adopt, there may be no rational reason to prefer married couples to couples who have entered some other formal relationship like a domestic partnership, but the state does have a basis for preferring as adoptive parents couples who have indicated a commitment to remain together.

92   Not surprisingly, none of the studies of gay and lesbian couples, including the few that examine the manner in which they handle finances, differentiates between those couples who would legally marry if they could and those who, like many heterosexual couples, would choose to remain single even if marriage were legally available.

93   The best available information about the economic behavior of gay and lesbian couples comes from Blumstein and Schwartz's pioneer study from the early 1980s of the handling of money by American couples. See Blumstein and Schwartz. *supra* note 51, at 94–111. This study included substantial but nonrandom samples of married and unmarried opposite-sex couples and of gay male and lesbian couples. The authors found that the great majority of married opposite-sex couples expected and favored the pooling of income and resources. Gay men and lesbians in couples had more diverse attitudes, with a significant minority of both women and men opposing pooling. Still, for those in relationships that had lasted more than two years, the proportion who favored pooling substantially exceeded the proportion who opposed it. Blumstein's samples of same-sex couples did not differentiate between those who would and would not have married if legal marriage had been available.

94   See Lesbian and Gay Marriage *supra* note 5, at 115, 127, 145, 153, 163, 208 (recorded interviews).

95   Jane Bryant Quinn observes that not all married heterosexual couples pool their resources. She cleverly observes two patterns for handling income and expenses even within married couples: "splitters" who keep their own separate accounts, and "poolers" who put everything into a common pot. Over time, she says, if the marriage goes well, "splitters usually turn into spoolers, splitting some, pooling some, and growing less antsy about who pays for what." Jane Bryant Quinn, Making the Most of Your Money 81 (1991). She does not rely on statistics.

96   See I.R.C. § 1(a) (1994).

97   For example, two single individuals living together who each earn $30,000 would pay $1248 less in total federal income taxes than two married individuals who earn the same amounts and filed a joint return. See Jonathan B. Forman, *What Can Be Done About Marriage Penalties?*, 30 Fam. L.Q. 1, 5 (1996). Similar differences apply to low-income earners who qualify for the earned Income Tax Credit. See Anne L. Alstott, *The Earned Income Tax Credit and the Limitations of Tax-Based Welfare Reform*, 108 Harv. L. Rev. 533, 559–64 (1995).

98   A fine recent critique can be found in Edward J. McCaffery, *Taxation and the Family: A Fresh Look at Behavioral Gender Biases in the Code*, 40 UCLA L. Rev. 983 (1993) [hereinafter McCaffery, *Taxation and the Family*] See also Edward J. McCaffery, *Slouching Towards Equality: Gender Discrimination, Market Efficiency, and Social Change*, 103 Yale L.J. 595, 617–19 (1993) [hereinafter McCaffery, *Slouching Towards Equality*].

99   See sources cited *supra* note 98.

100   *See* 42 U.S.C. § 1382(b) (1994).

101   42 U.S.C. § 1382c(f)(1) (1994). An unusual section in the statute establishing the program of Supplemental Security Income provides that if a man and woman "hold themselves out as married," they will be treated for purposes of the SSI program as if they were married. 42 U.S.C. § 1382c(d)(2) (1994). Federal laws recognize the unmarried couple only when those laws work to the couple's financial disadvantage.

102   *See* 20 U.S.C. § 1087 pp, 1087nn(b)(1)(A) (1994).

103   See Paul Drizner, Comment, *Medicaid's Unhealthy Side Effect: The Financial Burdens on At-Home Spouses of Institutionalized Recipients*, 18 Loy. U. Chi. LJ 1031, 1036–47 (1987).

104   42 U.S.C. § 402(b)–(c). See U.S. Social Security Administration. Social Security Handbook, § 305 (12th edn 1995). In much the same manner, a divorced spouse not fully covered through her own employment will be covered through her former spouse on reaching the requisite age. See *id.*

105   See *id.* § 401.

106   See I.R.C. §§ 1041, 2523 (1996); see also Patricia, A. Cain, *Same-Sex Couples and the Federal Tax Laws*, 1 L. & Sexuality 97, 123–29 (1991).

107   I.R.C. § 1041 (a)–(c) (1996).

108   See I.R.C. § 2056 (1996).

109   I.R.C. §§ 105, 213 (1996).

110   See Cain, *supra* note 106.

111   See *supra* note 98 and accompanying text.

112   See *supra* note 98 and accompanying text.

113   See Marjorie E. Kornhauser, *Love, Money and the IRS: Family, Income-Sharing, and the Joint Income-Tax Return*, 45 Hastings L.J. 63, 73–80 (1993).

114   See *id.*

115   See Elrod and Walker, *supra* note 49, at 695 (table). The states are Arizona, California, Idaho, Louisiana, Nevada, New Mexico, Texas, Washington, and Wisconsin.

116   See Roger A. Cunningham *et al.*, The Law of Property § 5.14, at 232–33 (2nd edn 1993); W.S. McClanahan, Community Property in the United States §§ 1:6, 1:8 (1982).

117   Though "owned" jointly, "control" over the earnings may lie initially with the earner. For example, a paycheck made out to an employee need not be endorsed by the spouse before being cashed.

118   See Cunningham *et al.*, *supra* note 116, § 5.15; McClanahan, *supra* note 116, § 1:07 (comparing common law and community property states).

119   Lawrence Waggoner believes that the two sets of rules serve to "reinforce the profoundly different symbolical and psychological feelings within the ongoing marriage." See Waggoner, *supra* note 29, at 27.

120   See generally Blumstein and Schwartz, *supra* note 51 (describing the personal and social characteristics motivating heterosexual relationships and comparing them to those motivating homosexual and lesbian relationships).

121   See Elrod and Walker, *supra* note 49, at 723–25.

122   See id. 716–21; Unif. Marriage & Divorce Act § 307, 9A U.L.A. 238 (1987).

123   See Elrod and Walker, *supra* note 49, at 725–28.

124   See, e.g., Grace Blumberg, *Marital Property Treatment of Pensions, Disability Pay, Workers' Compensation and Other Wage Substitutes: An Insurance or Replacement Analysis*, 33 UCLA L. Rev. 1250, 1251 (1986); Elizabeth A. Cheadle, *The Development of Sharing Principles in Common Law Marital Property States*, 28 UCLA L. Rev. 1269 (1981). Some common law states have translated this beginning point into a formal statutory presumption. *See, e.g.*, Ohio Rev. Code Ann. § 3105.171(A) (Anderson Supp. 1995).

125   See, e.g. Marsha Garrison, *Good Intentions Gone Awry: The Impact of New York's Equitable Distribution Law on Divorce Outcomes*, 57 Brook. L. Rev. 621 (1991).

126   See Ira Ellman *et al.*, Family Law 253–57 (1991).

127   See Unif. Marriage & Divorce Act § 307(a), 9A U.L.A. 239 (1987), adopted in many states.

128   See Linda D. Elrod and Robert G. Spector, *A Review of the Year in Family Law*, 29 Fam. L.Q. 741, 774 tbl. 5 (1996). A few states treat the professional degree earned during the marriage as property subject to equitable division. See, e.g., O'Brien v. O'Brien, 489 N.E.2d 712 (N.Y. 1985). In some others, compensatory payments much like alimony may be ordered by the court. See, e.g., Mahoney v. Mahoney, 453 A.2d 527 (N.J. 1982). In California, a community property state, special legislation permits a court to order a divorcing spouse to reimburse the other spouse for the costs of tuition and education. See Cal. Fam. Code § 2641 (West 1994).

129   See Elrod and Spector, *supra* note 128, at 770 tbl. 1; 2 Clark, *supra* note 18, 220–334.

130   See Leonore Wettzman, The Divorce Revolution: the unexpected social and economic consequences for women and children in America 33 (1985).

131   See Ann L. Estin, *Maintenance, Alimony and the Rehabilitation of Family Care*, 71 N.C. L. Rev. 721, 745–46 (1993). For heterosexual married couples today in which the wife has not been in the labor force, the alimony and property division rules facilitate at least modestly the division of labor within couples – one developing material wealth, one providing care for the family or pursuing nonwealthgaining activities. See Ira M. Ellman, *The Theory of Alimony*, 77 Cal. L. Rev. 1 (1989); but see Jana B. Singer, *Alimony and Efficiency: The Gendered Costs and Benefits of the Economic Justification for Alimony*, 82 Geo. L.J. 2423 (1994).

132   See Ralph C. Brashier, *Disinheritance and the Modern Family*, 45 Case W. Res. L. Rev. 83, 99–104 (1994); Lawrence Waggoner, *Spousal Rights in Our Multiple Marriage Society: The Revised Uniform Probate Code*, 26 Real Prop., Probate & Tr. J. 683, 720

(1994); see also Unif. Prob. Code § 2–102, 8 U.L.A. 59 (1982) (dividing the marital assets on a 50–50 basis).

133　See Brashier, *supra* note 132, at 97. The elective share rule can produce anomalous results in common law states in some cases in which a person dies shortly after marriage to a person who already has substantial assets of his or her own.

134　See Ellman *et al.*, *supra* note 126, at 662–87; Marjorie M. Shultz, *Contractual Ordering of Marriage: A New Model for State Policy*, 70 Cal. L. Rev. 204, 280–88 (1982). Eighteen states have adopted the Uniform Premarital Agreement Act. See Note, *Till Divorce Do Us Part: The Validity of Antenuptial Agreements in Michigan*, 38 Wayne L. Rev. 1919, 1921 n.3 (1992). Such agreements are apparently fairly common among wealthy persons who have children and who remarry late in life and who want to preserve for their children the assets they have acquired up to that point in their lives.

135　Waggoner, *supra* note 29, at 62–63.

136　See, e.g., Wallace v. Rappleye, 103 Ill. 229, 249 (1882).

137　See, e.g., Hewitt v. Hewitt, 394 N.E.2d 1204 (Ill. 1979).

138　On the demographic changes, see Arlen Thornton, *Cohabitation and Marriage in the 1980s*, 25 Demography 497 (1988); Waggoner, *supra* note 29, at 63.

139　See Marvin v. Marvin, 557 P.2d 106 (Cal. 1976) (holding that courts should enforce contracts between unmarried partners); Morone v. Morone, 413 N.E.2d 1154 (N.Y. 1980); *see also* Ellen Kandoian, *Cohabitation, Common Law Marriage, and the Possibility of a Shared Moral Life*, 75 Geo. L.J. 1829 (1987).

140　Only a few states have appellate decisions on the question whether such contracts will be honored for same-sex couples. See, e.g., Jones v. Daly, 176 Cal. Rptr. 130 (1981).

141　In the *Marvin* case, the California Supreme Court invited enforcing implied contracts and other traditional equitable remedies. See *Marvin*, 557 P.2d at 122–23. In *Morone*, the New York Court of Appeals held that its courts would enforce express but not implied contracts. See *Morone*, 413 N.E.2d at 1156.

142　See Shuraleff v. Donnelly, 817 P.2d 764 (Ore. Ct. App. 1991); Worden v. Worden, 676 P.2d 1037 (Wash. Ct. App. 1984). Even in these cases, the courts have refused to adopt as a general rule a principle of equal division such as they impose on divorcing couples.

143　See Blumstein and Schwartz, *supra* note 51.

144　See Grace G. Blumberg, *New Models of Marriage and Divorce*, in Contemporary Marriage: Comparative Perspectives on a Changing Institution 349, 354 (Kingsley Davis ed., 1985).

145　See *supra* note 94 and accompanying text.

146　In *American Couples*, Blumstein and Schwartz do not indicate the correlation between willingness to pool and income level, but they do report that, among gay men, when one partner has much more income than the other, he typically asserts considerable control over the expenditure of income and shares decisionmaking less. See Blumstein and Schwartz, *supra* note 51, at 105, 59–60. These high-earning men seem in the best position to protect themselves by insisting on agreements about keeping assets separate.

147　CF. Herma Hill Kaye, *Equality and Difference: A Perspective on No-Fault Divorce and Its Aftermath*, 56 U. Cin. L. Rev. 1 (1987).

148　Martha A. Fineman, The Illusion of Equality: the rhetoric and reality of divorce reform 4 (1992); June Carbone, *Equality and Difference: Reclaiming Motherhood as a Central Focus of Family Law*, 17 L. & Soc. Inquiry 471 (1992).

149　See Garrison, *supra* note 125, at 671.

150　See Fineman, *supra* note 148, at 36–37; *see also* David Chambers. Making Fathers Pay 37–68 (1979).

151   For a review of views about the functions of alimony and the social position of women, see June Carbone and Margaret Brinig, *Rethinking Marriage: Feminist Ideology, Economic Change, and Divorce Reform,* 65 Tul. L. Rev. 953, 987–1004 (1991).

152   CF. Jones v. Daly, 176 Cal. Rptr. 130 (1981) (concluding without adequate foundation that a relationship between two men, one of whom was old and rich and the other young and economically dependant, rested primarily on sex as the consideration).

153   In many states, judges may consider marital "fault" in dividing property or awarding alimony. See 2 Clark *supra* note 18, § 16.3, at 194–96 (property); *id.* § 17.5, at 267–69 (alimony); Elrod and Walker, *supra* note 49, at 534. Judges rarely get the opportunity to exercise their discretion because, in the overwhelming majority of cases, parties settle before a hearing, but the prospect that a judge will take fault into account can affect the bargaining process between partners.

154   See, e.g., Haw. Rev. Stat §§ 87–4, 393–7, 393–21 (1993).

155   2 Stuart M. Speiser *et al.*, Recovery for Wrongful Death and Injury § 10.2 (3rd edn 1992).

156   See 1 Clark, *supra* note 18, § 7.3, at 444–48. For a recent example of a hospital recovering from a wife for services provided to a spouse, even after the couple had separated, see Forsyth Memorial Hosp. Inc. v. Chisholm, 22 Fam. L. Rep: (BNA) 1185 (N.C. Feb. 2, 1996).

157   See Cunningham *et al.*, *supra* note 116, § 5.16, at 242–43; McClanahan, *supra* note 116, §§ 4:31–4:36.

158   As to wrongful death, see, e.g., Speiser *et al.*, *supra* note 155, § 10:21.

159   Hundreds of gay male and lesbian couples in San Francisco have registered their relationships as domestic partners under the city's Domestic Partnership Act. See San Francisco, Ca., Admin. Code §§ 62.1–62.8 (1991). In order to register, couples must affirm that they accept responsibility for each others' "basic living expenses." San Francisco, Ca., Admin. Code § 62.2(a) (1991).

160   See *supra* notes 11–12.

161   On the flexibility of marriage as an institution through time, see John Modell, *Historical Reflections on American Marriage*, in Contemporary Marriage: comparative perspectives on a changing institution 181 (Kingsley Davis ed., 1985).

162   See the discussion of various commentators in Elizabeth S. Scott, *Rehabilitating Liberalism in Modern Divorce Law*, 1994 Utah L. Rev. 687, 708–19; see also June Carbone, *Income Sharing: Redefining Family in Terms of Community*, 31 Hous. L. Rev. 359 (1994).

163   A substantial number of cities, including New York, San Francisco, Minneapolis, and Ann Arbor have adopted registration for unmarried couples by local ordinance. The California legislature passed a bill to permit state registration of unmarried couples, but the bill was vetoed by Governor Wilson. CA A.B. 2810, 1993–94 Reg. Sess.

164   See, e.g., *supra* text accompanying notes 34, 35, 75, 139–42. For a recent general discussion of the recognition of nonmarital relationships in the United States, see Jana B. Singer, *The Privatization of Family Law*, 1992 Wis. L. Rev. 1443, 1447–56.

165   See the Danish Registered Partnership Act, No. 372 (1989); Norwegian Act on Registered Partnerships for Homosexual Couples (1993).

166   See *supra* text accompanying note 2.

167   Nitya Duclos, *Some Complicating Thoughts on Same-Sex Marriage*, 1 L. & Sexuality 31, 55, 58 (1991).

168   *Id.* at 59.

169   *Id.* at 55.

170   See *supra* text accompanying notes 100–01.

171   See Weston, *supra* note 46, at 209–10; Homer, *supra* note 11, at 530; Jaff, *supra* note 90, at 238–42.

172   I've always been surprised that there were not more three and more person cohabiting units among gay men and lesbians, since homosexual people are, after all, already flouting convention when living together in pairs.

173   Justifiable limits could, for example, be placed on the number of spouses one could bring into the country on a privileged basis. Rules could be fashioned for the division of assets among three or four people who are splitting.

174   See Nan D. Hunter, *Marriage, Law and Gender: A Feminist Inquiry*, 1 L. & Sexuality 9, 12 (1991).